D1284170

LOUISA MAY ALCOTT

Selected Fiction

LOUISA MAY ALCOTT

Selected Fiction

With an Introduction by
MADELEINE B. STERN

Edited by
Daniel Shealy,
Madeleine B. Stern,
and
Joel Myerson

THE UNIVERSITY OF GEORGIA PRESS
Athens and London

Published in 2001 by the University of Georgia Press
Athens, Georgia 30602
© 1990 by Joel Myerson, Daniel Shealy, and Madeleine B. Stern
Introduction © 1990 by Madeleine B. Stern

The paper in this book meets the guidelines for
permanence and durability of the Committee on
Production Guidelines for Book Longevity of the
Council on Library Resources.

Printed in the United States of America
05 04 03 02 01 P 5 4 3 2 1

Library of Congress Cataloging-in-Publication Data
Alcott, Louisa May, 1832–1888.
[Novels. Selections]
Louisa May Alcott : selected fiction / with an introduction by
Madeleine B. Stern ; edited by Daniel Shealy,
Madeleine B. Stern, and Joel Myerson.
p. cm.
ISBN 0-8203-2313-6 (pbk.: alk. paper)
1. New England—Social life and customs—Fiction. 2. Women—
New England—Fiction.
I. Shealy, Daniel. II. Stern, Madeleine B., 1912–
III. Myerson, Joel.
IV. Title.
PS1016.S54   2001
813´.4—dc21   00-054502

British Library Cataloging-in-Publication Data available

The original hardcover version of this book was published
in 1990 by Little, Brown and Company.

Contents

Contents

Domesticity
The Roots of *Little Women*

The Little Women *Trilogy*

The Youth's Companion
America's Best-Loved Author of Juveniles

Fiction and Reform

Fiction and Autobiography

Acknowledgments

ALL THREE editors are grateful to the staffs of the American Antiquarian Society, the Boston Public Library, Harvard University Libraries (Widener and Houghton), Orchard House, Cooper Library of the University of South Carolina, and Atkins Library of the University of North Carolina at Charlotte for making available the original printings of the texts for *Louisa May Alcott: Selected Fiction*. We also wish to thank Armida Gilbert and Juanita Honeycutt for their help in preparing the texts for this volume. Once again, we are grateful to Christina Ward, who gave us much help and encouragement in seeing the book through press. Daniel Shealy is grateful to Frederik N. Smith, Chairman of the Department of English of the University of North Carolina at Charlotte. Madeleine B. Stern acknowledges the unceasing support of her partner, Dr. Leona Rostenberg, who originally discovered many of Alcott's pseudonymous works. Joel Myerson acknowledges the support of Carol McGinnis Kay, Dean of the College of Humanities and Social Sciences of the University of South Carolina.

A Note on the Texts

THIS BOOK reprints works by Louisa May Alcott that first appeared in newspapers, magazines, and books. All items were signed with Alcott's name unless otherwise noted. We have given publication information for the text used in reprinting at the beginning of each item.

In preparing these works for publication, we have made emendations only where the text would be obviously in error or unclear without them. For example, we have corrected obvious spelling and typographical errors, inserted words and punctuation marks for clarity, and provided missing single or double quotation marks. We have let stand nineteenth-century spellings (such as "to-day") and inconsistencies in capitalization, hyphenation, and commas in series. Alcott was careless in preparing her manuscripts for publication, and nineteenth-century compositors were not particularly careful in setting type from even the best-prepared copy; we have in general modernized or "corrected" these texts as little as possible.

Introduction

Madeleine B. Stern

*L*ITERARY SOURCES, lie generally in the mind and heart of the writer of fiction, and this is especially true of Louisa May Alcott. "I turn my adventures into bread and butter,"[1] she observed, knowing they were the adventures of her mind and heart as well as the experiences of the life she lived. And so, her life and her work are intriguingly interrelated. Out of the adventures that were her literary sources, Alcott, one of the most prolific authors, produced an immense variety of fiction. In her day, and for generations after her death, it attracted an enormous and a diverse readership. Now, for the first time, the wide range of fiction she created has been gathered together in a single volume. Its perusal suggests that this nineteenth-century New England spinster shaped her experiences not only into bread and butter but into stories often timeless and universal.

EARLY EXPERIMENTS IN ROMANCE

The path from the imaginary to the credible, from the romantic to the real, was long and involved, but its beginnings can be clearly traced. "My first story was printed, and $5 paid for it," Alcott recorded in her journal in 1852. "It was written in Concord when I was sixteen. Great rubbish! Read it aloud to sisters, and when they praised it, not knowing the author, I proudly announced her name."[2] Alcott's first published story appeared on 8 May 1852, in the *Olive Branch,* a Boston paper devoted to Christianity, general information, agriculture, and polite literature. Entitled "The Rival Painters. A Tale of Rome" and published anonymously, it was a triangular

---

1. *The Journals of Louisa May Alcott,* ed. Joel Myerson and Daniel Shealy (Boston: Little, Brown, 1989), p. 182 (April and May 1872) [hereinafter *Journals*].

2. Ibid., p. 67 (1852).

[xi]

love story about the rival painters Guido and Count Ferdinand, both of whom courted the beautiful Madeline. Madeline's father was a pragmatist who determined to give his daughter to him who "hath painted a picture the most perfect in grace, and beauty of form, design and coloring."[3] The Count painted a portrait of Madeline, but Guido, a wiser student of character, sketched his mother, and won the prize.

By 1848, when "The Rival Painters" was written, Louisa Alcott obviously had some knowledge of art, some further knowledge of human nature, and an abiding devotion to her mother. All these were sources for a story woven when the sixteen-year-old girl lived in Concord, Massachusetts, with a family consisting of an idealistic, head-in-the-clouds, transcendentalist father, Bronson Alcott, a long-suffering, hardworking, human rights–loving mother, Abby May Alcott, and three sisters, one of whom already showed an interest in art.

During the short time between her birth in Germantown, Pennsylvania, on 29 November 1832, and the writing of "The Rival Painters," Alcott had already experienced extremes of emotion that would be reflected in her narratives. Although she had not officially attended her father's Temple School in Boston, she had been the beneficiary of his advanced views on education, and they too would filter into her stories. The six months the family had spent in the Fruitlands community, established in Harvard, Massachusetts, by her father and the reformer Charles Lane, had introduced her to the glories of running wild, as well as to the peculiarities of unorthodox behavior and the miseries of family tension. By the time the Alcotts had a temporary residence in Concord, Louisa Alcott had been exposed to several varieties of human experience. She was not yet fully aware of the family's poverty and probably not yet conscious of her own rebellion against the doctrine of self-denial that was an Alcott tenet. But she was on her way to such realizations. Meanwhile, walks in the woods with neighbor Henry David Thoreau, visits to Ralph Waldo Emerson's home and library, much reading of Dickens, and plays written with her sister Anna and performed for the neighbors in a Concord barn — all provided the warmth of wholesomeness and the excitement of intellectual adventure that compensated in some measure for poverty and self-denial and that, one day, when portrayed in *Little Women,* would endear her to the reading world.[4]

3. Unless otherwise indicated, all quotations are from Alcott's fiction, principally the stories and excerpts in this anthology.

4. It is of interest that Alcott included in *Little Women* a sample of *The Pickwick Portfolio,* an early family newspaper produced by the four sisters, containing a portion of another of her romantic tales, "The Masked Marriage."

The family poverty reached a peak in the early 1850s. Living in Boston, Mrs. Alcott opened an employment office, Anna and Louisa taught, sister Lizzie was housekeeper, young May went to school, and "father wrote and talked when he could get classes or conversations." As Louisa wrote in her journal: "Our poor little home had much love and happiness in it,"[5] but the "love and happiness" did not altogether make up for the hardship and the poverty. Perhaps the tales of romance did, for they continued to flow from her pen.

One of them, "The Rival Prima Donnas," is of peculiar interest on several counts: for the first time Alcott adopted a pseudonym as a byline; it appeared in still another Boston weekly that would air her contributions for several years to come; and with the strong thread of romance she now entwined the scarlet thread of the sensational. By 1854, when "The Rival Prima Donnas" made its bow, Alcott had tried her hand at many types of employment to replenish the empty family cupboard. She had tutored and taught, sewed and laundered, and even, for seven harrowing weeks in Dedham, Massachusetts, gone into domestic service. Especially she had written. In the garret above the third floor in the Alcott home on Boston's Pinckney Street, she had sought from the life without as well as the life within sources for her tales. Her rival prima donnas were modeled after the great sopranos Jenny Lind, and Henriette Sontag, whom she had heard at Boston's Music Hall. Resemblance to life ended there, for Alcott embroidered a story of violence and vengeance in which one singer crushes her competitor to death by means of an iron ring set upon her head. In the end, the hero-villain who has instigated the tragedy is filled with remorse, and the actual perpetrator of the crime becomes suddenly insane. Vengeance and insanity would reappear in the oeuvre of the stagestruck author, who even attempted a dramatization of this flamboyant romance.[6] Meanwhile, on 11 November 1854, "The Rival Prima Donnas" adorned the *Saturday Evening Gazette,* a weekly edited by the younger William Warland Clapp, an authority on a subject close to Alcott's heart, the American theater. She would remain faithful to the *Gazette* for the next five years. "The Rival Prima Donnas," her first story in its pages, had a byline curiously inappropriate to the narrative: "Flora Fairfield."

That byline would have been far more suitable for Alcott's first book, which, like her first published story, "The Rival Painters," had been composed in her teens. The family, then living in Concord, had reason to be

---

5. *Journals,* p. 67 (1852).

6. For the dramatization of "The Rival Prima Donnas," as well as for all biographical details, see Madeleine B. Stern, *Louisa May Alcott* (Norman: University of Oklahoma Press, 1985), pp. 73, 74, 76–79.

grateful to their generous and illustrious neighbor Ralph Waldo Emerson, and, to tutor his children, Louisa opened a little school in the barn of the Alcott home, Hillside. For Emerson's daughter Ellen, who responded eagerly to her lessons, Alcott wove a series of romantic fables about flowers, garnering her facts and fancies from knowledge imparted to her by Henry David Thoreau and from such literary sources as Friedrich Wilhelm Carové's *Story without an End,* to which her father had written a preface. Now her dramatis personae consisted of Thistledown and Lily-Bell, Dr. Dewdrop, Violet, and the Frost King. She had kept the scribbled records of those tales, and some years later her father, perhaps at Mrs. Emerson's suggestion, consulted with the Boston publisher George Briggs about bringing them out in book form. In December 1854, fifteen hundred copies were issued, subsidized by a benefactor, Miss Wealthy Stevens. The book was dedicated to Ellen Emerson. Its monetary rewards were meager. Alcott reported in her journal that, "owing to Mr Briggs' dishonesty," she received only a very small sum, thirty-two or thirty-five dollars. Nonetheless, she also reported that "the principal event of the winter is the appearance of my book 'Flower Fables.' . . . I feel quite proud that the little tales that I wrote for Ellen E. when I was sixteen should now bring money and fame. . . . people began to think that topsey-turvey Louisa would amount to something after all, since she could do so well as housemaid, teacher, seamstress, and story-teller."[7]

One of the first copies of *Flower Fables,* if not the first, was presented by Louisa to her mother with a letter dated 25 December 1854: "Into your Christmas stocking I have put my 'firstborn,' knowing that you will accept it with all its faults . . . and look upon it merely as an earnest of what I may yet do; for, . . . I hope to pass in time from fairies and fables to men and realities."[8]

That passage was about to begin. Arrayed in her "glory-cloak" (an "old green and red party wrap" she wore when she wrote), sitting in a Boston garret, surrounded by papers and a pile of apples, Alcott wrote indefatigably, and always she experimented. Having tried her ink-stained fingers at the romantic, she attempted now, for the *Saturday Evening Gazette,* a series of stories that owed more to everyday life than to realms of the wildly impossible.

7. *Journals,* pp. 72, 73 ("Notes and Memoranda" 1854, 1 January and April 1855).

8. *The Selected Letters of Louisa May Alcott,* ed. Joel Myerson and Daniel Shealy (Boston: Little, Brown, 1987), p. 11 [hereinafter *Selected Letters*].

EARLY EXPERIMENTS IN REALISM

Only two years after her melodramatic "Rival Prima Donnas" made its debut, Alcott submitted to the *Saturday Evening Gazette* the story of two far more credible rivals, "The Lady and the Woman." The straightforward, independent Kate Loring makes a pointed contrast to the languid belle Amelia Langdon, and their story represents not only the author's early feminist inclinations but her ability to draw protagonists true to life. The reactions of the lady and the woman to a country flood pinpoint their characters. In the end the fretful, useless, and beautiful Amelia, who has tried to captivate Edward Windsor, loses him to Kate. Meanwhile Kate's character, "strong enough to stand alone, and give, not ask, support," has been skillfully depicted until it is possible to see in her an early prototype of Jo March.

Another romance based upon reality uses as its principal character the child-wife Effie, and as its pivotal episode an attempted suicide. "Love and Self-Love" is, like much of Alcott's fiction, a morality tale based upon life, upon her own life, for the author had recently experienced and overcome a desire to commit suicide. In October 1858 she wrote in her journal: "Went to Boston on my usual hunt for employment, as I . . . seem to be the only bread-winner just now." She added: "My fit of despair was soon over, for it seemed so cowardly to run away before the battle was over I could n't do it. So I said firmly, 'There *is* work for me, and I'll have it,' and went home resolved to take Fate by the throat and shake a living out of her."[9] In a letter to her family she explained that "fit of despair" more clearly: "Last week was a busy, anxious time, & my courage most gave out, for every one was so busy, & cared so little whether I got work or jumped into the river that I thought seriously of doing the latter. In fact did go over the Mill Dam & look at the water."[10] Alcott's heroine Effie does more than look at the water. Believing that her husband, Basil Ventnor, loves another, she attempts to drown herself. After that "despairing deed," we are informed, "the *child* Effie lay dead beneath the ripples of the river, but the *woman* rose up from that bed of suffering." Ventnor's fatherly feelings are transformed ultimately into a man's passion; he learns that love is greater than self-love, and the unlikely pair have a true marriage.

In November 1859 Alcott wrote in her journal:

> Hurrah! My story was accepted; and Lowell asked if it was not a translation from the German, it was so unlike most tales. I felt

9. *Journals,* p. 90 (October 1858).
10. *Selected Letters,* p. 34 ([October 1858]).

much set up, and my fifty dollars will be very happy money. People seem to think it a great thing to get into the "Atlantic;" but I've not been pegging away all these years in vain, and may yet have books and publishers and a fortune of my own. Success has gone to my head, and I wander a little. Twenty-seven years old, and very happy.[11]

By twenty-seven Alcott had converted the resources of a wild imagination into fiction and had also learned to borrow from life. As she would comment in "A Modern Cinderella," "Reality" was turning "Romance out of doors."[12] She had begun to craft herself into a writer.

SENSATIONALISM: THE THRILLERS

She had experimented with romance; she had experimented with realism. When she learned to combine the two, she would produce the autobiographical domestic novel that would metamorphose both her life and her literary style. *Little Women,* however, would not be written until 1868. Meanwhile, Louisa May Alcott was flirting with more daring fictional techniques than she had as yet attempted. She might mock "that class of light literature in which the passions have a holiday, and when the author's invention fails, a grand catastrophe clears the stage of one half the *dramatis personae.*" Yet the so-called sensation story presented a challenge to a developing writer, and, more important, it "paid the butcher's bill, . . . put down a new carpet, and . . . proved [a] blessing . . . in the way of groceries and gowns."[13] The weekly story papers that would one day provide "comforts" for the March family — the *Weekly Volcano* and the *Blarneystone Banner* — were modeled after *Frank Leslie's Illustrated Newspaper* and the *Flag of Our Union.* At the rate of fifty or seventy-five dollars a tale, they now supplied similar comforts for the Alcott family at the same time as they provided the author with opportunities for emotional catharsis and literary, or subliterary, experimentation.

In narratives revolving around macabre themes — family curses, madness, revenge, mesmerism, murder, addiction to opium — Louisa Alcott between 1862 and 1868 exercised her inventiveness. For her sensation stories she created strong and passionate heroines who were usually victorious

---

11. *Journals,* p. 95 (November 1859).

12. In another Alcott experiment in realism, "Mark Field's Success," the hero searches for "better work than weaving romances," for he has tired of "phantoms, their fictitious joys and sorrows."

13. Louisa May Alcott, *Little Women or Meg, Jo, Beth and Amy* (New York: Collier, 1975), pp. 300, 302.

in their power struggles with men. She injected into her shockers her own frustrations and fury, as well as her readings in exotic and Gothic romances. Having begun to master the technique of telling a story, she produced an amazing number of page turners as enticing for their characterizations as for their plots and themes.

Alcott painted her scarlet portraits secretly and published her shockers clandestinely over the pseudonym of "A. M. Barnard" or anonymously.[14] She disdained them, or professed to disdain them, knowing that neither her father nor her "intellectual god," the revered Ralph Waldo Emerson, would ever tolerate them. Their attitudes she would one day bestow upon Professor Bhaer in *Little Women*. Meanwhile she shared them, but only to a degree, for, despite her disparagement of her "rubbish," she found it impossible to resist the lure of the exotic and the sensational.

"Hope's Debut," here reprinted for the first time, was contributed in 1867 to the New York story paper *Frank Leslie's Chimney Corner*.[15] In it even the forbidden theme of incest is made tolerable. Set against the theatrical background that fascinated the stagestruck author, "Hope's Debut" presents as its lead the eighteen-year-old Hope Scott performing Ophelia to Jacques Le Brun's Hamlet, and later Cordelia to his Lear. We are informed that "many called them lovers," but their relationship becomes a thwarted romance when Hope learns the true identity of Jacques Le Brun, who is none other than her father. Undaunted, they plan "a starring tour together," and the joys of reunion for father and daughter supersede those of the budding romance. Did Alcott's ambivalent feelings for her own father influence her shaping of the father-daughter relationships in her thrillers? An autobiographical origin for her incestuous hints, though tenuous, invites conjecture.

Whatever subtleties existed in "Hope's Debut" were thrown to the winds in "Thrice Tempted." Here Alcott stirred in a witch's caldron the ingredients of a poisoned brew: revenge and guilt, sleepwalking and the horrors of live burial. In a triangular romance, the "slight, dark girl" Ruth, "with no beauty but much strength of character in her face," loses her lover to the charmer Laura. Twice Ruth saves her rival, once from plague, once from fire, but the third time, aware that Laura may still be alive (her forehead is damp), she nonetheless allows her to be buried. During a sleepwalking fit, Ruth, haunted by her guilt, confesses it but will never find

---

14. The Alcott sensational stories were originally identified in Leona Rostenberg, "Some Anonymous and Pseudonymous Thrillers of Louisa M. Alcott," *Papers of the Bibliographical Society of America* (1943), 131–140.

15. See *Journals*, p. 139 (March 1865): "Leslie asked me to be a regular contributor to . . . 'The Chimney Corner,' . . . & bespoke two tales at once $50 each."

forgiveness. In "Thrice Tempted," written at Frank Leslie's request and never before reprinted, Alcott let down her literary tresses. Her exercise in depicting revenge and guilt might have served, half a century later, as a Freudian case history.

During the 1860s, while she was exploiting the sensational genre, one of the author's favorite themes was the influence of narcotics, either in the form of opium addiction or hashish experimentation. The source for her fascination with the derivative of *cannabis sativa* is clearly traceable. The nineteenth-century pharmacopoeia included laudanum, or tincture of opium, and when, after her brief experience as a Civil War nurse, Alcott succumbed to severe illness, she was prescribed the customary narcotics. Indeed, hashish was available to all at only six cents a stick. And so, when Alcott describes, in a short shocker entitled "Perilous Play," the "heavenly dreaminess," the trance followed by an unnatural and wild excitement when "every nerve was overstrained, every pulse beating like a trip-hammer," she writes from experience. The experiment with hashish — "that Indian stuff which brings one fantastic visions" — is pivotal to the plot of her narrative; in fact, it *is* the plot. The cast of characters includes the femme fatale so often featured by Alcott, the daughter of a Spanish mother and an English father, whose eyes are "Southern," whose cheeks are "clear olive," and whose lips are "like a pomegranate flower."

Although "Perilous Play" was not published until February 1869 in *Frank Leslie's Chimney Corner,* it had been written the previous year. It earned only twenty-five dollars, doubtless because of its comparative brevity, but in every way — characterization, plot development, theme — the story was and is a gem. It is also probably the last thriller Alcott would contribute to the gaudy story papers of her day. After 1868 she would be engrossed, for the most part, in quite different literary genres.

THE CIVIL WAR AND REALISM

Early in her career Alcott had seesawed between the romantic and the plausible. During her productive 1860s she continued this dual experimentation. Even while she was sketching her shockers against bizarre and exotic backgrounds, she was painting pictures from life. Most of her experiments in realism between 1863 and 1868 were outgrowths of the Civil War and her own experience in that war. The delirium of her illness and the laudanum she was prescribed may have provided her with motifs for her thrillers, but it was the war itself, especially the hospital where she nursed and the soldiers whom she knew, that gave her source and substance for her realistic fiction.

By the outset of the war, Alcott's life had already been filled with episodes and convictions related to slavery and its ramifications. An escaped slave had briefly been harbored in the Alcott home in Concord; Louisa had heard of Jonathan Walker, whose hand had been branded with the initials *S.S.* for "slave stealer"; her father had joined with members of a Vigilance Committee to rescue the fugitive Anthony Burns; in the momentous month of April 1861, when war was declared, the daughters of the martyred abolitionist John Brown came to board with the Alcotts. Long before she served as army nurse, the crusade against slavery was in her blood, and her own experiences yielded sources for stories about it.

Alcott adopted two principal methods for narrating war-related tales. Still intrigued by the lurid, she sometimes combined threads of the melodramatic with threads of realism. "M.L." is ostensibly a suspense tale about the identity of an escaped slave whose hand is branded with his master's initials and who turns out to be the son of a Cuban planter and a beautiful quadroon. Actually it is a story about miscegenation and racial conflict. It is literally a romance about reality, in which a white heroine persists in her love of a mulatto hero and seeks to join a "brotherhood which makes the whole world kin." Rejected by an *Atlantic Monthly* fearful of offending the South with an antislavery tale, "M.L." earned twenty dollars from the *Boston Commonwealth*, where it ran in January and February 1863.

In other war stories Alcott tried to convey the genuine with more precision.[16] Even in "The Blue and the Gray," which concerns the presence of a Rebel soldier in a Union hospital and includes an attempted poisoning, there is less of the unreal and more of the real: the hospital background, the nurse, the death that "in a hospital, makes no stir." In her narratives of hospital life, Alcott could rely upon her own experience.

During her six weeks at the Union Hotel Hospital in Georgetown, D.C., Alcott was witness to and participant in the daily hospital routine. She was the percipient observer of the wounded and the dying, the nurses and the doctors, the food and the living conditions. All these she reported in letters home, "letters written on inverted tin kettles, in my pantry, while waiting for gruel to warm or poultices to cool, for boys to wake and be

16. Alcott's aim at realism is indicated in her war story "My Contraband," about which she wrote to Thomas Wentworth Higginson: "I knew that my contraband did not talk as he should, for even in Washington I had no time to study the genuine dialect, & when the story was written here I had no one to tell me how it should be" (*Selected Letters*, p. 96 (12 November [1863])). The story was entitled "The Brothers" when it appeared in the *Atlantic Monthly*, in November 1863.

tormented, on stairs, in window seats & other sequestered spots favorable to literary inspiration."[17] Out of those letters, none of which has survived, she shaped the first-person narrative not of a Flora Fairfield or an A. M. Barnard but of yet another literary self, "Nurse Tribulation Periwinkle." In a light, breezy style that made gruesome facts more shocking, she reported the dialogue she had heard, the private histories confided to her. Her patients lived again — the young sergeant who, having lost his right hand, was learning to write with the left; the blacksmith from Virginia wounded in the chest whom she helped to die. This cast of characters bore no relation to the romantic protagonists and the exotic world she had invented in so many tales; they were related to the life of a nation at war. The life was there in her sketches, the odors and bloody bandages, the stretchers carrying the armless and the legless, the rations of army bread and muddy coffee, the cold, dirty ward, the "chaos" that "reigned along with the rats." Here too were reflected those "secesh principles" that still "flourished even under the respectable nose of Father Abraham," even during a Civil War that would end slavery.

Alcott's life as army nurse was shortened by her grave illness, but after her recovery she was able to "arrange my letters in a printable shape & put them in the [Boston] Commonwealth."[18] "Hospital Sketches" ran there in four installments between May and June 1863, and the author received not only forty dollars but letters of praise and offers of book publication from James Redpath and Roberts Brothers, both of Boston. She chose the former because he was a fiery abolitionist, and in August, *Hospital Sketches* was ready "in its new dress. I had added several chapters to it & it was quite a neat little affair."[19] The "neat little affair" garnered considerable praise from the press for its quiet humor and graphic descriptions. In Alcott's double authorial life, the realism of Nurse Tribulation Periwinkle seemed to be as popular a literary commodity as the sensationalism of A. M. Barnard. As for herself, she commented in her journal: "I find I've done a good thing without knowing it."[20]

EXPERIMENTS IN THE NOVEL

Most of Alcott's fiction was more consciously contrived. Indeed, long before she had produced *Hospital Sketches* or served as army nurse, she had embarked upon experimentations with the novel that would fascinate her

17. *Selected Letters,* p. 95 (LMA to Mary Elizabeth Waterman, 6 November 1863).
18. *Journals,* p. 118 (April 1863).
19. Ibid., p. 120 (August 1863).
20. Ibid., p. 122 ("Notes and Memoranda" 1863).

for the remainder of her life. The first experiment was begun in August 1860 when she was twenty-seven. She reported it in her journal: "Genius burned so fiercely that for four weeks I wrote all day and planned nearly all night, being quite possessed by my work. I was perfectly happy, and seemed to have no wants. Finished the book, or a rough draught of it, and put it away to settle. . . . Daresay nothing will ever come of it; but it *had* to be done, and I'm the richer for a new experience."[21]

Alcott insisted that *Moods* had been written "from my own life & experience," "my own observation, experience & instinct." In it, she explained, "I've freed my mind upon a subject that always makes trouble, namely, Love. But being founded upon fact, & the characters drawn from life it may be of use as all experiences are." Alcott's first novel is less a depiction of "the effect of a moody person's moods" than it is a not completely coherent disquisition upon wrong marriages, "unmated pairs trying to live their legal lie decorously to the end at any cost."[22] This theme she elaborated in metaphysical self-analyses and lengthy dialogues.

The "unmated" or poorly mated pairs in *Moods* consist of the heroine Sylvia and Geoffrey Moor, Ottila and Adam Warwick. The resemblance of these characters to life, despite the author's protestations, is remote; they seem rather to hail from the pages of her sensational thrillers: Adam, "untamed by any law but that of [his] own will"; Ottila, the "affluent beauty" endowed with "eyes full of slumberous fire, and . . . passionate yet haughty mouth"; Moor, who "betrayed in every gesture the unconscious grace of the gentleman born"; Sylvia, passionate, restless, sensitive, torn between warring temperaments. From the emotional relationships of this quartet emerge Alcott's conclusions on unhappy marriages, "the tragedies of our day." In the end Adam Warwick dies at sea (in a style reminiscent of the feminist Margaret Fuller) after he has served in the Roman Revolution; Sylvia wills herself to die, somewhat in the manner of Louisa's sister Lizzie Alcott's end.

The author labored over this first novel for several years, remodeling, reworking, writing and rewriting "like a thinking machine in full operation."[23] At the request of publisher Aaron K. Loring of Boston, she cut ten chapters from the manuscript, a revision she came to repent. As she would write in *Little Women* of Jo's first novel: "With Spartan firmness, the young authoress laid her first-born on the table, and chopped it up as

21. Ibid., pp. 99–100 (August 1860).

22. Ibid., p. 133 (November 1864); *Selected Letters,* p. 107 (LMA to Annie Maria Lawrence, 3 February 1865), and pp. 109–110 (LMA to Mr. Ayer, 19 March 1865).

23. *Journals,* p. 132 (October 1864). The writer Caroline Healy Dall, after reading the manuscript of *Moods,* sent it to publisher Loring.

ruthlessly as any ogre. In the hope of pleasing every one, she took every one's advice; and like the old man and his donkey in the fable suited nobody."[24] Actually, although young Henry James berated "the author's ignorance of human nature, and her self-confidence in spite of this ignorance," *Harper's Weekly* found "the conflict of passion in noble characters . . . drawn with great delicacy and skill."[25] In due course the author received an initial payment of $236 from Loring and a five-pound advance from the English publisher George Routledge.

Alcott was not yet done with *Moods*. She was already becoming a compulsive reviser, using and reusing early stories for latter-day purposes, and *Moods* would obsess her for some time. Eventually she would publish a radically altered version of her first novel. Moreover, the interrelations of the *Moods* quartet foreshadowed the sexual acrobatics of another quartet in *A Modern Mephistopheles*; the homespun chapter titled "The Golden Wedding" in *Moods* looked forward to the domesticities of *Little Women*; and the slight glimmerings of Thoreau found in the character of Adam Warwick presaged his reappearance as David Sterling in *Work*.

It is difficult to realize that Alcott was writing *Moods* and *Work* almost simultaneously. The former is a novel constructed around her observations of failed marriages; the latter is a series of episodes connected by her protagonist and based almost entirely upon her own life. *Work* is not only an autobiographical distillation but a revamping of some of her earlier writings, including *Hospital Sketches*. The novel was begun in 1861 with quite a different title — *Success*. In typical fashion, Alcott added to it or reworked it from time to time, tapping her life for her literature. In the summer of 1863 she explained her purpose to James Redpath, publisher of *Hospital Sketches*: "This . . . was begun with the design of putting some [of] my own experiences into a story illustrating the trials of young women who want employment & find it hard to get. . . . The story is made up of various essays this girl makes, her failures & succeses [*sic*] told in chapters merry or sad, & various characters all more or less from life are introduced to help or hinder her."[26]

---

24. Alcott, *Little Women*, p. 304.

25. James's review appeared in *North American Review* (July 1865), 276–281, reprinted in *Critical Essays on Louisa May Alcott*, ed. Madeleine B. Stern (Boston: G. K. Hall, 1984), pp. 69–73; *Harper's Weekly* (21 January 1865), 35, reprinted in *Critical Essays on Louisa May Alcott*, p. 66. A variant version of the chapter "The Golden Wedding" appeared in the *Boston Commonwealth* (29 April and 6 May 1864) as "A Golden Wedding: and What Came of It."

26. *Selected Letters*, p. 87 ([July? 1863]). Another novel drawn from life by Alcott is her unfinished *Diana and Persis*, "an art novel, with May's romance for its thread." Based

The characters so introduced include Henry David Thoreau, transformed into David Sterling, and the Unitarian minister Theodore Parker in the role of Thomas Power. As for herself, Alcott became Christie Devon as she reshaped fragments of her own life into narratives that trace her character development. Alcott had been a domestic; the chapter "Servant" recalls her degradation. Alcott had performed in amateur theatricals, especially delighting in renditions of Dickens's dramatized novels; the chapter "Actress" features the histrionics of Christie Devon. The heroine's transmutations are reflected in segments entitled "Governess," "Companion," and "Seamstress." Christie proudly rejects Philip Fletcher with the remark: "I am as well-born as you in spite of my poverty"; she befriends the repentant Rachel, who "once went astray"; she contemplates drowning herself; she is deeply influenced by the minister Thomas Power, who made "religion . . . a visible and vital thing." Christie meets the gardener David Sterling, who, like Thoreau, "does not seek society." His portrait is clearly etched from Alcott's Concord neighbor: "broad-shouldered, brown-bearded, with an old hat and coat, trousers tucked into hs boots, fresh mould on the hand." Of course, Christie and David love and marry (the ceremony is performed by Mr. Power); David enlists in the Civil War; Christie serves as army nurse; the beloved husband dies. A final chapter, "At Forty," pictures Christie twenty years after she has set out to seek her fortune and gives the author the opportunity of advancing the cause of "a new emancipation" in women's solidarity.

One chapter of *Success* (*Work*) has special fascination, for it incorporates directly into this autobiographical novel a sensational romance ("A Nurse's Story") that Alcott contributed anonymously to *Frank Leslie's Chimney Corner* in 1865. Both the five-part serial and the chapter in the novel recount the melodramatic story of a family afflicted with the curse of inherited insanity. The "Companion" chapter is not so extraneous to the autobiography of Alcott's alter ego Christie as might appear, when it is recalled that at one time Alcott had cared for a young friend who had suffered "a temporary fit of insanity."[27]

Success, revised and reentitled *Work,* did not see publication until De-

---

upon her younger sister's artistic pursuits abroad and her marriage, the novel also reflects the author's ambivalent feelings toward her sister, who "always had the cream of things, and deserved it." See *Journals,* p. 211 (December 1878, "Notes and Memoranda" 1878) and p. 209 (April 1878). See also Louisa May Alcott, *Diana and Persis,* ed. Sarah Elbert (New York: Arno, 1978).

27. Ednah Dow Cheney, *Louisa May Alcott: Her Life, Letters, and Journals* (Boston: Roberts Brothers, 1889), p. 111 [hereinafter Cheney]. "A Nurse's Story" ran in *Frank Leslie's Chimney Corner* 2, 9, 16, 23, and 30 December 1865 and 6 January 1866.

cember 1872, when it began its serial appearance in the *Christian Union,* to be reprinted in book form in 1873. The author's 1873 accounting included five thousand dollars from Roberts Brothers for her autobiographical novel.[28] Her life had indeed become a tale to be told.

Bearing only slight resemblance to *Moods* and less to *Work,* still another novel preoccupied Alcott during this period. In *A Modern Mephistopheles* — begun in the mid-1860s and published in 1877 — she characteristically made use of earlier narratives, which she revised and reshaped for her purpose. In addition, she combined in that extraordinary story several of her literary selves: the explorer of sensational horrors of the mind; the pursuer of Goethe's intellectual affirmations; the dispenser of sweetness and light. An amalgam of many sources, *A Modern Mephistopheles* is uncharacteristic of its author only to those who are ignorant of her multifaceted creativity.

As with many of her experiments in the novel, *A Modern Mephistopheles* had a long history.[29] In August 1866, after her return from abroad, Alcott wrote a lengthy narrative at the request of Elliott, Thomes and Talbot of Boston, publishers of her pseudonymous thrillers. Its title was "A Modern Mephistopheles or The Fatal Love Chase," a heavily plotted narrative whose fate was recorded in her journal: "Elliott would not have it, saying it was too long & too sensational! So I put it away."[30] In October and November of the same year another Alcott shocker appeared, in *Frank Leslie's Illustrated Newspaper,* a five-part serial entitled "The Freak of a Genius,"[31] a story revolving around the false authorship of a book and the relationship between two men, one young, one older. When the need arose, Alcott would return to both those sources and borrow something from each.

Meanwhile her delight in Goethe, which began in her early days when Emerson had given her a copy of *Wilhelm Meister,* intensified — along with her continuing interest in power struggles between men and women and between men and men. In 1876, when the author of *Little Women* and *Little Men* had become universally known, her major publisher, Roberts Brothers of Boston, launched a No Name Series of anonymous books by well-known writers. The head of the firm, Thomas Niles, plied his star author for a contribution, and she obliged by reworking her old sensation

28. *Journals,* p. 189 ("Notes and Memoranda" 1873).

29. See Louisa May Alcott, *A Modern Mephistopheles and Taming a Tartar* (New York: Praeger, 1987).

30. *Journals,* p. 153 (September 1866).

31. "The Freak of a Genius," *Frank Leslie's Illustrated Newspaper* (20, 27 October, 3, 10, 17 November 1866).

stories into the framework of a Faustian tale. In January and February 1877, Alcott stayed at Boston's Bellevue Hotel and, as she noted in her journal, "wrote 'A Modern Mephistopheles' for the No Name Series. It has been simmering ever since I read Faust last year. Enjoyed doing it, being tired of providing moral pap for the young."[32]

As a creative artist, she took from her principal literary source, Goethe's *Faust,* as well as from her own sensational narratives, only what suited her purpose. Her purpose clearly was to modernize Mephistopheles and retell the tale of a power struggle. This she does with uncanny skill. In a Faustian pact, Felix Canaris, the victim of unfulfilled ambition, sells his liberty to the modern Mephistopheles, Jasper Helwyze, in return for literary fame. The power-hungry Helwyze, modern in the sense that he is less magician than psychologist, is indeed wise in his knowledge of Hell. The themes of enslavement and of struggle against enslavement are enriched by the introduction of the two women: Olivia, a variant of Goethe's Martha, is a mellow beauty, opulent and stately, reminiscent also of Ottila in *Moods*; Gladys, based upon Goethe's Margareta, is a simple, incorruptible maiden who eventually becomes Alcott's *dea ex machina* by saving Felix's soul before her own death; in some ways she suggests Sylvia, the heroine of *Moods*. The erotic quartet play out their roles. In a remarkable chapter Alcott paints her own version of the witches' Walpurgisnacht orgy of *Faust*. The orgy in *A Modern Mephistopheles* consists of innocent *tableaux vivants* performed by Gladys after hashish has been administered to her by Helwyze. In the course of her hashish dreams he interrogates her, thus becoming guilty of Hawthorne's unpardonable sin by violating "the sanctity of a human soul, robbing it . . . of its most secret and most precious thoughts," prying into "its mysterious depths . . . from a cold, philosophical curiosity." In an ironic end, it is Gladys who, dying in childbirth, conquers; Helwyze is paralyzed; Felix confronts life on his own. If the characters, the power struggles, and the Walpurgis Night of *A Modern Mephistopheles* are outcomes of Alcott's delving into darkness, its moral finale stems directly from her sojourn in realms of sweetness and light.

When the tale was published in the No Name Series in 1877, few penetrated its anonymity. *A Modern Mephistopheles* was generally found "thrilling, weird, and intense," although *Godey's Lady's Book* pontificated that "the characters . . . move in an atmosphere of their own, . . . With advancing years and a larger experience the author may make her mark."[33]

---

32. *Journals,* p. 204 (January, February 1877).

33. *Woman's Journal* (19 May 1877), 160; *Godey's Lady's Book* (July 1877), 86, reprinted in *Critical Essays on Louisa May Alcott,* p. 204.

At the end of her life Alcott put an end to the guesswork as to authorship and publicly acknowledged her book, which, she averred, she liked "better than 'Work' or 'Moods.' "[34]

Yet, as late as the 1880s, *Moods* still engrossed her. In November 1881, Alcott remarked in her journal: "Wrote a Preface to the new edition of 'Moods.' "[35] The reception and interpretation of her first novel had apparently troubled the author from time to time during her long and concentrated writing career. It demanded revision. The preface to the new edition elucidates Alcott's immediate intentions and indirectly casts light upon her development as a novelist:

> When "Moods" was first published, an interval of some years having then elapsed since it was written, it was so altered, to suit the taste and convenience of the publisher, that the original purpose of the story was lost sight of, and marriage appeared to be the theme instead of an attempt to show the mistakes of a moody nature, guided by impulse, not principle. . . .
>
> As the observation and experience of the woman have confirmed much that the instinct and imagination of the girl felt and tried to describe, I wish to give my first novel, with all its imperfections on its head, a place among its more successful sisters; for into it went the love, labor, and enthusiasm that no later book can possess.
>
> Several chapters have been omitted, several of the original ones restored; and those that remain have been pruned of as much fine writing as could be done without destroying the youthful spirit of the little romance. At eighteen death seemed the only solution for Sylvia's perplexities; but thirty years later, having learned the possibility of finding happiness after disappointment, and making love and duty go hand in hand, my heroine meets a wiser if less romantic fate than in the former edition.[36]

For the most part, Alcott's preface is accurate. Her revised Sylvia is clearly a creature of moods and contradictions, pliable clay for life's molding. Although Moor and Warwick are comparatively unchanged, there is far less metaphysics in the new version than in the original, and the emphasis is upon "wholesome, homely realities" in place of "romantic

34. LMA to Thomas Niles (6 May 1887) in Cheney, p. 379.
35. *Journals*, p. 231 (November 1881).
36. Louisa May Alcott, *Moods. A Novel* (Boston: Roberts Brothers, 1891), pp. [v]–vi. The preface is dated Concord, January 1882.

dreams." By revising some chapters, rearranging others, and adding or deleting sections, Alcott reshaped both her novel and her heroine. Now, when Sylvia lies "in the shadow of death," she feels "an earnest desire to atone, to rise above obstacles and turn the seeming defeat into a sweet success." "It seemed cowardly to die, and she asked for life . . . and when she rose a stronger and more patient soul shone through the frail body like the flame that makes the lamp transparent." If a reader of the new *Moods* harbored any doubts about the author's intentions, they were dispelled by the final affirmation: "Sylvia . . . turned from the painted romance to the more beautiful reality, to live, not dream, a long and happy life, unmarred by the moods that nearly wrecked her youth; for now she had learned to live by principle, not impulse, and this made it both sweet and possible for love and duty to go hand in hand."

The writer who in August 1860 had been so possessed by her theme that she had produced a "rough draught" of her first novel in four intense weeks had, during the twenty years that followed, clearly undergone a metamorphosis. The spinner of romance and sensationalism, author of "The Rival Prima Donnas" and "Thrice Tempted," had also been a confronter of reality, author of *Hospital Sketches*. Her forays into the gaudy and extravagant had been matched, sometimes almost simultaneously, by ventures into the true and the wholesome. Between the first edition of *Moods* and its revision Alcott had attempted still another experiment — literary domesticity — and the novel entitled *Little Women*, unlike her romances and sensation stories, had earned her worldwide popularity. Its success had also imposed upon her the obligation of supplying a demanding public with a constant flow of literature in the same genre. The "painted romance" of *Moods* I had been transformed into the "beautiful reality" of *Moods* II because, in between the two versions, Alcott had produced the masterpiece called *Little Women*.

DOMESTICITY: THE ROOTS OF *LITTLE WOMEN*

Unlike *Moods, Work,* and *A Modern Mephistopheles,* over which Alcott labored for long periods, the two parts of *Little Women* were written each in two months, sometimes at the rate of one chapter a day, and apparently without revision. Actually, all her life had been groundwork for this adaptation of tempered realism to domesticity. It is not remarkable that this "girls' story" in which the Alcott family was encapsulated was written so speedily. Louisa Alcott had not only lived this story but had made several earlier attempts to tell it. The roots of *Little Women* are traceable to the author's literary beginnings. Indeed, in a family newspaper that the Alcott girls ran under various names, the *Olive Leaf,* the *Pickwick Portfolio,* the

Portfolio, between 1849 and 1853, is a brief narrative entitled "Two scenes in a family," in which the Marches (though not so named) are adumbrated.[37] In 1856 Alcott sent to the Boston *Saturday Evening Gazette* a tale entitled "The Sisters' Trial," in which the March family is even more recognizable. Here four sisters sit as trial proofs, so to speak, for the full-length portraits that would adorn *Little Women:* Agnes becomes an actress; Ella works as governess; Amy — even the name is the same — studies art abroad; and Nora, an early Jo March, remains at home to write. This account of a year in the lives of four sisters, which earned six dollars, persisted in the author's memory. Four years later she produced another variation on the family theme, another foreshadowing.

Alcott recorded in her journal in March 1860, shortly before her sister Anna's marriage to John Pratt: "Wrote 'A Modern Cinderella,' with Nan for the heroine and John for the hero."[38] "A Modern Cinderella," published in the *Atlantic Monthly* in October, would culminate years later in the chapter "The First Wedding" in Part II of *Little Women.* The earlier version dilates upon the romance of Anna and John Lord, the hardworking clerk whose "honest eyes" and "helpful hands" evidence his goodness. But the story is even more interesting for its portraits of the artist sister, here named Laura, who copies Raphael and looks picturesque, and of sister Di, who loses herself in the delights of Goethe, corks her inkstand to go "at housework as if it were a five-barred gate," and determines to write to support the family. "Her will, like a battering-ram, would knock down the obstacles her wits could not surmount." Di, trying to learn the "worth of self-denial," prefigures the crises of Jo March as clearly as she recalls the struggles of her creator.

In October 1867 Alcott "agreed with Fuller to be editor for $500 a year. Read MSS. write 1 story each month & an editorial. On the strength of this engagement went to Boston, took a room No 6 Hayward Place, furnished it & set up housekeeping for myself."[39] For the editorial section of Horace B. Fuller's juvenile periodical, *Merry's Museum* — "Merry's Monthly Chat with His Friends" — Alcott in January 1868 supplied a story about an incident involving an impoverished German family that she would transfer to the chapter "A Merry Christmas" in Part I of *Little Women.* The episode concerns the sisters' giving their breakfast to a poor family at the request of their mother. Actually, the story as it is related in

37. Printed in Appendix B of *Journals,* pp. 338–341.

38. *Journals,* p. 98 (March 1860).

39. Ibid., p. 158 (October 1867). The story Alcott contributed to the October 1867 issue was "Living in an Omnibus," which introduced the Hummels, the impoverished German family who would shortly reappear in *Little Women.*

Merry's Museum is more autobiographical than in *Little Women*. In the former version, the first person is used, and the sisters are named Nan, Lu, Beth, and May. The poor family, nameless in *Merry's,* is called Hummel in *Little Women.* The most interesting variation concerns the girls' reactions to their mother's suggestion that they give their breakfast away. In "Merry's Monthly Chat," it is the narrator who thinks, "I wish we'd eaten it up," and it is Nan who nobly exclaims, "I'm so glad you came before we began." In *Little Women* it is Jo March who is given Nan's generous reaction: "I'm so glad you came before we began!"

Much of Alcott's fiction was not only based in fact but "simmered," as she liked to put it, often for years, in her mind. The characters of *Little Women* had been sketched before their full-length portraits were painted, its episodes tried out. The very poem "In the Garret," in which she epitomized the four sisters, Meg, Jo, Beth, and Amy, and which she used in the penultimate chapter of *Little Women,* had made a prior appearance in a most unlikely medium, the *Flag of Our Union,* where her pseudonymous thrillers had been published.[40]

And so, it is entirely credible that it took Louisa Alcott only four months to complete both parts of *Little Women.* It had not only been lived before; some of it had been written before.

THE *LITTLE WOMEN* TRILOGY

Little Women, Little Men, and *Jo's Boys* were of course not planned as a trilogy. Even Part II of *Little Women* was, when Part I was published, merely a hope, since Part I ends: "So grouped, the curtain falls upon Meg, Jo, Beth, and Amy. Whether it ever rises again, depends upon the reception given to the first act of the domestic drama called *Little Women.*" It was the reading public who made Part II of *Little Women* a reality and who eventually extended the novel into a trilogy.

That this happened, that *Little Women* became perhaps the most popular American fiction in its genre, a book that has never since its first appearance in 1868 gone out of print, provides clues to the nature of the domestic drama it narrates, to the taste of the reading public it captivated, and to the skills of its author.

The Alcotts wrote the story of the Marches, and in that transmutation the local became the universal. The great facts, as Alcott had learned from Emerson, are the near ones, and so in time a worldwide readership was able to identify with the New England family who lived in the pages of *Little Women.* As the minister Cyrus Bartol would comment: "She un-

40. In *Flag of Our Union* (18 March 1865).

latches the door to one house, and . . . all find it is their own house which they enter."[41] Who was Meg but Anna Alcott, simple, wholesome, loving; who was Beth but Lizzie, a cricket on the hearth; and Amy, simpering, parading her little elegancies, deciding upon a bottle of cologne for Marmee's birthday because it was cheap and she would have money left to buy pencils for herself — surely Amy was a photographic image of May Alcott. If Father was muted, his eccentricities glossed over, Marmee was glorified, the stout defender of human rights. But it was Jo, especially Jo — Jo the rebel, tall, thin, brown, with sharp eyes and long, thick hair, odd, blunt ways, and a fiery spirit — who captured the popular imagination and captures it still.

With such a cast of characters Alcott had only to unroll her own past for the Marches to appropriate. Whether real — as most were — or imaginary, all the incidents in the lives of the Marches seem *remembered* episodes: the role of *Pilgrim's Progress* in their childhood; the plays in the barn; the family post office; the *Pickwick Portfolio*; dramatizing the well-thumbed novels of Dickens; Amy's punishment for bringing pickled limes to school; Amy's fall through the ice; Meg's bedazzlement by the finery at Annie Moffat's "Vanity Fair"; Jo's selling her hair. Were they fact or fiction? It scarcely mattered, because they were all so real. As Alcott wrote in her journal on 26 August 1868: "Proof of whole book came. It reads better than I expected. Not a bit sensational, but simple and true, for we really lived most of it; and if it succeeds that will be the reason of it."[42]

By the end of October it was clear that there was "much interest in my little women, who seem to find friends by their truth to life."[43] Publisher Thomas Niles of Roberts Brothers requested a second volume for the spring. On 1 November Alcott noted in her journal: "Began the second part of 'Little Women.' I can do a chapter a day, and in a month I mean to be done. A little success is so inspiring that I now find my 'Marches' sober, nice people, and as I can launch into the future, my fancy has more play. Girls write to ask who the little women marry, as if that was the only end and aim of a woman's life. I *won't* marry Jo to Laurie to please any one."[44]

Part II of *Little Women* is set three years after Part I. Most of its major episodes were borrowings from the Alcott past: Meg's wedding and Beth's

41. Quoted in Stern, *Louisa May Alcott*, p. [xv].
42. *Journals,* p. 166 (26 August 1868).
43. Ibid., p. 167 (30 October 1868).
44. Ibid., p. 167 (1 November 1868).

death (the two events that had changed Louisa Alcott's life[45]); Amy's European voyage and Laurie's proposal; and, especially, Jo's sensational stories and their appearance in the *Blarneystone Banner*, "The Duke's Daughter" paying the butcher's bill, "A Phantom Hand" putting down a new carpet. Alcott carried out her intention of refusing to marry Jo to Laurie; instead she united her heroine with the authoritarian German professor Bhaer, who disapproved of her sensational stories and persuaded her to change her style. As Alcott explained to a correspondent: " 'Jo' should have remained a literary spinster but so many enthusiastic young ladies wrote to me clamorously demanding that she should marry Laurie, *or* somebody, that I didnt dare to refuse & out of perversity went & made a funny match for her. I expect vials of wrath to be poured out upon my head."[46] There is no doubt that Jo, being a genuine human being, is less a rebel at the end of *Little Women* than she is at the beginning. Nonetheless, she is *remembered* as a rebel, for that is the aura cast upon her by the author. As one critic has put it: "Jo is a unique creation: the one young woman in 19th-century fiction who maintains her individual independence, who gives up no part of her autonomy as payment for being born a woman — and who gets away with it. Jo is the tomboy dream come true, the dream of growing up into full humanity with all its potentialities instead of into limited femininity."[47]

"I am 'Jo,' " Alcott wrote years later to a reader in Holland.[48] Alcott had painted a self-portrait as well as a family portrait in *Little Women*, using what Jo March liked — "good strong words that mean something." Inversely, Jo March was Louisa Alcott, asking in *Little Women*: "What *can* there be in a simple little story . . . to make people praise it so?" to which her father replies: "There is truth in it, Jo, that's the secret; humor and pathos make it alive, and you have found your style at last."

During the next twenty years of her life Alcott would try to sustain the style she had found at last. Her motivation derived less perhaps from inclination than from sales figures — Roberts Brothers alone issued *Little Women* in 177 printings before the turn of the century.[49] From time to time the author was lured into other forms of literary experimentation, but

45. See ibid., p. 91 (November 1858): "The past year has brought us the first death and betrothal, — two events that change my life."

46. *Selected Letters*, p. 125 (LMA to Elizabeth Powell, 20 March [1869]).

47. Elizabeth Janeway, "Meg, Jo, Beth, Amy and Louisa," *New York Times Book Review* (29 September 1968), 24, 44, 46, reprinted in *Critical Essays on Louisa May Alcott*, pp. 97–98.

48. *Selected Letters*, p. 194 (LMA to Mrs. H. Koorders-Boeke, 7 August 1875).

49. See Joel Myerson and Daniel Shealy, "The Sales of Louisa May Alcott's Books," forthcoming in *Harvard Library Bulletin*.

nonetheless, for her insistent public, she added seven novels to what would come to be called the Little Women Series. Of these, one, *Little Men,* is a sequel to *Little Women,* and another, *Jo's Boys,* is a sequel to the sequel. Thus *Little Women* became a trilogy as well as a series.

Little Men was written quickly, as was *Little Women,* but most of it was written not in Boston or Concord but in Rome. In April 1870 Alcott embarked upon her second trip abroad, a journey that symbolized the changes in her life caused by the success of *Little Women.* Now, instead of serving as companion to an invalid, as she had on her first trip, she was a lion on grand tour. By November she arrived in Rome, where the tragic news of her brother-in-law's sudden death reached her. Determined to produce a book that would help support Anna's two boys, she plunged into work on her sequel to *Little Women.*[50]

Seated in her balcony on the Piazza Barberini, Alcott looked out at a Triton in a Roman square, but in her mind's eye she saw a group of boys in an atypical American school. At the end of *Little Women,* Jo had inherited an estate from Aunt March. That estate now became a school called Plumfield, where a dozen or so boys and a few girls learned less to study than to live. Modeled in part after her father's progressive Temple School in Boston, where the pioneer kindergartner Elizabeth Peabody and the great feminist Margaret Fuller had taught, Plumfield was portrayed as a decidedly "odd" institution never overburdened by rules or homework. Learning was viewed as a by-product of living; the rights of children were respected. "Latin, Greek, and mathematics were all very well, but . . . self-knowledge, self-help, and self-control were more important." Each boy at Plumfield was endowed with some fault awaiting help: Ned his bragging, Nat his weakness, Stuffy his appetite, Dan his wildness. Their stories gently rambled along in the episodic style the author had mastered.

Plumfield of course was benevolently run by the wise Professor Bhaer and the former Jo March. She was "Aunt Jo" now, "a genial, comfortable kind of person" with "a merry sort of face that never seemed to have forgotten . . . childish ways." If her own wildness had receded, Aunt Jo could see it reassert itself in her "wild boy" Dan, whose full story would not be told until the sequel to the sequel was written.

In May 1871 Alcott, on her way home, stopped in London, where *Little Men* was published just in advance of its American appearance. When the author returned to Boston she was greeted by her father and Thomas Niles, who "came to meet me with a great red placard of 'Little Men'

50. For a more detailed discussion of *Little Men,* see Louisa May Alcott, *Little Men* (New York: New American Library, 1986), pp. 330–346.

pinned up in the carriage."[51] The novel helped pay for "the furnace and all the bills"[52] and was critically well received. Despite its occasional sugary pietism, *Little Men* brought a fresh approach and an innovative philosophy to the subject of pedagogy. More important, it returned Jo March to the spotlight, now in the role of matriarch to a group of very natural boys. For this reason modern critics have discovered in *Little Men* not only an arresting educational ideology, but a provocative feminist slant, seeing the tomboy Jo March transmuted into a kind of "cosmic mother."[53] The ritual sacrifice in the chapter "Pranks and Plays" has even been compared with the incident of "The Doll-Burners" in D. H. Lawrence's *Sons and Lovers*.[54] Like *Little Women, Little Men* titillates the minds of scholars as it "touches the universal heart."[55] It is no *Little Women,* no reenactment; yet the book is rich because the life behind the book was rich.

Unlike its two predecessors, *Jo's Boys* was years in the writing. Although its cast of characters remained more or less steadfast, the author of the third book in the *Little Women* trilogy was by no means the same as the author of the first. By 1882, when she was ready to take up the thread she had dropped in Rome more than ten years before, Alcott had suffered the death of her mother and the more tragic death of May. Neither woman would be used as a pivotal character in *Jo's Boys.* The arrival of May's daughter, Lulu Nieriker, in September 1880 had complicated Alcott's life. In addition, the passage of time and the decline of her health had tempered the enthusiasm even of a compulsive writer. These were reasons enough for Alcott to put off the writing of *Jo's Boys.* But an even more basic reason contributed to the postponement: innate reluctance. By bringing the March saga to an end, the author was aware that she would also ring down the curtain on the Alcotts.[56]

It was not until October 1882 that Alcott went to Boston's Bellevue Hotel and began *Jo's Boys.* On the twenty-fourth of the month a telegram informed her that her father had had a paralytic stroke. "Home at once &

51. *Journals,* p. 178 (June 1871).

52. Ibid., p. 182 (January 1872).

53. See, for example, Nina Auerbach, *Communities of Women: An Idea in Fiction* (Cambridge: Harvard University Press, 1978), pp. 55–64, 68–73, 199–201, reprinted in *Critical Essays on Louisa May Alcott,* pp. 129–140.

54. Grover Smith, "The Doll-Burners: D. H. Lawrence and Louisa Alcott," *Modern Language Quarterly* (March 1958), 28–32, reprinted in *Critical Essays on Louisa May Alcott,* pp. 160–165.

55. Cheney, p. 190.

56. For a more detailed discussion of *Jo's Boys,* see Louisa May Alcott, *Jo's Boys* (New York: New American Library, 1987), pp. 279–296.

found him stricken down."[57] Bronson Alcott would linger another six years, adding not only to his daughter's anxious cares but to her writer's block. After a few false starts she wrote to the editor of *St. Nicholas,* Mary Mapes Dodge: "About 'Jo's Boys,' I can only say that it is not written, & I see no prospect of its being done for some time. A few chapters were started, but I made my boys *too old* so must begin anew."[58] Prompted frequently by her publisher Thomas Niles, who assured her that "that book . . . is needed to keep up the enthusiasm & renew the demand for 'Little Men' & 'Little Women,' "[59] Alcott "began again on 'Jo's Boys.' . . . Wrote two hours for three days, then had a violent attack of vertigo & was ill for a week."[60] The pattern repeated itself until finally, in March 1886, her "head worked like a steam engine & would not stop. Planned 'Jo's Boys' to the end & longed to get up & write it. Told Dr W[esselhoeft]. that he had better let me get the ideas *out* then I could rest. He very wisely agreed. . . . So I began as soon as able, & . . . had some pleasant hours when I forgot my body & lived in my mind."[61]

She lived too in the past, drawing threads from *Little Women* and *Little Men* to weave into the new narrative. In July 1886, nearly four years after she had begun, she wrote in her journal: "Finish 'Jo's Boys' & take it to T. N[iles]. . . . Two new chapters were needed, so I wrote them, & gladly corked my inkstand."[62] As she informed her publisher, "The book is not a child's book, as the lads are nearly all over twenty."[63] The Plumfield of *Little Men* had become Laurence College, donated by the Laurie of *Little Women,* now Amy's philanthropic husband. It was a coeducational school that insisted upon egalitarianism and attracted not only many of Jo's boys but "eager girls from the West, the awkward freedman or woman from the South, or the wellborn student whose poverty made this college a possibility when other doors were barred." As in the Plumfield of *Little Men,* academic studies seldom interfered with the basic business at hand, the pursuit of "health and real wisdom." Private theatricals, Dickensian allusions, and exercise all had their place at Laurence College, a domain

57. *Journals,* p. 235 (October 1882).

58. LMA to Mary Mapes Dodge [Fall 1883], quoted in Madeleine B. Stern's Afterword to Alcott, *Jo's Boys,* p. 284; see also Daniel Shealy, "The Author-Publisher Relationships of Louisa May Alcott" (Ph.D. diss., University of South Carolina, 1985).

59. Thomas Niles to LMA, 25 August 1883, quoted in Stern's Afterword to Alcott, *Jo's Boys,* p. 284; see also Shealy, "The Author-Publisher Relationships of Louisa May Alcott."

60. *Journals,* p. 245 (December 1884).

61. Ibid., pp. 272–273 (27 March 1886).

62. Ibid., p. 277 (July 1886).

63. *Selected Letters,* p. 298 (LMA to Thomas Niles, [June?] 1886).

presided over by Professor Bhaer, who still combined lofty ethical standards with German sentimentality.

An opening chapter encapsulating the history of the original Plumfield students sets the stage for what follows after the passage of ten years, and, as in *Little Men,* episodes interrelated but complete in themselves are skillfully recounted: "Emil's Thanksgiving," "Dan's Christmas," "Nat's New Year," "Demi Settles," "Plays at Plumfield." The girls play significant roles in the story of *Jo's Boys* — Josie and her theatrical ambitions, Daisy and her homing instincts, Nan and her medical bent. Indeed, in the end, Nan, the physician who chooses to remain single, becomes Alcott's feminist torchbearer.

Despite *Jo's Boys*'s cheerful platitudes and occasional condescensions, the simple domestic scenes of the novel still have appeal. It is largely through the character of Jo March that those scenes cohere and have verisimilitude. The matronly Mrs. Bhaer champions work and plain fare, the old-fashioned virtues, self-knowledge and self-control, but although she has become something of a reforming preacher, there is much of Jo March left in her. She still "carelessly" rumples "up her hair"; she still "gets into a vortex" of creative inspiration; and, famous though she has become, she still identifies with her boys.

Especially she identifies with Daniel Kean, the "wild boy" of *Little Men,* whose role in the sequel is highly significant. Dan has farmed sheep in Australia and mined in California, has shot a buffalo and rides a horse given him by Black Hawk. The Montana Indians, whom he looks upon as his brothers, call him "Dan Fire Cloud." Bold and adventurous, he is still a wanderer, still a firebrand. Dan, perhaps like his creator, becomes the victim of his own hubris. In the end he dies a hero's death defending his chosen people, the Indians. The spirit of the "wild boy" Dan brings us almost full circle back to the spirit of Jo March, the independent rebel of *Little Women.*

But Alcott was ending her trilogy, not beginning it. "It is a strong temptation to the weary historian," she wrote in her final chapter,

> to close the present tale with an earthquake which should engulf Plumfield and its environs so deeply in the bowels of the earth that no youthful Schliemann could ever find a vestige of it. But as that somewhat melodramatic conclusion might shock my gentle readers, I will refrain. . . . And . . . having endeavored to suit every one by many weddings, few deaths, and as much prosperity as the eternal fitness of things will permit, let the music stop, the lights die out, and the curtain fall forever on the March family.

THE YOUTH'S COMPANION: AMERICA'S BEST-LOVED AUTHOR OF JUVENILES

When she raised the curtain on the Marches, Alcott had been an experimenter whose pen might produce a sensational narrative or a realistic war sketch, a flowery fable or a metaphysical story about marriage. By the time she rang the curtain down she had been channeled into the wholesome, domestic narrative for young readers and was acclaimed as author not only of the *Little Women* trilogy and series, but of a host of stories and story collections designed for childhood and youth. A. M. Barnard and Tribulation Periwinkle had been more or less effaced, and in their place had emerged a "Youth's Companion" hailed as America's best-loved author of juvenile literature.

She did not always take kindly to the role, though she relished its rewards. As she wrote to a correspondent in 1878: "Though I do not enjoy writing 'moral tales' for the young, I do it because it pays well."[64] Between 1872, when the first volume of *Aunt Jo's Scrap-Bag* was published, and the year of her death, 1888, when *A Garland for Girls* appeared, Alcott wrote dozens of short stories, most of which are imbued with ethical and moral lessons. She was writing for the young at a time when the expression of sentiment was unabashed, when a prolonged deathbed scene was enthusiastically received and, although sex was hidden, love was enshrined.[65] And so Alcott wove into her tales for the young cheerful platitudes on the eternal verities. She served her age the fare it expected, and she served it with professional competence.

In her guise as youth's companion, however, she did far more. As a result, her narratives for young people often appeal to an adult readership as well. The line between morality and reform is often hard to draw, and Alcott slipped frequently from one to the other. Always she delved into her own past to create fictions for her demanding audience. The clamor for her stories was so great — she published twelve collections of them between 1872 and her death — that she frequently either reprinted her narratives from periodicals or revamped them from previously published sketches. Alcott liked to be paid twice for the same work.

64. Ibid., p. 232 (LMA to Miss Churchill, 25 December [1878?]).

65. In *Jack and Jill* (Boston: Little, Brown, 1928), pp. 267–268, Alcott wrote: "It is often said that there should be no death or grief in children's stories. It is not wise to dwell on the dark and sad side of these things; but they have also a bright and lovely side, and since even the youngest, dearest, and most guarded child cannot escape some knowledge of the great mystery, is it not well to teach them in simple, cheerful ways that affection sweetens sorrow, and a lovely life can make death beautiful?"

Emerson said of her, "She is a natural source of stories. . . . She is and is to be, the poet of children. She knows their angels."[66] The first volume of *Aunt Jo's Scrap-Bag* appeared over the Roberts Brothers imprint in 1872; the sixth and last would appear ten years later. In each a few new tales were included along with reprints. "Our lives are patchwork," as Aunt Pen says in "Patty's Patchwork" (from the first volume of the series), and Alcott's scrap bags of stories pieced together those patches of life that she chose to delineate for her youthful readers. In some of them (as in "A Jolly Fourth") she was content simply to evoke a time and a place, writing her own fictional notes on life in nineteenth-century New England. In others (as in "My Girls") she waved the banner of feminism. Indeed, "My Girls," outlining the careers of specific young women in medicine, art, philanthropy, the theater, law, and education, is comparable to Alcott's earlier essay "Happy Women,"[67] about women in the professions.

Many of Aunt Jo's narratives were mined from her own life. The artist in "My Girls" is clearly based upon her sister May, and the young lads in "My Boys" are the "kindred souls" for whom the author had formed warm attachments: Sergeant Bain, whom she had nursed during the Civil War; Alf Whitman, the "yellow-haired laddie" with whom she had acted Dickensian roles; and Ladislas Wisniewski, whom she had met in 1865 when she traveled abroad as companion to an invalid and who, with Alf, served as a model for Laurie in *Little Women*.

Alcott followed her *Scrap-Bags* with other collections designed for young readers, among them *Spinning-Wheel Stories,* in which she assembled a series of tales she had contributed to *St. Nicholas,* old-time narratives based upon her country's history or her own. The moral tucked into each did not unduly interfere with fiction that reanimated historical America, even Bronson Alcott's early days, which she described in "Eli's Education."

Having told her tales for so many children all over the world, Aunt Jo found it natural, with the arrival of May's daughter, Lulu Nieriker, to tell special stories for her. Alcott's sister May had pursued her art studies in Europe, where she had met a young Swiss, Ernest Nieriker; they married in March 1878. On 29 December 1879, May died in childbirth, bequeathing her daughter to Louisa. During the child's early years Alcott played the role not only of mother but of spinner of tales. Those tales were written out, and the tiny books were tied up in little birchbark covers for the delight of the child. They were also bound in more durable style by

---

66. Quoted in Stern, *Louisa May Alcott,* p. [xv].
67. Louisa May Alcott, "Happy Women," *New York Ledger* (11 April 1868).

Roberts Brothers. As Alcott wrote to her publisher in July 1885: "I want to know if it is too late to do it and if it is worth doing; namely, to collect some of the little tales I tell Lulu . . . and call it 'Lulu's Library'? I have several tiny books written down for L.; and as I can do no great work, it occurred to me that I might venture to copy these if it would do for a Christmas book for the younger set."[68] Eventually three volumes of *Lulu's Library* were published, collections of stories spurring children to give rather than to take (as in "A Christmas Dream, and How It Came True"), or painting (in "Sophie's Secret") the benevolent character of Lulu's young aunt Sophie Nieriker.

In the final anthology prepared before her death, Alcott returned full circle to her past. In December 1886, ill and obviously in decline, she moved to Dr. Rhoda Lawrence's nursing home in Roxbury, Massachusetts. The following May she wrote to the editor of *St. Nicholas* describing her plan for *A Garland for Girls:* "The idea is some eight or ten tales for girls, with flowery names as a sort of emblem of the moral or meaning of the stories."[69] Under the emblem of "Pansies" that are for thoughts, she produced one of the most interesting of those tales, for it records her attitude toward books — books as solace, books as spurs to romance, taste in books as an index to character. The flowery names in this last book were suggested by the flowers sent to her by her friends — scarlet poppies or green wheat, mayflowers or water lilies. Now, at the end of her life, she turned back to her starting point, for what was *A Garland for Girls* but another collection of *Flower Fables*? In her end was also her beginning.

FICTION AND REFORM

Most of Alcott's writings, sentimental or sensational, realistic or domestic, designed for adults or for children, reflect the reforms that fermented in nineteenth-century New England. She was part of an age that loved the "newness," that seeded one crusade after another: antislavery and woman's rights, cold baths and Graham bread, Bloomer dress and communal societies. Her family passed on to her a legacy of iconoclasm. The blood of two generations of abolitionists flowed through her veins. Plain living and high thinking sustained the Alcotts through their years of poverty and affluence, and these ideals punctuate the oeuvre of Louisa Alcott. As her alter ego Jo March asserts in *Little Women,* replying to Amy's comment "I don't like reformers": "I do like them, and I shall be one if I can."

Antislavery and feminism especially were part of the Alcott canon. In

68. *Selected Letters,* p. 290 (LMA to Thomas Niles, 13 July 1885).
69. Ibid., p. 310 (LMA to Mary Mapes Dodge, 4 May [1887]).

1881 Louisa wrote to Thomas Niles, "I can remember when Anti slavery was in just the same state that Suffrage is now, and take more pride in the very small help we Alcotts could give than in all the books I ever wrote or ever shall write."[70] But it was in her books that she gave the most lasting help to those causes. In her Civil War sketches and stories she endorsed abolition; in most of her narratives, as early as "The Lady and the Woman," she expressed her feminist convictions, implicitly in some, including *Little Women,* more explicitly in others, including *Work.*

In Alcott's eyes, oppression was wrong; brotherhood and sisterhood were right. The wrongs of blacks and of women were outgrowths of a false society, and it was against that false society that she inveighed, notably in her books for young people. Basically, pervading all her reform efforts, including her position on racial and sexual egalitarianism, was her deep-seated revulsion at the shams of nineteenth-century American society. She championed the genuine against the pretentious, the honest against the false, simplicity against folderol. This stand dictated her attitude toward education and society, food and dress, health and sex. It led her sometimes to write the "moral pap" she disdained, for, if she deemed it necessary to her purpose, she did not hesitate to insert platitudinous pills into her narratives. On the other hand, it also led her to the portraiture of the three-dimensional Old-Fashioned Girl.

In *An Old-Fashioned Girl,* the heroine, Polly, carries a standard emblazoned with common sense and simplicity, and she affords a sharp contrast to her fashionable cousin Fanny. Polly exposes the inanities of elegant dress (the hair piled on top of the head with a fringe or fuzz around the forehead), the uselessness of fashionable schools where "young ladies were so busy with their French, German, and Italian, that there was no time for good English." Especially she exposes the triviality of flirtation and "playing at love," for which she would substitute sexual egalitarianism or independent spinsterhood. Indeed, Alcott uses Polly as a mouthpiece for one of her favorite concepts, that of a "sisterhood" of independent girls, each with a "purpose to execute, a talent to develop, an ambition to achieve."[71]

Five years after *An Old-Fashioned Girl* had pointed its moral, the author published a variation on her theme in *Eight Cousins.* Now Polly reappears as Rose, the delightful object of Uncle Alec's experiment in common sense. Like Polly, Rose champions dress reform, preferring a "freedom suit" to "whalebones" and "metal gate-posts," and milk, oatmeal, and brown

---

70. Ibid., p. 253 (LMA to Thomas Niles, 19 February 1881).

71. Alcott's old-fashioned girl, Polly, had an earlier appearance as Debby in "Debby's Début," *Atlantic Monthly* (August 1863). Debby levels her shots against a tight-laced, dyspeptic, and double-standard age.

bread to "hot bread and fried stuff." She burgeons under the influence of Uncle Alec's three great remedies: sun, fresh air, and cold water.

By the mid-1870s Alcott's popularity was such that three publishers engaged in a bidding war for rights to *Eight Cousins*. A sequel was in order in which, as she wrote to a Dutch admirer, "the cousins are adults," adding: "Young girls in America do not get a good education in various respects, even though much is taught to them. They know nothing of health care, or of housekeeping, and are presented into society too early. My story is intended to encourage a better plan of child-rearing, and my heroine shows that such a plan is feasible."[72]

The heroine of *Rose in Bloom* is the result of that "better plan." She does not lose her independence when she falls in love with Mac, who believes that "it is very unreasonable in us to ask women to be saints, and then expect them to feel honored when we offer them our damaged hearts." Rose's heroes are "Garrison fighting for his chosen people; Howe restoring lost senses to the deaf, the dumb, and blind; Sumner unbribable, when other men were bought and sold." She herself becomes a philanthropist working to establish comfortable homes for poor but respectable women. When *Rose in Bloom* appeared, in 1876, Alcott was ahead of her time in her general attitude toward independent women and egalitarian marriage. Indeed, the novel evoked a shocked comment from the *Nation*: "Mac's declaration and subsequent courtship take us to the utmost verge of fiction for minors."[73]

In the last volume of the *Little Women* trilogy Alcott espoused not only feminism and educational reform but another cause that touched her closely — the rights of authors. In the chapter "Jo's Last Scrape" she vented her animosity at the tribe of autograph fiends and lion hunters who had disturbed her privacy since the publication of *Little Women*. In one day Mrs. Jo is inundated with twelve requests for autographs along with a poetic effusion beginning, "Oh, were I a heliotrope, / I would play poet, / And blow a breeze of fragrance / To you; and none should know it." A group of admirers from Oshkosh demands a view of the author; a young ladies' seminary camps on her lawn; an intruder requests a pair of her stockings to sew into a rug being made from a vest of Emerson's, a pair of trousers from Oliver Wendell Holmes, and a dress of Harriet Beecher Stowe's. Despite her tongue-in-cheek style, Alcott was serious. In 1885 she had written to a correspondent: "If you can teach your five hundred pupils to love books but to let authors rest in peace, you will give them a useful

72. *Selected Letters*, p. 194 (LMA to Mrs. H. Koorders-Boeke, 7 August 1875).
73. *Nation* (21 December 1876), 373, reprinted in *Critical Essays on Louisa May Alcott*, p. 170.

lesson and earn the gratitude of the long suffering craft, whose lives are made a burden to them by the modern lion hunter and autograph fiend."[74] In *Jo's Boys* she reiterated that plea: "There ought to be a law to protect unfortunate authors. . . . To me it is a more vital subject than international copyright; for time is money, peace is health, and I lose both with no return but less respect for my fellow-creatures and a wild desire to fly into the wilderness." When critics objected to "Jo's Last Scrape," Alcott commented: "If it is not good taste to put this part of Jo's life in print all the rest is a mistake also, for the best liked episodes are the real ones."[75]

Whether Alcott's reform preachments are or are not the best-liked episodes of her narratives, they open a window upon the world that generated them. In addition, they are the result of her background and her upbringing, and they reflect her beliefs and her convictions. Like so much in Alcott's fiction, they stem from the life she lived. Her autobiography pervades her fiction.

FICTION AND AUTOBIOGRAPHY

Alcott's novels and short stories made extensive use of her own experiences or observations. Tracing the factual sources of her fiction provides excitement for the literary detective, and, more important, throws light upon the manner in which fact was transformed into fiction. Sources from life can be found embedded even in Alcott's most unrealistic romances. Her wildly sensational thrillers hark back to episodes in her life — her addiction to the stage, her briefly contemplated suicide, the opiates prescribed for her after her illness during the Civil War. In almost every one of her literary phases the searcher after connections can find them in her life.

Probably it was in *Little Women* that Alcott embodied most of her life, even while she glossed over its hardships and poverty. There she captured her relations with May in Jo's ambivalence toward Amy ("Your wishes are always granted — mine never"); there she delineated a family that, "rich or poor," would "keep together and be happy in one another"; and there she accurately recounted in Jo's career her own literary struggles.

Alcott's first published story, "The Rival Painters," is mentioned in *Little Women,* although it is assigned not to the Boston *Olive Branch* but to a fictitious *Spread Eagle.* What better description of *Flower Fables* can be found than the one in the chapter "Jo Meets Apollyon": "Jo's book was the pride of her heart, and was regarded by her family as a literary sprout of great promise. It was only half a dozen little fairy tales, but Jo had

74. *Selected Letters,* p. 296 (LMA to Viola Price, 18 December 1885).
75. Ibid., p. 300 (LMA to Thomas Niles, 3 October [1886]).

worked over them patiently, putting her whole heart into her work, hoping to make something good enough to print." The story of the Alcott sensational thrillers is here in *Little Women,* along with the "pictorial sheet" where they appeared, emblazoned with "melodramatic illustration[s]." Even the struggle over *Moods* is recalled: "Having copied her novel for the fourth time, read it to all her confidential friends, and submitted it with fear and trembling to three publishers, she at last disposed of it, on condition that she would cut it down one third, and omit all the parts which she particularly admired." The contradictory criticism evoked by Alcott's first novel is evoked by Jo's: "The parts that were taken straight out of real life are denounced as impossible and absurd, and the scenes that I made up out of my own silly head are pronounced 'charmingly natural.' "

Despite the undoubted prevalence of autobiographical detail in the Alcott oeuvre, there is a distinct danger in categorically interpreting her life from her work. To conclude, as one biographer has done — principally on the basis of the sensation stories — that Alcott was a "depressed and sullen . . . withdrawn, hostile introvert" who led a "miserable and lonely girlhood" and whose "devils of guilt" vied with her "deep fear of men" is not only assumption but presumption.[76] Alcott's character and life can be reconstructed far more accurately from letters and journals than from her fiction, where they have been reshaped and often altered for literary purposes.

Three patently autobiographical stories reinforce this conclusion. "Transcendental Wild Oats" was published in the *Independent* on 18 December 1873; its story had been lived thirty years before. In June 1843 Bronson Alcott wrote to his brother from Fruitlands: "This dell is the canvas on which I will paint . . . a worthy picture for mankind."[77] The "dell" was located on Prospect Hill in Harvard, the setting for a communal experiment in Utopian living. For six months, from June 1843 to January 1844, the Alcott family remained there with the English reformer Charles Lane and other seekers after a new Eden. The experiment, which involved abjuration of cotton (a product of slavery) and of wool (the property of the sheep), as well as of sugar, molasses, flesh, and the entire dairy kingdom, was doomed to failure. The harsh life of self-denial was combined with general ignorance of farming. The sojourn in Fruitlands ended only after Lane had aroused much dissension, the Alcotts had considered separating as a family, and Bronson had sought death through starvation.

76. See Martha Saxton, *Louisa May: A Modern Biography of Louisa May Alcott* (Boston: Houghton Mifflin, 1977), pp. 7, 9, 10, and passim.

77. Bronson Alcott to Junius S. Alcott, 18 June 1843, in *The Letters of A. Bronson Alcott,* ed. Richard L. Herrnstadt (Ames: Iowa State University Press, 1969), pp. 102–103.

Louisa Alcott, who was ten years old at the time, was aware of much that was tragic in the Fruitlands experience. Yet, years later, when she came to write her autobiographical account of it, she produced a mildly satirical narrative, largely from the point of view of her mother, and, after she had glossed it over with humor, she turned it into a morality at the end. In "Transcendental Wild Oats" — even the title is tongue-in-cheek — Charles Lane appears as Timon Lion, who prefers "being" to "doing"; Bronson Alcott is given the role of Abel Lamb, a philosopher who "revelled in the Newness"; and Abby Alcott is Sister Hope, "unconverted but faithful to the end." Other members of the "Consociate Society" are amusingly touched off, and the regime of life is sketched — rising at dawn, bathing, consuming fruit and unleavened bread, farming without manure but with a yoke of oxen, one of which turns out to be a cow. Ann Page, who taught the Alcott girls at Fruitlands, is disguised as Jane Gage, "a stout lady of mature years" who "wrote verses copiously" and departed the scene after she had been unable to resist the temptation of eating fish.

Tragedy follows tragicomedy for the "forsaken little family." Abel Lamb, despairing and desolate, "turned his face to the wall, and waited . . . for death." Thanks to his wife's encouragement, he is able to conquer his hopelessness, and, we are told, "the love that outlives all else refused to die."

In "Transcendental Wild Oats" Timon Lion remarks: "Truth lies at the bottom of a well." Without doubt there is some truth in Alcott's narrative, but far from all the truth. Surely there is more truth in the journal entry she wrote at Fruitlands on 10 December 1843: "I did my lessons, and walked in the afternoon. Father read to us in dear Pilgrim's Progress. Mr. L[ane]. was in Boston, and we were glad. In the eve father and mother and Anna and I had a long talk. I was very unhappy, and we all cried. Anna and I cried in bed, and I prayed God to keep us all together."[78]

"Transcendental Wild Oats" turns a disturbing, tragic experience into a humorous satire that ends in uplifting thought. As usual, Alcott shaped her source to her purpose. She wrote not autobiography but autobiographical fiction.

The same holds true for another story based upon Alcott's early life, an experience equally devastating. She was nineteen when it took place, and she faced it alone. In the winter of 1851 the Alcotts had moved to 50 High Street, Boston, where Abby, working as city missionary among the poor, opened an employment office, or, as Bronson described it in a letter

---

78. *Journals*, p. 47 (10 December 1843).

to his mother, "a confusing business below."[79] When the Honorable James Richardson of Dedham appeared there in search of a companion for his sister, Louisa decided to take the position herself. Richardson was a lawyer, an orator, and the president of a local fire insurance company. Louisa needed work desperately. After seven harrowing weeks in domestic service she was given four dollars in payment. She described the experience tersely in her journal: "I go to Dedham as a servant & try it for a month, but get starved & frozen & give it up. $4,oo."[80]

This was the episode that, more than twenty years later, she converted into a narrative for the *Independent* entitled "How I Went Out to Service." As in "Transcendental Wild Oats," the author's touch is light, almost — but not quite — concealing the fury that boils beneath. In the fictional version Louisa takes the position not out of economic need but because she is searching for some "right task," and if she does not find it, her "bottled energies" will explode. Richardson, here named the Reverend Josephus or Mr. R., promises light labor in a stately mansion, although the pay is never stipulated. Approaching that "mansion," the future author of sensational romances "felt as if about to enter one of those delightfully dangerous houses we read of in novels." Her hopes are quickly shattered. She is expected to perform endless services for Josephus, including attendance in his study, where he reads "philosophic, metaphysical, and sentimental rubbish" to her. When she issues an ultimatum, announcing that she has come to work for his sister, not for him, all the housework devolves upon her, including digging paths through the snow, splitting the kindling, and sifting the ashes. She finally balks at the demand that she black Josephus's boots — "humiliating work for a woman." After a precipitate departure she opens the purse pressed into her hand by Mr. R.'s timid sister: "I have had a good many bitter minutes in my life; but one of the bitterest came to me as I stood there in the windy road, with the sixpenny pocket-book open before me, and looked from my poor chapped, grimy, chill-blained hands to the paltry sum that was considered reward enough for all the hard and humble labor they had done."

This is not quite the same as "I go to Dedham as a servant . . . but get starved & frozen & give it up. $4,oo," but it is effective and touching. Alcott was conscious of how she had converted the episode into fiction,

79. Bronson Alcott to Mrs. Anna Alcott, 19 October 1851, in *The Letters of A. Bronson Alcott,* p. 162.

80. *Journals,* p. 65 ("Notes and Memoranda" 1851). For details of the episode, see Louisa May Alcott, *Behind a Mask: The Unknown Thrillers of Louisa May Alcott,* ed. Madeleine B. Stern (New York: William Morrow, 1975), pp. ix–xi. For another treatment of the subject by Alcott, see the chapter "Servant" in *Work.*

for she described it as a "serio-comico experience," which is precisely what she had made it for readers of the *Independent*. Just as she had done in "Transcendental Wild Oats," she could not resist tagging it with an uplifting moral: "More than once . . . I have been grateful for that serio-comico experience," she wrote, "since it has taught me many lessons. One of the most useful of these has been the power of successfully making a companion, not a servant, of those whose aid I need, and helping to gild their honest wages with the sympathy and justice which can sweeten the humblest and lighten the hardest task." The fiction writer's record of the often painful past was highly selective.

It was even more selective in "Recollections of My Childhood," a brief autobiographical reminiscence written for the *Youth's Companion* but not published until after the author's death. This last narrative in the Alcott anthology brings us back to her beginnings, or rather to what she chose to remember of her beginnings.

Playing with books in her father's "study" and scribbling on blank pages are seen, at the end of her life, as portents and influences, "since books have been my greatest comfort . . . and scribbling a very profitable amusement." Similarly, Alcott remembers her fall into the Frog Pond and her rescue by a black boy as the beginning of her friendship with all blacks.[81] A luster is cast upon the happy Concord days, the plays in the barn, the "sentimental period" that began at fifteen with readings in Goethe and hero worship of Emerson. The "trials of life" when the family moved to Boston are glossed over. Alcott simply remarks that "money is never plentiful in a philosopher's house," a highly bowdlerized version of the statement in her 1851 journal: "Poor as rats & apparently quite forgotten by every one but the Lord."[82]

In her autobiographical fiction Alcott is perhaps more romantic than realistic. Truth is here, but it appears by innuendo, and her omissions are eloquent. Even in 1888, however, she remembered the persona of her childhood: "I always thought I must have been a deer or a horse in some former state, because it was such a joy to run." In her 1843 journal she had put it: "I ran in the wind and played be a horse."[83]

Little Louy Alcott turned into Flora Fairfield, Tribulation Periwinkle, A. M. Barnard, and *the* Miss Alcott. She also turned into the Sylvia of *Moods,* the Christie of *Work,* and of course the Jo March of *Little Women.* Between "The Rival Painters" and "Recollections of My Childhood" she

81. This incident is also related in "Poppy's Pranks," in *Aunt Jo's Scrap-Bag: An Old-Fashioned Thanksgiving.*

82. *Journals,* p. 65 ("Notes and Memoranda" 1851).

83. Ibid., p. 45 (14 September 1843).

created a long parade of heroines — and heroes too — who played their roles in an astounding variety of genres. She moved easily from the romantic to the realistic, from the sensational to the domestic, using as sources the life around her and within her. All was grist for her indefatigable mill, from her family and friends to the events and reforms of her day, and all this material is converted into narratives that range from the wildly imaginative to the moral and homiletic, from the fanciful to the simple and true.

Building "Castles in the Air," Jo March voices her dreams in *Little Women*: "I'd have a stable full of Arabian steeds, rooms piled with books, and I'd write out of a magic inkstand." Out of her own magic inkstand Louisa May Alcott wrote the multifaceted fiction that still quickens the mind and touches the heart.

LOUISA MAY ALCOTT

Selected Fiction

Early Experiments in Romance

The Rival Painters

A Tale of Rome

Olive Branch, 8 May 1852. Published anonymously

FAREWELL, MY SON, go trustingly forth, carve thine own fortunes by untiring efforts, and it will be doubly enriched by the memory of those years of patient toil that gained so much happiness for thee. The world is bright and beautiful to a young heart, but its light and loveliness pass away. Set not, therefore, too great value upon its riches. Walk calmly in the quiet path that leads to thy duty, envying none, loving all, and a purer and more lasting joy will be thine, than the praise and homage a flattering world can give thee. Fear nothing but sin and temptation; follow only the dictates of thine own innocent heart. Be faithful to thy friends, forgiving to thine enemies, true to thyself, and earnest in thy love to God, and with a mother's blessing on thy head, fare thee well."

And with nothing but a deep love for his beautiful art, and a heart filled with pure and lovely feelings, Guido, a young Florentine painter, left his quiet home for the great city of Rome where all his hopes and desires were centered. There in the studio of some great master, he would seek honor and wealth for himself, and a luxurious home for his mother, who with all a woman's patient constancy, had toiled to gain enough to place her son where his exalted genius might be guided and taught, till he could gain all that she so fondly hoped; and when the time came, freely gave up all that made life pleasant to her — cheerfully bade farewell to her noble son, and in her lonely room toiled on that he might lack nothing to cheer and help him on his way. Nor was all the mother's self-sacrificing love unappreciated or unfelt; it kept her son from temptation, and cheered him on to greater efforts, that he might repay with unfailing care and tenderness, the sacrifice so nobly made. Nothing could stay or turn him aside, while his mother's words lingered in his ear. No harm could fall on a head made sacred by her blessing, and no evil enter a heart filled with such holy love.

And so 'mid all the allurements of a luxurious city he passed unharmed, and labored steadily on till he won his way among the first of the highborn young artists, who crowded the studios of the great masters, and as time went on, honor and wealth seemed waiting for him, but not happiness.

The kind old painter, with whom he had spent so many happy years, had a fair young daughter whom he had loved long and silently, happy that he could be near one so good and beautiful. He never thought of asking more till a fellow-student, possessed of wealth and rank, comely in person, and courtly in manner, sought her hand, and then only, when he feared it was too late, did he gain courage to plead his love so well and earnestly that the old painter could not refuse to leave the choice to his daughter.

"Tell me truly, Madeline," he said, "and he you love shall be thine, with my blessing. But pause and consider; young Ferdinand hath wealth, rank, a splendid home, and a heart full of love for thee; Guido has nothing — nay blush not so proudly, my child! I mean no *earthly* riches; he hath a noble soul and a rare talent for painting, but in this cold world these are uncared for, where gold and honors are prized more highly. Judge for yourself, Madeline, which will bring thee most happiness, the pomp and show of a countess, or an humble painter's home, subject to all the care and sorrow poverty brings. Wealth or love — few maidens would pause; and yet 'tis a hard choice — both so noble and comely; I wonder not at your indecision."

The image of the pale young painter came oftenest to the girl's heart, all his silent acts of kindness, his humble, self-denying life, and most of all his deep and earnest love for herself — and the gay gallant Count, was forgotten. A flower from Guido was more highly prized than all the costly gifts her titled suitor laid at her feet; but she knew her father longed to see her the wife of some high-born lord; his own life had been darkened by hours of poverty and sorrow, and he fondly hoped to spare her that pain which he had borne unmurmuringly. So with a daughter's self-denying love, she answered —

"Father, as a painter's daughter, my life has been one of perfect happiness; why not as a wife? The count loves the beautiful art only as a means of gaining honor, and even *that* love will soon pass away, and some trifling thing succeed it. Guido is poor, and his art is his all. I know the deep, earnest love he bears for all that is great and good; beauty and purity he worships with a true painter's steadfastness, and while he humbly toils for bread, the noble genius which lies hidden now, will awake, and hallowed by such a purpose, will bring him honor, and wealth. But I am young, father, and the world is new to me; judge as your own wise love counsels, and by that judgment will I abide."

"So let it be, Madeline! and if I do not greatly err, our choice will be the same," he replied, as he passed out and left a loving heart behind, struggling with the gentle memories that thronged so tenderly about it. But with a woman's strength, all thoughts of love were banished, and she waited to fulfil her duty, hard though it might be.

"Seniors," said the old painter, when he joined the rivals, who together sought to learn their fate, "my daughter leaves the choice to me, and as a father, I would ask what you would give up to win her love? Maidens are fond and foolish things, and would be hardly won; my lord, how highly do *you* prize the love of a simple girl?"

"More than life, liberty, wealth or honor," replied the Count, with a glance at his humble rival who possessed so little to sacrifice.

"And you Guido," said the old man.

The bright blood mounted to the pale face, and the clear light glowed deeper in his dark eye as he answered with a low, sad voice, "I would give up that which is more precious than life or liberty; that for which I would toil and suffer long years — that for which I would most gladly give the little of honor, wealth or happiness that I possess; all these were trifles, useless and vain, if that one thing were not gained."

"And this is what?" asked the wondering painter.

"Your daughter! her happiness is more to me than all the earth can offer. Let her bestow her love where she will, and God protect him who is so blest as to possess it. My deepest, truest joy will be the knowledge of her own. Cold and selfish were the hearts that did not find pure happiness in the joy of those they truly love. My rival hath all that can make life fair and beautiful; I would not bring a cloud to darken her bright sky; but when all the blessings that the world can give are hers, I would only ask a passing thought of one, whose earnest life and abiding love, will ever link all bright and happy memories with her."

"It is enough! hear my decision: — Three weeks hence is the Carnival; he who before that time hath painted a picture the most perfect in grace, and beauty of form, design and coloring, to him will I give my daughter. Strange as it may seem, I feel a painter's pride in bestowing my only earthly wealth on one worthy the glorious art that wins her. Three weeks hence at the gallery of ---, we meet again; 'till then, farewell."

And as the two rivals turned away, his eye rested proudly on

Guido, as he whispered with a smile, "He is worthy of her, and will succeed."

The hours went by, and rumors of the strange trial between the rival painters were rife through the city. Many were the wondering thoughts of the people; gay jests went round, and happy visions of fame from the hand of the painters filled many a fair lady's heart.

The beautiful Madeline sat alone, and strove to banish the thoughts that would come, bringing a picture, she would not look upon, and so the time went on, the days were spent, and the Carnival was in progress.

Gallery after gallery filled, and still the crowd poured on till the dim old halls were brilliant with the fair and noble of the gay city; the sunlight stole softly in through the richly stained windows, throwing strange, bright hues on the old pictures within, and the air was heavy with the fragrance of the flowers twined round statue and pillar.

Two dark mysterious curtains hung side by side, and before them stood the rival painters — a strange contrast. The young count, his proud face glowing with joy; his costly garments glittering with embroidery, and his plumed cap, heavy with jewels, stood proudly forth, and many a light heart beat, and fair cheek flushed, as his dark eye glanced over the galleries, bright as an Eastern garden with the loveliest flowers of Rome.

But they soon turned from him to his rival, and lingered there. His humble dress and threadbare mantle were unheeded for the noble face that looked so pale in the dark shadows where he stood; but a ray of sunlight lay softly on the long, dark locks that fell heavily round his face, and all unconscious of the eyes upon him, he stood looking calmly on the sweet face of a Madonna above.

A crowd of the first painters stood around a canopied seat, conversing with the father, who listened, silently watching the dial as it fast approached the appointed hour; beside him sat Madeline; the long veil folded so closely could not hide the lovely face that blushed beneath; and the hand that clasped the victor's wreath, trembled with the emotions of hope and fear that made the dark eyes fill with tears, and the gentle heart beat wildly.

As the twelve silvery chimes died away, the count sprang forward and exultingly flung back the curtain. A long breathless pause, and then loud and long sounded the applause, till the vaulted roof rung again.

It was Madeline — beautiful as love could make her. Beneath the picture, traced in golden letters, were courtly words of love and flattery, and before it the count knelt gracefully, and with uncovered head.

Then the pale young painter lifted his dark curtain, and not a sound broke the deep stillness as with fascinated eyes they gazed. Tears were on many a cheek, for the simple word "Mother" traced below, brought back to many a careless heart, the long-forgotten hours of innocence and youth; it was strangely beautiful. The silvered hair lay softly round the gentle face, and the mild dark eyes seemed looking down on her son with all a mother's fondness, while the golden light that fell from the high window seemed to shut the world of sin and shadows from them.

The silence was broken by a burst of applause that shook the old walls, and often as it died away 'twas again renewed; plumed caps waved, and flowers fell at his feet. Still, with folded hands he stood, heedless of all, for his thoughts were far away, and he saw only the gentle face before him, heard only her low, sweet voice, felt only her hand laid in blessing on his head, and all else was forgotten.

Then clear and deep above the murmuring crowd, sounded the voice of the old painter, saying — "Guido of Florence hath won the prize, and more than this he hath gained our love and honor, for one whose holy affections prized above the young, and lovely; the face that first smiled upon him, the heart that first loved. I ask no greater wealth for my child than the love of so noble a son. She is thine, Guido, with my blessing."

And 'mid a burst of triumphant music the wreath fell upon his head, and Madeline upon his breast. The noblest painters crowded round him, fair ladies scattered flowers in his path, and even his rival, shrouding his own fair picture, flung a bright wreath over the other, and with tears on his proud face, stood humbly before it, while gentle memories came stealing back, bringing a quiet joy, long unknown to his ambitious heart; and he rose up a better man for the holy lesson he had learned.

And while noble painters, and beautiful women paid their homage to the humble artist, and the deep-toned music rolled through the bright halls, high above all, the calm soft face looked proudly down on the form, whose unfailing love for her, had gained him the honor and love he so richly deserved.

The Rival Prima Donnas

Boston *Saturday Evening Gazette,* 11 November 1854. By "Flora Fairfield"

I

THE OPERA-HOUSE was filling fast with a gay and brilliant audience, empty boxes grew bright with lovely women, jewels sparkled, plumes waved, and fans began to move: the lively murmur of conversation filled the air, and all was in that state of pleasant confusion which precedes the first notes of the orchestra.

But on this night something of greater interest than usual seemed to possess the audience, all seemed to talk with eagerness of some important event about to take place, and opera-glasses were levelled with untiring curiosity, at one particular box, just above the stage the curtains of which were closely drawn.

"My dear Giulio," said Lord N. to his friend Count P., "what is the meaning of the great interest every one seems to feel in yonder box, what fair divinity is there enshrined? I am a stranger here, so pray explain, for I am curious as a woman."

"Listen then," replied the Count, "and perhaps you too may share in the excitement of those about you. That box belongs to Beatrice, our fair Prima-Donna, whose place Theresa the young debutante takes to-night; she has long been the pride and favorite of the public as much for the blameless life she leads, as for her beauty and unequalled voice, and until to-night no one has ventured to usurp her place, but suddenly an unknown singer has appeared, who by her loveliness and talent has won friends, and they desire she should make her first appearance here well knowing that if she succeed in pleasing our fastidious judges, that her fortune will be made elsewhere. And Beatrice instead of striving to out-rival her, has generously yielded up the stage entirely, that nothing might be wanting to secure a favorable reception, for the young artiste. To-night therefore is to decide the success of one Prima-Donna, and perhaps the banishment of another, for if Theresa be successful she will doubtless be engaged and Beatrice must go elsewhere, and thus all are anxious to see how each will bear her part in the coming trial."

"Now I shall indeed share your interest," replied Lord N., "but tell me more of this Beatrice who generously yields her place to a rival; few women would so calmly step aside, and let another win the laurels she might have gained; is it not somewhat strange?"

"Nay, not so strange as one might fancy, Arthur," said his friend, "for it is whispered and with truth, I fear, that she will bestow the hand so many have sought in vain, upon the handsome painter yonder; he is a worthy person, but not a fitting husband for a true-hearted woman like Beatrice; he is gay, careless, and fickle too; I fear she is tender and confiding, loving with an Italian's passionate devotion, if he be true, and taking an Italian's quick revenge, if he prove false; therefore I pity her and hope she will place her happiness in better hands, but hush! the overture begins, and I must join my sister."

The two friends parted, the curtain rose, and amid a breathless silence, the young cantatrice appeared, beautiful indeed but pale and trembling with suppressed emotion.

Slight was the applause that greeted her; that she was yet to win; but a few kind faces smiled upon her and with an effort she began, faintly and low at first, but as the music swelled, her voice grew stronger till it rang clear and sweet as a silver clarion through the vast house and as if carried away by the resolution to win confidence and approbation from those who seemed to look so coldly on her, she sang on, till the enthusiasm she felt sent a bright glow to her pale cheek, a deeper light to her eye and a richer music to her wonderful voice. Stiller and stiller grew the multitude before her, and when the last clear notes died lingeringly away they still sat spell bound, till a garland fell at her feet and a woman's glad voice cried "Encore! Encore!"

At that sound every eye was turned to the mysterious box, the curtains were flung back, and radiant in beauty stood the generous Beatrice, as forgetful of all but the trembling singer before her she clapped her white hands and cast the flowers from her own bosom at her wondering rival's feet.

Then from pit to gallery thundered the applause and showered the bouquets till overcome by her own victory the cantatrice was borne from the stage and the curtain fell.

When it rose again the Opera went on, the box of Beatrice was deserted, and the young painter had vanished from the crowd. They now stood together on the vine-covered balcony of her splendid home and the summer moonlight falling on their faces revealed the happy tears that shone in Beatrice's dark eyes and the forced smile upon her lover's lips as he looked down upon her saying in a troubled voice:

"I fear you will repent your choice, Beatrice, what can I give you in return for all you lose in thus becoming mine? you will miss the pleasant flattery of the world and pine for the homage that has so long been yours, you will soon sigh to be again the queen of many hearts, the loved, admired and happy woman whose power so many felt and owned; it is yet not too late, remember I can give you nothing but a painter's home which you will soon grow weary of and long again for the brilliant life you leave so gladly now."

"How little do you know me, Claude," said Beatrice, "have I not tried the world and found its flattering homage false? have I not sought for happiness in wealth and fame and sought in vain until I found it in your love? what then do I leave but all I am most weary of, and what do I gain but all I prize and cherish most on the earth? the painter's home I will make beautiful with the useless wealth I have won, and the painter's heart I will make happy by all the blessings a woman's love can give! Then do not fear for me, what *can* I lose in leaving a careless world for a husband and a home?"

And as she spoke she laid her proud head trustingly upon his breast, little dreaming of the bitter disappointment her fond words brought to the false heart where all her hope and faith were placed. As thus they stood a sound broke on the silent air and soon along the moonlit street her carriage drawn by a shouting crowd, with torches gleaming round her and flowers falling thick and fast, came Theresa the successful Prima Donna, and Beatrice looked smiling down, hidden by the vines, and watched the bright train as with joyful cries, and waving garlands, it swept by.

"See, Claude, how soon I am forgotten by these admiring followers of mine; they bore me home in triumph once as they are bearing young Theresa now, and one day she will be forgotten for another, as I am even here, then may she find a faithful friend, that never will forsake her, and a heart that never can forget; success and fame be hers, and happiness like mine when she is weary of the world," she said, as the last sound died away.

"But must you leave me now, Claude," she added fondly as the young man threw his mantle round him and prepared to go.

"I must, for it grows late, and I must be early at my studio tomorrow, therefore goodnight, love and pleasant dreams," replied the painter, bending down to kiss the fair face lifted to his own, and as he did so from his breast a little paper fell unheeded to the ground. They parted, and with fond hopes stirring in her heart she watched his tall figure, till it vanished in the distance, and then she was alone with her own happy thoughts.

Long she sat musing in the silvery moonlight, while the cool night wind fanned her cheek and rustled softly through the blooming vines, that rustled round her. At length the echo of the distant clocks as they rang twelve, dispelled her pleasant dreams, and as she rose to leave the balcony before her lay the paper that had fallen from her lover's breast.

"It is some tender song from Claude; he dared not give it me, but left it at my feet to read when he was gone. Dear Claude, how fond and faithful he has ever been," thought Beatrice, as with an eager hand she raised the note and hastened to the lighted room beyond, where with a joyous smile she opened it and read these words:

"My Claude, if I succeed and all goes well, then come to me at midnight, when I am alone, and let me hear from your dear lips alone the praise I value far beyond the flattery of the world. For your sake only do I thus seek wealth and fame that I may become more worthy of the generous love you have given to THERESA."

Pale and paler grew the reader's face as each word met her startled gaze; white and still as a marble statue she stood till all was read, and then sank down like one smitten by a heavy blow; not a sigh or a tear escaped her as she lay there amid the ruins of her young heart's hope and joy, her sorrow was too deep for tears, and she would only seek to realize the bitter truth that came thus suddenly upon her; she had loved fervently, and trusted with a woman's perfect faith — and now, in one short moment, all was changed, love forgotten, faith betrayed, and bright hopes vanished like a dream, while all the light and loveliness of life seemed gone forever, and when at length she rose a sudden blight seemed to have fallen on her, for the face so lately radiant with love and joy was now pale and haggard, her dark eyes shone with a troubled light, and her white lips moved but made no sound — still in her grief and deep despair, she struggled to be calm, and a faint smile shone upon her pallid face as she read the fatal note once more and whispered: "It may *not* be true; some enemy to Claude's peace and my own, may have placed it there; and yet he was so cold tonight and seemed to leave me so gladly — ah, it all comes back upon me now, and he whom I have loved so fondly has deserted me at last — but no, I *will* not doubt him yet; I will believe him true till I can prove his falsehood plainly; but, alas, how can I know and whom can I trust now?"

and with a bitter sigh she bent her face upon her hands, while doubts, hopes and fears came thronging thick and fast — suddenly she started up saying hurriedly:

"There is one way left and that is my last hope. I cannot live in doubt and will know all to-night," and with a hasty step she vanished in an inner room.

The silver clock in the deserted chamber was just striking half-past twelve, as from a private door beneath the balcony there emerged a slender figure muffled in a cloak whose face was hidden by the dark plumes of his hat; for a moment he lingered in the shadow of the door and then with a light quick step passed down the quiet street.

In a luxurious apartment where silver lamps shed a soft light on velvet couch and gleaming mirror, where the cool night wind floated in heavy with the breath of flowers all was beautiful and bright, and still, sat Theresa the young cantatrice and at her feet the painter Claude, jewels still glittered in her hair and on the graceful robe she wore, the garlands and bouquets she had won lay scattered round her; never had she looked so beautiful as then, when joy and triumph sparkled in her eyes, and glowed upon her cheek as with a fond proud smile she looked upon the painter saying:

"Am I not worthy of you now, Claude? have I not shown my love to be as strong as yours? I am no longer poor, unknown and friendless, but a glorious future lies before me, fame and wealth I will soon win, and what greater happiness do I ask, than to share all with you! But you are sad, dear Claude, and this night should be one of joy alone; then why so gloomy; tell me all and let Theresa charm your grief away."

"What sorrow would not vanish in the light of such a smile," replied the painter gazing passionately into the lovely face that bent above him. "Can you doubt my joy that you have won from others love and admiration like my own? it is not that which makes me sad, it is the memory of Beatrice, forgive me if I speak a name you cannot wish to hear, and do not doubt my constancy to you: my love for her died long ago, and now I only pity, but to-night the image of her in her bitter grief, when she learns all, *will* rise before me even here, she has loved me as few women love, and my heart rebukes me for the sorrow I must give her in return; each generous deed she does for you, each gentle word she speaks, but makes me seem more false and cruel still, and almost turns my pity into love again."

A dark frown gathered on Theresa's face and her eyes flashed scornfully upon her lover as he spoke and when he turned away forgetful for a moment even of her, she rose proudly up and stood before him, saying, with a haughty smile upon her lips:

"If Beatrice be still so dear to you, I fear there is no place in your heart for me, therefore choose now between us, for I will have no rival in your love. If Beatrice be dearest, then go and share with her the quiet home she longs for and in her calm affection may you find the happiness you seek, but if your many vows be true and Theresa most beloved, then come and tread with me the path that lies before us, share with me the wealth and fame I go to win, and in the gay brilliant world find all that makes love pleasant, and happiness in my fond faithful love, both are before you, therefore choose and let all doubts be ended here forever."

With wonder, love, and admiration stirring in his heart the painter gazed upon her as she spoke, and when she stood silently before him with her white arms folded proudly on her breast, her clear eyes shining on him with a deeper light than the jewels flashing in her hair, while on her lips there played a smile half scornful and half fond, he would have paused no longer in his choice, but a tender face rose up before him with dark reproachful eyes that seemed to warn and win him back; he thought of Beatrice, her generous trusting love, her faith in him, her wild sorrow and despair when she should find that faith betrayed, and his heart whispered that no joy, no peace would brighten life for him while haunted by the memory of wrong, and falsehood such as this, and as these thoughts passed through his mind, his better angel for the moment triumphed, he seized his cloak and turned to go, saying half aloud, "I cannot break her heart, *she* is my truest love, I will not wrong her thus," but the words died on his lips, for there before him stood Theresa with the proud light banished from her eyes which now shone on him through bright tears as with a tender pleading smile she stretched those fair arms toward him whispering softly.

"Have you chosen, dearest Claude?" The cloak dropped from his hand, Beatrice was forgotten, and his only answer was to lay her bright head on his breast, and whisper as he folded her closer still, "Yes, I *have* chosen, and nothing now can part us more." As thus they stood, Theresa, with a sudden cry and a face white with terror, pointed trembling to the window through which the moonlight dimly shone as the drooping curtains pointed to and fro.

"Did you see it, Claude?" she whispered fearfully, "a wild, pale face, with gleaming eyes looked in upon us through the leaves, and as you turned it vanished; oh, do not leave me, for it may return."

"Fear nothing, dearest, I am here to guard you, nay, do not tremble so, 'twas but your fancy or a passing shadow, sit here, and let me sing to you, for now my only joy is to cheer and watch above *you*."

And all night long the quiet moon looked down upon the happy lovers, as they sat, forgetful of the world, wrapt in a blissful dream of love and joy.

And all night long the same quiet moon shone on a broken hearted woman, as she paced her splendid chamber with clasped hands and tearless eyes, struggling with her bitter sorrow and despair, in a stern silence far more terrible to see than the wildest, saddest tears a woman ever shed.

II

The noonday sunlight, shining through crimson curtains, cast a rosy glow on the pale cheek of the painter Claude, as with a look of troubled joy he stood before his easel, from which Theresa's face looked back upon him.

"I cannot give these lips the proud, bright smile she wears, and yet if I had never looked on her this would seem most beautiful to me," he murmured, half aloud, as he bent nearer still to gaze upon his lovely work.

"It *is* most beautiful, dear Claude," echoed a low voice at his side, and turning with a guilty start he met the dark eyes of Beatrice, bent on him with a strange, searching look, before which his own gaze fell.

"Why have you never let me see this lovely face before? Did you fear I should grow jealous, Claude? If so, you wronged me, for I well know the love you bear me, and I shall never doubt it more," said Beatrice. A dark smile passed across her face as she watched her lover, standing pale and silent by her side, fearing to look upon her he had so wronged.

But, as she looked, with a sudden effort he shook off the spell that held him silent, and in a voice he strove in vain to render gay replied:

"Then you can trust me to look daily on a face like this, and, never fear that it may touch me to love you less. Ah, Beatrice, you do not truly love me, or some jealous fear would stir your woman's heart, and waken tender doubts of me, if I should love another you would soon forget me."

"Never: I should not forget you, nor forgive you, if you were false, but tell me, Claude, you do not love Theresa? She is younger, lovelier than I, but she will never be to you all I will be, can never cling to you with half the faith and constancy that I have done. Look in my face, dear Claude, and answer truly, *do* you love Theresa?" A sudden light flashed in her eyes, a sudden passion trembled in her voice as Beatrice thus spoke, and with a fond, imploring glance looked up into the face he half averted as he answered hastily:

"Foolish Beatrice, you can doubt me then, but do not fear, Theresa is no more to me than yonder picture, a lovely thing to look upon, and then forget."

"Nay, Claude, look in my face, and as you love me answer, if she be dearest, tell me truly, but, oh deceive me not, choose now between us,

Theresa with her beauty, or Beatrice with all her love, speak, Claude, I will pardon all for the truth's sake," urged Beatrice, still looking with strange earnestness into her lover's changing face.

He turned away, and for a moment struggled with the wish to tell her all, and trust her generous love to pardon him, but his eye fell on Theresa's lovely face, as it smiled upon him from his easel, he remembered that he had already chosen, and now as then passion conquered, he thought only of Theresa, but with a false smile on his lips he turned to Beatrice, softly saying as he drew her to his side:

"Banish these doubts, and let no fear of another cloud your joy, dearest, look up and smile again, for I have made my choice."

"You have, you have! and I am not the chosen one. Oh! Claude, false to the last," murmured Beatrice in a low, broken voice, as she bent her face upon her hands, for she read his heart, and her last hope was gone. The painter only caught his whispered name, and casting one fond glance at the fatal picture, he looked down upon the bended head that rested for a moment upon his breast, with mingled pity, shame, and triumph stirring in his heart.

A sudden tap at the studio door broke the silence, and as her lover left the room Beatrice raised her face, and pressed her hands upon her breast, as if to still her bitter grief, white lips whispered:

"May God forgive him for this cruel wrong. I sought to win him to a generous confession of his fault, and that should have atoned for all but 'tis in vain; he would deceive me to the last, and turn the pure devoted love I bore him into scorn and pity for his weakness and the double falsehood he has shown. Oh, Claude! I could have borne to trust your love, but not to see my tender trust so cruelly betrayed: but hush! he comes, I cannot steal away, and so will look my last, and then depart forever."

And as his steps drew near, she stilled her sorrow, dashed away the tears that lay upon her cheek, and sinking on a couch, half unconscious what she did, began with trembling fingers to make a garland of some rare flowers heaped in a vase that stood beside her.

The painter frowned as he saw her thus employed, for the flowers were destined for another, but concealing his anger he gaily said, as he resumed his palette and brush: "These were gathered for you dear Beatrice — you see they are roses, Love's own flowers, then will you not wear them to-night for my sake?"

"Shall I not rather weave them into a garland for the lovely Theresa, for whom they are fitter ornaments than for me. I will crown her with roses, that the world may see I neither fear nor envy her: think not I slight your gift, Claude, but I know it will give you pleasure to see it resting on her beautiful head," said Beatrice, with a bitter smile, bending still lower to her task to hide her sorrow-stricken face. Claude cast a quick, fearful glance upon her as she spoke, but there was no sign of anger or suspicion on her half averted face, over which the crimson drapery cast a warm bright glow, and with a sigh of relief he gently replied:

"I shall, indeed, delight in seeing a wreath of your weaving on your rival's head, for it will only prove to the world more plainly still, how generous and noble a heart beats in your breast. Beatrice, this will, indeed, be a garland fit for a queen," he added, looking with admiration at the graceful band of flowers she had woven with her utmost skill: "but put in no more roses, or you will *crush* instead of crown her, Beatrice, for this wreath, light as it is, will fall heavily from the height whence you will drop it on her head: it might be a pleasant death for one to die, crushed with flowers in our hour of joy, but we cannot lose Theresa yet, so weave the garland lightly, and you can add no other charm to your lovely work."

And with these words upon his lips, he turned away and soon seemed unconscious of all but the beautiful face before him.

Beatrice did not speak, but as her lover's words fell on her ear she started, and some dreadful thought seemed to flash into her mind, for her cheek grew paler still, a fierce dark smile shot across her face, her eyes gleamed with a sudden light, and her lips moved silently, as if she muttered spells above the flowers she wove, her lover seemed to have forgotten even her, and as he bent eagerly to his work, she watched the color deepen in his cheek, the smile rise to his lips, the sparkle to his eye, as with a rapid, skilful hand, he gave fresh beauty to the fair face of her rival, and as she watched, sterner and darker grew her face, sadder and heavier the load of grief upon her heart, stronger and deeper the wild thoughts that stirred in her troubled brain. At length she rose, folded her mantle round her, and with the flower crown in her hand, glided to the painter's side saying:

"I must leave you now, Claude, but we shall *meet to-night*."

He started like one in a dream, and with a hasty word and a careless glance bid her farewell, then seeming to remember that he had a part to play he took her hand, saying, in a tender voice, "Farewell, dear Beatrice, I fear I have been but a dull companion, but Theresa leaves us soon and would think little of my skill, if her picture were not done.

"I shall not fail to join you to-night, for I long to see the flower crown given; so adieu till then."

And bending down to shun the gaze of her clear dark eyes he softly kissed her cheek, as she passed out — he turned to his work, saying, half aloud, as he bent to touch with his own the smiling lips of Theresa:

"My part has been well played; Beatrice trusts me blindly still, and now one kiss from these beautiful lips shall be my best reward." As he lifted his head a dark shadow flitted away from the half open door and vanished in the gloomy gallery beyond.

It was Beatrice!

Never had the Opera House been so full as now, gallery after gallery filled, and still the crowd poured in, for the fame of the lovely singer had flown far and wide, and hundreds gathered there to wonder and admire.

The purple curtains were undrawn in the box of Beatrice, but the painter Claude stood with folded arms in the shadow of the gallery opposite, and watched with a strange interest all that passed before him; he turned often from the gay brilliant throng to look with sorrow and regret towards that still dark curtain, behind which sat the woman he had so wronged and deceived; all her fond tender words, and loving acts of kindness, came freshly to his memory that night; her trusting love had never seemed so beautiful as now, when he had lost all right to seek or claim it, for that night he had vowed to fly with her fair rival, and it was now too late to sigh and sorrow for the true heart he had cast away.

The curtain rose, and the rustling crowd were still as music filled the air, and Norma, the white-robed priestess, glided in among her vestals with the sacred oak leaves in her hand; never had Theresa looked so beautiful as now, for love, ambition, joy and triumph lent a radiant beauty to her face, a statelier grace to her fair form, and a deeper, richer music to her magical voice, which echoed with a strange sweet melody through the vast house, and seemed to grow more fresh and beautiful as she poured forth in music all the sorrow, jealousy and love of the unhappy Norma, whom she personated with such tenderness and passion.

The painter still lingered in the shadow, but his eyes no longer rested on the lonely box; they never moved now from the fair enchantress, who in all her sorrow and despair seemed to sing for him alone, her eye often turned to meet his with a glance of love and pride that seemed to say, "All this I do for your dear sake, and all my triumph will I share with you;" the memory of Beatrice had vanished like a dream beneath the spell of such an hour, and all was now forgotten but love and the beautiful Theresa.

Meanwhile, behind the drooping curtains of the Prima Donna's box, sat one who could have acted Norma, the deceived, deserted woman, with a truth and power that would have thrilled the hearts that beat so quickly now. Beatrice sat in the purple shadow like a marble statue, pale, still, and cold, her hands clasped tightly on her breast, and her dark gleaming eyes fixed on her lover's face, where through a narrow opening it could be seen, while before her lay the rose-crown she had woven for her rival; and so, amid the music, light and bursts of joyful applause she sat unmoved, and never turned her steadfast gaze from the face that looked with such fond passion and delight upon the happy singer, who was acting just below her all the bitter grief and desolation she so keenly felt.

At length the opera ended, the priestess's doom was spoken, the fatal veil was folded around her, and with her wild, sad farewell lingering on the air, she was borne away, and all was over; but soon, amid the welcoming shouts of those who had sat spellbound by her power, she re-appeared, no longer pale and sorrow stricken but radiant with smiles, and bright in youthful joy and loveliness as with folded hands she bowed before the admiring throng who carpeted her path with flowers, and vented their delight in joyful cries and echoing applause.

Suddenly there was a pause, and a deep stillness fell on the excited multitude as every eye turned from the lovelier singer to a fairer, stranger sight. The curtains were thrown wide apart, and the stately form of Beatrice stood proudly forth glittering with a strange magnificence; jewels sparkled on her velvet robe, and shone like stars in her dark hair; a deep changing color glowed upon her cheek, and a wild brilliance flashed in her dark eyes as they glanced rapidly about the up-turned faces looking into hers.

"Look up, look up, Theresa, and receive the crown," cried a distant voice, that she well knew; and lifting her wondering eyes, the lovely singer shuddered as she met the dark glance that flashed upon her from the haggard face of the rival she had wronged, and in that glance each read the other's meaning; and while Theresa bowed her head in shame and fear, Beatrice, with a sudden smile, raised her white arms high above her head, and stood a moment gracefully holding a flower crown, while her eye sought out some distant object; then the garland *fell,* and high above the tumultuous applause, that shook the walls, roared the death-shriek of Theresa, and Beatrice, pointing to her as she lay amid the flowers, with the *iron* crown concealed among the roses on her blood-stained hair, cried in a voice that never ceased to echo in one guilty hearer's ear: "You bid me crown her, Claude; see, I have done it! better to 'die *crushed with flowers,*' than live to be what you have rendered me;" and with a wild, fearful laugh, she vanished from the sight of the horror-stricken crowd!

Years passed away, and in a lonely convent lived and died a sad grey-haired man, worn and wasted with remorse, and in a quiet home for the insane, dwelt a beautiful, pale woman, who constantly wove garlands, and, like a swan, died singing mournfully — and these were BEATRICE and CLAUDE.

The Frost-King
or,
The Power of Love

From *Flower Fables* (Boston: George W. Briggs, 1855)

*T*HREE LITTLE FAIRIES sat in the fields eating their breakfast; each among the leaves of her favorite flower, Daisy, Primrose, and Violet, were happy as Elves need be.

The morning wind gently rocked them to and fro, and the sun shone warmly down upon the dewy grass, where butterflies spread their gay wings, and bees with their deep voices sung among the flowers; while the little birds hopped merrily about to peep at them.

On a silvery mushroom was spread the breakfast; little cakes of flower-dust lay on a broad green leaf, beside a crimson strawberry, which, with sugar from the violet, and cream from the yellow milkweed, made a fairy meal, and their drink was the dew from the flowers' bright leaves.

"Ah me," sighed Primrose, throwing herself languidly back, "how warm the sun grows! give me another piece of strawberry, and then I must hasten away to the shadow of the ferns. But while I eat, tell me, dear Violet, why are you all so sad? I have scarce seen a happy face since my return from Rose Land; dear friend, what means it?"

"I will tell you," replied little Violet, the tears gathering in her soft eyes. "Our good Queen is ever striving to keep the dear flowers from the power of the cruel Frost-King; many ways she tried, but all have failed. She has sent messengers to his court with costly gifts; but all have returned sick for want of sunlight, weary and sad; we have watched over them, heedless of sun or shower, but still his dark spirits do their work, and we are left to weep over our blighted blossoms. Thus have we striven, and in vain; and this night our Queen holds council for the last time. Therefore are we sad, dear Primrose, for she has toiled and cared for us, and we can do nothing to help or advise her now."

"It is indeed a cruel thing," replied her friend; "but as we cannot help it, we must suffer patiently, and not let the sorrows of others disturb our happiness. But, dear sisters, see you not how high the sun is getting? I have my locks to curl, and my robe to prepare for the evening; therefore I must be gone, or I shall be brown as a withered leaf in this warm light." So, gathering a tiny mushroom for a parasol, she flew away; Daisy soon followed, and Violet was left alone.

Then she spread the table afresh, and to it came fearlessly the busy ant and bee, gay butterfly and bird; even the poor blind mole and humble worm were not forgotten; and with gentle words she gave to all, while each learned something of their kind little teacher; and the love that made her own heart bright shone alike on all.

The ant and bee learned generosity, the butterfly and bird contentment, the mole and worm confidence in the love of others; and each went to their home better for the little time they had been with Violet.

Evening came, and with it troops of Elves to counsel their good Queen, who, seated on her mossy throne, looked anxiously upon the throng below, whose glittering wings and rustling robes gleamed like many-colored flowers.

At length she rose, and amid the deep silence spoke thus: —

"Dear children, let us not tire of a good work, hard though it be and wearisome; think of the many little hearts that in their sorrow look to us for help. What would the green earth be without its lovely flowers, and what a lonely home for us! Their beauty fills our hearts with brightness, and their love with tender thoughts. Ought we then to leave them to die uncared for and alone? They give to us their all; ought we not to toil unceasingly, that they may bloom in peace within their quiet homes? We have tried to gain the love of the stern Frost-King, but in vain; his heart is hard as his own icy land; no love can melt, no kindness bring it back to sunlight and to joy. How then may we keep our frail blossoms from his cruel spirits? Who will give us counsel? Who will be our messenger for the last time? Speak, my subjects."

Then a great murmuring arose, and many spoke, some for costlier gifts, some for war; and the fearful counselled patience and submission.

Long and eagerly they spoke, and their soft voices rose high.

Then sweet music sounded on the air, and the loud tones were hushed, as in wondering silence the Fairies waited what should come.

Through the crowd there came a little form, a wreath of pure white violets lay among the bright locks that fell so softly round the gentle face, where a deep blush glowed, as, kneeling at the throne, little Violet said: —

"Dear Queen, we have bent to the Frost-King's power, we have borne gifts unto his pride, but have we gone trustingly to him and spoken fearlessly of his evil deeds? Have we shed the soft light of unwearied love around his cold heart, and with patient tenderness shown him how bright and beautiful love can make even the darkest lot?

"Our messengers have gone fearfully, and with cold looks and courtly words offered him rich gifts, things he cared not for, and with equal pride has he sent them back.

"Then let me, the weakest of your band, go to him, trusting in the love I know lies hidden in the coldest heart.

"I will bear only a garland of our fairest flowers; these will I wind about him, and their bright faces, looking lovingly in his, will bring sweet thoughts to his dark mind, and their soft breath steal in like gentle words. Then, when he sees them fading on his breast, will he not sigh that there is no warmth there to keep them fresh and lovely? This will I do, dear Queen, and never leave his dreary home, till the sunlight falls on flowers fair as those that bloom in our own dear land."

Silently the Queen had listened, but now, rising and placing her hand on little Violet's head, she said, turning to the throng below: —

"We in our pride and power have erred, while this, the weakest and lowliest of our subjects, has from the innocence of her own pure heart counselled us more wisely than the noblest of our train. All who will aid our brave little messenger, lift your wands, that we may know who will place their trust in the Power of Love."

Every fairy wand glistened in the air, as with silvery voices they cried, "Love and little Violet."

Then down from the throne, hand in hand, came the Queen and Violet, and till the moon sank did the Fairies toil, to weave a wreath of the fairest flowers. Tenderly they gathered them, with the night-dew fresh upon their leaves, and as they wove chanted sweet spells, and whispered fairy blessings on the bright messengers whom they sent forth to die in a dreary land, that their gentle kindred might bloom unharmed.

At length it was done; and the fair flowers lay glowing in the soft starlight, while beside them stood the Fairies, singing to the music of the wind-harps: —

We are sending you, dear flowers,
Forth alone to die,
Where your gentle sisters may not weep
O'er the cold graves where you lie;

But you go to bring them fadeless life
  In the bright homes where they dwell,
And you softly smile that 't is so,
  As we sadly sing farewell.
O plead with gentle words for us,
  And whisper tenderly
Of generous love to that cold heart,
  And it will answer ye;
And though you fade in a dreary home,
  Yet loving hearts will tell
Of the joy and peace that you have given:
  Flowers, dear flowers, farewell!

The morning sun looked softly down upon the broad green earth, which like a mighty altar was sending up clouds of perfume from its breast, while flowers danced gayly in the summer wind, and birds sang their morning hymn among the cool green leaves. Then high above, on shining wings, soared a little form. The sunlight rested softly on the silken hair, and the winds fanned lovingly the bright face, and brought the sweetest odors to cheer her on.

Thus went Violet through the clear air, and the earth looked smiling up to her, as, with the bright wreath folded in her arms, she flew among the soft, white clouds.

On and on she went, over hill and valley, broad rivers and rustling woods, till the warm sunlight passed away, the winds grew cold, and the air thick with falling snow. Then far below she saw the Frost-King's home. Pillars of hard, gray ice supported the high, arched roof, hung with crystal icicles. Dreary gardens lay around, filled with withered flowers and bare, drooping trees; while heavy clouds hung low in the dark sky, and a cold wind murmured sadly through the wintry air.

With a beating heart Violet folded her fading wreath more closely to her breast, and with weary wings flew onward to the dreary palace.

Here, before the closed doors, stood many forms with dark faces and harsh, discordant voices, who sternly asked the shivering little Fairy why she came to them.

Gently she answered, telling them her errand, beseeching them to let her pass ere the cold wind blighted her frail blossoms. Then they flung wide the doors, and she passed in.

Walls of ice, carved with strange figures, were around her; glittering icicles hung from the high roof, and soft, white snow covered the hard floors. On a throne hung with clouds sat the Frost-King; a crown of crystals bound his white locks, and a dark mantle wrought with delicate frostwork was folded over his cold breast.

His stern face could not stay little Violet, and on through the long hall she went, heedless of the snow that gathered on her feet, and the bleak wind that blew around her; while the King with wondering eyes looked on the golden light that played upon the dark walls as she passed.

The flowers, as if they knew their part, unfolded their bright leaves, and poured forth their sweetest perfume, as, kneeling at the throne, the brave little Fairy said, —

"O King of blight and sorrow, send me not away till I have brought back the light and joy that will make your dark home bright and beautiful again. Let me call back to the desolate gardens the fair forms that are gone, and their soft voices blessing you will bring to your breast a never failing joy. Cast by your icy crown and sceptre, and let the sunlight of love fall softly on your heart.

"Then will the earth bloom again in all its beauty, and your dim eyes will rest only on fair forms, while music shall sound through these dreary halls, and the love of grateful hearts be yours. Have pity on the gentle flower-spirits, and do not doom them to an early death, when they might bloom in fadeless beauty, making us wiser by their gentle teachings, and the earth brighter by their lovely forms. These fair flowers, with the prayers of all Fairy Land, I lay before you; O send me not away till they are answered."

And with tears falling thick and fast upon their tender leaves, Violet laid the wreath at his feet, while the golden light grew ever brighter as it fell upon the little form so humbly kneeling there.

The King's stern face grew milder as he gazed on the gentle Fairy, and the flowers seemed to look beseechingly upon him; while their fragrant voices sounded softly in his ear, telling of their dying sisters, and of the joy it gives to bring happiness to the weak and sorrowing. But he drew the dark mantle closer over his breast and answered coldly, —

"I cannot grant your prayer, little Fairy; it is my will the flowers should die. Go back to your Queen, and tell her that I cannot yield my power to please these foolish flowers."

Then Violet hung the wreath above the throne, and with weary feet went forth again, out into the cold, dark gardens, and still the golden shadows followed her, and wherever they fell, flowers bloomed and green leaves rustled.

Then came the Frost-Spirits, and beneath their cold wings the flowers died, while the Spirits bore Violet to a low, dark cell, saying as they left her, that their King was angry that she had dared to stay when he had bid her go.

So all alone she sat, and sad thoughts of her happy home came back to her, and she wept bitterly. But soon came visions of the gentle flowers dying in their forest homes, and their voices ringing in her ear, imploring her to save them. Then she wept no longer, but patiently awaited what might come.

Soon the golden light gleamed faintly through the cell, and she heard little voices calling for help, and high up among the heavy cobwebs hung poor little flies struggling to free themselves, while their cruel enemies sat in their nets, watching their pain.

With her wand the Fairy broke the bands that held them, tenderly bound up their broken wings, and healed their wounds; while they lay in the warm light, and feebly hummed their thanks to their kind deliverer.

Then she went to the ugly brown spiders, and in gentle words told them, how in Fairy Land their kindred spun all the elfin cloth, and in return the Fairies gave them food, and then how happily they lived among the cool green leaves, spinning garments for their neighbors. "And you too," said she, "shall spin for me, and I will give you better food than helpless insects. You shall live in peace, and spin your delicate threads into a mantle for the stern King; and I will weave golden threads amid the gray, that when folded over his cold heart gentle thoughts may enter in and make it their home."

And while she gayly sung, the little weavers spun their silken threads, the flies on glittering wings flew lovingly above her head, and over all the golden light shone softly down.

When the Frost-Spirits told their King, he greatly wondered, and often stole to look at the sunny little room where friends and enemies worked peacefully together. Still the light grew brighter, and floated out into the cold air, where it hung like bright clouds above the dreary gardens, whence all the Spirits' power could not drive it; and green leaves budded on the naked trees, and flowers bloomed; but the Spirits heaped snow upon them, and they bowed their heads and died.

At length the mantle was finished, and amid the gray threads shone golden ones, making it bright; and she sent it to the King, entreating him to wear it, for it would bring peace and love to dwell within his breast.

But he scornfully threw it aside, and bade his Spirits take her to a colder cell, deep in the earth; and there with harsh words they left her.

Still she sang gayly on, and the falling drops kept time so musically, that the King in his cold ice-halls wondered at the low, sweet sounds that came stealing up to him.

Thus Violet dwelt, and each day the golden light grew stronger; and from among the crevices of the rocky walls came troops of little velvet-coated moles, praying that they might listen to the sweet music, and lie in the warm light.

"We lead," said they, "a dreary life in the cold earth; the flower-roots are dead, and no soft dews descend for us to drink, no little seed or leaf can we find. Ah, good Fairy, let us be your servants: give us but a few crumbs of your daily bread, and we will do all in our power to serve you."

And Violet said, Yes; so day after day they labored to make a pathway through the frozen earth, that she might reach the roots of the withered flowers; and soon, wherever through the dark galleries she went, the soft light fell upon the roots of flowers, and they with new life spread forth in the warm ground, and forced fresh sap to the blossoms above. Brightly they bloomed and danced in the soft light, and the Frost-Spirits tried in vain to harm them, for when they came beneath the bright clouds their power to do evil left them.

From his dark castle the King looked out on the happy flowers, who nodded gayly to him, and in sweet odors strove to tell him of the good little Spirit, who toiled so faithfully below, that they might live. And when he turned from the brightness without, to his stately palace, it seemed so cold and dreary, that he folded Violet's mantle round him, and sat beneath the faded wreath upon his ice-carved throne, wondering at the strange warmth that came from it; till at length he bade his Spirits bring the little Fairy from her dismal prison.

Soon they came hastening back, and prayed him to come and see how lovely the dark cell had grown. The rough floor was spread with deep green moss, and over wall and roof grew flowery vines, filling the air with their sweet breath; while above played the clear, soft light, casting rosy shadows on the glittering drops that lay among the fragrant leaves; and beneath the vines stood Violet, casting crumbs to the downy little moles who ran fearlessly about and listened as she sang to them.

When the old King saw how much fairer she had made the dreary cell than his palace rooms, gentle thoughts within whispered him to grant her prayer, and let the little Fairy go back to her friends and home; but the Frost-Spirits breathed upon the flowers and bid him see how frail they were, and useless to a King. Then the stern, cold thoughts came back again, and he harshly bid her follow him.

With a sad farewell to her little friends she followed him, and before the throne awaited his command. When the King saw how pale and sad the gentle face had grown, how thin her robe, and weak her wings, and yet how lovingly the golden shadows fell around her and brightened as they lay upon the wand, which, guided by patient love, had made his once desolate home so bright, he could not be cruel to the one who had done so much for him, and in kindly tone he said, —

"Little Fairy, I offer you two things, and you may choose between them. If I will vow never more to harm the flowers you may love, will you go back to your own people and leave me and my Spirits to work our will on all the other flowers that bloom? The earth is broad, and we can find them in any land, then why should you care what happens to their kindred if your own are safe? Will you do this?"

"Ah!" answered Violet sadly, "do you not know that beneath the flowers' bright leaves there beats a little heart that loves and sorrows like our own? And can I, heedless of their beauty, doom them to pain and grief, that I might save my own dear blossoms from the cruel foes to which I leave them? Ah no! sooner would I dwell for ever in your darkest cell, than lose the love of those warm, trusting hearts."

"Then listen," said the King, "to the task I give you. You shall raise up for me a palace fairer than this, and if you can work that miracle I will grant your prayer or lose my kingly crown. And now go forth, and begin your task; my Spirits shall not harm you, and I will wait till it is done before I blight another flower."

Then out into the gardens went Violet with a heavy heart; for she had toiled so long, her strength was nearly gone. But the flowers whispered their gratitude, and folded their leaves as if they blessed her; and when she saw the garden filled with loving friends, who strove to cheer and thank her for her care, courage and strength returned; and raising up thick clouds of mist, that hid her from the wondering flowers, alone and trustingly she began her work.

As time went by, the Frost-King feared the task had been too hard for the Fairy; sounds were heard behind the walls of mist, bright shadows seen to pass within, but the little voice was never heard. Meanwhile, the golden light had faded from the garden, the flowers bowed their heads, and all was dark and cold as when the gentle Fairy came.

And to the stern King his home seemed more desolate and sad; for he missed the warm light, the happy flowers, and, more than all, the gay voice and bright face of little Violet. So he wandered through his dreary palace, wondering how he had been content to live before without sunlight and love.

And little Violet was mourned as dead in Fairy-Land, and many tears were shed, for the gentle Fairy was beloved by all, from the Queen down to the humblest flower. Sadly they watched over every bird and blossom which she had loved, and strove to be like her in kindly words and deeds. They wore cypress wreaths, and spoke of her as one whom they should never see again.

Thus they dwelt in deepest sorrow, till one day there came to them an unknown messenger, wrapped in a dark mantle, who looked with wondering eyes on the bright palace, and flower-crowned Elves, who kindly welcomed him, and brought fresh dew and rosy fruit to refresh the weary stranger. Then he told them that he came from the Frost-King, who begged the Queen and all her subjects to come and see the palace little Violet had built; for the veil of mist would soon be withdrawn, and as she could not make a fairer home than the ice-castle, the King wished her kindred near to comfort and to bear her home. And while the Elves wept, he told them how patiently she had toiled, how her fadeless love had made the dark cell bright and beautiful.

These and many other things he told them; for little Violet had won the love of many of the Frost-Spirits, and even when they killed the flowers she had toiled so hard to bring to life and beauty, she spoke gentle words to them, and sought to teach them how beautiful is love. Long stayed the messenger, and deeper grew his wonder that the Fairy could have left so fair a home, to toil in the dreary palace of his cruel master, and suffer cold and weariness, to give life and joy to the weak and sorrowing. When the Elves had promised they would come, he bade farewell to happy Fairy-Land, and flew sadly home.

At last the time arrived, and out in his barren garden, under a canopy of dark clouds, sat the Frost-King before the misty wall, behind which were heard low, sweet sounds, as of rustling trees and warbling birds.

Soon through the air came many-colored troops of Elves. First the Queen, known by the silver lilies on her snowy robe and the bright crown in her hair, beside whom flew a band of Elves in crimson and gold, making sweet music on their flower-trumpets, while all around, with smiling faces and bright eyes, fluttered her loving subjects.

On they came, like a flock of brilliant butterflies, their shining wings and many-colored garments sparkling in the dim air; and soon the leafless trees were gay with living flowers, and their sweet voices filled the gardens with music. Like his subjects, the King looked on the lovely Elves, and no longer wondered that little Violet wept and longed for her home. Darker and more desolate seemed his stately home, and when the Fairies asked for flowers, he felt ashamed that he had none to give them.

At length a warm wind swept through the gardens, and the mist-clouds passed away, while in silent wonder looked the Frost-King and the Elves upon the scene before them.

Far as eye could reach were tall green trees, whose drooping boughs made graceful arches, through which the golden light shone softly, making bright shadows on the deep green moss below, where the fairest flowers waved in the cool wind, and sang, in their low, sweet voices, how beautiful is Love.

Flowering vines folded their soft leaves around the trees, making green pillars of their rough trunks. Fountains threw their bright waters to the roof, and flocks of silver-winged birds flew singing among the flowers, or brooded lovingly above their nests. Doves with gentle eyes cooed among the green leaves, snow-white clouds floated in the sunny sky, and the golden light, brighter than before, shone softly down.

Soon through the long aisles came Violet, flowers and green leaves rustling as she passed. On she went to the Frost-King's throne, bearing two crowns, one of sparkling icicles, the other of pure white lilies, and kneeling before him, said, —

"My task is done, and, thanks to the Spirits of earth and air, I have made as fair a home as Elfin hands can form. You must now decide. Will you be King of Flower-Land, and own my gentle kindred for your loving friends? Will you possess unfading peace and joy, and the grateful love of all the green earth's fragrant children? Then take this crown of flowers. But if you can find no pleasure here, go back to your own cold home, and dwell in solitude and darkness, where no ray of sunlight or of joy can enter.

"Send forth your Spirits to carry sorrow and desolation over the happy earth, and win for yourself the fear and hatred of those who would so gladly love and reverence you. Then take this glittering crown, hard and cold as your own heart will be, if you will shut out all that is bright and beautiful. Both are before you. Choose."

The old King looked at the little Fairy, and saw how lovingly the bright shadows gathered round her, as if to shield her from every harm; the timid birds nestled in her bosom, and the flowers grew fairer as she looked upon them; while her gentle friends, with tears in their bright eyes, folded their hands beseechingly, and smiled on her.

Kind thoughts came thronging to his mind, and he turned to look at the two palaces. Violet's, so fair and beautiful, with its rustling trees, calm, sunny skies, and happy birds and flowers, all created by her patient love and care. His own, so cold and dark and dreary, his empty gardens where no flowers could bloom, no green trees dwell, or gay birds sing, all desolate and dim; — and while he gazed, his own Spirits, casting off their dark mantles, knelt before him and besought him not to send them forth to blight the things the gentle Fairies loved so much. "We have served you long and faithfully," said they, "give us now our freedom, that we may learn to be beloved by the sweet flowers we have harmed so long. Grant the little Fairy's prayer; and let her go back to her own dear home. She has taught us that Love is mightier than Fear. Choose the Flower crown, and we will be the truest subjects you have ever had."

Then, amid a burst of wild, sweet music, the Frost-King placed the Flower crown on his head, and knelt to little Violet; while far and near, over the broad green earth, sounded the voices of flowers, singing their thanks to the gentle Fairy, and the summer wind was laden with perfumes, which they sent as tokens of their gratitude; and wherever she went, old trees bent down to fold their slender branches round her, flowers laid their soft faces against her own, and whispered blessings; even the humble moss bent over the little feet, and kissed them as they passed.

The old King, surrounded by the happy Fairies, sat in Violet's lovely home, and watched his icy castle melt away beneath the bright sunlight; while his Spirits, cold and gloomy no longer, danced with the Elves, and waited on their King with loving eagerness. Brighter grew the golden light, gayer sang the birds, and the harmonious voices of grateful flowers, sounding over the earth, carried new joy to all their gentle kindred.

> *Brighter shone the golden shadows;*
>   *On the cool wind softly came*
> *The low, sweet tones of happy flowers,*
>   *Singing little Violet's name.*
> *'Mong the green trees was it whispered,*
>   *And the bright waves bore it on*
> *To the lonely forest flowers,*
>   *Where the glad news had not gone.*

> *Thus the Frost-King lost his kingdom,*
>   *And his power to harm and blight.*
> *Violet conquered, and his cold heart*
>   *Warmed with music, love, and light;*
> *And his fair home, once so dreary,*
>   *Gay with lovely Elves and flowers,*
> *Brought a joy that never faded*
>   *Through the long bright summer hours.*

> *Thus, by Violet's magic power,*
>   *All dark shadows passed away,*

And o'er the home of happy flowers
   The golden light for ever lay.
Thus the Fairy mission ended,
   And all Flower-Land was taught
The "Power of Love," by gentle deeds
   That little Violet wrought.

As Sunny Lock ceased, another little Elf came forward; and this was the tale "Silver Wing" told.

Early Experiments in Realism

The Lady and the Woman

Boston *Saturday Evening Gazette,* Quarto Series, 4 October 1856

*W*HAT STYLE OF WOMAN do you admire then, since your dislike for the 'strong minded!' is so great, Mr. Windsor?"

"That I can hardly tell you, Miss Kate; for I am not sure that I know myself; but I fancy that, like most men, I admire such as claim our protection and support, giving us in return affection and obedience. Beautiful and tender creatures, submissive to our will, confident in our judgment; and lenient to our faults — to be cherished in sunshine and sheltered in storms. I have given little thought to the subject in my busy life, but that's a hasty sketch. Does it meet your approbation?"

"Not at all. You have given your idol a heart, but no head. An affectionate or accomplished idiot is not my ideal of a woman. I would have her strong enough to stand alone, and give, not ask, support. Brave enough to think and act, as well as feel. Keen-eyed enough to see her own and others' faults, and wise enough to find a cure for them. I would have her humble, though self-reliant, gentle, though strong; man's companion, not his plaything; able and willing to face storms, as well as sunshines, and share life's burdens as they come."

"Such a character, Miss Kate, would be hard to find, and might perhaps, though lovely in thought, prove repulsive and unwomanly in reality. If these 'strong minded' ladies who are clamoring so fiercely for their rights are samples, however bad, of the style you desire, I can never hope or wish to see it perfected. A masculine woman is both unnatural and unlovely; and you surely cannot admire such."

"You are right; they are as utterly disagreeable as the effeminate men who are a disgrace to manhood. Ah, Mr. Windsor, there are two sides to the question and much to be set right on both. Give the brothers and sisters of our great family an equal share of the pleasures, duties, benefits, and rewards of life, and in time you will see the beautiful result. With a truer knowledge of each other, there will come a nobler justice for all; and what are now discordant fragments, will become a harmonious whole.

> *As unto the bow the cord is,*
> *So unto the man is woman,*
> *Though she bends him, she obeys him,*
> *Though she draws him, yet she follows;*
> *Useless each without the other.*

And Hiawatha's Indian philosophy was a very true one to my thinking."

"What is your opinion upon the subject, Miss Amelia?" asked the gentleman, addressing a handsome languid lady who with veils, shawls, fans and smelling bottles, filled one corner of the carriage.

"Oh, I agree with you entirely, Mr. Windsor, and nothing would induce me to adopt Kate's ideas, they are so dreadfully peculiar. I am willing to be led, and quite content with my share of good gifts. Somebody says, 'Man is the head and woman the heart,' and it's quite true, I dare say."

"It is like putting to sea without a rudder, Amelia," said her energetic friend. "Hearts are often shipwrecked, passions and feelings are an unruly crew. So let me advise you to take head as pilot, for you may find, as I have done, that the voyage of life is not quite a pleasure trip."

"Be that as it may, I shall float comfortably along till a stronger hand than mine comes to hold the helm for me; for I'm no sailor, and never mean to be if I must become one of those odious creatures Kate thinks so fine. I never saw one yet that was not utterly disagreeable." And the lady's fine eyes rested thoughtfully upon the gentleman before her, as if considering his fitness for the post of pilot to the "Amelia."

"I have seen a woman fill a father's, as well as a mother's place, and guide four wilful boys with a firm though gentle hand, and yet no one ever thought her unwomanly, or breathed a word against a character as beautiful as it was uncommon," said the pale faced lad at Mr. Windsor's side, with a glance of grateful affection at his sister Kate.

The elder gentleman did not see the look, but said, musingly, "I should like to know such a woman."

"Perhaps you may," replied the boy, significantly; and then they rode on in silence, for a while, each lost in thought.

The young party, journeying together, had met at a certain country place, much frequented by city visitors, and were now making a two days' pilgrimage to a distant mountain, which no summer sojourner at L——could leave unseen.

Edward Windsor, the leader of the excursion, was a young gentleman of family and fortune; handsome, generous hearted and agreeable; a favorite wherever he went, and no where more so than at L——, where quite a rivalry existed among the young ladies, each anxious to find favor in his eyes. Some from real admiration for the many good and noble qualities he possessed; some from a lower regard for his wealth and position; and others from mere love of conquest; so had the young gentleman possessed much vanity, this universal favor might have done him harm.

Careless of the honors he unconsciously won, he laughed good naturedly at the amiable syrens by whom he was surrounded, and, though courteous and kind to all, distinguished none above the rest; but as the pleasant circle was about to separate early in Autumn, he found himself regretting, secretly, the departure of one friend, in whose society he had enjoyed so much, that he almost decided to secure it, if possible, not for the winter, but for life.

This desire grew stronger as he thought of it, but a certain beautiful face smiled so bewitchingly upon him, when he came, and grew so sorrowful when he departed, that he sometimes fancied his happiness would be best secured by obtaining the heart belonging to the handsome face.

Kate Loring, though with no pretensions to beauty, possessed a certain life and vigor which gave a fresh and peculiar charm to her intelligent face, and contrasted pleasantly with the inanimate countenances about her.

She had read and thought much on many subjects sadly unfashionable, and though enjoying the various amusements of her young companions with the zest of a gay and cheerful nature, yet, when they were over, she could find in conversation, books, or her own thoughts, pleasant and profitable occupation for the hours which others spent in idleness or frivolous gossip.

Left at eighteen, with four younger brothers, she had filled the double place of parents and sister as few girls could have done, and was rewarded, for many anxieties and sacrifices, by the love and admiration of the lads, who looked upon "sister Kate" as unsurpassable in beauty, worth, or wisdom.

Her early trials had strengthened an originally strong character, till she possessed a decision and energy seldom seen in so young a woman. Her straightforward truthfulness and independence won the confidence of the most timid, while her womanly tenderness, and the softer virtues she possessed, though unobtrusively displayed, made many warm and faithful friends wherever she went.

Coming to L—— with her invalid brother, for country air and exercise, she straightway set to work to accomplish her purpose, never stopping to ask what people might think; or if any one else did the like. So while others were wasting the summer days by lounging on sofas, flirting in shaded parlors, or driving out in state, and on the sultry nights dancing in crowded rooms, she was up at dawn, walking or riding miles away among the hills, getting a healthy bloom upon her cheek, and fresh vigor of body and soul.

People stared, wondered, laughed, and then admired her. Some contented themselves with that, but others followed her example, and found in her a companion whose friendship grew in value as they learned to know her worth.

Alfred, Kate's brother, was a quiet lad, still feeble from a long illness, busy with his studies, and devoted to "sister Kate," his nurse and dearest friend.

Miss Amelia Langdon, the languid lady, was a beauty and a belle, accomplished in all the graceful arts of fascination and coquetry, but with little else to interest or charm. ·

She had set her heart upon the captivation of Mr. Windsor, and few thought there was any doubt of her success, for he admired her beauty and had paid her many kind attentions; though some said it was only since she had conceived such a warm attachment for Kate Loring. However, be that as it might, the two young ladies and the gentleman were great friends.

Toward sunset the party of travellers reached the village where they intended to pass the night. But the innkeeper, with many regrets, told them that his house was filled already with parties going and returning from the mountain, therefore they must go further on to a certain farm-house, two miles or more away, where they might be comfortably accommodated. So on they went, and were most hospitably received by the young farmer's wife, who was accustomed to entertain stray travellers to the mountain.

"May be you'd like to go a piece up the ravine; it's quite famous hereabouts, and well worth seeing, if you're fond of rocks and water, ladies and gentlemen," said their hostess, as they rose from her bountifully spread table.

Thanking her, the party strolled out to while away the twilight in a voyage of discovery. They climbed up the rocky way, following the babbling brook that dashed foaming down the deep ravine, whose sides were fringed with pines and carpeted with delicate ferns and moss. The higher they went the wilder it grew, and when they reached the rustic bridge which spanned the waterfall, the rocky glen, the broad green meadows, and the distant mountains, lay before them beautiful with evening lights and shadows.

"This stream reminds me of *your* style of woman, Miss Kate," said

Mr. Windsor, as, leaning on the rude railing of the bridge, he glanced from Miss Amelia, who was reclining gracefully upon a mossy bank gently swaying a green brake to and fro while gazing dreamily upon the scene before her, to Kate, who stood erect, on a projecting crag, with folded arms, and the red light streaming full upon her thoughtful face and gleaming eyes. There was something in her attitude and smile which made her beautiful as she looked down and answered, pointing to a little pool below them in a meadow:

"And that reminds me of yours, Mr. Windsor. See how placidly it lies, reflecting whatever shape may fall upon it, but with no life, no motion of its own. It may be clear and pleasant for awhile, but summer heats will dry its shallow waters, and winter frosts will freeze them. Winds may ruffle it, and weeds may choke whatever secret spring it possesses, and soon it will be gone or changed to a dark and stagnant pool, unlovely and unhealthful."

"Dear me, Kate, what strange ideas and tastes you have. I am sure the pretty pond in that nice meadow is far preferable to this noisy stream and these rough rocks. Don't you agree with me, Mr. Windsor?" Miss Amelia asked, grouping herself and her rustic parasol in a still more graceful attitude.

"Let me hear the other side, and then perhaps I can answer you better," he replied, looking up at the slender figure standing out in bold relief against the darkening sky.

Kate laughed a merry laugh, that echoed musically among the rocks, and said, glancing from the dell to the faces lifted to her own,

"Ah, you may smile, and think me a romantic girl, but I'll defend my beautiful bright stream, and prove its great superiority to any shallow pool, however clear. If my brook is strong and rapid, it is kind and gentle too; for see how it stays to bathe the little mosses and the maidens' hair that fringe the basins where it lingers for awhile, and then flows on, leaving all greener and more lovely than before. Like the generous deeds that beautify a noble life, trees, flowers and ferns all bend and gather round it, as toward a friend. Listen to its cheerful voice, and see with what bloom and freshness it fills this dell, so gloomy and so silent but for my light hearted brook."

"Spring rains and melting snows may render it a terrible and a destructive thing, Miss Kate. How then?"

"Like all strong natures, if it be not well and wisely governed it will carry ruin in its reckless course, but if controlled and turned to worthy purposes, the torrent grows more quiet, but not less deep and strong, and turns the mill wheel yonder, filling whole meadows with its music and its verdure, and, quietly surmounting every obstacle, leads a useful and a happy life, till, changing slowly to a noble river, it rolls serenely to the sea."

Kate's clear voice ceased, and for a moment nothing broke the silence but the dash of water, as if the stream leaped up to thank her for her sympathy and praise, and then flowed singing on with one more happy memory to swell the music of its cheerful voice.

"If I were sure that I possessed the power of governing as well as loving and admiring, then, like you, I should prefer the free mountain stream, Miss Kate," Mr. Windsor said, with a glance that deepened the color in her cheek.

"Shall we go now? the dew is falling and we must be off betimes to-morrow. Let me assist you down," he added, offering his hand.

But she sprung lightly from her perch, saying gaily,

"No, thank you; waterfalls need no help in tumbling over rocks. Devote yourself to the placid lake, for the least jar ruffles its tranquillity you know," and with her brother on her arm, Kate's active figure vanished down the winding path.

"What a dear strange creature she is, isn't she?" said Miss Amelia, as she rose with a charming sigh of pity for her friend's oddity.

"She is a very fine one I think," answered Mr. Windsor, taking her parasol and shawl with a queer smile lurking about his mouth.

"Well, yes, not beautiful, you know, but striking, perhaps, and she might be very agreeable if she were not so sadly masculine," Miss Amelia said, while a smile spread over her companion's face, and he laughed quietly to himself under cover of the deepening twilight, as she clung to his arm in affected terror at the steep descent, shrieking at toads, half-fainting at a snake, and bewailing stones, dirt and dew, till they reached the house and she sank utterly exhausted into the large cushioned chair prepared for Alfred.

Kate silently pillowed her head upon her shoulder, and filled the quiet room with the music of her cheerful voice, as she chatted, laughed and sang, exerting herself as much to entertain her brother as she had ever done to please a group of gay, admiring friends.

"Well, I must say, 'Lisha," said Mrs. Mills, as she came from the parlor where she had been to carry lights; "I must say, though the little lady is a sight the prettiest, and the smartest dressed, the tall one is worth a heap of such; for while the pretty one is dozing in the big chair where she ain't no right to be, the other one is chirping away in there, like a bird, to cheer up her brother's spirits, while she's dropping with sleep herself, I know. I declare it does a body's heart good to hear her say, 'Thank you, ma'am,' or look into her nice bright face, and I shouldn't wonder if the young gentleman thought so too."

Kate was just leaving the room to make Alfred comfortable for the night, so Mrs. Mills's outburst was plainly heard. The "young gentleman" nodded approvingly, and looked into the "nice bright face," which grew nicer and brighter with a blush and a smile as it went hastily away.

When she came down again to wake her friend, Kate found Mr. Windsor leaning over the great chair, chatting in a low voice with Amelia, who looked as if sleep was one of the lost arts.

As he looked up, Mr. Windsor saw a troubled, anxious expression flit across Kate's face. It was gone again instantly, and though Amelia wondered how any one could be tired when she felt so fresh herself, Kate never alluded, in self-defense, to their different modes of spending the evening, but waited till the young lady had settled her flounces and collected the various articles without which she never moved, and then with a quiet "good night," Kate went away.

Mr. Windsor sat a while meditating on the blush, smile and look, without coming to any very satisfactory conclusion, for the truth was, he found his regards for Kate increasing very rapidly. He had been first attracted by her faithfulness to her brother and the intelligent vivacity of her conversation; but he soon felt the real nobility of her character, and loved her in spite of himself.

For, like the best of mortals, he had his prejudices and weaknesses, and one of them was a great dislike of anything peculiar, or in the slightest degree unfeminine, according to his notion of the word. So, though always graceful and refined in word and manner, Kate's blunt sincerity, her quiet disregard for the false and foolish opinions of the world, and her peculiar ideas on many subjects, kept him in constant fear lest by some rash action or unwomanly sentiment she should dispel the charm which he now found in her society.

He often wished that she possessed some of Amelia's beauty, the fascination of which he daily felt; though at the same time, he was obliged to confess that there was a great lack of something in the young lady which he never found in Kate. So, wavering often in purpose though always true at heart, he watched and waited, hoping to find in Kate that union of gentleness and strength which makes a true womanly character.

His meditation ended just where it begun, and he strolled away to bed, leaving Mrs. Mills in a state of great curiosity to discover which of the ladies caused his thoughtful mood. As he leaned from his chamber window looking anxiously at the cloudy sky, Amelia's voice sounded from the room adjoining his, saying, with a drowsy laugh:

"I suppose you don't care to know what Mr. Windsor was saying to me when you came in?"

"Yes I do, if you choose to tell me," Kate answered with her usual straightforwardness.

"Ah, but I don't choose; only if you hear some day that we are engaged, you need not contradict it. But don't ask any questions, for I shall say no more, so good night to you!" and one of the young ladies laughed; and the other sighed.

The listener longed to know which did the latter, but having so far verified the old proverb in hearing no good of himself, he hastily withdrew, muttering something which sounded very like "baggage," which epithet, as there was only a carpet bag in the pantry, must have been applied to the truthful Miss Amelia, whose voice went murmuring on though he knocked his boots about to warn them of his neighborhood.

Presently it ceased, and giving a last look at the sky, he was about to close the window, when the sound of quiet weeping caught his ear. The wind had risen, and rain began to fall, but through these sounds the low sobs came distinctly every now and then, as of some one trying vainly to stifle their emotions.

Mr. Windsor stood motionless, longing to speak but feeling that he had no right to offer sympathy unasked, or venture to intrude it upon a private grief. But which could it be? he thought. Not Kate; she never wept, they said. Amelia often did, and he had seen her water the grave of a dead bird with copious showers; but not with such tears as were falling now. Yet what could either have to weep for? He longed to know that it was Kate, selfish as it seemed, and so sat listening till it ceased, and a light step passed his door and entered Alfred's room beyond his own. He heard the murmur of voices, and soon the continuous sound as if of some one reading.

"Alf must be ill," he thought, and remembering Kate's weariness, he hastily assumed his coat and went to offer his services as nurse or watcher.

The boy's door was open, and pausing in the gloom of the low passage, the young man looked at the group within with an interest that held him there in silence several minutes. Kate sat at her brother's bedside, reading in a low tone, hoping thus to soothe him to sleep. One arm lay over the pillow, gently caressing the restless head that tossed to and fro, the other hand shaded her eyes whose lids dropped heavily. Her black hair, loosened from its bands, lay on her shoulders, making her pale face paler, and over her whole countenance there was an air of patient weariness and sorrow, that touched the watcher's heart, and made the quiet, drooping figure in the dimly lighted room more beautiful than the animated one, bright with sunset radiance, which had been before him until now. The boy's eyes never wandered from her long, and a look of grateful love shone over his thin face as the music of her voice fell soothingly upon his ear, till restlessness and pain seemed chased away by the simple magic of her presence.

A tap disturbed them, and Mr. Windsor begged to share or lighten her long watch.

"The fatigue of the long ride and the sultriness of the night have made Alf restless, and I am reading him to sleep; that is all. Many thanks, but I need no help," Kate said, but in the unconscious tremor of her voice and the downcast eyes that never met his own, Mr. Windsor read all he desired to know; and gently taking the book from her hand, he led her to the door simply saying she must rest, for he had taken possession and would not be refused.

"Did you ever have a sister, Mr. Windsor?" Alf asked, abruptly, as Kate's door closed.

"No, Alf; neither brother nor sister."

"Then I pity you, that's all; brothers are well enough, but a sister like our Kate is a blessing worth having, sir."

"I hope you are grateful for it," said Mr. Windsor, laying down the book, seeing that the lad seemed disposed to talk, and feeling no inclination to check him, the subject being what it was.

"I should be a brute if I were not, remembering all she has done for us. Did she ever tell you about our life at home, sir?"

"No; but I should like to hear of it," answered Mr. Windsor, with great animation.

"Of course she didn't; I might have known that; for she couldn't speak of it without telling some of her own good deeds, and that she never does," said the boy, pleased with the other's interest, and eager to sound his sister's praises.

"Why you see, sir," he went on, "when father died, we found ourselves poorer than we had ever dreamed of being. Ned and Harry thought they must give up going to college, and that made them cross enough to wear out the patience of a saint; but it didn't Kate's. She just took the little fortune Aunt Mary left her, sent the boys off happy, put Will and I to school, settled things in the old house that we might always have a home to come to, and then, when all was done, we found that in making our happiness she had destroyed her own; for Mr. Elliott, when he found she was no longer rich, left her like a villain, and nearly broke her heart. I suppose I ought not to mention this, but my blood is up whenever I think of it, and Kate never speaks of it, so I must free my mind and vent my rage now and then. Yes, sir, he left her, and how many girls of eighteen, I wonder, would have borne it as she did? Her 'contempt killed her love,' she said, and though she altered very much, she never spoke of it, but went straight on, thinking, planning, working, for us good-for-nothing boys, when she needed help herself. That's nearly seven years ago, and now, instead of being a rich, happy wife, she is only our dear sister Kate. And people may call her poor and plain as much as they like; I know her worth; and, by Jove, sir, if ever I get on my legs again, if I don't make other people know it too, and don't pay part of the debt I owe her, I don't deserve to have any legs, and hope I sha'n't," cried the boy, thumping his pillow energetically to hide the tears in his eyes.

"Never think her poor or plain, for she is rendered beautiful and rich by her own virtue," Mr. Windsor said, earnestly, with an averted face — adding, more quietly: "I thank you for this, Alf, and now let me see you asleep, and then I shall have kept my promise to your sister."

And utterly unconscious of a single line he read on till the boy slept soundly, and nothing broke the midnight silence but the patter of the rain upon the roof. Then he stole away to dream of the quiet figure until dawn.

All night the rain fell heavily, and in the morning, instead of continuing their pilgrimage, the young party were forced to wait patiently till the storm should cease. After many consultations, and observations of the sky whose sullen appearance gave no hope, they settled down to spend the time as best they might.

Miss Amelia, after great lamentation, made herself comfortable on her cushioned throne, amusing herself and displaying her white jewelled hands to advantage among the beads and many colored silks of which she was crocheting some dainty article, while holding gracious audiences with Mr. Windsor and Alfred, and laughing at Kate, who had completed her conquest of Mrs. Mills by relieving her of the children, whose wants, mishaps, and uproars seriously impeded the progress of her household duties.

But though Miss Amelia laughed, Mr. Windsor thought Kate had never looked so well, as he watched the gentle wiles she used to win the friendship of the little ones, and saw her sitting on the floor building block houses, with the baby cooing in her lap, or the other three hopping merrily about her, shouting at the splendid towers she raised so patiently for them to demolish; putting their chubby faces close to hers, and showing by every artless look and word their love and admiration for the "nice kind lady," who possessed the power to make a rainy day such a festival of fun for them.

Miss Amelia looked quite disagreeable in spite of all her beauty, when she pushed away an admiring urchin who ventured to lay hands upon the trinkets at her side, saying with a sharpness quite astonishing:

"Oh, go away, child, your hands are shockingly dirty. Go to Miss Loring, for mercy sake; one victim is enough, I'm sure."

And as the rebuffed young gentleman indignantly went back to his old friend, the lady's voice sank into its usual musical drawl, and with her sweetest smile she renewed the conversation. But Mr. Windsor soon deserted, and joining the noisy group in the corner, found himself so comfortable that he stayed till dinner time.

As the afternoon wore on and still the rain poured down, Miss Amelia's patience was exhausted, and after a few fretful exclamations she retired to her room where, in a nap and a novel, she found some relief from her ennui.

Kate begged some sewing of Mrs. Mills, as a favor, but her quick eye had discovered that, like many farmers' wives, the poor young woman was so burdened with work that her health was giving way, and her children suffering for the care she could not give them.

So leaving her hostess to a few hours' rest, with her little ones about her, Kate sat stitching pinafores with an energy and dispatch that showed her zeal; Alfred worked on an unfinished sketch, Mr. Windsor read aloud, and the time slipped so pleasantly away, that it was dusk before they had thought of weariness.

"Hark!" said Kate, suddenly dropping her work. "What is that?"

They listened, and a loud continuous roar like distant thunder was plainly heard.

"It is the brook, but it sounds very near," said Mr. Windsor, going to the window. A sudden exclamation brought his companions to his side, and they saw a dark flood rushing by where an hour ago there had been a grassy road.

"This is a wild freak of your Undine's, Miss Kate. See how it washes away that bank opposite. I'm afraid the bridge will go, and then we are prisoners here, unless a boat can be found. How do you like this adventure, Alf?" said Mr. W.

"Would you be so kind as to step out a minute, sir? I'd like a word with you if you please," said the farmer, at this moment showing his anxious face at the door.

Mr. Windsor followed him to a back door, and there a wild and somewhat alarming sight presented itself. The old house stood upon a little mound. On one side flowed the stream, on the other a green lane wound over a bridge from the road below. The brook now came foaming down from the fall, bearing with it stones, trees, and the ruins of the rustic bridge: At a narrow bend close to the house a mass of rubbish had collected, half choking up the stream, which had risen higher and higher, till it overflowed and poured along the lane, forcing its passage through every obstacle, till the barn was separated from them by the deep gully the water had worn in the sandy soil.

"You see, sir, if the dam above the fall should give way, we ain't as safe as we might be," said the farmer, as they stood watching the furious stream and listening to its increasing roar.

"But it's pretty firm, and if the 'spillins' don't give way, we shall do. I jest would say that if it does, the barn may go; so if you'll lend a hand I'll get the horses over here into the shed. I'll wade across and fetch 'em over if you'll take 'em on this side for they may give trouble, and it's got to be done quick, for the water is deepening every minute."

Mr. Windsor was ready instantly, and, standing on the bank, watched the farmer make his way across. The rain poured down in sheets and the roar of the fall grew every moment louder, while the black stream whirled swiftly by carrying all before it.

Mr. Mills had just descended into the water, leading one of the horses, when a large timber shot down the current with such velocity that, before a warning cry could be uttered, the farmer was carried away by it and the terrified horse was careering wildly from the stream to the barn.

A loud shout brought the anxious faces at the windows in a crowd to the door, and Kate, putting back her brother, sprung down to the bank to find Mr. Windsor, pale and dripping, with the young farmer lying senseless across his knee with blood flowing from a deep cut on the forehead and one leg doubled under him in a strange, unnatural way, that made her sick to see.

Never stopping to scream, faint, or cry, Kate, without a word, supported the wounded head on her shoulder, while Mr. Windsor, with the strength of excitement, lifted the man in his arms, and carried him through the trembling group into the house, and laid him on his bed.

"Amelia, take these children and quiet them while Mrs. Mills and I attend to her husband," Kate said, trying to make herself heard through the screams of the babies and the poor woman's loud cries, for " 'Lisha to speak one word to her."

But Amelia was preparing to faint on Alfred's shoulder, and would have done so, if Kate had not gone to her, saying, in her decided voice, with a slight shake to rouse the young lady's faculties,

"Listen to me, Amelia; this is not the time to faint. Be a woman and keep these children quietly out of the way for their mother's sake. Mind me, and forget yourself, there is no danger yet."

Amelia obeyed like a child, and receiving the little ones as if she were afraid of them, administered a few vague pats and scraps of comfort. But the children refused to be consoled by such means, and roared louder than ever; till, at a signal from his sister, Alfred carried them off to another room, and peace was restored.

"Can you hold the bath while I bathe his forehead, Amelia? Mrs. Mills is trembling so she cannot stand," Kate asked, as her friend showed her frightened face at the door.

"Oh, I couldn't, the sight of blood makes me so faint. Do come away, Kate, how can you do it!" whimpered Miss Amelia, hastily retreating.

"Let me help you if I can," said Mr. Windsor, coming to the bed, instead of following the weeping lady to console and comfort her, as she hoped he would.

Kate's hands were as cold as ice, but firmer than those that met her own; and though her lips and cheek were white, she never trembled nor turned away from the ghastly sight before her, but with a light, skillful touch bound up the wound, and soon brought back the life and color to the poor man's face. He muttered feebly, as he looked into the pitying countenance above him.

"You're very good, Miss, and I don't know what we'd have done without you. Don't cry, Jane, it's all right now; she'll bring me round in a minute."

"You must have a doctor, sir, directly. I'll saddle one of the horses and go for him," said Mr. Windsor, as he hurried away. But as he came struggling up the bank with the first one, Kate stood there, and simply saying,

"I will help you, for no time must be lost and it's dangerous work alone." She took the bridle from his hand, led the animal into the shed, and was back again in time to receive the others, as, one by one, he led them over.

When all were safe they paused a moment to take breath, for the wind blew fiercely, and the rain fell faster than ever. As they stood thus, a sudden rush far up the dell warned them that the dam, the farmer spoke of, had probably given way. Their fear proved true, for before the young man could cross, the swollen torrent came thundering down bringing destruction and dismay. For as it swept by, the opposite bank gave way, and the old barn fell with a crash into the stream, turning its course dangerously toward the house.

One after the other Mr. Windsor led the horses to the water's edge, but none would venture in, and the treacherous bottom, the swift current, and the logs constantly dashing by added to the gloom; the wind and rain might have deterred even braver swimmers.

"I must go on foot, then," he said, "but I dislike leaving you all here in such apparent danger, for another turn might take the house. This accident to Mills is most unfortunate, however it's not time to talk; I'll get a lantern and be off."

But when the group within doors learned of his decision, they opposed it with so many arguments and lamentations that he was thoroughly perplexed as to what was best. Even Mr. Mills called faintly from his bed —

"Don't leave the women, sir, for me, I'll get on somehow till morning, or till the danger's over, for the storm can't last much longer. Stand by 'em, sir, for heaven's sake, and let the boy go if any one does."

Kate had stood listening silently, but now said decidedly as she drew near them —

"Alf must not stir, it would be going to his death, but *I* can and will; say no more, but let me set out instantly."

"You, Miss Kate? It's perfectly impossible," cried Mr. Windsor and the rest, in an astonished chorus.

"Listen a minute," she answered, quietly, "and you will see the plan is a reasonable one. Mr. Mills must have a doctor, and we must have help. You, Mr. Windsor, ought not to leave them. Alf is out of the question, and Mrs. Mills must stay to comfort her husband and her children. Who, then, remains to go but Amelia or me? one of us must, I leave it to you to say which it shall be."

The person addressed glanced from the breathless beauty sitting in her disordered finery, speechless with amazement and terror, to the energetic figure before him, standing calm and collected amid the tumult within and without, courage in her eye and the glow of her generous purpose shining in her face, inspiring confidence and hope in a single glance.

He caught the smile that lingered on her lips as she watched him, and divining its meaning he answered with a frank laugh —

"You are right, Miss Kate, the strong-minded wins the day, so if any safe means can be found by which to cross the stream, I suppose we must let you go, rash as it seems."

"But, my dear Miss, the rain and the dreadful roads!"

"Oh Kate! alone at night, how dare you!"

"Let *me* go, sister, I can stand it!"

[48]

"You're a brave girl, and we shan't forget, Miss," were a few of the exclamations that went on around her, as Kate wrapped herself up in the hooded cloak Mrs. Mills gave her, and bidding them be of good cheer, lit her lantern and went out into the storm.

Mr. Windsor followed her with a singularly bright and earnest face, considering the time and place, and after some search found a heavy beam wedged between the banks and firm enough to bear her weight.

"Miss Kate, I fear I am doing wrong in permitting this," he said, as she paused a moment looking over the wild stream into the gloom beyond.

"It is two lonely miles, and the storm does not abate. Have you no fear, and can I not dissuade you from it?"

"Fear is one of the soft, lady-like qualities I am so unfortunate as not to possess," Kate answered with a little bitterness in her tone. But it was gone as she bent to take the lantern, with the old smile on her lips, though something glistened softly in her eye as she said cheerfully —

"Do not try to keep me, for I ought to go. Only take care of Alfred, and put some courage into poor Amelia. Now each to our work — you to watch, and I to wander; so good bye."

And with a wave of her hand she set out lonely upon her journey. When half-way across the perilous bridge she paused suddenly and nearly fell, startled by a loud scream from Amelia, who was watching from the porch.

Alfred unceremoniously pushed her in and shut the door in her face, while Mr. Windsor sprung forward as he saw the dark figure waver for a moment.

But a cheery voice cried "all was well," and in silence they watched the light flicker over the black water and glide away till it was lost in the windings of the road.

And now, when it was too late to call her back, both the young men wondered how they had ever let her go, and fancied every possible and impossible accident which could befall her. The two long miles through lonely wood, the overflowed roads and broken bridges, the rain, the darkness, and the hour, all haunted them, till they would have followed, but for their promise to stand by the helpless creatures left to their protection.

Restless and anxious, they went to and fro, often looking, with a cheering word, into the room where the wounded man lay suffering, while his wife, surrounded by the sleeping children, tended him with every comfort her loving heart could offer.

Then they wandered out again to look for Kate, long before she could return, to quiet the restless horses, to listen to the whistling of the wind, and watch the dangerous eddies of the stream. The banks were washing rapidly away, and the little mound on which the house stood seemed hourly to contract and bring the stream still nearer to the walls.

With logs and stones they strove to turn its course, but little could be done. So hour after hour dragged on and no help came. The darkness and the storm increased, and as they sat together in the little shed, anxiously waiting, each followed silently in thought the lonely figure with the flickering light. Wondering where it might be then, pushing bravely on, or resting by the way? Or was the light extinguished, and the face which had so lately smiled on them turned unavailingly to them for help, bewildered in some gloomy spot; or was it lifted calmly to the pitiless sky as black waves bore it on lifeless and still after the treacherous fall and the brief struggle were past.

As they thought thus they unconsciously looked into each other's faces for some cheering hope, but found none, and sat pale and silent listening to the tumult round them.

"It is nearly eleven, Alfred, and she must be lost; but hark, what's that?" Mr. Windsor said, as the sudden surge of water sounded under them, and the shed shook violently. "Out with the horses, quick! the bank below has gone, and we shall have it over our heads in an instant," he shouted, through the crash of falling stones and earth.

The shed stood a few rods from the house, and as they watched it settling to its fall, Alfred said, with a hopeless glance toward the distant town,

"If she is not here soon it will be too late. A few stout arms on the other side could turn the flood and save poor Mills from further damage. I wonder no one thinks of him. What shall we do, sir, and where can Kate have lost herself?"

His only answer was the noise of the shed as it went down, and standing on the door-step they looked upon the conflict that went on below, as the stream tossed and tumbled foaming over the ruins, coming nearer and nearer as the bank gave way.

"We must warn them within there, and devise some way to get them safely over the rocks, if the house begins to go," Mr. Windsor said, with a last despairing look into the gloom.

But as he turned away a dozen lights came flashing up the hill, voices echoed cheerily, and figures were seen hastening to their aid. With one shout of welcome the two stood watching, with eager eyes and hurried breath, the movements of the approaching party. One light came swiftly on before the rest and passed just opposite the dangerous curve that widened every moment, and Kate's voice sounded loud and clear above the din, saying —

"The house is in danger; dig just here, and turn the stream from the bank. Bend to it heartily and all will be safe in an hour."

"The bridge you spoke of, alas, is gone. How are we to cross?" another voice inquired, as the clash of shovels and the quick rattle of earth told how well Kate was obeyed.

"Down with that tree then, we can cross on that," she said. "Here is the axe, Doctor, I will hold the lantern for you. Alfred, Mr. Windsor, are you there? Keep at a distance and we will be with you soon."

"By Jove, sir, my sister is splendid to-night. Look at her work!" cried Alfred, pale with excitement, as he held fast by his friend's shoulder, and leaned forward eagerly.

Mr. Windsor did not answer, but his eye never moved from the dark figure near the tree with the dull light of the lantern shining on it, showing glimpses of a face as resolute if not as calm as when he saw it last.

The shovels clattered and the axe rang, till the rocks echoed back the sound, and soon the tree fell crashing down across the stream. The young men sprang to clear the rocks away, and presently, with a last word of encouragement to the men who worked as if for a wage, Kate came slowly over the rough bridge into her brother's arms.

"Say, Alf, dear, never stop to kiss me now, I'm safe and much must be done before you all are too. So come in from the rain and let us see to Mr. Mills," she said, after one embrace, as close and warm as it was brief, and then followed by the village doctor and her friend she hastened in.

With a face glowing with exercise, eyes brilliant with excitement, garments dripping, and hair fluttering in the wind, Kate came into the full glaze of the lights lit up to guide her home, and Amelia with a little scream of rapture ran into her arms crying out,

"Oh, Kate, my dear, brave girl, have you come back at last, and neither drowned nor murdered by the way? How glad, how grateful we all are for this, and how I wish I were like you."

The long hours spent in danger, and alone, had not been without some good to one head and heart, both better than they seemed when once roused to action. So Miss Amelia clung to Kate, and sobbed out her admiration, gratitude and excitement, on her bosom.

Kate looked down upon her friend, with a smile half merry and half sad, wondering, while she soothed, if this pale faced dishevelled creature, so woebegone and weak, could be the beautiful and graceful Amelia she had sometimes envied when certain eyes looked admiringly upon her. She did not see the glance now shining on herself from those same eyes, for suddenly the lights and faces danced before her, and she knew nothing more until she found herself lying on the sofa, with some one gently chafing her cold hands.

"Do not let him know I was so foolish as to faint, Alfred, for he would only laugh at me, and I tried so hard to keep up for you all, so do not tell him," she said, half unconsciously expressing her first thought.

"Tell who, dear Kate," said Mr. Windsor, pressing the hands he held, and bending nearer to look earnestly into her face.

She looked up at him, with a startled glance, and her cheek grew crimson as the cushion where it lay. But after a brief pause she answered frankly.

"You, Mr. Windsor."

"And why think so unkindly of me, Kate."

"Forgive me if it seemed so, but I would not have you think me weak, both because I value your opinion, and desire to *be* all that I may *seem.*"

"I never thought you weak and never can; for the beautiful strong nature, womanly and true, which you so well described and I so longed to see, I have found to-night in you, dear Kate."

And as he spoke the young man kissed the hands that lay so passively and Kate sat erect with all her lost bloom glowing in her face. But she did not speak, for Alfred now came hurrying in with a cordial and a mandate from the doctor for her instant retirement and rest, if she would escape the consequences of her long exposure to the storm.

She quietly submitted, and leaning on her brother whose pride and tenderness were beautiful to see, she went away to dream as she had never done before, leaving Mr. Windsor standing with the wet cloak on his arm, but in thoughts so pleasant that he never stirred till his reverie was broken by the sudden exit of Miss Amelia and the entrance of the doctor, who, having dressed the wounds, had some preparation to make before attending to the broken leg.

"How is the young lady, sir?" he asked, unrolling his bandages. "A pretty wild night's work for her, though not so bad a one as your poor Mills has had."

"She has retired according to your advice, Doctor, but I hope no serious consequences need be apprehended, sir."

"Oh no, a good night's rest will set her up. But I tell you what, sir, there aint many ladies who would have done what she did," said the old man, with great animation. "Why, do you know she got lost, and went a mile into the woods, and found her way out again; and, what's more, come all the way back without a word of complaint or sign of fear, though it's not an easy walk, I can tell you, such a night as this."

"Where did she find you, and how did you collect so many men to help us?" asked Mr. Windsor, with an eagerness that far outdid the doctor's who answered willingly,

"Well, this was the way, sir: We were assembled as usual around the tavern fire, as we always do stormy nights, and were talking over matters and things, when the door opened, and in came the young lady, white as a ghost and dripping like a mermaid, but as calm and cool as the best of us, and in half a dozen words she told us your fix. At first nobody stirred. being kind of dumbfounded like at the sight of her and the suddenness of the whole thing. Besides, between you and me, Elisha Mills aint liked over and above well hereabouts; so, thinking the women had been scared about nothing, we were rather slow in moving.

"When she saw that, her eyes flashed and the color come; and looking straight at me, she said,

'If you're a man, sir, you will come instantly, for Mr. Mills is suffering for your help. As for the rest, let it be said of them that a woman and a stranger came miles alone through such a storm as this to ask in vain their aid for an unfortunate neighbor, who was powerless to save his wife and children from the flood that threatened to lay his home in ruins. Let them stay. I do not ask their help, unless, remembering their own homes, they can give it, freely and like men.'

"By George, sir, there wasn't one of us that didn't grow as red as that pillow, and turned out with a will. And when they heard what she had left and come through, there was a regular stir, and each was trying to do and offer most. But she wouldn't rest, or ride, or be carried, and kept the whole way through, thick and thin. She's a fine girl, sir, and you've a good right to be proud of such a sister." And the enthusiastic old doctor wiped his hot face and shook hands heartily with the young gentleman, who answered, smiling,

"She is not my sister, sir, but I'm prouder of her than if she were."

"Oh, your wife, is she? Lord bless me, I never thought of that; but what on earth possessed you to let her go?"

"Neither wife nor sister, doctor, so I had no right to keep her; though I tried; but she was the only one who had the courage and could be spared, and I was compelled to stay, you see."

"Oh, but I see, I see! It's all right; you'll weather most any storm with her at the helm; and I give you joy, sir," said the doctor; with a knowing and an approving smile, as he looked into his companion's telltale face, and hurried away with a merry twinkle in his eye.

At midnight the storm began to abate; and the sun came cheerily up, looking through his veil of mist upon the scene which had lately been so terrible and wild. The stream flowed more quietly, and the ravine looked green and sparkling as the sunshine fell on leaves and mosses bright with rain drops.

"Has Miss Loring appeared yet?" Mr. Windsor inquired of Mrs. Mills, as he came down from his chamber with as light a step and gay a face as if the past night had been one of great festivity and pleasure.

Mrs. Mills, comforted by her husband's quiet sleep and the doctor's kind assurances of a speedy recovery, was moving busily about, that all should be in order for her guests, and, looking up from her work, said eagerly, with tears in her eyes,

"Yes sir, she is out somewhere with the folks, and oh, sir, would you tell her how grateful 'Lisha and I are for all her goodness to us? We are to you all, sir, but specially to her who done so much, and now won't let me thank her for it."

"I'll tell her with *all my heart,* Mrs. Mills," said her guest, as he hurried away, leaving her, with a suddenly enlightened face, to nod her head wisely at the fire as she put the kettle on.

Mr. Windsor found Kate standing on the temporary bridge the men had constructed, watching them as they worked as sturdily as if her words were still ringing in their ears, and they were bound to prove them false.

They had all shouldered their shovels and gone home. Alfred and Amelia were waiting, and Mrs. Mills was in despair about her cooling breakfast, before the two figures, which had been seen going slowly into the ravine, came as slowly back, wondering at the hour and penitent for their forgetfulness.

Miss Amelia looked eagerly for any suspicious symptoms in either of the faces, which seemed utterly unconscious of her scrutiny; but Kate was calm and cheerful as usual, and Mr. Windsor, though a little absent, so like himself, that she felt assured nothing had happened to overthrow her hopes, and was content.

At noon the carriage and horses were conveyed across the quietest part of the stream; and, with many kind wishes on both sides, the young party took leave. Mr. Windsor was detained a moment behind the rest by Mrs. Mills, who insisted on restoring the little roll he had left in her hand at parting, saying as she looked after Kate,

"I couldn't take it, sir, for she, the excellent young lady, left some under 'Lisha's pillar, because she knew I wouldn't take it; and I shouldn't now, but he said she seemed so pleased with her little trick, not knowing he was awake and watching of her, and we don't wish to spoil her pleasure. Just tell her this, and don't ask me to take another mite. I'm heartily obliged but I couldn't do it. So good bye, and a pleasant journey, sir."

He shook her rough hand warmly, and went away, but the roll came back into Jenny's pocket when she had watched the carriage out of sight.

"What an eventful pilgrimage ours has been," said Alfred, as they drew near their journey's end, and the mountain rose up close before them.

"I shall soon set out upon a more eventful one," replied Mr. Windsor, with a glance at Miss Amelia, who was apparently sleeping peacefully behind her veil.

"I wish we were going with you, for I like this style of travelling, amazingly. Are you going alone?" asked Alfred.

"No, your sister Kate has promised to go with me."

"My sister Kate?" began the boy in great surprise, but a single glance explained the mystery, and, with a face of perfect satisfaction and delight, he gave a hand to sister and friend, saying,

"I thought you'd find the woman you so much desired to see close at your side, if you only chose to look, Mr. Windsor, and I give my consent and heartily."

"The lady says she has decided not to go, sir, as she has met some friends here, and prefers to stay with them," said a waiter, coming to them, as they stood waiting for Amelia at the foot of the mountain.

"I don't believe she was asleep, and so heard all we said in the carriage; that's a good joke," cried Alfred. "And that accounts for her willingness to stay behind with the Morgans whom she hates. I'm glad of it for I don't fancy dragging up the mountain with her on my arm."

"Poor Amelia!" said Kate with a sigh of generous pity for her friend's disappointment.

"Kate, was the falsehood she told you the cause of your tears last night," said Mr. Windsor, smiling at the look of wonder and confusion in the face before him, as he heard the low assent which Kate's truthful tongue could not refuse to utter.

"And now I hope you are satisfied, for I have proved myself womanly and weak on two occasions. But if we are going let us hasten. Come Edward, I am waiting for you."

Kate stood above them on the first green slope of the mountain side, and as she spoke the name that never seemed so musical to its owner's ears before, she stretched her hand to him. And from the figure bathed in light and the earnest face turned toward the distant peak, there seemed to come a voice softly saying, "Come up higher."

It touched the heart not yet grown cold and worldly, and looking up at her, with mingled reverence and love, her friend answered, half playfully half seriously,

"You are standing now where I would have you, dearest Kate, above me in the sunshine, leading me by your gentle hand, out of the shadows here below, along the narrow path that winds through light and darkness like our lives, up to the purer air and sunlight of the distant mountain top."

"No, this is not my place, I would not be above you as I now am, nor yet below, like poor Amelia in the garden. But *here* where every woman should be, at her husband's side, walking together through life's light and shadow," Kate replied, as she came and held her hand to his with a smile serene and beautiful as the mellow Autumn sunshine glowing on her face.

He held it fast in both of his, and so they journeyed upward side by side.

Love and Self-Love

Atlantic Monthly Magazine, March 1860

*F*RIENDLESS, WHEN YOU are gone? But, Jean, you surely do not mean that Effie has no claim on any human creature, beyond the universal one of common charity?" I said, as she ceased, and lay panting on her pillows, with her sunken eyes fixed eagerly upon my own.

"Ay, Sir, I do; for her grandfather has never by word or deed acknowledged her, or paid the least heed to the letter her poor mother sent him from her dying bed seven years ago. He is a lone old man, and this child is the last of his name; yet he will not see her, and cares little whether she be dead or living. It's a bitter shame, Sir, and the memory of it will rise up before him when he comes to lie where I am lying now."

"And you have kept the girl safe in the shelter of your honest home all these years? Heaven will remember that, and in the great record of good deeds will set the name of Adam Lyndsay far below that of poor Jean

Burns," I said, pressing the thin hand that had succored the orphan in her need.

But Jean took no honor to herself for that charity, and answered simply to my words of commendation.

"Sir, her mother was my foster-child; and when she left that stern old man for love of Walter Home, I went, too, for love of her. Ah, dear heart! she had sore need of me in the weary wanderings which ended only when she lay down by her dead husband's side and left her bairn to me. Then I came here to cherish her among kind souls where I was born; and here she has grown up, an innocent young thing, safe from the wicked world, the comfort of my life, and the one thing I grieve at leaving when the time that is drawing very near shall come."

"Would not an appeal to Mr. Lyndsay reach him now, think you? Might not Effie go to him herself? Surely, the sight of such a winsome creature would touch his heart, however hard."

But Jean rose up in her bed, crying, almost fiercely, —

"No, Sir! no! My child shall never go to beg a shelter in that hard man's house. I know too well the cold looks, the cruel words, that would sting her high spirit and try her heart, as they did her mother's. No, Sir, — rather than that, she shall go with Lady Gower."

"Lady Gower? What has she to do with Effie, Jean?" I asked, with increasing interest.

"She will take Effie as her maid, Sir. A hard life for my child! but what can I do?" And Jean's keen glance seemed trying to read mine.

"A waiting-maid? Heaven forbid!" I ejaculated, as a vision of that haughty lady and her three wild sons swept through my mind.

I rose, paced the room in silence for a little time, then took a sudden resolution, and, turning to the bed, exclaimed, —

"Jean, I will adopt Effie. I am old enough to be her father; and she shall never feel the want of one, if you will give her to my care."

To my surprise, Jean's eager face wore a look of disappointment as she listened, and with a sigh replied, —

"That's a kind thought, Sir, and a generous one; but it cannot be as you wish. You may be twice her age, but still too young for that. How could Effie look into that face of yours, so bonnie, Sir, for all it is so grave, and, seeing never a wrinkle on the forehead, nor a white hair among the black, how could she call you father? No, it will not do, though so kindly meant. Your friends would laugh at you, Sir, and idle tongues might speak ill of my bairn."

"Then what can I do, Jean?" I asked, regretfully.

"Make her your wife, Sir."

I turned sharply and stared at the woman, as her abrupt reply reached my ear. Though trembling for the consequences of her boldly spoken wish, Jean did not shrink from my astonished gaze; and when I saw the wistfulness of that wan face, the smile died on my lips, checked by the tender courage which had prompted the utterance of her dying hope.

"My good Jean, you forget that Effie is a child, and I a moody, solitary man, with no gifts to win a wife or make home happy."

"Effie is sixteen, Sir, — a fair, good lassie for her years; and you — ah, Sir, *you* may call yourself unfit for wife and home, but the poorest, saddest creature in this place knows that the man whose hand is always open, whose heart is always pitiful, is not the one to live alone, but to win and to deserve a happy home and a true wife. Oh, Sir, forgive me, if I have been too bold; but my time is short, and I love my child so well, I cannot leave the desire of my heart unspoken, for it is my last."

As the words fell brokenly from her lips, and tears streamed down her pallid cheek, a great pity took possession of me, the old longing to find some solace for my solitary life returned again, and peace seemed to smile on me from little Effie's eyes.

"Jean," I said, "give me till to-morrow to consider this new thought. I fear it cannot be; but I have learned to love the child too well to see her thrust out from the shelter of your home to walk through this evil world alone. I will consider your proposal, and endeavor to devise some future for the child which shall set your heart at rest. But before you urge this further, let me tell you that I am not what you think me. I am a cold, selfish man, often gloomy, often stern, — a most unfit guardian for a tender creature like this little girl. The deeds of mine which you call kind are not true charities; it frets me to see pain, and I desire my ease above all earthly things. You are grateful for the little I have done for you, and deceive yourself regarding my true worth; but of one thing you may rest assured, — I am an honest man, who holds his name too high to stain it with a false word or a dishonorable deed."

"I do believe you, Sir," Jean answered, eagerly. "And if I left the child to you, I could die this night in peace. Indeed, Sir, I never should have dared to speak of this, but for the belief that you loved the girl. What else could I think, when you came so often and were so kind to us?"

"I cannot blame you, Jean; it was my usual forgetfulness of others which so misled you. I was tired of the world, and came hither to find peace in solitude. Effie cheered me with her winsome ways, and I learned to look on her as the blithe spirit whose artless wiles won me to forget a bitter past and a regretful present." I paused; and then added, with a smile,

"But, in our wise schemes, we have overlooked one point: Effie does not love me, and may decline the future you desire me to offer her."

A vivid hope lit those dim eyes, as Jean met my smile with one far brighter, and joyfully replied, —

"She *does* love you, Sir; for you have given her the greatest happiness she has ever known. Last night she sat looking silently into the fire there with a strange gloom on her bonnie face, and, when I asked what she was dreaming of, she turned to me with a look of pain and fear, as if dismayed at some great loss, but she only said, 'He is going, Jean! What shall I do?'

"Poor child! she will miss her friend and teacher, when I'm gone; and I shall miss the only human creature that has seemed to care for me for years," I sighed, — adding, as I paused upon the threshold of the door, "Say nothing of this to Effie till I come to-morrow, Jean."

I went away, and far out on the lonely moor sat down to think. Like a weird magician, Memory led me back into the past, calling up the hopes and passions buried there. My childhood, — fatherless and motherless, but not unhappy; for no wish was ungratified, no idle whim denied. My boyhood, — with no shadows over it but those my own wayward will called up. My manhood, — when the great joy of my life arose, my love for Agnes, a midsummer dream of bloom and bliss, so short-lived and so sweet! I felt again the pang that wrung my heart when she coldly gave me back the pledge I thought so sacred and so sure, and the music of her marriage-bells tolled the knell of my lost love. I seemed to hear them still wafted across the purple moor through the silence of those fifteen years.

My life looked gray and joyless as the wide waste lying hushed around me, unblessed with the verdure of a single hope, a single love; and as I looked down the coming years, my way seemed very solitary, very dark.

Suddenly a lark soared upward from the heath, cleaving the silence with its jubilant song. The sleeping echoes woke, the dun moor seemed to smile, and the blithe music fell like dew upon my gloomy spirit, wakening a new desire.

"What this bird is to the moor might little Effie be to me," I thought within myself, longing to possess the cheerful spirit which had power to gladden me.

"Yes," I mused, "the old home will seem more solitary now than ever; and if I cannot win the lark's song without a golden fetter, I will give it one, and while it sings for love of me it shall not know a want or fear."

Heaven help me! I forgot the poor return I made my lark for the sweet liberty it lost.

All that night I pondered the altered future Jean had laid before me, and the longer I looked the fairer it seemed to grow. Wealth I cared nothing for; the world's opinion I defied; ambition had departed, and passion I believed lay dead; — then why should I deny myself the consolation which seemed offered to me? I would accept it; and as I resolved, the dawn looked in at me, fresh and fair as little Effie's face.

I met Jean with a smile, and, as she read its significance aright, there shone a sudden peace upon her countenance, more touching than her grateful words.

Effie came singing from the burn-side, as unconscious of the change which awaited her as the flowers gathered in her plaid and crowning her bright hair.

I drew her to my side, and in the simplest words asked her if she would go with me when Jean's long guardianship was ended. Joy, sorrow, and surprise stirred the sweet composure of her face, and quickened the tranquil beating of her heart. But as I ceased, joy conquered grief and wonder; for she clapped her hands like a glad child, exclaiming, —

"Go with you, Sir? Oh, if you knew how I long to see the home you have so often pictured to me, you would never doubt my willingness to go."

"But, Effie, you do not understand. Are you willing to go with me as my wife?" I said, — with a secret sense of something like remorse, as I uttered that word, which once meant so much to me, and now seemed such an empty title to bestow on her.

The flowers dropped from the loosened plaid, as Effie looked with a startled glance into my face; the color left her cheeks, and the smile died on her lips, but a timid joy lit her eye, as she softly echoed my last words, —

"Your wife? It sounds very solemn, though so sweet. Ah, Sir, I am not wise or good enough for that!"

A child's humility breathed in her speech, but something of a woman's fervor shone in her uplifted countenance, and sounded in the sudden tremor of her voice.

"Effie, I want you as you are," I said, — "no wiser, dear, — no better. I want your innocent affection to appease the hunger of an empty heart, your blithe companionship to cheer my solitary home. Be still a child to me, and let me give you the protection of my name."

Effie turned to her old friend, and, laying her young face on the pillow close beside the worn one grown so dear to her, asked, in a tone half pleading, half regretful, —

"Dear Jean, shall I go so far away from you and the home you gave me when I had no other?"

"My bairn, I shall not be here, and it will never seem like home with old Jean gone. It is the last wish I shall ever know, to see you safe with this good gentleman who loves my child. Go, dear heart, and be happy; and Heaven bless and keep you both!"

Jean held her fast a moment, and then, with a whispered prayer, put her gently away. Effie came to me, saying, with a look more eloquent than her meek words, —

"Sir, I will be your wife, and love you very truly all my life."

I drew the little creature to my breast, and felt a tender pride in knowing she was mine. Something in the shy caress those soft arms gave touched my cold nature with a generous warmth, and the innocence of that confiding heart was an appeal to all that made my manhood worth possessing.

Swiftly those few weeks passed, and when old Jean was laid to her last sleep, little Effie wept her grief away upon her husband's bosom, and soon learned to smile in her new English home. Its gloom departed when she came, and for a while it was a very happy place. My bitter moods seemed banished by the magic of the gentle presence that made sunshine there, and I was conscious of a fresh grace added to the life so wearisome before.

I should have been a father to the child, watchful, wise, and tender; but old Jean was right, — I was too young to feel a father's calm affection or to know a father's patient care. I should have been her teacher, striving to cultivate the nature given to my care, and fit it for the trials Heaven sends to all. I should have been a friend, if nothing more, and given her those innocent delights that make youth beautiful and its memory sweet.

I was a master, content to give little, while receiving all she could bestow.

Forgetting her loneliness, I fell back into my old way of life. I shunned the world, because its gayeties had lost their zest. I did not care to travel, for home now possessed a charm it never had before. I knew there was an eager face that always brightened when I came, light feet that flew to welcome me, and hands that loved to minister to every want of mine. Even when I sat engrossed among my books, there was a pleasant consciousness that I was the possessor of a household sprite whom a look could summon and a gesture banish. I loved her as I loved a picture or a flower, — a little better than my horse and hound, — but far less than I loved my most unworthy self.

And she, — always so blithe when I was by, so diligent in studying my desires, so full of simple arts to win my love and prove her gratitude, — she never asked for any boon, and seemed content to live alone with me in that still place, so utterly unlike the home she had left. I had not learned to read that true heart then. I saw those happy eyes grow wistful when I went, leaving her alone; I missed the roses from her cheek, faded for want of gentler care; and when the buoyant spirit which had been her chiefest charm departed, I fancied, in my blindness, that she pined for the free air of the Highlands, and tried to win it back by transient tenderness and costly gifts. But I had robbed my lark of heaven's sunshine, and it could not sing.

I met Agnes again. She was a widow, and to my eye seemed fairer than when I saw her last, and far more kind. Some soft regret seemed shining on me from those lustrous eyes, as if she hoped to win my pardon for that early wrong. I never could forget the deed that darkened my best years, but the old charm stole over me at times, and, turning from the meek child at my feet, I owned the power of the stately woman whose smile seemed a command.

I meant no wrong to Effie, but, looking on her as a child, I forgot the higher claim I had given her as a wife, and walking blindly on my selfish way, I crushed the little flower I should have cherished in my breast.

"Effie, my old friend Agnes Vaughan is coming here to-day; so make yourself fair, that you may do honor to my choice; for she desires to see you, and I wish my Scotch harebell to look lovely to this English rose," I said, half playfully, half earnestly, as we stood together looking out across the flowery lawn, one summer day.

"Do you like me to be pretty, Sir?" she answered, with a flush of pleasure on her upturned face. "I will try to make myself fair with the gifts you are always heaping on me; but even then I fear I shall not do you honor, nor please your friend, I am so small and young."

A careless reply was on my lips, but, seeing what a long way down the little figure was, I drew it nearer, saying, with a smile, which I knew would make an answering one, —

"Dear, there must be the bud before the flower; so never grieve, for your youth keeps my spirit young. To me you may be a child forever; but you must learn to be a stately little Madam Ventnor to my friends."

She laughed a gayer laugh than I had heard for many a day, and soon departed, intent on keeping well the promise she had given. An hour later, as I sat busied among my books, a little figure glided in, and stood before me with its jewelled arms demurely folded on its breast. It was Effie, as I had never seen her before. Some new freak possessed her, for with her girlish dress she seemed to have laid her girlhood by. The brown locks were gathered up, wreathing the small head like a coronet; aërial lace and silken vesture shimmered in the light, and became her well. She looked and moved a fairy queen, stately and small.

I watched her in a silent maze, for the face with its shy blushes and downcast eyes did not seem the childish one turned frankly to my own an hour ago. With a sigh I looked up at Agnes's picture, the sole ornament of that room, and when I withdrew my gaze the blooming vision had departed. I should have followed it to make my peace, but I fell into a fit of bitter musing, and forgot it till Agnes's voice sounded at my door.

She came with a brother, and seemed eager to see my young wife; but Effie did not appear, and I excused her absence as a girlish freak, smiling at it with them, while I chafed inwardly at her neglect, forgetting that I might have been the cause.

Pacing down the garden paths with Agnes at my side, our steps were arrested by a sudden sight of Effie fast asleep among the flowers. She looked a flower herself, lying with her flushed cheek pillowed on her arm, sunshine glittering on the ripples of her hair, and the changeful lustre of her dainty dress. Tears moistened her long lashes, but her lips smiled, as if in the blissful land of dreams she had found some solace for her grief.

"A 'Sleeping Beauty' worthy the awakening of any prince!" whispered Alfred Vaughan, pausing with admiring eyes.

A slight frown swept over Agnes's face, but vanished as she said, with that low-toned laugh that never seemed unmusical before, —

"We must pardon Mrs. Ventnor's seeming rudeness, if she welcomes us with graceful scenes like this. A child-wife's whims are often prettier than the world's formal ways; so do not chide her, Basil, when she wakes."

I was a proud man then, touched easily by trivial things. Agnes's pitying manner stung me, and the tone in which I wakened Effie was far harsher than it should have been. She sprang up; and with a gentle dignity most new to me received her guests, and played the part of hostess with a grace that well atoned for her offence.

Agnes watched her silently as she went before us with young Vaughan, and even I, ruffled as my temper was, felt a certain pride in the loving creature who for my sake conquered her timidity and strove to do me honor. But neither by look nor word did I show my satisfaction, for Agnes demanded the constant service of lips and eyes, and I was only too ready to devote them to the woman who still felt her power and dared to show it.

All that day I was beside her, forgetful in many ways of the gentle courtesies I owed the child whom I had made my wife. I did not see the wrong then, but others did, and the deference I failed to show she could ask of them.

In the evening, as I stood near Agnes while she sang the songs we both remembered well, my eye fell on a mirror that confronted me, and in it I saw Effie bending forward with a look that startled me. Some strong emotion controlled her, for with lips apart and eager eyes she gazed keenly at the countenances she believed unconscious of her scrutiny.

Agnes caught the vision that had arrested the half-uttered compliment upon my lips, and, turning, looked at Effie with a smile just touched with scorn.

The color rose vividly to Effie's cheek, but her eyes did not fall, — they sought my face, and rested there. A half-smile crossed my lips; with a sudden impulse I beckoned, and she came with such an altered countenance I fancied that I had not seen aright.

At my desire she sang the ballads she so loved, and in her girlish voice there was an undertone of deeper melody than when I heard them first among her native hills; for the child's heart was ripening fast into the woman's.

Agnes went, at length, and I heard Effie's sigh of relief when we were left alone, but only bid her "go and rest," while I paced to and fro, still murmuring the refrain of Agnes's song.

The Vaughans came often, and we went often to them in the summer-home they had chosen near us on the river-bank. I followed my own wayward will, and Effie's wistful eyes grew sadder as the weeks went by.

One sultry evening, as we strolled together on the balcony, I was seized with a sudden longing to hear Agnes sing, and bid Effie come with me for a moonlight voyage down the river.

She had been very silent all the evening, with a pensive shadow on her face and rare smiles on her lips. But as I spoke, she paused abruptly, and, clenching her small hands, turned upon me with defiant eyes, — crying, almost fiercely, —

"No, I will not go to listen to that woman's songs. I hate her! yes, more than I can tell! for, till she came, I thought you loved me; but now you think of her alone, and chide me when I look unhappy. You treat me like a child; but I am not one. Oh, Sir, be more kind, for I have only you to love!" — and as her voice died in that sad appeal, she clasped her hands before her face with such a burst of tears that I had no words to answer her.

Disturbed by the sudden passion of the hitherto meek girl, I sat down on the wide steps of the balcony and essayed to draw her to my knee, hoping she would weep this grief away as she had often done a lesser sorrow. But she resisted my caress, and, standing erect before me, checked her tears, saying, in a voice still trembling with resentment and reproach, —

"You promised Jean to be kind to me, and you are cruel; for when I ask for love, you give me jewels, books, or flowers, as you would give a pettish child a toy, and go away as if you were weary of me. Oh, it is not right, Sir! and I cannot, no, I will not bear it!"

If she had spared reproaches, deserved though they were, and humbly pleaded to be loved, I should have been more just and gentle; but her indignant words, the sharper for their truth, roused the despotic spirit of the man, and made me sternest when I should have been most kind.

"Effie," I said, looking coldly up into her troubled face, "I have given you the right to be thus frank with me; but before you exercise that right, let me tell you what may silence your reproaches and teach you to know me better. I desired to adopt you as my child; Jean would not consent to that, but bid me marry you, and so give you a home, and win for myself a companion who should make that home less solitary. I could protect you in no other way, and I married you. I meant it kindly, Effie; for I pitied you, — ay, and loved you, too, as I hoped I had fully proved."

"You have, Sir, — oh, you have! But I hoped I might in time be more to you than a dear child," sighed Effie, while softer tears flowed as she spoke.

"Effie, I told Jean I was a hard, cold man," — and I was one as those words passed my lips. "I told her I was unfitted to make a wife happy. But she said you would be content with what I could offer; and so I gave you all I had to bestow. It was not enough; yet I cannot make it more. Forgive me, child, and try to bear your disappointments as I have learned to bear mine."

Effie bent suddenly, saying, with a look of anguish, "Do you regret that I am your wife, Sir?"

"Heaven knows I do, for I cannot make you happy," I answered, mournfully.

"Let me go away where I can never grieve or trouble you again! I will, — indeed, I will, — for anything is easier to bear than this. Oh, Jean, why did you leave me when you went?" — and with that despairing cry Effie stretched her arms into the empty air as if seeking that lost friend.

My anger melted, and I tried to soothe her, saying gently, as I laid her tear-wet cheek to mine, —

"My child, death alone must part us two. We will be patient with each other, and so may learn to be happy yet."

A long silence fell upon us both. My thoughts were busy with the thought of what a different home mine might have been, if Agnes had been true; and Effie — God only knows how sharp a conflict passed in that young heart! I could not guess it till the bitter sequel of that hour came.

A timid hand upon my own aroused me, and, looking down, I met such an altered face, it touched me like a mute reproach. All the passion had died out, and a great patience seemed to have arisen there. It looked so meek and wan, I bent and kissed it; but no smile answered me as Effie humbly said, —

"Forgive me, Sir, and tell me how I can make you happier. For I am truly grateful for all you have done for me, and will try to be a docile child to you."

"Be happy yourself, Effie, and I shall be content. I am too grave and old to be a fit companion for you, dear. You shall have gay faces and young friends to make this quiet place more cheerful. I should have thought of that before. Dance, sing, be merry, Effie, and never let your life be darkened by Basil Ventnor's changeful moods."

"And you?" she whispered, looking up.

"I will sit among my books, or seek alone the few friends I care to see, and never mar your gayety with my gloomy presence, dear. We must begin at once to go our separate ways; for, with so many years between us, we can never find the same paths pleasant very long. Let me be a father to you, and a friend, — I cannot be a lover, child."

Effie rose and went silently away; but soon came again, wrapped in her mantle, saying, as she looked down at me, with something of her former cheerfulness, —

"I am good now. Come and row me down the river. It is too beautiful a night to be spent in tears and naughtiness."

"No, Effie, you shall never go to Mrs. Vaughan's again, if you dislike her so. No friendship of mine need be shared by you, if it gives you pain."

"Nothing shall pain me any more," she answered, with a patient sigh. "I will be your merry girl again, and try to love Agnes for your sake. Ah! do come, *father,* or I shall not feel forgiven."

Smiling at her April moods, I obeyed the small hands clasped about my own, and through the fragrant linden walk went musing to the river-side.

Silently we floated down, and at the lower landing-place found Alfred Vaughan just mooring his own boat. By him I sent a message to his sister, while we waited for her at the shore.

Effie stood above me on the sloping bank, and as Agnes entered the green vista of the flowery path, she turned and clung to me with sudden fervor, kissed me passionately, and then stole silently into the boat.

The moonlight turned the waves to silver, and in its magic rays the face of my first love grew young again. She sat before me with water-lilies in her shining hair, singing as she sang of old, while the dash of falling oars kept time to her low song. As we neared the ruined bridge, whose single arch still cast its heavy shadow far across the stream, Agnes bent toward me, softly saying, —

"Basil, you remember this?"

How could I forget that happy night, long years ago, when she and I went floating down the same bright stream, two happy lovers just betrothed? As she spoke, it all came back more beautiful than ever, and I forgot the silent figure sitting there behind me. I hope Agnes had forgotten, too; for, cruel as she was to me, I never wished to think her hard enough to hate that gentle child.

"I remember, Agnes," I said, with a regretful sigh. "My voyage has been a lonely one since then."

"Are you not happy, Basil?" she asked, with a tender pity thrilling her low voice.

"Happy?" I echoed, bitterly, — "how can I be happy, remembering what might have been?"

Agnes bowed her head upon her hands, and silently the boat shot into the black shadow of the arch. A sudden eddy seemed to sway us slightly from our course, and the waves dashed sullenly against the gloomy walls; a moment more and we glided into calmer waters and unbroken light. I looked up from my task to speak, but the words were frozen on my lips by a cry from Agnes, who, wild-eyed and pale, seemed pointing to some phantom which I could not see. I turned, — the phantom was Effie's empty seat. The shining stream grew dark before me, and a great pang of remorse wrung my heart as that sight met my eyes.

"Effie!" I cried, with a cry that rent the stillness of the night, and sent the name ringing down the river. But nothing answered me, and the waves rippled softly as they hurried by. Far over the wide stream went my despairing glance, and saw nothing but the lilies swaying as they slept, and the black arch where my child went down.

Agnes lay trembling at my feet, but I never heeded her, — for Jean's dead voice sounded in my ear, demanding the life confided to my care. I listened, benumbed with guilty fear, and, as if summoned by that weird cry, there came a white flash through the waves, and Effie's face rose up before me.

Pallid and wild with the agony of that swift plunge, it confronted me. No cry for help parted the pale lips, but those wide eyes were luminous with a love whose fire that deathful river could not quench.

[67]

Like one in an awful dream, I gazed till the ripples closed above it. One instant the terror held me, — the next I was far down in those waves, so silver fair above, so black and terrible below. A brief, blind struggle passed before I grasped a tress of that long hair, then an arm, and then the white shape, with a clutch like death. As the dividing waters gave us to the light again, Agnes flung herself far over the boat-side and drew my lifeless burden in; I followed, and we laid it down, a piteous sight for human eyes to look upon. Of that swift voyage home I can remember nothing but the still face on Agnes's breast, the sight of which nerved my dizzy brain and made my muscles iron.

For many weeks there was a darkened chamber in my house, and anxious figures gliding to and fro, wan with long vigils and the fear of death. I often crept in to look upon the little figure lying there, to watch the feverish roses blooming on the wasted cheek, the fitful fire burning in the unconscious eyes, to hear the broken words so full of pathos to my ear, and then to steal away and struggle to forget.

My bird fluttered on the threshold of its cage, but Love lured it back, for its gentle mission was not yet fulfilled.

The *child* Effie lay dead beneath the ripples of the river, but the *woman* rose up from that bed of suffering like one consecrated to life's high duties by the bitter baptism of that dark hour.

Slender and pale, with serious eyes and quiet steps, she moved through the home which once echoed to the glad voice and dancing feet of that vanished shape. A sweet sobriety shaded her young face, and a meek smile sat upon her lips, but the old blithesomeness was gone.

She never claimed her childish place upon my knee, never tried the winsome wiles that used to chase away my gloom, never came to pour her innocent delights and griefs into my ear, or bless me with the frank affection which grew very precious when I found it lost.

Docile as ever, and eager to gratify my lightest wish, she left no wifely duty unfulfilled. Always near me, if I breathed her name, but vanishing when I grew silent, as if her task were done. Always smiling a cheerful farewell when I went, a quiet welcome when I came. I missed the April face that once watched me go, the warm embrace that greeted me again, and at my heart the sense of loss grew daily deeper as I felt the growing change.

Effie remembered the words I had spoken on that mournful night; remembered that our paths must lie apart, — that her husband was a friend, and nothing more. She treasured every careless hint I had given, and followed it most faithfully. She gathered gay, young friends about her, went out into the brilliant world, and I believed she was content.

If I had ever felt she was a burden to the selfish freedom I desired, I was punished now, for I had lost a blessing which no common pleasure could replace. I sat alone, and no blithe voice made music in the silence of my room, no bright locks swept my shoulder, and no soft caress assured me that I was beloved.

I looked for my household sprite in girlish garb, with its free hair and sunny eyes, but found only a fair woman, graceful in rich attire, crowned with my gifts, and standing afar off among her blooming peers. I could not guess the solitude of that true heart, nor see the captive spirit gazing at me from those steadfast eyes.

No word of the cause of that despairing deed passed Effie's lips, and I had no need to ask it. Agnes was silent, and soon left us, but her brother was a frequent guest. Effie liked his gay companionship, and I denied her nothing, — nothing but the one desire of her life.

So that first year passed; and though the ease and liberty I coveted were undisturbed, I was not satisfied. Solitude grew irksome, and study ceased to charm. I tried old pleasures, but they had lost their zest, — renewed old friendships, but they wearied me. I forgot Agnes, and ceased to think her fair. I looked at Effie, and sighed for my lost youth.

My little wife grew very beautiful to me, for she was blooming fast into a gracious womanhood. I felt a secret pride in knowing she was mine, and watched her as I fancied a fond brother might, glad that she was so good, so fair, so much beloved. I ceased to mourn the plaything I had lost, and something akin to reverence mingled with the deepening admiration of the man.

Gay guests had filled the house with festal light and sound one winter's night, and when the last bright figure had vanished from the threshold of the door, I still stood there, looking over the snow-shrouded lawn, hoping to cool the fever of my blood, and ease the restless pain that haunted me.

I shut out the keen air and wintry sky, at length, and silently ascended to the deserted rooms above. But in the soft gloom of a vestibule my steps were stayed. Two figures, in a flowery alcove, fixed my eye. The light streamed full upon them, and the fragrant stillness of the air was hardly stirred by their low tones.

Effie was there, sunk on a low couch, her face bowed upon her hands; and at her side, speaking with impassioned voice and ardent eyes, leaned Alfred Vaughan.

The sight struck me like a blow, and the sharp anguish of that moment proved how deeply I had learned to love.

"Effie, it is a sinful tie that binds you to that man; he does not love you, and it should be broken, — for this slavery will wear away the life now grown so dear to me."

The words, hot with indignant passion, smote me like a wintry blast, but not so coldly as the broken voice that answered them: —

"He said death alone must part us two, and, remembering that, I cannot listen to another love."

Like a guilty ghost I stole away, and in the darkness of my solitary room struggled with my bitter grief, my new-born love. I never blamed my wife, — that wife who had heard the tender name so seldom, she could scarce feel it hers. I had fettered her free heart, forgetting it would one day cease to be a child's. I bade her look upon me as a father; she had learned the lesson well; and now what right had I to reproach her for listening to a lover's voice, when her husband's was so cold? What mattered it that slowly, almost unconsciously, I had learned to love her with the passion of a youth, the power of a man? I had alienated that fond nature from my own, and now it was too late.

Heaven only knows the bitterness of that hour; — I cannot tell it. But through the darkness of my anguish and remorse that newly kindled love burned like a blessed fire, and, while it tortured, purified. By its light I saw the error of my life: self-love was written on the actions of the past, and I knew that my punishment was very just. With a child's repentant tears, I confessed it to my Father, and He solaced me, showed me the path to tread, and made me nobler for the blessedness and pain of that still hour.

Dawn found me an altered man; for in natures like mine the rain of a great sorrow melts the ice of years, and their hidden strength blooms in a late harvest of patience, self-denial, and humility. I resolved to break the tie which bound poor Effie to a joyless fate; and gratitude for a selfish deed, which wore the guise of charity, should no longer mar her peace. I would atone for the wrong I had done her, the suffering she had endured; and she should never know that I had guessed her tender secret, nor learn the love which made my sacrifice so bitter, yet so just.

Alfred came no more; and as I watched the growing pallor of her cheek, her patient effort to be cheerful and serene, I honored that meek creature for her constancy to what she deemed the duty of her life.

I did not tell her my resolve at once, for I could not give her up so soon. It was a weak delay, but I had not learned the beauty of a perfect self-forgetfulness; and though I clung to my purpose steadfastly, my heart still cherished a desperate hope that I might be spared this loss.

In the midst of this secret conflict, there came a letter from old Adam Lyndsay, asking to see his daughter's child; for life was waning slowly, and he desired to forgive, as he hoped to be forgiven when the last hour came. The letter was to me, and, as I read it, I saw a way whereby I might be spared the hard task of telling Effie she was to be free. I feared my new-found strength would desert me, and my courage fail, when, looking on the woman who was dearer to me than my life, I tried to give her back the liberty whose worth she had learned to know.

Effie should go, and I would write the words I dared not speak. She would be in her mother's home, free to show her joy at her release, and smile upon the lover she had banished.

I went to tell her; for it was I who sought her now, who watched for her coming and sighed at her departing steps, — I who waited for her smile and followed her with wistful eyes. The child's slighted affection was atoned for now by my unseen devotion to the woman.

I gave the letter, and she read it silently.

"Will you go, love?" I asked, as she folded it.

"Yes, — the old man has no one to care for him but me, and it is so beautiful to be loved."

A sudden smile touched her lips, and a soft dew shone in the shadowy eyes, which seemed looking into other and tenderer ones than mine. She could not know how sadly I echoed those words, nor how I longed to tell her of another man who sighed to be forgiven.

"You must gather roses for these pale cheeks among the breezy moorlands, dear. They are not so blooming as they were a year ago. Jean would reproach me for my want of care," I said, trying to speak cheerfully, though each word seemed a farewell.

"Poor Jean! how long it seems since she kissed them last!" sighed Effie, musing sadly, as she turned her wedding-ring.

My heart ached to see how thin the hand had grown, and how easily that little fetter would fall off when I set my captive lark at liberty.

I looked till I dared look no longer, and then rose, saying, —

"You will write often, Effie, for I shall miss you very much."

She cast a quick look into my face, asking, hurriedly, —

"Am I to go alone?"

"Dear, I have much to do and cannot go; but you need fear nothing; I shall send Ralph and Mrs. Prior with you, and the journey is soon over. When will you go?"

It was the first time she had left me since I took her from Jean's arms, and I longed to keep her always near me; but, remembering the task I had to do, I felt that I must seem cold till she knew all.

"Soon, — very soon, — to-morrow; — let me go to-morrow, Sir. I long to be away!" she cried, some swift emotion banishing the calmness of her usual manner, as she rose, with eager eyes and a gesture full of longing.

"You shall go, Effie," was all I could say; and with no word of thanks, she hastened away, leaving me so calm without, so desolate within.

The same eagerness possessed her all that day; and the next she went away, clinging to me at the last as she had clung that night upon the river-bank, as if her grateful heart reproached her for the joy she felt at leaving my unhappy home.

A few days passed, bringing me the comfort of a few sweet lines from Effie, signed "Your child." That sight reminded me, that, if I would do an honest deed, it should be generously done. I read again the little missive she had sent, and then I wrote the letter which might be my last; — with no hint of my love, beyond the expression of sincerest regard and never-ceasing interest in her happiness; no hint of Alfred Vaughan; for I would not wound her pride, nor let her dream that any eye had seen the passion she so silently surrendered, with no reproach to me and no shadow on the name I had given into her keeping. Heaven knows what it cost me, and Heaven, through the suffering of that hour, granted me an humbler spirit and a better life.

It went, and I waited for my fate as one might wait for pardon or for doom. It came at length, — a short, sad letter, full of meek obedience to my will, of penitence for faults I never knew, and grateful prayers for my peace.

My last hope died then, and for many days I dwelt alone, living over all that happy year with painful vividness. I dreamed again of those fair days, and woke to curse the selfish blindness which had hidden my best blessing from me till it was forever lost.

How long I should have mourned thus unavailingly I cannot tell. A more sudden, but far less grievous loss befell me. My fortune was nearly swept away in the general ruin of a most disastrous year.

This event roused me from my despair and made me strong again, — for I must hoard what could be saved, for Effie's sake. She had known a cruel want with me, and she must never know another while she bore my name. I looked my misfortune in the face and ceased to feel it one; for the diminished fortune was still ample for my darling's dower, and now what need had I of any but the simplest home?

Before another month was gone, I was in the quiet place henceforth to be mine alone, and nothing now remained for me to do but to dissolve the bond that made my Effie mine. Sitting over the dim embers of my solitary hearth, I thought of this, and, looking round the silent room, whose only ornaments were the things made sacred by her use, the utter desolation struck so heavily upon my heart, that I bowed my head upon my folded arms, and yielded to the tender longing that could not be repressed.

The bitter paroxysm passed, and, raising my eyes, the clearer for that stormy rain, I beheld Effie standing like an answer to my spirit's cry.

With a great start, I regarded her, saying, at length, in a voice that sounded cold, for my heart leaped up to meet her, and yet must not speak, —

"Effie, why are you here?"

Wraith-like and pale, she stood before me, with no sign of emotion but the slight tremor of her frame, and answered my greeting with a sad humility: —

"I came because I promised to cleave to you through health and sickness, poverty and wealth, and I must keep that vow till you absolve me from it. Forgive me, but I knew misfortune had befallen you, and, remembering all you had done for me, came, hoping I might comfort when other friends deserted you."

"Grateful to the last!" I sighed, low to myself, and, though deeply touched, replied with the hard-won calmness that made my speech so brief, —

"You owe me nothing, Effie, and I most earnestly desired to spare you this."

Some sudden hope seemed born of my regretful words, for, with an eager glance, she cried, —

"Was it that desire which prompted you to part from me? Did you think I should shrink from sharing poverty with you who gave me all I own?"

"No, dear, — ah, no!" I said, "I knew your grateful spirit far too well for that. It was because I could not make your happiness, and yet had robbed you of the right to seek it with some younger and some better man."

"Basil, what man? Tell me; for no doubt shall stand between us now!"

She grasped my arm, and her rapid words were a command.

I only answered, "Alfred Vaughan."

Effie covered up her face, crying, as she sank down at my feet, —

"Oh, my fear! my fear! Why was I blind so long?"

I felt her grief to my heart's core; for my own anguish made me pitiful, and my love made me strong. I lifted up that drooping head and laid it down where it might never rest again, saying, gently, cheerily, and with a most sincere forgetfulness of self, —

"My wife, I never cherished a harsh thought of you, never uttered a reproach when your affections turned from a cold, neglectful guardian, to find a tenderer resting-place. I saw your struggles, dear, your patient grief, your silent sacrifice, and honored you more truly than I can tell. Effie, I robbed you of your liberty, but I will restore it, making such poor reparation as I can for this long year of pain; and when I see you blest in a happier home, my keen remorse will be appeased."

As I ceased, Effie rose erect and stood before me, transformed from a timid girl into an earnest woman. Some dormant power and passion woke; she turned on me a countenance aglow with feeling, soul in the eye, heart on the lips, and in her voice an energy that held me mute.

"I feared to speak before," she said, "but now I dare anything, for I have heard you call me 'wife,' and seen that in your face which gives me hope. Basil, the grief you saw was not for the loss of any love but yours; the conflict you beheld was the daily struggle to subdue my longing spirit to your will; and the sacrifice you honor but the renunciation of all hope. I stood between you and the woman whom you loved, and asked of death to free me from that cruel lot. You gave me back my life, but you withheld the gift that made it worth possessing. You desired to be freed from the affection which only wearied you, and I tried to conquer it; but it would not die. Let me speak now, and then I will be still forever! Must our ways lie apart? Can I never be more to you than now? Oh, Basil! oh, my husband! I have loved you very truly from the first! Shall I never know the blessedness of a return?"

Words could not answer that appeal. I gathered my life's happiness close to my breast, and in the silence of a full heart felt that God was very good to me.

Soon all my pain and passion were confessed. Fast and fervently the tale was told; and as the truth dawned on that patient wife, a tender peace transfigured her uplifted countenance, until to me it seemed an angel's face.

"I am a poor man now," I said, still holding that frail creature fast, fearing to see her vanish, as her semblance had so often done in the long vigils I had kept, — "a poor man, Effie, and yet very rich, for I have my treasure back again. But I am wiser than when we parted; for I have learned that love is better than a world of wealth, and victory over self a nobler conquest than a continent. Dear, I have no home but this. Can you be happy here, with no fortune but the little store set apart for you, and the knowledge that no want shall touch you while I live?"

And as I spoke, I sighed, remembering all I might have done, and dreading poverty for her alone.

But with a gesture, soft, yet solemn, Effie laid her hands upon my head, as if endowing me with blessing and with gift, and answered, with her steadfast eyes on mine, —

"You gave me your home when I was homeless; let me give it back, and with it a proud wife. I, too, am rich; for that old man is gone and left me all. Take it, Basil, and give me a little love."

I gave not little, but a long life of devotion for the good gift God had bestowed on me, — finding in it a household spirit the daily benediction of whose presence banished sorrow, selfishness, and gloom, and, through the influence of happy human love, led me to a truer faith in the Divine.

Sensationalism
The Thrillers

Hope's Debut

Frank Leslie's Chimney Corner, 6 April 1867. Published anonymously

I

*T*HERE WAS AN UNUSUAL commotion in the green-room that evening. Actors and actresses stood about, talking eagerly, the stage-manager ran to and fro with an ireful countenance, and even the sleepy scene-shifters looked somewhat excited. "Hamlet" was to be performed with great splendor in compliment to a famous tragedian who had made the part peculiarly his own; but it was not this alone which produced the unwonted excitement. While Laertes, Polonius, and Horatio laughed and swore alternately over the affair, a group of "supes" discussed it with feminine volubility.

"My dear creature, haven't you heard the fun?" cried one court-lady to a new comer who had been delayed by being ordered to assume a dress too small for her plump proportions.

"No, tell me quickly, prithee," replied the other, who affected the theatrical modes of speech.

"Why, Miss St. James has just sent word that she won't play; so we must act 'Hamlet' with the part of Ophelia left out."

"No great loss, as St. James plays it. Is she sick?"

"No, sulky; Le Brun has offended her by finding fault with her style and slighting her passion; so she revenges herself by failing him at the last minute after all his trouble in drilling her and giving her hints as to proper costume. She didn't even send a doctor's certificate. Won't she have to pay for this prank, though!" and the young lady uttered the words with an air of intense satisfaction.

"She has been such a pet of old Vincent's, she thinks she can do what she likes and he'll forgive her. How does he take this?"

"He's raging; her day is over, and she'll pack to-morrow as sure as she lives. He sent to her house, commanding her to come or forfeit her engagement; but she wasn't there, and he is in a towering passion, for he has taken such pains to get this up in style, it's enough to try a saint to have it fail."

"What does Le Brun say?"

"Nothing; he just walks the stage and looks daggers. I wouldn't be St. James for any money; next time he sees her, there'll be lightning in his eyes if there isn't thunder on his tongue. He will play magnificently to-night if he plays at all; he always does after a flurry."

"But what on earth will they do?"

"Don't know; Vincent will do Pheely himself rather than give up. I wish I could play it, for I should die happy if I could play once with Le Brun."

"So would I — hush, here he is! What is up now?"

Sudden silence fell upon the chattering group, as Vincent, the manager, and Le Brun, the tragedian, entered together. Approaching the girls, the manager, looking like a very fretful porcupine, demanded abruptly:

"Where's Miss Smythe?"

"Here, sir," and the most garrulous of the set advanced with a side-long glance at Le Brun, who was more than usually tragical, and consequently doubly fascinating in the eyes of the young ladies.

"When you came a year ago, you wanted to play all Shakespeare's heroines, and said you knew the parts. Now come and do your best as Ophelia."

"Lord, sir, I've forgotten every word, and if I hadn't, I should never dare to play with Mr. Le Brun."

"You can 'wing' it, and as for daring, you'd dare anything for the chance. Come, no airs, we are in a deuce of a scrape, and you must help us out. It's only to walk through the part and mind the business."

Miss Smythe hesitated and had the actor said a word, she would have yielded; but he stopped silent, looking both haughty and angry. The ominous silence and the fire of the wonderful black eyes daunted her, and she said decidedly:

"Mr. Vincent, I can't and I won't. You wouldn't let me play the part when I wanted to and was ready to do it, and now I really cannot make a fool of myself to please any one. It's not my plan to do St. James's work when she's in a pet, and you must get some one else to help you out with your scrape."

Miss Smythe was angry with herself as well as with actor and manager, for though dying to play the part, she knew it was entirely beyond her power, and she had too much vanity to run the risk of "making a fool of herself." What Mr. Vincent would have said or done remained a mystery, for just as he seemed about to issue some imperative order, a meekfaced girl spoke up:

"Please, sir, Hope Scott would do it beautifully. She knows it all, she's pretty and clever, and longs to try that line."

"Then where the deuce *is* Hope Scott?" testily demanded the distracted manager.

"A dressin' Mrs. Blount for the Queen. Shall I bring her, sir?" asked the meek girl, who evidently had some grateful reason for her good will.

"Yes, there's hardly time to get her ready. Off with you. She is the pale girl with the fine eyes who came last month, isn't she?" asked Vincent, wiping his heated face and sighing a sigh of relief.

"Yes, sir, she's high and mighty, but kind, and a real lady. She's always sitting over in that corner, studying her old Shakespeare, and she says that some day she'll play what she likes, for she knows she's got the power in her," answered another girl.

"She'll play to-night, power or no power," said Vincent, grimly.

"With pleasure, sir," replied a clear voice, behind him.

Every one turned and looked, but saw only a slender, pale girl, with brown rippling hair, straight dark brows and a pair of splendid eyes — an actor's most important nature.

"Good! well said — thank you, my dear," cried Mr. Vincent, heartily, while Le Brun smiled the brief bright smile that made his dark face beautiful.

"You know the part?" he asked, with a tone and look of interest that made Miss Smythe groan with envy.

"Every word," was the prompt reply.

"You have no fear?"

"Not a particle."

"Can you be ready in twenty minutes?"

"In ten, if necessary."

"How about the dress?"

"Miss St. James left hers — I can wear it."

"Excellent, do your best, I shall not forget the service," and with a bow that would have made Miss Smythe happy for life, Le Brun departed.

"The presumption of some people *is* amazing," exclaimed that amiable creature.

"The envy of other people is more so," said the meek girl, jerking up again.

"She'll fail to a dead certainty," croaked Polonius.

"Won't Tilly Smythe be sorry if she don't," laughed Horatio.

"I like her pluck," added Laertes, with an air of patronage, as the three walked away together.

Hope heard none of these remarks and prophecies; she was busy dressing for her part with quickly beating heart, and lips that trembled slightly as they rapidly rehearsed the little she had to say in that first scene. The play begun and went smoothly on after a brief speech from the manager, apologizing for the non-appearance of Miss St. James (for whom he invented a sudden indisposition), and requesting the indulgence of the audience, for the young lady who had kindly volunteered to sustain the part.

A slight interest was felt before the curtain in the unknown young lady who was to appear, but there was quite a stir behind the scenes as the moment drew near when Hope must enter. Actors and actresses crowded about the wings, and even Le Brun, who usually retired to his dressing-room when not playing, lingered to watch the girl's *début*. The instant she was called, she appeared, looking as calm and steady as if only a lady-in-waiting. By desire of Le Brun, the characters had been dressed as befitted the age they represented, and Miss St. James had received a polite request to play Ophelia in a costume more proper for a Danish girl than the modern white satin gown and fashionably dressed hair, with the ever-lasting string of mock pearls in it. But that willful lady had protested that the new costume did not suit her style, and nothing would induce her to wear it. It did suit Hope's style and become her well. It was something new, she wore it gracefully and satisfied the eye by the innocent, girlish beauty of the young Ophelia. She seemed to have caught the spirit of the part, and in spite of all suggestions in the dressing-room, had followed the hints Le Brun had offered Miss St. James in Hope's hearing.

Her golden brown hair hung in thick clusters about face and shoulders, fastened only by the fillet which is the mark of the maidenhood in Denmark as in Scotland. A long robe, guiltless of crinoline, gathered at the waist by a wide, rich girdle, donned her slender figure, and a little fur-trimmed tunic with hanging sleeves was in perfect keeping with a land and season wherein Horatio speaks of "an eager and a nipping air," and Hamlet says " 'Tis very cold."

Speaking to no one, Hope gave her hand to Laertes, and, entering with him, went through the little scene with an air of sisterly solicitude and affection which gave interest to an interview which is usually listened to with indifference if not impatience. She had evidently conceived an idea of the part, and had the courage and skill to execute it.

When Polonius spoke to his son, Hope did not stand like a statue, nor "retire up" to twine her handkerchief or smooth her hair, but like a tender-hearted girl about to lose her brother, she lingered near him, as if loth to let him go; and when he went, her farewell was so full of feeling that the touch of nature was felt by all.

While her father questioned her, she answered with an artless hesitation and a soft trouble in her eye, very maidenly and true to life.

Tilly Smythe vowed, she actually blushed when she uttered the words:

> *He hath of late made many tenders*
> *Of his affection to me,*

and Laertes, who, by the way, was somewhat in love with Hope, felt a slight pang of jealousy as he listened to her innocent confessions, made with a look and tone that added life and meaning to the few brief words.

When she left the stage the audience testified their approval by a round of applause.

Mr. Vincent received her with an emphatic

"Very well, my dear — very well, indeed. You'll make a 'star' in time," and Le Brun took the trouble to give her another smile as he went on himself.

Thus encouraged, Hope exerted herself to the utmost, and surprised every one by the unexpected power she displayed. The ease and polish of a finished actress, of course, was wanting, but grace and beauty covered a multitude of sins, and there was something novel and charming in the unhackneyed freshness and simplicity of the girl. Even old play-goers felt the influence of this, and found themselves delighted with the new rendering of well-known phrases, the unstudied costumes and genuine feeling of this young actress. This was peculiarly observable whenever Le Brun was on the stage with her.

In the scene where Ophelia returns the gifts of Hamlet, the love, grief and fear painted in her face made it more eloquent than her timid words, and, so quick is genius to feel the touch of a kindred power, Le Brun never played that scene more perfectly, betraying his unhappy passion in spite of the feigned madness that deceived the royal spy, and bidding the girl farewell with tender eyes and lips that belied the wild words they uttered. Some said there were real tears on Ophelia's cheeks as she left the stage mourning for her lost lover; real blushes certainly were there, for the color was plainly seen to come and go when in the play-scene Hamlet lay at her feet and often took her hand, keeping up the by-play with the fidelity of a true actor.

Tilly Smythe was not the only lady curious to know what he said when he looked up whispering with a smile that made Ophelia droop her eyes and color deeply. Had Tilly heard she would have turned pale with envy in spite of her rouge, for this was the whisper:

"I have often longed to see my ideal of Ophelia, and at last my wish is gratified."

Hope made no answer, but a shy glance from the downcast eyes plainly betrayed that her ideal of Hamlet was before her, for though a man of forty, Le Brun looked ten years younger, especially on the stage, and in that part.

In the mad scene, Hope surprised every one by the pathos of her voice, the truth of her acting. When she made the mimic grave with her veil, strewing it with flowers as she sang, the house was still as death; and as she vanished, with her last mournful "God be with you," many eyes were full, and many hands bore witness to the fact that "One touch of nature makes the whole world kin."

"Will you be kind enough to remain as you are till the play is over?" said Le Brun, as she passed him on her way to the green-room.

"If you wish it, sir; I always wait for little Bella, because she has no one to go home with her, and I have my old servant. You will find me here when you want me," she answered quietly, and went on.

Soon after a continued round of applause told her that the green curtain had fallen, and presently Le Brun appeared looking very tired, but very kind, saying, as he took her hand:

"Come."

"Where, sir?"

"Before the curtain; you have shared the labor — you shall also share the reward."

"I am already rewarded; indeed I'd rather not; it would be presumption in me to go out when I have done so little," and she shrunk back from his hold.

"They call for you; I wish it. Please come."

Few ever resisted that tone of gentle command, that enchanting smile, or the persuasive touch of the handsome hand.

Hope yielded, and a moment after found herself before the curtain. Though half bewildered by the novel situation, and her own emotions, she was conscious of the gentle deference of Le Brun's manner during that brief episode, for courteously gathering up the bouquets meant for himself, he laid them in her arms, as if to publicly acknowledge the favor she had done him.

This touched her deeply, and some secret cause made it doubly sweet to receive such honor from his hand.

How she reached the green-room she never knew, but once there, she dropped into a seat, and letting the flowers stray down upon the floor, she covered up her face, weeping with a vehemence which startled him.

Sending every one away, Le Brun stood silently beside her, till she was quiet again and looking up, said, with much of her usual compassion:

"I am very silly; but this was all so unexpected and exciting, I was not prepared for it."

"Then I am doubly grateful for the effort so freely and kindly made in my behalf. Are you going now?" he asked, as she took up a little shawl.

"No; Bella is in the farce; I shall rest and wait for her. She will soon be through."

"Can I bring you anything; you must be very tired."

"Thanks; Barbara will get me some water; I need nothing else," and she leaned her pale cheek against the wall with a look of weariness that touched Le Brun.

He went away, but soon returned with a fur-lined cloak over his arm and a bottle of wine in his hand, the aroma of which proved its age and purity.

"Now I shall make you comfortable, and take care of you till Barbara comes. Will you drink a little toast with me? it will do us both good."

She smiled, and let him do as he liked, to the great amazement of two or three observers, for Hope was usually cold as ice to the gentlemen of the company.

Filling two glasses, Le Brun said, laughing, yet with a very friendly expression and tone:

"Here is happiness and success to the successor of St. James."

"Here is success to the purpose of my life," and with sudden color in her cheeks, sudden fire in her eye, Hope drank the wine.

Something in her face and manner increased the interest he already felt, and held him there in spite of weariness and her evident desire to be alone. Lifting the old Shakespeare that lay on the seat, after he had put the cloak about her shoulders, he turned the well-worn leaves, saying inquiringly:

"This is your favorite book it seems?"

"Yes; I care for no other; that is a whole library in itself, and a better master than I can find elsewhere."

"You love your profession then?"

"Heartily, not for itself, but for the help it is to me."

Again the swift-rising light and warmth touched her face, making it lovely with the irresistible beauty of deep feeling.

Le Brun's keen eyes softened as he watched her, and his melancholy countenance grew mild, as if some tender memory warmed his heart. Almost abruptly he broke the little pause that followed her last words.

"You will take St. James's place? Vincent is done with her, and wishes you to try her line. You will do this, at least till my engagement ends, I trust?"

"Can I? ought I to undertake so much?" she began, with timidity contending against a strong desire to accept the generous offer.

"You certainly can, and I sincerely hope that you will. You wrong no one by so doing, as Vincent will not receive St. James on any terms. Your style of acting suits me excellently, and as you are a beginner, it will be the easier to carry out my ideas, for you will perhaps allow me to make suggestions now and then, and that few already-established players have permitted me to do as freely as I like."

"I shall gratefully receive any suggestions you may make, and will heartily do my best to please you while you remain. After that I cannot promise."

"But is it wise to throw up a good engagement when they are so difficult for young aspirants to obtain? If five-and-twenty years' seniority can give weight to counsel, let me advise you to accept mine to remain here."

Hope received this speech in a singular manner. She fixed her eyes on his face with a quick look, that brightened as she gazed, saying low, as if to herself:

"Twenty-five and eighteen are forty-three; that's not right, but then mistakes are easily made."

A smile and frown passed over Le Brun's face for his career had brought him many romances, and for a moment he fancied that another foolish girl had lost her heart to one whose own was barred against all womankind. But something about Hope seemed to repel the fancy and increased his interest.

The smile banished the frown, and as Barbara appeared, he offered his hand, saying kindly, yet seriously:

"You are a year older than I thought, but do not count my age by years; I am seventy in feeling. Good-night. I shall see you in the morning."

II

For three weeks Hope played nightly with Le Brun and made amazing progress, being thoroughly up in the text of the various parts, and possessing a woman's aptitude for acquiring ease, polish, and the necessary proficiency in the arts of her profession. Le Brun supported her finely, lending the prestige of his name and interest to her success, and aiding her by suggestion, teaching and commendation.

She was very happy and seemed to grow more blithe and beautiful each day, as if at last she had found her place and won the desire of her life. She *had,* in truth; but it was not the success which others saw that made her so content — it was a secret victory harder to win than any visible prize. Of course green-room gossip was rife about the two, and many called them lovers, for Le Brun's friendship and Hope's happiness could have no other explanation to ordinary observers. Rumors flew about the city, and all manner of conjectures, hints, and assertions were discussed, at which the tragedian frowned and the girl smiled; yet neither changed their life nor altered their regard for one another, whereat the gossips wondered more and more, and chattered with redoubled vigor.

Le Brun's long engagement ended at last, closing with "Lear." Hope had played it more than once, but that night she excelled herself, for it was his benefit, and every power of mind and body was heartily exerted in his service.

As every one knows, Cordelia is a short part, and most players hurry through it as if it was of little consequence. But Hope saw and felt its beauty, understood its power, and made it what it should be — daughterly, tender and true, hovering about the poor old king as if he were indeed her father.

She was already a favorite, and that night's effort added much to her growing reputation. The consciousness of this inspired her with unwonted spirit, and gave unwonted grace to every act, especially the last.

As the play ended, Lear, of course, was called for, and as usual, led Cordelia with him, for Le Brun never failed to do her this little honor. A shower of bouquets greeted him, but before he could stoop to gather them, Hope swept them up in her tunic and offered them to him with a look and gesture which gave a double charm to the act, for it seemed not only the woman's tribute to the great tragedian, but a daughter's service to her father.

It was beautifully done, and the audience, quick to catch any hint of romance or of genuine feeling, applauded her enthusiastically. Forced by the deed, and encumbered by his floral wealth, Le Brun was hastily retreating, followed by the girl, when, just as the curtain was withdrawn to admit them, there was a cry from the front, a rending sound above their heads, and with an upward look, Hope sprang forward just in time to drag her friend from the impending danger. It was an instant's work, but she paid dearly for it, for in the act, down crashed a chandelier from its worn fastening, and, with the shiver of glass and metal, stretched Hope senseless on the stage.

A swift uprising filled the house with tumult; a crowd of gentlemen from before and actors from behind the curtain hurried toward the ruin. The cry of "Fire!" was promptly checked by turning off the gas that supplied the chandelier, and the poor girl was borne away to the green-room.

All had seen the impulsive spring toward, not from the danger, and this unpremeditated action won heartier applause than Hope had ever received from her best rendering of more heroic deeds.

Pale and breathless she lay on the green-room couch, surrounded by a motley crowd, till Le Brun, who ruled wherever he went, sent all away but Barbara, motherly Mrs. Blount and himself. A physician soon appeared, and finding a broken arm, a wounded head and bruised shoulder, ordered her to be removed at once.

"She lives just out of town; it is too far to carry the poor child to-night; take her to my hotel close by. I am responsible for all expenses," said Le Brun, in his commanding tone.

But old Barbara, who guarded her young mistress like a dragon, would not hear of this arrangement, and insisted upon taking her home, till Dr. Hay, guessing how matters stood, suggested the hospital, not far distant.

Le Brun was indignant, but Barbara decided at once, and ordered the girl to be taken there. No one dared oppose her, and when Hope recovered consciousness she found herself occupying a comfortable bed in the casualty ward of an hospital. Barbara sat beside her, and a mild-faced nurse was chafing her cold hand, but Le Brun was no longer there.

"Is he safe?" were her first words, as her eyes roved anxiously about the long room, with its double row of curtained-beds.

"Quite safe, thanks to you, deary. Don't talk; you are hurt and must be still," replied Barbara, with a tenderness never shown to any one but her little mistress.

"Has he gone?" was the next feeble question.

"Yes, child; we've just got him away. It's against the rules to have him here, but he would stay till you were comfortable. Now go to sleep and forget all about it," said the old woman, soothingly.

"Why am I here?" asked Hope, wonderingly.

Barbara told her, and a grateful smile passed over her pale lips as she said, softly:

"He was very kind, but it is better to be here. Will he come again?"

"In the morning; but you'll not be well enough to see him unless you keep very quiet. He begged us to take the best care of you, deary, so mind and go to sleep, else you'll see no company tomorrow."

Hope meekly obeyed, and as she watched beside her, old Barbara shook her head, muttering as if ill pleased:

"It's getting worse and worse; she never cared for any one before, and he's not a man to be thwarted of his will. I'll do my best, but the Lord only knows how it will end."

Several days passed, but Le Brun did not appear. Hope waited, watched, and wondered, but never thought of doubting Barbara's assurances that he sent every day, but could not come till she was better.

Anxious to spare her darling from what she believed to be an unwise love, the old woman had frankly told Le Brun her fear, and begged him to see the girl no more. Conscious that his regard never could assume a tenderer guise, he promised, and faithfully kept his word till all anxiety for Hope was over; then being bound by an engagement in a distant city, he begged to be allowed to say farewell to his little friend. Barbara relented, on condition that he would not betray that it was a last interview, and one evening Hope was gladdened by the sight of the long-desired friend.

Ignorant of Barbara's well-meant treason, the girl made no effort to conceal her delight, but stretched her one hand toward him with a joyful exclamation which caused several of her neighbors to peep from behind their curtains and watch the meeting curiously.

Feeling the separation more than he dared to own even to himself, and generally anxious to spare the girl all further pain, Le Brun assumed a cheerful air, and greeted her with the friendly warmth so seldom shown to any but herself. Holding the little hand in his, he strewed the coverlid with exquisite flowers, saying, playfully:

"You gave me yours the other night, so I return them with more thanks than I have words to express. My child, you saved my life. How shall I repay the debt?"

As he uttered the last words his gay manner changed to one of deep feeling, and he put the pale hand to his lips.

"Indeed you owe me nothing. It is I who am in debt to you for much, and I am truly glad to serve you at the cost of a little pain. I am nearly well, so you need not look remorseful, for I shall soon be up again."

"God grant it. Are you comfortable, well served and petted here in this place? If I had not been thwarted by this good woman you would have been better cared for in cheerier quarters. Tell me truly, can I do nothing to make your imprisonment lighter?"

"I need nothing, thank you; they are very kind, and Barbara is like a mother to me. I never knew how pleasant an hospital was till I came here, for I have every comfort and many luxuries, as you see."

Hope pointed to a basket of hot-house grapes and a bottle of old wine, little dreaming whose generous hand had bestowed the costly comforts, for Barbara never told her of the daily visits, gifts, and messages which went on between hotel and hospital. Le Brun exchanged a look with her, and his smile was sadder than he knew as he remembered that this was to be the last interview for months, perhaps for ever. His solitary heart clung to the girl who had been his pupil, friend, and comrade, making his life happier for that short time than it had been for years.

More than once of late he had thought of adopting the orphan and training her to be his support in public, his comfort and delight in private; but Barbara's confidence had put these pleasant hopes to flight and made separation necessary. All he could do was to make generous provision for Hope's illness and extort from Barbara a promise to apply to him in any trouble, claiming the right to befriend Hope in return for her favors to him.

Longing to stay, yet conscious that he should go, he lingered till the girl's heightened color and the feverish lustre of her eyes warned him away. As he rose she caught his arm, saying eagerly and with an anxious look that haunted him long afterward:

"I shall see you again?"

"Oh, yes; I think Mrs. Barbara will not repulse me if I come. Vincent is waiting for you, so get well and go back to find how excellent a hit you made in that last play, which nearly proved a tragedy to both of us."

Hope said "Good-by" with a smile, but as he turned away, something in her wistful eyes made his own fill, and, obeying an irresistible impulse, he bent down and kissed her, saying, as if to excuse the act:

"My child, I am old enough to be your father. God bless and keep you, little Hope!"

With that he was gone, and the girl was left to hide her face in her pillow, weeping happy tears. Barbara followed him away, and Hope was alone in her nook when the curtains of the bed next to her own were carefully withdrawn and a face looked out — a woman's face, bearing traces of past beauty, but wan and haggard now, as if with much mental and physical suffering. Fixing her hollow eyes on Hope, she whispered, with startling abruptness:

"Who was that man?"

"Le Brun, the actor."

"He is your lover?"

"No, my best friend."

"Will he come again?"

"Without doubt. Do you know him?"

"No."

And the face disappeared as suddenly as it came.

"Is she delirious?" whispered Hope, as the nurse came to her side, glass in hand.

"At times; she has suffered much, poor soul, but is quite harmless," and administering a soothing draught, the nurse passed on.

As the sound of her step died away the face appeared again, half hidden in the dark, disheveled hair that hung about it. Silently the haggard eyes surveyed the girl, till, remembering that the woman was harmless, she said, in a gentle, pitiful tone:

"What can I do for you, neighbor?"

"Tell me your name," was the reply, in the same shrill whisper.

"Hope Scott."

"You are an actress?"

"Yes."

"And an orphan?"

"No, I think not."

"Where are your parents, then?"

"What right have you to ask me that?"

"Wake at midnight when the ward is still and I will answer you."

With this singular reply the strange face vanished again as Barbara drew near, and Hope soon forgot everything but the flowers she gathered up to cherish long with tender care as the last gifts of her friend, for he did not come again.

Three days after Hope left the hospital and went, no one knew whither, for Mr. Vincent received a brief note stating that she had quitted her old home and the stage, for the season was nearly over, and she required rest and change of air. With this meagre hint the gossips were forced to be content, for no further tidings came and no trace of her remained.

Neglected Tilly revenged herself by slandering her fortunate rival, and insisting that Hope was with Le Brun, for after playing a very short engagement he had suddenly gone abroad.

Out of these facts a charming little romance was concocted, and for a time believed; but the absent one was soon forgotten, and before many months had gone few remembered Hope Scott and her brief success.

Summer passed and the vacation was over; the company of the old— ——Theatre returned to their places, and the season was about to begin, when Mr. Vincent received another note from Hope, urgently desiring to know Le Brun's address. He could not give it, but replied that the tragedian was engaged to play early in the season, and doubtless would soon report himself. At the same time the manager offered her the place she last filled in his *corps dramatique,* and begged her to accept it, at least during Le Brun's stay.

She answered this letter in person, looking so changed that all who saw her felt that some sharp experience had come to her during that absence. In reply to questions she simply said she had been in the country with Barbara and had been ill. Nothing more could be drawn from her; but when Le Brun's name was mentioned she denied having seen him, and eagerly inquired when he would return.

Few believed her story, for in spite of her efforts to preserve her usual composure she became visibly excited when he was spoken of and waited for his coming with an eagerness which it was impossible to conceal.

People shook their heads at this, spoke of her as "poor girl," and some treated her with virtuous coldness, especially Tilly Smythe, who let no opportunity slip of wounding Hope by some of the many slights a malicious woman can inflict upon a rival.

This was easily done, for Hope accepted Vincent's offer conditionally, agreeing to play when Le Brun came, but not before. Meanwhile she daily appeared at the theatre to inquire for him and afford food for fresh scandal by the undisguised anxiety which possessed her.

She saw and felt the change which had come over her former comrades, and though deeply wounded, concealed her pain, waiting patiently for her friend's return, as if that event would end some trial daily growing heavier to bear.

Going to the theatre one morning during rehearsal, she glided to the manager's table with her usual question.

"Mr. Vincent, have you heard from him?"

"He is here," was the welcome answer.

"You have seen him?" she cried, clasping her hands.

"Yes, last night; he plays on Monday."

"Did he speak of me?" she whispered, eagerly.

"No, my dear; we were full of business."

"He knows I am here?"

"In speaking of the company I mentioned you, of course."

"What did he say?"

"Not a word."

Vincent spoke with evident reluctance, and glanced at the girl's pale face with an expression of concern, for the fatherly soul pitied her. She saw the look and understood it; but, controlling her agitation, steadily returned the look, as she said: ·

"Please give me his address."

"My dear, is it best? Won't it be wiser to wait till he comes or sends to you?"

Old Vincent spoke in the kindness of his heart and out of a firm belief that Hope had suffered some neglect or wrong at the actor's hands. He changed his mind an instant afterward, for, with an indignant flush, kindling eyes, and voice that trembled with intensity of feeling, she said, audibly:

"You are mistaken, sir. I have borne much in silence, but soon I may speak out and prove how much you wrong me. Till then, for the sake of the daughters whom you love, believe my story and tell me where to find my friend."

"By Jupiter, I will!" heartily began the manager, but Miss Smythe interrupted him by saying, as she looked over her shoulder with the stage air of scorn:

"Miss Scott, if that *is* your name, may I trouble you to rehearse your part in a lower tone: you disturb us, for we don't find 'Love's Labor Lost' as interesting as Mr. Vincent."

"I beg your pardon; and tomorrow will give you a new version of 'Love's Labor Won,' " was the quick reply.

Then, as Vincent whispered the address in her ear, Hope left the stage with a look and gesture that would have made a hit before the footlights.

III

Le Brun sat alone, looking much older and more worn than half a year of life should make a man without some suffering to deepen the lines time leaves behind. Leaning his head upon his hand, he sat absorbed in thoughts both sweet and bitter, to judge by the varying expression of his face. He was going over a conversation held that morning with a brother actor, who had told him all the rumors afloat concerning Hope and himself. His first anger and disgust was over, and after much serious meditation he had resolved to end all gossip and make Hope happy in the way which would most effectually accomplish this end.

"Poor little girl, she has borne enough," he said. "I have tried to forget her, but I cannot; if she still loves me, and can forget my age, forgive my melancholy, and be content with the paternal affection and protection I can give her I'll marry her and right her in the eyes of this uncharitable world."

As his purpose was confirmed by being shaped into words, a note was handed him, and impatiently tearing it open, he found it was from Hope. Only a line begging him to come to her at once. Without losing a moment he obeyed. When he tapped at Hope's door she opened it, and as if unable to restrain her joy, threw herself into his arms, exclaiming tenderly:

"At last! at last! I thought you would never come!"

"Dear child, how could I know you needed me? Barbara promised to send to me in any trouble, and I gave her my address. Why did you not let me know?"

"She lost the paper and never told me till long afterward. Sit here and listen, for I have much to say, and oh, forgive me if I am wrong in what I do."

She would have placed him in a seat, but gently resisting, he drew her to him, saying earnestly:

"Spare yourself the pain of telling all you have suffered. I know everything, and am come to claim the right to protect you from slander, poverty, and loneliness. Hope, forgive the past, and be my wife."

He thought to see her blush, or weep, or cling to him with timid joy, but, to his amazement, she tore herself away, pale and panic-stricken, as if some hope was suddenly destroyed, some happy certainty taken from her in a moment.

"Your wife!" she cried, in a tone of intense dismay. "You say you know everything, yet ask this of me! No, no, you are blind still, you do not guess the truth. You think I speak of foolish gossip, and generously try to protect me. I care nothing for that, now you are found. Father, father, I am your daughter; oh, receive and love me for my mother's sake."

As the words broke from her, Hope stretched her hands imploringly toward him with a face of joyful expectancy, a gesture of ardent longing. Like one bewildered, Le Brun drew back, saying, with a startled look, a tone of mingled incredulity and pain.

"My daughter! I have none — neither wife nor child. Why do you speak of this and open the old wound?"

"Hear me and believe me, for as God lives, I speak the truth. Read this, look at that picture, and ask your own heart if it does not plead for me."

She put a worn paper, a little miniature, into his hands and stood before him with hope, truth, and tenderness shining in her face. He read, looked, turned to her, and opening his arms, took her home to the shelter of a father's love.

Soon, with the melancholy gone forever which had overshadowed him so long, Le Brun sat listening to his daughter as she told the story of the long search now crowned with success.

"To prove that I am no imposter, I will go back to the past, and recall a time you will remember well. The time when you and poor mamma were married, both so young, and you already winning fame upon the stage. She told me this, told me how you loved her, and how happy you were till she grew jealous, and destroyed your peace. She did not play, but watched you, never growing tired of your power and skill, till a lovely actress came. It made mamma unhappy to see you play the lover to another woman, and to discover that this woman tried to change the mimic passion to a real one."

"Poor Margaret, I did my best to prove the folly of her sad delusion, but she would not trust me, and so this misery came to both. Go on, my darling, to the time when I was left alone."

"Poor father, that was hard. Mamma grieved sorely, and longed bitterly to see you and be forgiven before she died."

"I do forgive her truly, tenderly, for my wrath was conquered long ago," sighed Le Brun.

"I tried to comfort her by assurances of this, and now she knows it, past doubt, thank God! She left you in a paroxysm of jealous passion, and hid herself for months, hoping to punish you and revenge her suffering by inflicting still greater pain on you. But when the time drew near for her little child to be born, her heart softened, and, fearing she might die, she wrote the truth, and left it, with that picture, for the baby, if it lived to want a father. It did live, but mamma's poor mind gave way, and for years she was worse than dead. I was born among strangers, and seeing her sad state, they sent me away to Barbara, for, thinking hers a hopeless case, it seemed better to let me believe myself an orphan."

"Poor baby, alone among strangers, and I wearing my heart out with vain longings for my wife and home, and little child."

"That is past now, so forget it, father dear. Barbara was very kind and faithful, and took me for her own on condition that no one told me of my unhappy mother or tried to find my father. I never knew the truth till two years ago. Barbara fell ill, and fearing to die with the secret on her mind, she told me all, and gave me the proofs of my identity. From that moment I resolved to find and reunite my parents if they lived. Barbara recovered, and against her will I tried to find mamma. She had escaped from the home where she was placed, and had vanished long ago. All my efforts were vain, and believing her dead, I gave heart and energy and time to searching for you."

"My little Hope, surely God led you to me when I was most desolate and heavy-hearted! How did you discover me? I changed my name, feeling that disgrace attached to the old one, and I came to the New World to begin a new life, if I could."

"It came about quite accidentally, nay, I'll say providentially, for it *did* lead me to you. I always wore my miniature, and wherever I went, watched faces, hoping to see one like it, for I soon felt sure that if you lived you had assumed another name. All my inquiries abroad failed, and I was in despair, when, happening to take up an American magazine at a railway station, I saw a picture of Le Brun, the tragedian. It was older, graver, sterner, and much changed by time, but still it struck me, and, comparing it with my portrait, the fancy strengthened to a firm belief. A brief sketch of your career accompanied the picture, half true, half false, as such things usually are; but a date, a name, a hint here and there, increased my eagerness to find and know you. Barbara was strongly prejudiced against you, and took mamma's part, though she knew neither. She was continually urging me to drop my fruitless search, and attend to my profession, for my father's power was in me, and I loved the stage, and longed to be an actress even when a child. Money was needed; this life permitted of frequent change, threw me among the sort of people most likely to know you, and I began it soon after I knew the truth. For the sake of peace and freedom, I never told Barbara of my new hope, never confided my purpose to her, but quietly managed to make an arrangement with a company coming over last year. Once here, I soon found a clue, and followed it till it led me to my father.''

"How, Hope? I disguised my name, blotted out my past, and let others deceive themselves in my age, wishing to be known only in my new character.''

"Ah, but instinct is a wonderful thing, as our Shakespeare says, and in spite of all disguises, I daily felt surer and surer that the melancholy Jacques Le Brun was Richard Ingram. A woman's eye is quick to catch hints, and her wit to unravel tangles when her heart is in the work. Many things helped me; your kindness, interest, and patience with an unknown girl; my own readiness to love, obey, and copy you; and, more than all, a glimpse of a token evidently hidden from all eyes. Do you remember the first night we played Romeo and Juliet?''

"Yes, child; and never was there a sweeter Juliet than my Hope. What happened then?''

"As you lay dead and I lay dying on your breast, I saw a little miniature that had slipped from your vest. It was the exact counterpart of that which always hung on my own neck. You knew nothing of its escape, and taking advantage of your forced helplessness, I examined it as closely as I dared in that little minute while the friar spoke and the curtain fell.''

"Little traitor, how you deceived me. This, then, was the cause of your sparkling eyes, your smiles, and the wistful look you gave me as you said 'Good-night.' Blind that I was! I fancied you loved me, dear, and love me now with all your heart.''

"Here is the picture still about your neck. Ah, father, it is as I thought — poor mamma's face, that you cherished so faithfully all those years.''

Hope had drawn it out, and both sat silent for a moment, looking down on the blooming countenance never to meet their eyes again. Softly closing it, she put it back, and leaning her soft cheek against his, answered the question his trembling lips had left half uttered.

"I found her at the hospital; she saw you, knew you, and through all the bewilderment of her poor darkened mind, felt that I was her child. In the silence of the night she told me the strange, sad story of her wanderings, her brief seasons of sanity, her long months of affliction, and of the fear which never left her that you would revenge yourself on her for her desertion. I tried to comfort her, to banish this dreadful fancy, and when you came again I hoped to heal the breach, to clear up the mystery, and make a happy end to this long grief. You did not return; Barbara deceived me, thinking I loved you, and when I told her my belief she was dismayed, for the address was lost, and poor mamma, who was in our keeping, would not listen to my prayers to be allowed to find you. She was very ill, and for a time I thought only of her, then you were gone, and I could only wait."

"You were well named, my little girl. Hope has been your support through many trials; now it shall be mine. What more? Tell me all; I can bear it."

With her arm about his neck, her tender eyes on his, and her voice full of daughterly compassion for the misery of those most dear to her, she softly said:

"A month ago she died. I tried to find you, that she might depart in peace, but Mr. Vincent could only tell me you were abroad, and coming soon. Mamma passed away before you came, praying for pardon with her last breath, and beseeching me to find and comfort you. I have found you, father; now let me be your consolation if I can."

He did not answer, but held her close, and the first bitterness of that revived affliction was sweetened by the consciousness that the daughter's devotion would beautifully atone for the mother's wrong. Soon he was himself again, and with Hope on his knee, tried to banish the tears from eyes unused to weep, by speaking of the present and putting by the memory of the past.

"And now, my child, we have only to make known our true relationship, to laugh at the gossips, and be happy in each other."

As he spoke, over Hope's April face passed a smile, as she looked proudly into the handsome face before her.

"Poor Tilly Smythe envied me my lover; now she will envy me my father, and be doubly spiteful because her malicious triumph will be changed to defeat when I go back to-morrow such a rich and happy girl."

"Why did you not speak out sooner, Hope? Why let me live on so near you, yet so blind to the truth? Why suffer from the gossip of idle tongues, when a word would silence them?" asked Le Brun, with a frown, as he remembered all he had heard that day.

"Who would believe me if I did speak, till you were here to support me? How did I know you would acknowledge me, having so much to forgive? At first I waited to be sure you were my father; then I feared to go to you, a stranger, with my story; so I was wary, and tried to make you care for me a little first. I meant to speak before you went away, but the accident delayed me; Barbara played me false, and then you were lost. Why did you hide yourself so long?"

"I believed the old woman's tale, and went away for your sake, thinking I should forget you. But my little pupil haunted me, and I began to fear I should be tempted to go back and selfishly make my lonely life happy at the cost of her peace. I was ill at ease; I did not love you, yet I wanted you, and so I put the sea between us, hoping to fall back into my former apathy. Now I understand it, and thank God for making such happiness both right and possible."

Hope sighed a sigh of supreme content, and asked, with a persuasive caress:

"Shall I act again with you, father? Say yes; it will be so charming to play together, and dare to let our love show itself, making the parts natural and true. I am a born actress; let me fulfill my destiny, at least while you remain an actor."

"I must fulfill my engagement to Vincent; then I shall take you away and keep you to myself for a time; after that we will set out on a starring tour together, for I am too proud of my Hope to hide her long. You will come back with me at once, for now you are found, I have a home and something to live for."

"Father, I have one more confession to make," began Hope, with hidden eyes and tell-tale color in her cheeks. "Do you remember the young gentleman who used to haunt the stage-box last year, to send flowers and poetry, and vex you by applauding everything I said and did?"

"I remember that you laughed at him then, and would have none of his gifts. He is still a lover, and no longer a slighted one. Is that the confession you would make, Hope?"

"Yes, father; he was sincere, and during those lonely months has been so kind, so humble, so faithful and true, I could not help loving him. I told him all my story, and he generously said he could not change his love. I bade him wait till you came, and ask no promise of me before your consent was won, and he has waited patiently. He is rich, well-born, and very proud, but neither my poverty, my misfortune nor my profession can daunt his affection, for the more forlorn I am the dearer I seem to become to him. See him, hear him, and make him happy. I shall never leave you, father, and in my heart there is room for two."

"Where is he?" was Le Brun's sole reply; but the benignant smile which accompanied it gave Hope courage to answer joyfully, "Here," and lead her love in to plead his suit.

A happy man was Le Brun when he saw the girl sumptuously settled with Barbara at his hotel — a proud father was he when he introduced "My daughter" at the theatre; and a decidedly inspired actor when he played with her before enthusiastic audiences, drawn together by this romantic episode in the tragedian's career.

The engagement was a long and brilliant one closing with a double benefit, when the house was packed and the pleasurable excitement of the hour enhanced by the fact that the play was the same which had nearly terminated fatally the year before. Again, at the end, Lear led Cordelia out, and when from the stage-box a delicate wreath of white flowers fell at the daughter's feet, the father laid it on her head with a look more tender than a smile, a gesture full of paternal pride, as if a blessing had been given with that bridal-garland from a lover's hand. Every one before and behind the curtain applauded heartily, except Tilly Smythe, who was enjoying hysterics in her dressing room.

Thrice Tempted

Frank Leslie's Chimney Corner, 20 July 1867. Published anonymously

*S*HE SAT ALONE in the dull, old-fashioned room, a slight, dark girl, with no beauty but much strength of character in her face, which, just then, wore an unwonted expression of happiness, for she was reading her first love-letter.

So absorbed was she that the entrance of another person was unobserved — a tall, brilliant girl, dressed with a taste and skill that enhanced her beauty, and bearing about her the indefinable air of one which instantly marks those who have been luxuriously nurtured from birth.

With noiseless steps and an arch smile on her lips she glided to the reader's side and glanced over her shoulder.

An expression of surprise rose to her face as she read the first words aloud:

"My own little Ruth!"

"Why, child, who writes to you in that style?" she added, hastily.

With a slight start Ruth turned the leaf, and at the bottom of the closely-written page pointed to a name, smiling a sudden smile, full of tender pride and happiness, as the other read the line: — "Yours always and entirely, Walter Strathsay."

"Upon my word, this is a revelation, and I must know all about it. Tell me the romance, Ruthie."

"I meant to have told you soon, but since you have forced my confidence, I need not wait. I am betrothed to Walter."

Slowly, quietly the girl spoke, and to many she would have seemed cold, but a nice observer would have seen her lips tremble, her eyes shine and in the low voice have detected an undertone of strong emotion.

Laura eyed her keenly, and laughed, with a touch of scorn in her laughter, as she answered:

"No need to tell me that, child; I want to know when and how it came about. You've never dropped a hint of it in your letters, and three months ago you solemnly assured me you should never marry."

"I thought I never should, but Walter came, and I changed my mind. I've nothing to tell except that his father was a friend of my father's and grandmamma asked him here when she heard of his return from the Crimea."

"He came, saw and conquered. It strikes me as very droll; but I wish you much joy, my dear."

"Why droll, Laura?"

"One never fancies you with a lover; you are so cool and quiet, so proud, so odd and unlike most girls."

"So plain and unattractive you mean," and Ruth's tone was sharp with pain, though she smiled as she finished the sentence.

"Well, if you don't mind, I agree to the addition. What sort of a man is this lover of yours? Show me his picture; I know you have one, for I never saw that charming chain on your neck before," and Laura put forth her hand to examine it.

"Guess before you look," cried Ruth, guarding her treasure, and speaking with unusual vivacity.

Lounging gracefully on the couch beside her, Laura answered with a sarcastic smile:

"I think he is much older than you, forty, perhaps; a rough, bronzed, gray-headed soldier, who has come home an invalid, and wants a kind, quiet little nurse to take care of him in his old age. He has money enough to be comfortable, and finding you alone, took pity on you, and when the old lady dies you will take her place. I am right, I fancy, by the odd look you wear. Now, let me see."

Drawing out a golden medallion, Ruth touched the spring, and in a pearl-set oval showed the portrait of a young and strikingly handsome man.

Laura uttered an exclamation, and then sat looking at it in silent admiration, while Ruth watched her with eyes full of triumph, and there was a touch of malice in her tone, as she asked:

"Does my lover suit your description?"

"He is my ideal of a lover and a hero! Tell me more; tell me everything. His age, his fortune, his family and all the story," answered Laura still holding the picture, and still gazing intently at the painted face, so full of manly beauty.

"He is five and twenty, has just come into the possession of a fine fortune, is the last of the ancient Scotch family of Strathsay, has fought gallantly, received many honors; and, he loves me tenderly."

As the last words were spoken and Ruth put out her hand to reclaim the likeness of her lover something in her voice made Laura look up and exclaim, in real astonishment:

"Bless the girl! how the 'grand passion' has improved her! Why, child, you look quite inspired with that color in your brown cheeks, and your black eyes all afire. It is a miracle; but such a man as this can work greater ones, I fancy."

Her eyes went back to the miniature, and a sigh rose to her lips, for among her many lovers she had not one like this.

Quickly repressing the involuntary betrayal of regret, she caught up the hand extended for the picture, and holding it fast, laughed mischievously as she examined the costly ring, turned inward for concealment.

"Diamonds, as I live! and such diamonds! seven beauties, and set in a style to win the heart of any woman! Upon my word, Ruthie, your Walter does things in a princely way. Why did you hide your splendor from me all day?"

"I didn't want to tell you just yet; neither did I want to take off my ring, because he put it on; so I hid it. But if it gives you pleasure to see pretty things, I can show you more, for Walter is indeed, princely in his love."

With an air of pride, Ruth opened the old escritoir, and produced a quaint casket, steel-bound and clasped. Placing it on her lap she opened it, and let in the light upon a heap of glittering ornaments.

"They are the Strathsay jewels. Walter brought them all to me, and left them that I might decide upon new settings, for these are very antique, you see. But I like them as they are, for the stones are fine, and the curious setting pleases me."

"Ruth, they are magnificent! I never saw anything like them. Look how they become my arms. Happy girl to have won such a prize," and Laura sighed again as she clasped another bracelet on her round, white arm.

"I don't think this a prize, though I admire the jewels like a woman. Walter is better than a thousand diamond mines, and I care very little for these things, except as his gifts."

"So like you; but then they are not suited to your style, and that makes a difference, you know. I've always wanted to own real old lace and jewels, for money won't always buy them. I wish ours was an ancient family, and not a very new one. Papa left me a comfortable fortune, but neither rank nor position: and after all, money and beauty are not so valuable as an ancient name and heirlooms like these."

"Yes; I've nothing but my name, yet I find that has won me what richer, handsomer girls have failed to win; and I envy no one."

Ruth smiled down into her lover's face and for a moment forgot everything but the happy moment when a word made her lonely life supremely blest.

Laura, sitting with a strew of jewels about her, frowned and bit her lips as her eye went from the casket and the picture to the letter and the girl who had suddenly eclipsed her in everything but beauty. As the thought came, she suddenly glanced at Ruth's unconscious face then, at her own reflected in the mirror, and as she looked, the frown passed, for the strong contrast reassured her and she felt that one weapon still remained to her.

The letter lay open at their feet, and her keen eye ran down the page reading words that deepened her admiration, increased her envy, and confirmed the purpose already formed in her selfish heart.

"When are you to be married?" she asked abruptly.

"In autumn, if grandmamma is better."

"Where is Mr. Strathsay now?"

"My colonel is in London for a day or two, but will return soon and you can see him."

"Is the old lady pleased with the affair?"

"Delighted; she says she always wished it."

"Is he going to leave the army?"

"Yes; the fighting is over, and we want him at home."

"Shall you live in Scotland?"

"If I like, and I think I do. Walter leaves it all to me; but his old uncle wants him a little while before he dies, and it is right that we should do our best for the man who does so much for us."

"What will he do?"

"He leaves Walter his fortune and title, for he will soon be the last of the family. It makes no difference to me, but the people want another Sir Walter, so I consent for his sake."

"Lady Strathsay!" was all Laura said, as she flung the jewels into the casket, glanced again at the picture and restored the letter, with a curious expression. Her friend did not see it, and said softly:

"I like 'Little Ruth' better, and no title can be sweeter to me than what he bid me call him after the old Scottish fashion, 'my laddie.' "

"Very romantic. Long may it last. Marry soon, my dear, or the delightful glamour will pass away and the charm be broken for ever."

"How bitterly you speak, Laura! Has anything happened to grieve you since we parted? I've been so absorbed in my own happiness I forgot to ask how you had fared. Among so many lovers, have you not found one to reward?"

As she spoke with friendly warmth, Ruth put away her treasures and turned to the beauty who lay looking at her with an expression which troubled her, she knew not why.

"No, I've no tender secret to confide in return for yours, neither am I unhappy — why should I be? I'm only tired; so play to me and soothe my weariness like a good creature, as you are."

Ruth gladly complied, and filled the room with music, for this was her one gift, and she was justly proud of it. As she played, Laura lay looking dreamily out into the summer sunshine that shone warm over garden, grove and lawn. So lying, her eyes suddenly grew intent, her languid head rose erect, her cheek flushed, and her voice was unnaturally low, as she begged Ruth to play a stormy overture.

The girl's back was toward her, so her movements were unseen. Leaving the couch, she stole to the long window, and hidden in the folds of the curtain, peeped out to watch the approach of the man whom she had seen leave his horse at the foot of the lawn and come rapidly yet quietly toward the house, as if anxious to enter unseen. She knew him at a glance, for the picture had not lied, and the original was as comely as the miniature.

Noiselessly he reached the other open window and slipped in. Unconscious, Ruth played on, and pausing an instant to put down hat and gloves, her lover eyed her with a smile that made the watcher's heart beat with a strange mixture of emotions.

As the last chord died under her hand, Ruth said, without turning:

"Do you like it, Laura?"

"Not so well as the song, 'Oh, Welcome Hame, my Laddie,' " replied a man's voice, and with a cry that was full of gladder music than any air she played, Ruth ran to meet her lover.

"So soon — so soon! I thought it would be days before you came, Walter," she said, clinging to him in a quiet rapture of delight.

"I thought so too; but the time seemed so interminable I could not bear it, and came down almost as soon as my letter, for I cannot keep away from my little sweetheart a whole week."

"I'm glad, very glad, for if London is dull, what must this quiet place be? How long can you stay?"

"Two or three days, dear. Then I must run up again to get this tedious army business over. Now come and tell me everything you've done. Ah, ha! been playing, my lady, have you, and trying on your trinkets. I'll take them back with me to have them reset, if you have decided."

"I've not changed my mind; I like them as they are. I did not take them out to play with, but to show to my friend. Laura has come, and wants so much to see you!"

"She does me honor; but I haven't the least desire to see her. I want you all to myself, little Ruth. Will she stay long?" asked Strathsay, leading the girl toward the door.

"Why, where is she? I forgot her entirely and she was here a minute before you came," cried Ruth, looking about her with sudden recollection.

"Gone like a shadow, it seems. So much the better. Come and see the dear old lady with me, and then let us go 'and be happy in rest."

They went away, arm-in-arm, leaving the room empty, for Laura had slipped out while the lovers were absorbed in each other.

Half an hour later, as they sat together in a flowery nook of the old garden, Ruth paused suddenly in something she was saying, for it was evident that Strathsay's attention wandered. Her eye followed his, and saw Laura in the grape walk, with her little Italian greyhound prancing beside her.

She looked very lovely, coming down the cool, green vista, her rosy muslins blowing in the balmy wind and her sunny-brown hair bound with a chaplet of young vine leaves. A book was in her hand, but she read little, and her fine eyes were fixed on the river that rolled below.

Grace is often more powerful than beauty, but when the two are united, few can resist the spell. Laura possessed both, and knew how to use them with the skill of an actress. Apparently unconscious, she went to and fro, artfully making every look, gesture, attitude and tone serve a purpose. Now, she walked with indolent ease, long lashes hiding the violet eyes, and lips smiling as at what she read. Then pausing, she displayed a fine arm by reaching to draw down a cluster of climbing roses, or drew attention to a slender waist by setting the flowers in her belt. The little greyhound frisked before her with a leaf from her book, and she pursued him with flying feet, chiding as she ran, and when the culprit crouched before her, she relented and petted the dainty creature with all manner of pretty words and caresses.

As if weary, she threw by her book, put down the dog, and dropping on a seat, half sat, half lay there in an attitude full of listless grace, and seemed to fall into a waking dream.

"Is that your friend?" asked Strathsay, forgetting to apologize for his absence.

"Yes, that is Laura."

"You never told me she was beautiful, Ruth."

"Indeed I did, and you said you hated beauties."

"So I do — mere dolls, such as one sees in society. That is no doll, but a very lovely girl. How long have you known her?"

"Only since last March. We met in town, and though she was a belle and I a nobody, she was kind to me, for my odd ways amused her. I asked her to come and see me in the summer, and here she is. Will you go and speak with her? I'll let you admire her, but no more. She has many lovers and does not need you, so beware."

As Ruth spoke, she rose and beckoned, but Strathsay drew her back, saying earnestly:

"Do you doubt me, dear?"

"No, but I know the power of beauty, and Laura has great skill in winning hearts. You are my all, and I cannot lose you, unworthy as I am to possess so much."

"Nay, I'll not go; if this girl is such a siren, I had better shun her for both our sakes, though upon my life, a touch of jealousy improves you, little Ruth."

He laughed as he spoke, and stroked the smooth cheek grown rosy with a sudden flush. The girl's dark eyes were full of tears, and a foreboding fear chilled her heart, as she answered with a troubled look:

"A strange feeling came over me just then, and all the sunshine seemed to vanish. You told me that you had known few women in your busy life, and that now every one you met seemed charming. I'm not even pretty, and though you love me now, I feel a sudden fear that I may lose you."

"Shall I swear and protest, or will you trust me entirely?" he asked, as if hurt by her doubt.

"I'll trust entirely. But Walter, a time may come when you will repent of your generosity to me; promise that if it should, you will frankly tell me. I can hear anything but deceit."

"I promise. Now forget this foolish fancy and take me to your friend; she sees us, and it is rude to leave her so long."

"Come then," and Ruth gave him her hand, trying to feel at ease; but a shadow had fallen on her sunshine, and her happy mood was gone.

Laura received Strathsay with a charming mixture of eagerness, timidity, and half-hidden admiration, which was very flattering. She had friends in the Crimea, and leading the conversation in that direction, irresistibly interested the young officer and brought out many exciting episodes and warlike reminiscences. She possessed the art of putting others at their ease, of making them do their best, and imparting to them a pleasurable consciousness that they charmed her as she did them. Ruth had none of this skill; cold and shy externally, few knew what a depth of passion and power lay below, for self-control had been early learned, and pride led her to conceal both pain and pleasure from all but a chosen few. As she watched her lover and her friend growing more and more absorbed in the conversation, Strathsay unconsciously betraying his admiration, and Laura freely expressing hers in praises of his bravery and interest in his fortunes, her heart grew heavier and heavier with the morning instinct, born of love. So strong grew this foreboding, that when she parted from Laura after a long evening of seeming harmony and gayety, she could not resist saying in a tone she tried to render playful:

"No poaching on my grounds; remember your power, and use it generously."

"What do you mean?" asked Laura, with well-feigned surprise.

"I mean that you must not take my one lover away, for the pleasure of adding another conquest to the many you have already won."

"Jealous creature, do you think he would be worth regretting if his love was so fickle that another could rob you of it? You insult him by the fear and me by the warning."

"Forgive me; I could not help it. I have been so poor, that my sudden riches make me suspicious and miserly. I will do better, and trust you both."

She did implicitly, for generous natures are easiest to deceive, and Laura's anger quieted Ruth's fears for a time. Strathsay's visit lengthened to a week, and so happily did the days pass, that Ruth scarcely heeded their flight, till some accidental trifle reminded her of the lapse of time. When she spoke of business to her lover, he told her it could be carried on by letter, and he should not leave her yet. At this she rejoiced and resigned herself to the new happiness, blindly trusting that all was well. Nothing could be more irreproachable than Laura's conduct, nothing more devoted than his to Ruth, and all three seemed frank and friendly in their daily intercourse. So another week went by, and then Ruth's trouble came again.

"Little girl, I must go to-morrow," abruptly began Strathsay as they sat alone one evening.

"Why so suddenly, Walter?"

"I've neglected my affairs too long, and must be off without delay."

"When will you return?"

"Can't say; you've had enough of me for a month at least, so I will leave you in peace."

"You know I have not. What is the matter? You look excited, yet sad; your voice is bitter and you turn your eyes away. Have I offended you, my laddie?" and the girl's tender face looked wistfully into his averted one, as her hand stole to his shoulder with an appealing touch.

An instant he sat silent, then turned to her, and with a deep flush on his bronzed cheek, but honest eyes fixed on her own, and steady voice full of humility, yet earnest with the truth, he said, rapidly:

"I promised not to deceive you, Ruth, and I will keep my word. With shame and contrition I confess that I go because I dare not stay."

"You love her, then?" faltered poor Ruth, pale and panic-stricken in a moment.

"No, I can truly say I do not yet, but I fear I may. She fascinates me by her beauty. Tell her to be less lovely and less kind; it will be better for us both. Indeed I do not love her, but her face haunts me, and makes me miserable because it is wrong. I have kept my word to you, and made you unhappy by the truth; but I am impetuous and weak, and fear that I may, in some unguarded moment, look or say more than I ought. Help me to be true to my real love and to cast off this unhappy delusion before it is too late."

"I will! Flee temptation, Walter. Leave me before a rash word mars our peace. Go away, and if it is a delusion you will forget it; if it is not, I can do my duty, and endure to see you happy even with Laura."

Both had spoken impulsively, and both were so absorbed that neither saw the shadow that flitted in and out behind them, or dreamed that Laura overheard their words.

Long they talked, each trying to be just and generous, and each conscious that the love they bore each other was true and deep, in spite of all delusions, doubts, or temptations.

On the morrow Strathsay went, and though Ruth watched eagerly, Laura betrayed no concern, but said good-by with her blithest smile, and gave him sundry trifling commissions, as if unconscious of his gravity, or the covert glances he gave at the beautiful face which haunted him against his will, and was to prove the phantom of his life.

Very dull and quiet were the days that followed Strathsay's departure, for he wrote but seldom, and the friends felt that they were friends no longer. Not a word was said, but the coldness increased, and neither made any effort to change it.

Fortunately for Ruth her invalid grandmother needed unusual care just then, and thus she was freed from the constraint of Laura's presence some hours of each day.

To her surprise Laura did not shorten her visit, but remained, and seemed happy in the quiet place, and the various amusements she devised for herself.

While Ruth sat with the old lady she walked, and always came home gay and rosy, with some little adventure to relate, or some report of the poor souls she had comforted, for she was charitable with that cheap charity which gives money, but neither sympathy nor care.

Ruth smiled at her caprices, especially the last one, till accident enlightened her.

Some three weeks after Strathsay's departure, old madam was one day possessed with a strong desire for a certain kind of jelly which no one could make but a former maid of her own, now married and living in the village.

Ruth was dispatched with the other, and as she approached the cottage, overtook a little lad carrying a letter with great care.

Being one of Martha's boys, she chatted with him as they walked, and in so doing her eye fell on the letter. There was nothing remarkable about it to other eyes, for it was simply directed to "Mrs. Martha Hale," in a plain, clear hand, and post-marked "London."

But Ruth looked long at it, and felt a curious interest in it, for the writing was wonderfully like Strathsay's, especially three letters in one corner, with a dash below.

The rest of the address was a little changed, but the letters were in his peculiar hand, "L.C.R.," and as she looked she involuntarily said to herself, "Laura Catharine Richmond."

Something in the child's manner struck her also, for as he saw her examining the letter, he dropped his hands beside him, saying, with a droll mixture of importance and anxiety:

"Mammy bids me always put 'em in my pocket, but it's all wet with berries, and I can't. Don't you tell you see it, else she'll scold."

"Why, Teddy?"

"Don't know, but she does if I ain't careful of her old letters, and she won't even give me the seals on 'em; they are pretty stags' heads, and I like 'em."

An intense desire to see the letter again seized Ruth on hearing that, and she managed to do so by interesting the child in a marvelous tale, till he forgot to hide his hand and the paper it held. No seal was visible, and she hoped her fear was groundless.

Coming to the cottage, Teddy hurried to find his mother, and Ruth gave her message. She was on her way home when a fine flower in a wayside field caused her to climb the bank to get it. As she sat in the long grass to rest, Laura passed in the path below.

Ruth was about to speak, when Laura took a letter from her pocket, tore off the cover, broke the seal of the enclosed envelope, and passed into the grove, reading eagerly as she went.

The instant she disappeared Ruth sprang down to the path, caught up the crumpled cover, and saw it was the same that Teddy had just taken to his mother.

There was no doubt now in her mind that Strathsay wrote to Laura, and a stern calmness came over Ruth as her quick wit cleared up the mystery of Laura's charitable freak of late. No tears, reproaches, or complaints, but an instant resolution to know all took possession of the girl, and that night she executed her purpose.

Laura was unusually gay and amiable, but went early to bed. Ruth watched till her light was out and she was unmistakably asleep, then, with soundless steps she entered the room, found the desk, possessed herself of the key, and returning to her own room, opened and searched the papers of this fair false friend. The letters were there, several from Strathsay, and two or three copies of those Laura had written, beginning with a brief note of thanks for the well-executed commissions, and a delicately expressed regret that Ruth's unhappy temper should disturb their pleasant friendship.

This had produced an explanation and defense from the lover, followed by further notes from Laura, hinting that Ruth loved to show her power and was proud of the prize she had won.

It was evident that she had told him Ruth was happy in his absence, contented with her narrow life, and in no haste to recall him.

Skillfully had she worked upon his pride and temper, overcoming honorable scruples, silencing self-reproachful condemnation, and mingling her falsehoods with such pity, sympathy, and half-confessed affection, that it was little wonder an ardent, impressionable man should be deceived and taught to think Ruth the cold, shallow-hearted, ambitious girl her false friend painted her.

His letters proved that he had not yielded without a struggle, and as she read, Ruth forgave him, for that last letter was full of remorse, doubts of the depth of the new passion, and regrets that he had ever seen the fair face which had robbed him of peace and self-respect. Ruth forgave and loved him still, believing him more sinned against than sinning; but such hatred and contempt for Laura sprang up within her, she trembled lest it should lead her to some rash act of retribution. When all was read, she safely restored the stolen desk and went back to a sleepless pillow, feeling as if a year had passed since that discovery was made.

Pale and quiet she rose next day, with a firm resolve to save Strathsay and unmask Laura.

Secretly they had wronged her, and as secretly would she revenge herself upon the chief sinner; the means she left to time and her own address.

"Jane tells me that fever has broken out in the village, so be careful how you and Laura go there, for it is a dangerous and malignant disease," said old madam next day, as her grandchild left her.

There was nothing in the words to startle Ruth, but she suddenly turned pale, for a black thought rose up in her mind, and like an evil spirit tempted her.

Laura would go to carry her reply; one of Martha's children lay sick; perhaps it was the fever; or if not already there, the air was full of it. She might take it, and then —

A host of conflicting emotions filled her mind, but out of the confusion rose the wish that Laura was dead and Strathsay all her own again. She sat and thought of this till her temples throbbed, and her heart beat quick with the guilty purpose stirring in it, for to that poor, passionate heart it seemed right to be revenged for the wrong so cruelly done it.

As Ruth's eyes roved restlessly to and fro they fell on Laura's figure going down the green lane to the town. She guessed her errand, and watched her tripping away, looking lovelier than ever as she glanced back with a smile, and then went on rejoicing in her treachery and conquest. Ruth set her teeth and clinched her hands, but never stirred till the girl was out of sight. Then, with a shiver, she dropped her head upon her arm, feeling the first bitterness of sin. In the act the miniature slid from her bosom and swung open before her, wearing to her eyes a reproachful look, that smote her heart. The memory of the past touched her better self, and, forgetting hatred in love, she put away the purpose that made her so unworthy of it.

Without pausing for a second thought, Ruth hurried after her friend, and reached her in time to tell her of the danger she incurred.

An expression of sudden shame passed over Laura's face as she turned back, warmly thanking the girl for the warning.

But it was given too late; she had been often among the cottages where the contagion had just broken out, and a week from that day Ruth watched beside her, listening to her incoherent ravings, thanking God that she had not yielded to the strong temptation, and that if Laura died it would not be through her. For many days the fever raged, then left her weak and wan as a shadow of her former self. Ruth nursed her faithfully, trying to stifle sinful regrets that she was spared for further harm. She could have forgiven her if any sign of penitence or sorrow had escaped her; but the utter falseness of her nature hardened Ruth's heart and left no room for any softer feeling than contempt.

Strathsay wrote seldom now, and knowing the cause, Ruth made no complaint. She could not deceive him, and so waited till she could put an end to his struggle and her own.

She watched if any note came from him to Laura; but her friend's maid was wrong, and Ruth discovered nothing till one night, as she lay apparently asleep on the couch in Laura's room, she saw her draw a paper from under her pillow, read it, kiss it, and then put it back, to drop asleep, little dreaming whose eyes were on her.

No need for Ruth to read the note; she knew whence it came; and sitting in the hush of midnight, she brooded over her misery till no sin, no sacrifice seemed too great, if it but won her back the heart she had lost.

As she sat thus gazing at the face whose beauty had been so fatal to her peace, a sudden gust of air from the half-opened window wafted the muslin drapery of the bed across the night-lamp burning near. Ruth would have risen to move the light, but the evil spell was on her, and she sat unmoved, watching with fascinated eyes the white curtains floating nearer and nearer the dangerous lamp.

Laura lay in a deep sleep, the house was lonely and the maids in distant rooms. She heard the rustle of the rising breeze, saw the quickened sweep of the bright drapery, but neither spoke nor stirred.

A dreadful calm possessed her, and when a sudden blaze lit the room, she only smiled — an awful smile — she saw it in the mirror and trembled at herself.

The flames shot up brighter and hotter as the woodwork caught; Laura woke suddenly, and stretching her arms through smoke and fire, cried feebly:

"Walter, save me! save me!"

He could not answer her, but he saved Ruth, for the sound of his name freed her from the evil spell that bound her. She tore Laura from the burning bed and fought the flames till they were conquered, finding a fierce delight in the excitement and danger. But when the peril was over and Laura soothed to sleep again, then Ruth felt weak and helpless as a child.

Burdened with the weight of the nearly-committed crime, and conscious of the power her unhappy love possessed to lead her into evil, she cried within herself:

"This must end; I can lead this life no longer for it will ruin me body and soul. Walter must decide between us, and the struggle cease."

In the gray dawn she wrote to her lover, bidding him come home, simply telling him she knew everything, and would forgive it if he would end both doubt and misery at once.

She sent the letter, told Laura what she had done, and besought her to make his happiness if she truly loved him, for there was no other claim upon him now.

Laura seemed annoyed at the act, but not humbled by the discovery of her own treason. She called Ruth "a romantic child," and promised to see what she could do for Walter. Her heartless words were daggers to Ruth, but she bore it patiently, longing to have all over and past doubt.

A line from Strathsay arrived, appointing a day for his return, but nothing more; and in this alacrity, this silence, Ruth read her fate.

As the time approached Laura grew restless and excited. She insisted on making a fine toilet though still too feeble to leave her room, and rouged her wan cheeks, that his eye should miss as little as possible of the beauty that won him.

"He is coming! I know his step along the garden path! Are you faint?" said Ruth, as Laura lay back in the deep chair with pale lips, and a look of pain in her face.

"I am only tired of waiting. Bring him to me quickly, Ruth," she answered, sitting erect, with the old smile, the old attitude and glance.

"Walter, let me say a few words first," said Ruth, as he came in, wearing an expression of mingled shame, sorrow, and relief, that wrung her heart. "I release you from the promise which has become a burden. I want a free heart or none. Choose for yourself beauty or love, and let the trial end at once. One word more — and believe me, I try to say it in a kind spirit. Let me warn you that a false friend may not make a true wife. Now go, and let it soon be over."

He faltered and looked at her with a searching glance; but she stood resolute and calm, as unable to express her sorrow as she had been to demonstrate her love, yet feeling both the deeper for that cause. He could not read the suffering heart. He thought her cold and careless, for with a few hurried words of gratitude and regret he left her.

A moment after a cry brought Ruth to his side. She found him distractedly chafing Laura's cold hand, and imploring her to speak to him. But no answer came, for there, in the full glare of the sunshine, with the false bloom on her wasted cheeks, the set smile on her breathless lips, lay Laura, dead.

The physicians seemed little surprised, saying she was very frail, and the fever had left her too weak for any excitement. So when all restoratives failed, she was made ready for her last sleep, and her friends came to carry her to her last home.

Ruth had longed for this — had prayed that one of them might die; but now, when in a moment the wicked wish was granted, she repented and forgave her enemy.

"Rest in peace, Laura. I pardon you as I hope to be pardoned," she said, softly, as, standing alone beside the coffin, she looked down upon the quiet face, so powerless to harm her now. Uttering the words, she bent to put away a lock of hair fallen from its place. In doing so her hand touched Laura's forehead, and a strange thrill shot through her, for it was *damp*. She put her hand on the heart, pulse and lips, but all were cold and still. She touched the brow again, but the first touch had wiped the slight dew from it, and it was now like ice. For several minutes Ruth stood white and motionless as the dead girl, while the old struggle, fiercer than ever, raged in her heart. Fear whispered that she was not dead. Pity pleaded for her, lying helplessly before her, and conscience sternly bade her do the right, forgetful of all else. But she would not listen, for Love cried out, passionately:

"Walter is my own again; she cannot separate us any more, or rob me of the one blessing of my life. Twice I have conquered temptation, and been generous only to be more wronged. Now, I will yield to it, and if a word could save this traitorous friend, I will not utter it."

Then, hardening her heart, Ruth shut out from her sight the face she hated, and left the doubt unsolved. She was the last who saw Laura; she never told the fear that haunted her; the girl was buried and the lovers took up their life again.

Strathsay seemed more bewildered than bereaved by the sudden check his infatuation had received. The charm was broken and when the first shock was over he never spoke of her, and seemed to wake from his short dream himself again.

Ruth uttered no reproach, but by every tender art showed how gladly she welcomed back the love, not lost but led astray. Strathsay soon seemed fonder than ever, trying eagerly to atone for the past. The future lay clear before her, and life would have been all sunshine but for the shadow of a single cloud. A vague sense of guilt weighed on her, growing heavier day by day, for the horrible fancy that Laura was not dead haunted her like a ghost. She had held her peace at first, fearing that the evil genius of her life should return to torment her again. She had kept her sinful vow till it was too late, and now the hidden memory became a spectre to mar her peace.

Months went on, the wedding-day was fixed, and in the excitement of that event, Ruth hoped she might forget. But it was in vain; the fear was always lying heavy at her heart, making her days wearisome with ceaseless anxiety, her nights terrible with dark dreams. She would not believe it anything but a wild fancy, yet felt that it was wearing upon her. She saw her cheeks grow thin, her eyes full of feverish unrest, her spirits failing, her life a daily struggle to cast off the gloom that poisoned her happiness. Her only comfort was in the hope that the approaching change might banish the hidden trouble.

Once Strathsay's wife, she believed that his love would banish every care and allay every haunting fear. She fancied that a time would come when she would dare to confide her foolish dread and see him smile at it. She clung to this hope, and often in those miserable nights, when the dead face confronted her in the darkness with a mute reproach in its dim eyes that scared sleep from her pillow, she would lie framing her confession into fitting words for his ear, mingling self-accusations with whispered prayers for pardon, and fond reminders that these trials and temptations were caused by her great love for him.

The night before her wedding day she lay down with the old fear stronger than ever, and fell into a deep sleep, filled with troubled dreams, which tormented her till dawn. Then she sprang up with a sense of unutterable relief, and for a while forgot herself in glad preparations for the approaching ceremony.

The day was fair and Ruth was happy, for the phantom fear was gone. A few friends came with good wishes, to celebrate the quiet nuptials; the hour arrived and all was ready, but Strathsay did not come.

They waited long, and still no bridegroom appeared. Messengers were sent to find him, but returned saying he had gone away at dawn and had not yet returned. Then Ruth's heart died within her, feeling that some affliction was in store for her, and she waited, racked with apprehensions that almost drove her wild. But still he did not come.

One by one the friends departed, wondering, and she was left alone with old madam and the clergyman. They tried to comfort her, but their words went by her like the wind.

Hour after hour she paced the room with eye, ear and mind strained to the utmost. Still Strathsay did not come.

Old madam slept at last, the good man went away, and friendly neighbors ceased to question and condole. She was utterly alone, and the red fire-light which she thought would have shone upon a happy wife now glimmered faintly on a pale, anxious woman with dead flowers on her breast and bridal garments mocking her desolation, as she sat waiting for the coming sorrow.

Suddenly Strathsay's step sounded in the hall, and, speechless with relief, she sprang to welcome him; but there was that in his face which drove her back. Haggard and wild it looked, as with white lips and eyes dilated with some secret horror, he stood gazing at her till she was cold with ominous dread.

She could not bear it long, and going to him, would have given him a tender greeting; but he shrank from her touch with averted head and hands outstretched to keep her off.

"Walter, what is it? Do not kill me with such looks — such dreadful silence! Tell me what has happened. I can bear anything but this!" she cried, clinging to him with a desperate hold.

A look of bitter pain swept over his face as his eyes met her imploring gaze. He held her close a moment, then put her from him with a shudder.

She sat where he placed her, without power to move or speak, while standing before her, with a countenance as hard and stern as rock, he said with an abrupt calmness, far more terrible than the wildest agitation:

"Ruth, last night I sat alone in this room after you left me; and while here a white figure with vacant eyes and pallid cheeks came gliding in and pausing there, it told a sad tale of deceit and wrong, of hidden sins and struggles, and confessed one crime which drove it like a restless ghost to betray its secrets when most fatal to its peace."

"It was Laura come back from her tomb to wrong and rob me again," cried Ruth, half unconscious of what she said as the old fear overwhelmed her anew.

"No, *it was you,* coming in your haunted sleep to tell the secret that is wearing your life away. It was awful to see you standing there with no light in your open eyes, no color in your expressionless face, and hear the tender words, meant to be spoken with repentant tears, uttered in unearthly tones by lips unconscious of their meaning, and then to see the self-accusing apparition glide away unmoved into the gloom, leaving such misery behind."

"Forgive me! — you will, you must, for it was you who drove me to this. I loved you better than my own soul, and she came between us. I have been sorely tempted, but for your sake I resisted more than once. Did I not set you free when my whole heart was bound up in you? Did I not relinquish everything for you and have I not proved how strong my love is by these sacrifices for your sake? Do not reproach me that I unconsciously betrayed the struggles I have endured, nor chide me that I rejoiced when Laura died. She is dead, and nothing but my feverish fancy would ever have doubted it."

Strathsay's calmness vanished as she rapidly poured out this appeal. The horror-stricken look returned to his eyes, and his voice sounded hoarsely through the silent room as he replied, with lips that whitened as he spoke:

"She *is* dead, thank God! but *was not when they buried her.* Ay, you may well fall on your knees and hide your guilty face, for you murdered her. Hear me, and cheat yourself with doubts no longer. Filled with alarm by your confession, and remembering the strange restlessness which has possessed you since her death, I went to-day to R——, where Laura lies. Alone I went into the tomb, but was brought out senseless; she had been buried alive! There was no doubt of it. She had turned in her coffin, and, too weak to break it, had perished miserably. May God forgive you, Ruth; I never can!"

"Oh! be merciful, Walter. I had suffered so much from her, I could not give you up. Be merciful, and do not cast me off when all the sin was for your dear sake," she cried, overcoming in her despair the horror and remorse that froze her blood.

But Strathsay never heeded her, and his stern purpose never wavered. He tore himself away with an aspect of deeper despair than her own, saying, solemnly, as he passed from her sight for ever:

"God pardon us both; our sins have wrought out their own punishment, and we must never meet again."

Perilous Play

Frank Leslie's Chimney Corner, 13 February 1869. Published anonymously

*I*F SOMEONE DOES NOT propose a new and interesting amusement, I shall die of ennui!" said pretty Belle Daventry, in a tone of despair. "I have read all my books, used up all my Berlin wools, and it's too warm to go to town for more. No one can go sailing yet, as the tide is out; we are all nearly tired to death of cards, croquet, and gossip, so what shall we do to while away this endless afternoon? Dr. Meredith, I command you to invent and propose a new game in five minutes."

"To hear is to obey," replied the young man, who lay in the grass at her feet, as he submissively slapped his forehead, and fell a-thinking with all his might.

Holding up her finger to preserve silence, Belle pulled out her watch and waited with an expectant smile. The rest of the young party, who were indolently scattered about under the elms, drew nearer, and brightened visibly, for Dr. Meredith's inventive powers were well-known, and something refreshingly novel might be expected from him. One gentleman did not stir, but then he lay within earshot, and merely turned his fine eyes from the sea to the group before him. His glance rested a moment on Belle's piquant figure, for she looked very pretty with her bright hair blowing in the wind, one plump white arm extended to keep order, and one little foot, in a distracting slipper, just visible below the voluminous folds of her dress. Then the glance passed to another figure, sitting somewhat apart in a cloud of white muslin, for an airy burnoose floated from head and shoulders, showing only a singularly charming face. Pale and yet brilliant, for the Southern eyes were magnificent, the clear olive cheeks contrasted well with darkest hair; lips like a pomegranate flower, and delicate, straight brows, as mobile as the lips. A cluster of crimson flowers, half falling from the loose black braids, and a golden bracelet of Arabian coins on the slender wrist were the only ornaments she wore, and became her better than the fashionable frippery of her companions. A book lay on her lap, but her eyes, full of a passionate melancholy, were fixed on the sea, which glittered round an island green and flowery as a summer paradise. Rose St. Just was as beautiful as her Spanish mother, but had inherited the pride and reserve of her English father; and this pride was the thorn which repelled lovers from the human flower. Mark Done sighed as he looked, and as if the sigh, low as it was roused her from her reverie, Rose flashed a quick glance at him, took up her book, and went on reading the legend of "The Lotus Eaters."

"Time is up now, Doctor," cried Belle, pocketing her watch with a flourish.

"Ready to report," answered Meredith, sitting up and producing a little box of tortoiseshell and gold.

"How mysterious! What is it? Let me see, first!" And Belle removed the cover, looking like an inquisitive child. "Only bonbons; how stupid! That won't do, sir. We don't want to be fed with sugarplums. We demand to be amused."

"Eat six of these despised bonbons, and you *will* be amused in a new, delicious and wonderful manner," said the young doctor, laying half a dozen on a green leaf and offering them to her.

"Why, what are they?" she asked, looking at him askance.

"Hashish; did you never hear of it?"

"Oh, yes; it's that Indian stuff which brings one fantastic visions, isn't it? I've always wanted to see and taste it, and now I will," cried Belle, nibbling at one of the bean-shaped comfits with its green heart.

"I advise you not to try it. People do all sorts of queer things when they take it. I wouldn't for the world," said a prudent young lady warningly, as all examined the box and its contents.

"Six can do no harm, I give you my word. I take twenty before I can enjoy myself, and some people even more. I've tried many experiments, both on the sick and the well, and nothing ever happened amiss, though the demonstrations were immensely interesting," said Meredith, eating his sugarplums with a tranquil air, which was very convincing to others.

"How shall I feel?" asked Belle, beginning on her second comfit.

"A heavenly dreaminess comes over one, in which they move as if on air. Everything is calm and lovely to them: no pain, no care, no fear of anything, and while it lasts one feels like an angel half asleep."

"But if one takes too much, how then?" said a deep voice behind the doctor.

"Hum! Well, that's not so pleasant, unless one likes phantoms, frenzies, and a touch of nightmare, which seems to last a thousand years. Ever try it, Done?" replied Meredith, turning toward the speaker, who was now leaning on his arm and looking interested.

"Never. I'm not a good subject for experiments. Too nervous a temperament to play pranks with."

"I should say ten would be about your number. Less than that seldom affects men. Ladies go off sooner, and don't need so many. Miss St. Just, may I offer you a taste of Elysium? I owe my success to you," said the doctor, approaching her deferentially.

"To me! And how?" she asked, lifting her large eyes with a slight smile.

"I was in the depths of despair when my eye caught the title of your book, and I was saved. For I remembered that I had hashish in my pocket."

"Are you a lotus-eater?" she said, permitting him to lay the six charmed bonbons on the page.

"My faith, no! I use it for my patients. It is very efficacious in nervous disorders, and is getting to be quite a pet remedy with us."

"I do not want to forget the past, but to read the future. Will hashish help me to do that?" asked Rose with an eager look, which made the young man flush, wondering if he bore any part in her hopes of that veiled future.

"Alas, no. I wish it could, for I, too, long to know my fate," he answered, very low, as he looked into the lovely face before him.

The soft glance changed to one of cool indifference and Rose gently brushed the hashish off her book, saying, with a little gesture of dismissal, "Then I have no desire to taste Elysium."

The white morsels dropped into the grass at her feet; but Dr. Meredith let them lie, and turning sharply, went back to sun himself in Belle's smiles.

"I've eaten all mine, and so has Evelyn. Mr. Norton will see goblins, I know, for he has taken quantities. I'm glad of it, for he don't believe in it, and I want to have him convinced by making a spectacle of himself for our amusement," said Belle, in great spirits at the new plan.

"When does the trance come on?" asked Evelyn, a shy girl, already rather alarmed at what she had done.

"About three hours after you take your dose, though the time varies with different people. Your pulse will rise, heart beat quickly, eyes darken and dilate, and an uplifted sensation will pervade you generally. Then these symptoms change, and the bliss begins. I've seen people sit or lie in one position for hours, rapt in a delicious dream, and wake from it as tranquil as if they had not a nerve in their bodies."

"How charming! I'll take some every time I'm worried. Let me see.

It's now four, so our trances will come about seven, and we will devote the evening to manifestations," said Belle.

"Come, Done, try it. We are all going in for the fun. Here's your dose," and Meredith tossed him a dozen bonbons, twisted up in a bit of paper.

"No, thank you; I know myself too well to risk it. If you are all going to turn hashish-eaters, you'll need someone to take care of you, so I'll keep sober," tossing the little parcel back.

It fell short, and the doctor, too lazy to pick it up, let it lie, merely saying, with a laugh, "Well, I advise any bashful man to take hashish when he wants to offer his heart to any fair lady, for it will give him the courage of a hero, the eloquence of a poet, and the ardor of an Italian. Remember that, gentlemen, and come to me when the crisis approaches."

"Does it conquer the pride, rouse the pity, and soften the hard hearts of the fair sex?" asked Done.

"I dare say now is your time to settle the fact, for here are two ladies who have imbibed, and in three hours will be in such a seraphic state of mind that 'No' will be an impossibility to them."

"Oh, mercy on us; what *have* we done? If that's the case, I shall shut myself up till my foolish fit is over. Rose, you haven't taken any; I beg you to mount guard over me, and see that I don't disgrace myself by any nonsense. Promise me you will," cried Belle, in half-real, half-feigned alarm at the consequences of her prank.

"I promise," said Rose, and floated down the green path as noiselessly as a white cloud, with a curious smile on her lips.

"Don't tell any of the rest what we have done, but after tea let us go into the grove and compare notes," said Norton, as Done strolled away to the beach, and the voices of approaching friends broke the summer quiet.

At tea, the initiated glanced covertly at one another, and saw, or fancied they saw, the effects of the hashish, in a certain suppressed excitement of manner, and unusually brilliant eyes. Belle laughed often, a silvery ringing laugh, pleasant to hear; but when complimented on her good spirits, she looked distressed, and said she could not help her merriment; Meredith was quite calm, but rather dreamy; Evelyn was pale, and her next neighbor heard her heart beat; Norton talked incessantly, but as he talked uncommonly well, no one suspected anything. Done and Miss St. Just watched the others with interest, and were very quiet, especially Rose, who scarcely spoke, but smiled her sweetest, and looked very lovely.

The moon rose early, and the experimenters slipped away to the grove, leaving the outsiders on the lawn as usual. Some bold spirit asked Rose to sing, and she at once complied, pouring out Spanish airs in a voice that melted the hearts of her audience, so full of fiery sweetness or tragic pathos was it. Done seemed quite carried away, and lay with his face in the grass, to hide the tears that would come; till, afraid of openly disgracing himself, he started up and hurried down to the little wharf, where he sat alone, listening to the music with a countenance which plainly revealed to the stars the passion which possessed him. The sound of loud laughter from the grove, followed by entire silence, caused him to wonder what demonstrations were taking place, and half resolve to go and see. But that enchanting voice held him captive, even when a boat put off mysteriously from a point nearby, and sailed away like a phantom through the twilight.

Half an hour afterward, a white figure came down the path, and Rose's voice broke in on his midsummer night's dream. The moon shone clearly now, and showed him the anxiety in her face as she said hurriedly, "Where is Belle?"

"Gone sailing, I believe."

"How could you let her go? She was not fit to take care of herself!"

"I forgot that."

"So did I, but I promised to watch over her, and I must. Which way did they go?" demanded Rose, wrapping the white mantle about her, and running her eye over the little boats moored below.

"You will follow her?"

"Yes."

"I'll be your guide then. They went toward the lighthouse; it is too far to row; I am at your service. Oh, say yes," cried Done, leaping into his own skiff and offering his hand persuasively.

She hesitated an instant and looked at him. He was always pale, and the moonlight seemed to increase this pallor, but his hat brim hid his eyes, and his voice was very quiet. A loud peal of laughter floated over the water, and as if the sound decided her, she gave him her hand and entered the boat. Done smiled triumphantly as he shook out the sail, which caught the freshening wind, and sent the boat dancing along a path of light.

How lovely it was! All the indescribable allurements of a perfect summer night surrounded them: balmy airs, enchanting moonlight, distant music, and, close at hand, the delicious atmosphere of love, which made itself felt in the eloquent silences that fell between them. Rose seemed to yield to the subtle charm, and leaned back on the cushioned seat with her beautiful head uncovered, her face full of dreamy softness, and her hands lying loosely clasped before her. She seldom spoke, showed no further anxiety for Belle, and soon seemed to forget the object of her search, so absorbed was she in some delicious thought which wrapped her in its peace.

Done sat opposite, flushed now, restless, and excited, for his eyes glittered; the hand on the rudder shook, and his voice sounded intense and passionate, even in the utterance of the simplest words. He talked continually and with unusual brilliancy, for, though a man of many accomplishments, he was too indolent or too fastidious to exert himself, except among his peers. Rose seemed to look without seeing, to listen without hearing, and though she smiled blissfully, the smiles were evidently not for him.

On they sailed, scarcely heeding the bank of black cloud piled up in the horizon, the rising wind, or the silence which proved their solitude. Rose moved once or twice, and lifted her hand as if to speak, but sank back mutely, and the hand fell again as if it had not energy enough to enforce her wish. A cloud sweeping over the moon, a distant growl of thunder, and the slight gust that struck the sail seemed to rouse her. Done was singing now like one inspired, his hat at his feet, hair in disorder, and a strangely rapturous expression in his eyes, which were fixed on her. She started, shivered, and seemed to recover herself with an effort.

"Where are they?" she asked, looking vainly for the island heights and the other boat.

"They have gone to the beach, I fancy, but we will follow." As Done leaned forward to speak, she saw his face and shrank back with a sudden flush, for in it she read clearly what she had felt, yet doubted until now. He saw the telltale blush and gesture, and said impetuously, "You know it now; you cannot deceive me longer, or daunt me with your pride! Rose, I love you, and dare tell you so tonight!"

"Not now — not here — I will not listen. Turn back, and be silent, I entreat you, Mr. Done," she said hurriedly.

He laughed a defiant laugh and took her hand in his, which was burning and throbbing with the rapid heat of his pulse.

"No, I *will* have my answer here, and now, and never turn back till you give it; you have been a thorny Rose, and given me many wounds. I'll be paid for my heartache with sweet words, tender looks, and frank confessions of love, for proud as you are, you do love me, and dare not deny it."

Something in his tone terrified her; she snatched her hand away and drew beyond his reach, trying to speak calmly, and to meet coldly the ardent glances of the eyes which were strangely darkened and dilated with uncontrollable emotion.

"You forget yourself. I shall give no answer to an avowal made in such terms. Take me home instantly," she said in a tone of command.

"Confess you love me, Rose."

"Never!"

"Ah! I'll have a kinder answer, or —" Done half rose and put out his hand to grasp and draw her to him, but the cry she uttered seemed to arrest him with a sort of shock. He dropped into his seat, passed his hand over his eyes, and shivered nervously as he muttered in an altered tone, "I meant nothing; it's the moonlight; sit down, I'll control myself — upon my soul I will!"

"If you do not, I shall go overboard. Are you mad, sir?" cried Rose, trembling with indignation.

"Then I shall follow you, for I *am* mad, Rose, with love — hashish!"

His voice sank to a whisper, but the last word thrilled along her nerves, as no sound of fear had ever done before. An instant she regarded him with a look which took in every sign of unnatural excitement, then she clasped her hands with an imploring gesture, saying, in a tone of despair, "Why did I come! How will it end? Oh, Mark, take me home before it is too late!"

"Hush! Be calm; don't thwart me, or I may get wild again. My thoughts are not clear, but I understand you. There, take my knife, and if I forget myself, kill me. Don't go overboard; you are too beautiful to die, my Rose!"

He threw her the slender hunting knife he wore, looked at her a moment with a far-off look, and trimmed the sail like one moving in a dream. Rose took the weapon, wrapped her cloak closely about her, and crouching as far away as possible, kept her eye on him, with a face in which watchful terror contended with some secret trouble and bewilderment more powerful than her fear.

The boat moved round and began to beat up against wind and tide; spray flew from her bow; the sail bent and strained in the gusts that struck it with perilous fitfulness. The moon was nearly hidden by scudding clouds, and one-half the sky was black with the gathering storm. Rose looked from threatening heavens to treacherous sea, and tried to be ready for any danger, but her calm had been sadly broken, and she could not recover it. Done sat motionless, uttering no word of encouragement, though the frequent flaws almost tore the rope from his hand, and the water often dashed over him.

"Are we in any danger?" asked Rose at last, unable to bear the silence, for he looked like a ghostly helmsman seen by the fitful light, pale now, wild-eyed, and speechless.

"Yes, great danger."

"I thought you were a skillful boatman."

"I am when I am myself; now I am rapidly losing the control of my will, and the strange quiet is coming over me. If I had been alone I should have given up sooner, but for your sake I've kept on."

"Can't you work the boat?" asked Rose, terror-struck by the changed tone of his voice, the slow, uncertain movements of his hands.

"No. I see everything through a thick cloud; your voice sounds far away, and my one desire is to lay my head down and sleep."

"Let me steer — I can, I must!" she cried, springing toward him and laying her hand on the rudder.

He smiled and kissed the little hand, saying dreamily, "You could not hold it a minute; sit by me, love; let us turn the boat again, and drift away together — anywhere, anywhere out of the world."

"Oh, heaven, what will become of us!" and Rose wrung her hands in real despair. "Mr. Done — Mark — dear Mark, rouse yourself and listen to me. Turn, as you say, for it is certain death to go on so. Turn, and let us drift down to the lighthouse; they will hear and help us. Quick, take down the sail, get out the oars, and let us try to reach there before the storm breaks."

As Rose spoke, he obeyed her like a dumb animal; love for her was stronger even than the instinct of self-preservation, and for her sake he fought against the treacherous lethargy which was swiftly overpowering him. The sail was lowered, the boat brought round, and with little help from the ill-pulled oars it drifted rapidly out to sea with the ebbing tide.

As she caught her breath after this dangerous maneuver was accomplished, Rose asked, in a quiet tone she vainly tried to render natural, "How much hashish did you take?"

"All that Meredith threw me. Too much; but I was possessed to do it, so I hid the roll and tried it," he answered, peering at her with a weird laugh.

"Let us talk; our safety lies in keeping awake, and I dare not let you sleep," continued Rose, dashing water on her own hot forehead with a sort of desperation.

"Say you love me; that would wake me from my lost sleep, I think. I have hoped and feared, waited and suffered so long. Be pitiful, and answer, Rose."

"I do; but I should not own it now."

So low was the soft reply he scarcely heard it, but he felt it and made a strong effort to break from the hateful spell that bound him. Leaning forward, he tried to read her face in a ray of moonlight breaking through the clouds; he saw a new and tender warmth in it, for all the pride was gone, and no fear marred the eloquence of those soft, Southern eyes.

"Kiss me, Rose, then I shall believe it. I feel lost in a dream, and you, so changed, so kind, may be only a fair phantom. Kiss me, love, and make it real."

As if swayed by a power more potent than her will, Rose bent to meet his lips. But the ardent pressure seemed to startle her from a momentary oblivion of everything but love. She covered up her face and sank down, as if overwhelmed with shame, sobbing through passionate tears, "Oh, what am I doing? I am mad, for I, too, have taken hashish."

What he answered she never heard, for a rattling peal of thunder drowned his voice, and then the storm broke loose. Rain fell in torrents, the wind blew fiercely, sky and sea were black as ink, and the boat tossed from wave to wave almost at their mercy. Giving herself up for lost, Rose crept to her lover's side and clung there, conscious only that they would bide together through the perils their own folly brought them. Done's excitement was quite gone now; he sat like a statue, shielding the frail creature whom he loved with a smile on his face, which looked awfully emotionless when the lightning gave her glimpses of its white immobility. Drenched, exhausted, and half senseless with danger, fear, and exposure, Rose saw at last a welcome glimmer through the gloom, and roused herself to cry for help.

"Mark, wake and help me! Shout, for God's sake — shout and call them, for we are lost if we drift by!" she cried, lifting his head from his breast, and forcing him to see the brilliant beacons streaming far across the troubled water.

He understood her, and springing up, uttered shout after shout like one demented. Fortunately, the storm had lulled a little; the lighthouse keeper heard and answered. Rose seized the helm, Done the oars, and with one frantic effort guided the boat into quieter waters, where it was met by the keeper, who towed it to the rocky nook which served as harbor.

The moment a strong, steady face met her eyes, and a gruff, cheery voice hailed her, Rose gave way, and was carried up to the house, looking more like a beautiful drowned Ophelia than a living woman.

"Here, Sally, see to the poor thing; she's had a rough time on't. I'll take care of her sweetheart — and a nice job I'll have, I reckon, for if he ain't mad or drunk, he's had a stroke of lightnin', and looks as if he wouldn't get his hearin' in a hurry," said the old man as he housed his unexpected guests and stood staring at Done, who looked about him like one dazed. "You jest turn in yonder and sleep it off, mate. We'll see to the lady, and right up your boat in the morning," the old man added.

"Be kind to Rose. I frightened her. I'll not forget you. Yes, let me sleep and get over this cursed folly as soon as possible," muttered this strange visitor.

Done threw himself down on the rough couch and tried to sleep, but every nerve was overstrained, every pulse beating like a trip-hammer, and everything about him was intensified and exaggerated with awful power. The thundershower seemed a wild hurricane, the quaint room a wilderness peopled with tormenting phantoms, and all the events of his life passed before him in an endless procession, which nearly maddened him. The old man looked weird and gigantic, his own voice sounded shrill and discordant, and the ceaseless murmur of Rose's incoherent wanderings haunted him like parts of a grotesque but dreadful dream.

All night he lay motionless, with staring eyes, feverish lips, and a mind on the rack, for the delicate machinery which had been tampered with revenged the wrong by torturing the foolish experimenter. All night Rose wept and sang, talked and cried for help in a piteous state of nervous excitement, for with her the trance came first, and the after-agitation was increased by the events of the evening. She slept at last, lulled by the old woman's motherly care, and Done was spared one tormenting fear, for he dreaded the consequences of this folly on her, more than upon himself.

As day dawned he rose, haggard and faint, and staggered out. At the door he met the keeper, who stopped him to report that the boat was in order, and a fair day coming. Seeing doubt and perplexity in the old man's eye, Done told him the truth, and added that he was going to the beach for a plunge, hoping by that simple tonic to restore his unstrung nerves.

He came back feeling like himself again, except for a dull headache, and a heavy sense of remorse weighing on his spirits, for he distinctly recollected all the events of the night. The old woman made him eat and drink, and in an hour he felt ready for the homeward trip.

Rose slept late, and when she woke soon recovered herself, for her dose had been a small one. When she had breakfasted and made a hasty toilet, she professed herself anxious to return at once. She dreaded yet longed to see Done, and when the time came armed herself with pride, feeling all a woman's shame at what had passed, and resolving to feign forgetfulness of the incidents of the previous night. Pale and cold as a statue she met him, but the moment he began to say humbly, "Forgive me, Rose," she silenced him with an imperious gesture and the command "Don't speak of it; I only remember that it was very horrible, and wish to forget it all as soon as possible."

"All, Rose?" he asked, significantly.

"Yes, *all*. No one would care to recall the follies of a hashish dream," she answered, turning hastily to hide the scarlet flush that would rise, and the eyes that would fall before his own.

"*I* never can forget, but I will be silent if you bid me."

"I do. Let us go. What will they think at the island? Mr. Done, give me your promise to tell no one, now or ever, that I tried that dangerous experiment. I will guard your secret also." She spoke eagerly and looked up imploringly.

"I promise," and he gave her his hand, holding her own with a wistful glance, till she drew it away and begged him to take her home.

Leaving hearty thanks and a generous token of their gratitude, they sailed away with a fair wind, finding in the freshness of the morning a speedy cure for tired bodies and excited minds. They said little, but it was impossible for Rose to preserve her coldness. The memory of the past night broke down her pride, and Done's tender glances touched her heart. She half hid her face behind her hand, and tried to compose herself for the scene to come, for as she approached the island, she saw Belle and her party waiting for them on the shore.

"Oh, Mr. Done, screen me from their eyes and questions as much as you can! I'm so worn out and nervous, I shall betray myself. You will help me?" And she turned to him with a confiding look, strangely at variance with her usual calm self-possession.

"I'll shield you with my life, if you will tell me why you took the hashish," he said, bent on knowing his fate.

"I hoped it would make me soft and lovable, like other women. I'm tired of being a lonely statue," she faltered, as if the truth was wrung from her by a power stronger than her will.

"And I took it to gain courage to tell my love. Rose, we have been near death together; let us share life together, and neither of us be any more lonely or afraid?"

He stretched his hand to her with his heart in his face, and she gave him hers with a look of tender submission, as he said ardently, "Heaven bless hashish, if its dreams end like this!"

The Civil War and Realism

M. L.

Boston *Commonwealth*, 24 and 31 January; 7, 14, and 22 February 1863

CHAPTER I

The sun set — but set not his hope:
Stars rose — his faith was earlier up:
He spoke, and words more soft than rain
Brought back the Age of Gold again:
His action won such reverence sweet,
As hid all measure of the feat.

*H*USH! LET ME listen."

Mrs. Snowdon ceased her lively gossip, obedient to the command, and leaning her head upon her hand. Claudia sat silent.

Like a breath of purer air, the music floated through the room, bringing an exquisite delight to the gifted few, and stirring the dullest nature with a sense of something nobler than it knew. Frivolous women listened mutely, pleasure seeking men confessed its charm, world-worn spirits lived again the better moments of their lives, and wounded hearts found in it a brief solace for the griefs so jealously concealed. At its magic touch the masks fell from many faces and a momentary softness made them fair: eye met eye with rare sincerity, false smiles faded, vapid conversation died abashed, and for a little space, Music, the divine enchantress, asserted her supremacy, wooing tenderly as any woman, ruling royally as any queen.

Like water in a desert place, Claudia's thirsty spirit drank in the silver sounds that fed her ear, and through the hush they came to her like a remembered strain. Their varying power swayed her like a wizard's wand, its subtle softness wrapped her senses in a blissful calm, its passion thrilled along her nerves like south winds full of an aroma fiery and sweet, its energy stirred her blood like martial music or heroic speech, — for this mellow voice seemed to bring her the low sigh of pines, the ardent breath of human lips, the grand anthem of the sea. It held her fast, and lifting her above the narrow bounds of time and place, blessed her with a loftier mood than she had ever known before, for midsummer light and warmth seemed born of it, and her solitary nature yearned to greet the genial influence as frost-bound grasses spring to meet the sun.

What the song was, she never heard, she never cared to know; to other ears it might be love lay, barcarole, or miserere for the dead, — to her it was a melody devout and sweet as saintliest hymn, for it had touched the chords of that diviner self whose aspirations are the flowers of life, it had soothed the secret pain of a proud spirit, it had stirred the waters of a lonely heart, and from their depths a new born patience rose with healing on its wings.

Silent she sat, one hand above her eyes, the other lying in her lap, unmoved since with her last words it rose and fell. The singer had been forgotten in the song, but as the music with triumphant swell soared upward and grew still, the spell was broken, the tide of conversation flowed again, and with an impatient sigh, Claudia looked up and saw her happy dream depart.

"Who is this man? you told me but I did not hear."

With the eagerness of a born gossip, Mrs. Snowdon whispered the tale a second time into her friend's ear.

"This man (as you would never call him had you seen him) is a Spaniard, and of noble family, I'm sure, though he denies it. He is poor, of course, — these interesting exiles always are, — he teaches music, and though an accomplished gentleman and as proud as if the 'blue blood' of all the grandees of Spain flowed in his veins, he will not own to any rank, but steadily asserts that he is 'plain Paul Frere, trying honestly to earn his bread, and nothing more.' Ah, you like that, and the very thing that disappoints me most, will make the man a hero in your eyes."

"Honesty is an heroic virtue, and I honor it wherever it is found. What further, Jessie?" and Claudia looked a shade more interested than when the chat began.

"Only that in addition to his charming voice, he is a handsome soul, beside whom our pale faced gentlemen look boyish and insipid to a mortifying degree. Endless romances are in progress, of which he may be the hero if he will, but unfortunately for his fair pupils the fine eyes of their master seem blind to any 'tremolo movements' but those set down in the book; and he hears them warble '*O mio Fernando*' in the tenderest of spoken languages as tranquilly as if it were a nursery song. He leads a solitary life, devoted to his books and art, and rarely mixes in the society of which *I* think him a great ornament. This is all I know concerning him, and if you ever care to descend from your Mount Blanc of cool indifference, I fancy this minstrel will repay you for the effort. Look! that is he, the dark man with the melancholy eyes; deign to give me your opinion of my modern 'Thaddeus.'"

Claudia looked, and, as she did so, vividly before her mind's eye rose a picture she had often pondered over when a child.

A painting of a tropical island, beautiful with the bloom and verdure of the South. An ardent sky, flushed with sunrise canopied the scene, palm trees lifted their crowned heads far into the fervid air, orange groves dropped dark shadows on the sward where flowers in rank luxuriance glowed like spires of flame, or shone like stars among the green. Bright hued birds swung on vine and bough, dainty gazelles lifted their human eyes to greet the sun, and a summer sea seemed to flow low-singing to the bloomy shore. The first blush and dewiness of dawn lay over the still spot, but looking nearer, the eye saw that the palm's green crowns were rent, the vines hung torn as if by ruthless gusts, and the orange boughs were robbed of half their wealth, for fruit and flowers lay thick upon the sodden earth. Far on the horizon's edge, a thunderous cloud seemed rolling westward, and on the waves an ominous wreck swayed with the swaying of the treacherous sea.

Claudia saw a face that satisfied her eye as the voice had done her ear, and yet its comeliness was not its charm. Black locks streaked an ample forehead, black brows arched finely over southern eyes as full of softness as of fire. No color marred the pale bronze of the cheek, no beard hid the firm contour of the lips, no unmeaning smile destroyed the dignity of a thoughtful countenance, on which nature's hand had set the seal wherewith she stamps the manhood that no art can counterfeit.

But as she searched it deeper, Claudia saw upon the forehead lines that seldom come to men of thirty, in the eye a shadow of some past despair and about the closely folded lips traces of an impetuous nature tamed by suffering and taught by time. Here, as in the picture, the tempest seemed to have gone by, but though a gracious day had come, the cloud had left a shade behind. Sweet winds came wooingly from off the shore, and the sea serenely smiled above the wreck, but a vague unrest still stirred the air, and an undertone of human woe still whispered through the surges' song.

"So Dante might have looked before his genius changed the crown of thorns into a crown of roses for the woman he loved," thought Claudia, then said aloud in answer to her friend's last words,

"Yes, I like that face, less for its beauty than its strength. I like that austere simplicity of dress, that fine unconsciousness of self, and more than all I like the courtesy with which he listens to the poorest, plainest, least attractive woman in the room. Laugh if you will, Jessie, I respect him more for his kindness to neglected Mary Low, than if for a fairer woman he had fought as many battles as Saint George. This is true courtesy, and it is the want of this reverence for womanhood in itself, which makes many of our so-called gentlemen what they are, and robs them of one attribute of real manliness."

"Heaven defend us! here is an Alpine avalanche of praise from our Diana! Come be made known to this Endymion before you can congeal again," cried Jessie; for Claudia's words were full of energy, and in her eye shone an interest that softened its cold brilliancy and gave her countenance the warmth which was the charm it needed most. Claudia went, and soon found herself enjoying the delights of conversation in the finer sense of that fine word. Paul Frere did not offer her the stale compliments men usually think it proper to bestow upon a woman, as if her mind were like a dainty purse too limited for any small coin of little worth, nor did he offer her the witty gossips current in society, which, like crisp bank bills, rustle pleasantly, and are accepted as a "counterfeit presentment," of that silver speech, which should marry sound to sense. He gave her sterling gold, that rang true to the ear, and bore the stamp of genuine belief, for unconsciously he put himself into his words, and made them what they should be — the interpreters of one frank nature to another.

He took the few pale phantoms custom has condemned to serve as subjects of discourse between a man and woman in a place like that, and giving them vitality and color, they became the actors of his thought, and made a living drama of that little hour. Yet he was no scholar erudite and polished by long study or generous culture. Adversity had been his college, experience his tutor, and life the book whose lessons stern and salutary he had learned with patient pain. Real wrong and suffering and want, had given him a knowledge no philosopher could teach, real danger and desolation had lifted him above the petty fears that take the heroism out of daily life, and a fiery baptism had consecrated heart and mind and soul to one great aim, beside which other men's ambitions seemed most poor. This was the secret charm he owned, this gave the simplicity that dignified his manner, the sincerity that won in his address; this proved the supremacy of character over culture, opulence and rank, and made him what he was — a man to command respect, and confidence and love.

Dimly Claudia saw, and vaguely felt all this in that brief interview; but when it ended, she wished it were to come again, and felt as if she had left the glare and glitter of the stage whereon she played her part, for a moment had put off her mask to sit down in the ruddy circle of a household fire where little shadows danced upon the walls, and tender tones made common speech divine.

"It will be gone to-morrow, this pleasure beautiful and brief, and I shall fall back into my old disappointment again, as I have always done before;" she sighed within herself. Yet when she sat alone in her own home, it seemed no longer solitary, and like a happy child she lulled herself to sleep with fitful snatches of a song she had never heard but once.

CHAPTER II

Claudia stood alone in the world, a woman of strong character and independent will; gifted with beauty, opulence and position, possessing the admiration and esteem of many, the affection of a few whose love was worth desiring. All these good gifts were hers, and yet she was not satisfied. Home ties she had never known, mother-love had only blessed her long enough to make its loss most keenly felt, the sweet confidence of sisterhood had never warmed her with its innocent delights, "father" and "brother" were unknown words upon her lips, for she had never known the beauty, and the strength of man's most sincere affection.

Many hands had knocked at the closed door, but knocked in vain, for the master had not come, and true to her finer instincts, Claudia would not make a worldly marriage, or try to cheat her hunger into a painted feast. She would have all or nothing, and when friends urged or lovers pleaded, she answered steadily:

"I cannot act a lie, and receive where I have nothing to bestow. If I am to know the blessedness of love, it will come to me, and I can wait."

Love repaid her loyalty at last. Through the close scented air of the conservatory where she had lived a solitary plant, there came a new influence, like a breath of ocean air, both strengthening and sweet. Then the past ceased to be a mournful memory; for over her lost hopes, the morning glories that had early died — over her eager desires, the roses that had never bloomed — over broken friendships, the nests whence all the birds were flown — a pleasant twilight seemed to fall, and across the sombre present came the ruddy herald of a future dawn. It brought the magic moment when the flower could bloom, the master's hand whose touch unbarred the door, the charmed voice that woke the sleeping princess, and sang to her of

That new world, which is the old.

In "plain Paul Frere," Claudia found her hero, recognized her king, although like Bruce he came in minstrel guise and accepted royally the alms bestowed.

Slowly, by rare interviews, the swift language of the eye, and music's many wiles, Paul caught deeper glimpses into Claudia's solitary life, and felt the charm of an earnest nature shining through the maidenly reserve that veiled it from his search. He sang to her, and singing, watched the still fire that kindled in her eye, the content that touched her lips with something softer than a smile, the warmth that stole so beautifully to her face, melting the pride that chilled it, banishing the weariness that saddened it, and filling it with light, and hope and bloom, as if at his command the woman's sorrows fell away and left a happy girl again. It was a dangerous power to wield, but with the consciousness of its possession came a sentiment that curbed a strong man's love of power, and left it subject to a just man's love of right.

He denied himself the happiness of ministering to Claudia the frequent feasts she loved, for it was offering her a wine more subtle than she knew, a wine whose potency her friend already felt. He seldom sung to her alone, but conversation was a rich reward for this renunciation, for in those hours, beautiful and brief, he found an interest that "grew by what it fed on," and soon felt that it was fast becoming sweeter to receive than to bestow.

Claudia was a student of like dangerous lore, for she too scanned her new friend warily and well; often with keen perceptions divining what she dared not seek, with swift instincts feeling what she could not see. Her first judgments had been just, her first impulse never changed. For each month of increasing friendship, was one of increasing honor and esteem.

This man who earned his bread, and asked no favors where he might have demanded many, who would accept no fictitious rank, listen to no flattering romance who bore the traces of a fateful past, yet showed no bitterness of spirit, but went his way steadfastly, living to some high end unseen by human eyes, yet all-sustaining in itself, — this man seemed to Claudia the friend she had desired, for here she found a character built up by suffering and time, an eager intellect aspiring for the true, and a valiant spirit looking straight and strong into the world.

To her ear the music of his life became more beautiful than any lay he sang, and on his shield her heart inscribed the fine old lines,

> *Lord of himself, though not of lands,*
> *And having nothing, yet hath all.*

CHAPTER III

One balmy night, when early flowers were blossoming in Claudia's garden, and the west wind was the almoner of their sweet charities, she sat looking with thoughtful eyes into the shadowy stillness of the hour.

Miss Blank, the mild nonentity who played propriety in Claudia's house, had been absorbed into the darkness of an inner room, where sleep might descend upon her weary eyelids without an open breach of that decorum which was the good soul's staff of life.

Paul Frere, leaning in the shadow, looked down upon the bent head whereon the May moon dropped a shining benediction; and as he looked, his countenance grew young again with hope, and fervent with a strong desire. Silence had fallen on them, for watching *her,* Paul forgot to speak, and Claudia was plucking leaf after leaf from a flower that had strayed from among the knot that graced her breast. One by one the crimson petals fluttered to the ground, and as she saw them fall a melancholy shadow swept across her face.

"What has the rose done that its life should be so short?" her friend asked as the last leaf left her hand.

As if the words recalled her to the present, Claudia looked at the dismantled stem, saying regretfully, "I forgot the flower, and now I have destroyed it with no skill to make it live again." She paused a moment, then added smiling as if at her own fancies, though the regretful cadence lingered in her voice. "This is my birth-night, and thinking of my past, the rose ceased to be a rose to me, and became a little symbol of my life. Each leaf I gathered seemed a year, and as it fell I thought how fast, how vainly, they had gone. They should have been fairer in aspirations, fuller of duties, richer in good deeds, happier in those hopes that make existence sweet, but now it is too late. Poor rose! Poor life!" and from the smiling lips there fell a sigh.

Paul took the relic of the rose, and with a gesture soft as a caress, broke from the stem a little bud just springing from its mossy sheath, saying with a glance as full of cheer as hers had been of despondency, "My friend, it never is too late. Out of the loneliest life may bloom a higher beauty than the lost rose knew. Let the first sanguine petals fall, their perfume will remain a pleasant memory when they are dead; but cherish the fairer flower that comes so late, nurture it with sunshine, baptise it with dew, and though the garden never knows it more, it may make summer in some shady spot and bless a household with its breath and bloom. I have no gift wherewith to celebrate this night, but let me give you back a happier emblem of the life to be, and with it a prophecy that when another six and twenty years are gone, no sigh will mar your smile as you look back and say 'Fair rose! Fair life!'"

Claudia looked up with traitorous eyes, and answered softly — "I accept the prophecy, and will fulfil it, if the black frost does not fall." Then with a wistful glance and all persuasive tone, she added, "You have forgotten one gift always in your power to bestow. Give it to me to-night, and usher in my happier years with music."

There was no denial to a request like that, and with a keen sense of delight Paul obeyed, singing as he had never sang before, for heart and soul were in the act, and all benignant influences lent their aid to beautify his gift. The silence of the night received the melody, and sent it whispering back like ripples breaking on the shore; the moonbeams danced like elves upon the keys, as if endowing human touch with their magnetic power; the west wind tuned its leafy orchestra to an airy symphony, and every odorous shrub and flower paid tribute to the happy hour.

With drooping lids and lips apart, Claudia listened, till on the surges of sweet sound her spirit floated far away into that blissful realm where human aspirations are fulfilled, where human hearts find their ideals, and renew again the innocent beliefs that made their childhood green.

Silence fell suddenly, startling Claudia from her dream. For a moment the radiance of the room grew dark before her eyes, then a swift light dawned, and in it she beheld the countenance of her friend transfigured by the power of that great passion which heaven has gifted with eternal youth. For a long moment nothing stirred, and across the little space that parted them the two regarded one another with wordless lips, but eyes whose finer language made all speech impertinent.

Paul bent on the woman whom he loved a look more tender than the most impassioned prayer, more potent than the subtlest appeal, more eloquent than the most fervent vow. He saw the maiden color flush and fade, saw the breath quicken and the lips grow tremulous, but the steadfast eyes never wavered, never fell, and through those windows of the soul, her woman's heart looked out and answered him.

There was no longer any doubt or fear or power to part them now, and with a gesture full of something nobler than pride, Paul stretched his hand to Claudia, and she took it fast in both her own.

To a believer in metempsychosis it would have been an easy task to decide the last shape Mrs. Snowdon had endowed with life, for the old fable of the "cat transformed into a woman," might have been again suggested to a modern Æsop.

Soft of manner, smooth of tongue, stealthy of eye, this feline lady followed out the instincts of her nature with the fidelity of any veritable puss. With demure aspect and pleasant purrings she secured the admiration of innocents who forgot that velvet paws could scratch, and the friendship of comfortable souls who love to pet and be amused. Daintily picking her way through the troubles of this life, she slipped into cozy corners where rugs were softest and fires warmest, gambolling delightfully while the cream was plentiful, and the caresses graciously bestowed. Gossips and scandal were the rats and mice she feasted on, the prey she paraded with ill-disguised exultation when her prowlings and pouncings had brought them to light. Many a smart robin had been fascinated by her power, or escaping left his plumes behind; many a meek mouse had implored mercy for its indiscretion but found none, and many a blithe cricket's music ended when she glided through the grass. Dark holes and corners were hunted by her keen eye, the dust of forgotten rumors was disturbed by her covert tread, and secrets were hunted out with most untiring patience.

She had her enemies, what puss has not? Sundry honest mastiffs growled when she entered their domains, but scorned to molest a weaker foe: sundry pugs barked valiantly till she turned on them and with un-sheathed claws administered a swift quietus to their wrath; sundry jovial squirrels cracked their jokes and flourished defiance, but skipped nimbly from her way, and chattered on a bough she could not climb. More than one friend had found the pantry pillaged, and the milk of human kindness lapped dry by an indefatigable tongue; and yet no meeker countenance lifted its pensive eyes in church, no voice more indignantly rebuked the short-comings of her race, and no greater martyr bewailed ingratitude when doors were shut upon her, and stern housewives shouted "scat!"

Wifehood and widowhood had only increased her love of freedom and confirmed her love of power. Claudia pitied her, and when others blamed, defended or excused, for her generous nature had no knowledge of duplicity or littleness of soul. Jessie seemed all candor, and though superficial, was full of winning ways and tender confidences that seemed sincere, and very pleasant to the others' lonely heart. So Jessie haunted her friend's house, rode triumphantly in her carriage, made a shield of her regard, and disported herself at her expense, till a stronger force appeared, and the widow's reign abruptly ended.

The May moon had shone on Claudia's betrothal, and the harvest moon would shine upon her marriage. The months passed like a happy dream, and the midsummer of her life was in its prime. The stir and tattle that went on about her was like an idle wind, for she had gone out of the common world and believed that she cared little for its censure or its praise. What mattered it that Paul was poor — was she not rich? What mattered it that she knew little of his past — had she not all the present and the future for her own? What did she care for the tongues that called him "fortune-hunter," and herself romantic? he possessed a better fortune than any she could give, and she was blessed with a romance that taught her wiser lessons than reality had ever done. So they went their way, undisturbed by any wind that blew. Paul still gave her lessons, still retained his humble home as if no change had befallen him, and Claudia with all her energies alert, bestirred herself to "set her house in order, and make ready for the bridegroom's coming." But as each night fell, patient Teacher, busy Housewife vanished, and two lovers met. The sun set on all their cares, and twilight shed a peace upon them softer than the dew, for Joy was the musician now, and Love the fairy hostess of the guests who made high festival of that still hour.

The months had dwindled to a week, and in the gloaming of a sultry day, Paul came early to his tryst. Claudia was detained by lingering guests, and with a frown at their delay, her lover paced the room till she should come. Pausing suddenly in his restless march, Paul drew a letter from his breast and read it slowly as if his thoughts had been busy with its contents. It was a letter of many pages, written in decided characters, worn as if with frequent reading, and as he turned it his face wore a look it had never shown to Claudia's eyes. With a sudden impulse he raised his right hand to the light and scanned it with strange scrutiny. Across the palm stretched a wide purple scar, the relic of some wound healed long ago, but not effaced by time. Claudia had once asked as she caressed it what blow had left so deep a trace, and he had answered with a sudden clenching of the hand, a sudden fire in the eye, "Claudia, it is the memorial of a victory I won ten years ago; it was a righteous battle, but its memory is bitter. Let it sleep; and believe me, it is an honest hand, or I could never look in your true face and give it you again."

She had been content, and never touched the sad past by a word, for she wholly trusted where she wholly loved.

As Paul looked thoughtfully at that right hand of his, the left dropped at his side, and from among the loosely held papers, a single sheet escaped, and fluttered noiselessly among the white folds of the draperies that swept the floor. The stir of departing feet roused him from his reverie; with a quick gesture he crushed the letter, and lit it at the Roman lamp that always burned for him. Slowly the fateful pages shrivelled and grew black; silently he watched them burn; and when the last flame flickered and went out, he gathered up the ashes and gave them to the keeping of the wind. Then all the shadows faded from his face, and left the old composure there.

Claudia's voice called from below, and with the ardor of a boy he sprang down to meet the welcome he was hungering for.

As the door closed behind him, from the gloom of that inner room Jessie Snowdon stole out and seized her prize. Listening with sharpened sense for any coming step, she swept the page with her keen eye, gathering its meaning before a dozen lines were read. The paper rustled with the tremor of her hand, and for a moment the room spun dizzily before her as she dropped into a seat, and sat staring straight into the air with a countenance where exultation and bewilderment were strangely blended. "Poor Claudia," was the first thought that took shape in her mind, but a harder one usurped its place, an ominous glitter shone in her black eyes, as she muttered with a wicked smile, "I owe him this, and he shall have it."

An hour later Paul and Claudia sat in that same spot together, not yet content, for opposite still lounged Jessie Snowdon, showing no symptoms of departure. Her cheek burned with a brilliant color, her black eyes glittered with repressed excitement, and in gesture, look and tone there was a peculiar sharpness as if every sense were unwontedly alert, every nerve unwontedly high strung. She was not loquacious, but seemed waiting till speech would take effect; for all her feline instincts were awake, and she must torture a little before she dealt the blow. She knew the lovers wished her gone, yet still sat watchful and wary, till the auspicious moment came.

Paul was restless, for his southern temperament, more keenly alive to subtle influences than colder natures, vaguely warned him of the coming blow, unwillingly yielded to the baleful power it could not comprehend, unconsciously betrayed that Jessie's presence brought disquiet, and so doing placed a weapon in her hand, which she did not fail to use. Her eye was on him constantly, with a glance that stirred him like an insult, while it held him like a spell. His courtesy was sorely tried, for whether he spoke or was mute, moved about the room or sat with averted face, he felt that eye still on him, with a look of mingled hatred, pity and contempt. He confronted it and bore it down; but when he turned, it rose again and haunted him with its aggressive shine. He fixed his regard on Claudia, and so forgot it for a time, but it was always there and proved itself no fancy of a tired brain.

Claudia was weary and grudged the quiet hour which always left her refreshed, when no unwelcome presence marred its charm. She was unutterably tired of Jessie, and if a wish could have secured her absence, she would have vanished with the speed of a stage sprite at the wizard's will.

"Is't the old pain, Paul? Let me play Desdemona, and bind my handkerchief about your forehead as I have done before," and Claudia's voice soothed the ear with its unspoken love.

Paul had leaned his head upon his hand, but as she spoke he lifted it and answered cheerfully, "I have no pain, but something in the atmosphere oppresses me. I fancy there is thunder in the air."

"There is" — and Jessie laughed a laugh that had no mirth in it, as she sat erect with sudden interest in her voice.

Paul swept aside the curtain, and looked out; the sky was cloudless and the evening star hung luminous and large on the horizon's edge.

"Ah, you think I am a false prophet, but wait an hour then look again. *I* see a fierce storm rolling up, though the cloud is 'no bigger than a man's hand' now."

As she spoke Jessie's eye glanced across the hand Paul had extended for the fan which Claudia was offering; he did not see the look, but unfurling the daintily carved toy, answered calmly as the stirred air cooled the fever of his cheek: "I cannot doubt you, Mrs. Snowdon, for you look truly sibylline to-night; but if you read the future with such a gifted eye, can you not find us a fairer future than your storm foretells?"

"Did you never know before that there was gipsy blood in my veins, and that I possessed the gipsy's power of second sight? Shall I use it, and tell your fortune like a veritable witch? May I, Claudia?"

Jessie's friend looked at her with a touch of wonder; for the flush was deepening on her cheek, the fire kindling in her eyes, and her whole aspect seemed to stir and brighten like a snake's before it springs.

"If Paul pleases I should like to hear your 'rede,' and we will cross your palm with silver by and by. Indeed I think the inspired phrenzy is descending upon you, Jessie, for you look like an electric battery fully charged, and I dare not touch you lest I should receive a shock," Claudia answered, smiling at the sudden change.

"I *am* a battery to-night, and you may have your shock whenever you please. Come, Mr. Frere, your sovereign consents, come and let me try my power — if you dare."

A slight frown contracted Paul's brows, and a disdainful smile flitted across his lips; but Claudia waited, and he silently obeyed. "Not that hand, fate lies only in the *right*."

"Jessie, take mine instead, our fortunes henceforth will be the same!" cried Claudia, with eager voice remembering the mark Paul never showed.

But Jessie only laughed the metallic laugh again, clear and sharp as the jangle of a bell; and with a gesture of something like defiance Paul stretched his right hand to her, while the disdainful smile still sat upon his lips. Jessie did not touch it, but bent and scanned it eagerly, though nothing could be seen but the wide scar across the shapely palm.

A dead silence fell upon the three. Paul stood composed and motionless, Jessie paled visibly, and the quick throb of her heart grew audible, but Claudia felt the pain of that rude scrutiny, and leaning toward them asked impatiently, "Sibyl, what do you read?"

Jessie swayed slowly backward, and looking up at the defiant face above her, answered in a whisper that cut the silence like a knife.

"I see two letters, — M. L."

Paul did not start, his countenance did not change, but the fan dropped shattered from his grasp — the only sign that he had heard. Claudia's eyes were on them, but she could not speak, and the sibilant whisper came again.

"I know it all, for *this* remained to tell the secret, and *I* am the master now. See here!" and with a peal of laughter Jessie threw the paper at his feet.

CHAPTER IV

Paul gave one glance at the crumpled sheet, then turned on her with a look that sent her trembling to the door, as a gust would sweep a thistle down before it. It was the look of a hunted creature driven to bay; wrath, abhorrence, and despair stirred the strong man's frame, looked out at his desperate eye, strengthened his uplifted arm, and had not his opponent been a woman some swift retribution would have fallen on her, for there was murder in his fiery blood.

Claudia sprang to his side, and at the touch of those restraining hands a stern pallor settled on his countenance, a hard won self-control quenched his passion, a bitter truth confronted his despair, and left him desolate but not degraded. His eye fixed on Jessie, and its hopelessness was more eloquent than a torrent of entreaties, its contempt more keen than the sharpest reproach.

"Go," he said with a strange hush in his voice, "I ask nothing of you, for I know you would be merciless to me; but if there be any compassion, any touch of nobleness in your nature you will spare your friend, remembering what she has been to you. Go, and mar my hard won reputation as you will, the world's condemnation I will not accept, my judge is *here*."

"There will be no need of silence a week hence when the marriage day comes round and there is no bridegroom for the bride. I foretold the storm, and it has come; heaven help you through it Claudia. Good night, pleasant dreams, and a fair to-morrow!"

Jessie Snowdon tried to look exultant, but her white lips would not smile, and though the victory was hers she crept away like one who has suffered a defeat.

Paul locked the door behind her, and turning, looked at Claudia with a world of anguish in his altered face. She moved as if to go to him, but a gesture arrested her, and uttering a broken exclamation Paul struck his scarred hand on the chimney piece with a force that left it bruised and bleeding, and dropping his hot forehead on the marble stood silent, struggling with a grief that had no solace.

Claudia paused a moment, mute and pale, watching the bowed figure and the red drops as they fell, then she went to him, and holding the wounded palm as if it were a suffering child, she laid her cheek to his, whispering tenderly; "Paul, you said this was an honest hand and I believe it still. There should not be a grain of dust between us two, — deal frankly with me now, and let me comfort you."

Paul lifted up his face wan with the tearless sorrow of a man, and gathering the beloved comforter close to his sore heart looked long into the countenance whose loving confidence had no reproach for him as yet. He held her fast for a little space, kissed her lips and forehead lingeringly, as if he took a mute farewell, then gently put her from him saying, as she sank into a seat —

"Claudia, I never meant to burden you with my unhappy past, believing that I did no wrong in burying it deep from human sight, and walking through the world as if it had never been. I see my error now, and bitterly I repent it. Put pity, prejudice, and pride away, and see me as I am. Hear and judge me, and by your judgment I will abide."

He paused, silently gathering calmness from his strength, and courage from his love; then, as if each word were wrung from him by a sharper pang than he had ever known before, he said slowly: "Claudia, those letters were once branded on my hand, they are the initials of a name — 'Maurice Lecroix.' Ten years ago he was my master, I his slave."

If Paul had raised his strong right arm and struck her, the act would not have daunted her with such a pale dismay, or shocked the power more rudely from her limbs. For an instant the tall shape wavered mistily before her and her heart stood still; then she girded up her energies, for with her own suffering came the memory of his, and, true woman through it all, she only covered up her face and cried: "Go on, I can bear it Paul!"

Solemnly and steadily, as if it were his dying shrift, Paul stood before the woman whom he loved and told the story of his life.

"My father — God forgive him — was a Cuban planter, my mother a beautiful Quadroon, mercifully taken early out of slavery to an eternal freedom. I never knew her but she bequeathed to me my father's love, and I possessed it till he died. For fifteen years I was a happy child, and forgot that I was a slave. Light tasks, kind treatment, and slight restraints so blinded me to the real hardships of my lot. I had a sister, heiress of my father's name and fortune, and she was my playmate all those years, sharing her pleasures and her pains with me, her small store of knowledge, her girlish accomplishments as she acquired them, and — more than all — the blessing of an artless love. I was her proud protector, her willing servitor, and in those childish days we were what heaven made us, brother and sister fond and free.

"I was fifteen when my father died, and the black blight fell upon me in a single night. He had often promised me my freedom — strange gift from a father to his son! — but like other duties it had been neglected till too late. Death came suddenly, and I was left a sadder orphan than poor Nathalie, for my heritage was a curse that cancelled all past love by robbing me of liberty.

"Nathalie and I were separated — she went to her guardian's protection, I to the auction block. Her last words were 'Be kind to Paul.' They promised; but when she was gone they sold me far away from my old home, and then I learned what it was to be a slave. Ah, Claudia, you shudder when I say those words; give your abhorrence to the man who dared to love you, but bestow a little pity on the desolate boy you never knew. I had a hard master, he a rebellious spirit to subdue; for I could not learn subjection, and my young blood burned within me at an insult or a blow. My father's kindness proved the direst misfortune that could have befallen me, for I had been lifted up into humanity and now I was cast back among the brutes; I had been born with a high heart and an eager spirit, they had been cherished fifteen years, now they were to be crushed and broken by inevitable fate.

"Year after year I struggled on, growing more desperate, and tugging more fiercely at my chain as each went by, bringing manhood but not the right to enjoy or make it mine. I tried to escape, but in vain, and each failure added to my despair. I tried to hear of Nathalie, but she had learned to look on me in another light, and had forgotten the sweet tie that bound us once. I tried to become a chattel and be content, but my father had given me his own free instincts, aspirations, and desires, and I could not change my nature though I were to be a slave forever.

"Five miserable years dragged by — so short to tell of, such an eternity to live! I was twenty, and no young man ever looked into the world more eager to be up and doing, no young man ever saw so black a future as that which appalled me with its doom. I would not accept it, but made a last resolve to try once more for liberty, and if I failed, to end the life I could no longer bear. Watchfully I waited, warily I planned, desperately I staked my last hope — and lost it. I was betrayed, and hunted down as ruthlessly as any wolf; but I tried to keep my vow; for as my pursuers clutched me I struck the blow that should have ended all, and the happiest moment of my life was that swift pang when the world passed from me with the exultant thought, 'I am free at last.'"

Paul paused, spent and breathless with rapid speech and strong emotion, and in the silence heard Claudia murmuring through a rain of tears: "Oh, my love! my love! was there no friend but death?"

That low cry was a stronger cordial to Paul's spirit than the rarest wine grape that ever grew. He looked yearningly across the narrow space that parted them, but though his eye blessed her for her pity, he did not pass the invisible barrier he had set up between them till her hand should throw it down or fix it there forever.

"These are bitter things for you to hear, dear heart. God knows they were bitter things to bear, but I am stronger for them now, and you the calmer for your tears. A little more and happier times are coming. I could not die, but came out of that 'valley of the shadow' a meeker soul; for though branded, buffetted, and bruised, I clung to life, blindly believing help must come, and it did. One day a shape passed before my eyes that seemed the angel of deliverance — it was Nathalie, and she was my master's guest. I gathered covertly that she was a gentle-woman, that she was mistress of her fortune now and soon to be a happy wife; and hearing these things I determined to make one appeal to her in my great need.

"I watched her, and one blessed night, defying every penalty, and waiting till the house was still, and her light burned alone as I had seen it many times before, I climbed the balcony and stood before her saying, 'I am Paul, help me in our father's name.' She did not recognize the blithe boy in the desperate man, but I told my misery, implored compassion and relief, I looked at her with her father's face, and nature pleaded better than my prayers, for she stretched her hands to me, saying, with tears as beautiful as those now shining on your cheek, 'Who should help you if not I? Be comforted and I will atone for this great neglect and wrong. Paul, have faith in me; I shall not fail.'

"Claudia, you loved me first for my great reverence for womankind; this is the secret of the virtue you commend, for when I was most desolate a woman succored me. Since then, in every little maid, I see the child who loved me when a boy, in every blooming girl, the Nathalie who saved me when a man, in every woman, high or low, the semblance of my truest friend, and do them honor in my sister's name."

"Heaven crown her with a happy life!" prayed Claudia, with fervent heart, and still more steadily her lover's voice went on.

"She kept her word, and did a just deed generously, for money flowed like water till I was free, then giving me a little store for present needs, she sent me out the richest man that walked the world. I left the Island, and went to and fro seeking for my place upon the earth. I never told my story, never betrayed my past, I have no sign of my despised race but my

Spanish hue, and taking my father's native country for my own I found no bar in swarthy skin, or the only name I had a right to bear. I seared away all traces of a master's claim, and smiled as the flame tortured me; for liberty had set her seal upon my forehead, and my flesh and blood were *mine*.

"Then I took the rights and duties of a man upon me, feeling their weight and worth, looking proudly on them as a sacred trust won by much suffering, to be used worthily and restored to their bestower richer for my stewardship. I looked about me for some work to do, for now I labored for myself, and industry was sweet. I was a stranger in a strange land, friendless and poor: but I had energy and hope, two angels walking with me night and day.

"Music had always been my passion; now I chose it as my staff of life. In hospitable Germany I made true friends who aided me, and doing any honest work by day, I gave my nights to study, trying to repair the loss of years.

"Southern trees grow rapidly, for their sap is stirred by whirlwinds and fed with ardent heats. Fast I struggled up, groping for the light that dawned more fairly as I climbed; and when ten years were gone I seemed to have been born anew. Paul the slave was dead and his grave grown green; Paul the man had no part in him beyond a mournful memory of the youth that pined and died too soon. The world had done me a great wrong, yet I asked no atonement but the liberty to prove myself a man: no favor but the right to bury my dead past and make my future what I would. Other men's ambitions were not mine, for twenty years had been taken from me and I had no time to fight for any but the highest prize. I was grateful for the boon heaven sent me, and felt that my work was to build up an honest life, to till the nature given me, and sow therein a late harvest, that my sheaf might yet be worthy the Great Reaper's hand. If there be any power in sincere desire, any solace in devout belief, — that strength, that consolation will be mine. Man's opprobrium may oppress me, woman's pity may desert me, suffering and wrong may still pursue me, — yet I am not desolate; for when all human charities have cast me off I know that a Diviner love will take me in."

To Paul's voice came the music of a fervent faith, in his eye burned the fire of a quenchless hope, and on his countenance there shone a pale serenity that touched it with the youth time cannot take away. Past and present faded from his sight, for in that moment his spirit claimed its birthright, and beyond the creature of his love, his heart beheld the aspiration of his life.

"Claudia, I never thought to know affection like your own; never thought I could deserve so great a blessing; but when it came to me in tenderest guise, pleading to be taken in, how could I bar the door to such a welcome visitant? I did not, and the strong sweet angel entered in to kindle on my lonely hearth a household fire that can never die. Heaven help me if the ministering spirit goes!"

Through all the story of his own despairs and griefs Paul had not faltered, but gone resolutely on, painting his sufferings lightly for Claudia's sake, but now when he remembered the affection she had cherished, the anguish she might feel, the confidence she might believe betrayed, a keen remorse assailed him, and his courage failed. He thought of Claudia lost, and with an exclamation of passionate regret paced the long room with restless feet — paused for a little, looking out into the magic stillness of the night, and came back calm again.

"When you first gave me the good gift you have a right to take again, I told you I was orphaned, friendless, poor; but I did not tell you why I was thus desolate, believing it was wiser to leave a bitter history untold. I thought I did no wrong, but I have learned that perfect peace is only found in perfect truth; and I accept the lesson, for I was too proud of my success, and I am cast down into the dust to climb again with steadier feet. I let you judge me as an equal, showing you my weaknesses, my wants, my passions, and beliefs, as any happier lover might have done; you found some spark of manhood there, for you loved me, and that act should have made me worthier of the gift — but it did not. Claudia forgive me; I was weak, but I struggled to be strong; for in the blissful months that have gone by, you showed me all your heart, enriched me with your confidence, and left no sorrow of your life untold — this brave sincerity became a mute reproach to me at last, for far down in *my* heart was a secret chamber never opened to your eye, for there my lost youth lay so stark and cold I dared not show you its dead face. But as the time came nearer when you were to endow me with the name which should go hand in hand with innocence and truth, this vague remorse for a silent wrong determined me to make confession of my past. I wrote it all, believing I could never tell it, as I have done to-night, learning that love can cast out fear. I wrote it, and brought it many times, but never gave it, for O, Claudia! O, my heart! I loved you more than honor, and I could not give you up!"

From sleeping garden and still night a breath of air sighed through the room, as mournful and as sweet as those impassioned words, but Claudia never lifted up her hidden face, or stirred to answer it, for she was listening to a more divine appeal, and taking counsel in the silence of her heart.

Paul watched her, and the shadow of a great fear fell upon his face.

"I brought this confession here to-night, resolved to give it and be satisfied; but you did not come to meet me, and while I waited my love tempted me; the strong moment passed, and I burned it, yielding the nobler purpose for the dearer peace. This single page, how dropped I cannot tell, betrayed me to that ———— woman, and her malice forced on me the part I was not brave enough to play alone.

"Now, Claudia all is told. Now, seeing what I have been, knowing what I desired to be, remembering mercifully what I am, try my crime and adjudge my punishment."

There was no need of that appeal, for judgment had been given long before the prayer came. Pride, and fear, and shame had dropped away, leaving the purer passion free; now justice and mercy took love by the hand and led it home. On Claudia's face there came a light more beautiful than any smile; on cheek and forehead glowed the fervor of her generous blood, in eye and voice spoke the courage of her steadfast heart, as she flung down the barrier, saying only: "Mine still, mine forever, Paul!" and with that tender welcome took the wronged man to the shelter of her love.

Tears hot and heavy as a summer rain baptised the new born peace, and words of broken gratitude sang its lullaby, as that strong nature cradled it with blessings and with prayers. Paul was the weaker now, and Claudia learned the greatness of past fear by the vehemence of present joy, as they stood together tasting the sweetness of a moment that enriched their lives.

"Love, do you remember what this gift may cost? Do you remember what I am henceforth to other eyes? Can you bear to see familiar faces growing strange to you, to meet looks that wound you with their pity, to hear words that sting you with their truth, and find a shadow falling on your life from me?"

As he spoke, Paul lifted up that face, "clear-shining after rain," but it did not alter, did not lose its full content, as Claudia replied with fervent voice: "I do remember that I cannot pay too much what is priceless; that when I was loveless and alone, there came a friend who never will desert me when all others fail; that from lowly places poets, philosophers, and kings have come; and when the world sneers at the name you give me, I can turn upon it saying with the pride that stirs me now: '*My* husband has achieved a nobler success than men you honor, has surmounted greater obstacles, has conquered sterner foes, and risen to be an "honest man." ' "

Paul proved that he was one by still arming her against himself, still warning her of the cruel prejudices which he had such sad cause to know and fear.

"Your generous nature blinds you to the trials I foresee, the disappointments I foretell. In your world there will be no place for me, when this is known, and I cannot ask you to come down from your high place to sit beside an outcast's fire. I have not lost your love, — that was the blow I feared; and still possessing it I can relinquish much, and yield the new title I was soon to know, if I may keep the dear old one of 'friend.' It is no longer in our power to keep this secret unknown, and strengthen our affection by it, as I once hoped. Think of this, Claudia, in a calmer mood, weigh well the present and the future cost, for now you have the power to make or mar your happiness.

"No loss of yours must be my gain, and I had rather never look into this face again than live to see it saddened by a vain regret for any act I might have saved you from by timely pain." "I will consider, I will prove myself before I take your peace into my hands; but, Paul, I know the answer that will come to all my doubts, I know I shall not change."

Claudia spoke steadily, for she knew herself; and when at length her lover went, her last words were, "Believe in me, I shall not change."

CHAPTER V

Slowly the clear flame of the lamp grew dim and died, softly Night sang her cradle hymn to hush the weary world, and solemnly the silence deepened as the hours went by, but Claudia with wakeful eyes trod to and fro, or sat an image of mute thought. She was not alone, for good and evil spirits compassed her about, making that still room the battle-field of a viewless conflict between man's law, and woman's love. All the worldly wisdom time had taught, now warned her of the worldly losses she might yet sustain, all the prejudices born of her position and strengthened by her education now assailed her with covert skill, all the pride grown with her growth now tempted her to forget the lover in the slave, and fear threatened her with public opinion, that grim ghost that haunts the wisest and the best. But high above the voice of pride, the sigh of fear, and the echo of "the world's dread laugh," still rose the whisper of her heart, undaunted, undismayed, and cried to her, —

"I was cold, and he cherished me beside his fire; hungry, and he gave me food; a stranger and he took me in."

Slowly the moon climbed the zenith and dropped into the West, slowly the stars paled one by one, and the gray sky kindled ruddily as dawn came smiling from the hills. Slowly the pale shadow of all worldliness passed from Claudia's mind, and left it ready for the sun, slowly the spectral doubts, regrets and fears vanished one by one, and through the twilight of that brief eclipse arose the morning of a fairer day.

As young knights watched their arms of old in chapels haunted by the memory of warrior or saint, and came forth eager for heroic deeds, so

Claudia in the early dawn braced on the armor consecrated by a night of prayerful vigil, and with valiant soul addressed herself to the duty which would bring her life's defeat or victory.

Paul found another Claudia than the one he left; for a woman steadfast and strong turned to him a countenance as full of courage as of cheer, when standing there again he looked deep into her eyes and offered her his hand as he had done on their betrothal night. Now, as then, she took it, and in a moment gave a sweet significance to those characters which were the only vestiges of his wrong, for bending she touched the scarred palm with her lips, and whispered tenderly, "My love, there is no anguish in that brand, no humiliation in that claim, and I accept the bondage of the master who rules all the world."

As he spoke, Paul looked a happier, more *contented* slave, than those fabulous captives the South boasts of, but finds it hard to show.

Claudia led him back into the lower world again by asking with a sigh — "Paul, why should Jessie Snowdon wish to wound me so? What cause have I given her for such dislike?"

A swift color swept across her lover's face, and the disdainful smile touched his lips again as he replied, "It is not a thing for me to tell; yet for the truth's sake I must. Jessie Snowdon wooed what Claudia won. Heaven knows I have no cause for vanity, yet I could not help seeing in her eyes the regard it took so long, to read in these more maidenly ones. I had no return to make, but gave all the friendship and respect I could to one for whom I had a most invincible distaste. There was no other cause for her dislike, yet I believe she hated me, or why should she speak with such malicious pleasure where a more generous woman would have held her peace? I have no faith in her, and by to-morrow I shall see in some changed face the first cloud of the storm she once foretold. Claudia, let us be married quietly, and go away until the gossips are grown weary, and we are forgotten."

Paul spoke with the sudden impulse of a nature sensitive and proud, but Claudia's energy was fully roused and she answered with indignant color. "No, nothing must be changed. I asked my friends to see me made a proud and happy wife; shall I let them think I am ashamed to stand before them with the man I love? Paul, if I cannot bear a few harsh words, a few cold looks, a little pain, for you, of what worth is my love, of what use is my strength, and how shall I prove a fit friend and help-meet to you in the heavier cares and sorrows heaven sends us all?"

"Claudia, you are the braver of the two! I should be stronger if I had much to give; but I am so poor, this weight of obligation robs me of my courage. I am a weak soul, love, for I cannot trust, and am still haunted by the fear that I shall one day read some sorrowful regret in this face, grown so wan with one night's watching for my sake."

Claudia dropped on her knee before him, and lifting up her earnest countenance, said, "Read it Paul, and never doubt again. You spoke once of atonement, — make it by conquering your pride and receiving as freely as I give; for believe me, it is as hard a thing greatly to accept, as it is bountifully to bestow. You are not poor, for there can be no mine and thine between us two; you are not weak, for I lean on your strength, and know it will not fail; you are not fearful now, for looking here, you see the wife who never can regret or know the shadow of a change." Paul brushed the brown locks back, and as he read it smiled again, for heart and eyes and tender lips confirmed the truth, and he was satisfied.

Jessie Snowdon's secret haunted her like Lady Macbeth's, and like that strong-minded woman, she would have told it in her sleep, if she had not eased herself by confiding it to a single friend. "Dear Maria" promised an eternal silence, but "dear Maria" was the well-known "little bird" who gave the whisper to the air. Rumor sowed it broadcast, gossips nurtured it, and Claudia reaped a speedy harvest of discomforts and chagrins.

She thought herself well armed for the "war of words;" but women's tongues forged weapons whose blows she could not parry, and men's censure or coarse pity pierced her shield, and wounded deeper than she dared to tell. Her "dear five hundred friends" each came to save her from social suicide, and her peaceful drawing-room soon became a chamber of the Inquisition, where a daily "Council of Ten" tormented her with warnings, entreaties — and reproaches, — harder trials for a woman to bear, than the old tortures of rack and thirst and fire.

She bore herself bravely through these troublous times, but her pillow received bitter tears, heard passionate prayers and the throbbing of an indignant heart, that only calmed itself by the power of its love. Paul never saw a tear or heard a sigh, — for him the steady smile sat on her lips, a cheerful courage filled her eye; but he read her pain in the meekness which now beautified her face, and silently the trial now drew them nearer than before.

There was no mother to gather Claudia to her breast with blessings and with prayers when the marriage morning dawned, no sister to hover near her, April-like, with smiles and tears, no father to give her proudly to the man she loved, and few friends to make it a blithe festival; but a happier bride had never waited for her bridegroom's coming than Claudia, as she looked out at the sunshine of a gracious day, and said within herself,

"Heaven smiles upon me with auspicious skies, and in the depths of my own heart I hear a sweeter chime than any wedding bells can ring, — feel a truer peace than human commendation can bestow. Oh father, whom I never knew! oh mother whom I wholly loved! be with me now, and bless me in this happy hour."

Paul came at last, fevered with the disquiet of much sleepless thought, and still disturbed by the gratitude of a generous nature, which believed itself unworthy of the gift relenting Fortune now bestowed. He saw a fair woman crowned for him, and remembering his past, looked at her, saying with troubled and agitated voice — "Claudia, it is not yet too late." But the white shape fluttered from him to the threshold of the door, and looking back, only answered, "come."

Music, the benignant spirit of their lives, breathed a solemn welcome as the solitary pair paced down the chancel, through the silken stir of an uprising throng. Down from the altar window, full of sacred symbols and rich hues, fell heaven's benediction in a flood of light, touching Paul's bent head with mellow rays, and bathing Claudia's bridal snow in bloom.

Silently that unconscious pair preached a better sermon than had ever echoed there, for it appealed to principles that never die, and made its text, "The love of liberty, the liberty of love."

Many a worldly man forgot his worldliness, and thinking of Paul's hard-won success, owned that he honored him. Many a frivolous woman felt her eye wet by sudden dew, her bosom stirred by sudden sympathy, as Claudia's clear, "I will," rose through the hush, and many a softened heart confessed the beauty of the deed it had condemned.

Stern bridegroom and pale bride, those two had come into the chapel's gloom; proud-eyed husband, blooming wife, those two made one, passed out into the sunlight on the sward, and down along that shining path they walked serenely into their new life.

The nine days wonder died away, and Paul and Claudia, listening to the murmur of the sea, forgot there was a world through all that happy month. But when they came again and took their places in the circle they had left, the old charm had departed; for prejudice, a sterner autocrat than the Czar of all the Russias, hedged them round with an invisible restraint, that seemed to shut them out from the genial intercourse they had before enjoyed. Claudia would take no hand that was not given as freely to her husband, and there were not many to press her own as cordially as they once had done. Then she began to realize the emptyness of her old life, for now she looked upon it with a clearer eye, and saw it would not stand the test she had applied.

This was the lesson she had needed, it taught her the value of true friendship, showed her the poverty of old beliefs, the bitterness of old desires, and strengthened her proud nature by the sharp discipline of pain.

Paul saw the loneliness that sometimes came upon her when her former pleasures ceased to satisfy, and began to feel that his forebodings would prove true. But they never did; for there came to them those good Samaritans who minister to soul as well as sense, these took them by the hand, and through their honor for her husband, gave to Claudia the crowning lesson of her life.

They led her out of the world of wealth, and fashion, and pretence, into that other world that lies above it, full of the beauty of great deeds, high thoughts and humble souls, who walk its ways, rich in the virtues that

Smell sweet, and blossom in the dust.

Like a child in fairyland she looked about her, feeling that here she might see again the aspirations of her youth, and find those happy visions true.

In this new world she found a finer rank than any she had left, for men whose righteous lives were their renown, whose virtues their estate, were peers of this realm, whose sovereign was Truth, whose ministers were Justice and Humanity, whose subjects all "who loved their neighbor better than themselves."

She found a truer chivalry than she had known before, for heroic deeds shone on her in the humblest guise, and she discovered knights of a nobler court than Arthur founded, or than Spenser sang. Saint Georges, valiant as of old, Sir Guyens devout and strong, and silver tongued Sir Launcelots without a stain, all fighting the good fight for love of God and universal right.

She found a fashion old as womanhood and beautiful as charity, whose votaries lived better poems than any pen could write; brave Britomarts redressing wrongs; meek Unas succoring the weak, high hearted Maids of Orleans steadfast through long martyrdoms of labor for the poor, all going cheerfully along the by-ways of the world, and leaving them the greener for the touch of their unwearied feet.

She found a religion that welcomed all humanity to its broad church, and made its priest the peasant of Judea who preached the Sermon on the Mount.

Then, seeing these things, Claudia felt that she had found her place, and putting off her "purple and fine linen," gave herself to earnest work, which is the strengthening wine of life. Paul was no longer friendless and without a home, for here he found a country, and a welcome to that brotherhood which makes the whole world kin; and like the pilgrims in that fable never old, these two "went on their way rejoicing," leaving the shores of "Vanity Fair" behind them, and through the "Valley of Humiliation" climbed the mountains whence they saw the spires of the "Celestial City" shining in the sun.

Slowly all things right themselves when founded on the truth. Time brought tardy honors to Paul, and Claudia's false friends beckoned her to come and take her place again, but she only touched the little heads, looked up into her husband's face, and answered with a smile of beautiful content — "I cannot give the substance for the shadow, — I cannot leave my world for yours. Put off the old delusions that blind you to the light, and come up here to me."

A Night

From *Hospital Sketches* (Boston: James Redpath, 1863)

*B*EING FOND of the night side of nature, I was soon promoted to the post of night nurse, with every facility for indulging in my favorite pastime of "owling." My colleague, a black-eyed widow, relieved me at dawn, we two taking care of the ward, between us, like the immortal Sairy and Betsey, "turn and turn about." I usually found my boys in the jolliest state of mind their condition allowed; for it was a known fact that Nurse Periwinkle objected to blue devils, and entertained a belief that he who laughed most was surest of recovery. At the beginning of my reign, dumps and dismals prevailed; the nurses looked anxious and tired, the men gloomy or sad; and a general "Hark!-from-the-tombs-a-doleful-sound" style of conversation seemed to be the fashion: a state of things which caused one coming from a merry, social New England town, to feel as if she had got into an exhausted receiver; and the instinct of self-preservation, to say nothing of a philanthropic desire to serve the race, caused a speedy change in Ward No. 1.

More flattering than the most gracefully turned compliment, more grateful than the most admiring glance, was the sight of those rows of faces, all strange to me a little while ago, now lighting up, with smiles of welcome, as I came among them, enjoying that moment heartily, with a womanly pride in their regard, a motherly affection for them all. The evenings were spent in reading aloud, writing letters, waiting on and amusing the men, going the rounds with Dr. P., as he made his second daily survey, dressing my dozen wounds afresh, giving last doses, and making them cozy for the long hours to come, till the nine o'clock bell rang, the gas was turned down, the day nurses went off duty, the night watch came on, and my nocturnal adventure began.

My ward was now divided into three rooms; and, under favor of the matron, I had managed to sort out the patients in such a way that I had what I called, "my duty room," my "pleasure room," and my "pathetic room," and worked for each in a different way. One, I visited, armed with a dressing tray, full of rollers, plasters, and pins; another, with books, flowers, games, and gossip; a third, with teapots, lullabies, consolation, and, sometimes, a shroud.

Wherever the sickest or most helpless man chanced to be, there I held my watch, often visiting the other rooms, to see that the general watchman of the ward did his duty by the fires and the wounds, the latter needing constant wetting. Not only on this account did I meander, but also to get fresher air than the close rooms afforded; for, owing to the stupidity of that mysterious "somebody" who does all the damage in the world, the windows had been carefully nailed down above, and the lower sashes could only be raised in the mildest weather, for the men lay just below. I had suggested a summary smashing of a few panes here and there, when frequent appeals to headquarters had proved unavailing, and daily orders to lazy attendants had come to nothing. No one seconded the motion, however, and the nails were far beyond my reach; for, though belonging to the sisterhood of "ministering angels," I had no wings, and might as well have asked for Jacob's ladder, as a pair of steps, in that charitable chaos.

One of the harmless ghosts who bore me company during the haunted hours, was Dan, the watchman, whom I regarded with a certain awe; for, though so much together, I never fairly saw his face, and, but for his legs, should never have recognized him, as we seldom met by day. These legs were remarkable, as was his whole figure, for his body was short, rotund, and done up in a big jacket, and muffler; his beard hid the lower part of his face, his hat-brim the upper; and all I ever discovered was a pair of sleepy eyes, and a very mild voice. But the legs! — very long, very thin, very crooked and feeble, looking like grey sausages in their tight coverings, without a ray of pegtopishness about them, and finished off with a pair of expansive, green cloth shoes, very like Chinese junks, with the sails down. This figure, gliding noiselessly about the dimly lighted rooms, was strongly suggestive of the spirit of a beer barrel mounted on cork-screws, haunting the old hotel in search of its lost mates, emptied and staved in long ago.

Another goblin who frequently appeared to me, was the attendant of the pathetic room, who, being a faithful soul, was often up to tend two or three men, weak and wandering as babies, after the fever had gone. The amiable creature beguiled the watches of the night by brewing jorums of a fearful beverage, which he called coffee, and insisted on sharing with me; coming in with a great bowl of something like mud soup, scalding hot, guiltless of cream, rich in an all-pervading flavor of molasses, scorch and tin pot. Such an amount of good will and neighborly kindness also went into the mess, that I never could find the heart to refuse, but always received it with thanks, sipped it with hypocritical relish while he remained, and whipped it into the slop-jar the instant he departed, thereby gratifying him, securing one rousing laugh in the doziest hour of the night, and no one was the worse for the transaction but the pigs. Whether they were "cut off untimely in their sins," or not, I carefully abstained from inquiring.

It was a strange life — asleep half the day, exploring Washington the other half, and all night hovering, like a massive cherubim, in a red rigolette, over the slumbering sons of man. I liked it, and found many things to amuse, instruct, and interest me. The snores alone were quite a study, varying from the mild sniff to the stentorian snort, which startled the echoes and hoisted the performer erect to accuse his neighbor of the deed, magnanimously forgive him, and, wrapping the drapery of his couch about him, lie down to vocal slumber. After listening for a week to this band of wind instruments, I indulged in the belief that I could recognize each by the snore alone, and was tempted to join the chorus by breaking out with John Brown's favorite hymn:

Blow ye the trumpet, blow!

I would have given much to have possessed the art of sketching, for many of the faces became wonderfully interesting when unconscious. Some grew stern and grim, the men evidently dreaming of war, as they gave orders, groaned over their wounds, or damned the rebels vigorously; some grew sad and infinitely pathetic, as if the pain borne silently all day, revenged itself by now betraying what the man's pride had concealed so well. Often the roughest grew young and pleasant when sleep smoothed the hard lines away, letting the real nature assert itself; many almost seemed to speak, and I learned to know these men better by night than through any intercourse by day. Sometimes they disappointed me, for faces that looked merry and good in the light, grew bad and sly when the shadows came; and though they made no confidences in words, I read their lives, leaving them to wonder at the change of manner this midnight magic wrought in their nurse. A few talked busily; one drummer boy sang sweetly, though no persuasions could win a note from him by day; and several depended on being told what they had talked of in the morning. Even my constitutionals in the chilly halls, possessed a certain charm, for the house was never still. Sentinels tramped round it all night long, their muskets glittering in the wintry moonlight as they walked, or stood before the doors, straight and silent, as figures of stone, causing one to conjure up romantic visions of guarded forts, sudden surprises, and daring deeds; for in these war times the hum drum life of Yankeedom has vanished, and the most prosaic feel some thrill of that excitement which stirs the nation's heart, and makes its capital a camp of hospitals. Wandering up and down these lower halls, I often heard cries from above, steps hurrying to and fro, saw surgeons passing up, or men coming down carrying a stretcher, where lay a long white figure, whose face was shrouded and whose fight was done. Sometimes I stopped to watch the passers in the street, the moonlight shining on the spire opposite, or the gleam of some vessel floating, like a white-winged sea-gull, down the broad Potomac, whose fullest flow can never wash away the red stain of the land.

The night whose events I have a fancy to record, opened with a little comedy, and closed with a great tragedy; for a virtuous and useful life untimely ended is always tragical to those who see not as God sees. My headquarters were beside the bed of a New Jersey boy, crazed by the horrors of that dreadful Saturday. A slight wound in the knee brought him there; but his mind had suffered more than his body; some string of that delicate machine was over strained, and, for days, he had been reliving in imagination, the scenes he could not forget, till his distress broke out in incoherent ravings, pitiful to hear. As I sat by him, endeavoring to soothe his poor distracted brain by the constant touch of wet hands over his hot forehead, he lay cheering his comrades on, hurrying them back, then counting them as they fell around him, often clutching my arm, to drag me from the vicinity of a bursting shell, or covering up his head to screen himself from a shower of shot; his face brilliant with fever; his eyes restless; his head never still; every muscle strained and rigid; while an incessant stream of defiant shouts, whispered warnings, and broken laments, poured from his lips with that forceful bewilderment which makes such wanderings so hard to overhear.

It was past eleven, and my patient was slowly wearying himself into fitful intervals of quietude, when, in one of these pauses, a curious sound arrested my attention. Looking over my shoulder, I saw a one-legged phantom hopping nimbly down the room; and, going to meet it, recognized a certain Pennsylvania gentleman, whose wound-fever had taken a turn for the worse, and, depriving him of the few wits a drunken campaign had left him, set him literally tripping on the light, fantastic toe "toward home," as he blandly informed me, touching the military cap which formed a striking contrast to the severe simplicity of the rest of his decidedly *undress* uniform. When sane, the least movement produced a roar of pain or a volley of oaths; but the departure of reason seemed to have wrought an agreeable change, both in the man and his manners; for, balancing himself on one leg, like a meditative stork, he plunged into an animated discussion of the war, the President, lager beer, and Enfield rifles, regardless of any suggestions of mine as to the propriety of returning to bed, lest he be court-martialed for desertion.

Anything more supremely ridiculous can hardly be imagined than this figure, scantily draped in white, its one foot covered with a big blue sock, a dingy cap set rakingly askew on its shaven head, and placid satisfaction beaming in its broad red face, as it flourished a mug in one hand, an old boot in the other, calling them canteen and knapsack, while it skipped and fluttered in the most unearthly fashion. What to do with the creature I didn't know; Dan was absent, and if I went to find him, the perambulator might festoon himself out of the window, set his toga on fire, or do some of his neighbors a mischief. The attendant of the room was sleeping like a near relative of the celebrated Seven, and nothing short of pins would rouse him; for he had been out that day, and whiskey asserted its supremacy in balmy whiffs. Still declaiming, in a fine flow of eloquence, the demented gentleman hopped on, blind and deaf to my graspings and entreaties; and I was about to slam the door in his face, and run for help, when a second and saner phantom, "all in white," came to the rescue, in the likeness of a big Prussian, who spoke no English, but divined the crisis, and put an end to it, by bundling the lively monoped into his bed, like a baby, with an authoritative command to "stay put," which received added weight from being delivered in an odd conglomeration of French and German, accompanied by warning wags of a head decorated with a yellow cotton night cap, rendered most imposing by a tassel like a bell-pull. Rather exhausted by his excursion, the member from Pennsylvania subsided; and, after an irrepressible laugh together, my Prussian ally and myself were returning to our places, when the echo of a sob caused us to glance along the beds. It came from one in the corner — such a little bed! — and such a tearful little face looked up at us, as we stopped beside it! The twelve years old drummer boy was not singing now, but sobbing, with a manly effort all the while to stifle the distressful sounds that would break out.

"What is it, Teddy?" I asked, as he rubbed the tears away, and checked himself in the middle of a great sob to answer plaintively:

"I've got a chill, ma'am, but I aint cryin' for that, 'cause I'm used to it. I dreamed Kit was here, and when I waked up he wasn't, and I couldn't help it, then."

The boy came in with the rest, and the man who was taken dead from the ambulance was the Kit he mourned. Well he might; for, when the wounded were brought from Fredericksburg, the child lay in one of the camps thereabout, and this good friend, though sorely hurt himself, would not leave him to the exposure and neglect of such a time and place; but, wrapping him in his own blanket, carried him in his arms to the transport, tended him during the passage, and only yielded up his charge when Death met him at the door of the hospital which promised care and comfort for the boy. For ten days, Teddy had shivered or burned with fever and ague, pining the while for Kit, and refusing to be comforted, because he had not been able to thank him for the generous protection, which, perhaps, had cost the giver's life. The vivid dream had wrung the childish heart with a fresh pang, and when I tried the solace fitted for his years, the remorseful fear that haunted him found vent in a fresh burst of tears, as he looked at the wasted hands I was endeavoring to warm:

"Oh! if I'd only been as thin when Kit carried me as I am now, maybe he wouldn't have died; but I was heavy, he was hurt worser than we knew, and so it killed him; and I didn't see him, to say good bye."

This thought had troubled him in secret; and my assurances that his friend would probably have died at all events, hardly assuaged the bitterness of his regretful grief.

At this juncture, the delirious man began to shout; the one-legged rose up in his bed, as if preparing for another dart; Teddy bewailed himself more piteously than before: and if ever a woman was at her wit's end, that distracted female was Nurse Periwinkle, during the space of two or three minutes, as she vibrated between the three beds, like an agitated pendulum. Like a most opportune reinforcement, Dan, the bandy, appeared, and devoted himself to the lively party, leaving me free to return to my post; for the Prussian, with a nod and a smile, took the lad away to his own bed, and lulled him to sleep with a soothing murmur, like a mammoth bumble bee. I liked that in Fritz, and if he ever wondered afterward at the dainties which sometimes found their way into his rations, or the extra comforts of his bed, he might have found a solution of the mystery in sundry persons' knowledge of the fatherly action of that night.

Hardly was I settled again, when the inevitable bowl appeared, and its bearer delivered a message I had expected, yet dreaded to receive:

"John is going, ma'am, and wants to see you, if you can come."

"The moment this boy is asleep; tell him so, and let me know if I am in danger of being too late."

My Ganymede departed, and while I quieted poor Shaw, I thought of John. He came in a day or two after the others; and, one evening, when I entered my "pathetic room," I found a lately emptied bed occupied by a large, fair man, with a fine face, and the serenest eyes I ever met. One of the earlier comers had often spoken of a friend, who had remained behind, that those apparently worse wounded than himself might reach a shelter first. It seemed a David and Jonathan sort of friendship. The man fretted for his mate, and was never tired of praising John — his courage, sobriety, self-denial, and unfailing kindliness of heart; always winding up with: "He's an out an' out fine feller, ma'am; you see if he aint."

I had some curiosity to behold this piece of excellence, and when he came, watched him for a night or two, before I made friends with him; for, to tell the truth, I was a little afraid of the stately looking man, whose bed had to be lengthened to accommodate his commanding stature; who seldom spoke, uttered no complaint, asked no sympathy, but tranquilly observed what went on about him; and, as he lay high upon his pillows, no picture of dying statesman or warrior was ever fuller of real dignity than this Virginia blacksmith. A most attractive face he had, framed in brown hair and beard, comely featured and full of vigor, as yet unsubdued by pain; thoughtful and often beautifully mild while watching the afflictions of others, as if entirely forgetful of his own. His mouth was grave and firm, with plenty of will and courage in its lines, but a smile could make it as sweet as any woman's; and his eyes were child's eyes, looking one fairly in the face, with a clear, straightforward glance, which promised well for such as placed their faith in him. He seemed to cling to life, as if it were rich in duties and delights, and he had learned the secret of content. The only time I saw his composure disturbed, was when my surgeon brought another to examine John, who scrutinized their faces with an anxious look, asking of the elder: "Do you think I shall pull through, sir?" "I hope so, my man." And, as the two passed on, John's eye still followed them, with an intentness which would have won a clearer answer from them, had they seen it. A momentary shadow flitted over his face; then came the usual serenity, as if, in that brief eclipse, he had acknowledged the existence of some hard possibility, and, asking nothing yet hoping all things, left the issue in God's hands, with that submission which is true piety.

The next night, as I went my rounds with Dr. P., I happened to ask which man in the room probably suffered most; and, to my great surprise, he glanced at John:

"Every breath he draws is like a stab; for the ball pierced the left lung, broke a rib, and did no end of damage here and there; so the poor lad can find neither forgetfulness nor ease, because he must lie on his wounded back or suffocate. It will be a hard struggle, and a long one, for he possesses great vitality; but even his temperate life can't save him; I wish it could."

"You don't mean he must die, Doctor?"

"Bless you, there's not the slightest hope for him; and you'd better tell him so before long; women have a way of doing such things comfortably, so I leave it to you. He won't last more than a day or two, at furthest."

I could have sat down on the spot and cried heartily, if I had not learned the wisdom of bottling up one's tears for leisure moments. Such an end seemed very hard for such a man, when half a dozen worn out, worthless bodies round him, were gathering up the remnants of wasted lives, to linger on for years perhaps, burdens to others, daily reproaches to themselves. The army needed men like John, earnest, brave, and faithful; fighting for liberty and justice with both heart and hand, true soldiers of the Lord. I could not give him up so soon, or think with any patience of so excellent a nature robbed of its fulfilment, and blundered into eternity by the rashness or stupidity of those at whose hands so many lives may be required. It was an easy thing for Dr. P. to say: "Tell him he must die," but a cruelly hard thing to do, and by no means as "comfortable" as he politely suggested. I had not the heart to do it then, and privately indulged the hope that some change for the better might take place, in spite of gloomy prophesies; so, rendering my task unnecessary. A few minutes later, as I came in again, with fresh rollers, I saw John sitting erect, with no one to support him, while the surgeon dressed his back. I had never hitherto seen it done; for, having simpler wounds to attend to, and knowing the fidelity of the attendant, I had left John to him, thinking it might be more agreeable and safe; for both strength and experience were needed in his case. I had forgotten that the strong man might long for the gentler tendance of a woman's hands, the sympathetic magnetism of a woman's presence, as well as the feebler souls about him. The Doctor's words caused me to reproach myself with neglect, not of any real duty perhaps, but of those little cares and kindnesses that solace homesick spirits, and make the heavy hours pass easier. John looked lonely and forsaken just then, as he sat with bent head, hands folded on his knee, and no outward sign of suffering, till, looking nearer, I saw great tears roll down and drop upon the floor. It was a new sight there; for, though I had seen many suffer, some swore, some groaned, most endured silently, but none wept. Yet it did not seem weak, only very touching, and straightway my fear vanished, my heart opened wide and took him in, as, gathering the bent head in my arms, as freely as if he had been a little child, I said, "Let me help you bear it, John."

Never, on any human countenance, have I seen so swift and beautiful a look of gratitude, surprise and comfort, as that which answered me more eloquently than the whispered —

"Thank you, ma'am, this is right good! this is what I wanted!"

"Then why not ask for it before?"

"I didn't like to be a trouble; you seemed so busy, and I could manage to get on alone."

"You shall not want it any more, John."

Nor did he; for now I understood the wistful look that sometimes followed me, as I went out, after a brief pause beside his bed, or merely a passing nod, while busied with those who seemed to need me more than he, because more urgent in their demands; now I knew that to him, as to so many, I was the poor substitute for mother, wife, or sister, and in his eyes no stranger, but a friend who hitherto had seemed neglectful; for, in his modesty, he had never guessed the truth. This was changed now; and, through the tedious operation of probing, bathing, and dressing his wounds, he leaned against me, holding my hand fast, and, if pain wrung further tears from him, no one saw them fall but me. When he was laid down again, I hovered about him, in a remorseful state of mind that would not let me rest, till I had bathed his face, brushed his "bonny brown hair," set all things smooth about him, and laid a knot of heath and heliotrope on his clean pillow. While doing this, he watched me with the satisfied expression I so liked to see; and when I offered the little nosegay, held it carefully in his great hand, smoothed a ruffled leaf or two, surveyed and smelt it with an air of genuine delight, and lay contentedly regarding the glimmer of the sunshine on the green. Although the manliest man among my forty, he said, "Yes, ma'am," like a little boy; received suggestions for his comfort with the quick smile that brightened his whole face; and now and then, as I stood tidying the table by his bed, I felt him softly touch my gown, as if to assure himself that I was there. Anything more natural and frank I never saw, and found this brave John as bashful as brave, yet full of excellencies and fine aspirations, which, having no power to express themselves in words, seemed to have bloomed into his character and made him what he was.

After that night, an hour of each evening that remained to him was devoted to his ease or pleasure. He could not talk much, for breath was precious, and he spoke in whispers; but from occasional conversations, I gleaned scraps of private history which only added to the affection and respect I felt for him. Once he asked me to write a letter, and as I settled pen and paper, I said, with an irrepressible glimmer of feminine curiosity, "Shall it be addressed to wife, or mother, John?"

"Neither, ma'am; I've got no wife, and will write to mother myself when I get better. Did you think I was married because of this?" he asked, touching a plain ring he wore, and often turned thoughtfully on his finger when he lay alone.

"Partly that, but more from a settled sort of look you have, a look which young men seldom get until they marry."

"I don't know that; but I'm not so very young, ma'am, thirty in May, and have been what you might call settled this ten years; for mother's a widow, I'm the oldest child she has, and it wouldn't do for me to marry until Lizzy has a home of her own, and Laurie's learned his trade; for we're not rich, and I must be father to the children and husband to the dear old woman, if I can."

"No doubt but you are both, John; yet how came you to go to war, if you felt so? Wasn't enlisting as bad as marrying?"

"No, ma'am, not as I see it, for one is helping my neighbor, the other pleasing myself. I went because I couldn't help it. I didn't want the glory or the pay; I wanted the right thing done, and people kept saying the men who were in earnest ought to fight. I was in earnest, the Lord knows! but I held off as long as I could, not knowing which was my duty; mother saw the case, gave me her ring to keep me steady, and said 'Go:' so I went."

A short story and a simple one, but the man and the mother were portrayed better than pages of fine writing could have done it.

"Do you ever regret that you came, when you lie here suffering so much?"

"Never, ma'am; I haven't helped a great deal, but I've shown I was willing to give my life, and perhaps I've got to; but I don't blame anybody, and if it was to do over again, I'd do it. I'm a little sorry I wasn't wounded in front; it looks cowardly to be hit in the back, but I obeyed orders, and it don't matter in the end, I know."

Poor John! it did not matter now, except that a shot in front might have spared the long agony in store for him. He seemed to read the thought that troubled me, as he spoke so hopefully when there was no hope, for he suddenly added:

"This is my first battle; do they think it's going to be my last?"

"I'm afraid they do, John."

It was the hardest question I had ever been called upon to answer; doubly hard with those clear eyes fixed on mine, forcing a truthful answer by their own truth. He seemed a little startled at first, pondered over the fateful fact a moment then shook his head, with a glance at the broad chest and muscular limbs stretched out before him:

"I'm not afraid, but it's difficult to believe all at once. I'm so strong it don't seem possible for such a little wound to kill me."

Merry Mercutio's dying words glanced through my memory as he spoke: "'Tis not so deep as a well, nor so wide as a church door, but 'tis enough." And John would have said the same could he have seen the ominous black holes between his shoulders, he never had; and, seeing the ghastly sights about him, could not believe his own wound more fatal than these, for all the suffering it caused him.

"Shall I write to your mother, now?" I asked, thinking that these sudden tidings might change all plans and purposes; but they did not; for the man received the order of the Divine Commander to march with the same unquestioning obedience with which the soldier had received that of the human one, doubtless remembering that the first led him to life, and the last to death.

"No, ma'am; to Laurie just the same; he'll break it to her best, and I'll add a line to her myself when you get done."

So I wrote the letter which he dictated, finding it better than any I had sent; for, though here and there a little ungrammatical or inelegant, each sentence came to me briefly worded, but most expressive; full of excellent counsel to the boy, tenderly bequeathing "mother and Lizzie" to his care, and bidding him good bye in words the sadder for their simplicity. He added a few lines, with steady hand, and, as I sealed it, said, with a patient sort of sigh, "I hope the answer will come in time for me to see it;" then, turning away his face, laid the flowers against his lips, as if to hide some quiver of emotion at the thought of such a sudden sundering of all the dear home ties.

These things had happened two days before; now John was dying, and the letter had not come. I had been summoned to many death beds in my life, but to none that made my heart ache as it did then, since my mother called me to watch the departure of a spirit akin to this in its gentleness and patient strength. As I went in, John stretched out both hands:

"I knew you'd come! I guess I'm moving on, ma'am."

He was; and so rapidly that, even while he spoke, over his face I saw the grey veil falling that no human hand can lift. I sat down by him, wiped the drops from his forehead, stirred the air about him with the slow wave of a fan, and waited to help him die. He stood in sore need of help — and I could do so little; for, as the doctor had foretold, the strong body rebelled against death, and fought every inch of the way, forcing him to draw each breath with a spasm, and clench his hands with an imploring look, as if he asked, "How long must I endure this, and be still!" For hours he suffered dumbly, without a moment's respite, or a moment's murmuring; his limbs grew cold, his face damp, his lips white, and, again and again, he tore the covering off his breast, as if the lightest weight added to his agony; yet through it all, his eyes never lost their perfect serenity, and the man's soul seemed to sit therein, undaunted by the ills that vexed his flesh.

One by one, the men woke, and round the room appeared a circle of pale faces and watchful eyes, full of awe and pity; for, though a stranger, John was beloved by all. Each man there had wondered at his patience, respected his piety, admired his fortitude, and now lamented his hard death; for the influence of an upright nature had made itself deeply felt, even in one little week. Presently, the Jonathan who so loved this comely David, came creeping from his bed for a last look and word. The kind soul was full of trouble, as the choke in his voice, the grasp of his hand, betrayed; but there were no tears, and the farewell of the friends was the more touching for its brevity.

"Old boy, how are you?" faltered the one.

"Most through, thank heaven!" whispered the other.

"Can I say or do anything for you anywheres?"

"Take my things home, and tell them that I did my best."

"I will! I will!"

"Good bye, Ned."

"Good bye, John, good bye!"

They kissed each other, tenderly as women, and so parted, for poor Ned could not stay to see his comrade die. For a little while, there was no sound in the room but the drip of water, from a stump or two, and John's distressful gasps, as he slowly breathed his life away. I thought him nearly gone, and had just laid down the fan, believing its help to be no longer needed, when suddenly he rose up in his bed, and cried out with a bitter cry that broke the silence, sharply startling every one with its agonized appeal:

"For God's sake, give me air!"

It was the only cry pain or death had wrung from him, the only boon he had asked; and none of us could grant it, for all the airs that blew were useless now. Dan flung up the window. The first red streak of dawn was warming the grey east, a herald of the coming sun; John saw it, and with the love of light which lingers in us to the end, seemed to read in it a sign of hope of help, for, over his whole face there broke that mysterious expression, brighter than any smile, which often comes to eyes that look their last. He laid himself gently down; and, stretching out his strong right arm, as if to grasp and bring the blessed air to his lips in a fuller flow, lapsed into a merciful unconsciousness, which assured us that for him suffering was forever past. He died then; for, though the heavy breaths still tore their way up for a little longer, they were but the waves of an ebbing tide that beat unfelt against the wreck, which an immortal voyager had deserted with a smile. He never spoke again, but to the end held my hand close, so close that when he was asleep at last, I could not draw it away. Dan helped me, warning me as he did so that it was unsafe for dead and living flesh to lie so long together; but though my hand was strangely cold and stiff, and four white marks remained across its back, even when warmth and color had returned elsewhere, I could not but be glad that, through its touch, the presence of human sympathy, perhaps, had lightened that hard hour.

When they had made him ready for the grave, John lay in state for half an hour, a thing which seldom happened in that busy place; but a universal sentiment of reverence and affection seemed to fill the hearts of all who had known or heard of him; and when the rumor of his death went through the house, always astir, many came to see him, and I felt a tender sort of pride in my lost patient; for he looked a most heroic figure, lying there stately and still as the statue of some young knight asleep upon his tomb. The lovely expression which so often beautifies dead faces, soon replaced the marks of pain, and I longed for those who loved him best to see him when half an hour's acquaintance with Death had made them friends. As we stood looking at him, the ward master handed me a letter, saying it had been forgotten the night before. It was John's letter, come just an hour too late to gladden the eyes that had longed and looked for it so eagerly: yet he had it; for, after I had cut some brown locks for his mother, and taken off the ring to send her, telling how well the talisman had done its work, I kissed this good son for her sake, and laid the letter in his hand, still folded as when I drew my own away, feeling that its place was there, and making myself happy with the thought, that, even in his solitary place in the "Government Lot," he would not be without some token of the love which makes life beautiful and outlives death. Then I left him, glad to have known so genuine a man, and carrying with me an enduring memory of the brave Virginia blacksmith, as he lay serenely waiting for the dawn of that long day which knows no night.

The Blue and the Gray

A Hospital Sketch

Putnam's Magazine, June 1868. Published anonymously

*D*ON'T BRING HIM in here; every corner is full — and I'm glad of it," added the nurse under her breath, eyeing with strong disfavor the gaunt figure lying on the stretcher in the doorway.

"Where *shall* we put him, then? They won't have him in either of the other wards on this floor. He's ordered up here, and here he must stay if he's put in the hall — poor devil!" said the foremost bearer, looking around the crowded room in despair.

The nurse's eye followed his, and both saw a thin hand beckoning from the end of the long ward.

"It's Murry; I'll see what he wants;" and Miss Mercy went to him with her quick, noiseless step, and the smile her grave face always wore for him.

"There's room here, if you turn my bed 'round, you see. Don't let them leave him in the hall," said Murry, lifting his great eyes to hers. Brilliant with the fever burning his strength away, and pathetic with the silent protest of life against death.

"It's like you to think of it; but he's a rebel," began Miss Mercy.

"So much more reason to take him in. I don't mind having him here; but it will distress me dreadfully to know that any poor soul was turned away, from the comfort of this ward especially."

The look he gave her made the words an eloquent compliment, and his pity for a fallen enemy reproached her for her own lack of it. Her face softened as she nodded, and glanced about the recess.

"You will have the light in your eyes, and only the little table between you and a very disagreeable neighbor," she said.

"I can shut my eyes if the light troubles them; I've nothing else to do now," he answered, with a faint laugh. "I was too comfortable before; I'd more than my share of luxuries; so bring him along, and it will be all right."

The order was given, and, after a brief bustle, the two narrow beds stood side by side in the recess under the organ-loft — for the hospital had been a church. Left alone for a moment, the two men eyed each other silently. Murry saw a tall, sallow man, with fierce black eyes, wild hair and beard, and a thin-lipped, cruel mouth. A ragged gray uniform was visible under the blanket thrown over him; and in strange contrast to the squalor of his dress, and the neglect of his person, was the diamond ring that shone on his unwounded hand. The right arm was bound up, the right leg amputated at the knee; and though the man's face was white and haggard with suffering, not a sound escaped him as he lay with his bold eyes fixed defiantly upon his neighbor.

John Clay, the new-comer, saw opposite him a small, wasted figure, and a plain face; yet both face and figure were singularly attractive, for suffering seemed to have refined away all the grosser elements, and left the spiritual very visible through that frail tenement of flesh. Pale-brown hair streaked the hollow temples and white forehead. A deep color burned in the thin cheeks still tanned by the wind and weather of a long campaign. The mouth was grave and sweet, and in the gray eyes lay an infinite patience touched with melancholy. He wore a dressing-gown, but across his feet lay a faded coat of army-blue. As the other watched him, he saw a shadow pass across his tranquil face, and for a moment he laid his wasted hand over the eyes that had been so full of pity. Then he gently pushed a mug of fresh water, and the last of a bunch of grapes, toward the exhausted rebel, saying, in a cordial tone,

"You look faint and thirsty; have 'em."

Clay's lips were parched, and his hand went involuntarily toward the cup; but he caught it back, and leaning forward, asked in a shrill whisper,

"Where are you hurt?"

"A shot in the side," answered Murry, visibly surprised at the man's manner.

"What battle?"

"The Wilderness."

"Is it bad?"

"I'm dying of wound-fever; there's no hope, they say."

That reply, so simple, so serenely given, would have touched almost any hearer; but Clay smiled grimly, and lay down as if satisfied, with his one hand clenched, and an exulting glitter in his eyes, muttering to himself,

"The loss of my leg comes easier after hearing that."

Murry saw his lips move, but caught no sound, and asked with friendly solicitude,

"Do you want any thing, neighbor?"

"Yes — to be let alone," was the curt reply, with a savage frown.

"That's easily done. I sha'n't trouble you very long, any way;" and, with a sigh, Murry turned his face away, and lay silent till the surgeon came up on his morning round.

"Oh, you're here, are you? It's like Mercy Carrol to take you in," said Dr. Fitz Hugh as he surveyed the rebel with a slight frown; for, in spite of his benevolence and skill, he was a stanch loyalist, and hated the South as he did sin.

"Don't praise me; he never would have been here but for Murry," answered Miss Mercy, as she approached with her dressing-tray in her hand.

"Bless the lad! he'll give up his bed next, and feel offended if he's thanked for it. How are you, my good fellow?" and the doctor turned to press the hot hand with a friendly face.

"Much easier and stronger, thank you, doctor," was the cheerful answer.

"Less fever, pulse better, breath freer — good symptoms. Keep on so for twenty-four hours, and by my soul, I believe you'll have a chance for your life, Murry," cried the doctor, as his experienced eye took note of a hopeful change.

"In spite of the opinion of three good surgeons to the contrary?" asked Murry, with a wistful smile.

"Hang every body's opinion! We are but mortal men, and the best of us make mistakes in spite of science and experience. There's Parker; we all gave him up, and the rascal is larking 'round Washington as well as ever to-day. While there's life, there's hope; so cheer up, my lad, and do your best for the little girl at home."

"Do you really think I may hope?" cried Murry, white with the joy of this unexpected reprieve.

"Hope is a capital medicine, and I prescribe it for a day at least. Don't build on this change too much, but if you are as well to-morrow as this morning, I give you my word I think you'll pull through."

Murry laid his hands over his face with a broken "Thank God for that!" and the doctor turned away with a sonorous "Hem!" and an air of intense satisfaction.

During this conversation Miss Mercy had been watching the rebel, who looked and listened to the others so intently that he forgot her presence. She saw an expression of rage and disappointment gather in his face as the doctor spoke; and when Murry accepted the hope held out to him, Clay set his teeth with an evil look, that would have boded ill for his neighbor had he not been helpless.

"Ungrateful traitor! I'll watch him, for he'll do mischief if he can," she thought, and reluctantly began to unbind his arm for the doctor's inspection.

"Only a flesh-wound — no bones broken — a good syringing, rubber cushion, plenty of water, and it will soon heal. You'll attend to that Miss Mercy; this stump is more in my line;" and Dr. Fitz Hugh turned to the leg, leaving the arm to the nurse's skilful care.

"Evidently amputated in a hurry, and neglected since. If you're not careful, young man, you'll change places with your neighbor here."

"Damn him!" muttered Clay in his beard, with an emphasis which caused the doctor to glance at his vengeful face.

"Don't be a brute, if you can help it. But for him, you'd have fared ill," began the doctor.

"But for him, I never should have been here," muttered the man in French, with a furtive glance about the room.

"You owe this to him?" asked the doctor, touching the wound, and speaking in the same tongue.

"Yes; but he paid for it — at least, I thought he had."

"By the Lord! if you are the sneaking rascal that shot him as he lay wounded in the ambulance, I shall be tempted to leave you to your fate!" cried the doctor, with a wrathful flash in his keen eyes.

"Do it, then, for it was I," answered the man defiantly; adding as if anxious to explain, "We had a tussle, and each got hurt in the thick of the skirmish. He was put in the ambulance afterward, and I was left to live or die, as luck would have it. I was hurt the worst; they should have taken me too; it made me mad to see him chosen, and I fired my last shot as he drove away. I didn't know whether I hit him or not; but when they told me I must lose my leg, I hoped I had, and now I am satisfied."

He spoke rapidly, with clenched hand and fiery eyes, and the two listeners watched him with a sort of fascination as he hissed out the last words, glancing at the occupant of the next bed. Murry evidently did not understand French; he lay with averted face, closed eyes, and a hopeful smile still on his lips, quite unconscious of the meaning of the fierce words uttered close beside him. Dr. Fitz Hugh had laid down his instruments and knit his black brows irefully while he listened. But as the man paused, the doctor looked at Miss Mercy, who was quietly going on with her work, though there was an expression about her handsome mouth that made her womanly face look almost grim. Taking up his tools, the doctor followed her example, saying slowly,

"If I didn't believe Murry was mending, I'd turn you over to Roberts, whom the patients dread as they do the devil. I must do my duty, and you may thank Murry for it."

"Does he know you are the man who shot him?" asked Mercy, still in French.

"No; I shouldn't stay here long if he did," answered Clay, with a short laugh.

"Don't tell him, then — at least, till after you are moved," she said, in a tone of command.

"Where am I going?" demanded the man.

"Anywhere out of my ward," was the brief answer, with a look that made the black eyes waver and fall.

In silence nurse and doctor did their work, and passed on. In silence Murry lay hour after hour, and silently did Clay watch and wait, till, utterly exhausted by the suffering he was too proud to confess, he sank into a stupor, oblivious alike of hatred, defeat, and pain. Finding him in this pitiable condition, Mercy relented, and, woman-like, forgot her contempt in pity. He was not moved, but tended carefully all that day and night; and when he woke from a heavy sleep, the morning sun shone again on two pale faces in the beds, and flashed on the buttons of two army-coats hanging side by side on the recess wall, on loyalist and rebel, on the blue and the gray.

Dr. Fitz Hugh stood beside Murry's cot, saying cheerily, "You are doing well, my lad — better than I hoped. Keep calm and cool, and, if all goes right, we'll have little Mary here to pet you in a week."

"Who's Mary?" whispered the rebel to the attendant who was washing his face.

"His sweetheart; he left her for the war, and she's waitin' for him back — poor soul!" answered the man, with a somewhat vicious scrub across the sallow cheek he was wiping.

"So he'll get well, and go home and marry the girl he left behind him, will he?" sneered Clay, fingering a little case that hung about his neck, and was now visible as his rough valet unbuttoned his collar.

"What's that — your sweetheart's picter?" asked Ben, the attendant, eyeing the gold chain anxiously.

"I've got none," was the gruff answer.

"So much the wus for you, then. Small chance of gettin' one here; our girls won't look at you, and you a'n't likely to see any of your own sort for a long spell, I reckon," added Ben, rasping away at the rebel's long-neglected hair.

Clay lay looking at Mercy Carrol as she went to and fro among the men, leaving a smile behind her, and carrying comfort wherever she turned, — a right womanly woman, lovely and lovable, strong yet tender, patient yet decided, skilful, kind, and tireless in the discharge of duties that would have daunted most women. It was in vain she wore the plain gray gown and long apron, for neither could hide the grace of her figure. It was in vain she brushed her luxuriant hair back into a net, for the wavy locks would fall on her forehead, and stray curls would creep out or glisten like gold under the meshes meant to conceal them. Busy days and watchful nights had not faded the beautiful bloom on her cheeks, or dimmed the brightness of her hazel eyes. Always ready, fresh, and fair, Mercy Carrol was regarded as the good angel of the hospital, and not a man in it, sick or well, but was a loyal friend to her. None dared to be a lover, for her little romance was known; and, though still a maid, she was a widow in their eyes, for she had sent her lover to his death, and over the brave man's grave had said, "Well done."

Ben watched Clay as his eye followed the one female figure there, and, observing that he clutched the case still tighter, asked again,

"What is that — a charm?"

"Yes — against pain, captivity, and shame."

"Strikes me it a'n't kep' you from any one of 'em," said Ben, with a laugh.

"I haven't tried it yet."

"How does it work?" Ben asked more respectfully, being impressed by something in the rebel's manner.

"You will see when I use it. Now let me alone;" and Clay turned impatiently away.

"You've got p'ison, or some deviltry, in that thing. If you don't let me look, I swear I'll have it took away from you;" and Ben put his big hand on the slender chain with a resolute air.

Clay smiled a scornful smile, and offered the trinket, saying coolly,

"I only fooled you. Look as much as you like; you'll find nothing dangerous."

Ben opened the pocket, saw a curl of gray hair, and nothing more.

"Is that your mother's?"

"Yes; my dead mother's."

It was strange to see the instantaneous change that passed over the two men as each uttered that dearest word in all tongues. Rough Ben gently reclosed and returned the case, saying kindly,

"Keep it; I wouldn't rob you on't for no money."

Clay thrust it jealously into his breast, and the first trace of emotion he had shown softened his dark face, as he answered, with a grateful tremor in his voice,

"Thank you. I wouldn't lose it for the world."

"May I say good morning, neighbor?" asked a feeble voice, as Murry turned a very wan but cheerful face toward him, when Ben moved on with his basin and towel.

"If you like," returned Clay, looking at him with those quick, suspicious eyes of his.

"Well, I do like; so I say it, and hope you are better," returned the cordial voice.

"Are you?"

"Yes, thank God!"

"Is it sure?"

"Nothing is sure, in a case like mine, till I'm on my legs again; but I'm certainly better. I don't expect *you* to be glad, but I hope you don't regret it very much."

"I don't." The smile that accompanied the words surprised Murry as much as the reply, for both seemed honest, and his kind heart warmed toward his suffering enemy.

"I hope you'll be exchanged as soon as you are able. Till then, you can go to one of the other hospitals, where there are many reb — I would say, Southerners. If you'd like, I'll speak to Dr. Fitz Hugh, and he'll see you moved," said Murry, in his friendly way.

"I'd rather stay here, thank you." Clay smiled again as he spoke in the mild tone that surprised Murry as much as it pleased him.

"You like to be in my corner, then?" he said, with a boyish laugh.

"Very much — for a while."

"I'm very glad. Do you suffer much?"

"I shall suffer more by and by, if I go on; but I'll risk it," answered Clay, fixing his feverish eyes on Murry's placid face.

"You expect to have a hard time with your leg?" said Murry, compassionately.

"With my soul."

It was an odd answer, and given with such an odd expression, as Clay turned his face away, that Murry said no more, fancying his brain a little touched by the fever evidently coming on.

They spoke but seldom to each other that day, for Clay lay apparently asleep, with a flushed cheek and restless head, and Murry tranquilly dreamed waking dreams of home and little Mary. That night, after all was still, Miss Mercy went up into the organ-loft to get fresh rollers for the morrow — the boxes of old linen, and such matters, being kept there. As she stood looking down on the thirty pale sleepers, she remembered that she had not played a hymn on the little organ for Murry, as she had promised that day. Stealing softly to the front, she peeped over the gallery, to see if he was asleep; if not, she would keep her word, for he was her favorite.

A screen had been drawn before the recess where the two beds stood, shutting their occupants from the sight of the other men. Murry lay sleeping, but Clay was awake, and a quick thrill tingled along the young woman's nerves as she saw his face. Leaning on one arm, he peered about the place with an eager, watchful air, and glanced up at the dark gallery, but did not see the startled face behind the central pillar. Pausing an instant, he shook his one clenched hand at the unconscious sleeper, and then drew out the locket cautiously. Two white mugs just alike stood on the little table between the beds, water in each. With another furtive glance about him, Clay suddenly stretched out his long arm, and dropped something from the locket into Murry's cup. An instant he remained motionless, with a sinister smile on his face; then, as Ben's step sounded beyond the screen, he threw his arm over his face, and lay, breathing heavily, as if asleep.

Mercy's first impulse was to cry out; her next, to fly down and seize the cup. No time was to be lost, for Murry might wake and drink at any moment. What was in the cup? Poison, doubtless; that was the charm Clay carried to free himself from "pain, captivity, and shame," when all other hopes of escape vanished. This hidden helper he gave up to destroy his enemy, who was to outlive his shot, it seemed. Like a shadow, Mercy glided down, forming her plan as she went. A dozen mugs stood about the room, all alike in size and color; catching up one, she partly filled it, and, concealing it under the clean sheet hanging on her arm, went toward the recess, saying audibly,

"I want some fresh water, Ben."

Thus warned of her approach, Clay lay with carefully-averted face as she came in, and never stirred as she bent over him, while she dexterously changed Murry's mug for the one she carried. Hiding the poisoned cup, she went away, saying aloud,

"Never mind the water, now, Ben. Murry is asleep, and so is Clay; they'll not need it yet."

Straight to Dr. Fitz Hugh's room she went, and gave the cup into his keeping, with the story of what she had seen. A man was dying, and there was no time to test the water then; but putting it carefully away, he promised to set her fears at rest in the morning. To quiet her impatience, Mercy went back to watch over Murry till day dawned. As she sat down, she caught the glimmer of a satisfied smile on Clay's lips, and looking into the cup she had left, she saw that it was empty.

"He is satisfied, for he thinks his horrible revenge is secure. Sleep in peace, my poor boy! you are safe while I am here."

As she thought this, she put her hand on the broad, pale forehead of the sleeper with a motherly caress, but started to feel how damp and cold it was. Looking nearer, she saw that a change had passed over Murry, for dark shadows showed about his sunken eyes, his once quiet breath was faint and fitful now, his hand deathly cold, and a chilly dampness had gathered on his face. She looked at her watch; it was past twelve, and her heart sunk within her, for she had so often seen that solemn change come over men's faces then, that the hour was doubly weird and woeful to her. Sending a message to Dr. Fitz Hugh, she waited anxiously, trying to believe that she deceived herself.

The doctor came at once, and a single look convinced him that he had left one death-bed for another.

"As I feared," he said; "that sudden rally was but a last effort of nature. There was just one chance for him, and he has missed it. Poor lad! I can do nothing; he'll sink rapidly, and go without pain."

"Can *I* do nothing?" asked Mercy, with dim eyes, as she held the cold hand close in both her own with tender pressure.

"Give him stimulants as long as he can swallow, and, if he's conscious, take any messages he may have. Poor Hall is dying hard, and I can help him; I'll come again in an hour and say good-by."

The kind doctor choked, touched the pale sleeper with a gentle caress, and went away to help Hall die.

Murry slept on for an hour, then woke, and knew without words that his brief hope was gone. He looked up wistfully, and whispered, as Mercy tried to smile with trembling lips that refused to tell the heavy truth.

"I know, I feel it; don't grieve yourself by trying to tell me, dear friend. It's best so; I can bear it, but I did want to live."

"Have you any word for Mary, dear?" asked Mercy, for he seemed but a boy to her since she had nursed him.

One look of sharp anguish and dark despair passed over his face, as he wrung his thin hands and shut his eyes, finding death terrible. It passed in a moment, and his pallid countenance grew beautiful with the pathetic patience of one who submits without complaint to the inevitable.

"Tell her I was ready, and the only bitterness was leaving her. I shall remember, and wait until she comes. My little Mary! oh, be kind to her, for my sake, when you tell her this."

"I will, Murry, as God hears me. I will be a sister to her while I live."

As Mercy spoke with fervent voice, he laid the hand that had ministered to him so faithfully against his cheek, and lay silent, as if content.

"What else? let me do something more. Is there no other friend to be comforted?"

"No; she is all I have in the world. I hoped to make her so happy, to be so much to her, for she's a lonely little thing; but God says 'No,' and I submit."

A long pause, as he lay breathing heavily, with eyes that were dimming fast fixed on the gentle face beside him.

"Give Ben my clothes; send Mary a bit of my hair, and — may I give you this? It's a poor thing, but all I have to leave you, best and kindest of women."

He tried to draw off a slender ring, but the strength had gone out of his wasted fingers, and she helped him, thanking him with the first tears he had seen her shed. He seemed satisfied, but suddenly turned his eyes on Clay, who lay as if asleep. A sigh broke from Murry, and Mercy caught the words,

"How could he do it, and I so helpless!"

"Do you know him?" she whispered, eagerly, as she remembered Clay's own words.

"I knew he was the man who shot me, when he came. I forgive him; but I wish he had spared me, for Mary's sake," he answered sorrowfully, not angrily.

"Can you really pardon him?" cried Mercy, wondering, yet touched by the words.

"I can. He will be sorry one day, perhaps; at any rate, he did what he thought his duty; and war makes brutes of us all sometimes, I fear. I'd like to say good-by; but he's asleep after a weary day, so don't wake him. Tell him I'm glad *he* is to live, and that I forgive him heartily."

Although uttered between long pauses, these words seemed to have exhausted Murry, and he spoke no more till Dr. Fitz Hugh came. To him he feebly returned thanks, and whispered his farewell — then sank into a stupor, during which life ebbed fast. Both nurse and doctor forgot Clay as they hung over Murry, and neither saw the strange intentness of his face, the half awe-struck, half remorseful look he bent upon the dying man.

As the sun rose, sending its ruddy beams across the silent ward, Murry looked up and smiled, for the bright ray fell athwart the two coats hanging on the wall beside him. Some passerby had brushed one sleeve of the blue coat across the gray, as if the inanimate things were shaking hands.

"It should be so — love our enemies; we should be brothers," he murmured faintly; and, with the last impulse of a noble nature, stretched his hand toward the man who had murdered him.

But Clay shrunk back, and covered his face without a word. When he ventured to look up, Murry was no longer there. A pale, peaceful figure lay on the narrow bed, and Mercy was smoothing the brown locks as she cut a curl for Mary and herself. Clay could not take his eyes away; as if fascinated by its serenity, he watched the dead face with gloomy eyes, till Mercy, having done her part, stooped and kissed the cold lips tenderly as she left him to his sleep. Then, as if afraid to be alone with the dead, he bid Ben put the screen between the beds, and bring him a book. His order was obeyed, but he never turned his pages, and lay with muffled head trying to shut out little Watts' sobs, as the wounded drummer-boy mourned for Murry.

Death, in a hospital, makes no stir, and in an hour no trace of the departed remained but the coat upon the wall, for Ben would not take it down, though it was his now. The empty bed stood freshly made, the clean cup and worn Bible lay ready for other hands, and the card at the bed's head hung blank for a new-comer's name. In the hurry of this event, Clay's attempted crime was forgotten for a time. But that evening Dr. Fitz Hugh told Mercy that her suspicions were correct, for the water *was* poisoned.

"How horrible! What shall we do?" she cried, with a gesture full of energetic indignation.

"Leave him to remorse," replied the doctor, sternly. "I've thought over the matter, and believe this to be the only thing we can do. I fancy the man won't live a week; his leg is in a bad way, and he is such a fiery devil, he gives himself no chance. Let him believe he killed poor Murry, at least for a few days. He thinks so now, and tries to rejoice; but if he has a human heart, he will repent."

"But he may not. Should we not tell of this? Can he not be punished?"

"Law won't hang a dying man, and I'll not denounce him. Let remorse punish him while he lives, and God judge him when he dies. Murry pardoned him; can we do less?"

Mercy's indignant face softened at the name, and for Murry's sake she yielded. Neither spoke of what they tried to think the act of a half-delirious man; and soon they could not refuse to pity him, for the doctor's prophecy proved true.

Clay was a haunted man, and remorse gnawed like a worm at his heart. Day and night he saw that tranquil face on the pillow opposite; day and night he saw the pale hand outstretched to him; day and night he heard the faint voice murmuring kindly, regretfully, "I forgive him; but I wish he had spared me, for Mary's sake."

As the days passed, and his strength visibly declined, he began to suspect that he must soon follow Murry. No one told him; for, though both doctor and nurse did their duty faithfully, neither lingered long at his bedside, and not one of the men showed any interest in him. No new patient occupied the other bed, and he lay alone in the recess with his own gloomy thoughts.

"It will be all up with me in a few days, won't it?" he asked abruptly, as Ben made his toilet one morning with unusual care, and such visible pity in his rough face that Clay could not but observe it.

"I heard the doctor say you wouldn't suffer much more. Is there any one you'd like to see, or leave a message for?" answered Ben, smoothing the long locks as gently as a woman.

"There isn't a soul in the world that cares whether I live or die, except the man who wants my money," said Clay, bitterly, as his dark face grew a shade paler at this confirmation of his fear.

"Can't you head him off some way, and leave your money to some one that's been kind to you? Here's the doctor — or, better still, Miss Carrol. Neither on 'em is rich, and both on 'em has been good friends to you, or you'd 'a' fared a deal wus than you have," said Ben, not without the hope that, in saying a good word for them, he might say one for himself also.

Clay lay thinking for a moment as his face clouded over, and then brightened again.

"Miss Mercy wouldn't take it, nor the doctor either; but I know who will, and by G—d, I'll do it!" he exclaimed, with sudden energy.

His eye happened to rest on Ben as he spoke, and, feeling sure that he was to be the heir, Ben retired to send Miss Mercy, that the matter might be settled before Clay's mood changed. Miss Carrol came, and began to cut the buttons off Murry's coat while she waited for Clay to speak.

"What's that for?" he asked, restlessly.

"The men want them, and Ben is willing, for the coat is very old and ragged, you see. Murry gave his good one away to a sicker comrade, and took this instead. It was like him — my poor boy!"

"I'd like to speak to you, if you have a minute to spare," began Clay, after a pause, during which he watched her with a wistful, almost tender expression unseen by her.

"I have time; what can I do for you?" Very gentle was Mercy's voice, very pitiful her glance, as she sat down by him, for the change in his manner, and the thought of his approaching death, touched her heart.

Trying to resume his former gruffness, and cold facial expression, Clay said, as he picked nervously at the blanket,

"I've a little property that I put into the care of a friend going North. He's kept it safe; and now, as I'll never want it myself, I'd like to leave it to —" He paused an instant, glanced quickly at Mercy's face, and seeing only womanly compassion there, added with an irrepressible tremble in his voice — "to little Mary."

If he had expected any reward for the act, any comfort for his lonely death-bed, he received both in fullest measure when he saw Mercy's beautiful face flush with surprise and pleasure, her eyes fill with sudden tears, and heard her cordial voice, as she pressed his hand warmly in her own.

"I wish I could tell you how glad I am for this! I thought you were better than you seemed; I was sure you had both heart and conscience, and that you would repent before you died."

"Repent of what?" he asked, with a startled look.

"Need I tell you?" and her eye went from the empty bed to his face.

"You mean that shot? But it was only fair, after all; we killed each other, and war is nothing but wholesale murder, any way." He spoke easily, but his eyes were full of trouble, and other words seemed to tremble on his lips.

Leaning nearer, Mercy whispered in his ear,

"I mean the other murder, which you would have committed when you poisoned the cup of water he offered you, his enemy."

Every vestige of color faded out of Clay's thin face, and his haggard eyes seemed fascinated by some spectre opposite, as he muttered slowly,

"How do you know?"

"I saw you;" and she told him all the truth.

A look of intense relief passed over Clay's countenance, and the remorseful shadow lifted as he murmured brokenly,

"Thank God, I didn't kill him! Now, dying isn't so hard; now I can have a little peace."

Neither spoke for several minutes; Mercy had no words for such a time, and Clay forgot her presence as the tears dropped from between the wasted fingers spread before his face.

Presently he looked up, saying eagerly, as if his fluttering breath and rapidly failing strength warned him of approaching death,

"Will you write down a few words for me, so Mary can have the money? She needn't know any thing about me, only that I was one to whom Murry was kind, and so I gave her all I had."

"I'll get my pen and paper; rest, now, my poor fellow," said Mercy, wiping the unheeded tears away for him.

"How good it seems to hear you speak so to *me!* How can you do it?" he whispered, with such grateful wonder in his dim eyes that Mercy's heart smote her for the past.

"I do it for Murry's sake, and because I sincerely pity you."

Timidly turning his lips to that kind hand, he kissed it, and then hid his face in his pillow. When Mercy returned, she observed that there were but seven tarnished buttons where she had left eight. She guessed who had taken it, but said nothing, and endeavored to render poor Clay's last hours as happy as sympathy and care could make them. The letter and will were prepared as well as they could be, and none too soon; for, as if that secret was the burden that bound Clay's spirit to the shattered body, no sooner was it lifted off, than the diviner part seemed ready to be gone.

"You'll stay with me; you'll help me die; and — oh, if I dared to ask it, I'd beg you to kiss me once when I am dead, as you did Murry. I think I could rest then, and be fitter to meet him, if the Lord lets me," he cried imploringly, as the last night gathered around him, and the coming change seemed awful to a soul that possessed no inward peace, and no firm hope to lean on through the valley of the shadow.

"I will — I will! Hold fast to me, and believe in the eternal mercy of God," whispered Miss Carrol, with her firm hand in his, her tender face bending over him as the long struggle began.

"Mercy," he murmured, catching that word, and smiling feebly as he repeated it lingeringly. "Mercy! yes, I believe in her; she'll save me, if any one can. Lord, bless and keep her forever and forever."

There was no morning sunshine to gladden his dim eyes as they looked their last, but the pale glimmer of the lamp shone full on the blue and the gray coats hanging side by side. As if the sight recalled that other death-bed, that last act of brotherly love and pardon, Clay rose up in his bed, and, while one hand clutched the button hidden in his breast, the other was outstretched toward the empty bed, as his last breath parted in a cry of remorseful longing,

"I will! I will! Forgive me, Murry, and let me say good-by!"

Experiments in the Novel

Dull, But Necessary

From *Moods*
(Boston: Loring, 1865; revised edition, Boston: Roberts Brothers, 1882)

WHOEVER CARES ONLY for incident and action in a book had better skip this chapter and read on; but those who take an interest in the delineation of character will find the key to Sylvia's here.

John Yule might have been a poet, painter, or philanthropist, for Heaven had endowed him with fine gifts; he was a prosperous merchant, with no ambition but to leave a fortune to his children and live down the memory of a bitter past. On the threshold of his life he stumbled and fell; for as he paused there, Providence tested and found him wanting. On one side Poverty offered the aspiring youth her meagre hand; but he was not wise enough to see the virtues hidden under her hard aspect, nor brave enough to learn the stern yet salutary lessons which labor, necessity, and patience teach, giving to those who serve and suffer the true success. On the other hand Opulence allured him with her many baits, and, silencing the voice of conscience, he yielded to temptation and wrecked his nobler self.

A loveless marriage was the price he paid for his ambition; not a costly one, he thought, till time taught him that whosoever mars the integrity of his own soul by transgressing the great laws of life, even by so much as a hair's breadth, entails upon himself and heirs the inevitable retribution which proves their worth and keeps them sacred. The tie that bound and burdened the unhappy twain, worn thin by constant friction, snapped at last, and in the solemn pause death made in his busy life, there rose before him those two ghosts who sooner or later haunt us all, saying with reproachful voices, "This I might have been" and "This I am." Then he saw the failure of his life. At fifty he found himself poorer than when he made his momentous choice; for the years that had given him wealth, position, children, had also taken from him youth, self-respect, and many a gift whose worth was magnified by loss. He endeavored to repair the fault so tardily acknowledged, but found it impossible to cancel it when remorse, imbittered effort, and age left him powerless to redeem the rich inheritance squandered in his prime.

If ever man received punishment for a self-inflicted wrong, it was John Yule, — a punishment as subtle as the sin; for in the children growing up about him every relinquished hope, neglected gift, lost aspiration, seemed to live again; yet on each and all was set the direful stamp of imperfection, which made them visible illustrations of the great law broken in his youth.

In Prudence, as she grew to womanhood, he saw his own practical tact and talent, nothing more. She seemed the living representative of the years spent in strife for profit, power, and place; the petty cares that fret the soul, the mercenary schemes that waste a life, the worldly formalities, frivolities, and fears, that so belittle character. All these he saw in this daughter's shape; and with pathetic patience bore the daily trial of an over-active, over-anxious, affectionate, but most prosaic child.

In Max he saw his ardor for the beautiful, his love of the poetic, his reverence for genius, virtue, heroism. But here too the subtle blight had fallen. This son, though strong in purpose, was feeble in performance; for some hidden spring of power was wanting, and the shadow of that earlier defeat chilled in his nature the energy which is the first attribute of all success. Max loved art, and gave himself to it; but, though studying all forms of beauty, he never reached its soul, and every effort tantalized him with fresh glimpses of the fair ideal which he could not reach. He loved the true, but high thoughts seldom blossomed into noble deeds; for when the hour came the man was never ready, and disappointment was his daily portion. A sad fate for the son, a far sadder one for the father who had bequeathed it to him from the irrecoverable past.

In Sylvia he saw, mysteriously blended, the two natures that had given her life, although she was born when the gulf between regretful husband and sad wife was widest. As if indignant Nature rebelled against the outrage done her holiest ties, adverse temperaments gifted the child with the good and ill of each. From her father she received pride, intellect, and will; from her mother passion, imagination, and the fateful melancholy of a woman defrauded of her dearest hope. These conflicting temperaments, with all their aspirations, attributes, and inconsistencies, were woven into a nature fair and faulty; ambitious, yet not self-reliant; sensitive, yet not keen-sighted. These two masters ruled soul and body, warring against each other, making Sylvia an enigma to herself and her life a train of moods.

A wise and tender mother would have divined her nameless needs, answered her vague desires, and through the medium of the most omnipotent affection given to humanity, have made her what she might have been. But Sylvia had never known mother-love, for her life came through death; and the only legacy bequeathed her was a ceaseless craving for affection, and the shadow of a tragedy that wrung from the pale lips, that grew cold against her baby cheek, the cry, "Free at last, thank God!"

Prudence could not fill the empty place, though the good-hearted housewife did her best. Neither sister understood the other, and each tormented the other through her very love. Prue unconsciously exasperated Sylvia, Sylvia unconsciously shocked Prue, and they hitched along together, each trying to do well, and each taking diametrically opposite measures to effect her purpose. Max briefly but truly described them when he said, "Sylvia trims the house with flowers, Prudence dogs her with a dustpan."

Mr. Yule was now a busy, silent man, who, having said one fatal "No" to himself, made it the satisfaction of his life to say a never varying "Yes" to his children. But though he left no wish of theirs ungratified, he seemed to have forfeited his power to draw and hold them to himself. He was more like an unobtrusive guest than a master in his house. His children loved, but never clung to him, because unseen, yet impassable, rose the barrier of an instinctive protest against the wrong done their dead mother, unconscious on their part but terribly significant to him.

Max had been years away, studying abroad; and though the brother and sister were tenderly attached, sex, tastes, and pursuits kept them too far apart, and Sylvia was solitary even in this social-seeming home. Dissatisfied with herself, she endeavored to make her life what it should be with the energy of an ardent, aspiring nature; and through all experiences, sweet or bitter, all varying moods, successes, and defeats, a sincere desire for happiness the best and highest was the little rushlight of her soul that never wavered or went out.

She had never known friendship in its truest sense, for next to love it is the most abused of words. She had called many "friend," but was still ignorant of that sentiment, cooler than passion, warmer than respect, more just and generous than either, which recognizes a kindred spirit in another, and, claiming its right, keeps it sacred by the wise reserve that is to friendship what the purple bloom is to the grape, a charm which once destroyed can never be restored. Love she dreaded, feeling that when it came its power would possess her wholly, and she had no wish to lose her freedom yet. Therefore she rejoiced over a more tranquil pleasure, and believed that she had found a friend in the neighbor who after long absence had returned to his old place.

Nature had done much for Geoffrey Moor, but the wise mother also gave him those teachers to whose hard lessons she often leaves her dearest children. Five years spent in the service of a sister, who through the sharp discipline of pain was fitting her meek soul for heaven, had given him an experience such as few young men receive. This fraternal devotion proved a blessing in disguise; it preserved him from any profanation of his youth, and the companionship of the helpless creature whom he loved had proved an ever present stimulant to all that was best and sweetest in the man. A single duty, faithfully performed, had set the seal of integrity upon his character, and given him grace to see at thirty the rich compensation he had received for the ambitions silently sacrificed at twenty-five. When his long vigil was over, he looked into the world to find his place again. But the old desires were dead, the old allurements had lost their charm, and while he waited for time to show him what good work he should espouse, no longing was so strong as that for a home, where he might bless and be blessed in writing that immortal poem, a virtuous and happy life.

Sylvia soon felt the power and beauty of this nature, and, remembering how well he had ministered to a physical affliction, often looked into the face whose serenity was a perpetual rebuke, longing to ask him to help and heal the mental ills that perplexed and burdened her. Moor soon divined the real isolation of the girl, read the language of her wistful eyes, felt that he could serve her, and invited confidence by the cordial alacrity with which he met her least advance.

But while he served, he learned to love her; for Sylvia, humble in her own conceit, and guarded by the innocence of an unspoiled youth, freely showed the regard she felt, with no thought of misapprehension, no fear of consequences, — unconscious that such impulsive demonstration made her only more attractive, that every manifestation of her frank esteem was cherished in her friend's heart of hearts, and that through her he was enjoying the blossom time of life. So, peacefully and pleasantly, the spring ripened into summer, and Sylvia's interest into an enduring friendship, full of satisfaction till a stronger influence came to waken and disturb her.

At Forty

From *Work: A Story of Experience* (Boston: Roberts Brothers, 1873)

NEARLY TWENTY YEARS since I set out to seek my fortune. It has been a long search, but I think I have found it at last. I only asked to be a useful, happy woman, and my wish is granted: for, I believe I *am* useful; I *know* I am happy."

Christie looked so as she sat alone in the flowery parlor one September afternoon, thinking over her life with a grateful, cheerful spirit. Forty to-day, and pausing at that half-way house between youth and age, she looked back into the past without bitter regret or unsubmissive grief, and forward into the future with courageous patience; for three good angels attended her, and with faith, hope, and charity to brighten life, no woman need lament lost youth or fear approaching age. Christie did not, and though her eyes filled with quiet tears as they were raised to the faded cap and sheathed sword hanging on the wall, none fell; and in a moment tender sorrow changed to still tenderer joy as her glance wandered to rosy little Ruth playing hospital with her dollies in the porch. Then they shone with genuine satisfaction as they went from the letters and papers on her table to the garden, where several young women were at work with a healthful color in the cheeks that had been very pale and thin in the spring.

"I think David is satisfied with me; for I have given all my heart and strength to his work, and it prospers well," she said to herself, and then her face grew thoughtful, as she recalled a late event which seemed to have opened a new field of labor for her if she chose to enter it.

A few evenings before she had gone to one of the many meetings of working-women, which had made some stir of late. Not a first visit, for she was much interested in the subject and full of sympathy for this class of workers.

There were speeches of course, and of the most unparliamentary sort, for the meeting was composed almost entirely of women, each eager to tell her special grievance or theory. Any one who chose got up and spoke; and whether wisely or foolishly each proved how great was the ferment now going on, and how difficult it was for the two classes to meet and help one another in spite of the utmost need on one side and the sincerest good-will on the other. The workers poured out their wrongs and hardships passionately or plaintively, demanding or imploring justice, sympathy, and help; displaying the ignorance, incapacity, and prejudice, which make their need all the more pitiful, their relief all the more imperative.

The ladies did their part with kindliness, patience, and often unconscious condescension, showing in their turn how little they knew of the real trials of the women whom they longed to serve, how very narrow a sphere of usefulness they were fitted for in spite of culture and intelligence, and how rich they were in generous theories, how poor in practical methods of relief.

One accomplished creature with learning radiating from every pore, delivered a charming little essay on the strong-minded women of antiquity; then, taking labor into the region of art, painted delightful pictures of the time when all would work harmoniously together in an Ideal Republic, where each did the task she liked, and was paid for it in liberty, equality, and fraternity.

Unfortunately she talked over the heads of her audience, and it was like telling fairy tales to hungry children to describe Aspasia discussing Greek politics with Pericles and Plato reposing upon ivory couches, or Hypatia modestly delivering philosophical lectures to young men behind a Tyrian purple curtain; and the Ideal Republic met with little favor from anxious seamstresses, type-setters, and shop-girls, who said ungratefully among themselves, "That's all very pretty, but I don't see how it's going to better wages among us *now*."

Another eloquent sister gave them a political oration which fired the revolutionary blood in their veins, and made them eager to rush to the State-house *en masse,* and demand the ballot before one-half of them were quite clear what it meant, and the other half were as unfit for it as any ignorant Patrick bribed with a dollar and a sup of whiskey.

A third well-wisher quenched their ardor like a wet blanket, by reading reports of sundry labor reforms in foreign parts; most interesting, but made entirely futile by differences of climate, needs, and customs. She closed with a cheerful budget of statistics, giving the exact number of needle-women who had starved, gone mad, or committed suicide during the past year; the enormous profits wrung by capitalists from the blood and muscles of their employés; and the alarming increase in the cost of living, which was about to plunge the nation into debt and famine, if not destruction generally.

When she sat down despair was visible on many countenances, and immediate starvation seemed to be waiting at the door to clutch them as they went out; for the impressible creatures believed every word and saw no salvation anywhere.

Christie had listened intently to all this; had admired, regretted, or condemned as each spoke; and felt a steadily increasing sympathy for all, and a strong desire to bring the helpers and the helped into truer relations with each other.

The dear ladies were so earnest, so hopeful, and so unpractically benevolent, that it grieved her to see so much breath wasted, so much good-will astray; while the expectant, despondent, or excited faces of the work-women touched her heart; for well she knew how much they needed help, how eager they were for light, how ready to be led if some one would only show a possible way.

As the statistical extinguisher retired, beaming with satisfaction at having added her mite to the good cause, a sudden and uncontrollable impulse moved Christie to rise in her place and ask leave to speak. It was readily granted, and a little stir of interest greeted her; for she was known to many as Mr. Power's friend, David Sterling's wife, or an army nurse who had done well. Whispers circulated quickly, and faces brightened as they turned toward her; for she had a helpful look, and her first words pleased them. When the president invited her to the platform she paused on the lowest step, saying with an expressive look and gesture:

"I am better here, thank you; for I have been and mean to be a working-woman all my life."

"Hear! hear!" cried a stout matron in a gay bonnet, and the rest indorsed the sentiment with a hearty round. Then they were very still, and then in a clear, steady voice, with the sympathetic undertone to it that is so magical in its effect, Christie made her first speech in public since she left the stage.

That early training stood her in good stead now, giving her self-possession, power of voice, and ease of gesture; while the purpose at her heart lent her the sort of simple eloquence that touches, persuades, and convinces better than logic, flattery, or oratory.

What she said she hardly knew: words came faster than she could utter them, thoughts pressed upon her, and all the lessons of her life rose vividly before her to give weight to her arguments, value to her counsel, and the force of truth to every sentence she uttered. She had known so many of the same trials, troubles, and temptations that she could speak understand-ingly of them; and, better still, she had conquered or outlived so many of them, that she could not only pity but help others to do as she had done. Having found in labor her best teacher, comforter, and friend, she could tell those who listened that, no matter how hard or humble the task at the beginning, if faithfully and bravely performed, it would surely prove a stepping-stone to something better, and with each honest effort they were fitting themselves for the nobler labor, and larger liberty God meant them to enjoy.

The women felt that this speaker was one of them; for the same lines were on her face that they saw on their own, her hands were no fine lady's hands, her dress plainer than some of theirs, her speech simple enough for all to understand; cheerful, comforting, and full of practical suggestion, illustrations out of their own experience, and a spirit of companionship that uplifted their despondent hearts.

Yet more impressive than any thing she said was the subtle magnetism of character, for that has a universal language which all can understand. They saw and felt that a genuine woman stood down there among them like a sister, ready with head, heart, and hand to help them help themselves; not offering pity as an alms, but justice as a right. Hardship and sorrow, long effort and late-won reward had been hers they knew; wifehood, motherhood, and widowhood brought her very near to them; and behind her was the background of an earnest life, against which this figure with health on the cheeks, hope in the eyes, courage on the lips, and the ardor of a wide benevolence warming the whole countenance stood out full of unconscious dignity and beauty; an example to comfort, touch, and inspire them.

It was not a long speech, and in it there was no learning, no statistics, and no politics; yet it was the speech of the evening, and when it was over no one else seemed to have any thing to say. As the meeting broke up Christie's hand was shaken by many roughened by the needle, stained with printer's ink, or hard with humbler toil; many faces smiled gratefully at her, and many voices thanked her heartily. But sweeter than any applause were the words of one woman who grasped her hand, and whispered with wet eyes:

"I knew your blessed husband; he was very good to me, and I've been thanking the Lord he had such a wife for his reward!"

Christie was thinking of all this as she sat alone that day, and asking herself if she should go on; for the ladies had been as grateful as the women; had begged her to come and speak again, saying they needed just such a mediator to bridge across the space that now divided them from those they wished to serve. She certainly seemed fitted to act as interpreter between the two classes; for, from the gentleman her father she had inherited the fine instincts, gracious manners, and unblemished name of an old and honorable race; from the farmer's daughter, her mother, came the equally valuable dower of practical virtues, a sturdy love of independence, and great respect for the skill and courage that can win it.

Such women were much needed and are not always easy to find; for even in democratic America the hand that earns its daily bread must wear some talent, name, or honor as an ornament, before it is very cordially shaken by those that wear white gloves.

"Perhaps this is the task my life has been fitting me for," she said. "A great and noble one which I should be proud to accept and help accomplish if I can. Others have finished the emancipation work and done it splendidly, even at the cost of all this blood and sorrow. I came too late to do any thing but give my husband and behold the glorious end. This new task seems to offer me the chance of being among the pioneers, to do the hard work, share the persecution, and help lay the foundation of a new emancipation whose happy success I may never see. Yet I had rather be remembered as those brave beginners are, though many of them missed the triumph, than as the late comers will be, who only beat the drums and wave the banners when the victory is won."

Just then the gate creaked on its hinges, a step sounded in the porch, and little Ruth ran in to say in an audible whisper:

"It's a lady, mamma, a very pretty lady: can you see her?"

"Yes, dear, ask her in."

There was a rustle of sweeping silks through the narrow hall, a vision of a very lovely woman in the door-way, and two daintily gloved hands were extended as an eager voice asked: "Dearest Christie, don't you remember Bella Carrol?"

Christie did remember, and had her in her arms directly, utterly regardless of the imminent destruction of a marvellous hat, or the bad effect of tears on violet ribbons. Presently they were sitting close together, talking with April faces, and telling their stories as women must when they meet after the lapse of years. A few letters had passed between them, but Bella had been abroad, and Christie too busy living her life to have much time to write about it.

"Your mother, Bella? how is she, and where?"

"Still with Augustine, and he you know is melancholy mad: very quiet, very patient, and very kind to every one but himself. His penances for the sins of his race would soon kill him if mother was not there to watch over him. And her penance is never to leave him."

"Dear child, don't tell me any more; it is too sad. Talk of yourself and Harry. Now you smile, so I'm sure all is well with him."

"Yes, thank heaven! Christie, I do believe fate means to spare us as dear old Dr. Shirley said. I never can be gay again, but I keep as cheerful and busy as I can, for Harry's sake, and he does the same for mine. We shall always be together, and all in all to one another, for we can never marry and have homes apart you know. We have wandered over the face of the earth for several years, and now we mean to settle down and be as happy and as useful as we can."

"That's brave! I am so glad to hear it, and so truly thankful it is possible. But tell me, Bella, what Harry means to do? You spoke in one of your first letters of his being hard at work studying medicine. Is that to be his profession?"

"Yes; I don't know what made him choose it, unless it was the hope that he might spare other families from a curse like ours, or lighten it if it came. After Helen's death he was a changed creature; no longer a wild boy, but a man. I told him what you said to me, and it gave him hope. Dr. Shirley confirmed it as far as he dared; and Hal resolved to make the most of his one chance by interesting himself in some absorbing study, and leaving no room for fear, no time for dangerous recollections. I was so glad, and mother so comforted, for we both feared that sad trouble would destroy him. He studied hard, got on splendidly, and then went abroad to finish off. I went with him; for poor August was past hope, and mamma would not let me help her. The doctor said it was best for me to be away, and excellent for Hal to have me with him, to cheer him up, and keep him steady with a little responsibility. We have been happy together in spite of our trouble, he in his profession, and I in him; now he is ready, so we have come home, and now the hardest part begins for me."

"How, Bella?"

"He has his work and loves it: I have nothing after my duty to him is done. I find I've lost my taste for the old pleasures and pursuits, and though I have tried more sober, solid ones, there still remains much time to hang heavy on my hands, and such an empty place in my heart, that even Harry's love cannot fill it. I'm afraid I shall get melancholy, — that is the beginning of the end for us, you know."

As Bella spoke the light died out of her eyes, and they grew despairing with the gloom of a tragic memory. Christie drew the beautiful, pathetic face down upon her bosom, longing to comfort, yet feeling very powerless to lighten Bella's burden.

But Christie's little daughter did it for her. Ruth had been standing near regarding the "pretty lady," with as much wonder and admiration as if she thought her a fairy princess, who might vanish before she got a good look at her. Divining with a child's quick instinct that the princess was in trouble, Ruth flew into the porch, caught up her latest and dearest treasure, and presented it as a sure consolation, with such sweet good-will, that Bella could not refuse, although it was only a fuzzy caterpillar in a little box.

"I give it to you because it is my nicest one and just ready to spin up. Do you like pussy-pillars, and know how they do it?" asked Ruth, emboldened by the kiss she got in return for her offering.

"Tell me all about it, darling," and Bella could not help smiling, as the child fixed her great eyes upon her, and told her little story with such earnestness, that she was breathless by the time she ended.

"At first they are only grubs you know, and stay down in the earth; then they are like this, nice and downy and humpy, when they walk; and when it's time they spin up and go to sleep. It's all dark in their little beds, and they don't know what may happen to 'em; but they are not afraid 'cause God takes care of 'em. So they wait and don't fret, and when it's right for 'em they come out splendid butterflies, all beautiful and shining like your gown. They are happy then, and fly away to eat honey, and live in the air, and never be creeping worms any more."

"That's a pretty lesson for me," said Bella softly, "I accept and thank you for it, little teacher; I'll try to be a patient 'pussy-pillar' though it *is* dark, and I don't know what may happen to me; and I'll wait hopefully till it's time to float away a happy butterfly."

"Go and get the friend some flowers, the gayest and sweetest you can find, Pansy," said Christie, and, as the child ran off, she added to her friend:

"Now we must think of something pleasant for you to do. It may take a little time, but I know we shall find your niche if we give our minds to it."

"That's one reason why I came. I heard some friends of mine talking about you yesterday, and they seemed to think you were equal to any thing in the way of good works. Charity is the usual refuge for people like me, so I wish to try it. I don't mind doing or seeing sad or disagreeable things, if it only fills up my life and helps me to forget."

"You will help more by giving of your abundance to those who know how to dispense it wisely, than by trying to do it yourself, my dear. I never advise pretty creatures like you to tuck up their silk gowns and go down into the sloughs with alms for the poor, who don't like it any better than you do, and so much pity and money are wasted in sentimental charity."

"Then what shall I do?"

"If you choose you can find plenty of work in your own class; for, if you will allow me to say it, they need help quite as much as the paupers, though in a very different way."

"Oh, you mean I'm to be strong-minded, to cry aloud and spare not, to denounce their iniquities, and demand their money or their lives?"

"Now, Bella, that's personal; for I made my first speech a night or two ago."

"I know you did, and I wish I'd heard it. I'd make mine to-night if I could do it half as well as I'm told you did," interrupted Bella, clapping her hands with a face full of approval.

But Christie was in earnest, and produced her new project with all speed.

"I want you to try a little experiment for me, and if it succeeds you shall have all the glory; I've been waiting for some one to undertake it, and I fancy you are the woman. Not every one could attempt it; for it needs wealth and position, beauty and accomplishments, much tact, and more than all a heart that has not been spoilt by the world, but taught through sorrow how to value and use life well."

"Christie, what is it? this experiment that needs so much, and yet which you think me capable of trying?" asked Bella, interested and flattered by this opening.

"I want you to set a new fashion: you know you can set almost any you choose in your own circle; for people are very like sheep, and will follow their leader if it happens to be one they fancy. I don't ask you to be a De Staël, and have a brilliant *salon:* I only want you to provide employment and pleasure for others like yourself, who now are dying of frivolity or *ennui.*"

"I should love to do that if I could. Tell me how."

"Well, dear, I want you to make Harry's home as beautiful and attractive as you can; to keep all the elegance and refinement of former times, and to add to it a new charm by setting the fashion of common sense. Invite all the old friends, and as many new ones as you choose; but have it understood that they are to come as intelligent men and women, not as pleasure-hunting beaux and belles; give them conversation instead of gossip; less food for the body and more for the mind; the healthy stimulus of the nobler pleasures they can command, instead of the harmful excitements of present dissipation. In short, show them the sort of society we need more of, and might so easily have if those who possess the means of culture cared for the best sort, and took pride in acquiring it. Do you understand, Bella?"

"Yes, but it's a great undertaking, and you could do it better than I."

"Bless you, no! I haven't a single qualification for it but the will to have it done. I'm 'strong-minded,' a radical, and a reformer. I've done all sorts of dreadful things to get my living, and I have neither youth, beauty, talent, or position to back me up; so I should only be politely ignored if I tried the experiment myself. I don't want you to break out and announce your purpose with a flourish; or try to reform society at large, but I *do* want you to devote yourself and your advantages to quietly insinuating a better state of things into one little circle. The very fact of your own want, your own weariness, proves how much such a reform is needed. There are so many fine young women longing for something to fill up the empty places that come when the first flush of youth is over, and the serious side of life appears; so many promising young men learning to conceal or condemn the high ideals and the noble purposes they started with, because they find no welcome for them. You might help both by simply creating a purer atmosphere for them to breathe, sunshine to foster instead of frost to nip their good aspirations, and so, even if you planted no seed, you might encourage a timid sprout or two that would one day be a lovely flower or a grand tree all would admire and enjoy."

As Christie ended with the figure suggested by her favorite work, Bella said after a thoughtful pause:

"But few of the women I know can talk about any thing but servants, dress, and gossip. Here and there one knows something of music, art, or literature; but the superior ones are not favorites with the larger class of gentlemen."

"Then let the superior women cultivate the smaller class of men who do admire intelligence as well as beauty. There are plenty of them, and you had better introduce a few as samples, though their coats may not be of the finest broadcloth, nor their fathers 'solid men.' Women lead in society, and when men find that they can not only dress with taste, but talk with sense, the lords of creation will be glad to drop mere twaddle and converse as with their equals. Bless my heart!" cried Christie, walking about the room as if she had mounted her hobby, and was off for a canter, "how people can go on in such an idiotic fashion passes my understanding. Why keep up an endless clatter about gowns and dinners, your neighbors' affairs, and your own aches, when there is a world full of grand questions to settle, lovely things to see, wise things to study, and noble things to imitate. Bella, you *must* try the experiment, and be the queen of a better society than any you can reign over now."

"It looks inviting, and I *will* try it with you to help me. I know Harry would like it, and I'll get him to recommend it to his patients. If he is as successful here as elsewhere they will swallow any dose he orders; for he knows how to manage people wonderfully well. He prescribed a silk dress to a despondent, dowdy patient once, telling her the electricity of silk was good for her nerves: she obeyed, and when well dressed felt so much better that she bestirred herself generally and recovered; but to this day she sings the praises of Dr. Carrol's electric cure."

Bella was laughing gaily as she spoke, and so was Christie as she replied:

"That's just what I want you to do with *your* patients. Dress up their minds in their best; get them out into the air; and cure their ills by the magnetism of more active, earnest lives."

They talked over the new plan with increasing interest; for Christie did not mean that Bella should be one of the brilliant women who shine for a little while, and then go out like a firework. And Bella felt as if she had found something to do in her own sphere, a sort of charity she was fitted for, and with it a pleasant sense of power to give it zest.

When Letty and her mother came in, they found a much happier looking guest than the one Christie had welcomed an hour before. Scarcely had she introduced them when voices in the lane made all look up to see old Hepsey and Mrs. Wilkins approaching.

"Two more of my dear friends, Bella: a fugitive slave and a laundress. One has saved scores of her own people, and is my pet heroine. The other has the bravest, cheeriest soul I know, and is my private oracle."

The words were hardly out of Christie's mouth when in they came; Hepsey's black face shining with affection, and Mrs. Wilkins as usual running over with kind words.

"My dear creeter, the best of wishes and no end of happy birthdays. There's a triflin' keepsake; tuck it away, and look at it byme by. Mis' Sterlin', I'm proper glad to see you lookin' so well. Aunt Letty, how's that darlin' child? I ain't the pleasure of your acquaintance, Miss, but I'm pleased to see you. The children all sent love, likewise Lisha, whose bones is better sense I tried the camfire and red flannel."

Then they settled down like a flock of birds of various plumage and power of song, but all amicably disposed, and ready to peck socially at any topic which might turn up.

Mrs. Wilkins started one by exclaiming as she "laid off" her bonnet:

"Sakes alive, there's a new picter! Ain't it beautiful?"

"Colonel Fletcher brought it this morning. A great artist painted it for him, and he gave it to me in a way that added much to its value," answered Christie, with both gratitude and affection in her face; for she was a woman who could change a lover to a friend, and keep him all her life.

It was a quaint and lovely picture of Mr. Greatheart, leading the fu-

gitives from the City of Destruction. A dark wood lay behind; a wide river
rolled before; Mercy and Christiana pressed close to their faithful guide,
who went down the rough and narrow path bearing a cross-hilted sword
in his right hand, and holding a sleeping baby with the left. The sun was
just rising, and a long ray made a bright path athwart the river, turned
Greatheart's dinted armor to gold, and shone into the brave and tender face
that seemed to look beyond the sunrise.

"There's just a hint of Davy in it that is very comforting to me," said
Mrs. Sterling, as she laid her old hands softly together, and looked up with
her devout eyes full of love.

"Dem women oughter bin black," murmured Hepsey, tearfully; for
she considered David worthy of a place with old John Brown and Colonel
Shaw.

"The child looks like Pansy, we all think," added Letty, as the little
girl brought her nosegay for Aunty to tie up prettily.

Christie said nothing, because she felt too much; and Bella was also
silent because she knew too little. But Mrs. Wilkins with her kindly tact
changed the subject before it grew painful, and asked with sudden interest:

"When be you a goin' to hold forth agin, Christie? Jest let me know
beforehand, and I'll wear my old gloves: I tore my best ones all to rags
clappin' of you; it was so extra good."

"I don't deserve any credit for the speech, because it spoke itself, and
I couldn't help it. I had no thought of such a thing till it came over me all
at once, and I was up before I knew it. I'm truly glad you liked it, but I
shall never make another, unless you think I'd better. You know I always
ask your advice, and what is more remarkable usually take it," said Christie, glad to consult her oracle.

"Hadn't you better rest a little before you begin any new task, my
daughter? You have done so much these last years you must be tired,"
interrupted Mrs. Sterling, with a look of tender anxiety.

"You know I work for two, mother," answered Christie, with the
clear, sweet expression her face always wore when she spoke of David. "I
am not tired yet: I hope I never shall be, for without my work I should
fall into despair or *ennui*. There is so much to be done, and it is so delightful
to help do it, that I never mean to fold my hands till they are useless.
I owe all I can do, for in labor, and the efforts and experiences that
grew out of it, I have found independence, education, happiness, and
religion."

"Then, my dear, you are ready to help other folks into the same
blessed state, and it's your duty to do it!" cried Mrs. Wilkins, her keen
eyes full of sympathy and commendation as they rested on Christie's cheer-

ful, earnest face. "Ef the sperrit moves you to speak, up and do it without no misgivin's. *I* think it was a special leadin' that night, and I hope you'll foller, for it ain't every one that can make folks laugh and cry with a few plain words that go right to a body's heart and stop there real comfortable and fillin'. I guess this is your next job, my dear, and you'd better ketch hold and give it the right turn; for it's goin' to take time, and women ain't stood alone for so long they'll need a sight of boostin'."

There was a general laugh at the close of Mrs. Wilkins's remarks; but Christie answered seriously: "I accept the task, and will do my share faithfully with words or work, as shall seem best. We all need much preparation for the good time that is coming to us, and can get it best by trying to know and help, love and educate one another, — as we do here."

With an impulsive gesture Christie stretched her hands to the friends about her, and with one accord they laid theirs on hers, a loving league of sisters, old and young, black and white, rich and poor, each ready to do her part to hasten the coming of the happy end.

"Me too!" cried little Ruth, and spread her chubby hand above the rest: a hopeful omen, seeming to promise that the coming generation of women will not only receive but deserve their liberty, by learning that the greatest of God's gifts to us is the privilege of sharing His great work.

A Modern Mephistopheles

From *A Modern Mephistopheles* (Boston: Roberts Brothers, 1877).
Published anonymously

I

WITHOUT, A MIDWINTER twilight, where wandering snowflakes eddied in the bitter wind between a leaden sky and frost-bound earth.

Within, a garret; gloomy, bare, and cold as the bleak night coming down.

★   ★   ★

A haggard youth knelt before a little furnace, kindling a fire, with an expression of quiet desperation on his face, which made the simple operation strange and solemn.

A pile of manuscript lay beside him, and in the hollow eyes that watched the white leaves burn was a tragic shadow, terrible to see, — for he was offering the first-born of heart and brain as sacrifice to a hard fate.

Slowly the charcoal caught and kindled, while a light smoke filled the room. Slowly the youth staggered up, and, gathering the torn sheets, thrust them into his bosom, muttering bitterly, "Of all my hopes and dreams, my weary work and patient waiting, nothing is left but this. Poor little book, we'll go together, and leave no trace behind."

Throwing himself into a chair, he laid his head down upon the table, where no food had been for days, and, closing his eyes, waited in stern silence for death to come and take him.

Nothing broke the stillness but the soft crackle of the fire, which began to flicker with blue tongues of flame, and cast a lurid glow upon the motionless figure with its hidden face. Deeper grew the wintry gloom without, ruddier shone the fateful gleam within, and heavy breaths began to heave the breast so tired of life.

Suddenly a step sounded on the stair, a hand knocked at the door, and when no answer came, a voice cried, "Open!" in a commanding tone, which won instant obedience, and dispelled the deathful trance fast benumbing every sense.

"The devil!" ejaculated the same imperious voice, as the door swung open, letting a cloud of noxious vapor rush out to greet the new-comer, — a man standing tall and dark against the outer gloom.

"Who is it? Oh! come in!" gasped the youth, falling back faint and dizzy, as the fresh air smote him in the face.

"I cannot, till you make it safe for me to enter. I beg pardon if I interrupt your suicide; I came to help you live, but if you prefer the other thing, say so, and I will take myself away again," said the stranger, pausing on the threshold, as his quick eye took in the meaning of the scene before him.

"For God's sake, stay!" and, rushing to the window, the youth broke it with a blow, caught up the furnace, and set it out upon the snowy roof, where it hissed and glowed like an evil thing, while he dragged forth his one chair, and waited, trembling, for his unknown guest to enter.

"For my own sake, rather: I want excitement; and this looks as if I might find it here," muttered the man with a short laugh, as he watched the boy, calmly curious, till a gust of fresh air swept through the room, making him shiver with its sharp breath.

"Jasper Helwyze, at your service," he added aloud, stepping in, and accepting courteously the only hospitality his poor young host could offer.

The dim light and shrouding cloak showed nothing but a pale, keen face, with dark penetrating eyes, and a thin hand, holding a paper on which the youth recognized the familiar words, "Felix Canaris."

"My name! You came to help me? What good angel sent you, sir?" he exclaimed, with a thrill of hope, — for in the voice, the eye, the hand that held the card with such tenacious touch, he saw and felt the influence of a stronger nature, and involuntarily believed in and clung to it.

"Your bad angel, you might say, since it was the man who damned your book and refused the aid you asked of him," returned the stranger, in a suave tone, which contrasted curiously with the vigor of his language. "A mere chance led me there to-day, and my eye fell upon a letter lying open before him. The peculiar hand attracted me, and Forsythe, being in the midst of your farewell denunciation, read it out, and told your story."

"And you were laughing at my misery while I was making ready to end it?" said the youth, with a scornful quiver of the sensitive lips that uttered the reproach.

"We all laugh at such passionate folly when we have outlived it. You will, a year hence; so bear no malice, but tell me briefly if you can forget poetry, and be content with prose for a time. In plain words, can you work instead of dream?"

"I can."

"Good! then come to me for a month. I have been long from home, and my library is neglected; I have much for you to do, and believe you are the person I want, if Forsythe tells the truth. He says your father was a Greek, your mother English, both dead, and you an accomplished, ambitious young man who thinks himself a genius, and will not forgive the world for doubting what he has failed to prove. Am I right?"

"Quite right. Add also that I am friendless, penniless, and hopeless at nineteen."

A brief, pathetic story, more eloquently told by the starvation written on the pinched face, the squalor of the scanty garments, and the despair in the desperate eye, than by the words uttered with almost defiant bluntness.

The stranger read the little tragedy at a glance, and found the chief actor to his taste; for despite his hard case he possessed beauty, youth, and the high aspirations that die hard, — three gifts often peculiarly attractive to those who have lost them all.

"Wait a month, and you may find that you have earned friends, money, and the right to hope again. At nineteen, one should have courage to face the world, and master it."

"Show me how, and I *will* have courage. A word of sympathy has already made it possible to live!" and, seizing the hand that offered help, Canaris kissed it with the impulsive grace and ardor of his father's race.

"When can you come to me?" briefly demanded Helwyze, gathering his cloak about him as he rose, warned by the waning light.

"At once, to-night, if you will! I possess nothing in the world but the poor clothes that were to have been my shroud, and the relics of the book with which I kindled my last fire," answered the youth, with eager eyes, and an involuntary shiver as the bitter wind blew in from the broken window.

"Come, then, else a mightier master than I may claim you before dawn, for it will be an awful night. Put out your funeral pyre, Canaris, wrap your shroud well about you, gather up your relics, and follow me. I can at least give you a warmer welcome than I have received," added Helwyze, with that sardonic laugh of his, as he left the room.

Before he had groped his slow way down the long stairs the youth joined him, and side by side they went out into the night.

A month later the same pair sat together in a room that was a dream of luxury. A noble library, secluded, warm, and still; the reposeful atmosphere that students love pervaded it; rare books lined its lofty walls: poets and philosophers looked down upon their work with immortal satisfaction on their marble countenances; and the two living occupants well became their sumptuous surroundings.

Helwyze leaned in a great chair beside a table strewn with books which curiously betrayed the bent of a strong mind made morbid by physical suffering. Doré's "Dante" spread its awful pages before him; the old Greek tragedies were scattered about, and Goethe's "Faust" was in his hand. An unimpressive figure at first sight, this frail-looking man, whose age it would be hard to tell; for pain plays strange pranks, and sometimes preserves to manhood a youthful delicacy in return for the vigor it destroys. But at a second glance the eye was arrested and interest aroused, for an indefinable expression of power pervaded the whole face, beardless, thin-lipped, sharply cut, and colorless as ivory. A stray lock or two of dark hair streaked the high brow, and below shone the controlling feature of this singular countenance, a pair of eyes, intensely black, and so large they seemed to burden the thin face. Violet shadows encircled them, telling of sleepless nights, days of languor, and long years of suffering, borne with stern patience. But in the eyes themselves all the vitality of the man's indomitable spirit seemed concentrated, intense and brilliant as a flame, which nothing could quench. By turns melancholy, meditative, piercing, or contemptuous, they varied in expression with startling rapidity, unless mastered by an art stronger than nature; attracting or repelling with a magnetism few wills could resist.

Propping his great forehead on his hand, he read, motionless as a statue, till a restless movement made him glance up at his companion, and fall to studying him with a silent scrutiny which in another would have softened to admiration, for Canaris was scarcely less beautiful than the Narcissus in the niche behind him.

An utter contrast to his patron, for youth lent its vigor to the well-knit frame, every limb of which was so perfectly proportioned that strength and grace were most harmoniously blended. Health glowed in the rich coloring of the classically moulded face, and lurked in the luxuriant locks which clustered in glossy rings from the low brow to the white throat. Happiness shone in the large dreamy eyes and smiled on the voluptuous lips; while an indescribable expression of fire and force pervaded the whole, redeeming its beauty from effeminacy.

A gracious miracle had been wrought in that month, for the haggard youth was changed into a wonderfully attractive young man, whose natural ease and elegance fitted him to adorn that charming place, as well as to enjoy the luxury his pleasure-loving senses craved.

The pen had fallen from his hand, and lying back in his chair with eyes fixed on vacancy, he seemed dreaming dreams born of the unexpected prosperity which grew more precious with each hour of its possession.

"Youth surely *is* the beauty of the devil, and that boy might have come straight from the witches' kitchen and the magic draught," thought Helwyze, as he closed his book, adding to himself with a daring expression, "Of all the visions haunting his ambitious brain not one is so wild and wayward as the fancy which haunts mine. Why not play fate, and finish what I have begun?"

A pause fell, more momentous than either dreamed; then it was abruptly broken.

"Felix, the time is up."

"It is, sir. Am I to go or stay?" and Canaris rose, looking half-bewildered as his brilliant castles in the air dissolved like mist before a sudden gust.

"Stay, if you will; but it is a quiet life for such as you, and I am a dull companion. Could you bear it for a year?"

"For twenty! Sir, you have been most kind and generous, and this month has seemed like heaven, after the bitter want you took me from. Let me show gratitude by faithful service, if I can," exclaimed the young man, coming to stand before his master, as he chose to call his benefactor, for favors were no burden yet.

"No thanks, I do it for my own pleasure. It is not every one who can have antique beauty in flesh and blood as well as marble; I have a fancy to keep my handsome secretary as the one ornament my library lacked before."

Canaris reddened like a girl, and gave a disdainful shrug; but vanity was tickled, nevertheless, and he betrayed it by the sidelong glance he stole towards the polished doors of glass reflecting his figure like a mirror.

"Nay, never frown and blush, man; 'beauty is its own excuse for being,' and you may thank the gods for yours, since but for that I should send you away to fight your dragons single-handed," said Helwyze, with a covert smile, adding, as he leaned forward to read the face which could wear no mask for him, "Come, you shall give me a year of your liberty, and I will help you to prove Forsythe a liar."

"You will bring out my book?" cried Canaris, clasping his hands as a flash of joy irradiated every lineament.

"Why not? and satisfy the hunger that torments you, though you try to hide it. I cannot promise success, but I *can* promise a fair trial; and if you stand the test, fame and fortune will come together. Love and happiness you can seek for at your own good pleasure."

"You have divined my longing. I do hunger and thirst for fame; I dream of it by night, I sigh for it by day; every thought and aspiration centres in that desire; and if I did not still cling to that hope, even the perfect home you offer me would seem a prison. I *must* have it; the success men covet and admire, suffer and strive for, and die content if they win it only for a little time. Give me this and I am yours, body and soul; I have nothing else to offer."

Canaris spoke with passionate energy, and flung out his hand as if he cast himself at the other's feet, a thing of little worth compared to the tempting prize for which he lusted.

Helwyze took the hand in a light, cold clasp, that tightened slowly as he answered with the look of one before whose will all obstacles go down, —

"Done! Now show me the book and let us see if we cannot win this time."

XII

Olivia came before the swallows; for the three words, "I miss you," would have brought her from the ends of the earth, had she exiled herself so far. She had waited for him to want and call her, as he often did when others wearied or failed him. Seldom had so long a time passed without some word from him; and endless doubts, fears, conjectures, had harassed her, as month after month went by, and no summons came. Now she hastened, ready for any thing he might ask of her, since her reward would be a glimpse of the only heaven she knew.

"Amuse Felix: he is falling in love with his wife, and it spoils both of them for my use. He says he has forgotten you. Come often, and teach him to remember, as penalty for his bad taste and manners," was the single order Helwyze gave; but Olivia needed no other; and, for the sake of coming often, would have smiled upon a far less agreeable man than Canaris.

Gladys tried to welcome the new guest cordially, as an unsuspicious dove might have welcomed a falcon to its peaceful cote; but her heart sunk when she found her happy quiet sorely disturbed, her husband's place deserted, and the old glamour slowly returning to separate them, in spite of all her gentle arts. For Canaris, feeling quite safe in the sincere affection which now bound him to his wife, was foolhardy in his desire to show Olivia how heart-whole he had become. This piqued her irresistibly, because Helwyze was looking on, and she would win *his* approval at any cost. So these three, from divers motives, joined together to teach poor Gladys how much a woman can suffer with silent fortitude and make no sign.

The weeks that followed seemed unusually gay and sunny ones; for April came in blandly, and Olivia made a pleasant stir throughout the house by her frequent visits, and the various excursions she proposed. Many of these Gladys escaped; for her pain was not the jealousy that would drive her to out-rival her rival, but the sorrowful shame and pity which made her long to hide herself, till Felix should come back and be forgiven. Helwyze naturally declined the long drives, the exhilarating rides in the bright spring weather, which were so attractive to the younger man, and sat at home watching Gladys, now more absorbingly interesting than ever. He could not but admire the patience, strength, and dignity of the creature; for she made no complaint, showed no suspicion, asked no advice, but went straight on, like one who followed with faltering feet, but unwavering eye, the single star in all the sky that would lead her right. A craving curiosity to know what she felt and thought possessed him, and he invited confidence by unwonted kindliness, as well as the unfailing courtesy he showed her.

But Gladys would not speak either to him or to her husband, who seemed wilfully blind to the slowly changing face, all the sadder for the smile it always wore when his eyes were on it. At first, Helwyze tried his gentlest arts; but, finding her as true as brave, was driven, by the morbid curiosity which he had indulged till it became a mania, to use means as subtle as sinful, — like a burglar, who, failing to pick a lock, grows desperate and breaks it, careless of consequences.

Taking his daily walk through the house, he once came upon Gladys watering the *jardinière,* which was her especial care, and always kept full of her favorite plants. She was not singing as she worked, but seriously busy as a child, holding in both hands her little watering-pot to shower the thirsty ferns and flowers, who turned up their faces to be washed with the silent delight which was their thanks.

"See how the dear things enjoy it! I feel as if they knew and watched for me, and I never like to disappoint them of their bath," she said, looking over her shoulder, as he paused beside her. She was used to this now, and was never surprised or startled when below stairs by his noiseless approach.

"They are doing finely. Did Moss bring in some cyclamens? They are in full bloom now, and you are fond of them, I think?"

"Yes, here they are: both purple and white, so sweet and lovely! See how many buds this one has. I shall enjoy seeing them come out, they unfurl so prettily;" and, full of interest, Gladys parted the leaves to show several baby buds, whose rosy faces were just peeping from their green hoods.

Helwyze liked to see her among the flowers; for there was something peculiarly innocent and fresh about her then, as if the woman forgot her griefs, and was a girl again. It struck him anew, as she stood there in the sunshine, leaning down to tend the soft leaves and cherish the delicate buds with a caressing hand.

"Like seeks like: you are a sort of cyclamen yourself. I never observed it before, but the likeness is quite striking," he said, with the slow smile which usually prefaced some speech which bore a double meaning.

"Am I?" and Gladys eyed the flowers, pleased, yet a little shy, of compliment from him.

"This is especially like you," continued Helwyze, touching one of the freshest. "Out of these strong sombre leaves rises a wraith-like blossom, with white, softly folded petals, a rosy color on its modest face, and a most sweet perfume for those whose sense is fine enough to perceive it. Most of all, perhaps, it resembles you in this, — it hides its heart, and, if one tries to look too closely, there is danger of snapping the slender stem."

"That is its nature, and it cannot help being shy. I kneel down and look up without touching it; then one sees that it has nothing to hide," protested Gladys, following out the flower fancy, half in earnest, half in jest, for she felt there was a question and a reproach in his words.

"Perhaps not; let us see, in my way." With a light touch Helwyze turned the reluctant cyclamen upward, and in its purple cup there clung a newly fallen drop, like a secret tear.

Mute and stricken, Gladys looked at the little symbol of herself, owning, with a throb of pain, that if in nothing else, they *were* alike in that.

Helwyze stood silent likewise, inhaling the faint fragrance while he softly ruffled the curled petals as if searching for another tear. Suddenly Gladys spoke out with the directness which always gave him a keen pleasure, asking, as she stretched her hand involuntarily to shield the more helpless flower, —

"Sir, why do you wish to read my heart?"

"To comfort it."

"Do I need comfort, then?"

"Do you not?"

"If I have a sorrow, God only can console me, and He only need know it. To you it should be sacred. Forgive me if I seem ungrateful; but you cannot help me, if you would."

"Do you doubt my will?"

"I try to doubt no one; but I fear — I fear many things;" and, as if afraid of saying too much, Gladys broke off, to hurry away, wearing so strange a look that Helwyze was consumed with a desire to know its meaning.

He saw no more of her till twilight, for Canaris took her place just then, reading a foreign book, which she could not manage; but, when Felix went out, he sought one of his solitary haunts, hoping she would appear.

She did; for the day closed early with a gusty rain, and the sunset hour was gray and cold, leaving no after-glow to tint the western sky and bathe the great room in ruddy light. Pale and noiseless as a spirit, Gladys went to and fro, trying to quiet the unrest that made her nights sleepless, her days one long struggle to be patient, just, and kind. She tried to sing, but the song died in her throat; she tried to sew, but her eyes were dim, and the flower under her needle only reminded her that "pansies were for thoughts," and hers, alas! were too sad for thinking; she took up a book, but laid it down again, since Felix was not there to finish it with her. Her own rooms seemed so empty, she could not return thither when she had looked for him in vain; and, longing for some human voice to speak to her, it was a relief to come upon Helwyze sitting in his lonely corner, — for she never now went to the library, unless duty called her.

"A dull evening, and dull company," he said, as she paused beside him, glad to have found something to take her out of herself, for a time at least.

"Such a long day! and such a dreary night as it will be!" she answered, leaning her forehead against the window-pane, to watch the drops fall, and listen to the melancholy wind.

"Shorten the one and cheer the other, as I do: sleep, dream, and forget."

"I cannot!" and there was a world of suffering in the words that broke from her against her will.

"Try my sleep-compeller as freely as I tried yours. See, these will give you one, if not all the three desired blessings, — quiet slumber, delicious dreams, or utter oblivion for a time."

As he spoke, Helwyze had drawn out a little *bonbonnière* of tortoise-shell and silver, which he always carried, and shaken into his palm half a dozen white comfits, which he offered to Gladys, with a benign expression born of real sympathy and compassion. She hesitated; and he added, in a tone of mild reproach, which smote her generous heart with compunction, —

"Since I may not even try to minister to your troubled mind, let me, at least, give a little rest to your weary body. Trust me, child, these cannot hurt you; and, strong as you are, you will break down if you do not sleep."

Without a word, she took them; and, as they melted on her tongue, first sweet, then bitter, she stood leaning against the rainy window-pane, listening to Helwyze, who began to talk as if he too had tasted the Indian drug, which "made the face of Coleridge shine, as he conversed like one inspired."

It seemed a very simple, friendly act; but this man had learned to know how subtly the mind works; to see how often an apparently impulsive action is born of an almost unconscious thought, an unacknowledged purpose, a deeply hidden motive, which to many seem rather the child than the father of the deed. Helwyze did not deceive himself, and owned that baffled desire prompted that unpremeditated offer, and was ready to avail itself of any self-betrayal which might follow its acceptance, for he had given Gladys hasheesh.

It could not harm; it might soothe and comfort her unrest. It surely would make her forget for a while, and in that temporary oblivion perhaps he might discover what he burned to know. The very uncertainty of its effect added to the daring of the deed; and, while he talked, he waited to see how it would affect her, well knowing that in such a temperament as hers all processes are rapid. For an hour he conversed so delightfully of Rome and its wonders, that Gladys was amazed to find Felix had come in, unheard for once.

All through dinner she brightened steadily, thinking the happy mood was brought by her prodigal's return, quite forgetting Helwyze and his bitter-sweet bonbons.

"I shall stay at home, and enjoy the society of my pretty wife. What have you done to make yourself so beautiful to-night? Is it the new gown?" asked Canaris, surveying her with laughing but most genuine surprise and satisfaction as they returned to the drawing-room again.

"It is not new: I made it long ago, to please you, but you never noticed it before," answered Gladys, glancing at the pale-hued dress, all broad, soft folds from waist to ankle, with its winter trimming of swan's down at the neck and wrists; simple, but most becoming to her flower-like face and girlish figure.

"What cruel blindness! But I see and admire it now, and honestly declare that not Olivia in all her splendor is arrayed so much to my taste as you, my Sancta Simplicitas."

"It is pleasant to hear you say so; but that alone does not make me happy: it must be having you at home all to myself again," she whispered, with shining eyes, cheeks that glowed with a deeper rose each hour, and an indescribably blest expression in a face which now was both brilliant and dreamy.

Helwyze heard what she said, and, fearing to lose sight of her, promptly challenged Canaris to chess, a favorite pastime with them both. For an hour they played, well matched and keenly interested, while Gladys sat by, already tasting the restful peace, the delicious dreams, promised her.

The clock was on the stroke of eight, the game was nearly over, when a quick ring arrested Helwyze in the act of making the final move. There was a stir in the hall, then, bringing with her a waft of fresh, damp air, Olivia appeared, brave in purple silk and Roman gold.

"I thought you were all asleep or dead; but now I see the cause of this awful silence," she cried. "Don't speak, don't stir; let me enjoy the fine tableau you make. Retsch's 'Game of Life,' quite perfect, and most effective."

It certainly was to an observer; for Canaris, flushed and eager, looked the young man to the life; Helwyze, calm but intent, with his finger on his lip, pondering that last fateful move, was an excellent Satan; and behind them stood Gladys, wonderfully resembling the wistful angel, with that new brightness on her face.

"Which wins?" asked Olivia, rustling toward them, conscious of having made an impressive entrance; for both men looked up to welcome her, though Gladys never lifted her eyes from the mimic battle Felix seemed about to lose.

"I do, as usual," answered Helwyze, turning to finish the game with the careless ease of a victor.

"Not this time;" and Gladys touched a piece which Canaris in the hurry of the moment was about to overlook. He saw its value at a glance, made the one move that could save him, and in an instant cried "Checkmate," with a laugh of triumph.

"Not fair, the angel interfered," said Olivia, shaking a warning finger at Gladys, who echoed her husband's laugh with one still more exultant, as she put her hand upon his shoulder, saying, in a low, intense voice never heard from her lips before, —

"I have won him; he is mine, and cannot be taken from me any more."

"Dearest child, no one wants him, except to play with and admire," began Olivia, rather startled by the look and manner of the lately meek, mute Gladys.

Here Helwyze struck in, anxious to avert Olivia's attention; for her undesirable presence disconcerted him, since her woman's wit might discover what it was easy to conceal from Canaris.

"You have come to entertain us, like the amiable enchantress that you are?" he asked, suggestively; for nothing charmed Olivia more than permission to amuse him, when others failed.

"I have a thought, — a happy thought, — if Gladys will help me. You have given me one living picture: I will give you others, and she shall sing the scenes we illustrate."

"Take Felix, and give us 'The God and the Bayadere,' " said Helwyze, glancing at the young pair behind them, he intent upon their conversation, she upon him. "No, I will have only Gladys. You will act and sing for us, I know?" and Olivia turned to her with a most engaging smile.

"I never acted in my life, but I will try. I think I should like it for I feel as if I could do any thing to-night;" and she came to them with a swift step, an eager air, as if longing to find some outlet for the strange energy which seemed to thrill every nerve and set her heart to beating audibly.

"You look so. Do you know all these songs?" asked Olivia, taking up the book which had suggested her happy thought.

"There are but four: I know them all. I will gladly sing them; for I set them to music, if they had none of their own already. I often do that to those Felix writes me."

"Come, then. I want the key of the great press, where you keep your spoils, Jasper."

"Mrs. Bland will give it you. Order what you will, if you are going to treat us to an Arabian Night's entertainment."

"Better than that. We are going to teach a small poet, by illustrating the work of a great one;" and, with a mischievous laugh, Olivia vanished, beckoning Gladys to follow.

The two men beguiled the time as best they might: Canaris playing softly to himself in the music-room; Helwyze listening intently to the sounds that came from behind the curtains, now dropped over a double door-way leading to the lower end of the hall. Olivia's imperious voice was heard, directing men and maids. More than once an excited laugh from Gladys jarred upon his ear; and, as minute after minute passed, his impatience to see her again increased.

Domesticity
The Roots of Little Women

The Sisters' Trial

Boston *Saturday Evening Gazette,* Quarto Series, 26 January 1856. By "M. L. A."

FOUR SISTERS SAT together round a cheerful fire on New Year's Eve. The shadow of a recent sorrow lay on the young faces over which the red flames flickered brightly as they lit up every nook of the quiet room, whose simple furniture and scanty decorations plainly showed that Poverty had entered there hand in hand with her sister, Grief.

The deep silence that had lasted long as each sat lost in sad memories of the past, or anxious thought for the future, was at length broken by Leonore, the eldest, a dark haired, dark eyed woman whose proud, energetic face was softened by a tender smile as she looked upon the young girls, saying cheerily:

"Come, sisters, we must not sit brooding gloomily over our troubles when we should be up and doing. To-night you know we must decide what work we will each choose by which to earn our bread, for this home will soon be ours no longer and we must find some other place to shelter us, and some honest labor to maintain ourselves by, that we may not be dependent on the charity of relatives, till our own exertions fail. Tell me what after your separate search you have each decided to do. Agnes, you come first. What among the pursuits left open to us have *you* chosen?"

The color deepened in Agnes' cheek and the restless light burned in her large eyes as she hastily replied, "*I* will be an actress. Nay do not start and look so troubled, Nora. I am fixed, and when you hear all, you will not oppose me, I feel sure. You know this has been the one wish of my life, growing with my growth, strengthening with my strength; haunting my thoughts by day, my dreams by night. I have longed for it, planned for it, studied for it secretly, for years, always hoping a time might come when I could prove to you that it was no idle fancy, but a real desire, and satisfy myself whether I have in truth the power to succeed, or whether I have cherished a false hope and been deluded by my vanity. I have thought of it seriously and earnestly during my search for employment, and see but one thing else that I can do. I *will* not chain myself to a needle and sew my own shroud for a scanty livelihood. Teaching, therefore, is all that remains. I dislike it, am unfitted for it, in every way, and cannot try it till everything else has failed.

"*You,* Nora, have your pen, Ella her music, Amy her painting; you all *love* them and can support yourselves well by them. *I* have only this one eager longing that haunts me like a shadow and seems to beckon me away to the beautiful brilliant life I feel that I was born to enjoy."

"Set yourself resolutely about some humbler work and this longing will fade away if you do not cherish it," said Leonore earnestly.

"It will not, I have tried in vain and now I will follow it over every obstacle till I have made the trial I desire.

"You are calm and cold, Nora, and cannot understand my feelings, therefore do not try to dissuade me, for an actress I must and *will* be," answered Agnes resolutely.

A look of sudden pain crossed Leonore's face at her sister's words, but it quickly passed and looking into her excited countenance she said gently, "How will you manage this? It is no easy thing for a young and unknown girl to take such a step alone; have you thought of this? and what are your plans?"

"Listen and I will tell you, for all is ready though you seem inclined to doubt it," replied Agnes, meeting her sisters' wondering glances with a look of triumph as she went on.

"Mrs. Vernon, whom our mother loved and respected, (actress though she is,) has known us long and been a friend to us in our misfortunes. I remembered this; after seeking vainly for some employment that I did not hate, I went to her, and telling all my hopes and wishes asked for her advice.

"She listened kindly and after questioning me closely and trying what little skill I have acquired, she said that if you consented she would take me with her to the West, train and teach me, and then try what I can do. There is an opening for me there, and under her protection and motherly care what need I fear? I should have told you this before but you bade us each to look and judge for ourselves before we asked for your advice, making this our first lesson in self-reliance which now is all we can depend on for support and guidance.

"Now what is your answer? Shall I go as I *wish* safely and properly with Mrs. Vernon, or as I *will,* alone and unprotected if you deny me your consent? Ah! do say yes, and you will make my life so beautiful and pleasant that I shall love and bless you forever."

As Agnes spoke, Leonore had thought rapidly of her sister's restless and unsatisfied life. Her unfitness for the drudgery she would be forced to if denied her wish. Of their mother's confidence in the kind friend who would be a faithful guardian to her and looking in the eager imploring face lifted to her own and reading there the real unconquerable passion that filled her sister's heart, she felt that hard experience alone could teach her wisdom, and time only could dispel her dream or fix and strengthen it forever. So she replied simply and seriously. "Yes, Agnes, you may go."

Agnes, prepared for argument and denial seemed bewildered by this ready acquiescence, till meeting Leonore's troubled glance fixed anxiously upon her, she saw there all the silent sorrow and reproach she would not speak, and coming to her side, Agnes said gratefully and with a fond caress, "You never shall have cause to repent your goodness to me, Nora, for I will be true to you and to myself whatever else may happen. So do not fear for me, the memory of *home* and *you,* dear girls, will keep me safe amid the trials and temptations of my future life."

Leonore did not answer but drew her nearer as if to cherish and protect her for the little time they yet could be together, and with dim eyes but a cheerful voice bade Ella tell *her* plans.

"*I,*" said the third sister, turning her placid face from the fire whose pleasant glow seemed shining from it, as if attracted there by kindred light and warmth, "I shall go to the South as governess to three little motherless girls. Aunt Elliott, who told me of it, assured me it would prove a happy home, and with my salary which is large I shall so gladly help you, and mite by mite lay by a little store that may in time grow large enough to buy our dear old home again. This is my future lot and I am truly grateful it is such a pleasant one."

"How can you be content with such a dreary life?" cried Agnes.

"Because it is my duty, and in doing that I know I shall find happiness," replied Ella. "For twenty years I have been shielded from the rough winds that visit so many, I have had my share of rest and pleasure and I trust they have done well their work of sweetening and softening my nature. Now life's harder lessons are to be learned and I am trying to receive them as I ought. Like you I will not be dependent on relatives rich in all but love to us, and so must endeavor to go bravely out into the world to meet whatever fate God sends me."

The light of a pure unselfish heart beamed in the speaker's gentle face and her simple child-like faith seemed to rebuke her sisters' restless doubts and longings.

"I come next," said Amy, a slender graceful girl of eighteen, "and my search has been most successful. While looking for pupils, I met again my dear friend Annie L——, who when she learned my troubles bade me look no farther but come and make my home with her. That I would not do till she agreed that I should take the place of her attendant and companion (for she is lame you know), and go with her to Europe for a year. Think how beautiful it will be to live in those lands I have so longed to see, and pass my days in sketching, painting and taking care of Annie, who is alone in the world and needs an affectionate friend to cheer the many weary hours that must come to one rich, talented, and young, but a cripple for life. I shall thus support myself by my own labor though it is one of love, and gain skill and knowledge in my art in the only school that can give it to me. This is my choice. Have I not done well, sisters?"

"You have indeed, but how can we let you go so far from us, dear Amy?" asked Leonore as they all looked fondly at her for she had been the pet and sunbeam of the household all her life and their hearts clung to her fearing to send her out so young to strive and struggle with the selfish world.

But she met their anxious gaze with a brave smile, saying: "Fear nothing for me, it is what I need, for I shall never know my own strength if it is never tried and with you it will not be, for you cherish me like a delicate flower. Now I shall be blown about and made to think and judge for myself as it's time I should. I shall not seem so far away as you now think for my letters will come to you like my voice from over the sea and it shall always be loving and merry that nothing may be changed as the year rolls on, and I may ever seem your own fond, foolish little Amy.

"Now, Nora, last not least, let us know in what part of the globe you will bestow yourself."

"I shall stay here, Amy," answered Leonore.

"Here!" echoed the sisters. "How can you when the house is sold and the gentleman coming to take possession so soon?"

"Just before our mother died," replied Leonore in a reverent voice, "she said to me in the silence of the night, 'Nora you are the guardian of your sisters now, be a watchful mother to them, and if you separate, as I fear you must, try to secure some little spot, no matter how poor, where you may sometimes meet and feel that you have a *home*. Promise me this, for I cannot rest in peace feeling that all the sweet ties that now bind you tenderly together are broken, and that you are growing up as strangers to each other scattered far apart.'

"I promised her, and this is why I longed so much to have you all remain in B——, that we might often meet and cheer each other on.

"But, as it cannot be, I have decided to remain here, for Mr. Morton is a kind old man, with no family but a maiden sister. They need few apartments, and when I told him how things were, and that I desired to hire one room, he willingly consented, and among those they wished left the rest to me. I chose this one, and here, surrounded by the few familiar things now left us, I shall live and by my pen support myself, or if that fails seek for needlework or teaching.

"It will be a quiet, solitary life, but tidings of *you* all will come to cheer me, and when another New Year shall come round, let us, if we can, meet here again to tell our wanderings and to spend it on the spot where have passed so many happy ones.

"This is my decision, here I shall live, and remember, dear girls, wherever you may be, that there is one nook in the dear old home where in sickness or sorrow you can freely come, ever sure of a joyful welcome, and in this troubled world one heart that is always open to take you in, one friend that can never desert you."

The sisters gathered silently about her as Leonore rose, and taking from a case three delicately painted miniatures of their mother, in a faltering voice, said, as she threw the simply woven chains of her own dark hair about their necks:

"This is my parting gift to you, and may the dear face Amy's hand has given us so freshly, prove a talisman to keep you ever worthy of our mother's love. God bless and bring us all together once again, better and wiser for our first lesson in the school of life."

The fire leaped up with a sudden glow, and from the hearthstone where a tenderly united family once had gathered fell now like a warm, bright blessing on the orphan sisters folded in each other's arms for the last time in the shelter of their home.

The year was gone, and Leonore sat waiting for the wanderers to come with a shadow on her face, and a secret sorrow at her heart.

The once poor room now wore an air of perfect comfort. Flowers bloomed in the deep windows sheltered from the outer cold by the warm folds of graceful curtains, green wreaths framed the picture faces on the walls, and a generous blaze burned red upon the hearth, flashing brightly over old familiar objects beautified and freshened by a tasteful hand.

A pleasant change seemed to have fallen on all but the thoughtful woman, in whose troubled face passion and pride seemed struggling with softer, nobler feelings as she sat there pale and silent in the cheerful room. As the twilight deepened, the inward storm passed silently away, leaving only a slight cloud behind as she paced anxiously to and fro, till well known footsteps sounded without, and Ella and Amy came hastening in.

They had returned a week before, but though much with Leonore in her pleasant home they had playfully refused to answer any questions till the appointed night arrived.

Time seemed to have passed lightly over Ella, for her face was bright and tranquil as of old, while some secret joy seemed measured in her heart, which, though it found no vent in words, shone in the clear light of her quiet eyes, sounded in the music of her voice, and deepened the sweet seriousness of her whole gentle nature.

Amy's single year of travel had brought with its culture and experience fresh grace and bloom to the slender girl who had blossomed suddenly into a lovely woman, frank and generous as ever, but softened and refined by the simple charms of early womanhood.

Gathered in their old places, the sisters, talking cheerfully, waited for Agnes. But at length she came slowly, and faintly her footsteps sounded on the stair, and when she entered such a change had fallen on her they could scarce believe it was the same bright creature who had left them but a year ago.

Worn and wasted, with dim eyes and pallid cheeks, she came back but a shadow of her former self.

Her sisters knew she had been ill, and guessed she had been unhappy, for a gradual change had taken place in her letters; from being full of overflowing hope and happiness, they had grown sad, desponding, and short. But she had never spoken of the cause, and now, though grieved and startled, they breathed not a word of questioning, but, concealing their alarm, tenderly welcomed her, and tried to banish her gloom.

Agnes endeavored with forced gayety to join them, but it soon deserted her, and after the first affectionate greetings, seemed to sink unconsciously into a deep and painful reverie.

The sisters glanced silently and anxiously at one another as they heard her heavy sighs, and saw the feverish color that now burned on her thin cheek as she sat gazing absently into the glowing embers.

None seemed willing to break the silence that had fallen on them till Amy said, with a pleasant laugh:

"As I probably have the least to tell I will begin. My life, since we parted, has been one of rich experience and real happiness; with friends and labor that I loved how could it well be otherwise?

"I have fared better in my trial than I ever hoped to, and have been blessed with health of body and peace of heart to enjoy the many pleasant things about me. A home in Italy more beautiful than I can tell you, a faithful friend in Annie, cultivated minds around me, and time to study and improve myself in all the things that I most love, — all these I have had, and hope I have improved them well. I have gained courage, strength and knowledge, and armed with these I have the will and power to earn with my pencil and brush an honest livelihood, and make my own way in this busy world which has always been a friendly one to me.

"I shall stay with Annie till her marriage with the artist whom we met abroad, about whom I have already told you. Then I shall find some quiet nook, and there sit down to live, love, and labor, while waiting what the future may bring forth for me."

"May it bring you all the happiness you so well deserve, my cheerful-hearted Amy," said Leonore, looking fondly and proudly at her young sister. "Your cheerful courage is a richer fortune to you than money can ever be, while your contented mind will brighten life with the truest happiness for one who can find sunshine everywhere.

"Now, Ella, let us know how you have fared, and what your future is?" continued Leonore.

"The past year has been one of mingled joy and sorrow," answered Ella. "The sorrow was the sudden loss of little Effie, the youngest and dearest of my pupils. It was a heavy grief to us all, and her father mourned most bitterly, till a new love, as strong and pure as that he bore the lost child, came to cheer and comfort him when most he needed it." Here, in the sudden glow on Ella's cheek, and the radiant smile that lit her face with a tenderer beauty, the sisters read the secret she had hidden from them until now, as in a low, glad voice she said:

"The joy I spoke of was that this love, so generous and deep, he offered to the humble girl who had tried to be a mother to his little child, and sorrowed like one when she went. Freely, gratefully did I receive it, for his silent kindness and the simple beauty of his life had long made him very dear to me, and I felt I had the power to be to him a true and loving friend.

"And now, no longer poor and solitary, I shall journey back to fill the place, not of a humble governess, but of a happy wife and mother in my beautiful southern home. Ah, sisters, this has been a rich and blessed year to me, far more than I have deserved."

And Ella bent her head upon her folded hands, too full of happiness for words.

Agnes had been strongly moved while Ella spoke, and when she ceased broke into bitter weeping, while her sisters gathered round her, vainly trying to compose and comfort her. But she did not heed them till her sudden grief had wept itself calm, then speaking like one in a dream, she said, abruptly:

"*My* year has been one of brilliant, bitter sorrow, such another I could not live through.

"When I first began my new life all seemed bright and pleasant to me. I studied hard, learned fast, and at last made the wished for trial, you know how successfully. For awhile I was in a dream of joy and triumph, and fancied all was smooth and sure before me. I had done much, I would do more, and not content to rise slowly and surely, I longed to be at once what years of patient labor alone can make me, I struggled on through the daily trials that thickened round me, often disheartened and disgusted at the selfishness and injustice of those around me, and the thousand petty annoyances that tried my proud, ambitious spirit.

"It was a hard life, and but for the great love I still cherished for the better part of it I should have left it long ago. But there were moments, hours, when I forgot my real cares and troubles in the false ones of the fair creations I was called upon to personate. Then I seemed to move in an enchanted world of my own, and *was* the creature that I *seemed*. Ah! that was glorious to feel that, my power, small as it was, could call forth tears and smiles and fill strange hearts with pity, joy, or fear.

"So time went on, and I was just beginning to feel that at last I was rising from my humble place, lifted by my own power and the kind favor I had won, when between me and my brightening fortune there came a friend, who brought me the happiest and bitterest hours of my whole life."

Here Agnes paused, and putting back her fallen hair from her wet cheek, looked wistfully into the anxious faces around her, and then, after a moment's pause, with an effort and in a hurried voice, went on,

"Among the many friends who admired and respected Mrs. Vernon and often visited her pleasant home, none was more welcome than the rich, accomplished Mr. Butler, (whose name you may remember in my letters). None came oftener, or stayed longer, he was with us at the theatre and paid a thousand kind attentions to my good friend and to me, in whom he seemed to take an interest from the first moment we met. Do not think me weak and vain; how could I help discovering it, when among many who looked coldly on me, or treated me with careless freedom, I found *him* always just, respectful, and ah! how kind? He had read and travelled much, and with his knowledge of the world, he taught, encouraged and advised me, making my hard life beautiful by his generous friendship.

"You know my nature, frank, and quick to love, touched by a gentle word or a friendly deed. I was deeply grateful for his many silent acts of kindness and the true regard he seemed to feel for me, and slowly, half unconsciously, my gratitude warmed into love. I never knew how strong and deep, until I learned too late that it was all in vain.

"One night (how well I can remember its least circumstance!) I was playing one of my best parts, and never had I played it better, for *he* was there, and I thought only of *his* approbation then. Toward the close of the evening I was waiting for my cue, when Mr. Butler and friend passed near the spot where I was standing, partially concealed by a deep shadow; I caught the sound of my own name, and then in a low, pained voice, as if replying to some question, Mr. Butler said,

" 'I respect, admire, yes, love her far too deeply, willfully to destroy her peace, but I am of a proud race and cannot make an *actress* my wife. Therefore I shall leave to-morrow before she can discover what I have lately learned, and although we shall never meet again, I shall always be her friend.'

"They passed on and the next moment I was on the stage, laughing merrily with a dizzy brain and an aching heart. Pride nerved me to control my wandering thoughts and to play out mechanically my part in the comedy that had so suddenly become the deepest tragedy to me.

"Actress as I thought myself, it needed all my skill to hide beneath a smiling face the pang that wrung my heart, and but for the many eyes upon us and the false bloom on my cheek I should have betrayed all, when he came to take his leave that night. Little dreaming what I suffered, he kindly, seriously said farewell, and so we parted forever. For days I struggled to conceal the secret grief that preyed upon me until it laid me on a sick bed, from which I rose as you now see me, broken in health and spirit, saddened by the disappointed hopes and dreams that lie in ruins round me, distrustful of myself, and weary of life."

With a desponding sigh Agnes laid her head on Leonore's bosom, as if she never cared to lift it up again.

Ella knew why she had wept so sadly while listening to the story of *her* happy love, and bending over her she spoke gently of the past and cheerfully of the future till the desponding gloom was banished and Agnes looked up with a face brightened by earnest feeling as she said in answer to Leonore's whispered question, "You will stay with us now, dearest?"

"Yes; I shall never tread the stage again, for though I love it with a lingering memory of the many happy hours spent there, the misery of that one night has taught me what a hollow mockery the life I had chosen *may* become. I have neither health nor spirit for it now, and its glare and glitter have lost their charms. I shall find some humble work and quietly pursuing it, endeavor to become what *he* would have me: not an actress, but a simple woman, trying to play well her part in life's great drama. And though we shall never meet again, he may one day learn that, no longer mistaking the shadow for the substance, I have left the fair, false life and taken up the real and true."

"Thank heaven for this change," cried Leonore. "Dear Agnes, this shall henceforth be your home, and here we will lead a cheerful, busy life, sharing joy and sorrow together as in our childhood, and journeying hand in hand thro' light and darkness to a happy, calm old age."

"Leonore, you must tell us your experiences now, or our histories are not complete," said Amy, after a little time.

"I have nothing to relate but what you already know," replied her sister. "My book was well received and made for me a place among those writers who have the power to please and touch the hearts of many. I have earned much with my pen, and have a little store laid by for future need. My life has been a quiet, busy one. I have won many friends whose kindness and affection have cheered my solitude and helped me on. What more can I say but that I heartily rejoice that all has gone so well with us, and we have proved that we possess the power to make our own way in the world and need ask charity of none. Our talismans have kept us safe from harm, and God has let us meet again without one gone."

"Leonore," said Agnes, looking earnestly into her sister's face, "you have not told us *all*; nay, do not turn away, there is some hidden heart-sorrow that you are silent of. I read it in the secret trouble of your eye, the pallor of your cheek, and most of all, in your quick sympathy for me. We have given you our confidence, ah! give us yours as freely, dearest Nora."

"I cannot, do not ask me," murmured Leonore, averting her face.

"Let nothing break the sweet ties that now bind you together, and do not be as strangers to each other when you should be closest friends," whispered Ella from the low seat at her knee.

Leonore seemed to struggle within herself, and many contending emotions swept across her face, but she longed for sympathy and her proud heart melted at the mild echo of her mother's words. So holding Agnes's hand fast in her own, as if their sorrow drew them nearer to each other, she replied with a regretful sigh, "Yes, I will tell you, for your quick eyes have discovered what I hoped to have hidden from your sight forever. It *is* a heart-sorrow, Agnes, deeper than your own, for you can still reverence and trust the friend you have lost, but I can only feel contempt for what I have so truly loved. You well remember cousin Walter, the frank, generous-hearted boy who was our dearest playmate and companion years ago? Soon after we had separated he returned from India with his parents, and though *they* took no heed of me, *he* sought me out, and simply, naturally took the place of friend and brother to me, as of old. I needed help just then, he gave it freely, and by his wise counsel and generous kindness, banished my cares and cheered me when most solitary and forlorn.

"I have always loved him, and pleasant memories of my happy past have kept his image fresh within my heart. Through the long years of his absence I have sighed for his return, longing to know if the promise of a noble manhood I remembered in the boy had been fulfilled. He came at last when I most wished him, and with secret pride and joy I found him all I had hoped, brave, generous, and sincere. Ah! I was very happy then, and as our friendship grew, slowly and silently the frank affection of the girl deepened into the woman's earnest love.

"I knew it was returned, for in every look and deed the sweet, protecting tenderness that had guarded me in my childish days, now showed itself more plainly still, and at length found vent in words, which few and simple as they were seemed to fill my life with a strange happiness and beauty.

"Agnes, you have called me cold, but if you knew the deep and fervent passion that has stirred my heart, softening and sweetening my stern nature, you could never wrong me so again. Unhappy as that love has been, its short experience has made me wiser, and when its first sharp disappointment has passed away, the memory of it will linger like the warm glow of a fire whose brightness has departed.

"Two months ago a change came over Walter; he was kind as ever, coming often to cheer my lonely life, filling my home with lovely things, and more than all with his own dear presence, but a cloud was on him and I could not banish it.

"At length a week passed and he did not come, but in his place a letter from his father saying 'that he disapproved of his son's love for me and had persuaded him to relinquish me for a wife more suited to his rank in life; therefore at his request he wrote to spare us the pain of parting.' I cannot tell what more was in that cold, insulting letter, for I burned it, saving only two faintly written words in Walter's well known hand, 'Farewell, Leonore;' that was enough for me; by what magic the great change was wrought I cared not to discover. All I thought or felt was that he had left me without a word of explanation, breaking his plighted word, and like a coward fearing to tell me freely and openly that he no longer loved me.

"I have not seen or heard from him since; though rumors of his approaching marriage, his departure for Europe and a sudden illness, have reached my ears, I believe none of them and struggling sternly to conceal my sorrow, have passed silently on leaving him without one word of entreaty or reproach to the keen regret his cruelty will one day cause him."

A proud indignant light burned in Leonore's eye and flushed her cheek as with a bitter smile she met her sisters' troubled glances saying,

"You need not pity *me, he* wants it most, for money can buy his truth and cast an evil spell on him, and a sordid father has the power to tempt and win him from his duty. None but *you* will ever know the secret sorrow that now bows my spirit but shall never break it; I shall soon banish the tender memories that haunt me, and hiding the deep wound he has caused me, be again the calm, cold Leonore.

"Oh! Walter! Walter! you have made the patient love that should have been the blessing of my life, its heaviest sorrow; may God forgive you as I try to do."

And as these words broke from her lips, Leonore clasped her hands before her face and hot tears fell like rain on Ella's head bent down upon her knee.

Agnes and Amy, blinded by the dimness of their own eyes, had not seen a tall dark man who had entered silently as Leonore last spoke and had stood spell bound till she ceased, then coming to her side the stranger said in a low, eager voice,

"Nora, will you hear me?"

With a quick start Leonore dashed away her tears and rose up pale and stately, looking full into the earnest, manly face before her and plainly reading there all she had doubted. Truth in the frank, reproachful eyes that met her own, tender sorrow in the trembling lips, and over all the light of the faithful, generous love which never had deserted her.

Her stern glance softened as she bowed a silent reply, and fell before his own as standing close beside her and looking steadily into her changing countenance, her cousin Walter laid his thin hand on her own saying in the friendly voice she had so longed to hear,

"Leonore, from the sick bed where I have lain through these long weary weeks, I have come to prove my truth, which had your pride allowed you to inquire into you never would have doubted, knowing me as I fondly hoped you did."

With a sudden motion Leonore drew a little worn and blistered paper from her bosom and laid it in his hand from which she coldly drew her own and fixed a keen look on his face, where not a shadow of shame or fear appeared, as he read it, silently glancing from the tear-stains to the eyes that looked so proudly on him with a quiet smile that brought a hot glow to her cheek as she asked quickly,

"Did *you* write those cruel words?"

"I did; nay, listen patiently before you judge me, Nora," he replied as she turned to leave him.

"Two months ago my father questioned me of *you*. I told him freely that I loved you and soon hoped to gladden his home with a daughter's gentle presence. But his anger knew no bounds and commanding me to beware how I thwarted his wishes, he bade me choose between utter poverty and you, or all his Indian wealth and my cousin Clara; I told him that my choice was already made, but he would not listen to me and bade me consider it well for one whole week and then decide before I saw you again. I yielded to calm his anger and for a week tried to win him to a wiser and kinder course, but all in vain; his will was iron and mine was no less firm, for, high above all selfish doubts and fears, all lures of rank and wealth, rose up my faithful love for you and nothing else could tempt me. That needed no golden fetters to render it more true, no idle show to make it richer, fonder than it is and ever will be.

"It was no virtue in me to resist, for nothing great enough was offered in exchange for that; poverty was wealth with *you* and who would waver between a false, vain girl and a true hearted woman?

"Ah, Nora, you will learn to know me now and see how deep a wrong you have done me. But to finish. When at the week's close I told my father that my purpose was unbroken he bade me leave his house forever and would have cursed me but his passion choked the sinful words ere they were spoken and he is saved that sorrow, when he thinks more kindly of me hereafter.

"I silently prepared to leave his house, which since my own mother's death has never been like home to me, and should have hastened joyfully to you, had not the fever already burning in my veins, augmented by anxiety and grief, laid me on my bed from which I am just risen, and where through those long nights and days I have been haunted even in delirium by your image, and the one longing wish to tell you why I did not come.

"When better, I sent messages and letters, but they never were delivered, for my father thinking sickness might have changed me, was still at my side to watch my actions and to tempt me to revoke my words. I have since learned that he wrote to you and guiding my unconscious hand traced the words that gave you the right to doubt me. But now I am strong again; nothing can separate us more, and I am here to bury the past and win your pardon for the sorrow I could not spare you. Now, Leonore, I am poor and friendless as yourself, with my fortune to make by the labor of my hands as you have done. You once wished this and said you never would receive the wealth I longed to give you; your wish is granted; I have nothing now to offer but a hand to work untiringly for you, and a heart to love and cherish you most tenderly forever. Will you take them, Nora?"

Leonore's proud head had sunk lower and lower as he spoke and when he ceased it rested on his shoulder, and her hand lay with an earnest, loving clasp in his as she whispered in a broken voice,

"Forgive me, Walter, for the wrong I have done you and teach me to be worthy the great sacrifice you have made for me."

The clock struck twelve and as its silvery echoes sounded through the quiet room, the old year with its joys and sorrows, hopes and fears floated away into the shadowing past bearing among its many records the simple one of the Sisters' Trial.

A Modern Cinderella

or, The Little Old Shoe

Atlantic Monthly Magazine, October 1860. Published anonymously

HOW IT WAS LOST

*A*MONG GREEN New England hills stood an ancient house, many-gabled, mossy-roofed, and quaintly built, but picturesque and pleasant to the eye; for a brook ran babbling through the orchard that encompassed it about, a garden-plot stretched upward to the whispering birches on the slope, and patriarchal elms stood sentinel upon the lawn, as they had stood almost a century ago, when the Revolution rolled that way and found them young.

One summer morning, when the air was full of country sounds, of mowers in the meadow, blackbirds by the brook, and the low of kine upon the hill-side, the old house wore its cheeriest aspect, and a certain humble history began.

"Nan!"

"Yes, Di."

And a head, brown-locked, blue-eyed, soft-featured, looked in at the open door in answer to the call.

"Just bring me the third volume of 'Wilhelm Meister,' — there's a dear. It's hardly worth while to rouse such a restless ghost as I, when I'm once fairly laid."

As she spoke, Di pushed up her black braids, thumped the pillow of the couch where she was lying, and with eager eyes went down the last page of her book.

"Nan!"

"Yes, Laura," replied the girl, coming back with the third volume for the literary cormorant, who took it with a nod, still too intent upon the "Confessions of a Fair Saint" to remember the failings of a certain plain sinner.

"Don't forget the Italian cream for dinner. I depend upon it; for it's the only thing fit for me this hot weather."

And Laura, the cool blonde, disposed the folds of her white gown more gracefully about her, and touched up the eyebrow of the Minerva she was drawing.

"Little daughter!"

"Yes, father."

"Let me have plenty of clean collars in my bag, for I must go at three; and some of you bring me a glass of cider in about an hour; — I shall be in the lower garden."

The old man went away into his imaginary paradise, and Nan into that domestic purgatory on a summer day, — the kitchen. There were vines about the windows, sunshine on the floor, and order everywhere; but it was haunted by a cooking-stove, that family altar whence such varied incense rises to appease the appetite of household gods, before which such dire incantations are pronounced to ease the wrath and woe of the priestess of the fire, and about which often linger saddest memories of wasted temper, time, and toil.

Nan was tired, having risen with the birds, — hurried, having many cares those happy little housewives never know, — and disappointed in a hope that hourly "dwindled, peaked, and pined." She was too young to make the anxious lines upon her forehead seem at home there, too patient to be burdened with the labor others should have shared, too light of heart to be pent up when earth and sky were keeping a blithe holiday. But she was one of that meek sisterhood who, thinking humbly of themselves, believe they are honored by being spent in the service of less conscientious souls, whose careless thanks seem quite reward enough.

To and fro she went, silent and diligent, giving the grace of willingness to every humble or distasteful task the day had brought her; but some malignant sprite seemed to have taken possession of her kingdom, for rebellion broke out everywhere. The kettles would boil over most obstreperously, — the mutton refused to cook with the meek alacrity to be expected from the nature of a sheep, — the stove, with unnecessary warmth of temper, would glow like a fiery furnace, — the irons would scorch, — the linens would dry, — and spirits would fail, though patience never.

Nan tugged on, growing hotter and wearier, more hurried and more hopeless, till at last the crisis came; for in one fell moment she tore her gown, burnt her hand, and smutched the collar she was preparing to finish in the most unexceptionable style. Then, if she had been a nervous woman, she would have scolded; being a gentle girl, she only "lifted up her voice and wept."

"Behold, she watereth her linen with salt tears, and bewaileth herself because of much tribulation. But, lo! help cometh from afar: a strong man bringeth lettuce wherewith to stay her, plucketh berries to comfort her withal, and clasheth cymbals that she may dance for joy."

The voice came from the porch, and, with her hope fulfilled, Nan looked up to greet John Lord, the house-friend, who stood there with a basket on his arm; and as she saw his honest eyes, kind lips, and helpful hands, the girl thought this plain young man the comeliest, most welcome sight she had beheld that day.

"How good of you, to come through all this heat, and not to laugh at my despair!" she said, looking up like a grateful child, as she led him in.

"I only obeyed orders, Nan; for a certain dear old lady had a motherly presentiment that you had got into a domestic whirlpool, and sent me as a sort of life-preserver. So I took the basket of consolation, and came to fold my feet upon the carpet of contentment in the tent of friendship."

As he spoke, John gave his own gift in his mother's name, and bestowed himself in the wide window-seat, where morning-glories nodded at him, and the old butternut sent pleasant shadows dancing to and fro.

His advent, like that of Orpheus in Hades, seemed to soothe all unpropitious powers with a sudden spell. The fire began to slacken, the kettles began to lull, the meat began to cook, the irons began to cool, the clothes began to behave, the spirits began to rise, and the collar was finished off with most triumphant success. John watched the change, and, though a lord of creation, abased himself to take compassion on the weaker vessel, and was seized with a great desire to lighten the homely tasks that tried her strength of body and soul. He took a comprehensive glance about the room; then, extracting a dish from the closet, proceeded to imbrue his hands in the strawberries' blood.

"Oh, John, you needn't do that; I shall have time when I've turned the meat, made the pudding, and done these things. See, I'm getting on finely now; — you're a judge of such matters; isn't that nice?"

As she spoke, Nan offered the polished absurdity for inspection with innocent pride.

"Oh that I were a collar, to sit upon that hand!" sighed John, — adding, argumentatively, "As to the berry question, I might answer it with a gem from Dr. Watts, relative to 'Satan' and 'idle hands,' but will merely say, that, as a matter of public safety, you'd better leave me alone; for such is the destructiveness of my nature, that I shall certainly eat something hurtful, break something valuable, or sit upon something crushable, unless you let me concentrate my energies by knocking off these young fellows' hats, and preparing them for their doom."

Looking at the matter in a charitable light, Nan consented, and went cheerfully on with her work, wondering how she could have thought ironing an infliction, and been so ungrateful for the blessings of her lot.

"Where's Sally?" asked John, looking vainly for the energetic functionary who usually pervaded that region like a domestic police-woman, a terror to cats, dogs, and men.

"She has gone to her cousin's funeral, and won't be back till Monday. There seems to be a great fatality among her relations; for one dies, or comes to grief in some way, about once a month. But I don't blame poor Sally for wanting to get away from this place now and then. I think I could find it in my heart to murder an imaginary friend or two, if I had to stay here long."

And Nan laughed so blithely, it was a pleasure to hear her.

"Where's Di?" asked John, seized with a most unmasculine curiosity all at once.

"She is in Germany with 'Wilhelm Meister'; but, though 'lost to sight, to memory dear'; for I was just thinking, as I did her things, how clever she is to like all kinds of books that I don't understand at all, and to write things that make me cry with pride and delight. Yes, she's a talented dear, though she hardly knows a needle from a crowbar, and will make herself one great blot some of these days, when the 'divine afflatus' descends upon her, I'm afraid."

And Nan rubbed away with sisterly zeal at Di's forlorn hose and inky pocket-handkerchiefs.

"Where is Laura?" proceeded the inquisitor.

"Well, I might say that *she* was in Italy; for she is copying some fine thing of Raphael's, or Michel Angelo's, or some great creature's or other; and she looks so picturesque in her pretty gown, sitting before her easel, that it's really a sight to behold, and I've peeped two or three times to see how she gets on."

And Nan bestirred herself to prepare the dish wherewith her picturesque sister desired to prolong her artistic existence.

"Where is your father?" John asked again, checking off each answer with a nod and a little frown.

"He is down in the garden, deep in some plan about melons, the beginning of which seems to consist in stamping the first proposition in Euclid all over the bed, and then poking a few seeds into the middle of each. Why, bless the dear man! I forgot it was time for the cider. Wouldn't you like to take it to him, John? He'd love to consult you; and the lane is so cool, it does one's heart good to look at it."

John glanced from the steamy kitchen to the shadowy path, and answered with a sudden assumption of immense industry, —

"I couldn't possibly go, Nan, — I've so much on my hands. You'll have to do it yourself. 'Mr. Robert of Lincoln' has something for your private ear; and the lane is so cool, it will do one's heart good to see you in it. Give my regards to your father, and, in the words of 'Little Mabel's' mother, with slight variations, —

> Tell the dear old body
> This day I cannot run,
> For the pots are boiling over
> And the mutton isn't done."

"I will; but please, John, go in to the girls and be comfortable; for I don't like to leave you here," said Nan.

"You insinuate that I should pick at the pudding or invade the cream, do you? Ungrateful girl, leave me!" And, with melodramatic sternness, John extinguished her in his broad-brimmed hat, and offered the glass like a poisoned goblet.

Nan took it, and went smiling away. But the lane might have been the Desert of Sahara, for all she knew of it; and she would have passed her father as unconcernedly as if he had been an apple-tree, had he not called out, —

"Stand and deliver, little woman!"

She obeyed the venerable highwayman, and followed him to and fro, listening to his plans and directions with a mute attention that quite won his heart.

"That hop-pole is really an ornament now, Nan; this sage-bed needs weeding, — that's good work for you girls; and, now I think of it, you'd better water the lettuce in the cool of the evening, after I'm gone."

To all of which remarks Nan gave her assent; though the hop-pole took the likeness of a tall figure she had seen in the porch, the sage-bed, curiously enough, suggested a strawberry ditto, the lettuce vividly reminded her of certain vegetable productions a basket had brought, and the bob-o-link only sung in his cheeriest voice, "Go home, go home! he is there!"

She found John — he having made a freemason of himself, by assuming her little apron — meditating over the partially spread table, lost in amaze at its desolate appearance; one half its proper paraphernalia having been forgotten, and the other half put on awry. Nan laughed till the tears ran over her cheeks, and John was gratified at the efficacy of his treatment; for her face had brought a whole harvest of sunshine from the garden, and all her cares seemed to have been lost in the windings of the lane.

"Nan, are you in hysterics?" cried Di, appearing, book in hand. "John, you absurd man, what are you doing?"

"I'm helpin' the maid of all work, please marm." And John dropped a curtsy with his limited apron.

Di looked ruffled, for the merry words were a covert reproach; and with her usual energy of manner and freedom of speech she tossed "Wilhelm" out of the window, exclaiming, irefully, —

"That's always the way; I'm never where I ought to be, and never think of anything till it's too late; but it's all Goethe's fault. What does he write books full of smart 'Phillinas' and interesting 'Meisters' for? How can I be expected to remember that Sally's away, and people must eat, when I'm hearing the 'Harper' and little 'Mignon'? John, how dare you come here and do my work, instead of shaking me and telling me to do it myself? Take that toasted child away, and fan her like a Chinese mandarin, while I dish up this dreadful dinner."

John and Nan fled like chaff before the wind, while Di, full of remorseful zeal, charged at the kettles, and wrenched off the potatoes' jackets, as if she were revengefully pulling her own hair. Laura had a vague intention of going to assist; but, getting lost among the lights and shadows of Minerva's helmet, forgot to appear till dinner had been evoked from chaos and peace was restored.

At three o'clock, Di performed the coronation-ceremony with her father's best hat; Laura re-tied his old-fashioned neckcloth, and arranged his white locks with an eye to saintly effect; Nan appeared with a beautifully written sermon, and suspicious ink-stains on the fingers that slipped it into his pocket; John attached himself to the bag; and the patriarch was escorted to the door of his tent with the triumphal procession which usually attended his out-goings and in-comings. Having kissed the female portion of his tribe, he ascended the venerable chariot, which received him with audible lamentation, as its rheumatic joints swayed to and fro.

"Good-bye, my dears! I shall be back early on Monday morning; so take care of yourselves, and be sure you all go and hear Mr. Emerboy preach to-morrow. My regards to your mother, John. Come, Solon!"

But Solon merely cocked one ear, and remained a fixed fact; for long experience had induced the philosophic beast to take for his motto the Yankee maxim, "Be sure you're right, then go ahead!" He knew things were not right; therefore he did not go ahead.

"Oh, by-the-way, girls, don't forget to pay Tommy Mullein for bringing up the cow: he expects it to-night. And, Di, don't sit up till daylight, nor let Laura stay out in the dew. Now, I believe, I'm off. Come, Solon!"

But Solon only cocked the other ear, gently agitated his mortified tail, as premonitory symptoms of departure, and never stirred a hoof, being well aware that it always took three "comes" to make a "go."

"Bless me! I've forgotten my spectacles. They are probably shut up in that volume of Herbert on my table. Very awkward to find myself without them ten miles away. Thank you, John. Don't neglect to water the lettuce, Nan, and don't overwork yourself, my little 'Martha.' Come" ———

At this juncture, Solon suddenly went off, like "Mrs. Gamp," in a sort of walking swoon, apparently deaf and blind to all mundane matters, except the refreshments awaiting him ten miles away; and the benign old pastor disappeared, humming "Hebron" to the creaking accompaniment of the bulgy chaise.

Laura retired to take her *siesta;* Nan made a small *carbonaro* of herself by sharpening her sister's crayons, and Di, as a sort of penance for past sins, tried her patience over a piece of knitting, in which she soon originated a somewhat remarkable pattern, by dropping every third stitch, and seaming *ad libitum.* If John had been a gentlemanly creature, with refined tastes, he would have elevated his feet and made a nuisance of himself by indulging in a "weed"; but being only an uncultivated youth, with a rustic regard for pure air and womankind in general, he kept his head uppermost, and talked like a man, instead of smoking like a chimney.

"It will probably be six months before I sit here again, tangling your threads and maltreating your needles, Nan. How glad you must feel to hear it!" he said, looking up from a thoughtful examination of the hard-working little citizens of the Industrial Community settled in Nan's work-basket.

"No, I'm very sorry; for I like to see you coming and going as you used to, years ago, and I miss you very much when you are gone, John," answered truthful Nan, whittling away in a sadly wasteful manner, as her thoughts flew back to the happy times when a little lad rode a little lass in the big wheel-barrow, and never spilt his load, — when two brown heads bobbed daily side by side to school, and the favorite play was "Babes in the Wood," with Di for a somewhat peckish robin to cover the small martyrs with any vegetable substance that lay at hand. Nan sighed, as she thought of these things, and John regarded the battered thimble on his fingertip with increased benignity of aspect as he heard the sound.

"When are you going to make your fortune, John, and get out of that disagreeable hardware concern?" demanded Di, pausing after an exciting "round," and looking almost as much exhausted as if it had been a veritable pugilistic encounter.

"I intend to make it by plunging still deeper into 'that disagreeable hardware concern'; for, next year, if the world keeps rolling, and John Lord is alive, he will become a partner, and then — and then" ———

The color sprang up into the young man's cheek, his eyes looked out with a sudden shine, and his hand seemed involuntarily to close, as if he saw and seized some invisible delight.

"What will happen then, John?" asked Nan, with a wondering glance.

"I'll tell you in a year, Nan, — wait till then." And John's strong hand unclosed, as if the desired good were not to be his yet.

Di looked at him, with a knitting-needle stuck into her hair, saying, like a sarcastic unicorn, —

"I really thought you had a soul above pots and kettles, but I see you haven't; and I beg your pardon for the injustice I have done you."

Not a whit disturbed, John smiled, as if at some mighty pleasant fancy of his own, as he replied, —

"Thank you, Di; and as a further proof of the utter depravity of my nature, let me tell you that I have the greatest possible respect for those articles of ironmongery. Some of the happiest hours of my life have been spent in their society; some of my pleasantest associations are connected with them; some of my best lessons have come to me from among them; and when my fortune is made, I intend to show my gratitude by taking three flat-irons rampant for my coat of arms."

Nan laughed merrily, as she looked at the burns on her hand; but Di elevated the most prominent feature of her brown countenance, and sighed despondingly, —

"Dear, dear, what a disappointing world this is! I no sooner build a nice castle in Spain, and settle a smart young knight therein, then down it comes about my ears; and the ungrateful youth, who might fight dragons, if he chose, insists on quenching his energies in a saucepan, and making a

Saint Lawrence of himself by wasting his life on a series of gridirons. Ah, if *I* were only a man, I would do something better than that, and prove that heroes are not all dead yet. But, instead of that, I'm only a woman, and must sit rasping my temper with absurdities like this." And Di wrestled with her knitting as if it were Fate, and she were paying off the grudge she owed it.

John leaned toward her, saying, with a look that made his plain face handsome, —

"Di, my father began the world as I begin it, and left it the richer for the useful years he spent here, — as I hope I may leave it some half-century hence. His memory makes that dingy shop a pleasant place to me; for there he made an honest name, led an honest life, and bequeathed to me his reverence for honest work. That is a sort of hardware, Di, that no rust can corrupt, and which will always prove a better fortune than any your knights can achieve with sword and shield. I think I am not quite a clod, or quite without some aspirations above money-getting; for I sincerely desire that courage which makes daily life heroic by self-denial and cheerfulness of heart; I am eager to conquer my own rebellious nature, and earn the confidence of innocent and upright souls; I have a great ambition to become as good a man and leave as green a memory behind me as old John Lord."

Di winked violently, and seamed five times in perfect silence; but quiet Nan had the gift of knowing when to speak, and by a timely word saved her sister from a thunder-shower and her stocking from destruction.

"John, have you seen Philip since you wrote about your last meeting with him?"

The question was for John, but the soothing tone was for Di, who gratefully accepted it, and perked up again with speed.

"Yes; and I meant to have told you about it," answered John, plunging into the subject at once. "I saw him a few days before I came home, and found him more disconsolate than ever, — 'just ready to go to the Devil,' as he forcibly expressed himself. I consoled the poor lad as well as I could, telling him his wisest plan was to defer his proposed expedition, and go on as steadily as he had begun, — thereby proving the injustice of your father's prediction concerning his want of perseverance, and the sincerity of his affection. I told him the change in Laura's health and spirits was silently working in his favor, and that a few more months of persistent endeavor would conquer your father's prejudice against him, and make him a stronger man for the trial and the pain. I read him bits about Laura from your own and Di's letters, and he went away at last as patient as Jacob, ready to serve another 'seven years' for his beloved Rachel."

"God bless you for it, John!" cried a fervent voice; and, looking up, they saw the cold, listless Laura transformed into a tender girl, all aglow with love and longing, as she dropped her mask, and showed a living countenance eloquent with the first passion and softened by the first grief of her life.

John rose involuntarily in the presence of an innocent nature whose sorrow needed no interpreter to him. The girl read sympathy in his brotherly regard, and found comfort in the friendly voice that asked, half playfully, half seriously, —

"Shall I tell him that he is not forgotten, even for an Apollo? that Laura the artist has not conquered Laura the woman? and predict that the good daughter will yet prove the happy wife?"

With a gesture full of energy, Laura tore her Minerva from top to bottom, while two great tears rolled down the cheeks grown wan with hope deferred.

"Tell him I believe all things, hope all things, and that I never can forget."

Nan went to her and held her fast, leaving the prints of two loving, but grimy hands upon her shoulders; Di looked on approvingly, for, though rather stony-hearted regarding the cause, she fully appreciated the effect; and John, turning to the window, received the commendations of a robin swaying on an elm-bough with sunshine on its ruddy breast.

The clock struck five, and John declared that he must go; for, being an old-fashioned soul, he fancied that his mother had a better right to his last hour than any younger woman in the land, — always remembering that "she was a widow, and he her only son."

Nan ran away to wash her hands, and came back with the appearance of one who had washed her face also: and so she had; but there was a difference in the water.

"Play I'm your father, girls, and remember it will be six months before 'that John' will trouble you again."

With which preface the young man kissed his former playfellows as heartily as the boy had been wont to do, when stern parents banished him to distant schools, and three little maids bemoaned his fate. But times were changed now; for Di grew alarmingly rigid during the ceremony; Laura received the salute like a grateful queen; and Nan returned it with heart and eyes and tender lips, making such an improvement on the childish fashion of the thing, that John was moved to support his paternal character by softly echoing her father's words, — "Take care of yourself, my little 'Martha.'"

Then they all streamed after him along the garden-path, with the endless messages and warnings girls are so prone to give; and the young man, with a great softness at his heart, went away, as many another John has gone, feeling better for the companionship of innocent maidenhood, and stronger to wrestle with temptation, to wait and hope and work.

"Let's throw a shoe after him for luck, as dear old 'Mrs. Gummage' did after 'David' and the 'willin' Barkis!' Quick, Nan! you always have old shoes on; toss one, and shout, 'Good luck!' " cried Di, with one of her eccentric inspirations.

Nan tore off her shoe, and threw it far along the dusty road, with a sudden longing to become that auspicious article of apparel, that the omen might not fail.

Looking backward from the hill-top, John answered the meek shout cheerily, and took in the group with a lingering glance: Laura in the shadow of the elms, Di perched on the fence, and Nan leaning far over the gate with her hand above her eyes and the sunshine touching her brown hair with gold. He waved his hat and turned away; but the music seemed to die out of the blackbird's song, and in all the summer landscape his eye saw nothing but the little figure at the gate.

"Bless and save us! here's a flock of people coming; my hair is in a toss, and Nan's without her shoe; run! fly, girls! or the Philistines will be upon us!" cried Di, tumbling off her perch in sudden alarm.

Three agitated young ladies, with flying draperies and countenances of mingled mirth and dismay, might have been seen precipitating themselves into a respectable mansion with unbecoming haste; but the squirrels were the only witnesses of this "vision of sudden flight," and, being used to ground-and-lofty tumbling, didn't mind it.

When the pedestrians passed, the door was decorously closed, and no one visible but a young man, who snatched something out of the road, and marched away again, whistling with more vigor of tone than accuracy of tune, "Only that, and nothing more."

HOW IT WAS FOUND

Summer ripened into autumn, and something fairer than

> *Sweet-peas and mignonette*
> *In Annie's garden grew.*

Her nature was the counterpart of the hill-side grove, where as a child she had read her fairy tales, and now as a woman turned the first pages of a more wondrous legend still. Lifted above the many-gabled roof, yet not cut off from the echo of human speech, the little grove seemed a green sanctuary, fringed about with violets, and full of summer melody and bloom. Gentle creatures haunted it, and there was none to make afraid; wood-pigeons cooed and crickets chirped their shrill roundelays, anemones and lady-ferns looked up from the moss that kissed the wanderer's feet. Warm airs were all afloat, full of vernal odors for the grateful sense, silvery birches shimmered like spirits of the wood, larches gave their green tassels to the wind, and pines made airy music sweet and solemn, as they stood looking heavenward through veils of summer sunshine or shrouds of wintry snow.

Nan never felt alone now in this charmed wood; for when she came into its precincts, once so full of solitude, all things seemed to wear one shape, familiar eyes looked at her from the violets in the grass, familiar words sounded in the whisper of the leaves, and she grew conscious that an unseen influence filled the air with new delights, and touched earth and sky with a beauty never seen before. Slowly these May-flowers budded in her maiden heart, rosily they bloomed, and silently they waited till some lover of such lowly herbs should catch their fresh aroma, should brush away the fallen leaves, and lift them to the sun.

Though the eldest of the three, she had long been overtopped by the more aspiring maids. But though she meekly yielded the reins of government, whenever they chose to drive, they were soon restored to her again; for Di fell into literature, and Laura into love. Thus engrossed, these two forgot many duties which even blue-stockings and *innamoratas* are expected to perform, and slowly all the homely humdrum cares that house-wives know became Nan's daily life, and she accepted it without a thought of discontent. Noiseless and cheerful as the sunshine, she went to and fro, doing the tasks that mothers do, but without a mother's sweet reward, holding fast the numberless slight threads that bind a household tenderly together, and making each day a beautiful success.

Di, being tired of running, riding, climbing, and boating, decided at last to let her body rest and put her equally active mind through what classical collegians term "a course of sprouts." Having undertaken to read and know *everything,* she devoted herself to the task with great energy, going from Sue to Swedenborg with perfect impartiality, and having different authors as children have sundry distempers, being fractious while they lasted, but all the better for them when once over. Carlyle appeared like scarlet-fever, and raged violently for a time; for, being anything but a "passive bucket," Di became prophetic with Mahomet, belligerent with Cromwell, and made the French Revolution a veritable Reign of Terror to her family. Goethe and Schiller alternated like fever and ague; Mephistopheles became her hero, Joan of Arc her model, and she turned her black eyes red over Egmont and Wallenstein. A mild attack of Emerson followed, during which she was lost in a fog, and her sisters rejoiced inwardly when she emerged informing them that

The Sphinx was drowsy,
Her wings were furled.

Poor Di was floundering slowly to her proper place; but she splashed up a good deal of foam by getting out of her depth, and rather exhausted herself by trying to drink the ocean dry.

Laura, after the "midsummer night's dream" that often comes to girls of seventeen, woke up to find that youth and love were no match for age and common sense. Philip had been flying about the world like a thistle-down for five-and-twenty years, generous-hearted, frank, and kind, but with never an idea of the serious side of life in his handsome head. Great, therefore, were the wrath and dismay of the enamored thistle-down, when the father of his love mildly objected to seeing her begin the world in a balloon with a very tender but very inexperienced aëronaut for a guide.

"Laura is too young to 'play house' yet, and you are too unstable to assume the part of lord and master, Philip. Go and prove that you have prudence, patience, energy, and enterprise, and I will give you my girl, — but not before. I must seem cruel, that I may be truly kind; believe this, and let a little pain lead you to great happiness, or show you where you would have made a bitter blunder."

The lovers listened, owned the truth of the old man's words, bewailed their fate, and — yielded, — Laura for love of her father, Philip for love of her. He went away to build a firm foundation for his castle in the air, and Laura retired into an invisible convent, where she cast off the world, and regarded her sympathizing sisters through a grate of superior knowl-edge and unsharable grief. Like a devout nun, she worshipped "St. Philip," and firmly believed in his miraculous powers. She fancied that her woes set her apart from common cares, and slowly fell into a dreamy state, professing no interest in any mundane matter, but the art that first attracted Philip. Crayons, bread-crusts, and gray paper became glorified in Laura's eyes; and her one pleasure was to sit pale and still before her easel, day after day, filling her portfolios with the faces he had once admired. Her sisters observed that every Bacchus, Piping Faun, or Dying Gladiator bore some likeness to a comely countenance that heathen god or hero never owned; and seeing this, they privately rejoiced that she had found such solace for her grief.

Mrs. Lord's keen eye had read a certain newly written page in her son's heart, — his first chapter of that romance, begun in Paradise, whose interest never flags, whose beauty never fades, whose end can never come till Love lies dead. With womanly skill she divined the secret, with motherly discretion she counselled patience, and her son accepted her advice, feeling, that, like many a healthful herb, its worth lay in its bitterness.

"Love like a man, John, not like a boy, and learn to know yourself before you take a woman's happiness into your keeping. You and Nan have known each other all your lives; yet, till this last visit, you never thought you loved her more than any other childish friend. It is too soon to say the words so often spoken hastily, — so hard to be recalled. Go back to your work, dear, for another year; think of Nan in the light of this new hope; compare her with comelier, gayer girls; and by absence prove the truth of your belief. Then, if distance only makes her dearer, if time only strengthens your affection, and no doubt of your own worthiness disturbs you, come back and offer her what any woman should be glad to take, — my boy's true heart."

John smiled at the motherly pride of her words, but answered with a wistful look.

"It seems very long to wait, mother. If I could just ask her for a word of hope, I could be very patient then."

"Ah, my dear, better bear one year of impatience now than a lifetime of regret hereafter. Nan is happy; why disturb her by a word which will bring the tender cares and troubles that come soon enough to such conscientious creatures as herself? If she loves you, time will prove it; therefore let the new affection spring and ripen as your early friendship has done, and it will be all the stronger for a summer's growth. Philip was rash, and has to bear his trial now, and Laura shares it with him. Be more generous, John; make *your* trial, bear *your* doubts alone, and give Nan the happiness without the pain. Promise me this, dear, — promise me to hope and wait."

The young man's eye kindled, and in his heart there rose a better chivalry, a truer valor, than any Di's knights had ever known.

"I'll try, mother," was all he said; but she was satisfied, for John seldom tried in vain.

"Oh, girls, how splendid you are! It does my heart good to see my handsome sisters in their best array," cried Nan, one mild October night, as she put the last touches to certain airy raiment fashioned by her own skilful hands, and then fell back to survey the grand effect.

Di and Laura were preparing to assist at an "event of the season," and Nan, with her own locks fallen on her shoulders, for want of sundry combs promoted to her sisters' heads, and her dress in unwonted disorder, for lack of the many pins extracted in exciting crises of the toilet, hovered like an affectionate bee about two very full-blown flowers.

"Laura looks like a cool Undine, with the ivy-wreaths in her shining hair; and Di has illuminated herself to such an extent with those scarlet leaves, that I don't know what great creature she resembles most," said Nan, beaming with sisterly admiration.

"Like Juno, Zenobia, and Cleopatra simmered into one, with a touch of Xantippe by way of spice. But, to my eye, the finest woman of the three is the dishevelled young person embracing the bed-post; for she stays at home herself, and gives her time and taste to making homely people fine, — which is a waste of good material, and an imposition on the public."

As Di spoke, both the fashion-plates looked affectionately at the gray-gowned figure; but, being works of art, they were obliged to nip their feelings in the bud, and reserve their caresses till they returned to common life.

"Put on your bonnet, and we'll leave you at Mrs. Lord's on our way. It will do you good, Nan; and perhaps there may be news from John," added Di, as she bore down upon the door like a man-of-war under full sail.

"Or from Philip," sighed Laura, with a wistful look.

Whereupon Nan persuaded herself that her strong inclination to sit down was owing to want of exercise, and the heaviness of her eyelids a freak of imagination; so, speedily smoothing her ruffled plumage, she ran down to tell her father of the new arrangement.

"Go, my dear, by all means. I shall be writing; and you will be lonely, if you stay. But I must see my girls; for I caught glimpses of certain surprising phantoms flitting by the door."

Nan led the way, and the two pyramids revolved before him with the rigidity of lay-figures, much to the good man's edification; for with his fatherly pleasure there was mingled much mild wonderment at the amplitude of array.

"Yes, I see my geese are really swans, though there is such a cloud between us that I feel a long way off, and hardly know them. But this little daughter is always available, always my 'cricket on the hearth.' "

As he spoke, her father drew Nan closer, kissed her tranquil face, and smiled content.

"Well, if ever I see picters, I see 'em now, and I declare to goodness it's as interestin' as play-actin', every bit. Miss Di, with all them boughs in her head, looks like the Queen of Sheby, when she went a-visitin' What's-his-name; and if Miss Laura a'n't as sweet as a lally-barster figger, I should like to know what is."

In her enthusiasm, Sally gambolled about the girls, flourishing her milk-pan like a modern Miriam about to sound her timbrel for excess of joy.

Laughing merrily, the two Mont Blancs bestowed themselves in the family ark, Nan hopped up beside Patrick, and Solon, roused from his lawful slumbers, morosely trundled them away. But, looking backward with a last "Good night!" Nan saw her father still standing at the door with smiling countenance, and the moonlight falling like a benediction on his silver hair.

"Betsey shall go up the hill with you, my dear, and here's a basket of eggs for your father. Give him my love, and be sure you let me know the next time he is poorly," Mrs. Lord said, when her guest rose to depart, after an hour of pleasant chat.

But Nan never got the gift; for, to her great dismay, her hostess dropped the basket with a crash, and flew across the room to meet a tall shape pausing in the shadow of the door. There was no need to ask who the new-comer was; for, even in his mother's arms, John looked over her shoulder with an eager nod to Nan, who stood among the ruins with never a sign of weariness in her face, nor the memory of a care at her heart, — for they all went out when John came in.

"Now tell us how and why and when you came. Take off your coat, my dear! And here are the old slippers. Why didn't you let us know you were coming so soon? How have you been? and what makes you so late to-night? Betsey, you needn't put on your bonnet. And — oh, my dear boy, *have* you been to supper yet?"

Mrs. Lord was a quiet soul, and her flood of questions was purred softly in her son's ear; for, being a woman, she *must* talk, and, being a mother, *must* pet the one delight of her life, and make a little festival when the lord of the manor came home. A whole drove of fatted calves were metaphorically killed, and a banquet appeared with speed.

John was not one of those romantic heroes who can go through three volumes of hairbreadth escapes without the faintest hint of that blessed institution, dinner; therefore, like "Lady Leatherbridge," he "partook copiously of everything," while the two women beamed over each mouthful with an interest that enhanced its flavor, and urged upon him cold meat and cheese, pickles and pie, as if dyspepsia and nightmare were among the lost arts.

Then he opened his budget of news and fed *them*.

"I was coming next month, according to custom; but Philip fell upon and so tempted me, that I was driven to sacrifice myself to the cause of friendship, and up we came to-night. He would not let me come here till we had seen your father, Nan; for the poor lad was pining for Laura, and hoped his good behavior for the past year would satisfy his judge and secure his recall. We had a fine talk with your father; and, upon my life, Phil seemed to have received the gift of tongues, for he made a most eloquent plea, which I've stored away for future use, I assure you. The dear old gentleman was very kind, told Phil he was satisfied with the success of his probation, that he should see Laura when he liked, and, if all went well, should receive his reward in the spring. It must be a delightful sensation to know you have made a fellow-creature as happy as those words made Phil to-night."

John paused, and looked musingly at the matronly tea-pot, as if he saw a wondrous future in its shine.

Nan twinkled off the drops that rose at the thought of Laura's joy, and said, with grateful warmth, —

"You say nothing of your own share in the making of that happiness, John; but we know it, for Philip has told Laura in his letters all that you have been to him, and I am sure there was other eloquence beside his own before father granted all you say he has. Oh, John, I thank you very much for this!"

Mrs. Lord beamed a whole midsummer of delight upon her son, as she saw the pleasure these words gave him, though he answered simply, —

"I only tried to be a brother to him, Nan; for he has been most kind to me. Yes, I said my little say to-night, and gave my testimony in behalf of the prisoner at the bar, a most merciful judge pronounced his sentence, and he rushed straight to Mrs. Leigh's to tell Laura the blissful news. Just imagine the scene when he appears, and how Di will open her wicked eyes and enjoy the spectacle of the dishevelled lover, the bride-elect's tears, the stir, and the romance of the thing. She'll cry over it to-night, and caricature it to-morrow."

And John led the laugh at the picture he had conjured up, to turn the thoughts of Di's dangerous sister from himself.

At ten Nan retired into the depths of her old bonnet with a far different face from the one she brought out of it, and John, resuming his hat, mounted guard.

"Don't stay late, remember, John!" And in Mrs. Lord's voice there was a warning tone that her son interpreted aright.

"I'll not forget, mother."

And he kept his word; for though Philip's happiness floated temptingly before him, and the little figure at his side had never seemed so dear, he ignored the bland winds, the tender night, and set a seal upon his lips,

[244]

thinking manfully within himself, "I see many signs of promise in her happy face; but I will wait and hope a little longer for her sake."

"Where is father, Sally?" asked Nan, as that functionary appeared, blinking owlishly, but utterly repudiating the idea of sleep.

"He went down the garding, miss, when the gentlemen cleared, bein' a little flustered by the goin's on. Shall I fetch him in?" asked Sally, as irreverently as if her master were a bag of meal.

"No, we will go ourselves." And slowly the two paced down the leaf-strewn walk.

Fields of yellow grain were waving on the hill-side, and sere corn-blades rustled in the wind, from the orchard came the scent of ripening fruit, and all the garden-plots lay ready to yield up their humble offerings to their master's hand. But in the silence of the night a greater Reaper had passed by, gathering in the harvest of a righteous life, and leaving only tender memories for the gleaners who had come so late.

The old man sat in the shadow of the tree his own hands planted; its fruitful boughs shone ruddily, and its leaves still whispered the low lullaby that hushed him to his rest.

"How fast he sleeps! Poor father! I should have come before and made it pleasant for him."

As she spoke, Nan lifted up the head bent down upon his breast, and kissed his pallid cheek.

"Oh, John, this is not sleep!"

"Yes, dear, the happiest he will ever know."

For a moment the shadows flickered over three white faces and the silence deepened solemnly. Then John reverently bore the pale shape in, and Nan dropped down beside it, saying, with a rain of grateful tears, —

"He kissed me when I went, and said a last 'good night!' "

For an hour steps went to and fro about her, many voices whispered near her, and skilful hands touched the beloved clay she held so fast; but one by one the busy feet passed out, one by one the voices died away, and human skill proved vain. Then Mrs. Lord drew the orphan to the shelter of her arms, soothing her with the mute solace of that motherly embrace.

"Nan, Nan! here's Philip! come and see!"

The happy call reëchoed through the house, and Nan sprang up as if her time for grief were past.

"I must tell them. Oh, my poor girls, how will they bear it? — they have known so little sorrow!"

But there was no need for her to speak; other lips had spared her the hard task. For, as she stirred to meet them, a sharp cry rent the air, steps rang upon the stairs, and two wild-eyed creatures came into the hush of that familiar room, for the first time meeting with no welcome from their father's voice.

With one impulse, Di and Laura fled to Nan, and the sisters clung together in a silent embrace, far more eloquent than words. John took his mother by the hand, and led her from the room, closing the door upon the sacredness of grief.

"Yes, we are poorer than we thought; but when everything is settled, we shall get on very well. We can let a part of this great house, and live quietly together until spring; then Laura will be married, and Di can go on their travels with them, as Philip wishes her to do. We shall be cared for; so never fear for us, John."

Nan said this, as her friend parted from her a week later, after the saddest holiday he had ever known.

"And what becomes of you, Nan?" he asked, watching the patient eyes that smiled when others would have wept.

"I shall stay in the dear old house; for no other place would seem like home to me. I shall find some little child to love and care for, and be quite happy till the girls come back and want me."

John nodded wisely, as he listened, and went away prophesying within himself, —

"She shall find something more than a child to love; and, God willing, shall be very happy till the girls come home and — cannot have her."

Nan's plan was carried into effect. Slowly the divided waters closed again, and the three fell back into their old life. But the touch of sorrow drew them closer; and, though invisible, a beloved presence still moved among them, a familiar voice still spoke to them in the silence of their softened hearts. Thus the soil was made ready, and in the depth of winter the good seed was sown, was watered with many tears, and soon sprang up green with the promise of a harvest for their after years.

Di and Laura consoled themselves with their favorite employments, unconscious that Nan was growing paler, thinner, and more silent, as the weeks went by, till one day she dropped quietly before them, and it suddenly became manifest that she was utterly worn out with many cares and the secret suffering of a tender heart bereft of the paternal love which had been its strength and stay.

"I'm only tired, dear girls. Don't be troubled, for I shall be up to-morrow," she said cheerily, as she looked into the anxious faces bending over her.

But the weariness was of many months' growth, and it was weeks before that "to-morrow" came.

Laura installed herself as nurse, and her devotion was repaid four-fold; for, sitting at her sister's bedside, she learned a finer art than that she had left. Her eye grew clear to see the beauty of a self-denying life, and in the depths of Nan's meek nature she found the strong, sweet virtues that made her what she was.

Then remembering that these womanly attributes were a bride's best dowry, Laura gave herself to their attainment, that she might become to another household the blessing Nan had been to her own; and turning from the worship of the goddess Beauty, she gave her hand to that humbler and more human teacher, Duty, — learning her lessons with a willing heart, for Philip's sake.

Di corked her inkstand, locked her bookcase, and went at housework as if it were a five-barred gate; of course she missed the leap, but scrambled bravely through, and appeared much sobered by the exercise. Sally had departed to sit under a vine and fig-tree of her own, so Di had undisputed sway; but if dish-pans and dusters had tongues, direful would have been the history of that crusade against frost and fire, indolence and inexperience. But they were dumb, and Di scorned to complain, though her struggles were pathetic to behold, and her sisters went through a series of messes equal to a course of "Prince Benreddin's" peppery tarts. Reality turned Romance out of doors; for, unlike her favorite heroines in satin and tears, or helmet and shield, Di met her fate in a big checked apron and dust-cap, wonderful to see; yet she wielded her broom as stoutly as "Moll Pitcher" shouldered her gun, and marched to her daily martyrdom in the kitchen with as heroic a heart as the "Maid of Orleans" took to her stake.

Mind won the victory over matter in the end, and Di was better all her days for the tribulations and the triumphs of that time; for she drowned her idle fancies in her wash-tub, made burnt-offerings of selfishness and pride, and learned the worth of self-denial, as she sang with happy voice among the pots and kettles of her conquered realm.

Nan thought of John, and in the stillness of her sleepless nights prayed Heaven to keep him safe, and make her worthy to receive and strong enough to bear the blessedness or pain of love.

Snow fell without, and keen winds howled among the leafless elms, but "herbs of grace" were blooming beautifully in the sunshine of sincere endeavor, and this dreariest season proved the most fruitful of the year; for love taught Laura, labor chastened Di, and patience fitted Nan for the blessing of her life.

Nature, that stillest, yet most diligent of housewives, began at last that "spring-cleaning" which she makes so pleasant that none find the heart to grumble as they do when other matrons set their premises a-dust. Her handmaids, wind and rain and sun, swept, washed, and garnished busily, green carpets were unrolled, apple-boughs were hung with draperies of bloom, and dandelions, pet nurslings of the year, came out to play upon the sward.

From the South returned that opera troupe whose manager is never in despair, whose tenor never sulks, whose prima donna never fails, and in the orchard *bonâ fide* matinées were held, to which buttercups and clovers crowded in their prettiest spring hats, and verdant young blades twinkled their dewy lorgnettes, as they bowed and made way for the floral belles.

May was bidding June good-morrow, and the roses were just dreaming that it was almost time to wake, when John came again into the quiet room which now seemed the Eden that contained his Eve. Of course there was a jubilee; but something seemed to have befallen the whole group, for never had they all appeared in such odd frames of mind. John was restless, and wore an excited look, most unlike his usual serenity of aspect.

Nan the cheerful had fallen into a well of silence and was not to be extracted by any hydraulic power, though she smiled like the June sky over her head. Di's peculiarities were out in full force, and she looked as if she would go off like a torpedo at a touch; but through all her moods there was a half-triumphant, half-remorseful expression in the glance she fixed on John. And Laura, once so silent, now sang like a blackbird, as she flitted to and fro; but her fitful song was always, "Philip, my king."

John felt that there had come a change upon the three, and silently divined whose unconscious influence had wrought the miracle. The embargo was off his tongue, and he was in a fever to ask that question which brings a flutter to the stoutest heart; but though the "man" had come, the "hour" had not. So, by way of steadying his nerves, he paced the room, pausing often to take notes of his companions, and each pause seemed to increase his wonder and content.

He looked at Nan. She was in her usual place, the rigid little chair she loved, because it once was large enough to hold a curly-headed playmate and herself. The old work-basket was at her side, and the battered thimble busily at work; but here lips wore a smile they had never worn before, the color of the unblown roses touched her cheek, and her downcast eyes were full of light.

He looked at Di. The inevitable book was on her knee, but its leaves were uncut; the strong-minded knob of hair still asserted its supremacy aloft upon her head, and the triangular jacket still adorned her shoulders in defiance of all fashions, past, present, or to come; but the expression of her brown countenance had grown softer, her tongue had found a curb, and in her hand lay a card with "Potts, Kettel, & Co." inscribed thereon, which she regarded with never a scornful word for the "Co."

He looked at Laura. She was before her easel, as of old; but the pale nun had given place to a blooming girl, who sang at her work, which was no prim Pallas, but a Clytie turning her human face to meet the sun.

"John, what are you thinking of?"

He stirred as if Di's voice had disturbed his fancy at some pleasant pastime, but answered with his usual sincerity, —

"I was thinking of a certain dear old fairy tale called 'Cinderella.' "

"Oh!" said Di; and her "Oh" was a most impressive monosyllable. "I see the meaning of your smile now; and though the application of the story is not very complimentary to all parties concerned, it is very just and very true."

She paused a moment, then went on with softened voice and earnest mien: —

"You think I am a blind and selfish creature. So I am, but not so blind and selfish as I have been; for many tears have cleared my eyes, and much sincere regret has made me humbler than I was. I have found a better book than any father's library can give me, and I have read it with a love and admiration that grew stronger as I turned the leaves. Henceforth I take it for my guide and gospel, and, looking back upon the selfish and neglectful past, can only say, Heaven bless your dear heart, Nan!"

Laura echoed Di's last words; for, with eyes as full of tenderness, she looked down upon the sister she had lately learned to know, saying, warmly, —

"Yes, 'Heaven bless your dear heart, Nan!' I never can forget all you have been to me; and when I am far away with Philip, there will always be one countenance more beautiful to me than any pictured face I may discover, there will be one place more dear to me than Rome. The face will be yours, Nan, — always so patient, always so serene; and the dearer place will be this home of ours, which you have made so pleasant to me all these years by kindnesses as numberless and noiseless as the drops of dew."

"Dear girls, what have I ever done, that you should love me so?" cried Nan, with happy wonderment, as the tall heads, black and golden, bent to meet the lowly brown one, and her sisters' mute lips answered her.

Then Laura looked up, saying, playfully, —

"Here are the good and wicked sisters; — where shall we find the Prince?"

"There!" cried Di, pointing to John; and then her secret went off like a rocket; for, with her old impetuosity, she said, —

"I have found you out, John, and am ashamed to look you in the face, remembering the past. Girls, you know, when father died, John sent us money, which he said Mr. Owen had long owed us and had paid at last? It was a kind lie, John, and a generous thing to do; for we needed it, but never would have taken it as a gift. I know you meant that we should never find this out; but yesterday I met Mr. Owen returning from the West, and when I thanked him for a piece of justice we had not expected of him, he gruffly told me he had never paid the debt, never meant to pay it, for it was outlawed, and we could not claim a farthing. John, I have laughed at you, thought you stupid, treated you unkindly; but I know you now, and never shall forget the lesson you have taught me. I am proud as Lucifer, but I ask you to forgive me, and I seal my real repentance so — and so."

With tragic countenance, Di rushed across the room, threw both arms about the astonished young man's neck and dropped an energetic kiss upon his cheek. There was a momentary silence; for Di finely illustrated her strong-minded theories by crying like the weakest of her sex. Laura, with "the ruling passion strong in death," still tried to draw, but broke her pet crayon, and endowed her Clytie with a supplementary orb, owing to the dimness of her own. And Nan sat with drooping eyes, that shone upon her work, thinking with tender pride, —

"They know him now, and love him for his generous heart."

Di spoke first, rallying to her colors, though a little daunted by her loss of self-control.

"Don't laugh, John, — I couldn't help it; and don't think I'm not sincere, for I am, — I am; and I will prove it by growing good enough to be your friend. That debt must all be paid, and I shall do it; for I'll turn my books and pen to some account, and write stories full of dear old souls like you and Nan; and some one, I know, will like and buy them, though they are not 'works of Shakespeare.' I've thought of this before, have felt I had the power in me; *now* I have the motive, and *now* I'll do it."

If Di had proposed to translate the Koran, or build a new Saint Paul's, there would have been many chances of success; for, once moved, her will, like a battering-ram, would knock down the obstacles her wits could not surmount. John believed in her most heartily, and showed it, as he answered, looking into her resolute face, —

"I know you will, and yet make us very proud of our 'Chaos,' Di. Let the money lie, and when you have made a fortune, I'll claim it with enormous interest; but, believe me, I feel already doubly repaid by the esteem so generously confessed, so cordially bestowed, and can only say, as we used to years ago, — 'Now let's forgive and so forget.' "

But proud Di would not let him add to her obligation, even by returning her impetuous salute; she slipped away, and, shaking off the last drops, answered with a curious mixture of old freedom and new respect, —

"No more sentiment, please, John. We know each other now; and when I find a friend, I never let him go. We have smoked the pipe of peace; so let us go back to our wigwams and bury the feud. Where were we when I lost my head? and what were we talking about?"

"Cinderella and the Prince."

As he spoke, John's eye kindled, and, turning, he looked down at Nan, who sat diligently ornamenting with microscopic stitches a great patch going on, the wrong side out.

"Yes, — so we were; and now taking pussy for the godmother, the characters of the story are well personated, — all but the slipper," said Di, laughing, as she thought of the many times they had played it together years ago.

A sudden movement stirred John's frame, a sudden purpose shone in his countenance, and a sudden change befell his voice, as he said, producing from some hiding-place a little worn-out shoe, —

"I can supply the slipper; — who will try it first?"

Di's black eyes opened wide, as they fell on the familiar object; then her romance-loving nature saw the whole plot of that drama which needs but two to act it. A great delight flushed up into her face, as she promptly took her cue, saying, —

"No need for us to try it, Laura; for it wouldn't fit us, if our feet were as small as Chinese dolls'; — our parts are played out; therefore 'Exeunt wicked sisters to the music of the wedding-bells.' " And pouncing upon the dismayed artist, she swept her out and closed the door with a triumphant bang.

John went to Nan, and, dropping on his knee as reverently as the herald of the fairy tale, he asked, still smiling, but with lips grown tremulous, —

"Will Cinderella try the little shoe, and — if it fits — go with the Prince?"

But Nan only covered up her face, weeping happy tears, while all the weary work strayed down upon the floor, as if it knew her holiday had come.

John drew the hidden face still closer, and while she listened to his eager words, Nan heard the beating of the strong man's heart, and knew it spoke the truth.

"Nan, I promised mother to be silent till I was sure I loved you wholly, — sure that the knowledge would give no pain when I should tell it, as I am trying to tell it now. This little shoe has been my comforter through this long year, and I have kept it as other lovers keep their fairer favors. It has been a talisman more eloquent to me than flower or ring; for, when I saw how worn it was, I always thought of the willing feet that came and went for others' comfort all day long; when I saw the little bow you tied, I always thought of the hands so diligent in serving any one who knew a want or felt a pain; and when I recalled the gentle creature who had worn it last, I always saw her patient, tender, and devout, — and tried to grow more worthy of her, that I might one day dare to ask if she would walk beside me all my life and be my 'angel in the house.' Will you, dear? Believe me, you shall never know a weariness or grief I have the power to shield you from."

Then Nan, as simple in her love as in her life, laid her arms about his neck, her happy face against his own, and answered softly, —

"Oh, John, I never can be sad or tired any more!"

Merry's Monthly Chat

Merry's Museum, January 1868. By "Cousin Tribulation"

A HAPPY NEW YEAR all round, and best wishes to every one, especially those who give old Merry a welcome in his new dress. Those who knew him years ago will, we hope, lend him a hand for old acquaintance's sake; and the young folks will find him such a pleasant companion, that they will open their doors to him, and make a little place on their library shelves for Uncle Merry, who, in spite of time, keeps his heart young, and dearly loves the children.

A new friend wishes to be admitted to the circle, and cousin Tribulation shall have a place.

DEAR MERRYS: — As a subject appropriate to the season, I want to tell you about a New Year's breakfast which I had when I was a little girl. What do you think it was? A slice of dry bread and an apple. This is how it happened, and it is a true story, every word.

As we came down to breakfast that morning, with very shiny faces and spandy clean aprons, we found father alone in the dining-room.

"Happy New Year, papa! Where is mother?" we cried.

"A little boy came begging, and said they were starving at home, so your mother went to see and — ah, here she is."

As Papa spoke, in came mamma, looking very cold, rather sad, and very much excited.

"Children, don't begin till you hear what I have to say," she cried; and we sat staring at her, with the breakfast untouched before us.

"Not far away from here lies a poor woman with a little new-born baby. Six children are huddled into one bed to keep from freezing, for they have no fire. There is nothing to eat over there; and the oldest boy came here to tell me they were starving this bitter cold day. My little girls, will you give them your breakfast, as a New Year's gift?"

We sat silent a minute, and looked at the nice, hot porridge, creamy milk, and good bread and butter; for we were brought up like English children, never drank tea or coffee, or ate anything but porridge for our breakfast.

"I wish we'd eaten it up," thought I, for I was rather a selfish child, and very hungry.

"I'm so glad you came before we began," said Nan, cheerfully.

"May I go and help carry it to the poor, little children?" asked Beth, who had the tenderest heart that ever beat under a pinafore.

"I can carry the lassy pot," said little May, proudly giving the thing that she loved best.

"You shall put on your things and help me, and when we come back, we'll get something to eat," said mother, beginning to pile the bread and butter into a big basket.

We were soon ready, and the procession set out. First, papa, with a basket of wood on one arm and coal on the other; mamma next, with a bundle of warm things and the teapot; Nan and I carried a pail of hot porridge between us, and each a pitcher of milk. Beth brought some cold meat, May the "lassy pot," and her old hood and boots: and Betsy, the girl, brought up the rear with a bag of potatoes and some meat.

Fortunately it was early, and we went along the back streets, so few people saw us, and no one laughed at the funny party.

What a poor, bare, miserable place it was, to be sure, — broken windows, no fire, ragged clothing, wailing baby, sick mother, and a pile of pale, hungry children cuddled under one quilt, trying to keep warm. How the big eyes stared and the blue lips smiled as we came in!

"Ah, mein Gott! it is the good angels that come to us!" cried the poor woman, with tears of joy.

"Funny angels, in woollen hoods and red mittens," said I; and they all laughed.

Then we fell to work, and in fifteen minutes, it really did seem as if fairies had been at work there. Papa made a splendid fire in the old fireplace and stopped up the broken window with his own hat and coat. Mamma set the shivering children round the fire, and wrapped the poor woman in warm things. Betsy and the rest of us spread the table, and fed the starving little ones.

"Das ist gute!" "Oh, nice!" "Der angel — Kinder!" cried the poor things as they ate and smiled and basked in the warm blaze. We had never been called "angel-children" before, and we thought it was very charming, especially I who had often been told I was "a regular Sancho." What fun it was! Papa, with a towel for an apron, fed the smallest child; mamma dressed the poor little new-born baby as tenderly as if it had been her own. Betsy gave the mother gruel and tea, and comforted her with assurances of better days for all. Nan, Lu, Beth and May flew about talking and laughing and trying to understand their funny, broken English. It was a very happy breakfast, though we didn't get any of it; and when we came away, leaving them all so comfortable, and promising to bring clothes and food by and by, I think there were not in all the city four merrier children than the hungry little girls who gave away their breakfast, and contented themselves with a bit of bread and an apple on New Year's day.

The Little Women *Trilogy*

———————

A Merry Christmas

Chapter 2 of *Little Women or, Meg, Jo, Beth and Amy*, 2 vols.
(Boston: Roberts Brothers, 1868–1869)

JO WAS THE FIRST to wake in the gray dawn of Christmas morning. No stockings hung at the fireplace, and for a moment she felt as much disappointed as she did long ago, when her little sock fell down because it was so crammed with goodies. Then she remembered her mother's promise, and slipping her hand under her pillow, drew out a little crimson-covered book. She knew it very well, for it was that beautiful old story of the best life ever lived, and Jo felt that it was a true guide-book for any pilgrim going the long journey. She woke Meg with a "Merry Christmas," and bade her see what was under her pillow. A green-covered book appeared, with the same picture inside, and a few words written by their mother, which made their one present very precious in their eyes. Presently Beth and Amy woke, to rummage and find their little books also, — one dove-colored, the other blue; and all sat looking at and talking about them, while the East grew rosy with the coming day.

In spite of her small vanities, Margaret had a sweet and pious nature, which unconsciously influenced her sisters, especially Jo, who loved her very tenderly, and obeyed her because her advice was so gently given.

"Girls," said Meg, seriously, looking from the tumbled head beside her to the two little night-capped ones in the room beyond, "mother wants us to read and love and mind these books, and we must begin at once. We used to be faithful about it; but since father went away, and all this war trouble unsettled us, we have neglected many things. You can do as you please; but *I* shall keep my book on the table here, and read a little every morning as soon as I wake, for I know it will do me good, and help me through the day."

Then she opened her new book and began to read. Jo put her arm round her, and, leaning cheek to cheek, read also, with the quiet expression so seldom seen on her restless face.

"How good Meg is! Come, Amy, let's do as they do. I'll help you with the hard words, and they'll explain things if we don't understand," whispered Beth, very much impressed by the pretty books and her sisters' example.

"I'm glad mine is blue," said Amy; and then the rooms were very still while pages were softly turned, and the winter sunshine crept in to touch the bright heads and serious faces with a Christmas greeting.

"Where is mother?" asked Meg, as she and Jo ran down to thank her for their gifts, half an hour later.

"Goodness only knows. Some poor creeter come a–beggin', and your ma went straight off to see what was needed. There never *was* such a woman for givin' away vittles and drink, clothes and firin'," replied Hannah, who had lived with the family since Meg was born, and was considered by them all more as a friend than a servant.

"She will be back soon, I guess; so do your cakes, and have everything ready," said Meg, looking over the presents which were collected in a basket and kept under the sofa, ready to be produced at the proper time. "Why, where is Amy's bottle of Cologne?" she added, as the little flask did not appear.

"She took it out a minute ago, and went off with it to put a ribbon on it, or some such notion," replied Jo, dancing about the room to take the first stiffness off the new army-slippers.

"How nice my handkerchiefs look, don't they? Hannah washed and ironed them for me, and I marked them all myself," said Beth, looking proudly at the somewhat uneven letters which had cost her such labor.

"Bless the child, she's gone and put 'Mother' on them instead of 'M. March;' how funny!" cried Jo, taking up one.

"Isn't it right? I thought it was better to do it so, because Meg's initials are 'M. M.,' and I don't want any one to use these but Marmee," said Beth, looking troubled.

"It's all right, dear, and a very pretty idea; quite sensible, too, for no one can ever mistake now. It will please her very much, I know," said Meg, with a frown for Jo, and a smile for Beth.

"There's mother; hide the basket, quick!" cried Jo, as a door slammed, and steps sounded in the hall.

Amy came in hastily, and looked rather abashed when she saw her sisters all waiting for her.

"Where have you been, and what are you hiding behind you?" asked

Meg, surprised to see, by her hood and cloak, that lazy Amy had been out so early.

"Don't laugh at me, Jo, I didn't mean any one should know till the time came. I only meant to change the little bottle for a big one, and I gave *all* my money to get it, and I'm truly trying not to be selfish any more."

As she spoke, Amy showed the handsome flask which replaced the cheap one; and looked so earnest and humble in her little effort to forget herself, that Meg hugged her on the spot, and Jo pronounced her "a trump," while Beth ran to the window, and picked her finest rose to ornament the stately bottle.

"You see I felt ashamed of my present, after reading and talking about being good this morning, so I ran round the corner and changed it the minute I was up; and I'm *so* glad, for mine is the handsomest now."

Another bang of the street-door sent the basket under the sofa, and the girls to the table eager for breakfast.

"Merry Christmas, Marmee! Lots of them! Thank you for our books; we read some, and mean to every day," they cried, in chorus.

"Merry Christmas, little daughters! I'm glad you began at once, and hope you will keep on. But I want to say one word before we sit down. Not far away from here lies a poor woman with a little new-born baby. Six children are huddled into one bed to keep from freezing, for they have no fire. There is nothing to eat over there; and the oldest boy came to tell me they were suffering hunger and cold. My girls, will you give them your breakfast as a Christmas present?"

They were all unusually hungry, having waited nearly an hour, and for a minute no one spoke; only a minute, for Jo exclaimed impetuously, —

"I'm so glad you came before we began!"

"May I go and help carry the things to the poor little children?" asked Beth, eagerly.

"*I* shall take the cream and the muffins," added Amy, heroically giving up the articles she most liked.

Meg was already covering the buckwheats, and piling the bread into one big plate.

"I thought you'd do it," said Mrs. March, smiling as if satisfied. "You shall all go and help me, and when we come back we will have bread and milk for breakfast, and make it up at dinner-time."

They were soon ready, and the procession set out. Fortunately it was early, and they went through back streets, so few people saw them, and no one laughed at the funny party.

A poor, bare, miserable room it was, with broken windows, no fire, ragged bed-clothes, a sick mother, wailing baby, and a group of pale, hungry children cuddled under one old quilt, trying to keep warm. How the big eyes stared, and the blue lips smiled, as the girls went in!

"Ach, mein Gott! it is good angels come to us!" cried the poor woman, crying for joy.

"Funny angels in hoods and mittens," said Jo, and set them laughing.

In a few minutes it really did seem as if kind spirits had been at work there. Hannah, who had carried wood, made a fire, and stopped up the broken panes with old hats, and her own shawl. Mrs. March gave the mother tea and gruel, and comforted her with promises of help, while she dressed the little baby as tenderly as if it had been her own. The girls, meantime, spread the table, set the children round the fire, and fed them like so many hungry birds; laughing, talking, and trying to understand the funny broken English.

"Das ist gute!" "Der angel-kinder!" cried the poor things, as they ate, and warmed their purple hands at the comfortable blaze. The girls had never been called angel children before, and thought it very agreeable, especially Jo, who had been considered "a Sancho" ever since she was born. That was a very happy breakfast, though they didn't get any of it; and when they went away, leaving comfort behind, I think there were not in all the city four merrier people than the hungry little girls who gave away their breakfasts, and contented themselves with bread and milk on Christmas morning.

"That's loving our neighbor better than ourselves, and I like it," said Meg, as they set out their presents, while their mother was up stairs collecting clothes for the poor Hummels.

Not a very splendid show, but there was a great deal of love done up in the few little bundles; and the tall vase of red roses, white chrysanthemums, and trailing vines, which stood in the middle, gave quite an elegant air to the table.

"She's coming! strike up, Beth, open the door, Amy. Three cheers for Marmee!" cried Jo, prancing about, while Meg went to conduct mother to the seat of honor.

Beth played her gayest march, Amy threw open the door, and Meg enacted escort with great dignity. Mrs. March was both surprised and touched; and smiled with her eyes full as she examined her presents, and read the little notes which accompanied them. The slippers went on at once, a new handkerchief was slipped into her pocket, well scented with Amy's Cologne, the rose was fastened in her bosom, and the nice gloves were pronounced "a perfect fit."

There was a good deal of laughing, and kissing, and explaining, in the simple, loving fashion which makes these home-festivals so pleasant at the time, so sweet to remember long afterward, and then all fell to work.

The morning charities and ceremonies took so much time, that the rest of the day was devoted to preparations for the evening festivities. Being still too young to go often to the theatre, and not rich enough to afford any great outlay for private performances, the girls put their wits to work, and, necessity being the mother of invention, made whatever they needed. Very clever were some of their productions; paste-board guitars, antique lamps made of old-fashioned butter-boats, covered with silver paper, gorgeous robes of old cotton, glittering with tin spangles from a pickle factory, and armor covered with the same useful diamond-shaped bits, left in sheets when the lids of tin preserve-pots were cut out. The furniture was used to being turned topsy-turvy, and the big chamber was the scene of many innocent revels.

No gentlemen were admitted; so Jo played male parts to her heart's content, and took immense satisfaction in a pair of russet-leather boots given her by a friend, who knew a lady who knew an actor. These boots, an old foil, and a slashed doublet once used by an artist for some picture, were Jo's chief treasures, and appeared on all occasions. The smallness of the company made it necessary for the two principal actors to take several parts apiece; and they certainly deserved some credit for the hard work they did in learning three or four different parts, whisking in and out of various costumes, and managing the stage besides. It was excellent drill for their memories, a harmless amusement, and employed many hours which otherwise would have been idle, lonely, or spent in less profitable society.

On Christmas night, a dozen girls piled on to the bed, which was the dress circle, and sat before the blue and yellow chintz curtains, in a most flattering state of expectancy. There was a good deal of rustling and whispering behind the curtain, a trifle of lamp-smoke, and an occasional giggle from Amy, who was apt to get hysterical in the excitement of the moment. Presently a bell sounded, the curtains flew apart, and the Operatic Tragedy began.

"A gloomy wood," according to the one play-bill, was represented by a few shrubs in pots, a green baize on the floor, and a cave in the distance. This cave was made with a clothes-horse for a roof, bureaus for walls; and in it was a small furnace in full blast, with a black pot on it, and an old witch bending over it. The stage was dark, and the glow of the furnace had a fine effect, especially as real steam issued from the kettle when the witch took off the cover. A moment was allowed for the first thrill to subside; then Hugo, the villain, stalked in with a clanking sword at his side, a slouched hat, black beard, mysterious cloak, and the boots. After pacing to and fro in much agitation, he struck his forehead, and burst out in a wild strain, singing of his hatred to Roderigo, his love for Zara, and his pleasing resolution to kill the one and win the other. The gruff tones of Hugo's voice, with an occasional shout when his feelings overcame him, were very impressive, and the audience applauded the moment he paused for breath. Bowing with the air of one accustomed to public praise, he stole to the cavern and ordered Hagar to come forth with a commanding "What ho! minion! I need thee!"

Out came Meg, with gray horse-hair hanging about her face, a red and black robe, a staff, and cabalistic signs upon her cloak. Hugo demanded a potion to make Zara adore him, and one to destroy Roderigo. Hagar, in a fine dramatic melody, promised both, and proceeded to call up the spirit who would bring the love philter: —

> *Hither, hither, from thy home,*
> *Airy sprite, I bid thee come!*
> *Born of roses, fed on dew,*
> *Charms and potions canst thou brew?*
> *Bring me here, with elfin speed,*
> *The fragrant philter which I need;*
> *Make it sweet, and swift and strong;*
> *Spirit, answer now my song!*

A soft strain of music sounded, and then at the back of the cave appeared a little figure in cloudy white, with glittering wings, golden hair, and a garland of roses on its head. Waving a wand, it sung: —

> *Hither I come,*
> *From my airy home,*
> *Afar in the silver moon;*
> *Take the magic spell,*
> *Oh, use it well!*
> *Or its power will vanish soon!*

and dropping a small gilded bottle at the witch's feet, the spirit vanished. Another chant from Hagar produced another apparition, — not a lovely one, for, with a bang, an ugly, black imp appeared, and having croaked a reply, tossed a dark bottle at Hugo, and disappeared with a mocking laugh. Having warbled his thanks, and put the potions in his boots, Hugo departed; and Hagar informed the audience that, as he had killed a few of her friends in times past, she has cursed him, and intends to thwart his plans, and be revenged on him. Then the curtain fell, and the audience reposed and ate candy while discussing the merits of the play.

A good deal of hammering went on before the curtain rose again; but when it became evident what a masterpiece of stage carpentering had been got up, no one murmured at the delay. It was truly superb! A tower rose to the ceiling; half-way up appeared a window with a lamp burning at it, and behind the white curtain appeared Zara in a lovely blue and silver dress, waiting for Roderigo. He came, in gorgeous array, with plumed cap, red cloak, chestnut love-locks, a guitar, and the boots, of course. Kneeling at the foot of the tower, he sung a serenade in melting tones. Zara replied, and after a musical dialogue, consented to fly. Then came the grand effect of the play. Roderigo produced a rope-ladder with five steps to it, threw up one end, and invited Zara to descend. Timidly she crept from her lattice, put her hand on Roderigo's shoulder, and was about to leap gracefully down, when, "alas, alas for Zara!" she forgot her train, — it caught on the window; the tower tottered, leaned forward, fell with a crash, and buried the unhappy lovers in the ruins!

A universal shriek arose as the russet boots waved wildly from the wreck, and a golden head emerged, exclaiming, "I told you so! I told you so!" With wonderful presence of mind Don Pedro, the cruel sire, rushed in, dragged out his daughter with a hasty aside, —

"Don't laugh, act as if it was all right!" and ordering Roderigo up, banished him from the kingdom with wrath and scorn. Though decidedly shaken by the fall of the tower upon him, Roderigo defied the old gentleman, and refused to stir. This dauntless example fired Zara; she also defied her sire, and he ordered them both to the deepest dungeons of the castle. A stout little retainer came in with chains, and led them away, looking very much frightened, and evidently forgetting the speech he ought to have made.

Act third was the castle hall; and here Hagar appeared, having come to free the lovers and finish Hugo. She hears him coming, and hides; sees him put the potions into two cups of wine, and bid the timid little servant "Bear them to the captives in their cells, and tell them I shall come anon." The servant takes Hugo aside to tell him something, and Hagar changes the cups for two others which are harmless. Ferdinando, the "minion," carries them away, and Hagar puts back the cup which holds the poison meant for Roderigo. Hugo, getting thirsty after a long warble, drinks it, loses his wits, and after a good deal of clutching and stamping, falls flat and dies; while Hagar informs him what she has done in a song of exquisite power and melody.

This was a truly thrilling scene; though some persons might have thought that the sudden tumbling down of a quantity of long hair rather marred the effect of the villain's death. He was called before the curtain, and with great propriety appeared leading Hagar, whose singing was considered more wonderful than all the rest of the performance put together.

Act fourth displayed the despairing Roderigo on the point of stabbing himself, because he has been told that Zara has deserted him. Just as the dagger is at his heart, a lovely song is sung under his window, informing him that Zara is true, but in danger, and he can save her if he will. A key is thrown in, which unlocks the door, and in a spasm of rapture he tears off his chains, and rushes away to find and rescue his lady-love.

Act fifth opened with a stormy scene between Zara and Don Pedro. He wishes her to go into a convent, but she won't hear of it; and, after a touching appeal, is about to faint, when Roderigo dashes in and demands her hand. Don Pedro refuses, because he is not rich. They shout and gesticulate tremendously, but cannot agree, and Roderigo is about to bear away the exhausted Zara, when the timid servant enters with a letter and a bag from Hagar, who has mysteriously disappeared. The letter informs the party that she bequeaths untold wealth to the young pair, and an awful doom to Don Pedro if he doesn't make them happy. The bag is opened, and several quarts of tin money shower down upon the stage, till it is quite glorified with the glitter. This entirely softens the "stern sire;" he consents without a murmur, all join in a joyful chorus, and the curtain falls upon the lovers kneeling to receive Don Pedro's blessing, in attitudes of the most romantic grace.

Tumultuous applause followed, but received an unexpected check; for the cot-bed on which the "dress circle" was built, suddenly shut up, and extinguished the enthusiastic audience. Roderigo and Don Pedro flew to the rescue, and all were taken out unhurt, though many were speechless with laughter. The excitement had hardly subsided when Hannah appeared, with "Mrs. March's compliments, and would the ladies walk down to supper."

This was a surprise, even to the actors; and when they saw the table they looked at one another in rapturous amazement. It was like "Marmee" to get up a little treat for them, but anything so fine as this was unheard of since the departed days of plenty. There was ice cream, actually two dishes of it, — pink and white, — and cake, and fruit, and distracting French bonbons, and in the middle of the table four great bouquets of hothouse flowers!

It quite took their breath away; and they stared first at the table and then at their mother, who looked as if she enjoyed it immensely.

"Is it fairies?" asked Amy.

"It's Santa Claus," said Beth.

"Mother did it;" and Meg smiled her sweetest, in spite of her gray beard and white eyebrows.

"Aunt March had a good fit, and sent the supper," cried Jo, with a sudden inspiration.

"All wrong; old Mr. Laurence sent it," replied Mrs. March.

"The Laurence boy's grandfather! What in the world put such a thing into his head? We don't know him," exclaimed Meg.

"Hannah told one of his servants about your breakfast party; he is an odd old gentleman, but that pleased him. He knew my father, years ago, and he sent me a polite note this afternoon, saying he hoped I would allow him to express his friendly feeling toward my children by sending them a few trifles in honor of the day. I could not refuse, and so you have a little feast at night to make up for the bread and milk breakfast."

"That boy put it into his head, I know he did! He's a capital fellow, and I wish we could get acquainted. He looks as if he'd like to know us; but he's bashful, and Meg is so prim she won't let me speak to him when we pass," said Jo, as the plates went round, and the ice began to melt out of sight, with ohs! and ahs! of satisfaction.

"You mean the people who live in the big house next door, don't you?" asked one of the girls. "My mother knows old Mr. Laurence, but says he's very proud, and don't like to mix with his neighbors. He keeps his grandson shut up when he isn't riding or walking with his tutor, and makes him study dreadful hard. We invited him to our party, but he didn't come. Mother says he's very nice, though he never speaks to us girls."

"Our cat ran away once, and he brought her back, and we talked over the fence, and were getting on capitally, all about cricket, and so on, when he saw Meg coming, and walked off. I mean to know him some day, for he needs fun, I'm sure he does," said Jo, decidedly.

"I like his manners, and he looks like a little gentleman, so I've no objection to your knowing him if a proper opportunity comes. He brought the flowers himself, and I should have asked him in if I had been sure what was going on up stairs. He looked so wistful as he went away, hearing the frolic, and evidently having none of his own."

"It's a mercy you didn't, mother," laughed Jo, looking at her boots. "But we'll have another play some time, that he *can* see. Maybe he'll help act; wouldn't that be jolly?"

"I never had a bouquet before; how pretty it is," and Meg examined her flowers with great interest.

"They *are* lovely, but Beth's roses are sweeter to me," said Mrs. March, sniffing at the half dead posy in her belt.

Beth nestled up to her, and whispered, softly, "I wish I could send my bunch to father. I'm afraid he isn't having such a merry Christmas as we are."

Secrets

Chapter 14 of *Little Women or, Meg, Jo, Beth and Amy,* 2 vols.
(Boston: Roberts Brothers, 1868–1869)

*J*O WAS VERY BUSY up in the garret, for the October days began to grow chilly, and the afternoons were short. For two or three hours the sun lay warmly in at the high window, showing Jo seated on the old sofa writing busily, with her papers spread out upon a trunk before her, while Scrabble, the pet rat, promenaded the beams overhead, accompanied by his oldest son, a fine young fellow, who was evidently very proud of his whiskers. Quite absorbed in her work, Jo scribbled away till the last page was filled, when she signed her name with a flourish, and threw down her pen, exclaiming, —

"There, I've done my best! If this don't suit I shall have to wait till I can do better."

Lying back on the sofa, she read the manuscript carefully through, making dashes here and there, and putting in many exclamation points, which looked like little balloons; then she tied it up with a smart red ribbon, and sat a minute looking at it with a sober, wistful expression, which plainly showed how earnest her work had been. Jo's desk up here was an old tin kitchen, which hung against the wall. In it she kept her papers, and a few books, safely shut away from Scrabble, who, being likewise of a literary turn, was fond of making a circulating library of such books as were left in his way, by eating the leaves. From this tin receptacle Jo produced another manuscript; and, putting both in her pocket, crept quietly down stairs, leaving her friends to nibble her pens and taste her ink.

She put on her hat and jacket as noiselessly as possible, and, going to the back entry window, got out upon the roof of a low porch, swung herself down to the grassy bank, and took a roundabout way to the road. Once there she composed herself, hailed a passing omnibus, and rolled away to town, looking very merry and mysterious.

If any one had been watching her, he would have thought her movements decidedly peculiar; for, on alighting, she went off at a great pace till she reached a certain number in a certain busy street; having found the place with some difficulty, she went into the door-way, looked up the dirty stairs, and, after standing stock still a minute, suddenly dived into the street, and walked away as rapidly as she came. This manœuvre she repeated several times, to the great amusement of a black-eyed young gentleman lounging in the window of a building opposite. On returning for the third time, Jo gave herself a shake, pulled her hat over her eyes, and walked up the stairs, looking as if she was going to have all her teeth out.

There was a dentist's sign, among others, which adorned the entrance, and, after staring a moment at the pair of artificial jaws which slowly opened and shut to draw attention to a fine set of teeth, the young gentleman put on his coat, took his hat, and went down to post himself in the opposite door-way, saying, with a smile and a shiver, —

"It's like her to come alone, but if she has a bad time she'll need some one to help her home."

In ten minutes Jo came running down stairs with a very red face, and the general appearance of a person who had just passed through a trying ordeal of some sort. When she saw the young gentleman she looked anything but pleased, and passed him with a nod; but he followed, asking with an air of sympathy, —

"Did you have a bad time?"

"Not very."

"You got through quick."

"Yes, thank goodness!"

"Why did you go alone?"

"Didn't want any one to know."

"You're the oddest fellow I ever saw. How many did you have out?"

Jo looked at her friend as if she did not understand him; then began to laugh, as if mightily amused at something.

"There are two which I want to have come out, but I must wait a week."

"What are you laughing at? You are up to some mischief, Jo," said Laurie, looking mystified.

"So are you. What were you doing, sir, up in that billiard saloon?"

"Begging your pardon, ma'am, it wasn't a billiard saloon, but a gymnasium, and I was taking a lesson in fencing."

"I'm glad of that!"

"Why?"

"You can teach me; and then, when we play Hamlet, you can be Laertes, and we'll make a fine thing of the fencing scene."

Laurie burst out with a hearty boy's laugh, which made several passers-by smile in spite of themselves.

"I'll teach you, whether we play Hamlet or not; it's grand fun, and will straighten you up capitally. But I don't believe that was your only reason for saying 'I'm glad,' in that decided way; was it, now?"

"No, I was glad you were not in the saloon, because I hope you never go to such places. Do you?"

"Not often."

"I wish you wouldn't."

"It's no harm, Jo, I have billiards at home, but it's no fun unless you have good players; so, as I'm fond of it, I come sometimes and have a game with Ned Moffat or some of the other fellows."

"Oh dear, I'm so sorry, for you'll get to liking it better and better, and will waste time and money, and grow like those dreadful boys. I did hope you'd stay respectable, and be a satisfaction to your friends," said Jo, shaking her head.

"Can't a fellow take a little innocent amusement now and then without losing his respectability?" asked Laurie, looking nettled.

"That depends upon how and where he takes it. I don't like Ned and his set, and wish you'd keep out of it. Mother won't let us have him at our house, though he wants to come, and if you grow like him she won't be willing to have us frolic together as we do now."

"Won't she?" asked Laurie, anxiously.

"No, she can't bear fashionable young men, and she'd shut us all up in bandboxes rather than have us associate with them."

"Well, she needn't get out her bandboxes yet; I'm not a fashionable party, and don't mean to be; but I do like harmless larks now and then, don't you?"

"Yes, nobody minds them, so lark away, but don't get wild, will you? or there will be an end of all our good times."

"I'll be a double distilled saint."

"I can't bear saints; just be a simple, honest, respectable boy, and we'll never desert you. I don't know what I *should* do if you acted like Mr. King's son; he had plenty of money, but didn't know how to spend it, and got tipsy, and gambled, and ran away, and forged his father's name, I believe, and was altogether horrid."

"You think I'm likely to do the same? Much obliged."

"No I don't — oh, *dear,* no! — but I hear people talking about money being such a temptation, and I sometimes wish you were poor; I shouldn't worry then."

"Do you worry about me, Jo?"

"A little, when you look moody or discontented, as you sometimes do, for you've got such a strong will if you once get started wrong, I'm afraid it would be hard to stop you."

Laurie walked in silence a few minutes, and Jo watched him, wishing she had held her tongue, for his eyes looked angry, though his lips still smiled as if at her warnings.

"Are you going to deliver lectures all the way home?" he asked, presently.

"Of course not; why?"

"Because if you are, I'll take a 'bus; if you are not, I'd like to walk with you, and tell you something very interesting."

"I won't preach any more, and I'd like to hear the news immensely."

"Very well, then; come on. It's a secret, and if I tell you, you must tell me yours."

"I haven't got any," began Jo, but stopped suddenly, remembering that she had.

"You know you have; you can't hide anything, so up and 'fess, or I won't tell," cried Laurie.

"Is your secret a nice one?"

"Oh, isn't it! all about people you know, and such fun! You ought to hear it, and I've been aching to tell this long time. Come! you begin."

"You'll not say anything about it at home, will you?"

"Not a word."

"And you won't tease me in private?"

"I never tease."

"Yes, you do; you get everything you want out of people. I don't know how you do it, but you are a born wheedler."

"Thank you; fire away!"

"Well, I've left two stories with a newspaper man, and he's to give his answer next week," whispered Jo, in her confidant's ear.

"Hurrah for Miss March, the celebrated American authoress!" cried Laurie, throwing up his hat and catching it again, to the great delight of two ducks, four cats, five hens, and half a dozen Irish children; for they were out of the city now.

"Hush! it won't come to anything, I dare say; but I couldn't rest till I had tried, and I said nothing about it, because I didn't want any one else to be disappointed."

"It won't fail! Why, Jo, your stories are works of Shakespeare compared to half the rubbish that's published every day. Won't it be fun to see them in print; and shan't we feel proud of our authoress?"

Jo's eyes sparkled, for it's always pleasant to be believed in; and a friend's praise is always sweeter than a dozen newspaper puffs.

"Where's *your* secret? Play fair, Teddy, or I'll never believe you again," she said, trying to extinguish the brilliant hopes that blazed up at a word of encouragement.

"I may get into a scrape for telling; but I didn't promise not to, so I will, for I never feel easy in my mind till I've told you any plummy bit of news I get. I know where Meg's glove is."

"Is that all?" said Jo, looking disappointed, as Laurie nodded and twinkled, with a face full of mysterious intelligence.

"It's quite enough for the present, as you'll agree when I tell you where it is."

"Tell, then."

Laurie bent and whispered three words in Jo's ear, which produced a comical change. She stood and stared at him for a minute, looking both surprised and displeased, then walked on, saying sharply, "How do you know?"

"Saw it."

"Where?"

"Pocket."

"All this time?"

"Yes; isn't that romantic?"

"No, it's horrid."

"Don't you like it?"

"Of course I don't; it's ridiculous; it won't be allowed. My patience! what would Meg say?"

"You are not to tell any one, mind that."

"I didn't promise."

"That was understood, and I trusted you."

"Well, I won't for the present, any way; but I'm disgusted, and wish you hadn't told me."

"I thought you'd be pleased."

"At the idea of anybody coming to take Meg away? No, thank you."

"You'll feel better about it when somebody comes to take you away."

"I'd like to see any one try it," cried Jo, fiercely.

"So should I!" and Laurie chuckled at the idea.

"I don't think secrets agree with me; I feel rumpled up in my mind since you told me that," said Jo, rather ungratefully.

"Race down this hill with me, and you'll be all right," suggested Laurie.

No one was in sight; the smooth road sloped invitingly before her, and, finding the temptation irresistible, Jo darted away, soon leaving hat and comb behind her, and scattering hair-pins as she ran. Laurie reached the goal first, and was quite satisfied with the success of his treatment; for his Atlanta came panting up with flying hair, bright eyes, ruddy cheeks, and no signs of dissatisfaction in her face.

"I wish I was a horse; then I could run for miles in this splendid air, and not lose my breath. It was capital; but see what a guy it's made me. Go, pick up my things, like a cherub as you are," said Jo, dropping down under a maple tree, which was carpeting the bank with crimson leaves.

Laurie leisurely departed to recover the lost property, and Jo bundled up her braids, hoping no one would pass by till she was tidy again. But some one did pass, and who should it be but Meg, looking particularly lady-like in her state and festival suit, for she had been making calls.

"What in the world are you doing here?" she asked, regarding her dishevelled sister with well-bred surprise.

"Getting leaves," meekly answered Jo, sorting the rosy handful she had just swept up.

"And hair-pins," added Laurie, throwing half a dozen into Jo's lap. "They grow on this road, Meg; so do combs and brown straw hats."

"You have been running, Jo; how could you? When *will* you stop such romping ways?" said Meg, reprovingly, as she settled her cuffs and smoothed her hair, with which the wind had taken liberties.

"Never till I'm stiff and old, and have to use a crutch. Don't try to make me grow up before my time, Meg; it's hard enough to have you change all of a sudden; let me be a little girl as long as I can."

As she spoke, Jo bent over her work to hide the trembling of her lips; for lately she had felt that Margaret was fast getting to be a woman, and Laurie's secret made her dread the separation which must surely come some time, and now seemed very near. He saw the trouble in her face, and drew Meg's attention from it by asking, quickly, "Where have you been calling, all so fine?"

"At the Gardiners; and Sallie has been telling me all about Belle Moffat's wedding. It was very splendid, and they have gone to spend the winter in Paris; just think how delightful that must be!"

"Do you envy her, Meg?" said Laurie.

"I'm afraid I do."

"I'm glad of it!" muttered Jo, tying on her hat with a jerk.

"Why?" asked Meg, looking surprised.

"Because, if you care much about riches, you will never go and marry a poor man," said Jo, frowning at Laurie, who was mutely warning her to mind what she said.

"I shall never 'go and marry' any one," observed Meg, walking on with great dignity, while the others followed, laughing, whispering, skipping stones, and "behaving like children," as Meg said to herself, though she might have been tempted to join them if she had not had her best dress on.

For a week or two Jo behaved so queerly, that her sisters got quite bewildered. She rushed to the door when the postman rang; was rude to Mr. Brooke whenever they met; would sit looking at Meg with a woe-begone face, occasionally jumping up to shake, and then to kiss her, in a very mysterious manner; Laurie and she were always making signs to one another, and talking about "Spread Eagles," till the girls declared they had both lost their wits. On the second Saturday after Jo got out of the window, Meg, as she sat sewing at her window, was scandalized by the sight of Laurie chasing Jo all over the garden, and finally capturing her in Amy's bower. What went on there, Meg could not see, but shrieks of laughter were heard, followed by the murmur of voices, and a great flapping of newspapers.

"What shall we do with that girl? She never *will* behave like a young lady," sighed Meg, as she watched the race with a disapproving face.

"I hope she won't; she is so funny and dear as she is," said Beth, who had never betrayed that she was a little hurt at Jo's having secrets with any one but her.

"It's very trying, but we never can make her *comme la fo*," added Amy, who sat making some new frills for herself, with her curls tied up in a very becoming way, — two agreeable things, which made her feel unusually elegant and lady-like.

In a few minutes Jo bounced in, laid herself on the sofa, and affected to read.

"Have you anything interesting there?" asked Meg, with condescension.

"Nothing but a story; don't amount to much, I guess," returned Jo, carefully keeping the name of the paper out of sight.

"You'd better read it loud; that will amuse us, and keep you out of mischief," said Amy, in her most grown-up tone.

"What's the name?" asked Beth, wondering why Jo kept her face behind the sheet.

"The Rival Painters."

"That sounds well; read it," said Meg.

With a loud "hem!" and a long breath, Jo began to read very fast. The girls listened with interest, for the tale was romantic, and somewhat pathetic, as most of the characters died in the end.

"I like that about the splendid picture," was Amy's approving remark, as Jo paused.

"I prefer the lovering part. Viola and Angelo are two of our favorite names; isn't that queer?" said Meg, wiping her eyes, for the "lovering part" was tragical.

"Who wrote it?" asked Beth, who had caught a glimpse of Jo's face.

The reader suddenly sat up, cast away the paper, displaying a flushed countenance, and, with a funny mixture of solemnity and excitement, replied in a loud voice, "Your sister!"

"You?" cried Meg, dropping her work.

"It's very good," said Amy, critically.

"I knew it! I knew it! oh, my Jo, I *am* so proud!" and Beth ran to hug her sister and exult over this splendid success.

Dear me, how delighted they all were, to be sure; how Meg wouldn't believe it till she saw the words, "Miss Josephine March," actually printed in the paper; how graciously Amy criticised the artistic parts of the story, and offered hints for a sequel, which unfortunately couldn't be carried out, as the hero and heroine were dead; how Beth got excited, and skipped and sung with joy; how Hannah came in to exclaim, "Sakes alive, well I never!" in great astonishment at "that Jo's doins;" how proud Mrs. March was when she knew it; how Jo laughed, with tears in her eyes, as she declared she might as well be a peacock and done with it; and how the "Spread Eagle" might be said to flap his wings triumphantly over the house of March, as the paper passed from hand to hand.

"Tell us about it." "When did it come?" "How much did you get for it?" "What *will* father say?" "Won't Laurie laugh?" cried the family, all in one breath, as they clustered about Jo; for these foolish, affectionate people made a jubilee of every little household joy.

"Stop jabbering, girls, and I'll tell you everything," said Jo, wondering if Miss Burney felt any grander over her "Evelina" than she did over her "Rival Painters." Having told how she disposed of her tales, Jo added, — "And when I went to get my answer the man said he liked them both, but didn't pay beginners, only let them print in his paper, and noticed the stories. It was good practice, he said; and, when the beginners improved, any one would pay. So I let him have the two stories, and today this was sent to me, and Laurie caught me with it, and insisted on seeing it, so I let him; and he said it was good, and I shall write more, and he's going to get the next paid for, and oh — I *am* so happy, for in time I may be able to support myself and help the girls.''

Jo's breath gave out here; and, wrapping her head in the paper, she bedewed her little story with a few natural tears; for to be independent, and earn the praise of those she loved, were the dearest wishes of her heart, and this seemed to be the first step toward that happy end.

Literary Lessons

Chapter 29 of *Little Women or, Meg, Jo, Beth and Amy,* 2 vols.
(Boston: Roberts Brothers, 1868–1869)

FORTUNE SUDDENLY SMILED upon Jo, and dropped a good-luck penny in her path. Not a golden penny, exactly, but I doubt if half a million would have given more real happiness than did the little sum that came to her in this wise.

Every few weeks she would shut herself up in her room, put on her scribbling suit, and "fall into a vortex," as she expressed it, writing away at her novel with all her heart and soul, for till that was finished she could find no peace. Her "scribbling suit" consisted of a black pinafore on which she could wipe her pen at will, and a cap of the same material, adorned with a cheerful red bow, into which she bundled her hair when the decks were cleared for action. This cap was a beacon to the inquiring eyes of her family, who, during these periods, kept their distance, merely popping in their heads semi-occasionally, to ask, with interest, "Does genius burn, Jo?" They did not always venture even to ask this question, but took an observation of the cap, and judged accordingly. If this expressive article of dress was drawn low upon the forehead, it was a sign that hard work was going on; in exciting moments it was pushed rakishly askew, and when despair seized the author it was plucked wholly off, and cast upon the floor.

At such times the intruder silently withdrew; and not until the red bow was seen gaily erect upon the gifted brow, did any one dare address Jo.

She did not think herself a genius by any means; but when the writing fit came on, she gave herself up to it with entire abandon, and led a blissful life, unconscious of want, care, or bad weather, while she sat safe and happy in an imaginary world, full of friends almost as real and dear to her as any in the flesh. Sleep forsook her eyes, meals stood untasted, day and night were all too short to enjoy the happiness which blessed her only at such times, and made these hours worth living, even if they bore no other fruit. The divine afflatus usually lasted a week or two, and then she emerged from her "vortex" hungry, sleepy, cross, or despondent.

She was just recovering from one of these attacks when she was prevailed upon to escort Miss Crocker to a lecture, and in return for her virtue was rewarded with a new idea. It was a People's Course, — the lecture on the Pyramids, — and Jo rather wondered at the choice of such a subject for such an audience, but took it for granted that some great social evil would be remedied, or some great want supplied by unfolding the glories of the Pharaohs, to an audience whose thoughts were busy with the price of coal and flour, and whose lives were spent in trying to solve harder riddles than that of the Sphinx.

They were early; and while Miss Crocker set the heel of her stocking, Jo amused herself by examining the faces of the people who occupied the seat with them. On her left were two matrons with massive foreheads, and bonnets to match, discussing Woman's Rights and making tatting. Beyond sat a pair of humble lovers artlessly holding each other by the hand, a sombre spinster eating peppermints out of a paper bag, and an old gentleman taking his preparatory nap behind a yellow bandanna. On her right, her only neighbor was a studious-looking lad absorbed in a newspaper.

It was a pictorial sheet, and Jo examined the work of art nearest her, idly wondering what unfortuitous concatenation of circumstances needed the melodramatic illustration of an Indian in full war costume, tumbling over a precipice with a wolf at his throat, while two infuriated young gentlemen, with unnaturally small feet and big eyes, were stabbing each other close by, and a dishevelled female was flying away in the background, with her mouth wide open. Pausing to turn a page, the lad saw her looking, and, with boyish good-nature, offered half his paper, saying, bluntly, "Want to read it? That's a first-rate story."

Jo accepted it with a smile, for she had never outgrown her liking for lads, and soon found herself involved in the usual labyrinth of love, mystery, and murder, — for the story belonged to that class of light literature in which the passions have a holiday, and when the author's invention fails, a grand catastrophe clears the stage of one-half the *dramatis personæ,* leaving the other half to exult over their downfall.

"Prime, isn't it?" asked the boy, as her eye went down the last paragraph of her portion.

"I guess you and I could do most as well as that if we tried," returned Jo, amused at his admiration of the trash.

"I should think I was a pretty lucky chap if I could. She makes a good living out of such stories, they say;" and he pointed to the name of Mrs. S. L. A. N. G. Northbury, under the title of the tale.

"Do you know her?" asked Jo, with sudden interest.

"No; but I read all her pieces, and I know a fellow that works in the office where this paper is printed."

"Do you say she makes a good living out of stories like this?" and Jo looked more respectfully at the agitated group and thickly-sprinkled exclamation points that adorned the page.

"Guess she does! she knows just what folks like, and gets paid well for writing it."

Here the lecture began, but Jo heard very little of it, for while Professor Sands was prosing away about Belzoni, Cheops, scarabei, and hieroglyphics, she was covertly taking down the address of the paper, and boldly resolving to try for the hundred dollar prize offered in its columns for a sensational story. By the time the lecture ended, and the audience awoke, she had built up a splendid fortune for herself (not the first founded upon paper), and was already deep in the concoction of her story, being unable to decide whether the duel should come before the elopement or after the murder.

She said nothing of her plan at home, but fell to work next day, much to the disquiet of her mother, who always looked a little anxious when "genius took to burning." Jo had never tried this style before, contenting herself with very mild romances for the "Spread Eagle." Her theatrical experience and miscellaneous reading were of service now, for they gave her some idea of dramatic effect, and supplied plot, language, and costumes. Her story was as full of desperation and despair as her limited acquaintance with those uncomfortable emotions enabled her to make it, and, having located it in Lisbon, she wound up with an earthquake, as a striking and appropriate *denouement.* The manuscript was privately despatched, accompanied by a note, modestly saying that if the tale didn't get the prize, which the writer hardly dared expect, she would be very glad to receive any sum it might be considered worth.

Six weeks is a long time to wait, and a still longer time for a girl to keep a secret; but Jo did both, and was just beginning to give up all hope of ever seeing her manuscript again, when a letter arrived which almost took her breath away; for, on opening it, a check for a hundred dollars fell into her lap. For a minute she stared at it as if it had been a snake, then she read her letter, and began to cry. If the amiable gentleman who wrote that kindly note could have known what intense happiness he was giving a fellow-creature, I think he would devote his leisure hours, if he has any, to that amusement; for Jo valued the letter more than the money, because it was encouraging; and after years of effort it was *so* pleasant to find that she had learned to do *something,* though it was only to write a sensation story.

A prouder young woman was seldom seen than she, when, having composed herself, she electrified the family by appearing before them with the letter in one hand, the check in the other, announcing that she had won the prize! Of course there was a great jubilee, and when the story came every one read and praised it; though after her father had told her that the language was good, the romance fresh and hearty, and the tragedy quite thrilling, he shook his head, and said in his unworldly way, —

"You can do better than this, Jo. Aim at the highest, and never mind the money."

"*I* think the money is the best part of it. What *will* you do with such a fortune?" asked Amy, regarding the magic slip of paper with a reverential eye.

"Send Beth and mother to the sea-side for a month or two," answered Jo promptly.

"Oh, how splendid! No, I can't do it, dear, it would be so selfish," cried Beth, who had clapped her thin hands, and taken a long breath, as if pining for fresh ocean breezes; then stopped herself, and motioned away the check which her sister waved before her.

"Ah, but you shall go, I've set my heart on it; that's what I tried for, and that's why I succeeded. I never get on when I think of myself alone, so it will help me to work for you, don't you see. Besides, Marmee needs the change, and she won't leave you, so you *must* go. Won't it be fun to see you come home plump and rosy again? Hurrah for Dr. Jo, who always cures her patients!"

To the sea-side they went, after much discussion; and though Beth didn't come home as plump and rosy as could be desired, she was much better, while Mrs. March declared she felt ten years younger; so Jo was satisfied with the investment of her prize-money, and fell to work with a cheery spirit, bent on earning more of those delightful checks. She did earn several that year, and began to feel herself a power in the house; for by the magic of a pen, her "rubbish" turned into comforts for them all. "The

Duke's Daughter" paid the butcher's bill, "A Phantom Hand" put down a new carpet, and "The Curse of the Coventrys" proved the blessing of the Marches in the way of groceries and gowns.

Wealth is certainly a most desirable thing, but poverty has its sunny side, and one of the sweet uses of adversity, is the genuine satisfaction which comes from hearty work of head or hand; and to the inspiration of necessity, we owe half the wise, beautiful, and useful blessings of the world. Jo enjoyed a taste of this satisfaction, and ceased to envy richer girls, taking great comfort in the knowledge that she could supply her own wants, and need ask no one for a penny.

Little notice was taken of her stories, but they found a market; and, encouraged by this fact, she resolved to make a bold stroke for fame and fortune. Having copied her novel for the fourth time, read it to all her confidential friends, and submitted it with fear and trembling to three publishers, she at last disposed of it, on condition that she would cut it down one-third, and omit all the parts which she particularly admired.

"Now I must either bundle it back into my tin-kitchen, to mould, pay for printing it myself, or chop it up to suit purchasers, and get what I can for it. Fame is a very good thing to have in the house, but cash is more convenient; so I wish to take the sense of the meeting on this important subject," said Jo, calling a family council.

"Don't spoil your book, my girl, for there is more in it than you know, and the idea is well worked out. Let it wait and ripen," was her father's advice; and he practised as he preached, having waited patiently thirty years for fruit of his own to ripen, and being in no haste to gather it, even now, when it was sweet and mellow.

"It seems to me that Jo will profit more by making the trial than by waiting," said Mrs. March. "Criticism is the best test of such work, for it will show her both unsuspected merits and faults, and help her to do better next time. We are too partial; but the praise and blame of outsiders will prove useful, even if she gets but little money."

"Yes," said Jo, knitting her brows, "that's just it; I've been fussing over the thing so long, I really don't know whether it's good, bad, or indifferent. It will be a great help to have cool, impartial persons take a look at it, and tell me what they think of it."

"I wouldn't leave out a word of it; you'll spoil it if you do, for the interest of the story is more in the minds than in the actions of the people, and it will be all a muddle if you don't explain as you go on," said Meg, who firmly believed that this book was the most remarkable novel ever written.

"But Mr. Allen says, 'Leave out the explanations, make it brief and dramatic, and let the characters tell the story,' " interrupted Jo, turning to the publisher's note.

"Do as he tells you; he knows what will sell, and we don't. Make a good, popular book, and get as much money as you can. By and by, when you've got a name, you can afford to digress, and have philosophical and metaphysical people in your novels," said Amy, who took a strictly practical view of the subject.

"Well," said Jo, laughing, "If my people *are* 'philosophical and metaphysical,' it isn't my fault, for I know nothing about such things, except what I hear father say, sometimes. If I've got some of his wise ideas jumbled up with my romance, so much the better for me. Now, Beth, what do you say?"

"I should so like to see it printed *soon*," was all Beth said, and smiled in saying it; but there was an unconscious emphasis on the last word, and a wistful look in the eyes that never lost their child-like candor, which chilled Jo's heart, for a minute, with a foreboding fear, and decided her to make her little venture "soon."

So, with Spartan firmness, the young authoress laid her first-born on her table, and chopped it up as ruthlessly as any ogre. In the hope of pleasing every one, she took every one's advice; and, like the old man and his donkey in the fable, suited nobody.

Her father liked the metaphysical streak which had unconsciously got into it, so that was allowed to remain, though she had her doubts about it. Her mother thought that there *was* a trifle too much description; out, therefore, it nearly all came, and with it many necessary links in the story. Meg admired the tragedy; so Jo piled up the agony to suit her, while Amy objected to the fun, and, with the best intentions in life, Jo quenched the sprightly scenes which relieved the sombre character of the story. Then, to complete the ruin, she cut it down one-third, and confidingly sent the poor little romance, like a picked robin, out into the big, busy world, to try its fate.

Well, it was printed, and she got three hundred dollars for it; likewise plenty of praise and blame, both so much greater than she expected, that she was thrown into a state of bewilderment, from which it took her some time to recover.

"You said, mother, that criticism would help me; but how can it, when it's so contradictory that I don't know whether I have written a promising book, or broken all the ten commandments," cried poor Jo, turning over a heap of notices, the perusal of which filled her with pride and joy one minute — wrath and dire dismay the next. "This man says 'An exquisite book, full of truth, beauty, and earnestness; all is sweet, pure, and healthy,' " continued the perplexed authoress. "The next, 'The theory of the book is bad, — full of morbid fancies, spiritualistic ideas, and unnatural characters.' Now, as I had no theory of any kind, don't believe in spiritualism, and copied my characters from life, I don't see how this critic *can* be right. Another says, 'It's one of the best American novels which has appeared for years' " (I know better than that); "and the next asserts that 'though it is original, and written with great force and feeling, it is a dangerous book.' 'Tisn't! Some make fun of it, some over-praise, and nearly all insist that I had a deep theory to expound, when I only wrote it for the pleasure and the money. I wish I'd printed it whole, or not at all, for I do hate to be so horridly misjudged."

Her family and friends administered comfort and commendation liberally; yet it was a hard time for sensitive, high-spirited Jo, who meant so well, and had apparently done so ill. But it did her good, for those whose opinion had real value, gave her the criticism which is an author's best education; and when the first soreness was over, she could laugh at her poor little book, yet believe in it still, and feel herself the wiser and stronger for the buffeting she had received.

"Not being a genius, like Keats, it won't kill me," she said stoutly; "and I've got the joke on my side, after all; for the parts that were taken straight out of real life, are denounced as impossible and absurd, and the scenes that I made up out of my own silly head, are pronounced 'charmingly natural, tender, and true.' So I'll comfort myself with that; and, when I'm ready, I'll up again and take another."

The Valley of the Shadow

Chapter 40 of *Little Women or, Meg, Jo, Beth and Amy,* 2 vols.
(Boston: Roberts Brothers, 1868–1869)

WHEN THE FIRST bitterness was over, the family accepted the inevitable, and tried to bear it cheerfully, helping one another by the increased affection which comes to bind households tenderly together in times of trouble. They put away their grief, and each did their part toward making that last year a happy one.

The pleasantest room in the house was set apart for Beth, and in it was gathered everything that she most loved — flowers, pictures, her piano, the little work-table, and the beloved pussies. Father's best books found their way there, mother's easy chair, Jo's desk, Amy's loveliest sketches; and every day Meg brought her babies on a loving pilgrimage, to make sunshine for Aunty Beth. John quietly set apart a little sum, that he might enjoy the pleasure of keeping the invalid supplied with the fruit she loved and longed for; old Hannah never wearied of concocting dainty dishes to tempt a capricious appetite, dropping tears as she worked; and, from across the sea, came little gifts and cheerful letters, seeming to bring breaths of warmth and fragrance from lands that know no winter.

Here, cherished like a household saint in its shrine, sat Beth, tranquil and busy as ever; for nothing could change the sweet, unselfish nature; and even while preparing to leave life, she tried to make it happier for those who should remain behind. The feeble fingers were never idle, and one of her pleasures was to make little things for the school children daily passing to and fro. To drop a pair of mittens from her window for a pair of purple hands, a needle-book for some small mother of many dolls, pen-wipers for young penmen toiling through forests of pot-hooks, scrap-books for picture-loving eyes, and all manner of pleasant devices, till the reluctant climbers up the ladder of learning found their way strewn with flowers, as it were, and came to regard the gentle giver as a sort of fairy god-mother, who sat above there, and showered down gifts miraculously suited to their tastes and needs. If Beth had wanted any reward, she found it in the bright little faces always turned up to her window, with nods and smiles, and the droll little letters which came to her, full of blots and gratitude.

The first few months were very happy ones, and Beth often used to look round, and say "How beautiful this is," as they all sat together in her sunny room, the babies kicking and crowing on the floor, mother and sisters working near, and father reading in his pleasant voice, from the wise old books, which seemed rich in good and comfortable words, as applicable now as when written centuries ago — a little chapel, where a paternal priest taught his flock the hard lessons all must learn, trying to show them that hope can comfort love, and faith make resignation possible. Simple sermons, that went straight to the souls of those who listened; for the father's heart was in the minister's religion, and the frequent falter in the voice gave a double eloquence to the words he spoke or read.

It was well for all that this peaceful time was given them as preparation for the sad hours to come; for, by and by, Beth said the needle was "so heavy," and put it down forever; talking wearied her, faces troubled her, pain claimed her for its own, and her tranquil spirit was sorrowfully perturbed by the ills that vexed her feeble flesh. Ah me! such heavy days, such long, long nights, such aching hearts and imploring prayers, when those who loved her best were forced to see the thin hands stretched out to them beseechingly, to hear the bitter cry, "Help me, help me!" and to feel that there was no help. A sad eclipse of the serene soul, a sharp struggle of the young life with death; but both were mercifully brief, and then, the natural rebellion over, the old peace returned more beautiful than ever. With the wreck of her frail body, Beth's soul grew strong; and, though she said little, those about her felt that she was ready, saw that the first pilgrim called was likewise the fittest, and waited with her on the shore, trying to see the Shining ones coming to receive her when she crossed the river.

Jo never left her for an hour since Beth had said, "I feel stronger when you are here." She slept on a couch in the room, waking often to renew the fire, to feed, lift, or wait upon the patient creature who seldom asked for anything, and "tried not to be a trouble." All day she haunted the room, jealous of any other nurse, and prouder of being chosen then than of any honor her life ever brought her. Precious and helpful hours to Jo, for now her heart received the teaching that it needed; lessons in patience were so sweetly taught her, that she could not fail to learn them; charity for all, the lovely spirit that can forgive and truly forget unkindness, the loyalty to duty that makes the hardest easy, and the sincere faith that fears nothing, but trusts undoubtingly.

Often when she woke, Jo found Beth reading in her well-worn little book, heard her singing softly, to beguile the sleepless night, or saw her lean her face upon her hands, while slow tears dropped through the transparent fingers; and Jo would lie watching her, with thoughts too deep for tears, feeling that Beth, in her simple, unselfish way, was trying to wean herself from the dear old life, and fit herself for the life to come, by sacred words of comfort, quiet prayers, and the music she loved so well.

Seeing this did more for Jo than the wisest sermons, the saintliest hymns, the most fervent prayers that any voice could utter; for, with eyes made clear by many tears, and a heart softened by the tenderest sorrow, she recognized the beauty of her sister's life — uneventful, unambitious, yet full of the genuine virtues which "smell sweet, and blossom in the dust"; the self-forgetfulness that makes the humblest on earth remembered soonest in heaven, the true success which is possible to all.

One night, when Beth looked among the books upon her table, to find something to make her forget the mortal weariness that was almost as hard to bear as pain, as she turned the leaves of her old favorite Pilgrim's

Progress, she found a little paper scribbled over, in Jo's hand. The name caught her eye, and the blurred look of the lines made her sure that tears had fallen on it.

"Poor Jo, she's fast asleep, so I won't wake her to ask leave; she shows me all her things, and I don't think she'll mind if I look at this," thought Beth, with a glance at her sister, who lay on the rug, with the tongs beside her, ready to wake up the minute the log fell apart.

MY BETH

Sitting patient in the shadow
  Till the blessed light shall come,
A serene and saintly presence
  Sanctifies our troubled home.
Earthly joys, and hopes, and sorrows,
  Break like ripples on the strand
Of the deep and solemn river
  Where her willing feet now stand.

Oh, my sister, passing from me,
  Out of human care and strife,
Leave me, as a gift, those virtues
  Which have beautified your life.
Dear, bequeath me that great patience
  Which has power to sustain
A cheerful, uncomplaining spirit
  In its prison-house of pain.

Give me, for I need it sorely,
  Of that courage, wise and sweet,
Which has made the path of duty
  Green beneath your willing feet.
Give me that unselfish nature,
  That with charity divine
Can pardon wrong for love's dear sake —
  Meek heart, forgive me mine!

Thus our parting daily loseth
  Something of its bitter pain,
And while learning this hard lesson,
  My great loss becomes my gain.
For the touch of grief will render
  My wild nature more serene,

Give to life new aspirations —
 A new trust in the unseen.

Henceforth, safe across the river,
 I shall see forever more
A beloved, household spirit
 Waiting for me on the shore.
Hope and faith, born of my sorrow,
 Guardian angels shall become,
And the sister gone before me,
 By their hands shall lead me home.

Blurred and blotted, faulty and feeble as the lines were, they brought a look of inexpressible comfort to Beth's face, for her one regret had been that she had done so little; and this seemed to assure her that her life had not been useless — that her death would not bring the despair she feared. As she sat with the paper folded between her hands, the charred log fell asunder. Jo started up, revived the blaze, and crept to the bedside, hoping Beth slept.

"Not asleep, but so happy, dear. See, I found this and read it; I knew you wouldn't care. Have I been all that to you, Jo?" she asked, with wistful, humble earnestness.

"Oh, Beth, so much, so much!" and Jo's head went down upon the pillow, beside her sister's.

"Then I don't feel as if I'd wasted my life. I'm not so good as you make me, but I *have* tried to do right; and now, when it's too late to begin even to do better, it's such a comfort to know that some one loves me so much, and feels as if I'd helped them."

"More than any one in the world, Beth. I used to think I couldn't let you go; but I'm learning to feel that I don't lose you; that you'll be more to me than ever, and death can't part us, though it seems to."

"I know it cannot, and I don't fear it any longer, for I'm sure I shall be your Beth still, to love and help you more than ever. You must take my place, Jo, and be everything to father and mother when I'm gone. They will turn to you — don't fail them; and if it's hard to work alone, remember that I don't forget you, and that you'll be happier in doing that, than writing splendid books, or seeing all the world; for love is the only thing that we can carry with us when we go, and it makes the end so easy."

"I'll try, Beth;" and then and there Jo renounced her old ambition, pledged herself to a new and better one, acknowledging the poverty of other desires, and feeling the blessed solace of a belief in the immortality of love.

So the spring days came and went, the sky grew clearer, the earth greener, the flowers were up fair and early, and the birds came back in time to say good-by to Beth, who, like a tired but trustful child, clung to the hands that had led her all her life, as father and mother guided her tenderly through the valley of the shadow, and gave her up to God.

Seldom, except in books, do the dying utter memorable words, see visions, or depart with beatified countenances; and those who have sped many parting souls know, that to most the end comes as naturally and simply as sleep. As Beth had hoped, the "tide went out easily"; and in the dark hour before the dawn, on the bosom where she had drawn her first breath, she quietly drew her last, with no farewell but one loving look and a little sigh.

With tears, and prayers, and tender hands, mother and sisters made her ready for the long sleep that pain would never mar again — seeing with grateful eyes the beautiful serenity that soon replaced the pathetic patience that had wrung their hearts so long, and feeling with reverent joy, that to their darling death was a benignant angel — not a phantom full of dread.

When morning came, for the first time in many months the fire was out, Jo's place was empty, and the room was very still. But a bird sang blithely on a budding bough, close by, the snow-drops blossomed freshly at the window, and the spring sunshine streamed in like a benediction over the placid face upon the pillow — a face so full of painless peace, that those who loved it best smiled through their tears, and thanked God that Beth was well at last.

A Fire Brand

From *Little Men: Life at Plumfield with Jo's Boys*
(Boston: Roberts Brothers, 1871)

"PLEASE, MA'AM, could I speak to you? It is something *very* important," said Nat, popping his head in at the door of Mrs. Bhaer's room.

It was the fifth head which had popped in during the last half-hour; but Mrs. Jo was used to it, so she looked up, and said briskly —

"What is it, my lad?"

Nat came in, shut the door carefully behind him, and said in an eager, anxious tone —

"Dan has come."

"Who is Dan?"

"He's a boy I used to know when I fiddled round the streets. He sold papers, and he was kind to me, and I saw him the other day in town, and told him how nice it was here, and he's come."

"But, my dear boy, that is rather a sudden way to pay a visit."

"Oh, it isn't a visit, he wants to stay if you will let him!" said Nat, innocently.

"Well, but I don't know about that," began Mrs. Bhaer, rather startled by the coolness of the proposition.

"Why, I thought you liked to have poor boys come and live with you, and be kind to 'em as you were to me," said Nat, looking surprised and alarmed.

"So I do, but I like to know something about them first. I have to choose them, because there are so many. I have not room for all. I wish I had."

"I told him to come because I thought you'd like it, but if there isn't room he can go away again," said Nat, sorrowfully.

The boy's confidence in her hospitality touched Mrs. Bhaer, and she could not find the heart to disappoint his hope, and spoil his kind little plan, so she said —

"Tell me about this Dan."

"I don't know any thing, only he hasn't got any folks, and he's poor, and he was good to me, so I'd like to be good to him if I could."

"Excellent reasons every one; but really, Nat, the house is full, and I don't know where I could put him," said Mrs. Bhaer, more and more inclined to prove herself the haven of refuge he seemed to think her.

"He could have my bed, and I could sleep in the barn. It isn't cold now, and I don't mind, I used to sleep anywhere with father," said Nat, eagerly.

Something in his speech and face made Mrs. Jo put her hand on his shoulder, and say in her kindest tone:

"Bring in your friend, Nat; I think we must find room for him without giving him your place."

Nat joyfully ran off, and soon returned followed by a most unprepossessing boy, who slouched in and stood looking about him, with a half bold, half sullen look, which made Mrs. Bhaer say to herself, after one glance:

"A bad specimen, I am afraid."

"This is Dan," said Nat, presenting him as if sure of his welcome.

"Nat tells me you would like to come and stay with us," began Mrs. Jo, in a friendly tone.

"Yes," was the gruff reply.

"Have you no friends to take care of you?"

"No."

"Say, 'No, ma'am,' " whispered Nat.

"Shan't neither," muttered Dan.

"How old are you?"

"About fourteen."

"You look older. What can you do?"

" 'Most any thing."

"If you stay here we shall want you to do as the others do, work and study as well as play. Are you willing to agree to that?"

"Don't mind trying."

"Well, you can stay a few days, and we will see how we get on together. Take him out, Nat, and amuse him till Mr. Bhaer comes home, when we will settle about the matter," said Mrs. Jo, finding it rather difficult to get on with this cool young person, who fixed his big black eyes on her with a hard, suspicious expression, sorrowfully unboyish.

"Come on, Nat," he said, and slouched out again.

"Thank you, ma'am," added Nat, as he followed him, feeling without quite understanding the difference in the welcome given to him and to his ungracious friend.

"The fellows are having a circus out in the barn; don't you want to come and see it?" he asked, as they came down the wide steps on to the lawn.

"Are they big fellows?" said Dan.

"No; the big ones are gone fishing."

"Fire away then," said Dan.

Nat led him to the great barn and introduced him to his set, who were disporting themselves among the half empty lofts. A large circle was marked out with hay on the wide floor, and in the middle stood Demi with a long whip, while Tommy, mounted on the much enduring Toby, pranced about the circle playing being a monkey.

"You must pay a pin a-piece, or you can't see the show," said Stuffy, who stood by the wheel-barrow in which sat the band, consisting of a pocket-comb blown upon by Ned, and a toy drum beaten spasmodically by Rob.

"He's company, so I'll pay for both," said Nat, handsomely, as he stuck two crooked pins in the dried mushroom which served as money-box.

With a nod to the company they seated themselves on a couple of boards, and the performance went on. After the monkey act, Ned gave them a fine specimen of his agility by jumping over an old chair, and running up and down ladders, sailor fashion. Then Demi danced a jig with a gravity beautiful to behold. Nat was called upon to wrestle with Stuffy, and speedily laid that stout youth upon the ground. After this, Tommy proudly advanced to turn a somersault, an accomplishment which he had acquired by painful perseverance, practising in private till every joint of his little frame was black and blue. His feats were received with great applause, and he was about to retire, flushed with pride and a rush of blood to the head, when a scornful voice in the audience was heard to say —

"Ho! that ain't any thing!"

"Say that again, will you?" said Tommy bristled up like an angry turkey-cock.

"Do you want to fight," said Dan, promptly descending from the barrel and doubling up his fists in a business-like manner.

"No, I don't;" and the candid Thomas retired a step, rather taken aback by the proposition.

"Fighting isn't allowed!" cried the others, much excited.

"You're a nice lot," sneered Dan.

"Come, if you don't behave, you shan't stay," said Nat, firing up at that insult to his friends.

"I'd like to see him do better than I did, that's all," observed Tommy, with a swagger.

"Clear the way, then," and without the slightest preparation Dan turned three somersaults one after the other and came up on his feet.

"You can't beat that, Tom; you always hit your head and tumble flat," said Nat, pleased at his friend's success.

Before he could say any more the audience were electrified by three more somersaults backwards, and a short promenade on the hands, head down, feet up. This brought down the house, and Tommy joined in the admiring cries which greeted the accomplished gymnast as he righted himself, and looked at them with an air of calm superiority.

"Do you think I could learn to do it without its hurting me very much?" Tom meekly asked, as he rubbed the elbows which still smarted after the last attempt.

"What will you give me if I'll teach you?" said Dan.

"My new jack-knife; it's got five blades, and only one is broken."

"Give it here then."

Tommy handed it over with an affectionate look at its smooth handle. Dan examined it carefully, then putting it into his pocket, walked off, saying with a wink —

"Keep it up till you learn, that's all."

A howl of wrath from Tommy was followed by a general uproar, which did not subside till Dan, finding himself in a minority, proposed that they should play stick-knife, and whichever won should have the treasure. Tommy agreed, and the game was played in a circle of excited faces, which all wore an expression of satisfaction, when Tommy won and secured the knife in the depth of his safest pocket.

"You come off with me, and I'll show you round," said Nat, feeling that he must have a little serious conversation with his friend in private.

What passed between them no one knew, but when they appeared again, Dan was more respectful to every one, though still gruff in his speech, and rough in his manner; and what else could be expected of the poor lad who had been knocking about the world all his short life with no one to teach him any better?

The boys had decided that they did not like him, and so they left him to Nat, who soon felt rather oppressed by the responsibility, but was too kind-hearted to desert him.

Tommy, however, felt that in spite of the jack-knife transaction, there was a bond of sympathy between them, and longed to return to the interesting subject of somersaults. He soon found an opportunity, for Dan, seeing how much he admired him, grew more amiable, and by the end of the first week was quite intimate with the lively Tom.

Mr. Bhaer when he heard the story and saw Dan, shook his head, but only said quietly —

"The experiment may cost us something, but we will try it."

If Dan felt any gratitude for his protection, he did not show it, and took without thanks all that was given him. He was ignorant, but very quick to learn when he chose; had sharp eyes to watch what went on about him; a saucy tongue, rough manners, and a temper that was fierce and sullen by turns. He played with all his might, and played well at almost all the games. He was silent and gruff before grown people, and only now and then was thoroughly social among the lads. Few of them really liked him, but few could help admiring his courage and strength, for nothing daunted him, and he knocked tall Franz flat on one occasion with an ease that caused all the others to keep at a respectful distance from his fists. Mr. Bhaer watched him silently, and did his best to tame the "Wild Boy," as they called him, but in private the worthy man shook his head, and said soberly, "I *hope* the experiment will turn out well, but I am a little afraid it may cost too much."

Mrs. Bhaer lost her patience with him half a dozen times a day, yet never gave him up, and always insisted that there was something good in the lad after all; for he was kinder to animals than to people, he liked to rove about in the woods, and, best of all, little Ted was fond of him. What the secret was no one could discover, but Baby took to him at once — gabbled and crowed whenever he saw him — preferred his strong back to ride on to any of the others — and called him "My Danny" out of his own little head. Teddy was the only creature to whom Dan showed any affection, and this was only manifested when he thought no one else could see it; but mothers' eyes are quick, and motherly hearts instinctively divine who love their babies. So Mrs. Jo soon saw and felt that there *was* a soft spot in rough Dan, and bided her time to touch and win him.

But an unexpected and decidedly alarming event upset all their plans, and banished Dan from Plumfield.

Tommy, Nat, and Demi began by patronizing Dan, because the other lads rather slighted him; but soon they each felt there was a certain fascination about the bad boy, and from looking down upon him they came to looking up, each for a different reason. Tommy admired his skill and courage; Nat was grateful for past kindness; and Demi regarded him as a sort of animated story book, for when he chose Dan could tell his adventures in a most interesting way. It pleased Dan to have the three favorites like him, and he exerted himself to be agreeable, which was the secret of his success.

The Bhaers were surprised, but hoped the lads would have a good influence over Dan, and waited with some anxiety, trusting that no harm would come of it.

Dan felt they did not quite trust him, and never showed them his best side, but took a wilful pleasure in trying their patience and thwarting their hopes as far as he dared.

Mr. Bhaer did not approve of fighting, and did not think it a proof of either manliness or courage for two lads to pommel one another for the amusement of the rest. All sorts of hardy games and exercises were encouraged, and the boys were expected to take hard knocks and tumbles without whining; but black eyes and bloody noses given for the fun of it were forbidden as a foolish and a brutal play.

Dan laughed at this rule, and told such exciting tales of his own valor, and the many frays that he had been in, that some of the lads were fired with a desire to have a regular good "mill."

"Don't tell, and I'll show you how," said Dan; and, getting half a dozen of the lads together behind the barn, he gave them a lesson in boxing, which quite satisfied the ardor of most of them. Emil, however, could not submit to be beaten by a fellow younger than himself, — for Emil was past fourteen, and a plucky fellow, — so he challenged Dan to a fight. Dan accepted at once, and the others looked on with intense interest.

What little bird carried the news to head-quarters no one ever knew, but, in the very hottest of the fray, when Dan and Emil were fighting like a pair of young bull-dogs, and the others with fierce, excited faces were cheering them on, Mr. Bhaer walked into the ring, plucked the combatants apart with a strong hand, and said, in the voice they seldom heard —

"I can't allow this, boys! Stop it at once; and never let me see it again. I keep a school for boys, not for wild beasts. Look at each other and be ashamed of yourselves."

"You let me go, and I'll knock him down again," shouted Dan, sparring away in spite of the grip on his collar.

"Come on, come on, I ain't thrashed yet!" cried Emil, who had been down five times, but did not know when he was beaten.

"They are playing be gladdy — what-you-call-'ems, like the Romans, Uncle Fritz," called out Demi, whose eyes were bigger than ever with the excitement of this new pastime.

"They were a fine set of brutes; but we have learned something since then I hope, and I cannot have you make my barn a Colosseum. Who proposed this?" asked Mr. Bhaer.

"Dan," answered several voices.

"Don't you know that it is forbidden?"

"Yes," growled Dan, sullenly.

"Then why break the rule?"

"They'll all be molly-coddles, if they don't know how to fight."

"Have you found Emil a molly-coddle? He doesn't look much like one," and Mr. Bhaer brought the two face to face. Dan had a black eye, and his jacket was torn to rags; but Emil's face was covered with blood from a cut lip and a bruised nose, while a bump on his forehead was already as purple as a plum. In spite of his wounds however, he still glared upon his foe, and evidently panted to renew the fight.

"He'd make a first-rater if he was taught," said Dan, unable to withhold the praise from the boy who made it necessary for him to do his best.

"He'll be taught to fence and box by and by, and till then I think he will do very well without any lessons in mauling. Go and wash your faces; and remember, Dan, if you break any more of the rules again, you will be sent away. That was the bargain; do your part and we will do ours."

The lads went off, and after a few more words to the spectators, Mr. Bhaer followed to bind up the wounds of the young gladiators. Emil went to bed sick, and Dan was an unpleasant spectacle for a week.

But the lawless lad had no thought of obeying, and soon transgressed again.

One Saturday afternoon as a party of the boys went out to play, Tommy said —

"Let's go down to the river, and cut a lot of new fish-poles."

"Take Toby to drag them back, and one of us can ride him down," proposed Stuffy, who hated to walk.

"That means *you*, I suppose; well, hurry up, lazy-bones," said Dan.

Away they went, and having got the poles were about to go home, when Demi unluckily said to Tommy, who was on Toby with a long rod in his hand —

"You look like the picture of the man in the bull-fight, only you haven't got a red cloth, or pretty clothes on."

"I'd like to see one; wouldn't you?" said Tommy shaking his lance.

"Let's have one; there's old Buttercup in the big meadow, ride at her Tom, and see her run," proposed Dan, bent on mischief.

"No, you mustn't," began Demi, who was learning to distrust Dan's propositions.

"Why not, little fuss-button?" demanded Dan.

"I don't think Uncle Fritz would like it."

"Did he ever say we must not have a bull-fight?"

"No, I don't think he ever did," admitted Demi.

"Then hold your tongue. Drive on, Tom, and here's a red rag to flap at the old thing. I'll help you to stir her up," and over the wall went Dan, full of the new game, and the rest followed like a flock of sheep; even Demi, who sat upon the bars, and watched the fun with interest.

Poor Buttercup was not in a very good mood, for she had been lately bereft of her calf, and mourned for the little thing most dismally. Just now she regarded all mankind as her enemies (and I do not blame her), so when the matadore came prancing towards her with the red handkerchief flying at the end of his long lance, she threw up her head, and gave a most appropriate "Moo!" Tommy rode gallantly at her, and Toby recognizing an old friend, was quite willing to approach; but when the lance came down on her back with a loud whack, both cow and donkey were surprised and disgusted. Toby backed with a bray of remonstrance, and Buttercup lowered her horns angrily.

"At her again, Tom; she's jolly cross, and will do it capitally!" called

Dan, coming up behind with another rod, while Jack and Ned followed his example.

Seeing herself thus beset, and treated with such disrespect, Buttercup trotted round the field, getting more and more bewildered and excited every moment, for whichever way she turned, there was a dreadful boy, yelling and brandishing a new and very disagreeable sort of whip. It was great fun for them, but real misery for her, till she lost patience and turned the tables in the most unexpected manner. All at once she wheeled short round, and charged full at her old friend Toby, whose conduct cut her to the heart. Poor slow Toby backed so precipitately, that he tripped over a stone, and down went horse, matadore, and all, in one ignominious heap, while distracted Buttercup took a surprising leap over the wall, and gal-loped wildly out of sight down the road.

"Catch her, stop her, head her off! run, boys, run!" shouted Dan, tearing after her at his best pace, for she was Mr. Bhaer's pet Alderney, and if any thing happened to her, Dan feared it would be all over with him. Such a running and racing and bawling and puffing as there was before she was caught! The fish-poles were left behind; Toby was trotted nearly off his legs in the chase; and every boy was red, breathless, and scared. They found poor Buttercup at last in a flower garden, where she had taken refuge, worn out with the long run. Borrowing a rope for a halter, Dan led her home, followed by a party of very sober young gentle-men, for the cow was in a sad state, having strained her shoulder in jump-ing, so that she limped, her eyes looked wild, and her glossy coat was wet and muddy.

"You'll catch it this time, Dan," said Tommy, as he led the wheezing donkey beside the maltreated cow.

"So will you, for you helped."

"We all did, but Demi," added Jack.

"He put it into our heads," said Ned.

"I told you not to do it," cried Demi, who was most broken-hearted at poor Buttercup's state.

"Old Bhaer will send me off, I guess. Don't care if he does," muttered Dan, looking worried in spite of his words.

"We'll ask him not to, all of us," said Demi, and the others assented with the exception of Stuffy, who cherished the hope that all the punish-ment might fall on one guilty head. Dan only said, "Don't bother about me;" but he never forgot it, even though he led the lads astray again, as soon as the temptation came.

When Mr. Bhaer saw the animal, and heard the story, he said very little, evidently fearing that he should say too much in the first moments of impatience. Buttercup was made comfortable in her stall, and the boys sent to their rooms till supper-time. This brief respite gave them time to think the matter over, to wonder what the penalty would be, and to try to imagine where Dan would be sent. He whistled briskly in his room, so that no one should think he cared a bit; but while he waited to know his fate, the longing to stay grew stronger and stronger, the more he recalled the comfort and kindness he had known here, the hardship and neglect he had felt elsewhere. He knew they tried to help him, and at the bottom of his heart he was grateful, but his rough life had made him hard and careless, suspicious and wilful. He hated restraint of any sort, and fought against it like an untamed creature, even while he knew it was kindly meant, and dimly felt that he would be the better for it. He made up his mind to be turned adrift again, to knock about the city as he had done nearly all his life; a prospect that made him knit his black brows, and look about the cosy little room with a wistful expression that would have touched a much harder heart than Mr. Bhaer's if he had seen it. It vanished instantly, however, when the good man came in, and said in his accustomed grave way —

"I have heard all about it, Dan, and though you have broken the rules again, I am going to give you one more trial, to please Mother Bhaer."

Dan flushed up to his forehead at this unexpected reprieve, but he only said in his gruff way —

"I didn't know there was any rule about bull fighting."

"As I never expected to have any at Plumfield, I never did make such a rule," answered Mr. Bhaer, smiling in spite of himself at the boy's excuse. Then he added gravely, "But one of the first and most important of our few laws is the law of kindness to every dumb creature on the place. I want everybody and every thing to be happy here, to love, and trust, and serve us, as we try to love and trust and serve them faithfully and willingly. I have often said that you were kinder to the animals than any of the other boys, and Mrs. Bhaer liked that trait in you very much, because she thought it showed a good heart. But you have disappointed us in that, and we are sorry, for we hoped to make you quite one of us. Shall we try again?"

Dan's eyes had been on the floor, and his hands nervously picking at the bit of wood he had been whittling as Mr. Bhaer came in, but when he heard the kind voice ask that question, he looked up quickly, and said in a more respectful tone than he had ever used before —

"Yes, please."

"Very well then, we will say no more, only you will stay at home from the walk to-morrow, as the other boys will, and all of you must wait on poor Buttercup till she is well again."

"I will."

"Now, go down to supper, and do your best, my boy, more for your own sake than for ours." Then Mr. Bhaer shook hands with him, and Dan went down more tamed by kindness, than he would have been by the good whipping which Asia had strongly recommended.

Dan did try for a day or two, but not being used to it, he soon tired and relapsed into his old wilful ways. Mr. Bhaer was called from home on business one day, and the boys had no lessons. They liked this, and played hard till bed-time, when most of them turned in and slept like dormice. Dan, however, had a plan in his head, and when he and Nat were alone, he unfolded it.

"Look here!" he said, taking from under his bed a bottle, a cigar, and a pack of cards, "I'm going to have some fun, and do as I used to with the fellows in town. Here's some beer, I got it of the old man at the station, and this cigar; you can pay for 'em, or Tommy will, he's got heaps of money, and I haven't a cent. I'm going to ask him in; no, you go, they won't mind you."

"The folks won't like it," began Nat.

"They won't know. Daddy Bhaer is away, and Mrs. Bhaer's busy with Ted; he's got croup or something, and she can't leave him. We shan't sit up late or make any noise, so where's the harm?"

"Asia will know if we burn the lamp long, she always does."

"No, she won't, I've got the dark lantern on purpose, it don't give much light, and we can shut it quick if we hear any one coming," said Dan.

This idea struck Nat as a fine one, and lent an air of romance to the thing. He started off to tell Tommy, but put his head in again to say —

"You want Demi, too, don't you?"

"No, I don't; the Deacon will roll up eyes and preach if you tell him. He will be asleep, so just tip the wink to Tom and cut back again."

Nat obeyed, and returned in a minute with Tommy half dressed, rather tousled about the head and very sleepy, but quite ready for fun as usual.

"Now, keep quiet, and I'll show you how to play a first-rate game called 'Poker,' " said Dan, as the three revellers gathered round the table, on which were set forth the bottle, the cigar, and the cards. "First we'll all have a drink, then we'll take a go at the 'weed,' and then we'll play. That's the way men do, and it's jolly fun."

The beer circulated in a mug, and all three smacked their lips over it, though Nat and Tommy did not like the bitter stuff. The cigar was worse still, but they dared not say so, and each puffed away till he was dizzy or choked, when he passed the "weed" on to his neighbor. Dan liked it, for it seemed like old times when he now and then had a chance to imitate the low men who surrounded him. He drank, and smoked, and swaggered as much like them as he could, and, getting into the spirit of the part he assumed, he soon began to swear under his breath for fear some one should hear him. "You mustn't; it's wicked to say 'Damn!' " cried Tommy, who had followed his leader so far.

"Oh, hang! don't you preach, but play away; it's part of the fun to swear."

"I'd rather say 'thunder——turtles,' " said Tommy, who had composed this interesting exclamation and was very proud of it.

"And I'll say 'The Devil;' that sounds well," added Nat, much impressed by Dan's manly ways.

Dan scoffed at their "nonsense," and swore stoutly as he tried to teach them the new game.

But Tommy was very sleepy, and Nat's head began to ache with the beer and the smoke, so neither of them was very quick to learn, and the game dragged. The room was nearly dark, for the lantern burned badly; they could not laugh loud nor move about much, for Silas slept next door in the shed-chamber, and altogether the party was dull. In the middle of a deal Dan stopped suddenly, called out, "Who's that?" in a startled tone, and at the same moment drew the slide over the light. A voice in the darkness said, tremulously, "I can't find Tommy," and then there was the quick patter of bare feet running away down the entry that led from the wing to the main house.

"It's Demi! he's gone to call some one; cut into bed, Tom, and don't tell!" cried Dan, whisking all signs of the revel out of sight, and beginning to tear off his clothes, while Nat did the same.

Tommy flew to his room and dived into bed, where he lay laughing till something burned his hand, when he discovered that he was still clutching the stump of the festive cigar, which he happened to be smoking when the revel broke up.

It was nearly out, and he was about to extinguish it carefully when Nursey's voice was heard, and fearing it would betray him if he hid it in the bed, he threw it underneath, after a final pinch which he thought finished it.

Nursey came in with Demi, who looked much amazed to see the red face of Tommy reposing peacefully upon his pillow.

"He wasn't there just now, because I woke up and could not find him anywhere," said Demi, pouncing on him.

"What mischief are you at now, bad child?" asked Nursey, with a good-natured shake, which made the sleeper open his eyes to say, meekly, —

"I only ran into Nat's room to see him about something. Go away, and let me alone; I'm awful sleepy."

Nursey tucked Demi in, and went off to reconnoitre, but only found two boys slumbering peacefully in Dan's room. "Some little frolic," she thought, and as there was no harm done she said nothing to Mrs. Bhaer, who was busy and worried over little Teddy.

Tommy was sleepy and telling Demi to mind his own business and not ask questions, he was snoring in ten minutes, little dreaming what was going on under his bed. The cigar did not go out, but smouldered away on the straw carpet till it was nicely on fire, and a hungry little flame went creeping along till the dimity bedcover caught, then the sheets, and then the bed itself. The beer made Tommy sleep heavily, and the smoke stupefied Demi, so they slept on till the fire began to scorch them, and they were in danger of being burned to death.

Franz was sitting up to study, and as he left the school-room he smelt the smoke, dashed up-stairs and saw it coming in a cloud from the left wing of the house. Without stopping to call any one, he ran into the room, dragged the boys from the blazing bed, and splashed all the water he could find at hand on to the flames. It checked but did not quench the fire, and the children, wakened on being tumbled topsy-turvy into a cold hall, began to roar at the top of their voices. Mrs. Bhaer instantly appeared, and a minute after Silas burst out of his room shouting "Fire!" in a tone that raised the whole house. A flock of white goblins with scared faces crowded into the hall, and for a minute every one was panic-stricken.

Then Mrs. Bhaer found her wits, bade Nursey see to the burnt boys, and sent Franz and Silas down-stairs for some tubs of wet clothes which she flung on to the bed, over the carpet, and up against the curtains, now burning finely, and threatening to kindle the walls.

Most of the boys stood dumbly looking on, but Dan and Emil worked bravely, running to and fro with water from the bath-room, and helping to pull down the dangerous curtains.

The peril was soon over, and ordering the boys all back to bed, and leaving Silas to watch lest the fire broke out again, Mrs. Bhaer and Franz went to see how the poor boys got on. Demi had escaped with one burn and a grand scare, but Tommy had not only most of his hair scorched off his head, but a great burn on his arm, that made him half crazy with the pain. Demi was soon made cosy, and Franz took him away to his own bed, where the kind lad soothed his fright and hummed him to sleep as cosily as a woman. Nursey watched over poor Tommy all night, trying to ease his misery, and Mrs. Bhaer vibrated between him and little Teddy with oil and cotton, paregoric and squills, saying to herself from time to time, as if she found great amusement in the thought, "I always *knew* Tommy would set the house on fire, and now he has done it!"

When Mr. Bhaer got home next morning he found a nice state of things. Tommy in bed, Teddy wheezing like a little grampus, Mrs. Jo quite used up, and the whole flock of boys so excited that they all talked at once, and almost dragged him by main force to view the ruins. Under his quiet management things soon fell into order, for every one felt that he was equal to a dozen conflagrations, and worked with a will at whatever task he gave them.

There was no school that morning, but by afternoon the damaged room was put to rights, the invalids were better, and there was time to hear and judge the little culprits quietly. Nat and Tommy told their parts in the mischief, and were honestly sorry for the danger they had brought to the dear old house and all in it. But Dan put on his devil-may-care look, and would not own that there was much harm done.

Now, of all things, Mr. Bhaer hated drinking, gambling, and swearing; smoking he had given up that the lads might not be tempted to try it, and it grieved and angered him deeply to find that the boy, with whom he had tried to be most forbearing, should take advantage of his absence to introduce these forbidden vices, and teach his innocent little lads to think it manly and pleasant to indulge in them. He talked long and earnestly to the assembled boys, and ended by saying, with an air of mingled firmness and regret —

"I think Tommy is punished enough, and that scar on his arm will remind him for a long time to let these things alone. Nat's fright will do for him, for he is really sorry, and does try to obey me. But you, Dan, have been many times forgiven, and yet it does no good. I cannot have my boys hurt by your bad example, nor my time wasted in talking to deaf ears, so you can say good-by to them all, and tell Nursey to put up your things in my little black bag."

"Oh! sir, where is he going?" cried Nat.

"To a pleasant place up in the country, where I sometimes send boys when they don't do well here. Mr. Page is a kind man, and Dan will be happy there if he chooses to do his best."

"Will he ever come back?" asked Demi.

"That will depend on himself; I hope so."

As he spoke, Mr. Bhaer left the room to write his letter to Mr. Page, and the boys crowded round Dan very much as people do about a man who is going on a long and perilous journey to unknown regions.

"I wonder if you'll like it," began Jack.

"Shan't stay if I don't," said Dan, coolly.

"Where will you go?" asked Nat.

"I may go to sea, or out west, or take a look at California," answered Dan, with a reckless air that quite took away the breath of the little boys.

"Oh, don't! stay with Mr. Page awhile and then come back here; do, Dan," pleaded Nat, much affected at the whole affair.

"I don't care where I go, or how long I stay, and I'll be hanged if I ever come back here," with which wrathful speech Dan went away to put up his things, every one of which Mr. Bhaer had given him.

That was the only good-by he gave the boys, for they were all talking the matter over in the barn when he came down, and he told Nat not to call them. The wagon stood at the door, and Mrs. Bhaer came out to speak to Dan, looking so sad that his heart smote him, and he said in a low tone —

"May I say good-by to Teddy?"

"Yes, dear; go in and kiss him, he will miss his Danny very much."

No one saw the look in Dan's eyes as he stooped over the crib, and saw the little face light up at first sight of him, but he heard Mrs. Bhaer say pleadingly —

"Can't we give the poor lad *one* more trial, Fritz?" and Mr. Bhaer answer in his steady way —

"My dear, it is not best, so let him go where he can do no harm to others, while they do good to him, and by and by he shall come back, I promise you."

"He's the only boy we ever failed with, and I am so grieved, for I thought there was the making of a fine man in him, spite of his faults."

Dan heard Mrs. Bhaer sigh, and he wanted to ask for *one more* trial himself, but his pride would not let him, and he came out with the hard look on his face, shook hands without a word, and drove away with Mr. Bhaer, leaving Nat and Mrs. Jo to look after him with tears in their eyes.

A few days afterwards they received a letter from Mr. Page, saying that Dan was doing well, whereat they all rejoiced. But three weeks later came another letter, saying that Dan had run away, and nothing had been heard of him, whereat they all looked sober, and Mr. Bhaer said —

"Perhaps I ought to have given him another chance."

Mrs. Bhaer, however, nodded wisely and answered, "Don't be troubled, Fritz; the boy will come back to us, I'm sure of it."

But time went on and no Dan came.

Ten Years Later

From *Jo's Boys, and How They Turned Out. A Sequel to "Little Men"*
(Boston: Roberts Brothers, 1886)

I F ANY ONE had told me what wonderful changes were to take place here in ten years, I would n't have believed it," said Mrs. Jo to Mrs. Meg, as they sat on the piazza at Plumfield one summer day, looking about them with faces full of pride and pleasure.

"This is the sort of magic that money and kind hearts can work. I am sure Mr. Laurence could have no nobler monument than the college he so generously endowed; and a home like this will keep Aunt March's memory green as long as it lasts," answered Mrs. Meg, always glad to praise the absent.

"We used to believe in fairies, you remember, and plan what we'd ask for if we could have three wishes. Does n't it seem as if mine had been really granted at last? Money, fame, and plenty of the work I love," said Mrs. Jo, carelessly rumpling up her hair as she clasped her hands over her head just as she used to do when a girl.

"I have had mine, and Amy is enjoying hers to her heart's content. If dear Marmee, John, and Beth were here, it would be quite perfect," added Meg, with a tender quiver in her voice; for Marmee's place was empty now.

Jo put her hand on her sister's, and both sat silent for a little while, surveying the pleasant scene before them with mingled sad and happy thoughts.

It certainly did look as if magic had been at work, for quiet Plumfield was transformed into a busy little world. The house seemed more hospitable than ever, refreshed with new paint, added wings, well-kept lawn and garden, and a prosperous air it had not worn when riotous boys swarmed everywhere and it was rather difficult for the Bhaers to make both ends meet. On the hill, where kites used to be flown, stood the fine college which Mr. Laurence's munificent legacy had built. Busy students were going to and fro along the paths once trodden by childish feet, and many young men and women were enjoying all the advantages that wealth, wisdom, and benevolence could give them.

Just inside the gates of Plumfield a pretty brown cottage, very like the Dove-cote, nestled among the trees, and on the green slope westward Laurie's white-pillared· mansion glittered in the sunshine; for when the rapid growth of the city shut in the old house, spoilt Meg's nest, and dared to put a soap-factory under Mr. Laurence's indignant nose, our friends emigrated to Plumfield, and the great changes began.

These were the pleasant ones; and the loss of the dear old people was sweetened by the blessings they left behind; so all prospered now in the little community, and Mr. Bhaer as president, and Mr. March as chaplain, of the college, saw their long-cherished dream beautifully realized. The sisters divided the care of the young people among them, each taking the part that suited her best. Meg was the motherly friend of the young women, Jo the confidante and defender of all the youths, and Amy the Lady Bountiful who delicately smoothed the way for needy students, and entertained them all so cordially that it was no wonder they named her lovely home Mount Parnassus, so full was it of music, beauty, and the culture hungry young hearts and fancies long for.

The original twelve boys had of course scattered far and wide during these years, but all that lived still remembered old Plumfield, and came wandering back from the four quarters of the earth to tell their various experiences, laugh over the pleasures of the past, and face the duties of the present with fresh courage; for such home-comings keep hearts tender and hands helpful with the memories of young and happy days. A few words will tell the history of each, and then we can go on with the new chapter of their lives.

Franz was with a merchant kinsman in Hamburg, a man of twenty-six now, and doing well. Emil was the jolliest tar that ever "sailed the ocean blue." His uncle sent him on a long voyage to disgust him with this adventurous life; but he came home so delighted with it that it was plain this was his profession, and the German kinsman gave him a good chance in his ships; so the lad was happy. Dan was a wanderer still; for after the geological researches in South America he tried sheep-farming in Australia, and was now in California looking up mines. Nat was busy with music at the Conservatory, preparing for a year or two in Germany to finish him off. Tom was studying medicine and trying to like it. Jack was in business with his father, bent on getting rich. Dolly was in college with Stuffy and Ned reading law. Poor little Dick was dead, so was Billy; and no one could mourn for them, since life would never be happy, afflicted as they were in mind and body.

Rob and Teddy were called the "Lion and the Lamb;" for the latter was as rampant as the king of beasts, and the former as gentle as any sheep that ever baaed. Mrs. Jo called him "my daughter," and found him the most dutiful of children, with plenty of manliness underlying the quiet manners and tender nature. But in Ted she seemed to see all the faults, whims, aspirations, and fun of her own youth in a new shape. With his tawny locks always in wild confusion, his long legs and arms, loud voice, and continual activity, Ted was a prominent figure at Plumfield. He had his moods of gloom, and fell into the Slough of Despond about once a week, to be hoisted out by patient Rob or his mother, who understood when to let him alone and when to shake him up. He was her pride and joy as well as torment, being a very bright lad for his age, and so full of all sorts of budding talent, that her maternal mind was much exercised as to what this remarkable boy would become.

Demi had gone through college with honor, and Mrs. Meg had set her heart on his being a minister, — picturing in her fond fancy the first sermon her dignified young parson would preach, as well as the long, useful, and honored life he was to lead. But John, as she called him now, firmly declined the divinity school, saying he had had enough of books, and needed to know more of men and the world, and caused the dear woman much disappointment by deciding to try a journalist's career. It was a blow; but she knew that young minds cannot be driven, and that experience is the best teacher; so she let him follow his own inclinations, still hoping to see him in the pulpit. Aunt Jo raged when she found that there was to be a reporter in the family, and called him "Jenkins" on the spot. She liked his literary tendencies, but had reason to detest official Paul Prys, as we shall see later. Demi knew his own mind, however, and tranquilly carried out his plans, unmoved by the tongues of the anxious mammas or the jokes of his mates. Uncle Teddy encouraged him, and painted a splendid career, mentioning Dickens and other celebrities who began as reporters and ended as famous novelists or newspaper men.

The girls were all flourishing. Daisy, as sweet and domestic as ever, was her mother's comfort and companion. Josie at fourteen was a most original young person, full of pranks and peculiarities, the latest of which was a passion for the stage, which caused her quiet mother and sister much anxiety as well as amusement. Bess had grown into a tall, beautiful girl, looking several years older than she was, with the same graceful ways and dainty tastes which the little Princess had, and a rich inheritance of both the father's and mother's gifts, fostered by every aid love and money could give. But the pride of the community was Naughty Nan; for, like so many restless, wilful children, she was growing into a woman full of the energy and promise that suddenly blossoms when the ambitious seeker finds the work she is fitted to do well. Nan began to study medicine at sixteen, and at twenty was getting on bravely; for now, thanks to other intelligent women, colleges and hospitals were open to her. She had never wavered in her purpose from the childish days when she shocked Daisy in the old willow by saying, "I don't want any family to fuss over. I shall have an office, with bottles and pestle things in it, and drive round and cure folks." The future foretold by the little girl the young woman was rapidly bringing to pass, and finding so much happiness in it that nothing could win her from the chosen work. Several worthy young gentlemen had tried to make her change her mind and choose, as Daisy did, "a nice little house and a family to take care of." But Nan only laughed, and routed the lovers by proposing to look at the tongue which spoke of adoration, or profession-ally felt the pulse in the manly hand offered for her acceptance. So all departed but one persistent youth, who was such a devoted Traddles it was impossible to quench him.

This was Tom, who was as faithful to his child sweetheart as she to her "pestle things," and gave a proof of fidelity that touched her very much. He studied medicine for her sake alone, having no taste for it, and a decided fancy for a mercantile life. But Nan was firm, and Tom stoutly kept on, devoutly hoping he might not kill many of his fellow-beings when he came to practise. They were excellent friends, however, and caused much amusement to their comrades by the vicissitudes of this merry love-chase.

Both were approaching Plumfield on the afternoon when Mrs. Meg and Mrs. Jo were talking on the piazza. Not together; for Nan was walking briskly along the pleasant road alone, thinking over a case that interested her, and Tom was pegging on behind to overtake her, as if by accident, when the suburbs of the city were past, — a little way of his, which was part of the joke.

Nan was a handsome girl, with a fresh color, clear eye, quick smile, and the self-poised look young women with a purpose always have. She was simply and sensibly dressed, walked easily, and seemed full of vigor, with her broad shoulders well back, arms swinging freely, and the elasticity of youth and health in every motion. The few people she met turned to look at her, as if it was a pleasant sight to see a hearty, happy girl walking countryward that lovely day; and the red-faced young man steaming along behind, hat off and every tight curl wagging with impatience, evidently agreed with them.

Presently a mild "Hullo!" was borne upon the breeze, and pausing, with an effort to look surprised that was an utter failure, Nan said affably, —

"Oh, is that you, Tom?"

"Looks like it. Thought you might be walking out to-day;" and Tom's jovial face beamed with pleasure.

"You knew it. How is your throat?" asked Nan in her professional tone, which was always a quencher to undue raptures.

"Throat? — oh, ah! yes, I remember. It is well. The effect of that prescription was wonderful. I'll never call homœopathy a humbug again."

"You were the humbug this time, and so were the unmedicated pellets I gave you. If sugar or milk can cure diphtheria in this remarkable manner, I'll make a note of it. O Tom, Tom, will you never be done playing tricks?"

"O Nan, Nan, will you never be done getting the better of me?" And the merry pair laughed at one another just as they did in the old times, which always came back freshly when they went to Plumfield.

"Well, I knew I should n't see you for a week if I did n't scare up some excuse for a call at the office. You are so desperately busy all the time I never get a word," explained Tom.

"You ought to be busy too, and above such nonsense. Really, Tom, if you don't give your mind to your lectures, you'll never get on," said Nan, soberly.

"I have quite enough of them as it is," answered Tom, with an air of disgust. "A fellow must lark a bit after dissecting corpuses all day. I can't stand it long at a time, though *some people* seem to enjoy it immensely."

"Then why not leave it, and do what suits you better? I always thought it a foolish thing, you know," said Nan, with a trace of anxiety in the keen eyes that searched for signs of illness in a face as ruddy as a Baldwin apple.

"You know why I chose it, and why I shall stick to it if it kills me. I may not *look* delicate, but I've a deep-seated heart complaint, and it will carry me off sooner or later; for only one doctor in the world can cure it, and she won't."

There was an air of pensive resignation about Tom that was both comic and pathetic; for he was in earnest, and kept on giving hints of this sort, without the least encouragement.

Nan frowned; but she was used to it, and knew how to treat him.

"She *is* curing it in the best and only way; but a more refractory patient never lived. Did you go to that ball, as I directed?"

"I did."

"And devote yourself to pretty Miss West?"

"Danced with her the whole evening."

"No impression made on that susceptible organ of yours?"

"Not the slightest. I gaped in her face once, forgot to feed her, and gave a sigh of relief when I handed her over to her mamma."

"Repeat the dose as often as possible, and note the symptoms. I predict that you will 'cry for it' by and by."

"Never! I'm sure it doesn't suit my constitution."

"We shall see. Obey orders!" sternly.

"Yes, Doctor," meekly.

Silence reigned for a moment; then, as if the bone of contention was forgotten in the pleasant recollections called up by familiar objects, Nan said, suddenly, —

"What fun we used to have in that wood! Do you remember how you tumbled out of the big nut-tree and nearly broke your collar-bone?"

"Don't I! and how you steeped me in wormwood till I was a fine mahogany color, and Aunt Jo wailed over my spoilt jacket," laughed Tom, a boy again in a minute.

"And how you set the house afire?"

"And you ran off for your band-box?"

"Do you ever say 'Thunder-turtles' now?"

"Do people ever call you 'Giddy-gaddy'?"

"Daisy does. Dear thing, I have n't seen her for a week."

"I saw Demi this morning, and he said she was keeping house for Mother Bhaer."

"She always does when Aunt Jo gets into a vortex. Daisy is a model housekeeper; and you could n't do better than make your bow to her, if you can't go to work and wait till you are grown up before you begin lovering."

"Nat would break his fiddle over my head if I suggested such a thing. No, thank you. Another name is engraved upon my heart as indelibly as the blue anchor on my arm. 'Hope' is my motto, and 'No surrender,' yours; see who will hold out longest."

"You silly boys think we must pair off as we did when children; but we shall do nothing of the kind. How well Parnassus looks from here!" said Nan, abruptly changing the conversation again.

"It is a fine house; but I love old Plum best. Would n't Aunt March stare if she could see the changes here?" answered Tom, as they both paused at the great gate to look at the pleasant landscape before them.

A sudden whoop startled them, as a long boy with a wild yellow head came leaping over a hedge like a kangaroo, followed by a slender girl, who stuck in the hawthorn, and sat there laughing like a witch. A pretty little lass she was, with curly dark hair, bright eyes, and a very expressive face. Her hat was at her back, and her skirts a good deal the worse for the brooks she had crossed, the trees she had climbed, and the last leap, which added several fine rents.

"Take me down, Nan, please. Tom, hold Ted; he's got my book, and I *will* have it," called Josie from her perch, not at all daunted by the appearance of her friends.

Tom promptly collared the thief, while Nan picked Josie from among the thorns and set her on her feet without a word of reproof; for having been a romp in her own girlhood, she was very indulgent to like tastes in others. "What's the matter, dear?" she asked, pinning up the longest rip, while Josie examined the scratches on her hands.

"I was studying my part in the willow, and Ted came slyly up and poked the book out of my hands with his rod. It fell in the brook, and before I could scrabble down he was off. You wretch, give it back this moment or I'll box your ears," cried Josie, laughing and scolding in the same breath.

Escaping from Tom, Ted struck a sentimental attitude, and with tender glances at the wet, torn young person before him, delivered Claude Melnotte's famous speech in a lackadaisical way that was irresistibly funny, ending with "Dost like the picture, love?" as he made an object of himself by tying his long legs in a knot and distorting his face horribly.

The sound of applause from the piazza put a stop to these antics, and the young folks went up the avenue together very much in the old style when Tom drove four in hand and Nan was the best horse in the team. Rosy, breathless, and merry, they greeted the ladies and sat down on the steps to rest, Aunt Meg sewing up her daughter's rags while Mrs. Jo smoothed the Lion's mane, and rescued the book. Daisy appeared in a moment to greet her friend, and all began to talk.

"Muffins for tea; better stay and eat 'em; Daisy's never fail," said Ted, hospitably.

"He's a judge; he ate nine last time. That's why he's so fat," added Josie, with a withering glance at her cousin, who was as thin as a lath.

"I must go and see Lucy Dove. She has a whitlow, and it's time to lance it. I'll tea at college," answered Nan, feeling in her pocket to be sure she had not forgotten her case of instruments.

"Thanks, I'm going there also. Tom Merryweather has granulated lids, and I promised to touch them up for him. Save a doctor's fee and be good practice for me. I'm clumsy with my thumbs," said Tom, bound to be near his idol while he could.

"Hush! Daisy does n't like to hear you saw-bones talk of your work. Muffins suit us better;" and Ted grinned sweetly, with a view to future favors in the eating line.

"Any news of the Commodore?" asked Tom.

"He is on his way home, and Dan hopes to come soon. I long to see my boys together, and have begged the wanderers to come to Thanksgiving, if not before," answered Mrs. Jo, beaming at the thought.

"They'll come, every man of them, if they can. Even Jack will risk losing a dollar for the sake of one of our jolly old dinners," laughed Tom.

"There's the turkey fattening for the feast. I never chase him now, but feed him well; and he's 'swellin' wisibly,' bless his drumsticks!" said Ted, pointing out the doomed fowl proudly parading in a neighboring field.

"If Nat goes the last of the month we shall want a farewell frolic for him. I suppose the dear old Chirper will come home a second Ole Bull," said Nan to her friend.

A pretty color came into Daisy's cheek, and the folds of muslin on her breast rose and fell with a quick breath; but she answered placidly, "Uncle Laurie says he has *real* talent, and after the training he will get abroad he can command a good living here, though he may never be famous."

"Young people seldom turn out as one predicts, so it is of little use to expect anything," said Mrs. Meg with a sigh. "If our children are good and useful men and women we should be satisfied; yet it's very natural to wish them to be brilliant and successful."

"They are like my chickens, mighty uncertain. Now, that fine-looking cockerel of mine is the stupidest one of the lot, and the ugly, long-legged chap is the king of the yard, he's so smart; crows loud enough to wake the Seven Sleepers; but the handsome one croaks, and is no end of a coward. *I* get snubbed; but you wait till I grow up, and then see;" and Ted looked so like his own long-legged pet that every one laughed at his modest prediction.

"I want to see Dan settled somewhere. 'A rolling stone gathers no moss,' and at twenty-five he is still roaming about the world without a tie to hold him, except this;" and Mrs. Meg nodded toward her sister.

"Dan will find his place at last, and experience is his best teacher. He is rough still, but each time he comes home I see a change for the better, and never lose my faith in him. He may never do anything great, or get rich; but if the wild boy makes an honest man, I'm satisfied," said Mrs. Jo, who always defended the black sheep of her flock.

"That's right, mother, stand by Dan! He's worth a dozen Jacks and Neds bragging about money and trying to be swells. You see if he does n't do something to be proud of and take the wind out of their sails," added Ted, whose love for his "Danny" was now strengthened by a boy's admiration for the bold, adventurous man.

"Hope so, I'm sure. He's just the fellow to do rash things and come to glory, — climbing the Matterhorn, taking a 'header' into Niagara, or finding a big nugget. That's his way of sowing wild oats, and perhaps it's better than ours," said Tom, thoughtfully; for he had gained a good deal of experience in that sort of agriculture since he became a medical student.

"Much better!" said Mrs. Jo, emphatically. "I'd rather send my boys off to see the world in that way than leave them alone in a city full of temptations, with nothing to do but waste time, money, and health, as so many are left. Dan has to work his way, and that teaches him courage, patience and self-reliance. I don't worry about him as much as I do about George and Dolly at college, no more fit than two babies to take care of themselves."

"How about John? He's knocking round town as a newspaper man, reporting all sorts of things, from sermons to prize-fights," asked Tom, who thought that sort of life would be much more to his own taste than medical lectures and hospital wards.

"Demi has three safeguards, — good principles, refined tastes, and a wise mother. He won't come to harm, and these experiences will be useful to him when he begins to write, as I'm sure he will in time," began Mrs. Jo in her prophetic tone; for she was anxious to have some of her geese turn out swans.

"Speak of Jenkins, and you'll hear the rustling of his paper," cried Tom, as a fresh-faced, brown-eyed young man came up the avenue, waving a newspaper over his head.

"Here's your 'Evening Tattler!' Latest edition! Awful murder! Bank clerk absconded! Powder-mill explosion, and great strike of the Latin School boys!" roared Ted, going to meet his cousin with the graceful gait of a young giraffe.

"The Commodore is in, and will cut his cable and run before the wind as soon as he can get off," called Demi, with "a nice derangement of nautical epitaphs," as he came up smiling over his good news.

Every one talked together for a moment, and the paper passed from hand to hand that each eye might rest on the pleasant fact that the "Brenda," from Hamburg, was safe in port.

"He'll come lurching out by to-morrow with his usual collection of marine monsters and lively yarns. I saw him, jolly and tarry and brown as a coffee-berry. Had a good run, and hopes to be second mate, as the other chap is laid up with a broken leg," added Demi.

"Wish I had the setting of it," said Nan to herself, with a professional twist of her hand.

"How's Franz?" asked Mrs. Jo.

"He's going to be married! There's news for you. The first of the flock, Aunty, so say good-by to him. Her name is Ludmilla Hildegard Blumenthal; good family, well-off, pretty, and of course an angel. The dear old boy wants uncle's consent, and then he will settle down to be a happy and an honest burgher. Long life to him!"

"I'm glad to hear it. I do so like to settle my boys with a good wife and a nice little home. Now, if all is right, I shall feel as if Franz was off my mind," said Mrs. Jo, folding her hands contentedly; for she often felt like a distracted hen with a large brood of mixed chickens and ducks upon her hands.

"So do I," sighed Tom, with a sly glance at Nan. "That's what a fellow needs to keep him steady; and it's the duty of nice girls to marry as soon as possible, isn't it, Demi?"

"If there are enough nice fellows to go round. The female population exceeds the male, you know, especially in New England; which accounts for the high state of culture we are in, perhaps," answered John, who was leaning over his mother's chair, telling his day's experiences in a whisper.

"It is a merciful provision, my dears; for it takes three or four women to get each man into, through, and out of the world. You are costly crea-tures, boys; and it is well that mothers, sisters, wives, and daughters love their duty and do it so well, or you would perish off the face of the earth," said Mrs. Jo, solemnly, as she took up a basket filled with dilapidated hose; for the good Professor was still hard on his socks, and his sons resembled him in that respect.

"Such being the case, there is a plenty for the 'superfluous women' to do, in taking care of these helpless men and their families. I see that more clearly every day, and am very glad and grateful that my profession will make me a useful, happy, and independent spinster."

Nan's emphasis on the last word caused Tom to groan, and the rest to laugh.

"I take great pride and solid satisfaction in you, Nan, and hope to see you very successful; for we do need just such helpful women in the world. I sometimes feel as if I'd missed my vocation and ought to have remained single; but my duty seemed to point this way, and I don't regret it," said Mrs. Jo, folding a large and very ragged blue sock to her bosom.

"Neither do I. What should I ever have done without my dearest Mum?" added Ted, with a filial hug which caused both to disappear behind the newspaper in which he had been mercifully absorbed for a few minutes.

"My darling boy, if you would wash your hands semi-occasionally, fond caresses would be less disastrous to my collar. Never mind, my precious touzle-head, better grass-stains and dirt than no cuddlings at all;" and Mrs. Jo emerged from that brief eclipse looking much refreshed, though her back hair was caught in Ted's buttons and her collar under one ear.

Here Josie, who had been studying her part at the other end of the piazza, suddenly burst forth with a smothered shriek, and gave Juliet's speech in the tomb so effectively that the boys applauded, Daisy shivered, and Nan murmured, "Too much cerebral excitement for one of her age."

"I'm afraid you'll have to make up your mind to it, Meg. That child is a born actress. We never did anything so well, not even the 'Witch's Curse,' " said Mrs. Jo, casting a bouquet of many-colored socks at the feet of her flushed and panting niece, when she fell gracefully upon the door-mat.

"It is a sort of judgment upon me for my passion for the stage when a girl. Now I know how dear Marmee felt when I begged to be an actress. I never can consent, and yet I may be obliged to give up my wishes, hopes, and plans again."

There was an accent of reproach in his mother's voice, which made Demi pick up his sister with a gentle shake, and the stern command to "drop that nonsense in public."

"Drop me, Minion, or I'll give you the 'Maniac Bride,' with my best *Ha-ha!*" cried Josie, glaring at him like an offended kitten.

Being set on her feet, she made a splendid courtesy, and dramatically proclaiming "Mrs. Woffington's carriage waits," swept down the steps and round the corner, trailing Daisy's scarlet shawl majestically behind her.

"Is n't she great fun? I could n't stop in this dull place if I had n't that child to make it lively for me. If ever she turns prim, I'm off; so mind how you nip her in the bud," said Teddy, frowning at Demi, who was now writing out short-hand notes on the steps.

"You two are a team, and it takes a strong hand to drive you, but I rather like it. Josie ought to have been my child, and Rob yours, Meg. Then your house would have been all peace and mine all Bedlam. Now I must go and tell Laurie the news. Come with me, Meg, a little stroll will do us good;" and sticking Ted's straw hat on her head, Mrs. Jo walked off with her sister, leaving Daisy to attend to the muffins, Ted to appease Josie, and Tom and Nan to give their respective patients a very bad quarter of an hour.

Positively Last Appearance

An excerpt from the concluding chapter of *Jo's Boys, and How They Turned Out. A Sequel to "Little Men"* (Boston: Roberts Brothers, 1886)

I T IS A strong temptation to the weary historian to close the present tale with an earthquake which should engulf Plumfield and its environs so deeply in the bowels of the earth that no youthful Schliemann could ever find a vestige of it. But as that somewhat melodramatic conclusion might shock my gentle readers, I will refrain, and forestall the usual question, "How did they end?" by briefly stating that all the marriages turned out well. The boys prospered in their various callings; so did the girls, for Bess and Josie won honors in their artistic careers, and in the course of time found worthy mates. Nan remained a busy, cheerful, independent spinster, and dedicated her life to her suffering sisters and their children, in which true woman's work she found abiding happiness. Dan never married, but lived, bravely and usefully, among his chosen people till he was shot defending them, and at last lay quietly asleep in the green wilderness he loved so well, with a lock of golden hair upon his breast, and a smile on his face which seemed to say that Aslauga's Knight had fought his last fight and was at peace. Stuffy became an alderman, and died suddenly of apoplexy after a public dinner. Dolly was a society man of mark till he lost his money, when he found congenial employment in a fashionable tailoring establishment. Demi became a partner, and lived to see his name above the door, and Rob was a professor at Laurence College; but Teddy eclipsed them all by becoming an eloquent and famous clergyman, to the great delight of his astonished mother. And now, having endeavored to suit every one by many weddings, few deaths, and as much prosperity as the eternal fitness of things will permit, let the music stop, the lights die out, and the curtain fall forever on the March family.

The Youth's Companion

America's Best-Loved Author of Juveniles

My Boys

From *Aunt Jo's Scrap-Bag* (6 vols.), vol. 1
(Boston: Roberts Brothers, 1872)

*F*EELING THAT I have been unusually fortunate in my knowledge of a choice and pleasing variety of this least appreciated portion of the human race, I have a fancy to record some of my experiences, hoping that it may awaken an interest in other minds, and cause other people to cultivate the delightful, but too often neglected boys, who now run to waste, so to speak.

I have often wondered what they thought of the peculiar treatment they receive, even at the hands of their nearest friends. While they are rosy, roly-poly little fellows they are petted and praised, adorned and adored, till it is a miracle that they are not utterly ruined. But the moment they outgrow their babyhood their trials begin, and they are regarded as nuisances till they are twenty-one, when they are again received into favor.

Yet that very time of neglect is the period when they most need all manner of helps, and ought to have them. I like boys and oysters raw; so, though good manners are always pleasing, I don't mind the rough outside burr which repels most people, and perhaps that is the reason why the burrs open and let me see the soft lining and taste the sweet nut hidden inside.

My first well-beloved boy was a certain Frank, to whom I clung at the age of seven with a devotion which I fear he did not appreciate. There were six girls in the house, but I would have nothing to say to them, preferring to tag after Frank, and perfectly happy when he allowed me to play with him. I regret to say that the small youth was something of a tyrant, and one of his favorite amusements was trying to make me cry by slapping my hands with books, hoop-sticks, shoes, any thing that came along capable of giving a good stinging blow. I believe I endured these marks of friendship with the fortitude of a young Indian, and felt fully repaid for a blistered palm by hearing Frank tell the other boys "She's a brave little thing, and you can't make her cry."

My chief joy was in romping with him in the long galleries of a piano manufactory behind our house. What bliss it was to mount one of the cars on which the workmen rolled heavy loads from room to room, and to go thundering down the inclined planes, regardless of the crash that usually awaited us at the bottom! If I could have played foot-ball on the Common with my Frank and Billy Babcock, life could have offered me no greater joy at that period. As the prejudices of society forbid this sport, I revenged myself by driving hoop all around the mall without stopping, which the boys could *not* do.

I can remember certain happy evenings, when we snuggled in sofa corners and planned tricks and ate stolen goodies, and sometimes Frank would put his curly head in my lap and let me stroke it when he was tired. What the girls did I don't recollect; their domestic plays were not to my taste, and the only figure that stands out from the dimness of the past is that jolly boy with a twinkling eye. This memory would be quite radiant but for one sad thing, — a deed that cut me to the soul then, and which I have never quite forgiven in all these years.

On one occasion I did something very naughty, and when called up for judgment fled to the dining-room, locked the door, and from my stronghold defied the whole world. I could have made my own terms, for it was near dinner-time and the family must eat; but, alas, for the treachery of the human heart! Frank betrayed me. He climbed in at the window, unlocked the door, and delivered me up to the foe. Nay, he even defended the base act, and helped bear the struggling culprit to imprisonment. That nearly broke my heart, for I believed *he* would stand by me as staunchly as I always stood by him. It was a sad blow, and I couldn't love or trust him any more. Peanuts and candy, ginger-snaps and car-rides were unavailing; even foot-ball could not reunite the broken friendship, and to this day I recollect the pang that entered my little heart when I lost my faith in the loyalty of my first boy.

The second attachment was of quite a different sort, and had a happier ending. At the mature age of ten, I left home for my first visit to a family of gay and kindly people in — well, why not say right out? — Providence. There were no children, and at first I did not mind this, as every one petted me, especially one of the young men named Christopher. So kind and patient, yet so merry was this good Christy that I took him for my private and particular boy, and loved him dearly, for he got me out of innumerable scrapes, and never was tired of amusing the restless little girl who kept the family in a fever of anxiety by her pranks. *He* never laughed at her mishaps and mistakes, never played tricks upon her like a certain William who composed the most trying nicknames, and wickedly goaded the wild visitor into all manner of naughtiness. Christy stood up for her through every thing; let her ride the cows, feed the pigs, bang on the piano, and race all over the spice mill, feasting on cinnamon and cloves; brought her down from housetops and fished her out of brooks; never scolded, and never seemed tired of the troublesome friendship of little Torment.

In a week I had exhausted every amusement and was desperately homesick. It has always been my opinion that I should have been speedily restored to the bosom of my family but for Christy, and but for him I should assuredly have ran away before the second week was out. He kept me, and in the hour of my disgrace stood by me like a man and a brother.

One afternoon, inspired by a spirit of benevolence, enthusiastic but short-sighted, I collected several poor children in the barn and regaled them on cake and figs, helping myself freely to the treasures of the pantry without asking leave, meaning to explain afterward. Being discovered before the supplies were entirely exhausted, the patience of the long-suffering matron gave out, and I was ordered to go to the garret to reflect upon my sins, and the pleasing prospect of being sent home with the character of the worst child ever known.

My sufferings were deep as I sat upon a fuzzy little trunk all alone in the dull garret, thinking how hard it was to do right, and wondering why I was scolded for feeding the poor when we were expressly bidden to do so. I felt myself an outcast, and bewailed the disgrace I had brought upon my family. Nobody could possibly love such a bad child; and if the mice were to come and eat me then and there, — a la Bishop Hatto, — it would only be a relief to my friends. At this dark moment I heard Christy say below, "She meant it kindly, so I wouldn't mind, Fanny;" and then up came my boy full of sympathy and comfort. Seeing the tragic expression of my face, he said not a word, but, sitting down in an old chair, took me on his knee and held me close and quietly, letting the action speak for itself. It did most eloquently; for the kind arm seemed to take me back from that dreadful exile, and the friendly face to assure me without words that I had not sinned beyond forgiveness.

I had not shed a tear before, but now I cried tempestuously, and clung to him like a shipwrecked little mariner in a storm. Neither spoke, but he held me fast and let me cry myself to sleep; for, when the shower was over, a pensive peace fell upon me, and the dim old garret seemed not a prison, but a haven of refuge, since my boy came to share it with me. How long I slept I don't know, but it must have been an hour, at least; yet my good Christy never stirred, only waited patiently till I woke up in the twilight and was not afraid because he was there. He took me down as meek as a mouse, and kept me by him all that trying evening, screening me from jokes, rebukes, and sober looks; and when I went to bed he came up to kiss me, and to assure me that this awful circumstance should not be reported at home. This took a load off my heart, and I remember fervently thanking him, and telling him I never would forget it.

I never have, though he died long ago, and others have probably forgotten all about the naughty prank. I often longed to ask him how he knew the surest way to win a child's heart by the patience, sympathy, and tender little acts that have kept his memory green for nearly thirty years.

Cy was a comrade after my own heart, and for a summer or two we kept the neighborhood in a ferment by our adventures and hair-breadth escapes. I think I never knew a boy so full of mischief, and my opportunities of judging have been manifold. He did not get into scrapes himself, but possessed a splendid talent for deluding others into them, and then morally remarking, "There, I told you so!" His way of saying "You dars'nt do this or that," was like fire to powder; and why I still live in the possession of all my limbs and senses is a miracle to those who know my youthful friendship with Cy. It was he who incited me to jump off of the highest beam in the barn to be borne home on a board with a pair of sprained ankles. It was he who dared me to rub my eyes with red peppers, and then sympathizingly led me home blind and roaring with pain. It was he who solemnly assured me that all the little pigs would die in agony if their tails were not cut off, and won me to hold thirteen little squealers while the operation was performed. Those thirteen innocent pink tails haunt me yet, and the memory of that deed has given me a truly Jewish aversion to pork.

I did not know him long, but he was a kindred soul, and must have a place in my list of boys. He is a big, brown man now, and having done his part in the war, is at work on his farm. We meet sometimes, and though we try to be dignified and proper, it is quite impossible; there is a sly twinkle in Cy's eye that upsets my gravity, and we always burst out laughing at the memory of our early frolics.

My Augustus! oh, my Augustus! my first little lover, and the most romantic of my boys. At fifteen I met this charming youth; and thought I had found my fate. It was at a spelling school in a little country town where I, as a stranger and visitor from the city, was an object of interest. Painfully conscious of this fact, I sat in a corner trying to look easy and elegant, with a large red bow under my chin, and a carnelian ring in full view. Among the boys and girls who frolicked about me, I saw one lad of seventeen with "large blue eyes, a noble brow, and a beautiful straight nose," as I described him in a letter to my sister. This attractive youth had a certain air of refinement and ease of manner that the others lacked; and when I found he was the minister's son, I felt that I might admire him without loss of dignity. "Imagine my sensations," as Miss Burney's Evelina says, when this boy came and talked to me, a little bashfully at first, but soon quite freely, and invited me to a huckleberry party next day. I had observed that he was one of the best spellers. I also observed that his language was quite elegant; he even quoted Byron, and rolled his eyes in a most engaging manner, not to mention that he asked who gave me my ring, and said he depended on escorting me to the berry pasture.

Dear me, how interesting it was! and when I found myself, next day, sitting under a tree in the sunny field (full of boys and girls, all more or less lovering), with the amiable Augustus at my feet, gallantly supplying me with bushes to strip while we talked about books and poetry, I really felt as if I had got into a novel, and enjoyed it immensely. I believe a dim idea that Gus was sentimental hovered in my mind, but I would not encourage it, though I laughed in my sleeve when he was spouting Latin for my benefit, and was uncertain whether to box his ears or simper later in the day, when he languished over the gate, and said he thought chestnut hair the loveliest in the world.

Poor, dear boy! how innocent and soft-hearted and full of splendid dreams he was, and what deliciously romantic times we had floating on the pond, while the frogs sung to his accordion, as he tried to say unutterable things with his honest blue eyes. It makes me shiver now to think of the mosquitoes and the damp; but it was Pauline and Claude Melnotte then, and when I went home we promised to be true to one another, and write every week during the year he was away at school.

We parted, — not in tears by any means; that sort of nonsense comes later, when the romance is less childish, — but quite jolly and comfortable, and I hastened to pour forth the thrilling tale to my faithful sister, who approved of the match, being a perfect "mush of sentiment" herself.

I fear it was not a very ardent flame, however, for Gus did not write every week, and I did not care a bit; nevertheless, I kept his picture and gave it a sentimental sigh when I happened to think of it, while he sent messages now and then, and devoted himself to his studies like an ambitious boy as he was. I hardly expected to see him again, but soon after the year was out, to my great surprise he called. I was so fluttered by the appearance of his card that I rather lost my head, and did such a silly thing that it makes me laugh even now. He liked chestnut hair, and, pulling out my combs, I rushed down, theatrically dishevelled, hoping to impress my lover with my ardor and my charms.

I expected to find little Gus; but, to my great confusion, a tall being with a beaver in his hand rose to meet me, looking so big and handsome and generally imposing, that I could not recover myself for several minutes, and mentally wailed for my combs, feeling like an untidy simpleton.

I don't know whether he thought me a little cracked or not, but he was very friendly and pleasant, and told me his plans, and hoped I would make another visit, and smoothed his beaver, and let me see his tail-coat, and behaved himself like a dear, conceited, clever boy. He did not allude to our love-passages, being shy, and I blessed him for it; for really, I don't know what rash thing I might have done under the exciting circumstances. Just as he was going, however, he forgot his cherished hat for a minute, put out both hands, and said heartily, with his old boyish laugh, —

"Now you will come, and we'll go boating and berrying, and all the rest of it again, won't we?"

The blue eyes were full of fun and feeling, too, I fancied, as I blushingly retired behind my locks and gave the promise. But I never went, and never saw my little lover any more, for in a few weeks he was dead of a fever, brought on by too much study, — and so ended the sad history of my fourth boy.

After this, for many years, I was a boyless being; but was so busy I did not feel my destitute condition till I went to the hospital during the war, and found my little sergeant. His story has been told elsewhere, but the sequel to it is a pleasant one, for Baby B. still writes to me now and then, asks advice about his future, and gladdens me with good news of his success as a business man in Kansas.

As if to atone for the former dearth, a sudden shower of most superior boys fell upon me, after I recovered from my campaign. Some of the very best sort it was my fortune to know and like, — real gentlemen, yet boys still, — and jolly times they had, stirring up the quiet old town with their energetic society.

There was W., a stout, amiable youth, who would stand in the middle of a strawberry patch, with his hands in his pockets, and let us feed him luxuriously. B., a delightful scapegrace, who came once a week to confess his sins, beat his breast in despair, vow awful vows of repentance, and then cheerfully depart, to break every one of them in the next twenty-four hours. S. the gentle-hearted giant; J. the dandy; sober, sensible B.; and E., the young knight without reproach or fear.

But my especial boy of the batch was A., — proud and cold and shy to other people, sad and serious sometimes when his good heart and tender conscience showed him his short-comings, but so grateful for sympathy and a kind word.

I could not get at him as easily as I could the other lads, but, thanks to Dickens, I found him out at last.

We played Dolphus and Sophy Tetterby in the "Haunted Man," at one of the school festivals; and during the rehearsals I discovered that my Dolphus was — permit the expression, oh, well-bred readers! — a trump. What fun we had, to be sure, acting the droll and pathetic scenes together, with a swarm of little Tetterbys skirmishing about us! From that time he has been my Dolphus and I his Sophy, and my yellow-haired laddie don't forget me, though he has a younger Sophy now, and some small Tetterbys of his own. He writes just the same affectionate letters as he used to do, though I, less faithful, am too busy to answer them.

But the best and dearest of all my flock was my Polish boy, Ladislas Wisniewski, — two hiccoughs and a sneeze will give you the name perfectly. Six years ago, as I went down to my early breakfast at our Pension in Vevey, I saw that a stranger had arrived. He was a tall youth, of eighteen or twenty, with a thin, intelligent face, and the charmingly polite manners of a foreigner. As the other boarders came in, one by one, they left the door open, and a draught of cold autumn air blew in from the stone corridor, making the new comer cough, shiver, and cast wistful glances toward the warm corner by the stove. My place was there, and the heat often oppressed me, so I was glad of an opportunity to move.

A word to Madame Vodoz effected the change; and at dinner I was rewarded by a grateful smile from the poor fellow, as he nestled into his warm seat, after a pause of surprise and a flush of pleasure at the small kindness from a stranger. We were too far apart to talk much, but, as he filled his glass, the Pole bowed to me, and said low in French, —

"I drink the good health to Mademoiselle."

I returned the wish, but he shook his head with a sudden shadow on his face, as if the words meant more than mere compliment to him.

"That boy is sick and needs care. I must see to him," said I to myself, as I met him in the afternoon, and observed the military look of his blue and white suit, as he touched his cap and smiled pleasantly. I have a weakness for brave boys in blue, and having discovered that he had been in the late Polish Revolution, my heart warmed to him at once.

That evening he came to me in the salon, and expressed his thanks in the prettiest broken English I ever heard. So simple, frank, and grateful was he that a few words of interest won his little story from him, and in half an hour we were friends. With his fellow-students he had fought through the last outbreak, had suffered imprisonment and hardship rather than submit, had lost many friends, his fortune and his health, and at twenty, lonely, poor, and ill, was trying bravely to cure the malady which seemed fatal.

"If I recover myself of this affair in the chest, I teach the music to acquire my bread in this so hospitable country. At Paris, my friends, all two, find a refuge, and I go to them in spring if I die not here. Yes, it is solitary, and my memories are not gay, but I have my work, and the good God remains always to me, so I content myself with much hope, and I wait."

Such genuine piety and courage increased my respect and regard immensely, and a few minutes later he added to both by one of the little acts that show character better than words.

He told me about the massacre, when five hundred Poles were shot down by Cossacks in the market-place, merely because they sung their national hymn.

"Play me that forbidden air," I said, wishing to judge of his skill, for I had heard him practising softly in the afternoon.

He rose willingly, then glanced about the room and gave a little shrug which made me ask what he wanted.

"I look to see if the Baron is here. He is Russian, and to him my national air will not be pleasing."

"Then play it. He dare not forbid it here, and I should rather enjoy that little insult to your bitter enemy," said I, feeling very indignant with every thing Russian just then.

"Ah, mademoiselle, it is true we are enemies, but we are also gentlemen," returned the boy, proving that *he* at least was one.

I thanked him for his lesson in politeness, and as the Baron was not there he played the beautiful hymn, singing it enthusiastically in spite of the danger to his weak lungs. A true musician evidently, for, as he sung his pale face glowed, his eyes shone, and his lost vigor seemed restored to him.

From that evening we were fast friends; for the memory of certain dear lads at home made my heart open to this lonely boy, who gave me in return the most grateful affection and service. He begged me to call him "Varjo," as his mother did. He constituted himself my escort, errand-boy, French teacher, and private musician, making those weeks infinitely pleasant by his winning ways, his charming little confidences, and faithful friendship.

We had much fun over our lessons, for I helped him about his English. With a great interest in free America, and an intense longing to hear about our war, the barrier of an unknown tongue did not long stand between us.

Beginning with my bad French and his broken English, we got on capitally; but he outdid me entirely, making astonishing progress, though he often slapped his forehead with the despairing exclamation, —

"I am imbecile! I never can will shall to have learn this beast of English!"

But he did, and in a month had added a new language to the five he already possessed.

His music was the delight of the house; and he often gave us little concerts with the help of Madam Teiblin, a German St. Cecelia, with a cropped head and a gentlemanly sack, cravat, and collar. Both were enthusiasts, and the longer they played the more inspired they got. The piano vibrated, the stools creaked, the candles danced in their sockets, and every one sat mute while the four white hands chased one another up and down the keys, and the two fine faces beamed with such ecstasy that we almost expected to see instrument and performers disappear in a musical whirlwind.

Lake Leman will never seem so lovely again as when Laddie and I roamed about its shores, floated on its bosom, or laid splendid plans for the future in the sunny garden of the old chateau. I tried it again last year, but the charm was gone, for I missed my boy with his fun, his music, and the frank, fresh affection he gave his "little mamma," as he insisted on calling the lofty spinster who loved him like half a dozen grandmothers rolled into one.

December roses blossomed in the gardens then, and Laddie never failed to have a posy ready for me at dinner. Few evenings passed without "confidences" in my corner of the salon, and I still have a pile of merry little notes which I used to find tucked under my door. He called them chapters of a great history we were to write together, and being a "*polisson*" he illustrated it with droll pictures, and a funny mixture of French and English romance.

It was very pleasant, but like all pleasant things in this world of change it soon came to an end. When I left for Italy we jokingly agreed to meet in Paris the next May, but neither really felt that we should ever meet again, for Laddie hardly expected to outlive the winter, and I felt sure I should soon be forgotten. As he kissed my hand there were tears in my boy's eyes, and a choke in the voice that tried to say cheerfully, —

"*Bon voyage,* dear and good little mamma. I do not say adieu, but *au revoir*."

Then the carriage rolled away, the wistful face vanished, and nothing remained to me but the memory of Laddie, and a little stain on my glove where a drop had fallen.

As I drew near Paris six months later, and found myself wishing that I might meet Varjo in the great, gay city, and wondering if there was any chance of my doing it, I never dreamed of seeing him so soon; but, as I made my way among the crowd of passengers that poured through the station, feeling tired, bewildered, and homesick, I suddenly saw a blue and white cap wave wildly in the air, then Laddie's beaming face appeared, and Laddie's eager hands grasped mine so cordially that I began to laugh at once, and felt that Paris was almost as good as home.

"Ah, ha! behold the little mamma, who did not thought to see again her bad son! Yes, I am greatly glad that I make the fine surprise for you as you come all weary to this place of noise. Give to me the billets, for I am still mademoiselle's servant and go to find the coffers."

He got my trunks, put me into a carriage, and as we rolled merrily away I asked how he chanced to meet me so unexpectedly. Knowing where I intended to stay, he had called occasionally till I notified Madame D. of the day and hour of my arrival, and then he had come to "make the fine surprise." He enjoyed the joke like a true boy, and I was glad to see how well he looked, and how gay he seemed.

"You are better?" I said.

"I truly hope so. The winter was good to me and I cough less. It is a small hope, but I do not enlarge my fear by a sad face. I yet work and save a little purse, so that I may not be a heaviness to those who have the charity to finish me if I fall back and yet die."

I would not hear of that, and told him he looked as well and happy as if he had found a fortune.

He laughed, and answered with his fine bow, "I have. Behold, you come to make the fête for me. I find also here my friends Joseph and Napoleon. Poor as mouses of the church, as you say, but brave boys, and we work together with much gayety."

When I asked if he had leisure to be my guide about Paris, for my time was short and I wanted to see *every thing,* he pranced, and told me he had promised himself a holiday, and had planned many excursions the most wonderful, charming, and gay. Then, having settled me at Madame's, he went blithely away to what I afterward discovered were very poor lodgings, across the river.

Next day began the pleasantest fortnight in all my year of travel. Laddie appeared early, elegant to behold in a new hat and buff gloves, and was immensely amused because the servant informed me that my big son had arrived.

I believe the first thing a woman does in Paris is to buy a new bonnet. I did, or rather stood by and let "my son" do it in the best of French, only whispering when he proposed gorgeous *chapeaus* full of flowers and feathers, that I could not afford it.

"Ah! we must make our economies, must we? See, then, this modest, pearl-colored one, with the crape rose. Yes, we will have that, and be most elegant for the Sunday promenade."

I fear I should have bought a pea-green hat with a yellow plume if he had urged it, so wheedlesome and droll were his ways and words. His good taste saved me, however, and the modest one was sent home for the morrow, when we were to meet Joseph and Napoleon and go to the concert in the Tuileries garden.

Then we set off on our day of sight-seeing, and Laddie proved himself an excellent guide. We had a charming trip about the enchanted city, a gay lunch at a café, and a first brief glimpse of the Louvre. At dinner-time I found a posy at my place; and afterward Laddie came and spent the evening in my little salon, playing to me, and having what he called "babblings and pleasantries." I found that he was translating "Vanity Fair" into Polish, and intended to sell it at home. He convulsed me with his struggles to put cockney English and slang into good Polish, for he had saved up a list of words for me to explain to him. Haystack and bean-pot were among them, I remember; and when he had mastered the meanings he fell upon the sofa exhausted.

Other days like this followed, and we led a happy life together; for my twelve years' seniority made our adventures quite proper, and I fearlessly went anywhere on the arm of my big son. Not to theatres or balls, however, for heated rooms were bad for Laddie, but pleasant trips out of the city in the bright spring weather, quiet strolls in the gardens, moonlight concerts in the Champs Elysées; or, best of all, long talks with music in the little red salon, with the gas turned low, and the ever-changing scenes of the Rue de Rivoli under the balcony.

Never were pleasures more cheaply purchased or more thoroughly enjoyed, for our hearts were as light as our purses, and our "little economies" gave zest to our amusements.

Joseph and Napoleon sometimes joined us, and I felt in my element with the three invalid soldier boys, for Napoleon still limped with a wound received in the war, Joseph had never recovered from his two years' imprisonment in an Austrian dungeon, and Laddie's loyalty might yet cost him his life.

Thanks to them, I discovered a joke played upon me by my "*polisson.*" He told me to call him "ma drogha," saying it meant "my friend," in Polish. I innocently did so, and he seemed to find great pleasure in it, for his eyes always laughed when I said it. Using it one day before the other

lads, I saw a queer twinkle in their eyes, and, suspecting mischief, demanded the real meaning of the words. Laddie tried to silence them, but
the joke was too good to keep, and I found to my dismay that I had been
calling him "my darling" in the tenderest manner.

How the three rascals shouted, and what a vain struggle it was to try
and preserve my dignity when Laddie clasped his hands and begged pardon, explaining that jokes were necessary to his health, and he never meant
me to know the full baseness of this "pleasantrie!" I revenged myself by
giving him some bad English for his translation, and telling him of it just
as I left Paris.

It was not all fun with my boy, however; he had his troubles, and in
spite of his cheerfulness he knew what heartache was. Walking in the quaint
garden of the Luxembourg one day, he confided to me the little romance
of his life. A very touching little romance as he told it, with eloquent eyes
and voice and frequent pauses for breath. I cannot give his words, but the
simple facts were these: —

He had grown up with a pretty cousin, and at eighteen was desperately
in love with her. She returned his affection, but they could not be happy,
for her father wished her to marry a richer man. In Poland, to marry without the consent of parents is to incur lasting disgrace; so Leonore obeyed,
and the young pair parted. This had been a heavy sorrow to Laddie, and
he rushed into the war hoping to end his trouble.

"Do you ever hear from your cousin?" I asked, as he walked beside
me, looking sadly down the green aisles where kings and queens had loved
and parted years ago.

"I only know that she suffers still, for she remembers. Her husband
submits to the Russians, and I despise him as I have no English to tell;"
and he clenched his hands with the flash of the eye and sudden kindling of
the whole face that made him handsome.

He showed me a faded little picture, and when I tried to comfort him,
he laid his head down on the pedestal of one of the marble queens who
guard the walk, as if he never cared to lift it up again.

But he was all right in a minute, and bravely put away his sorrow
with the little picture. He never spoke of it again, and I saw no more
shadows on his face till we came to say good-by.

"You have been so kind to me, I wish I had something beautiful to
give you, Laddie," I said, feeling that it would be hard to get on without
my boy.

"This time it is for always; so, as a parting souvenir, give to me the
sweet English good-by."

As he said this, with a despairing sort of look, as if he could not spare even so humble a friend as myself, my heart was quite rent within me, and, regardless of several prim English ladies, I drew down his tall head and kissed him tenderly, feeling that in this world there were no more meetings for us. Then I ran away and buried myself in an empty railway carriage, hugging the little cologne bottle he had given me.

He promised to write, and for five years he has kept his word, sending me from Paris and Poland cheery, bright letters in English, at my desire, so that he might not forget. Here is one as a specimen.

MY DEAR AND GOOD FRIEND, — What do you think of me that I do not write so long time? Excuse me, my good mamma, for I was so busy in these days I could not do this pleasant thing. I write English without the fear that you laugh at it, because I know it is more agreeable to read the own language, and I think you are not excepted of this rule. It is good of me, for the expressions of love and regard, made with faults, take the funny appearance; they are *ridicule,* and instead to go to the heart, they make the laugh. Never mind, I do it.

You cannot imagine yourself how *stupide* is Paris when you are gone. I fly to my work, and make no more fêtes, — it is too sad alone. I tie myself to my table and my Vanity (not of mine, for I am not vain, am I?). I wish some chapters to finish themselfs *vite,* that I send them to Pologne and know the end. I have a little question to ask you (of Vanity as always). I cannot translate this, no one of *dictionnaires* makes me the words, and I think it is *jàrgon de prison,* this little period. Behold: —

"*Mopy, is that your snum?*"
"*Nubble your dad and gully the dog,*" *&c.*

So funny things I cannot explain myself, so I send to you, and you reply sooner than without it, for you have so kind interest in my work you do not stay to wait. So this is a little hook for you to make you write some words to your son who likes it so much and is fond of you.

My doctor tells me my lungs are soon to be re-established; so you may imagine yourself how glad I am, and of more courage in my future. You may one day see your Varjo in Amerique, if I study commerce as I wish. So then the last time of seeing ourselves is *not* the last. Is that to please you? I suppose the grand *histoire* is finished, *n' est ce pas?* You will then send it to me care of M. Gryhomski Austriche, and he will give to me in clandestine way at Varsovie, otherwise it will be confiscated at the frontier by the stupid Russians.

Now we are dispersed in two sides of world far apart, for soon I go home to Pologne and am no more *"juif errant."* It is now time I work at my life in some useful way, and I do it.

As I am your *grand fils,* it is proper that I make you my compliment of happy Christmas and New Year, is it not? I wish for you so many as they may fulfil long human life. May this year bring you more and more good hearts to love you (the only real happiness in the hard life), and may I be as now, yours for always,

"VARJO."

A year ago he sent me his photograph and a few lines. I acknowledged the receipt of it, but since then not a word has come, and I begin to fear that my boy is dead. Others have appeared to take his place, but they don't suit, and I keep his corner always ready for him if he lives. If he is dead, I am glad to have known so sweet and brave a character, for it does one good to see even as short-lived and obscure a hero as my Polish boy, whose dead December rose embalms for me the memory of Varjo, the last and dearest of my boys.

It is hardly necessary to add, for the satisfaction of inquisitive little women, that Laddie was the original of Laurie, as far as a pale pen and ink sketch could embody a living, loving boy.

My Girls

From *Aunt Jo's Scrap-Bag* (6 vols.), vol. 4
(Boston: Roberts Brothers, 1878)

ONCE UPON a time I wrote a little account of some of the agreeable boys I had known, whereupon the damsels reproached me with partiality, and begged me to write about them. I owned the soft impeachment, and promised that I would not forget them if I could find any thing worth recording.

That was six years ago, and since then I have been studying girls whenever I had an opportunity, and have been both pleased and surprised to see how much they are doing for themselves now that their day has come.

Poor girls always had my sympathy and respect, for necessity soon makes brave women of them if they have any strength or talent in them; but the well-to-do girls usually seemed to me like pretty butterflies, leading easy, aimless lives when the world was full of work which ought to be done.

Making a call in New York, I got a little lesson, which caused me to change my opinion, and further investigation proved that the rising generation was wide awake, and bound to use the new freedom well. Several young girls, handsomely dressed, were in the room, and I thought, of course, that they belonged to the butterfly species; but on asking one of them what she was about now school was over, I was much amazed to hear her reply, "I am reading law with my uncle." Another said, "I am studying medicine;" a third, "I devote myself to music," and the fourth was giving time, money, and heart to some of the best charities of the great city.

So my pretty butterflies proved to be industrious bees, making real honey, and I shook hands with sincere respect, though they did wear jaunty hats; my good opinion being much increased by the fact that not one was silly enough to ask for an autograph.

Since then I have talked with many girls, finding nearly all intent on some noble end, and as some of them have already won the battle, it may be cheering to those still in the thick of the fight, or just putting on their armor, to hear how these sisters prospered in their different ways.

Several of them are girls no longer; but as they are still unmarried, I like to call them by their old name, because they are so young at heart, and have so beautifully fulfilled the promise of their youth, not only by doing, but being excellent and admirable women.

A is one in whom I take especial pride. Well-born, pretty, and bright, she, after a year or two of society, felt the need of something more satisfactory, and, following her taste, decided to study medicine. Fortunately she had a father who did not think marriage the only thing a woman was created for, but was ready to help his daughter in the work she had chosen, merely desiring her to study as faithfully and thoroughly as a man, if she undertook the profession that she might be an honor to it. A *was* in earnest, and studied four years, visiting the hospitals of London, Paris, and Prussia; being able to command private lessons when the doors of public institutions were shut in her face because she was a woman. More study and work at home, and then she had the right to accept the post of resident physician in a hospital for women. Here she was so successful that her outside practice increased rapidly, and she left the hospital to devote herself to patients of all sorts, beloved and valued for the womanly sympathy and cheerfulness that went hand in hand with the physician's skill and courage.

When I see this woman, young still, yet so independent, successful, and contented, I am very proud of her; not only because she has her own house, with a little adopted daughter to make it home-like, her well-earned reputation, and a handsome income, but because she has so quietly and persistently carried out the plan of her life, undaunted by prejudice, hard work, or the solitary lot she chose. She may well be satisfied; for few women receive so much love and confidence, few mothers have so many children to care for, few physicians are more heartily welcomed and trusted, few men lead a freer, nobler life, than this happy woman, who lives for others and never thinks of any fame but that which is the best worth having, a place in the hearts of all who know her.

B is another of my successful girls; but her task has been a harder one than A's, because she was as poor as she was ambitious. B is an artist, loving beauty more than any thing else in the world; ready to go cold and hungry, shabby and lonely, if she can only see, study, and try to create the loveliness she worships. It was so even as a child; for flowers and fairies grew on her slate when she should have been doing sums, painted birds and butterflies perched on her book-covers, Flaxman's designs, and familiar faces appeared on the walls of her little room, and clay gods and goddesses were set upon the rough altar of her moulding board, to be toiled over and adored till they were smashed in the "divine despair" all true artists feel.

But winged things will fly sooner or later, and patient waiting, persistent effort, only give sweetness to the song and strength to the flight when the door of the cage opens at last. So, after years of hard work with pencil and crayon, plaster and clay, oil and water colors, the happy hour came for B when the dream of her life was realized; for one fine spring day, with a thousand dollars in her pocket and a little trunk holding more art materials than clothes, she sailed away, alone, but brave and beaming, for a year in England.

She knew now what she wanted and where to find it, and "a heavenly year" followed, though to many it would have seemed a very dull one. All day and every day but the seventh was spent in the National Gallery, copying Turner's pictures in oil and water colors. So busy, so happy, so wrapt up in delightsome work, that food and sleep seemed impertinencies, friends were forgotten, pleasuring had no charms, society no claims, and life was one joyful progress from the blue Giudecca to the golden Sol de

Venezia, or the red glow of the old Temeraire. "Van Tromp entering the mouth of the Texel" was more interesting to her than any political event transpiring in the world without; ancient Rome eclipsed modern London, and the roar of a great city could not disturb the "Datur Hora Quieti" which softly grew into beauty under her happy brush.

A spring-tide trip to Stratford, Warwick, and Kenilworth was the only holiday she allowed herself; and even this was turned to profit; for, lodging cheaply at the Shakespearian baker's, she roamed about, portfolio in hand, booking every lovely bit she saw, regardless of sun or rain, and bringing away a pictorial diary of that week's trip which charmed those who beheld it, and put money in her purse.

When the year was out, home came the artist, with half her little fortune still unspent, and the one trunk nearly as empty as it went, but there were two great boxes of pictures, and a golden saint in a coffin five feet long, which caused much interest at the Custom House, but was passed duty-free after its owner had displayed it with enthusiastic explanations of its charms.

"They are only attempts and studies, you know, and I dare say you'll all laugh at them; but I feel that I *can* in time *do* something, so my year has not been wasted," said the modest damsel, as she set forth her work, glorifying all the house with Venetian color, English verdure, and, what was better still, the sunshine of a happy heart.

But to B's great surprise and delight, people did *not* laugh; they praised and bought, and ordered more, till, before she knew it, several thousand dollars were at her command, and the way clear to the artist-life she loved.

To some who watched her, the sweetest picture she created was the free art-school which B opened in a very humble way; giving her books, copies, casts, time, and teaching to all who cared to come. For with her, as with most who *earn* their good things, the generous desire to share them with others is so strong it is sure to blossom out in some way, blessing as it has been blessed. Slowly, but surely, success comes to the patient worker, and B, being again abroad for more lessons, paints one day a little still life study so well that her master says she "does him honor," and her mates advise her to send it to the Salon. Never dreaming that it will be accepted, B, for the joke of it, puts her study in a plain frame, and sends it, with the eight thousand others, only two thousand of which are received.

To her amazement the little picture is accepted, hung "on the line" and noticed in the report. Nor is that all, the Committee asked leave to exhibit it at another place, and desired an autobiographical sketch of the artist. A more deeply gratified young woman it would be hard to find than

B, as she now plans the studio she is to open soon, and the happy independent life she hopes to lead in it, for she has earned her place, and, after years of earnest labor, is about to enter in and joyfully possess it.

There was C, — alas, that I must write *was!* beautiful, gifted, young, and full of the lovely possibilities which give some girls such an indescribable charm. Placed where it would have been natural for her to have made herself a young queen of society, she preferred something infinitely better, and so quietly devoted herself to the chosen work that very few guessed she had any.

I had known her for some years before I found it out, and then only by accident; but I never shall forget the impression it made upon me. I had called to get a book, and something led me to speak of the sad case of a poor girl lately made known to me, when C, with a sudden brightening of her whole face, said, warmly, "I wish I had known it, I could have helped her."

"You? what can a happy creature like you know about such things?" I answered, surprised.

"That is my work." And in a few words which went to my heart, the beautiful girl, sitting in her own pretty room, told me how, for a long time, she and others had stepped out of their safe, sunshiny homes to help and save the most forlorn of our sister women. So quietly, so tenderly, that only those saved knew who did it, and such loyal silence kept, that, even among the friends, the names of these unfortunates were not given, that the after life might be untroubled by even a look of reproach or recognition.

"Do not speak of this," she said. "Not that I am ashamed; but we are able to work better in a private way, and want no thanks for what we do."

I kept silence till her share of the womanly labor of love, so delicately, dutifully done, was over. But I never saw that sweet face afterward without thinking how like an angel's it must have seemed to those who sat in darkness till she came to lift them up.

Always simply dressed, this young sister of charity went about her chosen task when others of her age and position were at play; happy in it, and unconsciously preaching a little sermon by her lovely life. Another girl, who spent her days reading novels and eating confectionery, said to me, in speaking of C, —

"Why doesn't she dress more? She is rich enough, and so handsome I should think she would."

Taking up the reports of several charities which lay on my table, I pointed to C's name among the generous givers, saying, —

"Perhaps *that* is the reason;" and my visitor went away with a new idea of economy in her frivolous head, a sincere respect for the beautiful girl who wore the plain suit and loved her neighbor *better* than herself.

A short life; but one so full of sweetness that all the bitter waters of the pitiless sea cannot wash its memory away, and I am sure that white soul won heaven sooner for the grateful prayers of those whom she had rescued from a blacker ocean.

D was one of a large family all taught at home, and all of a dramatic turn; so, with a witty father to write the plays, an indulgent mother to yield up her house to destruction, five boys and seven girls for the *corps dramatique,* it is not to be wondered at that D set her heart on being an actress.

Having had the honor to play the immortal Pillicoddy on that famous stage, I know whereof I write, and what glorious times that little company of brothers and sisters had safe at home. But D burned for a larger field, and at length found a chance to appear on the real boards with several of her sisters. Being very small and youthful in appearance they played children's parts, fairies in spectacles and soubrettes in farce or vaudeville. Once D had a benefit, and it was a pretty sight to see the long list of familiar names on the bill; for the brothers and sisters all turned out and made a jolly play of "Parents and Guardians," as well as a memorable sensation in the "Imitations" which they gave.

One would think that the innocent little girls might have come to harm singing in the chorus of operas, dancing as peasants, or playing "Nan the good-for-nothing." But the small women were so dignified, well-mannered, and intent on their duties that no harm befell them. Father and brothers watched over them; there were few temptations for girls who made "Mother" their confidante, and a happy home was a safe refuge from the unavoidable annoyances to which all actresses are exposed.

D tried the life, found it wanting, left it, and put her experiences into a clever little book, then turned to less pleasant but more profitable work. The father, holding a public office, was allowed two clerks; but, finding that his clear-headed daughter could do the work of both easily and well, gave her the place, and she earned her thousand a year, going to her daily duty looking like a school girl; while her brain was busy with figures and statistics which would have puzzled many older heads.

This she did for years, faithfully earning her salary, and meanwhile playing her part in the domestic drama; for real tragedy and comedy came into it as time went on; the sisters married or died, brothers won their way up, and more than one Infant Phenomenon appeared on the household stage.

But through all changes my good D was still "leading lady," and now, when the mother is gone, the other birds all flown, she remains in the once overflowing nest, the stay and comfort of her father, unspoiled by either poverty or wealth, unsaddened by much sorrow, unsoured by spinsterhood. A wise and witty little woman, and a happy one too, though the curly locks are turning gray; for the three Christian graces, faith, hope, and charity, abide with her to the end.

Of E I know too little to do justice to her success; but as it has been an unusual one, I cannot resist giving her a place here, although I never saw her, and much regret that now I never can, since she has gone to plead her own cause before the wise Judge of all.

Her story was told me by a friend, and made so strong an impression upon me that I wrote down the facts while they were fresh in my mind. A few words, added since her death, finish the too brief record of her brave life.

At fourteen, E began to read law with a legal friend. At eighteen she began to practise, and did so well that this friend offered her half his business, which was very large. But she preferred to stand alone, and in two years had a hundred cases of all sorts in different courts, and never lost one.

In a certain court-room, where she was the only woman present, her bearing was so full of dignity that every one treated her with respect. Her opponent, a shrewd old lawyer, made many sharp or impertinent remarks, hoping to anger her and make her damage her cause by some loss of self-control. But she merely looked at him with such a wise, calm smile, and answered with such unexpected wit and wisdom, that the man was worsted and young Portia won her suit, to the great satisfaction of the spectators, men though they were.

She used to say that her success was owing to hard work, — too hard, I fear, if she often studied eighteen hours a day. She asked no help or patronage, only fair play, and one cannot but regret that it ever was denied a creature who so womanfully proved her claim to it.

A friend says, "she was a royal girl, and did all her work in a royal way. She broke down suddenly, just as she had passed the last hostile outpost; just as she had begun to taste the ineffable sweetness of peace and rest, following a relative life-time of battle and toil."

But, short as her career has been, not one brave effort is wasted, since she has cleared the way for those who come after her, and proved that women have not only the right but the ability to sit upon the bench as well as stand at the bar of justice.

Last, but by no means least, is F, because her success is the most wonderful of all, since every thing was against her from the first, as you will see when I tell her little story.

Seven or eight years ago, a brave woman went down into Virginia with a friend, and built a schoolhouse for the freed people, who were utterly forlorn; because, though the great gift of liberty was theirs, it was so new and strange they hardly understood how to use it. These good women showed them, and among the first twenty children who began the school, which now has hundreds of pupils, white as well as black, came little F.

Ignorant, ragged and wild, yet with such an earnest, resolute face that she attracted the attention of her teachers at once, and her eagerness to learn touched their hearts; for it was a hard fight with her to get an education, because she could only be spared now and then from corn-planting, pulling fodder, toting water, oyster-shucking or grubbing the new land.

She must have made good use of those "odd days," for she was among the first dozen who earned a pictorial pocket-handkerchief for learning the multiplication table, and a proud child was F when she bore home the prize. Rapidly the patient little fingers learned to write on the first slate she ever saw, and her whole heart went into the task of reading the books which opened a new world to her.

The instinct of progression was as strong in her as the love of light in a plant, and when the stone was lifted away, she sprang up and grew vigorously.

At last the chance to go North and earn something, which all freed people desire, came to F; and in spite of many obstacles she made the most of it. At the very outset she had to fight for a place in the steamer, since the captain objected to her being admitted to the cabin on account of her color; though any lady could take her black maid in without any trouble. But the friend with whom she travelled insisted on F's rights, and won them by declaring that if the child was condemned to pass the night on deck, she would pass it with her.

F watched the contest with breathless interest, as well she might; for this was her first glimpse of the world outside the narrow circle where her fourteen years had been spent. Poor little girl! there seemed to be no place for her anywhere; and I cannot help wondering what her thoughts were, as she sat alone in the night, shut out from among her kind for no fault but the color of her skin.

What could she think of "white folks'" religion, intelligence, and courtesy? Fortunately she had one staunch friend beside her to keep her faith in human justice alive, and win a little place for her among her fellow beings. The captain for very shame consented at last, and F felt that she was truly free when she stepped out of the lonely darkness of the night into the light and shelter of the cabin, a harmless little girl, asking only a place to lay her head.

That was the first experience, and it made a deep impression on her; but those that followed were pleasanter, for nowhere in the free North was she refused her share of room in God's world.

I saw her in New York, and even before I learned her story I was attracted to the quiet, tidy, door-girl by the fact that she was always studying as she sat in the noisy hall of a great boarding-house, keeping her books under her chair and poring over them at every leisure moment. Kindly people, touched by her patient efforts, helped her along; and one of the prettiest sights I saw in the big city was a little white girl taking time from her own sports to sit on the stairs and hear F recite. I think Bijou Heron will never play a sweeter part than that, nor have a more enthusiastic admirer than F was when we went together to see the child-actress play "The Little Treasure" for charity.

To those who know F it seems as if a sort of miracle had been wrought, to change in so short a time a forlorn little Topsy into this intelligent, independent, ambitious girl, who not only supports and educates herself, but sends a part of her earnings home, and writes such good letters to her mates that they are read aloud in school. Here is a paragraph from one which was a part of the Christmas festival last year: —

"I have now seen what a great advantage it is to have an education. I begin to feel the good of the little I know, and I am trying hard every day to add more to it. Most every child up here from ten to twelve years old can read and write, colored as well as white. And if you were up here, I think you would be surprised to see such little bits of children going to school with their arms full of books. I do hope you will all learn as much as you can; for an Education is a great thing."

I wonder how many white girls of sixteen would do any better, if as well, as this resolute F, bravely making her way against fate and fortune, toward the useful, happy womanhood we all desire. I know she will find friends, and I trust that if she ever knocks at the door of any college, asking her sisters to let her in, they will not disgrace themselves by turning their backs upon her; but prove themselves worthy of their blessings, by showing them Christian gentlewomen.

Here are my six girls; doctor, artist, philanthropist, actress, lawyer, and freedwoman; only a few among the hundreds who work and win, and receive their reward, seen of men or only known to God. Perhaps some other girl reading of these may take heart again, and travel on cheered by their example; for the knowledge of what has been done often proves wonderfully inspiring to those who long to do.

I felt this strongly when I went to a Woman's Congress not long ago; for on the stage was a noble array of successful women, making the noblest use of their talents in discussing all the questions which should interest and educate their sex. I was particularly proud of the senators from Massachusetts, and, looking about the crowded house to see how the audience stirred and glowed under their inspiring words, I saw a good omen for the future.

Down below were grown people, many women, and a few men; but up in the gallery, like a garland of flowers, a circle of girlish faces looked down eager-eyed; listening, with quick smiles and tears, to the wit or eloquence of those who spoke, dropping their school books to clap heartily when a good point was made, and learning better lessons in those three days than as many years of common teaching could give them.

It was close and crowded down below, dusty and dark; but up in the gallery the fresh October air blew in, mellow sunshine touched the young heads, there was plenty of room to stir, and each day the garland seemed to blossom fuller and brighter, showing how the interest grew. There they were, the future Mary Livermores, Ednah Cheneys, Julia Howes, Maria Mitchells, Lucy Stones, unconsciously getting ready to play their parts on the wider stage which those pioneers have made ready for them, before gentler critics, a wiser public, and more enthusiastic friends.

Looking from the fine gray heads which adorned the shadowy platform, to the bright faces up aloft, I wanted to call out, —

"Look, listen, and learn, my girls; then, bringing your sunshine and fresh air, your youth and vigor, come down to fill nobly the places of these true women, and earn for yourselves the same success which will make their names long loved and honored in the land."

Eli's Education

From *Spinning-Wheel Stories* (Boston: Roberts Brothers, 1884)

MANY YEARS AGO, a boy of sixteen sat in a little room in an old farm-house up among the Connecticut hills, writing busily in a book made of odd bits of paper stitched together, with a cover formed of two thin boards. The lid of a blue chest was his desk, the end of a tallow candle stuck into a potato was his lamp, a mixture of soot and vinegar his ink, and a quill from the gray goose his pen. A "Webster's Spelling-book," "Dilworth's New Guide to the English Tongue," "Daboll's Arithmetic," and the "American Preceptor," stood on the chimney-piece over his head, with the "Assembly Catechism," and New Testament, in the place of honor. This was his library; and now and then a borrowed "Pilgrim's Progress," "Fox's Book of Martyrs," or some stray volume, gladdened his heart; for he passionately loved books, and scoured the neighborhood for miles around to feed this steadily increasing hunger. Every penny he could earn or save went to buy a song or a story from the peddlers who occasionally climbed the hill to the solitary farm-house. When others took a noon-spell, he read under the trees or by the fire. He carried a book in his pocket, and studied as he went with the cows to and from the pasture, and sat late in his little room, ciphering on an old slate, or puzzling his young brain over some question which no one could answer for him.

His father had no patience with him, called him a shiftless dreamer, and threatened to burn the beloved books. But his mother defended him, for he was her youngest and the pride of her heart; so she let him scribble all over her floors before she scrubbed them up, dipped extra thick candles for his use, saved every scrap of paper to swell his little store, and firmly believed that he would turn out the great man of the family. His brothers joked about his queer ways, but in his sisters he found firm friends and tender comforters for all his woes. So he struggled along, working on the farm in summer and in a clock shop during the winter, with such brief spells of schooling as he could get between whiles, improving even these poor opportunities so well that he was letter-writer for all the young people in the neighborhood.

Now, he was writing in his journal very slowly, but very well, shaping his letters with unusual grace and freedom; for the wide snow-banks were his copy-books in winter, and on their white pages he had learned to sweep splendid capitals or link syllables handsomely together. This is what he wrote that night, with a sparkle in the blue eyes and a firm folding of the lips that made the boyish face resolute and manly.

> I am set in my own mind that I get learning. I see not how, but my will is strong, and mother hopes for to make a scholar of me. So, please God, we shall do it.

Then he shut the little book and put it carefully away in the blue chest, with pen and ink, as if they were very precious things; piously said his prayers, and was soon asleep under the homespun coverlet, dreaming splendid dreams, while a great bright star looked in at the low window, as if waiting to show him the road to fortune.

And God did please to help the patient lad; only the next evening came an opportunity he had never imagined. As he sat playing "Over the Hills and Far Away" on the fiddle that he had himself made out of maple-wood, with a bow strung from the tail of the old farm horse, a neighbor came in to talk over the fall pork and cider, and tell the news.

"Ef you want ter go over the hills and far away, Eli, here's the chance. I see a man down to Woodtick who was askin' ef I knew any likely young chap who'd like to git 'scribers for a pious book he wants to sell. He'd pay for the job when the names is got and the books give out. That's ruther in your line, boy, so I calk'lated your daddy would spare you, as you ain't much of a hand at shuckin' corn nor cartin' pummace."

"Haw! haw!" laughed the big brothers, Ambrose Vitruvius and Junius Solomon, as neighbor Terry spoke with a sly twinkle in his eye.

But the sisters, Miranda and Pamela, smiled for joy, while the good mother stopped her busy wheel to listen eagerly. Eli laid down his fiddle and came to the hearth where the others sat, with such a wide-awake expression on his usually thoughtful face that it was plain that he liked the idea.

"I'll do it, if father'll let me," he said, looking wistfully at the industrious man, who was shaving axe-handles for the winter wood-chopping, after his day's work was over.

"Wal, I can spare you for a week, mebby. It's not time for the clock shop yet, and sence you've heerd o' this, you won't do your chores right, so you may as wal see what you can make of peddlin'."

"Thank you, sir; I'll give you all I get, to pay for my time," began Eli, glowing with pleasure at the prospect of seeing a little of the world; for one of his most cherished dreams was to cross the blue hills that hemmed him in, and find what lay beyond.

"Guess I can afford to give you all you'll make this trip," answered his father, in a tone that made the brothers laugh again.

"Boys, don't pester Eli. Every one has n't a call to farmin', and it's wal to foller the leadin's of Providence when they come along," said the mother, stroking the smooth, brown head at her knee; for Eli always went to her footstool with his sorrows and his joys.

So it was settled, and next day the boy, in his home-spun and home-made Sunday best, set off to see his employer and secure the job. He got it, and for three days trudged up and down the steep roads, calling at every house with a sample of his book, the Rev. John Flavel's treatise on "Keeping the Heart." Eli's winning face, modest manner, and earnest voice served him well, and he got many names; for books were scarce in those days, and a pious work was a treasure to many a good soul who found it difficult to keep the heart strong and cheerful in troublous times.

Then the books were to be delivered, and, anxious to save his small earnings, Eli hired no horse to transport his load, but borrowed a stout, green shawl from his mother, and, with his pack on his back, marched bravely away to finish his task. His wages were spent in a new prayer-book for his mother, smart handkerchief-pins for the faithful sisters, and a good store of paper for himself.

This trip was so successful that he was seized with a strong desire to try a more ambitious and extended one; for these glimpses of the world showed him how much he had to learn, and how pleasantly he could pick up knowledge in these flights.

"What be you a-brewdin' over now, boy? Gettin' ready for the clock shop? It's 'most time for winter work, and Terry says you do pretty wal at puttin' together," said the farmer, a day or two after the boy's return, as they sat at dinner, all helping themselves from the large pewter platter heaped with pork and vegetables.

"I was wishin' I could go South with Gad Upson. He's been twice with clocks and notions, and wants a mate. Hoadley fits him out and pays him a good share if he does well. Could n't I go along? I hate that old shop, and I know I can do something better than put together the insides of cheap clocks."

Eli spoke eagerly, and gave his mother an imploring look which brought her to second the motion at once, her consent having been already won.

The brothers stared as if Eli had proposed to go up in a balloon, for to them the South seemed farther off than Africa does nowadays. The father had evidently been secretly prepared, for he showed no surprise, and merely paused a moment to look at his ambitious son with a glance in which amusement and reproach were mingled.

"When a hen finds she's hatched a duck's egg, it's no use for her to cackle; that ducklin' will take to the water in spite on her, and paddle off, nobody knows where. Go ahead, boy, and when you get enough of junketin' 'round the world, come home and fall to work."

"Then I *may* go?" cried Eli, upsetting his mug of cider in his excitement.

His father nodded, being too busy eating cabbage with a wide-bladed green-handled knife to speak just then. Eli, red and speechless with delight and gratitude, could only sit and beam at his family till a sob drew his attention to sister Pamela, whose pet he was.

"Don't, Pam, don't! I'll come back all right, and bring you news and all the pretty things I can. I *must* go; I feel as if I could n't breathe, shut up here winters. I s'pose it's wicked, but I can't help it," whispered Eli, with his arm around his buxom eighteen-year old sister, who laid her head on his shoulder and held him tight.

"Daughter, it's sinful to repine at the ways of Providence. I see a leadin' plain in this, and ef *I* can be chirk when my dear boy is goin', 'pears to me you ought to keep a taut rein on your feelin's, and not spile his pleasure."

The good mother's eyes were full of tears as she spoke, but she caught up the end of her short gown and wiped them quickly away to smile on Eli, who thanked her with a loving look.

"It's so lonesome when he's not here. What will we do evenings without the fiddle, or Eli to read a piece in some of his books while we spin?" said poor Pam, ashamed of her grief, yet glad to hide her tears by affecting to settle the long wooden bodkin that held up her coils of brown hair.

"Obed Finch will be comin' along, I guess likely, and he'll read to you out uv Eli's book about keepin' the heart, and you'll find your'n gone 'fore you know it," said Junius Solomon, in a tone that made pretty Pam blush and run away, while the rest laughed at her confusion.

So it was settled, and when all was ready, the boy came home to show his equipment before he started. A very modest outfit, — only two tin trunks slung across the shoulders, filled with jewelry, combs, lace, essences, and small wares.

"I hate to have ye go, son, but it's better than to be mopin' to hum, gettin' desperut for books and rilin' father. We'll all be workin' for ye, so be chipper and do wal. Keep steddy, and don't disgrace your folks. The Lord bless ye, my dear boy, and hold ye in the holler of his hand!"

Her own rough hand was on his head as his mother spoke, with wet eyes, and the tall lad kissed her tenderly, whispering, with a choke in his throat: —

"Good-by, mammy dear; I'll remember."

Then he tramped away to join his mate, turning now and then to nod and smile and show a ruddy face full of happiness, while the family watched him out of sight with mingled hopes and doubts and fears.

Mails were slow in those days, but at length a letter came; and here it is, — a true copy of one written by a boy in 1820: —

Norfolk, Va., December 4th.

HONORED PARENTS: I write to inform you I am safe here and to work. Our business is profitable, and I am fast learning the Quirks and Turns of trade. We are going to the eastern shore of Va., calculating to be gone six weeks. The inhabitants are sociable and hospitable, and you need not fear I shall suffer, for I find many almost fathers and mothers among these good folks.

Taking our trunks, we travel through the country, entering the houses of the rich and poor, offering our goods, and earning our wages by the sweat of our brows. How do you think we look? Like two Awkward, Homespun, Tugging Yankee peddlers? No, that is not the case. By people of breeding we are treated with politeness and gentility, and the low and vulgar we do not seek. For my part, I enjoy travelling more than I expected. Conversation with new folks, observing manners and customs, and seeing the world, does me great good.

I never met a real gentleman till I came here. Their hospitality allows me to see and copy their fine ways of acting and speaking, and they put the most Bashful at ease. Gad likes the maids and stays in the kitchen most times. I get into the libraries and read when we put up nights, and the ladies are most kind to me everywhere.

I'm so tall they can't believe I'm only sixteen. They are n't as pretty as our rosy-faced girls, but their ways are elegant, and so are their clothes, tell Pam.

When I think how kind you were to let me come, I am full

of gratitude. I made some verses, one day, as I waited in a hovel for the rain to hold up.

> To conduce to my own and parents' good,
>   Was why I left my home;
> To make their cares and burdens less,
>   And try to help them some.
> 'T was my own choice to earn them cash,
>   And get them free from debt;
> Before that I am twenty-one
>   It shall be done, I bet.
> My parents they have done for me
>   What I for them can never do,
> So if I serve them all I may,
>   Sure God will help me through.
> My chief delight, therefore, shall be
>   To earn them all I can,
> Not only now, but when that I
>   At last am my own man.

These are the genuine Sentiments of your son, who returns thanks for the many favors you have heaped upon him, and hopes to repay you by his best Endeavors. Accept this letter and the inclosed small sum as a token of his love and respect.

Your dutiful son,
ELI.

Tell the girls to write.

In reply to this, came a letter from the anxious mother, which shows not only the tender, pious nature of the good woman, but also how much need of education the boy had, and how well he was doing for himself: —

AFFECTIONATE SON: We was very glad to receave your letter. I feal very anctious about you this winter, and how you are a doing. You cannot know a mother's concern for her boy wen he is fur away. Do not git into bad habbits. Take the Bible for your rule and guide to vartue. I pray for your prosperity in all spiritall and temporrall things, and leave you in the care of Him who gave you breath and will keep you safe.

We are all well, and your father enjoys his helth better than last year. I visited Uncle Medad a spell last week. I am provided with a horse and shay to ride to meatin. Mr. Eben Welton took our cow and give us his old horse. Captain Stephen Harrington was excommunicated last Sabbath. Pamely goes away to learn dressmakin soon. I mistrust Mirandy will take up with Pennel Haskell; he is likely, and comes frequent. I wish you had been here a Christmas. We had a large company to dinner, and I got some wheat flower and made a fine chicken pye. Eli, I hope you attend meatin when you can. Do not trifle away the holy day in vane pleasures, but live to the glory of God, and in the fear of your parents. Father sold the white colt. He was too spirity, and upsat Ambrose and nigh broke his head. His nose is still black. Dear son: I miss you every time I set a platter in your place. Is your close warm and suffitient? Put your stockin round your throat if sore. Do you git good cyder to drink? Take the Pennyryal if you feal wimbly after a long spell of travil. The girls send love. No more now. Wright soon.

Your mother,
HANNAH GARDENER.

P.S. — Liddy Finch is married. Our pigs give us nine hunderd pound of prime pork.

Many such letters went to and fro that winter, and Eli faithfully reported all his adventures. For he had many, and once or twice was in danger of losing his life.

On one occasion, having parted from his mate for a day or two, wishing to try his luck alone, our young peddler found himself, late in the afternoon, approaching the Dismal Swamp. A tempest arose, adding to the loneliness and terror of the hour. The cypresses uprooted by the blast fell now and then across the road, endangering the poor boy's head. A sluggish stream rolled through tangled junipers and beds of reeds, and the fen on either side was full of ugly creatures, lizards, snakes, and toads; while owls, scared by the storm, flew wildly about and hooted dismally. Just at the height of the tumult, Eli saw three men coming toward him, and gladly hastened to meet them, hoping to have their company or learn of them where he could find a shelter. But their bad faces daunted him, and he would have hurried by without speaking if they had not stopped him, roughly demanding his name and business.

The tall stripling was brave, but his youthful face showed him to be but a boy, and the consciousness of a well-filled purse in his pocket made him anxious to escape. So he answered briefly, and tried to go on. But two men held him, in spite of his struggles, while the third rifled his pockets, broke open his trunks, and took all that was of any value in the way of watches and jewelry. They they left him, with a cruel joke about a good journey, and made off with their booty. It was the first time poor Eli had met with such a mishap, and as he stood in the rain looking at his wares scattered about the road, he felt inclined to throw himself into the creek, and forget his woes there among the frogs and snakes. But he had a stout heart, and soon decided to make the best of it, since nothing could be done to mend the matter. Gathering up his bedraggled laces, scattered scent-bottles, and dirty buttons, pins, and needles, he trudged sadly on, feeling that for him this was indeed a Dismal Swamp.

"I told you we'd better stick together, but you wanted to be so dre'd-ful smart, and go travellin' off alone in them out'n the way places. Might 'a' known you'd get overhauled somers. I always did think you was a gump, Eli, and now I'm sure on 't," was all the comfort Gad gave him when they met, and the direful tale was told.

"What shall I do now?" asked the poor lad. "My notions are n't worth selling, and my money's gone. I'll have to pay Hoadley somehow."

"You'd better foot it home and go to choppin' punkins for the cows, or help your marm spin. I vow I never did see such a chap for gettin' into a mess," scolded Gad, who was a true Yankee, and made a successful trader, even in a small way.

"We'll sleep on it," said Eli, gently, and went to bed very low in his mind.

Perhaps a few tears wet his pillow as he lay awake, and the prayers his mother taught him were whispered in the silence of the night; for hope revived, comfort came, and in the morning his serene face and sensible plan proved to his irate friend that the "gump" had a wise head and a manly heart, after all.

"Gad, it is just the time for the new almanacs, and Allen wants men to sell 'em. I thought it was small business before, but beggars must n't be choosers, so I'm going right off to offer for the job 'round here. It will do for a start, and if I'm smart, Allen will give me a better chance maybe."

"That's a fust-rate plan. Go ahead, and I'll say a good word for you. Allen knows me, and books is in your line, so I guess you'll do wal if you keep out'n the mashes," answered Gad, with great good will, having slept off his vexation.

The plan did go well, and for weeks the rosy-faced, gentle-voiced youth might have been seen mildly offering the new almanacs at doors and shops, and at street corners, with a wistful look in his blue eyes, and a courtesy of manner that attracted many customers and earned many a dollar. Several mates, envying his fine handwriting and pitying his hard luck, took lessons in penmanship of him and paid him fairly, whereat he rejoiced over the hours spent at home, flat on the kitchen floor, or flourishing splendid capitals on the snow-banks, when his nose was blue with cold and his hands half-frozen.

When the season for the yellow-covered almanacs was over, Eli, having won the confidence of his employer, was fitted out with more notions, and again set forth on his travels, armed, this time, and in company with his townsman. He prospered well, and all winter trudged to and fro, seemingly a common peddler, but really a student, making the world his book, and bent on learning all he could. Travel taught him geography and history, for he soon knew every corner of Virginia; looked longingly at the ancient walls of William and Mary College, where Jefferson and Monroe studied; where young George Washington received his surveyor's commission, and in his later years served as Chancellor. In Yorktown, he heard all about the siege of 1781; saw Lord Cornwallis's lodgings and the cave named for him; met pleasant people, whose fine speech and manners he carefully copied; read excellent books wherever he could find them, and observed, remembered, and stored away all that he saw, heard, and learned, to help and adorn his later life.

By spring he set out for home, having slowly saved enough to repay Hoadley for the lost goods. But as if Providence meant to teach him another lesson, and make him still more prudent, humble, and manly, a sad adventure befell him on his way.

While waiting for the coaster that was to take them home, he one day went in swimming with Gad; for this was one of the favorite pastimes of the Connecticut boys, who on Saturday nights congregated by the score at a pond called Benson's Pot, and leaped from the spring-board like circus tumblers, turning somersaults into the deep water below.

It was too early for such sport now; the water was very cold, and poor Gad, taken with cramp, nearly drowned Eli by clinging to his legs as he went down. Freeing himself with difficulty, Eli tried to save his friend; but the current swept the helpless man away, and he was lost. Hurriedly dressing, Eli ran for aid, but found himself regarded with suspicion by those to whom he told his story; for he was a stranger in the place and certain peddlers who had gone before had left a bad name behind them.

To his horror, he was arrested, accused of murder, and would have been tried for his life, if Mr. Allen of Norfolk had not come to testify to his good character, and set him free. Poor Gad's body was found and buried, and after a month's delay, Eli set out again, alone, heavy-hearted, and very poor, for all his own little savings had been consumed by various expenses. Mr. Hoadley's money was untouched, but not increased, as he hoped to have it; and rather than borrow a penny of it, Eli landed bare-footed. His boots were so old he threw them overboard, and spent his last dollar for a cheap pair of shoes to wear when he appeared at home, for they were not stout enough to stand travel. So, like Franklin with his rolls, the lad ate crackers and cheese as he trudged through the city, and set out for the far-away farm-house among the hills.

A long journey, but a pleasant one, in spite of his troubles; for spring made the world lovely, habit made walking no hardship, and all he had seen in his wanderings passed before him at will, like a panorama full of color and variety.

Letters had gone before, but it was a sad homecoming, and when all was told, Eli said: —

"Now, father, I'll go to work. I've had my wish and enjoyed it a sight; and would go again, but I feel as if I ought to work, as long as I can't pay for my time."

"That's hearty, son, and I'm obleeged to ye. Hear what mother's got to say, and then do whichever you prefer," answered the farmer, with a nod toward his wife, who, with the girls, seemed full of some pleasant news which they longed to tell.

"I've sold all the cloth we made last winter for a good sum, and father says you may hev the spendin' on 't. It will be enough to pay your board down to Uncle Tillotson's while you study with him, so 's 't you kin be gettin' ready for college next year. I've sot my heart on 't, and you mus n't disapp'int me and the girls," said the good woman, with a face full of faith and pride in her boy, in spite of all mishaps.

"Oh, mammy, how good you be! It don't seem as if I ought to take it. But I *do* want to go!" cried Eli, catching her round the neck in an ecstasy of boyish delight and gratitude.

Here Miranda and Pamela appeared, bringing their homely gifts of warm hose, and new shirts made from wool and flax grown by the father, and spun and woven by the accomplished housewife.

A very happy youth was Eli when he again set off to the city, with his humble outfit and slender purse, though father still looked doubtful, and the brothers were more sure than ever that Eli was a fool to prefer dry books to country work and fun.

A busy year followed, Eli studying, as never boy studied before, with the excellent minister, who soon grew proud of his best pupil. Less prep-aration was needed in those days, and perhaps more love and industry went to the work; for necessity is a stern master, and poor boys often work wonders if the spark of greatness is there.

Eli had his wish in time, and went to college, mother and sisters making it possible by the sale of their handiwork; for the girls were famous spinners, and the mother the best weaver in the country around. How willingly they toiled for Eli! — rising early and sitting late, cheering their labor with loving talk of the dear lad's progress, and an unfailing faith in his future success. Many a long ride did that good mother take to the city, miles away, with a great roll of cloth on the pillion behind her to sell, that she might pay her son's college bills. Many a coveted pleasure did the faithful sisters give up that they might keep Eli well clothed, or send him some country dainty to cheer the studies which seemed to them painfully hard and mysteriously precious. Father began to take pride in the ugly duckling now, and brothers to brag of his great learning. Neighbors came in to hear his letters, and when vacation brought him home, the lads and lasses regarded him with a certain awe; for his manners were better, his language purer, than theirs, and the new life he led refined the country boy till he seemed a gentleman.

The second year he yielded to temptation, and got into debt. Being anxious to do credit to his family, of whom he was secretly a little ashamed about this time, he spent money on his clothes, conscious that he was a comely youth with a great love of beauty, and a longing for all that cultivates and embellishes character and life. An elegant gentleman astonished the hill folk that season, by appearing at the little church in a suit such as the greatest rustic dandy never imagined in his wildest dreams, — the tall white hat with rolling brim, Marseilles vest with watch-chain and seals festooned across it, the fine blue coat with its brass buttons, and the nankeen trousers strapped over boots so tight that it was torture to walk in them. Armed with a cane in the well-gloved hand, an imposing brooch in the frills of the linen shirt, Eli sauntered across the green, the observed of all observers, proudly hoping that the blue eyes of a certain sweet Lucinda were fixed admiringly upon him.

The boys were the first to recover from the shock, and promptly resented the transformation of their former butt into a city beau, by jeering openly and affecting great scorn of the envied splendor. The poor jackdaw, somewhat abashed at the effect of his plumes, tried to prove that he felt no superiority, by being very affable, which won the lasses, but failed to soften the hearts of the boys; and when he secured the belle of the village for the Thanksgiving drive and dance, the young men resolved that pride should have a fall.

Arrayed in all his finery, Eli drove pretty Lucinda in a smart borrowed wagon to the tavern where the dance was held. Full of the airs and graces he had learned at college, the once bashful, awkward Eli was the admired of all eyes, as he pranced down the long contra-dance in the agonizing

[348]

boots, or played "threading the needle" without the least reluctance on the part of the blushing girls to pay the fine of a kiss when the players sung the old rhyme: —

The needle's eye no one can pass;
The thread that runs so true —
It has caught many a pretty lass,
And now it has caught you.

But his glory was short-lived; for some enemy maliciously drew out the linchpin from the smart wagon, and as they were gayly driving homeward over the hills, the downfall came, and out they both went, to the great damage of Eli's city suit, and poor Lucinda's simple finery.

Fortunately, no bones were broken, and picking themselves up, they sadly footed it home, hoping the mishap would remain unknown. But the rogues took care that Eli should not escape, and the whole neighborhood laughed over the joke; for the fine hat was ruined, and the costly coat split down the back, in the ignominious tumble.

Great was the humiliation of the poor student; for not only was he ridiculed, but Lucinda would not forgive him, and the blue eyes smiled upon another; worst of all, he had to confess his debts and borrow money of his father to pay them. He meekly bore the stern rebuke that came with the hard-earned dollars, but the sight of the tears his mother shed, even while she comforted him, filled him with remorse. He went back to his books, in a homespun suit, a sadder and a wiser boy, and fell to work as if resolved to wash out past errors and regain the confidence he had lost.

All that winter the wheels turned and the loom jangled, that the rolls of cloth might be increased; and never was the day too cold, the way too long, for the good mother's pious pilgrimage.

That summer, a man came home to them, shabby enough as to his clothes, but so wonderfully improved in other ways, that not only did the women folk glow with tender pride, but father and brothers looked at him with respect, and owned at last there was something in Eli. "No vacation for me," he said; "I must work to pay my debts; and as I am not of much use here, I'll try my old plan, and peddle some money into my empty pockets."

It was both comic and pathetic to see the shoulders that had worn the fine broadcloth burdened with a yoke, the hands that had worn kid gloves grasping the tin trunks, and the dapper feet trudging through dust and dew in cow-hide boots. But the face under the old straw hat was a manlier one than that which the tall beaver crowned, and the heart under the rough vest was far happier than when the gold chain glittered above it. He did so well that when he returned to college his debts were paid, and the family faith in Eli restored.

That was an eventful year; for one brother married, and one went off to seek his fortune, the father mortgaging his farm to give these sons a fair start in life. Eli was to be a minister, and the farmer left his fortunes in the hands of his wife, who, like many another good mother, was the making of the great man of the family, and was content with that knowledge, leaving him the glory.

The next year, Eli graduated with honor, and went home, to be received with great rejoicing, just twenty-one, and a free man. He had longed for this time, and planned a happy, studious life, preparing to preach the gospel in a little parsonage of his own. But suddenly all was changed; joy turned to sorrow, hope to doubt, and Eli was called to relinquish liberty for duty, — to give up his own dreams of a home, to keep a roof over the heads of the dear mother and the faithful sisters. His father died suddenly, leaving very little for the women folk besides the independence that lay in the skill of their own thrifty hands. The elder brothers could not offer much help, and Eli was the one to whom the poor souls turned in their hour of sorrow and anxiety.

"Go on, dear, and don't pester yourself about us. We can find food and firin' here as long as the old farm is ours. I guess we can manage to pay off the mortgage by-and-by. It don't seem as if I *could* turn out, after livin' here ever sense I was married, and poor father so fond on 't."

The widow covered her face with her apron, and Eli put his arms about her, saying manfully, as he gave up all his fondest hopes for her dearer sake: —

"Cheer up, mother, and trust to me. I should be a poor fellow if I allowed you and the girls to want, after all you've done for me. I can get a school, and earn instead of spend. Teaching and studying can go together. I'm sure I should n't prosper if I shirked my duty, and I won't." The three sad women clung to him, and the brothers, looking at his brave, bright face, felt that Eli was indeed a man to lean on and to love in times like this.

"Well," thought the young philosopher, "the Lord knows what is best for me, and perhaps this is a part of my education. I'll try to think so, and hope to get some good out of a hard job."

In this spirit he set about teaching, and prospered wonderfully, for his own great love of learning made it an easy and delightful task to help others as he had longed to be helped. His innocent and tender nature made all children love him, and gave him a remarkable power over them; so when the first hard months were past, and his efforts began to bear fruit, he found that what had seemed an affliction was a blessing, and that teaching was his special gift. Filial duty sweetened the task, a submissive heart found happiness in self-sacrifice, and a wise soul showed him what a noble and lovely work it was to minister to little children, — for of such is the kingdom of heaven.

For years Eli taught, and his school grew famous; for he copied the fashions of other countries, invented new methods, and gave himself so entirely to his profession that he could not fail of success. The mortgage was paid off, and Eli made frequent pilgrimages to the dear old mother, whose staff and comfort he still was. The sisters married well, the brothers prospered, and at thirty, the schoolmaster found a nobler mate than pretty Lucinda, and soon had some little pupils of his very own to love and teach.

There his youth ends; but after the years of teaching he began to preach at last, not in one pulpit, but in many all over the land, diffusing good thoughts now as he had peddled small wares when a boy; still learning as he went, still loving books and studying mankind, still patient, pious, dutiful, and tender, a wise and beautiful old man, till, at eighty, Eli's education ended.

A Christmas Dream, and How It Came True

From *Lulu's Library* (3 vols.), vol. 1, *A Christmas Dream*
(Boston: Roberts Brothers, 1886)

I'M SO TIRED of Christmas I wish there never would be another one!" exclaimed a discontented-looking little girl, as she sat idly watching her mother arrange a pile of gifts two days before they were to be given.

"Why, Effie, what a dreadful thing to say! You are as bad as old Scrooge; and I'm afraid something will happen to you, as it did to him, if you don't care for dear Christmas," answered mamma, almost dropping the silver horn she was filling with delicious candies.

"Who was Scrooge? What happened to him?" asked Effie, with a glimmer of interest in her listless face, as she picked out the sourest lemon-drop she could find; for nothing sweet suited her just then.

"He was one of Dickens's best people, and you can read the charming story some day. He hated Christmas until a strange dream showed him how dear and beautiful it was, and made a better man of him."

"I shall read it; for I like dreams, and have a great many curious ones myself. But they don't keep me from being tired of Christmas," said Effie, poking discontentedly among the sweeties for something worth eating.

"Why are you tired of what should be the happiest time of all the year?" asked mamma, anxiously.

"Perhaps I should n't be if I had something new. But it is always the same, and there is n't any more surprise about it. I always find heaps of goodies in my stocking. Don't like some of them, and soon get tired of those I do like. We always have a great dinner, and I eat too much, and feel ill next day. Then there is a Christmas tree somewhere, with a doll on top, or a stupid old Santa Claus, and children dancing and screaming over bonbons and toys that break, and shiny things that are of no use. Really, mamma, I've had so many Christmases all alike that I don't think I *can* bear another one." And Effie laid herself flat on the sofa, as if the mere idea was too much for her.

Her mother laughed at her despair, but was sorry to see her little girl so discontented, when she had everything to make her happy, and had known but ten Christmas days.

"Suppose we don't give you *any* presents at all, — how would that suit you?" asked mamma, anxious to please her spoiled child.

"I should like one large and splendid one, and one dear little one, to remember some very nice person by," said Effie, who was a fanciful little body, full of odd whims and notions, which her friends loved to gratify, regardless of time, trouble, or money; for she was the last of three little girls, and very dear to all the family.

"Well, my darling, I will see what I can do to please you, and not say a word until all is ready. If I could only get a new idea to start with!" And mamma went on tying up her pretty bundles with a thoughtful face, while Effie strolled to the window to watch the rain that kept her in-doors and made her dismal.

"Seems to me poor children have better times than rich ones. I can't go out, and there is a girl about my age splashing along, without any maid to fuss about rubbers and cloaks and umbrellas and colds. I wish I was a beggar-girl."

"Would you like to be hungry, cold, and ragged, to beg all day, and sleep on an ash-heap at night?" asked mamma, wondering what would come next.

"Cinderella did, and had a nice time in the end. This girl out here has a basket of scraps on her arm, and a big old shawl all round her, and does n't seem to care a bit, though the water runs out of the toes of her boots. She goes paddling along, laughing at the rain, and eating a cold potato as if it tasted nicer than the chicken and ice-cream I had for dinner. Yes, I do think poor children are happier than rich ones."

"So do I, sometimes. At the Orphan Asylum to-day I saw two dozen merry little souls who have no parents, no home, and no hope of Christmas beyond a stick of candy or a cake. I wish you had been there to see how happy they were, playing with the old toys some richer children had sent them."

"You may give them all mine; I'm so tired of them I never want to see them again," said Effie, turning from the window to the pretty baby-house full of everything a child's heart could desire.

"I will, and let you begin again with something you will not tire of, if I can only find it." And mamma knit her brows trying to discover some grand surprise for this child who did n't care for Christmas.

Nothing more was said then; and wandering off to the library, Effie found "A Christmas Carol," and curling herself up in the sofa corner, read it all before tea. Some of it she did not understand; but she laughed and cried over many parts of the charming story, and felt better without knowing why.

All the evening she thought of poor Tiny Tim, Mrs. Cratchit with the pudding, and the stout old gentleman who danced so gayly that "his legs twinkled in the air." Presently bedtime arrived.

"Come, now, and toast your feet," said Effie's nurse, "while I do your pretty hair and tell stories."

"I'll have a fairy tale to-night, a very interesting one," commanded Effie, as she put on her blue silk wrapper and little fur-lined slippers to sit before the fire and have her long curls brushed.

So Nursey told her best tales; and when at last the child lay down under her lace curtains, her head was full of a curious jumble of Christmas elves, poor children, snow-storms, sugar-plums, and surprises. So it is no wonder that she dreamed all night; and this was the dream, which she never quite forgot.

She found herself sitting on a stone, in the middle of a great field, all alone. The snow was falling fast, a bitter wind whistled by, and night was coming on. She felt hungry, cold, and tired, and did not know where to go nor what to do.

"I wanted to be a beggar-girl, and now I am one; but I don't like it, and wish somebody would come and take care of me. I don't know who I am, and I think I must be lost," thought Effie, with the curious interest one takes in one's self in dreams.

But the more she thought about it, the more bewildered she felt. Faster fell the snow, colder blew the wind, darker grew the night; and poor Effie made up her mind that she was quite forgotten and left to freeze alone. The tears were chilled on her cheeks, her feet felt like icicles, and her heart died within her, so hungry, frightened, and forlorn was she. Laying her head on her knees, she gave herself up for lost, and sat there with the great flakes fast turning her to a little white mound, when suddenly the sound of music reached her, and starting up, she looked and listened with all her eyes and ears.

Far away a dim light shone, and a voice was heard singing. She tried to run toward the welcome glimmer, but could not stir, and stood like a small statue of expectation while the light drew nearer, and the sweet words of the song grew clearer.

> From our happy home
> Through the world we roam
> One week in all the year,
> Making winter spring
> With the joy we bring,
> For Christmas-tide is here.
>
> Now the eastern star
> Shines from afar
> To light the poorest home;
> Hearts warmer grow,
> Gifts freely flow,
> For Christmas-tide has come.
>
> Now gay trees rise
> Before young eyes,
> Abloom with tempting cheer;
> Blithe voices sing,
> And blithe bells ring,
> For Christmas-tide is here.
>
> Oh, happy chime,
> Oh, blessèd time,
> That draws us all so near!
> "Welcome, dear day,"

A Christmas Dream, and How It Came True

All creatures say,
For Christmas-tide is here.

A child's voice sang, a child's hand carried the little candle; and in the circle of soft light it shed, Effie saw a pretty child coming to her through the night and snow. A rosy, smiling creature, wrapped in white fur, with a wreath of green and scarlet holly on its shining hair, the magic candle in one hand, and the other outstretched as if to shower gifts and warmly press all other hands.

Effie forgot to speak as this bright vision came nearer, leaving no trace of footsteps in the snow, only lighting the way with its little candle, and filling the air with the music of its song.

"Dear child, you are lost, and I have come to find you," said the stranger, taking Effie's cold hands in his, with a smile like sunshine, while every holly berry glowed like a little fire.

"Do you know me?" asked Effie, feeling no fear, but a great gladness, at his coming.

"I know all children, and go to find them; for this is my holiday, and I gather them from all parts of the world to be merry with me once a year."

"Are you an angel?" asked Effie, looking for the wings.

"No; I am a Christmas spirit, and live with my mates in a pleasant place, getting ready for our holiday, when we are let out to roam about the world, helping make this a happy time for all who will let us in. Will you come and see how we work?"

"I will go anywhere with you. Don't leave me again," cried Effie, gladly.

"First I will make you comfortable. That is what we love to do. You are cold, and you shall be warm; hungry, and I will feed you; sorrowful, and I will make you gay."

With a wave of his candle all three miracles were wrought, — for the snow-flakes turned to a white fur cloak and hood on Effie's head and shoulders; a bowl of hot soup came sailing to her lips, and vanished when she had eagerly drunk the last drop; and suddenly the dismal field changed to a new world so full of wonders that all her troubles were forgotten in a minute.

Bells were ringing so merrily that it was hard to keep from dancing. Green garlands hung on the walls, and every tree was a Christmas tree full of toys, and blazing with candles that never went out.

In one place many little spirits sewed like mad on warm clothes, turning off work faster than any sewing-machine ever invented, and great piles were made ready to be sent to poor people. Other busy creatures packed money into purses, and wrote checks which they sent flying away on the wind, — a lovely kind of snow-storm to fall into a world below full of poverty.

Older and graver spirits were looking over piles of little books, in which the records of the past year were kept, telling how different people had spent it, and what sort of gifts they deserved. Some got peace, some disappointment, some remorse and sorrow, some great joy and hope. The rich had generous thoughts sent them; the poor, gratitude and contentment. Children had more love and duty to parents; and parents renewed patience, wisdom, and satisfaction for and in their children. No one was forgotten.

"Please tell me what splendid place this is?" asked Effie, as soon as she could collect her wits after the first look at all these astonishing things.

"This is the Christmas world; and here we work all the year round, never tired of getting ready for the happy day. See, these are the saints just setting off; for some have far to go, and the children must not be disappointed."

As he spoke the spirit pointed to four gates, out of which four great sleighs were just driving, laden with toys, while a jolly old Santa Claus sat in the middle of each, drawing on his mittens and tucking up his wraps for a long cold drive.

"Why, I thought there was only one Santa Claus, and even he was a humbug," cried Effie, astonished at the sight.

"Never give up your faith in the sweet old stories, even after you come to see that they are only the pleasant shadow of a lovely truth."

Just then the sleighs went off with a great jingling of bells and pattering of reindeer hoofs, while all the spirits gave a cheer that was heard in the lower world, where people said, "Hear the stars sing."

"I never will say there isn't any Santa Claus again. Now, show me more."

"You will like to see this place, I think, and may learn something here perhaps."

The spirit smiled as he led the way to a little door, through which Effie peeped into a world of dolls. Baby-houses were in full blast, with dolls of all sorts going on like live people. Waxen ladies sat in their parlors elegantly dressed; black dolls cooked in the kitchens; nurses walked out with the bits of dollies; and the streets were full of tin soldiers marching, wooden horses prancing, express wagons rumbling, and little men hurrying to and fro. Shops were there, and tiny people buying legs of mutton, pounds of tea, mites of clothes, and everything dolls use or wear or want.

But presently she saw that in some ways the dolls improved upon the manners and customs of human beings, and she watched eagerly to learn why they did these things. A fine Paris doll driving in her carriage took up a black worsted Dinah who was hobbling along with a basket of clean clothes, and carried her to her journey's end, as if it were the proper thing to do. Another interesting china lady took off her comfortable red cloak and put it round a poor wooden creature done up in a paper shift, and so badly painted that its face would have sent some babies into fits.

"Seems to me I once knew a rich girl who did n't give her things to poor girls. I wish I could remember who she was, and tell her to be as kind as that china doll," said Effie, much touched at the sweet way the pretty creature wrapped up the poor fright, and then ran off in her little gray gown to buy a shiny fowl stuck on a wooden platter for her invalid mother's dinner.

"We recall these things to people's minds by dreams. I think the girl you speak of won't forget this one." And the spirit smiled, as if he enjoyed some joke which she did not see.

A little bell rang as she looked, and away scampered the children into the red-and-green school-house with the roof that lifted up, so one could see how nicely they sat at their desks with mites of books, or drew on the inch-square blackboards with crumbs of chalk.

"They know their lessons very well, and are as still as mice. We make a great racket at our school, and get bad marks every day. I shall tell the girls they had better mind what they do, or their dolls will be better scholars than they are," said Effie, much impressed, as she peeped in and saw no rod in the hand of the little mistress, who looked up and shook her head at the intruder, as if begging her to go away before the order of the school was disturbed.

Effie retired at once, but could not resist one look in at the window of a fine mansion, where the family were at dinner, the children behaved so well at table, and never grumbled a bit when their mamma said they could not have any more fruit.

"Now, show me something else," she said, as they came again to the low door that led out of Doll land.

"You have seen how we prepare for Christmas; let me show you where we love best to send our good and happy gifts," answered the spirit, giving her his hand again.

"I know. I've seen ever so many," began Effie, thinking of her own Christmases.

"No, you have never seen what I will show you. Come away, and remember what you see to-night."

Like a flash that bright world vanished, and Effie found herself in a part of the city she had never seen before. It was far away from the gayer places, where every store was brilliant with lights and full of pretty things, and every house wore a festival air, while people hurried to and fro with merry greetings. It was down among the dingy streets where the poor lived, and where there was no making ready for Christmas.

Hungry women looked in at the shabby shops, longing to buy meat and bread, but empty pockets forbade. Tipsy men drank up their wages in the bar-rooms; and in many cold dark chambers little children huddled under the thin blankets, trying to forget their misery in sleep.

No nice dinners filled the air with savory smells, no gay trees dropped toys and bonbons into eager hands, no little stockings hung in rows beside the chimney-piece ready to be filled, no happy sounds of music, gay voices, and dancing feet were heard; and there were no signs of Christmas anywhere.

"Don't they have any in this place?" asked Effie, shivering, as she held fast the spirit's hand, following where he led her.

"We come to bring it. Let me show you our best workers." And the spirit pointed to some sweet-faced men and women who came stealing into the poor houses, working such beautiful miracles that Effie could only stand and watch.

Some slipped money into the empty pockets, and sent the happy mothers to buy all the comforts they needed; others led the drunken men out of temptation, and took them home to find safer pleasures there. Fires were kindled on cold hearths, tables spread as if by magic, and warm clothes wrapped round shivering limbs. Flowers suddenly bloomed in the chambers of the sick; old people found themselves remembered; sad hearts were consoled by a tender word, and wicked ones softened by the story of Him who forgave all sin.

But the sweetest work was for the children; and Effie held her breath to watch these human fairies hang up and fill the little stockings without which a child's Christmas is not perfect, putting in things that once she would have thought very humble presents, but which now seemed beautiful and precious because these poor babies had nothing.

"That is so beautiful! I wish I could make merry Christmases as these good people do, and be loved and thanked as they are," said Effie, softly, as she watched the busy men and women do their work and steal away without thinking of any reward but their own satisfaction.

"You can if you will. I have shown you the way. Try it, and see how happy your own holiday will be hereafter."

As he spoke, the spirit seemed to put his arms about her, and vanished with a kiss.

"Oh, stay and show me more!" cried Effie, trying to hold him fast.

"Darling, wake up, and tell me why you are smiling in your sleep," said a voice in her ear; and opening her eyes, there was mamma bending over her, and morning sunshine streaming into the room.

"Are they all gone? Did you hear the bells? Was n't it splendid?" she asked, rubbing her eyes, and looking about her for the pretty child who was so real and sweet.

"You have been dreaming at a great rate, — talking in your sleep, laughing, and clapping your hands as if you were cheering some one. Tell me what was so splendid," said mamma, smoothing the tumbled hair and lifting up the sleepy head.

Then, while she was being dressed, Effie told her dream, and Nursey thought it very wonderful; but mamma smiled to see how curiously things the child had thought, read, heard, and seen through the day were mixed up in her sleep.

"The spirit said I could work lovely miracles if I tried; but I don't know how to begin, for I have no magic candle to make feasts appear, and light up groves of Christmas trees, as he did," said Effie, sorrow-fully.

"Yes, you have. We will do it! we will do it!" And clapping her hands, mamma suddenly began to dance all over the room as if she had lost her wits.

"How? how? You must tell me, mamma," cried Effie, dancing after her, and ready to believe anything possible when she remembered the adventures of the past night.

"I've got it! I've got it! — the new idea. A splendid one, if I can only carry it out!" And mamma waltzed the little girl round till her curls flew wildly in the air, while Nursey laughed as if she would die.

"Tell me! tell me!" shrieked Effie.

"No, no; it is a surprise, — a grand surprise for Christmas day!" sung mamma, evidently charmed with her happy thought. "Now, come to breakfast; for we must work like bees if we want to play spirits to-morrow. You and Nursey will go out shopping, and get heaps of things, while I arrange matters behind the scenes."

They were running downstairs as mamma spoke, and Effie called out breathlessly, —

"It won't be a surprise; for I know you are going to ask some poor children here, and have a tree or something. It won't be like my dream;

for they had ever so many trees, and more children than we can find any-where."

"There will be no tree, no party, no dinner, in this house at all, and no presents for you. Won't that be a surprise?" And mamma laughed at Effie's bewildered face.

"Do it. I shall like it, I think; and I won't ask any questions, so it will all burst upon me when the time comes," she said; and she ate her breakfast thoughtfully, for this really would be a new sort of Christmas.

All that morning Effie trotted after Nursey in and out of shops, buying dozens of barking dogs, woolly lambs, and squeaking birds; tiny tea-sets, gay picture-books, mittens and hoods, dolls and candy. Parcel after parcel was sent home; but when Effie returned she saw no trace of them, though she peeped everywhere. Nursey chuckled, but would n't give a hint, and went out again in the afternoon with a long list of more things to buy; while Effie wandered forlornly about the house, missing the usual merry stir that went before the Christmas dinner and the evening fun.

As for mamma, she was quite invisible all day, and came in at night so tired that she could only lie on the sofa to rest, smiling as if some very pleasant thought made her happy in spite of weariness.

"Is the surprise going on all right?" asked Effie, anxiously; for it seemed an immense time to wait till another evening came.

"Beautifully! better than I expected; for several of my good friends are helping, or I could n't have done it as I wish. I know you will like it, dear, and long remember this new way of making Christmas merry."

Mamma gave her a very tender kiss, and Effie went to bed.

The next day was a very strange one; for when she woke there was no stocking to examine, no pile of gifts under her napkin, no one said "Merry Christmas!" to her, and the dinner was just as usual to her. Mamma vanished again, and Nursey kept wiping her eyes and saying: "The dear things! It's the prettiest idea I ever heard of. No one but your blessed ma could have done it."

"Do stop, Nursey, or I shall go crazy because I don't know the se-cret!" cried Effie, more than once; and she kept her eye on the clock, for at seven in the evening the surprise was to come off.

The longed-for hour arrived at last, and the child was too excited to ask questions when Nurse put on her cloak and hood, led her to the car-riage, and they drove away, leaving their house the one dark and silent one in the row.

"I feel like the girls in the fairy tales who are led off to strange places and see fine things," said Effie, in a whisper, as they jingled through the gay streets.

"Ah, my deary, it *is* like a fairy tale, I do assure you, and you *will* see finer things than most children will to-night. Steady, now, and do just as I tell you, and don't say one word whatever you see," answered Nursey, quite quivering with excitement as she patted a large box in her lap, and nodded and laughed with twinkling eyes.

They drove into a dark yard, and Effie was led through a back door to a little room, where Nurse coolly proceeded to take off not only her cloak and hood, but her dress and shoes also. Effie stared and bit her lips, but kept still until out of the box came a little white fur coat and boots, a wreath of holly leaves and berries, and a candle with a frill of gold paper round it. A long "Oh!" escaped her then; and when she was dressed and saw herself in the glass, she started back, exclaiming, "Why, Nursey, I look like the spirit in my dream!"

"So you do; and that's the part you are to play, my pretty! Now whist, while I blind your eyes and put you in your place."

"Shall I be afraid?" whispered Effie, full of wonder; for as they went out she heard the sound of many voices, the tramp of many feet, and, in spite of the bandage, was sure a great light shone upon her when she stopped.

"You need n't be; I shall stand close by, and your ma will be there."

After the handkerchief was tied about her eyes, Nurse led Effie up some steps, and placed her on a high platform, where something like leaves touched her head, and the soft snap of lamps seemed to fill the air.

Music began as soon as Nurse clapped her hands, the voices outside sounded nearer, and the tramp was evidently coming up the stairs.

"Now, my precious, look and see how you and your dear ma have made a merry Christmas for them that needed it!"

Off went the bandage; and for a minute Effie really did think she was asleep again, for she actually stood in "a grove of Christmas trees," all gay and shining as in her vision. Twelve on a side, in two rows down the room, stood the little pines, each on its low table; and behind Effie a taller one rose to the roof, hung with wreaths of popcorn, apples, oranges, horns of candy, and cakes of all sorts, from sugary hearts to gingerbread Jumbos. On the smaller trees she saw many of her own discarded toys and those Nursey bought, as well as heaps that seemed to have rained down straight from that delightful Christmas country where she felt as if she was again.

"How splendid! Who is it for? What is that noise? Where is mamma?"

cried Effie, pale with pleasure and surprise, as she stood looking down the brilliant little street from her high place.

Before Nurse could answer, the doors at the lower end flew open, and in marched twenty-four little blue-gowned orphan girls, singing sweetly, until amazement changed the song to cries of joy and wonder as the shining spectacle appeared. While they stood staring with round eyes at the wilderness of pretty things about them, mamma stepped up beside Effie, and holding her hand fast to give her courage, told the story of the dream in a few simple words, ending in this way: —

"So my little girl wanted to be a Christmas spirit too, and make this a happy day for those who had not as many pleasures and comforts as she has. She likes surprises, and we planned this for you all. She shall play the good fairy, and give each of you something from this tree, after which every one will find her own name on a small tree, and can go to enjoy it in her own way. March by, my dears, and let us fill your hands."

Nobody told them to do it, but all the hands were clapped heartily before a single child stirred; then one by one they came to look up wonderingly at the pretty giver of the feast as she leaned down to offer them great yellow oranges, red apples, bunches of grapes, bonbons, and cakes, till all were gone, and a double row of smiling faces turned toward her as the children filed back to their places in the orderly way they had been taught.

Then each was led to her own tree by the good ladies who had helped mamma with all their hearts; and the happy hubbub that arose would have satisfied even Santa Claus himself, — shrieks of joy, dances of delight, laughter and tears (for some tender little things could not bear so much pleasure at once, and sobbed with mouths full of candy and hands full of toys). How they ran to show one another the new treasures! how they peeped and tasted, pulled and pinched, until the air was full of queer noises, the floor covered with papers, and the little trees left bare of all but candles!

"I don't think heaven can be any gooder than this," sighed one small girl, as she looked about her in a blissful maze, holding her full apron with one hand, while she luxuriously carried sugar-plums to her mouth with the other.

"Is that a truly angel up there?" asked another, fascinated by the little white figure with the wreath on its shining hair, who in some mysterious way had been the cause of all this merry-making.

"I wish I dared to go and kiss her for this splendid party," said a lame child, leaning on her crutch, as she stood near the steps, wondering how it seemed to sit in a mother's lap, as Effie was doing, while she watched the happy scene before her.

Effie heard her, and remembering Tiny Tim, ran down and put her arms about the pale child, kissing the wistful face, as she said sweetly, "You may; but mamma deserves the thanks. She did it all; I only dreamed about it."

Lame Katy felt as if "a truly angel" was embracing her, and could only stammer out her thanks, while the other children ran to see the pretty spirit, and touch her soft dress, until she stood in a crowd of blue gowns laughing as they held up their gifts for her to see and admire.

Mamma leaned down and whispered one word to the older girls; and suddenly they all took hands to dance round Effie, singing as they skipped.

It was a pretty sight, and the ladies found it hard to break up the happy revel; but it was late for small people, and too much fun is a mistake. So the girls fell into line, and marched before Effie and mamma again, to say good-night with such grateful little faces that the eyes of those who looked grew dim with tears. Mamma kissed every one; and many a hungry child-ish heart felt as if the touch of those tender lips was their best gift. Effie shook so many small hands that her own tingled; and when Katy came she pressed a small doll into Effie's hand, whispering, "You did n't have a single present, and we had lots. Do keep that; it's the prettiest thing I got."

"I will," answered Effie, and held it fast until the last smiling face was gone, the surprise all over, and she safe in her own bed, too tired and happy for anything but sleep.

"Mamma, it *was* a beautiful surprise, and I thank you so much! I don't see how you did it; but I like it best of all the Christmases I ever had, and mean to make one every year. I had my splendid big present, and here is the dear little one to keep for love of poor Katy; so even that part of my wish came true."

And Effie fell asleep with a happy smile on her lips, her one humble gift still in her hand, and a new love for Christmas in her heart that never changed through a long life spent in doing good.

Sophie's Secret

From *Lulu's Library* (3 vols.), vol. 3, *Recollections*
(Boston: Roberts Brothers, 1889)

I

A PARTY OF YOUNG girls, in their gay bathing-dresses, were sitting on the beach waiting for the tide to rise a little higher before they enjoyed the daily frolic which they called "mermaiding."

"I wish we could have a clam-bake; but we have n't any clams, and don't know how to cook them if we had. It's such a pity all the boys have gone off on that stupid fishing excursion," said one girl, in a yellow-and-black striped suit which made her look like a wasp.

"What is a clam-bake? I do not know that kind of fête," asked a pretty brown-eyed girl, with an accent that betrayed the foreigner.

The girls laughed at such sad ignorance, and Sophie colored, wishing she had not spoken.

"Poor thing! she has never tasted a clam. What *should* we do if we went to Switzerland?" said the wasp, who loved to tease.

"We should give you the best we had, and not laugh at your ignorance, if you did not know all our dishes. In *my* country, we have politeness, though not the clam-bake," answered Sophie, with a flash of the brown eyes which warned naughty Di to desist.

"We might row to the light-house, and have a picnic supper. Our mammas will let us do that alone," suggested Dora from the roof of the bath-house, where she perched like a flamingo.

"That's a good idea," cried Fanny, a slender brown girl who sat dabbling her feet in the water, with her hair streaming in the wind. "Sophie should see that, and get some of the shells she likes so much."

"You are kind to think of me. I shall be glad to have a necklace of the pretty things, as a souvenir of this so charming place and my good friend," answered Sophie, with a grateful look at Fanny, whose many attentions had won the stranger's heart.

"Those boys have n't left us a single boat, so we must dive off the rocks, and that is n't half so nice," said Di, to change the subject, being ashamed of her rudeness.

"A boat is just coming round the Point; perhaps we can hire that, and have some fun," cried Dora, from her perch. "There is only a girl in it; I'll hail her when she is near enough."

Sophie looked about her to see where the *hail* was coming from; but the sky was clear, and she waited to see what new meaning this word might have, not daring to ask for fear of another laugh.

While the girls watched the boat float around the farther horn of the crescent-shaped beach, we shall have time to say a few words about our little heroine.

She was a sixteen-year-old Swiss girl, on a visit to some American friends, and had come to the seaside for a month with one of them who was an invalid. This left Sophie to the tender mercies of the young people; and they gladly welcomed the pretty creature, with her fine manners, foreign ways, and many accomplishments. But she had a quick temper, a funny little accent, and dressed so very plainly that the girls could not resist criticising and teasing her in a way that seemed very ill-bred and unkind to the new-comer.

Their free and easy ways astonished her, their curious language bewildered her; and their ignorance of many things she had been taught made her wonder at the American education she had heard so much praised. All had studied French and German; yet few read or spoke either tongue correctly, or understood her easily when she tried to talk to them. Their music did not amount to much, and in the games they played, their want of useful information amazed Sophie. One did not know the signs of the zodiac; another could only say of cotton that "it was stuff that grew down South;" and a third was not sure whether a frog was an animal or a reptile, while the handwriting and spelling displayed on these occasions left much to be desired. Yet all were fifteen or sixteen, and would soon leave school "finished," as they expressed it, but not *furnished,* as they should have been, with a solid, sensible education. Dress was an all-absorbing topic, sweetmeats their delight; and in confidential moments sweethearts were discussed with great freedom. Fathers were conveniences, mothers comforters, brothers plagues, and sisters ornaments or playthings according to their ages. They were not hard-hearted girls, only frivolous, idle, and fond of fun; and poor little Sophie amused them immensely till they learned to admire, love, and respect her.

Coming straight from Paris, they expected to find that her trunks contained the latest fashions for demoiselles, and begged to see her dresses with girlish interest. But when Sophie obligingly showed a few simple, but pretty and appropriate gowns and hats, they exclaimed with one voice, —

"Why, you dress like a little girl! Don't you have ruffles and lace on your dresses; and silks and high-heeled boots and long gloves and bustles and corsets, and things like ours?"

"I *am* a little girl," laughed Sophie, hardly understanding their dismay. "What should I do with fine toilets at school? My sisters go to balls in silk and lace; but I — not yet."

"How queer! Is your father poor?" asked Di, with Yankee bluntness.

"We have enough," answered Sophie, slightly knitting her dark brows.

"How many servants do you keep?"

"But five, now that the little ones are grown up."

"Have you a piano?" continued undaunted Di, while the others affected to be looking at the books and pictures strewn about by the hasty unpacking.

"We have two pianos, four violins, three flutes, and an organ. We love music, and all play, from papa to little Franz."

"My gracious, how swell! You must live in a big house to hold all that and eight brothers and sisters."

"We are not peasants; we do not live in a hut. *Voilà,* this is my home." And Sophie laid before them a fine photograph of a large and elegant house on lovely Lake Geneva.

It was droll to see the change in the faces of the girls as they looked, admired, and slyly nudged one another, enjoying saucy Di's astonishment, for she had stoutly insisted that the Swiss girl was a poor relation.

Sophie meanwhile was folding up her plain piqué and muslin frocks, with a glimmer of mirthful satisfaction in her eyes, and a tender pride in the work of loving hands now far away.

Kind Fanny saw a little quiver of the lips as she smoothed the blue corn-flowers in the best hat, and put her arm around Sophie, whispering, —

"Never mind, dear, they don't mean to be rude; it's only our Yankee way of asking questions. I like *all* your things, and that hat is perfectly lovely."

"Indeed, yes! Dear mamma arranged it for me. I was thinking of her and longing for my morning kiss."

"Do you do that every day?" asked Fanny, forgetting herself in her sympathetic interest.

"Surely, yes. Papa and mamma sit always on the sofa, and we all have the hand-shake and the embrace each day before our morning coffee. I do not see that here," answered Sophie, who sorely missed the affectionate respect foreign children give their parents.

"Have n't time," said Fanny, smiling too, at the idea of American parents sitting still for five minutes in the busiest part of the busy day to kiss their sons and daughters.

"It is what you call old-fashioned, but a sweet fashion to me; and since I have not the dear warm cheeks to kiss, I embrace my pictures often. See, I have them all." And Sophie unfolded a Russia-leather case, displaying with pride a long row of handsome brothers and sisters with the parents in the midst.

More exclamations from the girls, and increased interest in "Wilhelmina Tell," as they christened the loyal Swiss maiden, who was now accepted as a companion, and soon became a favorite with old and young.

They could not resist teasing her, however, — her mistakes were so amusing, her little flashes of temper so dramatic, and her tongue so quick to give a sharp or witty answer when the new language did not perplex her. But Fanny always took her part, and helped her in many ways. Now they sat together on the rock, a pretty pair of mermaids with wind-tossed hair, wave-washed feet, and eyes fixed on the approaching boat.

The girl who sat in it was a great contrast to the gay creatures grouped so picturesquely on the shore, for the old straw hat shaded a very anxious face, the brown calico gown covered a heart full of hopes and fears, and the boat that drifted so slowly with the incoming tide carried Tilly Reed like a young Columbus toward the new world she longed for, believed in, and was resolved to discover.

It was a weather-beaten little boat, yet very pretty; for a pile of nets lay at one end, a creel of red lobsters at the other, and all between stood baskets of berries and water-lilies, purple marsh rosemary and orange butterfly-weed, shells and great smooth stones such as artists like to paint little sea-views on. A tame gull perched on the prow; and the morning sunshine glittered from the blue water to the bluer sky.

"Oh, how pretty! Come on, please, and sell us some lilies," cried Dora, and roused Tilly from her waking dream.

Pushing back her hat, she saw the girls beckoning, felt that the critical moment had come, and catching up her oars, rowed bravely on, though her cheeks reddened and her heart beat, for this venture was her last hope, and on its success depended the desire of her life. As the boat approached, the watchers forgot its cargo to look with surprise and pleasure at its rower, for she was not the rough country lass they expected to see, but a really splendid girl of fifteen, tall, broad-shouldered, bright-eyed, and blooming, with a certain shy dignity of her own and a very sweet smile, as she nodded and pulled in with strong, steady strokes. Before they could offer help, she had risen, planted an oar in the water, and leaping to the shore, pulled her boat high up on the beach, offering her wares with wistful eyes and a very expressive wave of both brown hands.

"Everything is for sale, if you'll buy," said she.

Charmed with the novelty of this little adventure, the girls, after scampering to the bathing-houses for purses and portemonnaies, crowded around the boat like butterflies about a thistle, all eager to buy, and to discover who this bonny fisher-maiden might be.

"Oh, see these beauties!" "A dozen lilies for me!" "All the yellow flowers for me, they'll be so becoming at the dance to-night!" "Ow! that lob bites awfully!" "Where do you come from?" "Why have we never seen you before?"

These were some of the exclamations and questions showered upon Tilly, as she filled little birch-bark panniers with berries, dealt out flowers, or dispensed handfuls of shells. Her eyes shone, her cheeks glowed, and her heart danced in her bosom; for this was a better beginning than she had dared to hope for, and as the dimes tinkled into the tin pail she used for her till, it was the sweetest music she had ever heard. This hearty welcome banished her shyness; and in these eager, girlish customers she found it easy to confide.

"I'm from the light-house. You have never seen me because I never came before, except with fish for the hotel. But I mean to come every day, if folks will buy my things, for I want to make some money, and this is the only way in which I can do it."

Sophie glanced at the old hat and worn shoes of the speaker, and dropping a bright half-dollar into the pail, said in her pretty way:

"For me all these lovely shells. I will make necklaces of them for my people at home as souvenirs of this charming place. If you will bring me more, I shall be much grateful to you."

"Oh, thank you! I'll bring heaps; I know where to find beauties in places where other folks can't go. Please take these; you paid too much for the shells;" and quick to feel the kindness of the stranger, Tilly put into her hands a little bark canoe heaped with red raspberries.

Not to be outdone by the foreigner, the other girls emptied their purses and Tilly's boat also of all but the lobsters, which were ordered for the hotel.

"Is that jolly bird for sale?" asked Di, as the last berry vanished, pointing to the gull who was swimming near them while the chatter went on.

"If you can catch him," laughed Tilly, whose spirits were now the gayest of the party.

The girls dashed into the water, and with shrieks of merriment swam away to capture the gull, who paddled off as if he enjoyed the fun as much as they.

Leaving them to splash vainly to and fro, Tilly swung the creel to her shoulder and went off to leave her lobsters, longing to dance and sing to the music of the silver clinking in her pocket.

When she came back, the bird was far out of reach and the girls diving from her boat, which they had launched without leave. Too happy to care what happened now, Tilly threw herself down on the warm sand to plan a new and still finer cargo for the next day.

Sophie came and sat beside her while she dried her curly hair, and in five minutes her sympathetic face and sweet ways had won Tilly to tell all her hopes and cares and dreams.

"I want schooling, and I mean to have it. I've got no folks of my own; and uncle has married again, so he does n't need me now. If I only had a little money, I could go to school somewhere, and take care of myself. Last summer I worked at the hotel, but I did n't make much, and had to have good clothes, and that took my wages pretty much. Sewing is slow work, and baby-tending leaves me no time to study; so I've kept on at home picking berries and doing what I could to pick up enough to buy books. Aunt thinks I'm a fool; but uncle, he says, 'Go ahead, girl, and see what you can do.' And I mean to show him!"

Tilly's brown hand came down on the sand with a resolute thump; and her clear young eyes looked bravely out across the wide sea, as if far away in the blue distance she saw her hope happily fulfilled.

Sophie's eyes shone approval, for she understood this love of independence, and had come to America because she longed for new scenes and greater freedom than her native land could give her. Education is a large word, and both girls felt that desire for self-improvement that comes to all energetic natures. Sophie had laid a good foundation, but still desired more; while Tilly was just climbing up the first steep slope which rises to the heights few attain, yet all may strive for.

"That is beautiful! You will do it! I am glad to help you if I may. See, I have many books; will you take some of them? Come to my room to-morrow and take what will best please you. We will say nothing of it, and it will make me a truly great pleasure."

As Sophie spoke, her little white hand touched the strong, sunburned one that turned to meet and grasp hers with grateful warmth, while Tilly's face betrayed the hunger that possessed her, for it looked as a starving girl's would look when offered a generous meal.

"I *will* come. Thank you so much! I don't know anything, but just blunder along and do the best I can. I got so discouraged I was real desperate, and thought I'd have one try, and see if I could n't earn enough to get books to study this winter. Folks buy berries at the cottages; so I just added flowers and shells, and I'm going to bring my boxes of butterflies, birds' eggs, and seaweeds. I've got lots of such things; and people seem to like spending money down here. I often wish I had a little of what they throw away."

Tilly paused with a sigh, then laughed as an impatient movement caused a silver clink; and slapping her pocket, she added gayly, —

"I won't blame 'em if they'll only throw their money in here."

Sophie's hand went involuntarily toward her own pocket, where lay a plump purse, for papa was generous, and simple Sophie had few wants. But something in the intelligent face opposite made her hesitate to offer as a gift what she felt sure Tilly would refuse, preferring to earn her education if she could.

"Come often, then, and let me exchange these stupid bills for the lovely things you bring. We will come this afternoon to see you if we may, and I shall like the butterflies. I try to catch them; but people tell me I am too old to run, so I have not many."

Proposed in this way, Tilly fell into the little trap, and presently rowed away with all her might to set her possessions in order, and put her precious earnings in a safe place. The mermaids clung about the boat as long as they dared, making a pretty tableau for the artists on the rocks, then swam to shore, more than ever eager for the picnic on Light-house Island.

They went, and had a merry time; while Tilly did the honors and showed them a room full of treasures gathered from earth, air, and water, for she led a lonely life, and found friends among the fishes, made playmates of the birds, and studied rocks and flowers, clouds and waves, when books were wanting.

The girls bought gulls' wings for their hats, queer and lovely shells, eggs and insects, seaweeds and carved wood, and for their small brothers, birch baskets and toy ships, made by Uncle Hiram, who had been a sailor.

When Tilly had sold nearly everything she possessed (for Fanny and

Sophie bought whatever the others declined), she made a fire of drift-wood on the rocks, cooked fish for supper, and kept them till moonrise, telling sea stories or singing old songs, as if she could not do enough for these good fairies who had come to her when life looked hardest and the future very dark. Then she rowed them home, and promising to bring loads of fruit and flowers every day, went back along a shining road, to find a great bundle of books in her dismantled room, and to fall asleep with wet eye-lashes and a happy heart.

II

For a month Tilly went daily to the Point with a cargo of pretty merchandise, for her patrons increased; and soon the ladies engaged her berries, the boys ordered boats enough to supply a navy, the children clamored for shells, and the girls depended on her for bouquets and garlands for the dances that ended every summer day. Uncle Hiram's fish was in demand when such a comely saleswoman offered it, so he let Tilly have her way, glad to see the old tobacco-pouch in which she kept her cash fill fast with well-earned money.

She really began to feel that her dream was coming true, and she would be able to go to the town and study in some great school, eking out her little fund with light work. The other girls soon lost their interest in her, but Sophie never did; and many a book went to the island in the empty baskets, many a helpful word was said over the lilies or wild honeysuckle Sophie loved to wear, and many a lesson was given in the bare room in the light-house tower which no one knew about but the gulls and the sea-winds sweeping by the little window where the two heads leaned together over one page.

"You will do it, Tilly, I am very sure. Such a will and such a memory will make a way for you; and one day I shall see you teaching as you wish. Keep the brave heart, and all will be well with you," said Sophie, when the grand breaking-up came in September, and the girls were parting down behind the deserted bath-houses.

"Oh, Miss Sophie, what should I have done without you? Don't think I have n't seen and known all the kind things you have said and done for me. I'll never forget 'em; and I do hope I'll be able to thank you some day," cried grateful Tilly, with tears in her clear eyes that seldom wept over her own troubles.

"I am thanked if you do well. Adieu; write to me, and remember always that I am your friend."

Then they kissed with girlish warmth, and Tilly rowed away to the lonely island; while Sophie lingered on the shore, her handkerchief fluttering in the wind, till the boat vanished and the waves had washed away their footprints on the sand.

III

December snow was falling fast, and the wintry wind whistled through the streets; but it was warm and cosey in the luxurious parlor where Di and Do were sitting making Christmas presents, and planning what they would wear at the party Fanny was to give on Christmas Eve.

"If I can get mamma to buy me a new dress, I shall have something yellow. It is always becoming to brunettes, and I'm so tired of red," said Di, giving a last touch to the lace that trimmed a blue satin *sachet* for Fanny.

"That will be lovely. I shall have pink, with roses of the same color. Under muslin it is perfectly sweet." And Dora eyed the sunflower she was embroidering as if she already saw the new toilet before her.

"Fan always wears blue, so we shall make a nice contrast. She is coming over to show me about finishing off my banner-screen; and I asked Sophie to come with her. I want to know what *she* is going to wear," said Di, taking a little sniff at the violet-scented bag.

"That old white cashmere. Just think! I asked her why she did n't get a new one, and she laughed and said she could n't afford it. Fan told me Sophie's father sent her a hundred dollars not long ago, yet she has n't got a thing that we know of. I do think she's mean."

"She bought a great bundle of books. I was there when the parcel came, and I peeped while she was out of the room, because she put it away in a great hurry. I'm afraid she *is* mean, for she never buys a bit of candy, and she wears shabby boots and gloves, and she has made over her old hat instead of having that lovely one with the pheasant's breast in it."

"She's very queer; but I can't help liking her, she's so pretty and bright and obliging. I'd give anything if I could speak three languages and play as she does."

"So would I. It seems so elegant to be able to talk to foreigners. Papa had some Frenchmen to dinner the other day, and they were so pleased to find they need n't speak English to Sophie. I could n't get on at all; and I was so mortified when papa said all the money he had spent on my languages was thrown away."

"I would n't mind. It's so much easier to learn those things abroad, she would be a goose if she did n't speak French better than we do. There's Fan! she looks as if something had happened. I hope no one is ill and the party spoiled."

As Dora spoke, both girls looked out to see Fanny shaking the snow from her seal-skin sack on the doorstep; then Do hastened to meet her, while Di hid the *sachet,* and was hard at work on an old-gold sofa cushion when the new-comer entered.

"What's the matter? Where's Sophie?" exclaimed the girls together, as Fan threw off her wraps and sat down with a tragic sigh.

"She will be along in a few minutes. I'm disappointed in her! I would n't have believed it if I had n't seen them. Promise not to breathe a word to a living soul, and I'll tell you something dreadful," began Fanny, in a tone that caused her friends to drop their work and draw their chairs nearer, as they solemnly vowed eternal silence.

"I've seen Sophie's Christmas presents, — all but mine; and they are just nothing at all! She has n't bought a thing, not even ribbons, lace, or silk, to make up prettily as we do. Only a painted shell for one, an acorn emery for another, her ivory fan with a new tassel for a third, and I suspect one of those nice handkerchiefs embroidered by the nuns for me, or her silver filigree necklace. I saw the box in the drawer with the other things. She's knit woollen cuffs and tippets for the children, and got some eight-cent calico gowns for the servants. I don't know how people do things in Switzerland, but I do know that if *I* had a hundred dollars in my pocket, I would be more generous than that!"

As Fanny paused, out of breath, Di and Do groaned in sympathy, for this was indeed a sad state of things; because the girls had a code that Christmas being the season for gifts, extravagance would be forgiven then as at no other time.

"I have a lovely smelling-bottle for her; but I've a great mind not to give it now," cried Di, feeling defrauded of the bracelet she had plainly hinted she would like.

"I shall heap coals of fire on her head by giving her *that*;" and Dora displayed a very useless but very pretty apron of muslin, lace, and carnation ribbon.

"It is n't the worth of the things. I don't care for that so much as I do for being disappointed in her; and I have been lately in more ways than one," said Fanny, listlessly taking up the screen she was to finish. "She used to tell me everything, and now she does n't. I'm sure she has some sort of a secret; and I do think *I* ought to know it. I found her smiling over a letter one day; and she whisked it into her pocket and never said a word about it. I always stood by her, and I do feel hurt."

"I should think you might! It's real naughty of her, and I shall tell her so! Perhaps she'll confide in you then, and you can just give *me* a hint; I always liked Sophie, and never thought of not giving *my* present," said Dora, persuasively, for both girls were now dying with curiosity to know the secret.

"I'll have it out of her, without any dodging or bribing. I'm not afraid of any one, and I shall ask her straight out, no matter how much she scowls at me," said dauntless Di, with a threatening nod.

"There she is! Let us see you do it now!" cried Fanny, as the bell rang, and a clear voice was heard a moment later asking if Mademoiselle was in.

"You shall!" and Di looked ready for any audacity.

"I'll wager a box of candy that you don't find out a thing," whispered Do.

"Done!" answered Di, and then turned to meet Sophie, who came in looking as fresh as an Alpine rose with the wintry wind.

"You dear thing! we were just talking of you. Sit here and get warm, and let us show you our gifts. We are almost done, but it seems as if it got to be a harder job each Christmas. Don't you find it so?"

"But no; I think it the most charming work of all the year," answered Sophie, greeting her friend, and putting her well-worn boots toward the fire to dry.

"Perhaps you don't make as much of Christmas as we do, or give such expensive presents. That would make a great difference, you know," said Di, as she lifted a cloth from the table where her own generous store of gifts was set forth.

"I had a piano last year, a set of jewels, and many pretty trifles from all at home. Here is one;" and pulling the fine gold chain hidden under her frills, Sophie showed a locket set thick with pearls, containing a picture of her mother.

"It must be so nice to be rich, and able to make such fine presents. I've got something for you; but I shall be ashamed of it after I see your gift to me, I'm afraid."

Fan and Dora were working as if their bread depended on it, while Di, with a naughty twinkle in her eye, affected to be rearranging her pretty table as she talked.

"Do not fear that; my gifts this year are very simple ones. I did not know your custom, and now it is too late. My comfort is that you need nothing, and having so much, you will not care for my — what you call — coming short."

Was it the fire that made Sophie's face look so hot, and a cold that gave a husky sort of tone to her usually clear voice? A curious expression came into her face as her eyes roved from the table to the gay trifles in her friend's hands; and she opened her lips as if to add something impulsively.

But nothing came, and for a moment she looked straight out at the storm as if she had forgotten where she was.

" 'Shortcoming' is the proper way to speak it. But never mind that, and tell me why you say 'too late'?" asked Di, bent on winning her wager.

"Christmas comes in three days, and I have no time," began Sophie.

"But with money one can buy plenty of lovely things in one day," said Di.

"No, it is better to put a little love and hard work into what we give to friends. I have done that with my trifles, and another year I shall be more ready."

There was an uncomfortable pause, for Sophie did not speak with her usual frankness, but looked both proud and ashamed, and seemed anxious to change the subject, as she began to admire Dora's work, which had made very little progress during the last fifteen minutes.

Fanny glanced at Di with a smile that made the other toss her head and return to the charge with renewed vigor.

"Sophie, will you do me a favor?"

"With much pleasure."

"Do has promised me a whole box of French bonbons, and if you will answer three questions, you shall have it."

"*Allóns,*" said Sophie, smiling.

"Have n't you a secret?" asked Di, gravely.

"Yes."

"Will you tell us?"

"No."

Di paused before she asked her last question, and Fan and Dora waited breathlessly, while Sophie knit her brows and looked uneasy.

"Why not?"

"Because I do not wish to tell it."

"Will you tell if we guess?"

"Try."

"You are engaged."

At this absurd suggestion Sophie laughed gayly, and shook her curly head.

"Do you think we are betrothed at sixteen in my country?"

"I *know* that is an engagement ring, — you made such a time about it when you lost it in the water, and cried for joy when Tilly dived and found it."

"Ah, yes, I was truly glad. Dear Tilly, never do I forget that kindness!" and Sophie kissed the little pearl ring in her impulsive way, while her eyes sparkled and the frown vanished.

[375]

"I *know* a sweetheart gave it," insisted Di, sure now she had found a clew to the secret.

"He did," and Sophie hung her head in a sentimental way that made the three girls crowd nearer with faces full of interest.

"Do tell us all about it, dear. It's *so* interesting to hear love-stories. What is his name?" cried Dora.

"Hermann," simpered Sophie, drooping still more, while her lips trembled with suppressed emotion of some sort.

"How lovely!" sighed Fanny, who was very romantic.

"Tell on, do! Is he handsome?"

"To me the finest man in all the world," confessed Sophie, as she hid her face.

"And you love him?"

"I adore him!" and Sophie clasped her hands so dramatically that the girls were a little startled, yet charmed at this discovery.

"Have you his picture?" asked Di, feeling that she had won her wager now.

"Yes," and pulling out the locket again, Sophie showed in the other side the face of a fine old gentleman who looked very like herself.

"It's your father!" exclaimed Fanny, rolling her blue eyes excitedly. "You are a humbug!" cried Dora. "Then you fibbed about the ring," said Di crossly.

"Never! It is mamma's betrothal ring; but her finger grew too plump, and when I left home she gave the ring to me as a charm to keep me safe. Ah, ha! I have my little joke as well as you, and the laugh is for me this time." And falling back among the sofa cushions, Sophie enjoyed it as only a gay girl could. Do and Fanny joined her; but Di was much disgusted, and vowed she *would* discover the secret and keep all the bonbons to herself.

"You are most welcome; but I will not tell until I like, and then to Fanny first. She will not have ridicule for what I do, but say it is well, and be glad with me. Come now and work. I will plait these ribbons, or paint a wild rose on this pretty fan. It is too plain now. Will you that I do it, dear Di?"

The kind tone and the prospect of such an ornament to her gift appeased Di somewhat; but the mirthful malice in Sophie's eyes made the other more than ever determined to be even with her by and by.

Christmas Eve came, and found Di still in the dark, which fact nettled her sadly, for Sophie tormented her and amused the other girls by pretended confidences and dark hints at the mystery which might never, never be disclosed.

Fan had determined to have an unusually jolly party; so she invited only her chosen friends, and opened the festivities with a Christmas tree, as the prettiest way of exchanging gifts and providing jokes for the evening in the shape of delusive bottles, animals full of candy, and every sort of musical instrument to be used in an impromptu concert afterward. The presents to one another were done up in secure parcels, so that they might burst upon the public eye in all their freshness. Di was very curious to know what Fan was going to give her, — for Fanny was a generous creature and loved to give. Di was a little jealous of her love for Sophie, and could n't rest till she discovered which was to get the finer gift.

So she went early and slipped into the room where the tree stood, to peep and pick a bit, as well as to hang up a few trifles of her own. She guessed several things by feeling the parcels; but one excited her curiosity intensely, and she could not resist turning it about and pulling up one corner of the lid. It was a flat box, prettily ornamented with sea-weeds like red lace, and tied with scarlet ribbons. A tantalizing glimpse of jeweler's cotton, gold clasps, and something rose-colored conquered Di's last scruples; and she was just about to untie the ribbons when she heard Fanny's voice, and had only time to replace the box, pick up a paper that had fallen out of it, and fly up the backstairs to the dressing-room, where she found Sophie and Dora surveying each other as girls always do before they go down.

"You look like a daisy," cried Di, admiring Dora with great interest, because she felt ashamed of her prying, and the stolen note in her pocket.

"And you like a dandelion," returned Do, falling back a step to get a good view of Di's gold-colored dress and black velvet bows.

"Sophie is a lily of the valley, all in green and white," added Fanny, coming in with her own blue skirts waving in the breeze.

"It does me very well. Little girls do not need grand toilets, and I am fine enough for a 'peasant,' " laughed Sophie, as she settled the fresh ribbons on her simple white cashmere and the holly wreath in her brown hair, but secretly longing for the fine dress she might have had.

"Why did n't you wear your silver necklace? It would be lovely on your pretty neck," said Di, longing to know if she had given the trinket away.

But Sophie was not to be caught, and said with a contented smile, "I do not care for ornaments unless some one I love gives me them. I had red roses for my *bouquet de corsage*; but the poor Madame Page was so *triste*, I left them on her table to remember her of me. It seemed so heartless to go and dance while she had only pain; but she wished it."

"Dear little Sophie, how good you are!" and warm-hearted Fan kissed the blooming face that needed no roses to make it sweet and gay.

Half an hour later, twenty girls and boys were dancing round the brilliant tree. Then its boughs were stripped. Every one seemed contented; even Sophie's little gifts gave pleasure, because with each went a merry or affectionate verse, which made great fun on being read aloud. She was quite loaded with pretty things, and had no words to express her gratitude and pleasure.

"Ah, you are all so good to me! and I have nothing beautiful for you. I receive much and give little, but I cannot help it! Wait a little and I will redeem myself," she said to Fanny, with eyes full of tears, and a lap heaped with gay and useful things.

"Never mind that now; but look at this, for here's still another offering of friendship, and a very charming one, to judge by the outside," answered Fan, bringing the white box with the sea-weed ornaments.

Sophie opened it, and cries of admiration followed, for lying on the soft cotton was a lovely set of coral. Rosy pink branches, highly polished and fastened with gold clasps, formed necklace, bracelets, and a spray for the bosom. No note or card appeared, and the girls crowded round to admire and wonder who could have sent so valuable a gift.

"Can't you guess, Sophie?" cried Dora, longing to own the pretty things.

"I should believe I knew, but it is too costly. How came the parcel, Fan? I think you must know all," and Sophie turned the box about, searching vainly for a name.

"An expressman left it, and Jane took off the wet paper and put it on my table with the other things. Here's the wrapper; do you know that writing?" and Fan offered the brown paper which she had kept.

"No; and the label is all mud, so I cannot see the place. Ah, well, I shall discover some day, but I should like to thank this generous friend at once. See now, how fine I am! I do myself the honor to wear them at once."

Smiling with girlish delight at her pretty ornaments, Sophie clasped the bracelets on her round arms, the necklace about her white throat, and set the rosy spray in the lace on her bosom. Then she took a little dance down the room and found herself before Di, who was looking at her with an expression of naughty satisfaction on her face.

"Don't you wish you knew who sent them?"

"Indeed, yes;" and Sophie paused abruptly.

"Well, *I* know, and *I* won't tell till I like. It's my turn to have a secret; and I mean to keep it."

"But it is not right," began Sophie, with indignation.

"Tell me yours, and I'll tell mine," said Di, teasingly.

"I will not! You have no right to touch my gifts, and I am sure you have done it, else how know you who sends this fine *cadeau?*" cried Sophie, with the flash Di liked to see.

Here Fanny interposed, "If you have any note or card belonging to Sophie, give it up at once. She shall not be tormented. Out with it, Di. I see your hand in your pocket, and I'm sure you have been in mischief."

"Take your old letter, then. I know what's in it; and if I can't keep my secret for fun, Sophie shall not have hers. That Tilly sent the coral, and Sophie spent her hundred dollars in books and clothes for that queer girl, who'd better stay among her lobsters than try to be a lady," cried Di, bent on telling all she knew, while Sophie was reading her letter eagerly.

"Is it true?" asked Dora, for the four girls were in a corner together, and the rest of the company busy pulling crackers.

"Just like her! I thought it was that; but she would n't tell. Tell us now, Sophie, for *I* think it was truly sweet and beautiful to help that poor girl, and let us say hard things of you," cried Fanny, as her friend looked up with a face and a heart too full of happiness to help overflowing into words.

"Yes; I will tell you now. It was foolish, perhaps; but I did not want to be praised, and I loved to help that good Tilly. You know she worked all summer and made a little sum. So glad, so proud she was, and planned to study that she might go to school this winter. Well, in October the uncle fell very ill, and Tilly gave all her money for the doctors. The uncle had been kind to her, she did not forget; she was glad to help, and told no one but me. Then I said, 'What better can I do with my father's gift than give it to the dear creature, and let her lose no time?' I do it; she will not at first, but I write and say, 'It must be,' and she submits. She is made neat with some little dresses, and she goes at last, to be so happy and do so well that I am proud of her. Is not that better than fine toilets and rich gifts to those who need nothing? Truly, yes! yet I confess it cost me pain to give up my plans for Christmas, and to seem selfish or ungrateful. Forgive me that."

"Yes, indeed, you dear generous thing!" cried Fan and Dora, touched by the truth.

"But how came Tilly to send you such a splendid present?" asked Di. "Should n't think you'd like her to spend your money in such things."

"She did not. A sea-captain, a friend of the uncle, gave her these lovely ornaments, and she sends them to me with a letter that is more precious than all the coral in the sea. I cannot read it; but of all my gifts *this* is the dearest and the best!"

Sophie had spoken eagerly, and her face, her voice, her gestures, made the little story eloquent; but with the last words she clasped the letter to her bosom as if it well repaid her for all the sacrifices she had made. They might seem small to others, but she was sensitive and proud, anxious to be loved in the strange country, and fond of giving, so it cost her many tears to seem mean and thoughtless, to go poorly dressed, and be thought hardly of by those she wished to please. She did not like to tell of her own generosity, because it seemed like boasting; and she was not sure that it had been wise to give so much. Therefore, she waited to see if Tilly was worthy of the trust reposed in her; and she now found a balm for many wounds in the loving letter that came with the beautiful and unexpected gift.

Di listened with hot cheeks, and when Sophie paused, she whispered regretfully, —

"Forgive me, I was wrong! I'll keep your gift all my life to remember you by, for you *are* the best and the dearest girl I know."

Then with a hasty kiss she ran away, carrying with great care the white shell on which Sophie had painted a dainty little picture of the mermaids waiting for the pretty boat that brought good fortune to poor Tilly, and this lesson to those who were hereafter her faithful friends.

Pansies

From *A Garland for Girls* (Boston: Roberts Brothers, 1888)

They are never alone that are accompanied with noble thoughts.
— SIR PHILIP SIDNEY.

I'VE FINISHED MY BOOK, and now what *can* I do till this tiresome rain is over?" exclaimed Carrie, as she lay back on the couch with a yawn of weariness.

"Take another and a better book; the house is full of them, and this is a rare chance for a feast on the best," answered Alice, looking over the pile of volumes in her lap, as she sat on the floor before one of the tall bookcases that lined the room.

"Not being a book-worm like you, I can't read forever, and you need n't sniff at 'Wanda,' for it's perfectly thrilling!" cried Carrie, regretfully turning the crumpled leaves of the Seaside Library copy of that interminable and impossible tale.

"We should read to improve our minds, and that rubbish is only a waste of time," began Alice, in a warning tone, as she looked up from "Romola," over which she had been poring with the delight one feels in meeting an old friend.

"I don't *wish* to improve my mind, thank you: I read for amusement in vacation time, and don't want to see any moral works till next autumn. I get enough of them in school. This is n't 'rubbish'! It's full of fine descriptions of scenery —"

"Which you skip by the page, I've seen you do it," said Eva, the third young girl in the library, as she shut up the stout book on her knee and began to knit as if this sudden outburst of chat disturbed her enjoyment of "The Dove in the Eagle's Nest."

"I do at first, being carried away by my interest in the people, but I almost always go back and read them afterward," protested Carrie. "You know *you* like to hear about nice clothes, Eva, and Wanda's were simply gorgeous; white velvet and a rope of pearls is one costume; gray velvet and a silver girdle another; and Idalia was all a 'shower of perfumed laces,' and scarlet and gold satin mask dresses, or primrose silk with violets, so lovely! I do revel in 'em!"

Both girls laughed as Carrie reeled off this list of elegances, with the relish of a French modiste.

"Well, I'm poor and can't have as many pretty things as I want, so it *is* delightful to read about women who wear white quilted satin dressing-gowns and olive velvet trains with Mechlin lace sweepers to them. Diamonds as large as nuts, and rivers of opals and sapphires, and rubies and pearls, are great fun to read of, if you never even get a look at real ones. I don't believe the love part does me a bit of harm, for we never see such languid swells in America, nor such lovely, naughty ladies; and Ouida scolds them all, so of course she does n't approve of them, and that's moral, I'm sure."

But Alice shook her head again, as Carrie paused, out of breath, and said in her serious way: "That's the harm of it all. False and foolish things are made interesting, and we read for that, not for any lesson there may be hidden under the velvet and jewels and fine words of your splendid men and women. Now, *this* book is a wonderful picture of Florence in old times, and the famous people who really lived are painted in it, and it has a true and clean moral that we can all see, and one feels wiser and better for reading it. I do wish you'd leave those trashy things and try something really good."

"I hate George Eliot, — so awfully wise and preachy and dismal! I really could n't wade through 'Daniel Deronda,' though 'The Mill on the Floss' was n't bad," answered Carrie, with another yawn, as she recalled the Jew Mordecai's long speeches, and Daniel's meditations.

"I know you'd like this," said Eva, patting her book with an air of calm content; for she was a modest, common-sense little body, full of innocent fancies and the mildest sort of romance. "I love dear Miss Yonge, with her nice, large families, and their trials, and their pious ways, and pleasant homes full of brothers and sisters, and good fathers and mothers. I'm never tired of them, and have read 'Daisy Chain' nine times at least."

"I used to like them, and still think them good for young girls, with our own 'Queechy' and 'Wide, Wide World,' and books of that kind. Now I'm eighteen I prefer stronger novels, and books by great men and women, because these are always talked about by cultivated people, and when I go into society next winter I wish to be able to listen intelligently, and know what to admire."

"That's all very well for you, Alice; you were always poking over books, and I dare say you will write them some day, or be a blue-stocking. But I've got another year to study and fuss over my education, and I'm going to enjoy myself all I can, and leave the wise books till I come out."

"But, Carrie, there won't be any time to read them; you'll be so busy with parties, and beaux, and travelling, and such things. I *would* take Alice's advice and read up a little now; it's so nice to know useful things, and be able to find help and comfort in good books when trouble comes, as Ellen Montgomery and Fleda did, and Ethel, and the other girls in Miss Yonge's stories," said Eva, earnestly, remembering how much the efforts of those natural little heroines had helped her in her own struggles for self-control and the cheerful bearing of the burdens which come to all.

"I don't want to be a priggish Ellen, or a moral Fleda, and I do detest bothering about self-improvement all the time. I know I ought, but I'd rather wait another year or two, and enjoy my vanities in peace just a *little* longer." And Carrie tucked Wanda under the sofa pillow, as if a trifle ashamed of her society, with Eva's innocent eyes upon her own, and Alice sadly regarding her over the rampart of wise books, which kept growing higher as the eager girl found more and more treasures in this richly stored library.

A little silence followed, broken only by the patter of the rain without, the crackle of the wood fire within, and the scratch of a busy pen from a curtained recess at the end of the long room. In the sudden hush the girls heard it and remembered that they were not alone.

"She must have heard every word we said!" and Carrie sat up with a dismayed face as she spoke in a whisper.

Eva laughed, but Alice shrugged her shoulders, and said tranquilly, "I don't mind. She would n't expect much wisdom from school-girls."

This was cold comfort to Carrie, who was painfully conscious of having been a particularly silly school-girl just then. So she gave a groan and lay down again, wishing she had not expressed her views quite so freely, and had kept Wanda for the privacy of her own room.

The three girls were the guests of a delightful old lady, who had known their mothers and was fond of renewing her acquaintance with them through their daughters. She loved young people, and each summer invited parties of them to enjoy the delights of her beautiful country house, where she lived alone now, being the childless widow of a somewhat celebrated man. She made it very pleasant for her guests, leaving them free to employ a part of the day as they liked, providing the best of company at dinner, gay revels in the evening, and a large house full of curious and interesting things to examine at their leisure.

The rain had spoiled a pleasant plan, and business letters had made it necessary for Mrs. Warburton to leave the three to their own devices after lunch. They had read quietly for several hours, and their hostess was just finishing her last letter when fragments of the conversation reached her ear. She listened with amusement, unconscious that they had forgotten her presence, finding the different views very characteristic, and easily explained by the difference of the homes out of which the three friends came.

Alice was the only daughter of a scholarly man and a brilliant woman; therefore her love of books and desire to cultivate her mind was very natural, but the danger in her case would be in the neglect of other things equally important, too varied reading, and a superficial knowledge of many authors rather than a true appreciation of a few of the best and greatest. Eva was one of many children in a happy home, with a busy father, a pious mother, and many domestic cares, as well as joys, already falling to the dutiful girl's lot. Her instincts were sweet and unspoiled, and she only needed to be shown where to find new and better helpers for the real trials of life, when the childish heroines she loved could no longer serve her in the years to come.

Carrie was one of the ambitious yet commonplace girls who wish to shine, without knowing the difference between the glitter of a candle which attracts moths, and the serene light of a star, or the cheery glow of a fire round which all love to gather. Her mother's aims were not high, and the two pretty daughters knew that she desired good matches for them, educated them for that end, and expected them to do their part when the time came. The elder sister was now at a watering-place with her mother, and Carrie hoped that a letter would soon come telling her that Mary was settled. During her stay with Mrs. Warburton she had learned a good deal, and was unconsciously contrasting the life here with the frivolous one at home, made up of public show and private sacrifice of comfort, dignity, and peace. Here were people who dressed simply, enjoyed conversation, kept up their accomplishments even when old, and were so busy, lovable, and charming, that poor Carrie often felt vulgar, ignorant, and mortified among them, in spite of their fine breeding and kindliness. The society Mrs. Warburton drew about her was the best, and old and young, rich and poor, wise and simple, all seemed genuine, — glad to give or receive, enjoy and rest, and then go out to their work refreshed by the influences of the place and the sweet old lady who made it what it was. The girls would soon begin life for themselves, and it was well that they had this little glimpse of really good society before they left the shelter of home to choose friends, pleasures, and pursuits for themselves, as all young women do when once launched.

The sudden silence and then the whispers suggested to the listener that she had perhaps heard something not meant for her ear; so she presently emerged with her letters, and said, as she came smiling toward the group about the fire, —

"How are you getting through this long, dull afternoon, my dears? Quiet as mice till just now. What woke you up? A battle of the books? Alice looks as if she had laid in plenty of ammunition, and you were preparing to besiege her."

The girls laughed, and all rose, for Madam Warburton was a stately old lady, and people involuntarily treated her with great respect, even in this mannerless age.

"We were only talking about books," began Carrie, deeply grateful that Wanda was safely out of sight.

"And we could n't agree," added Eva, running to ring the bell for the man to take the letters, for she was used to these little offices at home, and loved to wait on Madam.

"Thanks, my love. Now let us talk a little, if you are tired of reading, and if you like to let me share the discussion. Comparing tastes in literature is always a pleasure, and I used to enjoy talking over books with my girl friends more than anything else."

As she spoke, Mrs. Warburton sat down in the chair which Alice rolled up, drew Eva to the cushion at her feet, and nodded to the others as they settled again, with interested faces, one at the table where the pile of chosen volumes now lay, the other erect upon the couch where she had been practising the poses "full of languid grace," so much affected by her favorite heroines.

"Carrie was laughing at me for liking wise books and wanting to improve my mind. Is it foolish and a waste of time?" asked Alice, eager to convince her friend and secure so powerful an ally.

"No, my dear, it is a very sensible desire, and I wish more girls had it. Only don't be greedy, and read too much; cramming and smattering is as bad as promiscuous novel-reading, or no reading at all. Choose carefully, read intelligently, and digest thoroughly each book, and then you make it your own," answered Mrs. Warburton, quite in her element now, for she loved to give advice, as most old ladies do.

"But how can we know *what* to read if we may n't follow our tastes?" said Carrie, trying to be interested and "intelligent" in spite of her fear that a "schoolmarmy" lecture was in store for her.

"Ask advice, and so cultivate a true and refined taste. I always judge people's characters a good deal by the books they like, as well as by the company they keep; so one should be careful, for this is a pretty good test. Another is, be sure that whatever will not bear reading *aloud* is not fit to read to one's self. Many young girls ignorantly or curiously take up books quite worthless, and really harmful, because under the fine writing and brilliant color lurks immorality or the false sentiment which gives wrong ideas of life and things which should be sacred. They think, perhaps, that no one knows this taste of theirs; but they are mistaken, for it shows itself in many ways, and betrays them. Attitudes, looks, careless words, and a morbid or foolishly romantic view of certain things, show plainly that the maidenly instincts are blunted, and harm done that perhaps can never be repaired."

Mrs. Warburton kept her eyes fixed upon the tall andirons as if gravely reproving them, which was a great relief to Carrie, whose cheeks glowed as she stirred uneasily and took up a screen as if to guard them from the fire. But conscience pricked her sharply, and memory, like a traitor, recalled many a passage or scene in her favorite books which she could not have read aloud even to that old lady, though she enjoyed them in private. Nothing very bad, but false and foolish, poor food for a lively fancy and young mind to feed on, as the weariness or excitement which always followed plainly proved, since one should feel refreshed, not cloyed, with an intellectual feast.

Alice, with both elbows on the table, listened with wide-awake eyes, and Eva watched the rain-drops trickle down the pane with an intent expression, as if asking herself if she had ever done this naughty thing.

"Then there is another fault," continued Mrs. Warburton, well knowing that her first shot had hit its mark, and anxious to be just. "Some book-loving lassies have a mania for trying to read *everything,* and dip into works far beyond their powers, or try too many different kinds of self-improvement at once. So they get a muddle of useless things into their heads, instead of well-assorted ideas and real knowledge. They must learn to wait and select; for each age has its proper class of books, and what is Greek to us at eighteen may be just what we need at thirty. One can get mental dyspepsia on meat and wine as well as on ice-cream and frosted cake, you know."

Alice smiled; and pushed away four of the eight books she had selected, as if afraid she *had* been greedy, and now felt that it was best to wait a little.

Eva looked up with some anxiety in her frank eyes as she said, "Now it is my turn. Must I give up my dear homely books, and take to Ruskin, Kant, or Plato?"

Mrs. Warburton laughed, as she stroked the pretty brown head at her knee.

"Not yet, my love, perhaps never, for those are not the masters you need, I fancy. Since you like stories about every-day people, try some of the fine biographies of real men and women about whom you should know something. You will find their lives full of stirring, helpful, and lovely experiences, and in reading of these you will get courage and hope and faith to bear your own trials as they come. True stories suit you, and are the best, for there we get real tragedy and comedy, and the lessons all must learn."

"Thank you! I will begin at once if you will kindly give me a list of such as would be good for me," cried Eva, with the sweet docility of one eager to be all that is lovable and wise in woman.

"Give us a list, and we will try to improve in the best way. You know what we need, and love to help foolish girls, or you would n't be so kind and patient with us," said Alice, going to sit beside Carrie, hoping for much discussion of this, to her, very interesting subject.

"I will, with pleasure; but I read few modern novels, so I may not be a good judge there. Most of them seem very poor stuff, and I cannot waste time even to *skim* them as some people do. I still like the old-fashioned ones I read as a girl, though you would laugh at them. Did any of you ever read 'Thaddeus of Warsaw'?"

"I have, and thought it very funny; so were 'Evelina' and 'Cecilia.' I wanted to try Smollett and Fielding, after reading some fine essays about them, but Papa told me I must wait," said Alice.

"Ah, my dears, in my day, Thaddeus was our hero, and we thought the scene where he and Miss Beaufort are in the Park a most thrilling one. Two fops ask Thaddeus where he got his boots, and he replies, with withering dignity, 'Where I got my sword, gentlemen.' I treasured the picture of that episode for a long time. Thaddeus wears a hat as full of black plumes as a hearse, Hessian boots with tassels, and leans over Mary, who languishes on the seat in a short-waisted gown, limp scarf, poke bonnet, and large bag, — the height of elegance then, but very funny now. Then William Wallace in 'Scottish Chiefs.' Bless me! we cried over him as much as you do over your 'Heir of Clifton,' or whatever the boy's name is. You would n't get through it, I fancy; and as for poor, dear, prosy Richardson, his letter-writing heroines would bore you to death. Just imagine a lover saying to a friend, 'I begged my angel to stay and sip one dish of tea. She sipped one dish and flew.' "

"Now, I'm sure that's sillier than anything the Duchess ever wrote with her five-o'clock teas and flirtations over plum-cake on lawns," cried Carrie, as they all laughed at the immortal Lovelace.

"I never read Richardson, but he could n't be duller than Henry James, with his everlasting stories, full of people who talk a great deal and amount to nothing. *I* like the older novels best, and enjoy some of Scott's and Miss Edgeworth's better than Howells's, or any of the modern realistic writers, with their elevators, and paint-pots, and every-day people," said Alice, who wasted little time on light literature.

"I'm glad to hear you say so, for I have an old-fashioned fancy that I'd rather read about people as they *were,* for that is history, or as they *might* and should be, for that helps us in our own efforts; not as they *are,* for that we know, and are all sufficiently commonplace ourselves, to be the better for a nobler and wider view of life and men than any we are apt to get, so busy are we earning daily bread, or running after fortune, honor, or some other bubble. But I must n't lecture, or I shall bore you, and forget that I am your hostess, whose duty it is to amuse."

As Mrs. Warburton paused, Carrie, anxious to change the subject, said, with her eyes on a curious jewel which the old lady wore, "I also like true stories, and you promised to tell us about that lovely pin some day. This is just the time for it, — please do."

"With pleasure, for the little romance is quite *apropos* to our present chat. It is a very simple tale, and rather sad, but it had a great influence on my life, and this brooch is very dear to me."

As Mrs. Warburton sat silent a moment, the girls all looked with in-

terest at the quaint pin which clasped the soft folds of muslin over the black
silk dress which was as becoming to the still handsome woman as the cap
on her white hair and the winter roses in her cheeks. The ornament was
in the shape of a pansy; its purple leaves were of amethyst, the yellow of
topaz, and in the middle lay a diamond drop of dew. Several letters were
delicately cut on its golden stem, and a guard pin showed how much its
wearer valued it.

"My sister Lucretia was a good deal older than I, for the three boys
came between," began Mrs. Warburton, still gazing at the fire, as if from
its ashes the past rose up bright and warm again. "She was a very lovely
and superior girl, and I looked up to her with wonder as well as adoration.
Others did the same, and at eighteen she was engaged to a charming man,
who would have made his mark had he lived. She was too young to marry
then, and Frank Lyman had a fine opening to practise his profession at the
South. So they parted for two years, and it was then that he gave her the
brooch, saying to her, as she whispered how lonely she should be without
him, 'This *pensée* is a happy, faithful *thought* of me. Wear it, dearest girl,
and don't pine while we are separated. Read and study, write much to me,
and remember, "They never are alone that are accompanied with noble
thoughts." ' "

"Was n't that sweet?" cried Eva, pleased with the beginning of the
tale.

"So romantic!" added Carrie, recalling the "amber amulet" one of her
pet heroes wore for years, and died kissing, after he had killed some fifty
Arabs in the desert.

"*Did* she read and study?" asked Alice, with a soft color in her cheek,
and eager eyes, for a budding romance was folded away in the depths of
her maidenly heart, and she liked a love story.

"I'll tell you what she did, for it was rather remarkable at that day,
when girls had little schooling, and picked up accomplishments as they
could. The first winter she read and studied at home, and wrote much to
Mr. Lyman. I have their letters now, and very fine ones they are, though
they would seem old-fashioned to you young things. Curious love letters, — full of advice, the discussion of books, report of progress, glad
praise, modest gratitude, happy plans, and a faithful affection that never
wavered, though Lucretia was beautiful and much admired, and the dear
fellow a great favorite among the brilliant Southern women.

"The second spring, Lucretia, anxious to waste no time, and ambitious to surprise Lyman, decided to go and study with old Dr. Gardener
at Portland. He fitted young men for college, was a friend of our father's,
and had a daughter who was a very wise and accomplished woman. That

was a very happy summer, and Lu got on so well that she begged to stay all winter. It was a rare chance, for there were no colleges for girls then, and very few advantages to be had, and the dear creature burned to improve every faculty, that she might be more worthy of her lover. She fitted herself for college with the youths there, and did wonders; for love sharpened her wits, and the thought of that happy meeting spurred her on to untiring exertion. Lyman was expected in May, and the wedding was to be in June; but, alas for the poor girl! the yellow-fever came, and he was one of the first victims. They never met again, and nothing was left her of all that happy time but his letters, his library, and the pansy."

Mrs. Warburton paused to wipe a few quiet tears from her eyes, while the girls sat in sympathetic silence.

"We thought it would kill her, that sudden change from love, hope, and happiness to sorrow, death, and solitude. But hearts don't break, my dears, if they know where to go for strength. Lucretia did, and after the first shock was over found comfort in her books, saying, with a brave, bright look, and the sweetest resignation, 'I must go on trying to be more worthy of him, for we shall meet again in God's good time and he shall see that I do not forget.'

"That was better than tears and lamentation, and the long years that followed were beautiful and busy ones, full of dutiful care for us at home after our mother died, of interest in all the good works of her time, and a steady, quiet effort to improve every faculty of her fine mind, till she was felt to be one of the noblest women in our city. Her influence was widespread; all the intelligent people sought her, and when she travelled she was welcome everywhere, for cultivated persons have a free-masonry of their own, and are recognized at once."

"Did she ever marry?" asked Carrie, feeling that no life could be quite successful without that great event.

"Never. She felt herself a widow, and wore black to the day of her death. Many men asked her hand, but she refused them all, and was the sweetest 'old maid' ever seen, — cheerful and serene to the very last, for she was ill a long time, and found her solace and stay still in the beloved books. Even when she could no longer read them, her memory supplied her with the mental food that kept her soul strong while her body failed. It was wonderful to see and hear her repeating fine lines, heroic sayings, and comforting psalms through the weary nights when no sleep would come, making friends and helpers of the poets, philosophers, and saints whom she knew and loved so well. It made death beautiful, and taught me how victorious an immortal soul can be over the ills that vex our mortal flesh.

"She died at dawn on Easter Sunday, after a quiet night, when she had given me her little legacy of letters, books, and the one jewel she had always worn, repeating her lover's words to comfort me. I had read the Commendatory Prayer, and as I finished she whispered, with a look of perfect peace, 'Shut the book, dear, I need study no more; I have hoped and believed, now I shall know;' and so went happily away to meet her lover after patient waiting."

The sigh of the wind was the only sound that broke the silence till the quiet voice went on again, as if it loved to tell the story, for the thought of soon seeing the beloved sister took the sadness from the memory of the past.

"I also found my solace in books, for I was very lonely when she was gone, my father being dead, the brothers married, and home desolate. I took to study and reading as a congenial employment, feeling no inclination to marry, and for many years was quite contented among my books. But in trying to follow in dear Lucretia's footsteps, I unconsciously fitted myself for the great honor and happiness of my life, and curiously enough I owed it to a book."

Mrs. Warburton smiled as she took up a shabby little volume from the table where Alice had laid it, and, quick to divine another romance, Eva said, like a story-loving child, "Do tell about it! The other was so sad."

"This begins merrily, and has a wedding in it, as young girls think all tales should. Well, when I was about thirty-five, I was invited to join a party of friends on a trip to Canada, that being the favorite jaunt in my young days. I'd been studying hard for some years, and needed rest, so I was glad to go. As a good book for an excursion, I took this Wordsworth in my bag. It is full of fine passages, you know, and I loved it, for it was one of the books given to Lucretia by her lover. We had a charming time, and were on our way to Quebec when my little adventure happened. I was in raptures over the grand St. Lawrence as we steamed slowly from Montreal that lovely summer day. I could not read, but sat on the upper deck, feasting my eyes and dreaming dreams as even staid maiden ladies will when out on a holiday. Suddenly I caught the sound of voices in earnest discussion on the lower deck, and, glancing down, saw several gentlemen leaning against the rail as they talked over certain events of great public interest at that moment. I knew that a party of distinguished persons were on board, as my friend's husband, Dr. Tracy, knew some of them, and pointed out Mr. Warburton as one of the rising scientific men of the day. I remembered that my sister had met him years ago, and much admired him both for his own gifts and because he had known Lyman. As other people were listening, I felt no delicacy about doing the same, for the conversation was an eloquent one, and well worth catching. So interested did I become that I forgot the great rafts floating by, the picturesque shores, the splendid river, and leaned nearer and nearer that no word might be lost, till my book slid out of my lap and fell straight down upon the head of one of the gentlemen, giving him a smart blow, and knocking his hat overboard."

"Oh, what *did* you do?" cried the girls, much amused at this unromantic catastrophe.

Mrs. Warburton clasped her hands dramatically, as her eyes twinkled and a pretty color came into her cheeks at the memory of that exciting moment.

"My dears, I could have dropped with mortification! What *could* I do but dodge and peep as I waited to see the end of this most untoward accident? Fortunately I was alone on that side of the deck, so none of the ladies saw my mishap, and, slipping along the seat to a distant corner, I hid my face behind a convenient newspaper, as I watched the little flurry of fishing up the hat by a man in a boat near by, and the merriment of the gentlemen over this assault of William Wordsworth upon Samuel Warburton. The poor book passed from hand to hand, and many jokes were made upon the 'fair Helen' whose name was written on the paper cover which protected it.

" 'I knew a Miss Harper once, — a lovely woman, but her name was not Helen, and she is dead, — God bless her!' I heard Mr. Warburton say, as he flapped his straw hat to dry it, and rubbed his head, which fortunately was well covered with thick gray hair at that time.

"I longed to go down and tell him who I was, but I had not the courage to face all those men. It really was *most* embarrassing; so I waited for a more private moment to claim my book, as I knew we should not land till night, so there was no danger of losing it.

" 'This is rather unusual stuff for a woman to be reading. Some literary lady doubtless. Better look her up, Warburton. You'll know her by the color of her stockings when she comes down to lunch,' said a jolly old gentleman, in a tone that made me 'rouge high,' as Evelina says.

" 'I shall know her by her intelligent face and conversation, if this book belongs to a lady. It will be an honor and a pleasure to meet a woman who enjoys Wordsworth, for in my opinion he is one of our truest poets,' answered Mr. Warburton, putting the book in his pocket, with a look and a tone that were most respectful and comforting to me just then.

"I hoped he would examine the volume, for Lucretia's and Lyman's names were on the fly leaf, and that would be a delightful introduction for me. So I said nothing and bided my time, feeling rather foolish when we all filed in to lunch, and I saw the other party glancing at the ladies at the table. Mr. Warburton's eye paused a moment as it passed from Mrs. Tracy to me, and I fear I blushed like a girl, my dears, for Samuel had very fine eyes, and I remembered the stout gentleman's unseemly joke about the stockings. Mine were white as snow, for I had a neat foot, and was fond of nice hose and well-made shoes. I am so still, as you see." Here the old lady displayed a small foot in a black silk stocking and delicate slipper, with the artless pride a woman feels, at any age, in one of her best points. The girls gratified her by a murmur of admiration, and, decorously re-adjusting the folds of her gown, she went on with the most romantic ep-isode of her quiet life.

"I retired to my state-room after lunch to compose myself, and when I emerged, in the cool of the afternoon, my first glance showed me that the hour had come, for there on deck was Mr. Warburton, talking to Mrs. Tracy, with my book in his hand. I hesitated a moment, for in spite of my age I was rather shy, and really it was not an easy thing to apologize to a strange gentleman for dropping books on his head and spoiling his hat. Men think so much of their hats, you know. I was spared embarrassment, however, for he saw me and came to me at once, saying, in the most cordial manner, as he showed the names on the fly leaf of my Wordsworth, 'I am sure we need no other introduction but the names of these two dear friends of ours. I am very glad to find that Miss Helen Harper is the little girl I saw once or twice at your father's house some years ago, and to meet her so pleasantly again.'

"That made everything easy and delightful, and when I had apolo-gized and been laughingly assured that he considered it rather an honor than otherwise to be assaulted by so great a man, we fell to talking of old times, and soon forgot that we were strangers. He was twenty years older than I, but a handsome man, and a most interesting and excellent one, as we all know. He had lost a young wife long ago, and had lived for science ever since, but it had not made him dry, or cold, or selfish. He was very young at heart for all his wisdom, and enjoyed that holiday like a boy out of school. So did I, and never dreamed that anything would come of it but a pleasant friendship founded on our love for those now dead and gone. Dear me! how strangely things turn out in this world of ours, and how the dropping of that book changed my life! Well, that was our introduc-tion, and that first long conversation was followed by many more equally charming, during the three weeks our parties were much together, as both were taking the same trip, and Dr. Tracy was glad to meet his old friend.

"I need not tell you how delightful such society was to me, nor how surprised I was when, on the last day before we parted, Mr. Warburton, who had answered many questions of mine during these long chats of ours, asked me a very serious one, and I found that I could answer it as he wished. It brought me great honor as well as happiness. I fear I was not worthy of it, but I tried to be, and felt a tender satisfaction in thinking that I owed it to dear Lucretia, in part at least; for my effort to imitate her made me fitter to become a wise man's wife, and thirty years of very sweet companionship was my reward."

As she spoke, Mrs. Warburton bowed her head before the portrait of a venerable old man which hung above the mantel-piece.

It was a pretty, old-fashioned expression of wifely pride and womanly tenderness in the fine old lady, who forgot her own gifts, and felt only humility and gratitude to the man who had found in her a comrade in intellectual pursuits, as well as a helpmeet at home and a gentle prop for his declining years.

The girls looked up with eyes full of something softer than mere curiosity, and felt in their young hearts how precious and honorable such a memory must be, how true and beautiful such a marriage was, and how sweet wisdom might become when it went hand in hand with love.

Alice spoke first, saying, as she touched the worn cover of the little book with a new sort of respect, "Thank you very much! Perhaps I ought not to have taken this from the corner shelves in your sanctum? I wanted to find the rest of the lines Mr. Thornton quoted last night, and did n't stop to ask leave."

"You are welcome, my love, for you know how to treat books. Yes, those in that little case are my precious relics. I keep them all, from my childish hymn-book to my great-grandfather's brass-bound Bible, for by and by when I sit 'Looking towards Sunset,' as dear Lydia Maria Child calls our last days, I shall lose my interest in other books, and take comfort in these. At the end as at the beginning of life we are all children again, and love the songs our mothers sung us, and find the one true Book our best teacher as we draw near to God."

As the reverent voice paused, a ray of sunshine broke through the parting clouds, and shone full on the serene old face turned to meet it, with a smile that welcomed the herald of a lovely sunset.

"The rain is over; there will be just time for a run in the garden before dinner, girls. I must go and change my cap, for literary ladies should not neglect to look well after the ways of their household and keep themselves tidy, no matter how old they may be." And with a nod Mrs. Warburton left them, wondering what the effect of the conversation would be on the minds of her young guests.

Alice went away to the garden, thinking of Lucretia and her lover, as she gathered flowers in the sunshine. Conscientious Eva took the Life of Mary Somerville to her room, and read diligently for half an hour, that no time might be lost in her new course of study, Carrie sent Wanda and her finery up the chimney in a lively blaze, and, as she watched the book burn, decided to take her blue and gold volume of Tennyson with her on her next trip to Nahant, in case any eligible learned or literary man's head should offer itself as a shining mark. Since a good marriage was the end of life, why not follow Mrs. Warburton's example, and make a really excellent one?

When they all met at dinner-time the old lady was pleased to see a nosegay of fresh pansies in the bosoms of her three youngest guests, and to hear Alice whisper, with grateful eyes, —

"We wear your flower to show you that we don't mean to forget the lesson you so kindly gave us, and to fortify ourselves with 'noble thoughts,' as you and she did."

Fiction and Reform

Polly's Troubles

From *An Old-Fashioned Girl*
(Boston: Roberts Brothers, 1870)

OLLY SOON FOUND that she was in a new world, a world where the manners and customs were so different from the simple ways at home, that she felt like a stranger in a strange land, and often wished that she had not come. In the first place, she had nothing to do but lounge and gossip, read novels, parade the streets, and dress; and before a week was gone, she was as heartily sick of all this, as a healthy person would be who attempted to live on confectionery. Fanny liked it, because she was used to it, and had never known anything better; but Polly had, and often felt like a little wood-bird shut up in a gilded cage. Nevertheless, she was much impressed by the luxuries all about her, enjoyed them, wished she owned them, and wondered why the Shaws were not a happier family. She was not wise enough to know where the trouble lay; she did not attempt to say which of the two lives was the right one; she only knew which she liked best, and supposed it was merely another of her "old-fashioned" ways.

Fanny's friends did not interest her much; she was rather afraid of them, they seemed so much older and wiser than herself, even those younger in years. They talked about things of which she knew nothing, and when Fanny tried to explain, she did n't find them interesting; indeed, some of them rather shocked and puzzled her; so the girls let her alone, being civil when they met, but evidently feeling that she was too "odd" to belong to their set. Then she turned to Maud for companionship, for her own little sister was excellent company, and Polly loved her dearly. But Miss Maud was much absorbed in her own affairs, for she belonged to a "set" also; and these mites of five and six had their "musicals," their parties, receptions, and promenades, as well as their elders; and the chief idea of their little lives seemed to be to ape the fashionable follies they should have been too innocent to understand. Maud had her tiny card-case, and paid calls, "like mamma and Fan"; her box of dainty gloves, her jewel-drawer, her crimping-pins, as fine and fanciful a wardrobe as a Paris doll, and a French maid to dress her. Polly could n't get on with her at first, for Maud did n't seem like a child, and often corrected Polly in her conversation and manners, though little mademoiselle's own were any-thing but perfect. Now and then, when Maud felt poorly, or had a "fwac-tious" turn, for she had "nerves" as well as mamma, she would go to Polly to be "amoosed," for her gentle ways and kind forbearance soothed the little fine lady better than anything else. Polly enjoyed these times, and told stories, played games, or went out walking, just as Maud liked, slowly and surely winning the child's heart, and relieving the whole house of the young tyrant who ruled it.

Tom soon got over staring at Polly, and at first did not take much notice of her, for, in his opinion, "girls did n't amount to much, any way"; and, considering the style of girl he knew most about, Polly quite agreed with him. He occasionally refreshed himself by teasing her, to see how she'd stand it, and caused Polly much anguish of spirit, for she never knew where he would take her next. He bounced out at her from behind doors, booed at her in dark entries, clutched her feet as she went up-stairs, startled her by shrill whistles right in her ear, or sudden tweaks of the hair as he passed her in the street; and as sure as there was company to dinner, he fixed his round eyes on her, and never took them off till she was reduced to a piteous state of confusion and distress. She used to beg him not to plague her; but he said he did it for her good; she was too shy, and needed toughening like the other girls. In vain she protested that she did n't want to be like the other girls in that respect; he only laughed in her face, stuck his red hair straight up all over his head, and glared at her, till she fled in dismay.

Yet Polly rather liked Tom, for she soon saw that he was neglected, hustled out of the way, and left to get on pretty much by himself. She often wondered why his mother did n't pet him as she did the girls; why his father ordered him about as if he was a born rebel, and took so little interest in his only son. Fanny considered him a bear, and was ashamed of him, but never tried to polish him up a bit; and Maud and he lived together like a cat and dog who did not belong to a "happy family." Grandma was the only one who stood by poor old Tom; and Polly more than once dis-covered him doing something kind for Madam, and seeming very much ashamed when it was found out. He was n't respectful at all; he called her "the old lady," and told her he "would n't be fussed over"; but when anything was the matter, he always went to "the old lady," and was very grateful for the "fussing." Polly liked him for this, and often wanted to speak of it; but she had a feeling that it would n't do, for in praising their affection, she was reproaching others with neglect; so she held her tongue, and thought about it all the more.

Grandma was rather neglected, too, and perhaps that is the reason why Tom and she were such good friends. She was even more old-fashioned than Polly; but people did n't seem to mind it so much in her, as her day was supposed to be over, and nothing was expected of her but to keep out of everybody's way, and to be handsomely dressed when she appeared "before people." Grandma led a quiet, solitary life up in her own rooms, full of old furniture, pictures, books, and relics of a past for which no one cared but herself. Her son went up every evening for a little call, was very kind to her, and saw that she wanted nothing money could buy; but he was a busy man, so intent on getting rich that he had no time to enjoy what he already possessed. Madam never complained, interfered, or suggested; but there was a sad sort of quietude about her, a wistful look in her faded eyes, as if she wanted something which money could not buy, and when children were near, she hovered about them, evidently longing to cuddle and caress them as only grandmothers can. Polly felt this; and, as she missed the home-petting, gladly showed that she liked to see the quiet old face brighten as she entered the solitary room, where few children came, except the phantoms of little sons and daughters, who, to the motherly heart that loved them, never faded or grew up. Polly wished the children would be kinder to grandma; but it was not for her to tell them so, although it troubled her a good deal, and she could only try to make up for it by being as dutiful and affectionate as if their grandma was her own.

Another thing that disturbed Polly was the want of exercise. To dress up and parade certain streets for an hour every day, to stand talking in doorways, or drive out in a fine carriage, was not the sort of exercise she liked, and Fan would take no other. Indeed, she was so shocked, when Polly, one day, proposed a run down the mall, that her friend never dared suggest such a thing again. At home, Polly ran and rode, coasted and skated, jumped rope and raked hay, worked in her garden and rowed her boat; so no wonder she longed for something more lively than a daily promenade with a flock of giddy girls, who tilted along in high-heeled boots, and costumes which made Polly ashamed to be seen with some of them. So she used to slip out alone sometimes, when Fanny was absorbed in novels, company, or millinery, and get fine brisk walks round the park, on the unfashionable side, where the babies took their airings; or she went inside, to watch the boys coasting, and to wish she could coast too, as she did at home. She never went far, and always came back rosy and gay.

One afternoon, just before dinner, she felt so tired of doing nothing, that she slipped out for a run. It had been a dull day; but the sun was visible now, setting brightly below the clouds. It was cold but still, and Polly trotted down the smooth, snow-covered mall, humming to herself, and trying not to feel homesick. The coasters were at it with all their might, and she watched them, till her longing to join the fun grew irresistible. On the hill, some little girls were playing with their sleds, — real little girls, in warm hoods and coats, rubber boots and mittens, — and Polly felt drawn toward them in spite of her fear of Fan.

"I want to go down, but I dars n't, it's so steep," said one of these "common children," as Maud called them.

"If you'll lend me your sled, and sit in my lap, I'll take you down all nice," answered Polly, in a confidential tone.

The little girls took a look at her, seemed satisfied, and accepted her offer. Polly looked carefully round to see that no fashionable eye beheld the awful deed, and finding all safe, settled her freight, and spun away down hill, feeling all over the delightsome excitement of swift motion which makes coasting such a favorite pastime with the more sensible portion of the child-world. One after another, she took the little girls down the hill and dragged them up again, while they regarded her in the light of a gray-coated angel, descended for their express benefit. Polly was just finishing off with one delicious "go" all by herself, when she heard a familiar whistle behind her, and before she could get off, up came Tom, looking as much astonished as if he had found her mounted on an elephant.

"Hullo, Polly! What'll Fan say to you?" was his polished salutation.

"Don't know, and don't care. Coasting is no harm; I like it, and I'm going to do it, now I've got a chance; so clear the lul-la!" And away went independent Polly, with her hair blowing in the wind, and an expression of genuine enjoyment, which a very red nose did n't damage in the least.

"Good for you, Polly!" And casting himself upon his sled, with the most reckless disregard for his ribs, off whizzed Tom after her, and came alongside just as she reined up "General Grant" on the broad path below. "Oh, won't you get it when we go home?" cried the young gentleman, even before he changed his graceful attitude.

"I shan't, if you don't go and tell; but of course you will," added Polly, sitting still, while an anxious expression began to steal over her happy face.

"I just won't, then," returned Tom, with the natural perversity of his tribe.

"If they ask me, I shall tell, of course; if they don't ask, I think there's no harm in keeping still. I should n't have done it, if I had n't known my mother was willing; but I don't wish to trouble your mother by telling of it. Do you think it was very dreadful of me?" asked Polly, looking at him.

"I think it was downright jolly; and I won't tell, if you don't want me to. Now, come up and have another," said Tom, heartily.

"Just one more; the little girls want to go, and this is their sled."

"Let 'em take it, 't is n't good for much; and you come on mine. Mazeppa's a stunner; you see if he is n't."

So Polly tucked herself up in front, Tom hung on behind in some mysterious manner, and Mazeppa proved that he fully merited his master's sincere if inelegant praise. They got on capitally now, for Tom was in his proper sphere, and showed his best side, being civil and gay in the bluff boy-fashion that was natural to him; while Polly forgot to be shy, and liked this sort of "toughening" much better than the other. They laughed and talked, and kept taking "just one more," till the sunshine was all gone, and the clocks struck dinner-time.

"We shall be late; let's run," said Polly, as they came into the path after the last coast.

"You just sit still, and I'll get you home in a jiffy;" and before she could unpack herself, Tom trotted off with her at a fine pace.

"Here's a pair of cheeks! I wish you'd get a color like this, Fanny," said Mr. Shaw, as Polly came into the dining-room after smoothing her hair.

"Your nose is as red as that cranberry sauce," answered Fan, coming out of the big chair where she had been curled up for an hour or two, deep in "Lady Audley's Secret."

"So it is," said Polly, shutting one eye to look at the offending feature. "Never mind; I've had a good time, anyway," she added, giving a little prance in her chair.

"I don't see much fun in these cold runs you are so fond of taking," said Fanny, with a yawn and a shiver.

"Perhaps you would if you tried it;" and Polly laughed as she glanced at Tom.

"Did you go alone, dear?" asked grandma, patting the rosy cheek beside her.

"Yes'm; but I met Tom, and we came home together." Polly's eyes twinkled when she said that, and Tom choked in his soup.

"Thomas, leave the table!" commanded Mr. Shaw, as his incorrigible son gurgled and gasped behind his napkin.

"Please, don't send him away, sir. I made him laugh," said Polly, penitently.

"What's the joke?" asked Fanny, waking up at last.

"I should n't think you'd make him laugh, when he's always making you cwy," observed Maud, who had just come in.

"What have you been doing now, sir?" demanded Mr. Shaw, as Tom emerged, red and solemn, from his brief obscurity.

"Nothing but coast," he said, gruffly, for papa was always lecturing him, and letting the girls do just as they liked.

"So's Polly; I saw her. Me and Blanche were coming home just now, and we saw her and Tom widing down the hill on his sled, and then he dwagged her ever so far!" cried Maud, with her mouthful.

"You did n't?" And Fanny dropped her fork with a scandalized face.

"Yes, I did, and liked it ever so much," answered Polly, looking anxious but resolute.

"*Did* any one see you?" cried Fanny.

"Only some little girls, and Tom."

"It was horridly improper; and Tom ought to have told you so, if you did n't know any better. I should be mortified to death if any of my friends saw you," added Fan, much disturbed.

"Now, don't you scold. It's no harm, and Polly shall coast if she wants to; may n't she, grandma?" cried Tom, gallantly coming to the rescue, and securing a powerful ally.

"My mother lets me; and if I don't go among the boys, I can't see what harm there is in it," said Polly, before Madam could speak.

"People do many things in the country that are not proper here," began Mrs. Shaw, in her reproving tone.

"Let the child do it if she likes, and take Maud with her. I should be glad to have one hearty girl in my house," interrupted Mr. Shaw, and that was the end of it.

"Thank you, sir," said Polly, gratefully, and nodded at Tom, who telegraphed back "All right!" and fell upon his dinner with the appetite of a young wolf.

"Oh, you sly-boots! you're getting up a flirtation with Tom, are you?" whispered Fanny to her friend, as if much amused.

"What!" and Polly looked so surprised and indignant, that Fanny was ashamed of herself, and changed the subject by telling her mother she needed some new gloves.

Polly was very quiet after that, and the minute dinner was over, she left the room to go and have a quiet "think" about the whole matter. Before she got half-way up stairs, she saw Tom coming after, and immediately sat down to guard her feet. He laughed, and said, as he perched himself on the post of the banisters, "I won't grab you, honor bright. I just wanted to say, if you'll come out to-morrow some time, we'll have a good coast."

"No," said Polly, "I can't come."

"Why not? Are you mad? I did n't tell." And Tom looked amazed at the change which had come over her.

"No; you kept your word, and stood by me like a good boy. I'm not mad, either; but I don't mean to coast any more. Your mother don't like it."

"That is n't the reason, *I* know. You nodded to me after she'd freed her mind, and you meant to go then. Come, now, what is it?"

"I shan't tell you; but I'm not going," was Polly's determined answer.

"Well, I did think you had more sense than most girls; but you have n't, and I would n't give a sixpence for you."

"That's polite," said Polly, getting ruffled.

"Well, I hate cowards."

"I ain't a coward."

"Yes, you are. You're afraid of what folks will say; ain't you now?"

Polly knew she was, and held her peace, though she longed to speak; but how could she?

"Ah, I knew you'd back out." And Tom walked away with an air of scorn that cut Polly to the heart.

"It's too bad! Just as he was growing kind to me, and I was going to have a good time, it's all spoilt by Fan's nonsense. Mrs. Shaw don't like it, nor grandma either, I dare say. There'll be a fuss if I go, and Fan will plague me; so I'll give it up, and let Tom think I'm afraid. Oh, dear! I never did see such ridiculous people."

Polly shut her door hard, and felt ready to cry with vexation, that her pleasure should be spoilt by such a silly idea; for, of all the silly freaks of this fast age, that of little people playing at love is about the silliest. Polly had been taught that it was a very serious and sacred thing; and, according to her notions, it was far more improper to flirt with one boy than to coast with a dozen. She had been much amazed, only the day before, to hear Maud say to her mother, "Mamma, must I have a beau? The girls all do, and say I ought to have Fweddy Lovell: but I don't like him as well as Hawry Fiske."

"Oh, yes; I'd have a little sweetheart, dear, it's so cunning," answered Mrs. Shaw. And Maud announced soon after that she was engaged to "Fweddy, 'cause Hawry slapped her" when she proposed the match.

Polly laughed with the rest at the time; but when she thought of it afterward, and wondered what her own mother would have said, if little

Kitty had put such a question, she did n't find it cunning or funny, but ridiculous and unnatural. She felt so now about herself; and when her first petulance was over, resolved to give up coasting and everything else, rather than have any nonsense with Tom, who, thanks to his neglected education, was as ignorant as herself of the charms of this new amusement for school-children. So Polly tried to console herself by jumping rope in the back-yard, and playing tag with Maud in the drying-room, where she likewise gave lessons in "nasgim-nics," as Maud called it, which did that little person good. Fanny came up sometimes to teach them a new dancing step, and more than once was betrayed into a game of romps, for which she was none the worse. But Tom turned a cold shoulder to Polly, and made it evident, by his cavalier manner, that he really did n't think her "worth a sixpence."

Another thing that troubled Polly was her clothes, for, though no one said anything, she knew they were very plain; and now and then she wished that her blue and mouse colored merinos were rather more trimmed, her sashes had bigger bows, and her little ruffles more lace on them. She sighed for a locket, and, for the first time in her life, thought seriously of turning up her pretty curls and putting on a "wad." She kept these discontents to herself, however, after she had written to ask her mother if she might have her best dress altered like Fanny's, and received this reply:

"No, dear; the dress is proper and becoming as it is, and the old fashion of simplicity the best for all of us. I don't want my Polly to be loved for her clothes, but for herself; so wear the plain frocks mother took such pleasure in making for you, and let the *panniers* go. The least of us have some influence in this big world; and perhaps my little girl can do some good by showing others that a contented heart and a happy face are better ornaments than any Paris can give her. You want a locket, deary; so I send one that my mother gave me years ago. You will find father's face on one side, mine on the other; and when things trouble you, just look at your talisman, and I think the sunshine will come back again."

Of course it did, for the best of all magic was shut up in the quaint little case that Polly wore inside her frock, and kissed so tenderly each night and morning. The thought that, insignificant as she was, she yet might do some good, made her very careful of her acts and words, and so anxious to keep heart contented and face happy, that she forgot her clothes, and made others do the same. She did not know it, but that good old fashion of simplicity made the plain gowns pretty, and the grace of unconscious-ness beautified their little wearer with the charm that makes girlhood sweetest to those who truly love and reverence it. One temptation Polly had already yielded to before the letter came, and repented heartily of afterward.

"Polly, I wish you'd let me call you Marie," said Fanny one day, as they were shopping together.

"You may call me Mary, if you like; but I won't have any *ie* put on to my name. I'm Polly at home, and I'm fond of being called so; but Marie is Frenchified and silly."

"I spell my own name with an *ie,* and so do all the girls."

"And what a jumble of Netties, Nellies, Hatties, and Sallies there is. How 'Pollie' would look spelt so!"

"Well, never mind; that was n't what I began to say. There's one thing you must have, and that is, bronze boots," said Fan, impressively.

"Why must I, when I've got enough without?"

"Because it's the fashion to have them, and you can't be finished off properly without. I'm going to get a pair, and so must you."

"Don't they cost a great deal?"

"Eight or nine dollars, I believe. I have mine charged; but it don't matter if you have n't got the money. I can lend you some."

"I've got ten dollars to do what I like with; but I meant to get some presents for the children." And Polly took out her purse in an undecided way.

"You can make presents easy enough. Grandma knows all sorts of nice contrivances. They'll do just as well; and then you can get your boots."

"Well; I'll look at them," said Polly, following Fanny into the store, feeling rather rich and important to be shopping in this elegant manner.

"Are n't they lovely? Your foot is perfectly divine in that boot, Polly. Get them for my party; you'll dance like a fairy," whispered Fan.

Polly surveyed the dainty, shining boot with the scalloped top, the jaunty heel, and the delicate toe, thought her foot did look very well in it, and after a little pause, said she would have them. It was all very delightful till she got home, and was alone; then, on looking into her purse, she saw one dollar and the list of things she meant to get for mother and the children. How mean the dollar looked all alone! and how long the list grew when there was nothing to buy the articles.

"I can't make skates for Ned, nor a desk for Will; and those are what they have set their hearts upon. Father's book and mother's collar are impossible now; and I'm a selfish thing to go and spend all my money for myself. How could I do it?" and Polly eyed the new boots reproachfully, as they stood in the first position as if ready for the party. "They *are* lovely; but I don't believe they will feel good, for I shall be thinking about my lost presents all the time," sighed Polly, pushing the enticing boots out of sight. "I'll go and ask grandma what I can do; for if I've got to make something for every one, I must begin right away, or I shan't get done;" and off she bustled, glad to forget her remorse in hard work.

Grandma proved equal to the emergency, and planned something for every one, supplying materials, taste, and skill in the most delightful manner. Polly felt much comforted; but while she began to knit a pretty pair of white bed-socks, to be tied with rose-colored ribbons, for her mother, she thought some very sober thoughts upon the subject of temptation; and if any one had asked her just then what made her sigh, as if something lay heavy on her conscience, she would have answered, "Bronze boots."

Uncles

From *Eight Cousins; or, the Aunt-Hill* (Boston: Roberts Brothers, 1875)

WHEN ROSE WOKE next morning, she was not sure whether she had dreamed what occurred the night before, or it had actually happened. So she hopped up and dressed, although it was an hour earlier than she usually rose, for she could not sleep any more, being possessed with a strong desire to slip down and see if the big portmanteau and packing-cases were really in the hall. She seemed to remember tumbling over them when she went to bed, for the aunts had sent her off very punctually, because they wanted their pet nephew all to themselves.

The sun was shining, and Rose opened her window to let in the soft May air fresh from the sea. As she leaned over her little balcony, watching an early bird get the worm, and wondering how she should like Uncle Alec, she saw a man leap the garden wall and come whistling up the path. At first she thought it was some trespasser, but a second look showed her that it was her uncle returning from an early dip into the sea. She had hardly dared to look at him the night before, because whenever she tried to do so she always found a pair of keen blue eyes looking at her. Now she could take a good stare at him as he lingered along, looking about him as if glad to see the old place again.

A brown, breezy man, in a blue jacket, with no hat on the curly head which he shook now and then like a water-dog; broad-shouldered, alert in his motions, and with a general air of strength and stability about him which pleased Rose, though she could not explain the feeling of comfort it gave her. She had just said to herself, with a sense of relief, "I guess I *shall* like him, though he looks as if he made people mind," when he lifted his eyes to examine the budding horse-chestnut overhead, and saw the eager face peering down at him. He waved his hand to her, nodded, and called out in a bluff, cheery voice, —

"You are on deck early, little niece."

"I got up to see if you had really come, uncle."

"Did you? Well, come down here and make sure of it."

"I'm not allowed to go out before breakfast, sir."

"Oh, indeed!" with a shrug. "Then I'll come aboard and salute," he added; and, to Rose's great amazement, Uncle Alec went up one of the pillars of the back piazza hand over hand, stepped across the roof, and swung himself into her balcony, saying, as he landed on the wide balustrade: "Have you any doubts about me now, ma'am?"

Rose was so taken aback, she could only answer with a smile as she went to meet him.

"How does my girl do this morning?" he asked, taking the little cold hand she gave him in both his big warm ones.

"Pretty well, thank you, sir."

"Ah, but it should be *very well*. Why is n't it?"

"I always wake up with a headache, and feel tired."

"Don't you sleep well?"

"I lie awake a long time, and then I dream, and my sleep does not seem to rest me much."

"What do you do all day?"

"Oh, I read, and sew a little, and take naps, and sit with auntie."

"No running about out of doors, or house-work, or riding, hey?"

"Aunt Plenty says I'm not strong enough for much exercise. I drive out with her sometimes, but I don't care for it."

"I'm not surprised at that," said Uncle Alec, half to himself, adding, in his quick way: "Who have you had to play with?"

"No one but Annabel Bliss, and she was *such* a goose I could n't bear her. The boys came yesterday, and seemed rather nice; but, of course, I could n't play with them."

"Why not?"

"I'm too old to play with boys."

"Not a bit of it: that's just what you need, for you've been molly-coddled too much. They are good lads, and you'll be mixed up with them more or less for years to come, so you may as well be friends and playmates at once. I will look you up some girls also, if I can find a sensible one who is not spoilt by her nonsensical education."

"Phebe is sensible, I'm sure, and I like her, though I only saw her yesterday," cried Rose, waking up suddenly.

"And who is Phebe, if you please?"

Rose eagerly told all she knew, and Uncle Alec listened, with an odd smile lurking about his mouth, though his eyes were quite sober as he watched the face before him.

"I'm glad to see that you are not aristocratic in your tastes, but I don't quite make out why you like this young lady from the poor-house."

"You may laugh at me, but I do. I can't tell why, only she seems so happy and busy, and sings so beautifully, and is strong enough to scrub and sweep, and has n't any troubles to plague her," said Rose, making a funny jumble of reasons in her efforts to explain.

"How do you know that?"

"Oh, I was telling her about mine, and asked if she had any, and she said, 'No, only I'd like to go to school, and I mean to some day.' "

"So she does n't call desertion, poverty, and hard work, troubles? She's a brave little girl, and I shall be proud to know her." And Uncle Alec gave an approving nod, that made Rose wish she had been the one to earn it.

"But what are these troubles of yours, child?" he asked, after a minute of silence.

"Please don't ask me, uncle."

"Can't you tell them to me as well as to Phebe?"

Something in his tone made Rose feel that it would be better to speak out and be done with it, so she answered, with sudden color and averted eyes, —

"The greatest one was losing dear papa."

As she said that, Uncle Alec's arm came gently round her, and he drew her to him, saying, in the voice so like papa's, —

"That *is* a trouble which I cannot cure, my child; but I shall try to make you feel it less. What else, dear?"

"I am so tired and poorly all the time, I can't do any thing I want to, and it makes me cross," sighed Rose, rubbing the aching head like a fretful child.

"That we *can* cure and we *will,*" said her uncle, with a decided nod that made the curls bob on his head, so that Rose saw the gray ones underneath the brown.

"Aunt Myra says I have no constitution, and never shall be strong," observed Rose, in a pensive tone, as if it was rather a nice thing to be an invalid.

"Aunt Myra is — ahem! — an excellent woman, but it is her hobby to believe that every one is tottering on the brink of the grave; and, upon my life, I believe she is offended if people don't fall into it! We will show her how to make constitutions and turn pale-faced little ghosts into rosy, hearty girls. That's my business, you know," he added, more quietly, for his sudden outburst had rather startled Rose.

"I had forgotten you were a doctor. I'm glad of it, for I do want to be well, only I hope you won't give me much medicine, for I've taken quarts already, and it does me no good."

As she spoke, Rose pointed to a little table just inside the window, on which appeared a regiment of bottles.

"Ah, ha! Now we'll see what mischief these blessed women have been at." And, making a long arm, Dr. Alec set the bottles on the wide railing before him, examined each carefully, smiled over some, frowned over others, and said, as he put down the last: "Now I'll show you the best way to take these messes." And, as quick as a flash, he sent one after another smashing down into the posy-beds below.

"But Aunt Plenty won't like it; and Aunt Myra will be angry, for she sent most of them!" cried Rose, half frightened and half pleased at such energetic measures.

"You are my patient now, and I'll take the responsibility. My way of giving physic is evidently the best, for you look better already," he said, laughing so infectiously that Rose followed suit, saying saucily, —

"If I don't like your medicines any better than those, I shall throw them into the garden, and then what will you do?"

"When I prescribe such rubbish, I'll give you leave to pitch it overboard as soon as you like. Now what is the next trouble?"

"I hoped you would forget to ask."

"But how can I help you if I don't know them? Come, let us have No. 3."

"It is very wrong, I suppose, but I do sometimes wish I had not *quite* so many aunts. They are all very good to me, and I want to please them; but they are so different, I feel sort of pulled to pieces among them," said Rose, trying to express the emotions of a stray chicken with six hens all clucking over it at once.

Uncle Alec threw back his head and laughed like a boy, for he could entirely understand how the good ladies had each put in her oar and tried to paddle her own way, to the great disturbance of the waters and the entire bewilderment of poor Rose.

"I intend to try a course of uncles now, and see how that suits your constitution. I'm going to have you all to myself, and no one is to give a word of advice unless I ask it. There is no other way to keep order aboard, and I am captain of this little craft, for a time at least. What comes next?"

But Rose stuck there, and grew so red, her uncle guessed what that trouble was.

"I don't think I *can* tell this one. It would n't be polite, and I feel pretty sure that it is n't going to be a trouble any more."

As she blushed and stammered over these words, Dr. Alec turned his eyes away to the distant sea, and said so seriously, so tenderly, that she felt every word and long remembered them, —

"My child, I don't expect you to love and trust me all at once, but I do want you to believe that I shall give my whole heart to this new duty; and if I make mistakes, as I probably shall, no one will grieve over them more bitterly than I. It is my fault that I am a stranger to you, when I want to be your best friend. That is one of my mistakes, and I never repented it more deeply than I do now. Your father and I had a trouble once, and I thought I never could forgive him; so I kept away for years. Thank God, we made it all up the last time I saw him, and he told me then, that if he was forced to leave her he should bequeath his little girl to me as a token of his love. I can't fill his place, but I shall try to be a father to her; and if she learns to love me half as well as she did the good one she has lost, I shall be a proud and happy man. Will she believe this and try?"

Something in Uncle Alec's face touched Rose to the heart, and when he held out his hand with that anxious, troubled look in his eyes, she was moved to put up her innocent lips and seal the contract with a confiding kiss. The strong arm held her close a minute, and she felt the broad chest heave once as if with a great sigh of relief; but not a word was spoken till a tap at the door made both start.

Rose popped her head through the window to say "come in," while Dr. Alec hastily rubbed the sleeve of his jacket across his eyes and began to whistle again.

Phebe appeared with a cup of coffee.

"Debby told me to bring this and help you get up," she said, opening her black eyes wide, as if she wondered how on earth "the sailor man" got there.

"I'm all dressed, so I don't need any help. I hope that is good and strong," added Rose, eying the steaming cup with an eager look.

But she did not get it, for a brown hand took possession of it as her uncle said quickly, —

"Hold hard, my lass, and let me overhaul that dose before you take it. Do you drink all this strong coffee every morning, Rose?"

"Yes, sir, and I like it. Auntie says it 'tones' me up, and I always feel better after it."

"This accounts for the sleepless nights, the flutter your heart gets into at the least start, and this is why that cheek of yours is pale yellow instead of rosy red. No more coffee for you, my dear, and by and by you'll see that I am right. Any new milk downstairs, Phebe?"

"Yes, sir, plenty, — right in from the barn."

"That's the drink for my patient. Go bring me a pitcherful, and another cup; I want a draught myself. This won't hurt the honeysuckles, for they have no nerves to speak of." And, to Rose's great discomfort, the coffee went after the medicine.

Dr. Alec saw the injured look she put on, but took no notice, and presently banished it by saying pleasantly, —

"I've got a capital little cup among my traps, and I'll give it to you to drink your milk in, as it is made of wood that is supposed to improve whatever is put into it, — something like a quassia cup. That reminds me; one of the boxes Phebe wanted to lug upstairs last night is for you. Knowing that I was coming home to find a ready-made daughter, I picked up all sorts of odd and pretty trifles along the way, hoping she would be able to find something she liked among them all. Early to-morrow we'll have a grand rummage. Here's our milk! I propose the health of Miss Rose Campbell — and drink it with all my heart."

It was impossible for Rose to pout with the prospect of a delightful boxful of gifts dancing before her eyes; so, in spite of herself, she smiled as she drank her own health, and found that fresh milk was not a hard dose to take.

"Now I must be off, before I am caught again with my wig in a toss," said Dr. Alec, preparing to descend the way he came.

"Do you always go in and out like a cat, uncle?" asked Rose, much amused at his odd ways.

"I used to sneak out of my window when I was a boy, so I need not disturb the aunts, and now I rather like it, for it's the shortest road, and it keeps me limber when I have no rigging to climb. Good-by till breakfast." And away he went down the water-spout, over the roof, and vanished among the budding honey-suckles below.

"Ain't he a funny guardeen?" exclaimed Phebe, as she went off with the cups.

"He is a very kind one, I think," answered Rose, following, to prowl round the big boxes and try to guess which was hers.

When her uncle appeared at sound of the bell, he found her surveying with an anxious face a new dish that smoked upon the table.

"Got a fresh trouble, Rosy?" he asked, stroking her smooth head.

"Uncle, *are* you going to make me eat oatmeal?" asked Rose, in a tragic tone.

"Don't you like it?"

"I de-test it!" answered Rose, with all the emphasis which a turned-up nose, a shudder, and a groan could give to the three words.

"You are not a true Scotchwoman, if you don't like the 'parritch.' It's a pity, for I made it myself, and thought we'd have such a good time with all that cream to float it in. Well, never mind." And he sat down with a disappointed air.

Rose had made up her mind to be obstinate about it, because she did heartily "detest" the dish; but as Uncle Alec did not attempt to make her obey, she suddenly changed her mind and thought she would.

"I'll try to eat it to please you, uncle; but people are always saying how wholesome it is, and that makes me hate it," she said, half ashamed at her silly excuse.

"I do want you to like it, because I wish my girl to be as well and strong as Jessie's boys, who are brought up on this in the good old fashion. No hot bread and fried stuff for them, and they are the biggest and bonniest lads of the lot. Bless you, auntie, and good morning!"

Dr. Alec turned to greet the old lady, and, with a firm resolve to eat or die in the attempt, Rose sat down.

In five minutes she forgot what she was eating, so interested was she in the chat that went on. It amused her very much to hear Aunt Plenty call her forty-year-old nephew "my dear boy;" and Uncle Alec was so full of lively gossip about all creation in general, and the Aunt-hill in particular, that the detested porridge vanished without a murmur.

"You will go to church with us, I hope, Alec, if you are not too tired," said the old lady, when breakfast was over.

"I came all the way from Calcutta for that express purpose, ma'am. Only I must send the sisters word of my arrival, for they don't expect me till to-morrow, you know, and there will be a row in church if those boys see me without warning."

"I'll send Ben up the hill, and you can step over to Myra's yourself; it will please her, and you will have plenty of time."

Dr. Alec was off at once, and they saw no more of him till the old barouche was at the door, and Aunt Plenty just rustling downstairs in her Sunday best, with Rose like a little black shadow behind her.

Away they drove in state, and all the way Uncle Alec's hat was more off his head than on, for every one they met smiled and bowed, and gave him as blithe a greeting as the day permitted.

It was evident that the warning had been a wise one, for, in spite of time and place, the lads were in such a ferment that their elders sat in momentary dread of an unseemly outbreak somewhere. It was simply impossible to keep those fourteen eyes off Uncle Alec, and the dreadful things that were done during sermon-time will hardly be believed.

Rose dared not look up after a while, for these bad boys vented their emotions upon her till she was ready to laugh and cry with mingled amusement and vexation. Charlie winked rapturously at her behind his mother's fan; Mac openly pointed to the tall figure beside her; Jamie stared fixedly over the back of his pew, till Rose thought his round eyes would drop out of his head; George fell over a stool and dropped three books in his excitement; Will drew sailors and Chinamen on his clean cuffs, and displayed them, to Rose's great tribulation; Steve nearly upset the whole party by burning his nose with salts, as he pretended to be overcome by his joy; even dignified Archie disgraced himself by writing in his hymn-book, "Is n't he *blue* and *brown?*" and passing it politely to Rose.

Her only salvation was trying to fix her attention upon Uncle Mac, — a portly, placid gentleman, who seemed entirely unconscious of the iniquities of the Clan, and dozed peacefully in his pew corner. This was the only uncle Rose had met for years, for Uncle Jem and Uncle Steve, the husbands of Aunt Jessie and Aunt Clara, were at sea, and Aunt Myra was a widow. Uncle Mac was a merchant, very rich and busy, and as quiet as a mouse at home, for he was in such a minority among the women folk he dared not open his lips, and let his wife rule undisturbed.

Rose liked the big, kindly, silent man who came to her when papa died, was always sending her splendid boxes of goodies at school, and often invited her into his great warehouse, full of teas and spices, wines and all sorts of foreign fruits, there to eat and carry away whatever she liked. She had secretly regretted that he was not to be her guardian; but since she had seen Uncle Alec she felt better about it, for she did not particularly admire Aunt Jane.

When church was over, Dr. Alec got into the porch as quickly as possible, and there the young bears had a hug all round, while the sisters shook hands and welcomed him with bright faces and glad hearts. Rose was nearly crushed flat behind a door in that dangerous passage from pew to porch; but Uncle Mac rescued her, and put her into the carriage for safe keeping.

"Now, girls, I want you all to come and dine with Alec; Mac also, of course. But I cannot ask the boys, for we did not expect this dear fellow till to-morrow, you know, so I made no preparations. Send the lads home, and let them wait till Monday, for really I was shocked at their behavior in church," said Aunt Plenty, as she followed Rose.

In any other place the defrauded boys would have set up a howl; as it was, they growled and protested till Dr. Alec settled the matter by saying, —

"Never mind, old chaps, I'll make it up to you to-morrow, if you sheer off quietly; if you don't, not a blessed thing shall you have out of my big boxes."

Coming Home

Chapter 1 of *Rose in Bloom. A Sequel to "Eight Cousins"*
(Boston: Roberts Brothers, 1876)

THREE YOUNG MEN stood together on a wharf one bright October day, awaiting the arrival of an ocean steamer with an impatience which found a vent in lively skirmishes with a small lad, who pervaded the premises like a will-o'-the-wisp, and afforded much amusement to the other groups assembled there.

"They are the Campbells, waiting for their cousin, who has been abroad several years with her uncle, the Doctor," whispered one lady to another, as the handsomest of the young men touched his hat to her as he passed, lugging the boy, whom he had just rescued from a little expedition down among the piles.

"Which is that?" asked the stranger.

"Prince Charlie, as he's called, — a fine fellow, the most promising of the seven; but a little fast, people say," answered the first speaker, with a shake of the head.

"Are the others his brothers?"

"No, cousins. The elder is Archie, a most exemplary young man. He has just gone into business with the merchant uncle, and bids fair to be an honor to his family. The other, with the eye-glasses and no gloves, is Mac, the odd one, just out of college."

"And the boy?"

"Oh, he is Jamie, the youngest brother of Archibald, and the pet of the whole family. Mercy on us! he'll be in if they don't hold on to him."

The ladies' chat came to a sudden end just there; for, by the time Jamie had been fished out of a hogshead, the steamer hove in sight and every thing else was forgotten. As it swung slowly round to enter the dock, a boyish voice shouted, —

"There she is! I see her and uncle and Phebe! Hooray for Cousin Rose!" and three small cheers were given with a will by Jamie, as he stood on a post waving his arms like a windmill, while his brother held on to the tail of his jacket.

Yes, there they were, — Uncle Alec swinging his hat like a boy, with Phebe smiling and nodding on one side, and Rose kissing both hands delightedly on the other, as she recognized familiar faces and heard familiar voices welcoming her home.

"Bless her dear heart, she's bonnier than ever! Looks like a Madonna, — doesn't she? — with that blue cloak round her, and her bright hair flying in the wind!" said Charlie excitedly, as they watched the group upon the deck with eager eyes.

"Madonnas don't wear hats like that. Rose hasn't changed much, but Phebe has. Why, she's a regular beauty!" answered Archie, staring with all his might at the dark-eyed young woman, with the brilliant color and glossy, black braids shining in the sun.

"Dear old uncle! doesn't it seem good to have him back?" was all Mac said; but he was not looking at "dear old uncle," as he made the fervent remark, for he saw only the slender blonde girl near by, and stretched out his hands to meet hers, forgetful of the green water tumbling between them.

During the confusion that reigned for a moment as the steamers settled to her moorings, Rose looked down into the three faces upturned to hers, and seemed to read in them something that both pleased and pained her. It was only a glance, and her own eyes were full; but through the mist of happy tears she received the impression that Archie was about the same, that Mac had decidedly improved, and that something was amiss with Charlie. There was no time for observation, however; for in a moment the shoreward rush began, and, before she could grasp her travelling bag, Jamie was clinging to her like an ecstatic young bear. She was with difficulty released from his embrace, to fall into the gentler ones of the elder cousins, who took advantage of the general excitement to welcome both blooming girls with affectionate impartiality. Then the wanderers were borne ashore in a triumphal procession, while Jamie danced rapturous jigs before them even on the gangway.

Archie remained to help his uncle get the luggage through the Custom House, and the others escorted the damsels home. No sooner were they shut up in a carriage, however, than a new and curious constraint seemed to fall upon the young people; for they realized, all at once, that their former playmates were men and women now. Fortunately, Jamie was quite free from this feeling of restraint, and, sitting bodkin-wise between the ladies, took all sorts of liberties with them and their belongings.

"Well, my mannikin, what do you think of us?" asked Rose, to break an awkward pause.

"You've both grown so pretty, I can't decide which I like best. Phebe is the biggest and brightest looking, and I was always fond of Phebe; but, somehow you are so kind of sweet and precious, I really think I *must* hug you again," and the small youth did it tempestuously.

"If you love me best, I shall not mind a bit about your thinking Phebe the handsomest, because she *is*. Isn't she, boys?" asked Rose, with a mischievous look at the gentlemen opposite, whose faces expressed a respectful admiration which much amused her.

"I'm so dazzled by the brilliancy and beauty that has suddenly burst upon me, I have no words to express my emotions," answered Charlie, gallantly dodging the dangerous question.

"I can't say yet, for I have not had time to look at any one. I will now, if you don't mind;" and, to the great amusement of the rest, Mac gravely adjusted his eye-glasses and took an observation.

"Well?" said Phebe, smiling and blushing under his honest stare, yet seeming not to resent it as she did the lordly sort of approval which made her answer the glance of Charlie's audacious blue eyes with a flash of her black ones.

"I think if you were my sister, I should be very proud of you, because your face shows what I admire more than its beauty, — truth and courage, Phebe," answered Mac, with a little bow, full of such genuine respect that surprise and pleasure brought a sudden dew to quench the fire of the girl's eyes, and soothe the sensitive pride of the girl's heart.

Rose clapped her hands just as she used to do when any thing delighted her, and beamed at Mac approvingly, as she said, —

"Now that's a criticism worth having, and we are much obliged. I was sure *you'd* admire my Phebe when you knew her: but I didn't believe you would be wise enough to see it at once; and you have gone up many pegs in my estimation, I assure you."

"I was always fond of mineralogy you remember, and I've been tapping round a good deal lately, so I've learned to know precious metals when I see them," Mac said with his shrewd smile.

"That is the last hobby, then? Your letters have amused us immensely; for each one had a new theory or experiment, and the latest was always the best. I thought uncle would have died of laughing over the vegetarian mania: it was so funny to imagine you living on bread and milk, baked apples, and potatoes roasted in your own fire," continued Rose, changing the subject again.

"This old chap was the laughing-stock of his class. They called him Don Quixote; and the way he went at windmills of all sorts was a sight to see," put in Charlie, evidently feeling that Mac had been patted on the head quite as much as was good for him.

"But in spite of that the Don got through college with all the honors. Oh, wasn't I proud when Aunt Jane wrote us about it! and didn't she rejoice that her boy kept at the head of his class, and won the medal!" cried Rose, shaking Mac by both hands in a way that caused Charlie to wish "the old chap" had been left behind with Dr. Alec.

"Oh come, that's all mother's nonsense. I began earlier than the other fellows and liked it better: so I don't deserve any praise. Prince is right, though: I did make a regular jack of myself; but, on the whole, I'm not sure that my wild oats weren't better than some I've seen sowed. Anyway, they didn't cost much, and I'm none the worse for them," said Mac, placidly.

"I know what 'wild oats' mean. I heard Uncle Mac say Charlie was sowing 'em too fast, and I asked mamma, so she told me. And I know that he was suspelled or expended, I don't remember which, but it was something bad, and Aunt Clara cried," added Jamie, all in one breath; for he possessed a fatal gift of making *malapropos* remarks, which caused him to be a terror to his family.

"Do you want to go on the box again?" demanded Prince, with a warning frown.

"No, I don't."

"Then hold your tongue."

"Well, Mac needn't kick me; for I was only" — began the culprit, innocently trying to make a bad matter worse.

"That will do," interrupted Charlie, sternly, and James subsided a crushed boy, consoling himself with Rose's new watch for the indignities he suffered at the hands of the "old fellows," as he vengefully called his elders.

Mac and Charlie immediately began to talk as hard as their tongues could wag, bringing up all sorts of pleasant subjects so successfully that peals of laughter made passers-by look after the merry load with sympathetic smiles.

An avalanche of aunts fell upon Rose as soon as she reached home, and for the rest of the day the old house buzzed like a beehive. Evening found the whole tribe collected in the drawing-rooms, with the exception of Aunt Peace, whose place was empty now.

Naturally enough, the elders settled into one group after a while, and the young fellows clustered about the girls, like butterflies round two attractive flowers. Dr. Alec was the central figure in one room and Rose in the other; for the little girl, whom they had all loved and petted, had bloomed into a woman; and two years of absence had wrought a curious change in the relative positions of the cousins, especially the three elder ones, who eyed her with a mixture of boyish affection and manly admiration that was both new and pleasant.

Something sweet yet spirited about her charmed them and piqued their curiosity; for she was not quite like other girls, and rather startled them now and then by some independent little speech or act, which made them look at one another with a sly smile, as if reminded that Rose was "uncle's girl."

Let us listen, as in duty bound, to what the elders are saying first; for they are already building castles in the air for the boys and girls to inhabit.

"Dear child! how nice it is to see her safely back, so well and happy and like her sweet little self!" said Aunt Plenty, folding her hands as if giving thanks for a great happiness.

"I shouldn't wonder if you found that you'd brought a firebrand into the family, Alec. Two, in fact; for Phebe is a fine girl, and the lads have found it out already, if I'm not mistaken," added Uncle Mac, with a nod toward the other room.

All eyes followed his, and a highly suggestive tableau presented itself to the paternal and maternal audience in the back parlor.

Rose and Phebe, sitting side by side on the sofa, had evidently assumed at once the places which they were destined to fill by right of youth, sex, and beauty; for Phebe had long since ceased to be the maid and become the friend, and Rose meant to have that fact established at once.

Jamie occupied the rug, on which Will and Geordie stood at ease, showing their uniforms to the best advantage; for they were now in a great school, where military drill was the delight of their souls. Steve posed gracefully in an arm-chair, with Mac lounging over the back of it; while Archie leaned on one corner of the low chimney-piece, looking down at Phebe as she listened to his chat with smiling lips, and cheeks almost as rich in color as the carnations in her belt.

But Charlie was particularly effective, although he sat upon a music-stool, that most trying position for any man not gifted with grace in the management of his legs. Fortunately Prince was, and had fallen into an easy attitude, with one arm over the back of the sofa, his handsome head bent a little, as he monopolized Rose, with a devoted air and a very becoming expression of contentment on his face.

Aunt Clara smiled as if well pleased; Aunt Jessie looked thoughtful; Aunt Jane's keen eyes went from dapper Steve to broad-shouldered Mac with an anxious glance; Mrs. Myra murmured something about her "blessed Caroline;" and Aunt Plenty said warmly, —

"Bless the dears! any one might be proud of such a bonny flock of bairns as that."

"I am all ready to play chaperon as soon as you please, Alec; for I suppose the dear girl will come out at once, as she did not before you went away. My services won't be wanted long, I fancy; for with her many advantages she will be carried off in her first season or I'm much mistaken," said Mrs. Clara, with significant nods and smiles.

"You must settle all those matters with Rose: I am no longer captain, only first mate now, you know," answered Dr. Alec, adding soberly, half to himself, half to his brother, — "I wonder people are in such haste to 'bring out' their daughters, as it's called. To me there is something almost pathetic in the sight of a young girl standing on the threshold of the world, so innocent and hopeful, so ignorant of all that lies before her, and usually so ill prepared to meet the ups and downs of life. We do our duty better by the boys; but the poor little women are seldom provided with any armor worth having; and, sooner or later, they are sure to need it, for every one must fight her own battle, and only the brave and strong can win."

"You can't reproach yourself with neglect of that sort, Alec, for you have done your duty faithfully by George's girl; and I envy you the pride and happiness of having such a daughter, for she is that to you," answered old Mac, unexpectedly betraying the paternal sort of tenderness men seldom feel for their sons.

"I've tried, Mac, and I *am* both proud and happy; but with every year my anxiety seems to increase. I've done my best to fit Rose for what may come, as far as I can foresee it; but now she must stand alone, and all my care is powerless to keep her heart from aching, her life from being saddened by mistakes, or thwarted by the acts of others. I can only stand by, ready to share her joy and sorrow, and watch her shape her life."

"Why, Alec, what is the child going to do, that you need look so solemn?" exclaimed Mrs. Clara, who seemed to have assumed a sort of right to Rose already.

"Hark! and let her tell you herself," answered Dr. Alec, as Rose's voice was heard saying very earnestly, —

"Now you have all told your plans for the future, why don't you ask us ours?"

"Because we know that there is only one thing for a pretty girl to do, — break a dozen or so of hearts before she finds one to suit, then marry and settle," answered Charlie, as if no other reply was possible.

"That may be the case with many, but not with us; for Phebe and I believe that it is as much a right and a duty for women to do something with their lives as for men; and we are not going to be satisfied with such frivolous parts as you give us," cried Rose, with kindling eyes. "I mean what I say, and you cannot laugh me down. Would *you* be contented to be told to enjoy yourself for a little while, then marry and do nothing more till you die?" she added, turning to Archie.

"Of course not: that is only a part of a man's life," he answered decidedly.

"A very precious and lovely part, but not *all,*" continued Rose; "neither should it be for a woman: for we've got minds and souls as well as hearts; ambition and talents, as well as beauty and accomplishments; and we want to live and learn as well as love and be loved. I'm sick of being told that is all a woman is fit for! I won't have any thing to do with love till I prove that I am something beside a housekeeper and baby-tender!"

"Heaven preserve us! here's woman's rights with a vengeance!" cried Charlie, starting up with mock horror, while the others regarded Rose with mingled surprise and amusement, evidently fancying it all a girlish outbreak.

"Ah, you needn't pretend to be shocked: you will be in earnest presently; for this is only the beginning of my strong-mindedness," continued Rose, nothing daunted by the smiles of good-natured incredulity or derision on the faces of her cousins. "I have made up my mind not to be cheated out of the real things that make one good and happy; and, just because I'm a rich girl, fold my hands and drift as so many do. I haven't lived with Phebe all these years in vain: I know what courage and self-reliance can do for one; and I sometimes wish I hadn't a penny in the world so that I could go and earn my bread with her, and be as brave and independent as she will be pretty soon.''

It was evident that Rose was in earnest now; for, as she spoke, she turned to her friend with such respect as well as love in her face that the look told better than any words how heartily the rich girl appreciated the virtues hard experience had given the poor girl, and how eagerly she desired to earn what all her fortune could not buy for her.

Something in the glance exchanged between the friends impressed the young men in spite of their prejudices; and it was in a perfectly serious tone that Archie said, —

"I fancy you'll find your hands full, cousin, if you want work; for I've heard people say that wealth has its troubles and trials as well as poverty.''

"I know it, and I'm going to try and fill my place well. I've got some capital little plans all made, and have begun to study my profession already,'' answered Rose, with an energetic nod.

"Could I ask what it is to be?'' inquired Charlie, in a tone of awe.

"Guess!'' and Rose looked up at him with an expression half-earnest, half-merry.

"Well, I should say that you were fitted for a beauty and a belle; but, as that is evidently not to your taste, I am afraid you are going to study medicine and be a doctor. Won't your patients have a heavenly time though? It will be easy dying with an angel to poison them.''

"Now, Charlie, that's base of you, when you know how well women have succeeded in this profession, and what a comfort Dr. Mary Kirk was to dear Aunt Peace. I did want to study medicine; but uncle thought it wouldn't do to have so many M.D.'s in one family, since Mac thinks of trying it. Besides, I seem to have other work put into my hands that I am better fitted for.''

"You are fitted for any thing that is generous and good; and I'll stand by you, no matter what you've chosen,'' cried Mac heartily; for this was a new style of talk from a girl's lips, and he liked it immensely.

"Philanthropy is a generous, good, and beautiful profession; and I've chosen it for mine because I have much to give. I'm only the steward of the fortune papa left me; and I think, if I use it wisely for the happiness of others, it will be more blest than if I keep it all for myself.''

Very sweetly and simply was this said, but it was curious to see how differently the various hearers received it.

Charlie shot a quick look at his mother, who exclaimed, as if in spite of herself, —

"Now, Alec, *are* you going to let that girl squander a fine fortune on all sorts of charitable nonsense and wild schemes, for the prevention of pauperism and crime?"

" 'They who give to the poor lend to the Lord,' and practical Christianity is the kind He loves the best," was all Dr. Alec answered; but it silenced the aunts, and caused even prudent Uncle Mac to think with sudden satisfaction of certain secret investments he had made, which paid him no interest but the thanks of the poor.

Archie and Mac looked well pleased, and promised their advice and assistance with the enthusiasm of generous young hearts. Steve shook his head, but said nothing; and the lads on the rug at once proposed founding a hospital for invalid dogs and horses, white mice and wounded heroes.

"Don't you think that will be a better way for a woman to spend her life, than in dancing, dressing, and husband-hunting, Charlie?" asked Rose, observing his silence and anxious for his approval.

"Very pretty for a little while, and very effective too; for I don't know any thing more captivating than a sweet girl in a meek little bonnet, going on charitable errands and glorifying poor people's houses with a delightful mixture of beauty and benevolence. Fortunately, the dear souls soon tire of it, but it's heavenly while it lasts."

Charlie spoke in a tone of mingled admiration and contempt, and smiled a superior sort of smile, as if he understood all the innocent delusions as well as the artful devices of the sex, and expected nothing more from them. It both surprised and grieved Rose, for it did not sound like the Charlie she had left two years ago. But she only said, with a reproachful look and a proud little gesture of head and hand, as if she put the subject aside since it was not treated with respect, —

"I am sorry you have so low an opinion of women: there *was* a time when you believed in them sincerely."

"I do still, upon my word I do! They haven't a more devoted admirer and slave in the world than I am. Just try me and see," cried Charlie, gallantly kissing his hand to the sex in general.

But Rose was not appeased, and gave a disdainful shrug, as she answered with a look in her eyes that his lordship did not like, —

"Thank you: I don't want admirers or slaves, but friends and helpers. I've lived so long with a wise, good man that I am rather hard to suit, perhaps; but I don't intend to lower my standard, and any one who cares for my regard must at least try to live up to it."

"Whew! here's a wrathful dove! Come and smooth her ruffled plumage, Mac. I'll dodge before I do further mischief," and Charlie strolled away into the other room, privately lamenting that Uncle Alec had spoiled a fine girl by making her strong-minded.

He wished himself back again in five minutes; for Mac said something that produced a gale of laughter, and when he took a look over his shoulder the "wrathful dove" was cooing so peacefully and pleasantly he was sorely tempted to return and share the fun. But Charlie had been spoiled by too much indulgence, and it was hard for him to own himself in the wrong even when he knew it. He always got what he wanted sooner or later; and, having long ago made up his mind that Rose and her fortune were to be his, he was secretly displeased at the new plans and beliefs of the young lady, but flattered himself that they would soon be changed when she saw how unfashionable and inconvenient they were.

Musing over the delightful future he had laid out, he made himself comfortable in the sofa corner near his mother, till the appearance of a slight refection caused both groups to melt into one. Aunt Plenty believed in eating and drinking; so the slightest excuse for festivity delighted her hospitable soul, and on this joyful occasion she surpassed herself.

It was during this informal banquet that Rose, roaming about from one admiring relative to another, came upon the three younger lads, who were having a quiet little scuffle in a secluded corner.

"Come out here and let me have a look at you," she said enticingly; for she predicted an explosion and public disgrace if peace was not speedily restored.

Hastily smoothing themselves down, the young gentlemen presented three flushed and merry countenances for inspection, feeling highly honored by the command.

"Dear me, how you two have grown! You big things! how dare you get ahead of me in this way?" she said, standing on tiptoe to pat the curly pates before her; for Will and Geordie had shot up like weeds, and now grinned cheerfully down upon her as she surveyed them in comic amazement.

"The Campbells are all fine, tall fellows; and we mean to be the best of the lot. Shouldn't wonder if we were six-footers, like Grandpa," observed Will proudly, looking so like a young Shanghae rooster, all legs and an insignificant head, that Rose kept her countenance with difficulty.

"We shall broaden out when we get our growth. We are taller than Steve now, a half a head, both of us," added Geordie, with his nose in the air.

Rose turned to look at Steve, and, with a sudden smile, beckoned to him. He dropped his napkin, and flew to obey the summons; for she was queen of the hour, and he had openly announced his deathless loyalty.

"Tell the other boys to come here. I've a fancy to stand you all in a row and look you over, as you did me that dreadful day when you nearly frightened me out of my wits," she said, laughing at the memory of it as she spoke.

They came in a body, and, standing shoulder to shoulder, made such an imposing array that the young commander was rather daunted for a moment. But she had seen too much of the world lately to be abashed by a trifle; and the desire to try a girlish test gave her courage to face the line of smiling cousins with dignity and spirit.

"Now I'm going to stare at you as you stared at me. It is my revenge on you seven bad boys for entrapping one poor little girl, and enjoying her alarm. I'm not a bit afraid of you now; so tremble and beware!"

As she spoke, Rose looked up into Archie's face and nodded approvingly; for the steady gray eyes met hers fairly, and softened as they did so, — a becoming change, for naturally they were rather keen than kind.

"A true Campbell, bless you!" she said, and shook his hand heartily as she passed on.

Charlie came next, and here she felt less satisfied, though scarcely conscious why; for, as she looked, there came a defiant sort of flash, changing suddenly to something warmer than anger, stronger than pride, making her shrink a little and say, hastily, —

"I don't find the Charlie I left; but the Prince is there still, I see."

Turning to Mac with a sense of relief, she gently took off his "winkers," as Jamie called them, and looked straight into the honest blue eyes that looked straight back at her, full of a frank and friendly affection that warmed her heart, and made her own eyes brighten as she gave back the glasses, saying, with a look and tone of cordial satisfaction, —

"*You* are not changed, my dear old Mac; and I'm so glad of that!"

"Now say something extra sweet to me, because I'm the flower of the the family," said Steve, twirling the blonde moustache, which was evidently the pride of his life.

Rose saw at a glance that Dandy deserved his name more than ever, and promptly quenched his vanities by answering, with a provoking laugh, —

"Then the name of the flower of the family is Cock's-comb."

"Ah, ha! who's got it now?" jeered Will.

"Let us off easy, please," whispered Geordie, mindful that their turn came next.

"You blessed beanstalks! I'm proud of you: only don't grow quite out of sight, or ever be ashamed to look a woman in the face," answered Rose, with a gentle pat on the cheek of either bashful young giant; for both were as red as peonies, though their boyish eyes were as clear and calm as summer lakes.

"Now me!" And Jamie assumed his manliest air, feeling that he did not appear to advantage among his tall kinsmen. But he went to the head of the class in every one's opinion when Rose put her arms round him, saying, with a kiss, —

"You must be my boy now; for all the others are too old, and I want a faithful little page to do my errands for me."

"I will, I will! and I'll marry you too, if you'll just hold on till I grow up!" cried Jamie, rather losing his head at this sudden promotion.

"Bless the baby, what is he talking about?" laughed Rose, looking down at her little knight, as he clung about her with grateful ardor.

"Oh, I heard the aunts say that you'd better marry one of us, and keep the property in the family; so I speak first, because you are very fond of me, and I *do* love curls."

Alas for Jamie! this awful speech had hardly left his innocent lips when Will and Geordie swept him out of the room like a whirlwind; and the howls of that hapless boy were heard from the torture-hall, where being shut into the skeleton-case was one of the mildest punishments inflicted upon him.

Dismay fell upon the unfortunates who remained: but their confusion was soon ended; for Rose, with a look which they had never seen upon her face before, dismissed them with the brief command, "Break ranks, — the review is over," and walked away to Phebe.

"Confound that boy! You ought to shut him up, or gag him!" fumed Charlie, irritably.

"He shall be attended to," answered poor Archie, who was trying to bring up the little marplot with the success of most parents and guardians.

"The whole thing was deuced disagreeable," growled Steve, who felt that he had not distinguished himself in the late engagement.

"Truth generally is," observed Mac dryly, as he strolled away with his odd smile.

As if he suspected discord somewhere, Dr. Alec proposed music at this crisis; and the young people felt that it was a happy thought.

"I want you to hear both my birds; for they have improved immensely, and I am very proud of them," said the Doctor, twirling up the stool and pulling out the old music-books.

"I had better come first, for after you have heard the nightingale you won't care for the canary," added Rose, wishing to put Phebe at her ease; for she sat among them looking like a picture, but rather shy and silent, remembering the days when her place was in the kitchen.

"I'll give you some of the dear old songs you used to like so much. This was a favorite, I think;" and sitting down she sang the first familiar air that came, and sang it well in a pleasant, but by no means finished, manner.

It chanced to be "The Birks of Aberfeldie," and vividly recalled the time when Mac was ill, and she took care of him. The memory was sweet to her, and involuntarily her eye wandered in search of him. He was not far away, sitting just as he used to sit when she soothed his most despondent moods, — astride of a chair with his head down on his arms, as if the song suggested the attitude. Her heart quite softened to him as she looked, and she decided to forgive *him* if no one else; for she was sure that he had no mercenary plans about her tiresome money.

Charlie had assumed a pensive air, and fixed his fine eyes upon her with an expression of tender admiration, which made her laugh in spite of all her efforts to seem unconscious of it. She was both amused and annoyed at his very evident desire to remind her of certain sentimental passages in the last year of their girl and boyhood, and to change what she had considered a childish joke into romantic earnest. This did not suit her; for, young as she was, Rose had very serious ideas of love, and had no intention of being beguiled into even a flirtation with her handsome cousin.

So Charlie attitudinized unnoticed, and was getting rather out of temper when Phebe began to sing; and he forgot all about himself in admiration of her. It took everyone by surprise: for two years of foreign training added to several at home had worked wonders; and the beautiful voice that used to warble cheerily over pots and kettles, now rang out melodiously or melted to a mellow music that woke a sympathetic thrill in those who listened. Rose glowed with pride as she accompanied her friend; for Phebe was in her own world now, — a lovely world where no depressing memory of poor-house or kitchen, ignorance or loneliness, came to trouble her; a happy world where she could be herself, and rule others by the magic of her sweet gift.

Yes, Phebe was herself now, and showed it in the change that came over her at the first note of music. No longer shy and silent, no longer the image of a handsome girl, but a blooming woman, alive and full of the eloquence her art gave her, as she laid her hands softly together, fixed her eye on the light, and just poured out her song as simply and joyfully as the lark does soaring toward the sun.

"My faith, Alec! that's the sort of voice that wins a man's heart out of his breast!" exclaimed Uncle Mac, wiping his eyes after one of the plaintive ballads that never grow old.

"So it would!" answered Dr. Alec, delightedly.

"So it has," added Archie to himself; and he was right: for, just at that moment, he fell in love with Phebe. He actually did, and could fix the time almost to a second: for, at a quarter past nine, he merely thought her a very charming young person; at twenty minutes past, he considered her the loveliest woman he ever beheld; at five and twenty minutes past, she was an angel singing his soul away; and at half after nine he was a lost man, floating over a delicious sea to that temporary heaven on earth where lovers usually land after the first rapturous plunge.

If any one had mentioned this astonishing fact, nobody would have believed it; nevertheless, it was quite true: and sober, business-like Archie suddenly discovered a fund of romance at the bottom of his hitherto well-conducted heart that amazed him. He was not quite clear what had happened to him at first, and sat about in a dazed sort of way; seeing, hearing, knowing nothing but Phebe: while the unconscious idol found something wanting in the cordial praise so modestly received, because Mr. Archie never said a word.

This was one of the remarkable things which occurred that evening; another was that Mac paid Rose a compliment, which was such an unprecedented fact, it produced a great sensation, though only one person heard it.

Everybody had gone but Mac and his father, who was busy with the Doctor. Aunt Plenty was counting the teaspoons in the dining-room, and Phebe was helping her as of old. Mac and Rose were alone, — he apparently in a brown study, leaning his elbows on the chimney-piece; and she lying back in a low chair, looking thoughtfully at the fire. She was tired; and the quiet was grateful to her: so she kept silence and Mac respectfully held his tongue. Presently, however, she became conscious that he was looking at her as intently as eyes and glasses could do it; and, without stirring from her comfortable attitude, she said, smiling up at him, —

"He looks as wise as an owl: I wonder what he's thinking about?"

"You, cousin."

"Something good, I hope?"

"I was thinking Leigh Hunt was about right when he said, 'A girl is the sweetest thing God ever made.' "

"Why, Mac!" and Rose sat bolt upright with an astonished face: this was such an entirely unexpected sort of remark for the philosopher to make.

Evidently interested in the new discovery, Mac placidly continued, "Do you know, it seems as if I never really saw a girl before, or had any idea what agreeable creatures they could be. I fancy you are a remarkably good specimen, Rose."

"No, indeed! I'm only hearty and happy; and being safe at home again may make me look better than usual perhaps: but I'm no beauty except to uncle."

" 'Hearty and happy,' — that must be it," echoed Mac, soberly investigating the problem. "Most girls are sickly or silly, I think I have observed; and that is probably why I am so struck with you."

"Of all queer boys you are the queerest! Do you really mean that you don't like or notice girls?" asked Rose, much amused at this new peculiarity of her studious cousin.

"Well, no: I am only conscious of two sorts, — noisy and quiet ones. I prefer the latter: but, as a general thing, I don't notice any of them much more than I do flies, unless they bother me; then I'd like to flap them away; but, as that won't do, I hide."

Rose leaned back and laughed till her eyes were full: it was so comical to hear Mac sink his voice to a confidential whisper at the last words, and see him smile with sinful satisfaction at the memory of the tormentors he had eluded.

"You needn't laugh: it's a fact, I assure you. Charlie likes the creatures, and they spoil him; Steve follows suit, of course. Archie is a respectful slave when he can't help himself. As for me, I don't often give them a chance; and, when I get caught, I talk science and dead languages till they run for their lives. Now and then I find a sensible one, and then we get on excellently."

"A sad prospect for Phebe and me," sighed Rose, trying to keep sober.

"Phebe is evidently a quiet one. I know she is sensible, or you wouldn't care for her. I can see that she is pleasant to look at, so I fancy I shall like her. As for you, I helped bring you up; therefore I am a little anxious to see how you turn out. I was afraid your foreign polish might spoil you, but I think it has not. In fact, I find you quite satisfactory so far, if you don't mind my saying it. I don't quite know what the charm is, though. Must be the power of inward graces, since you insist that you have no outward ones."

Mac was peering at her with a shrewd smile on his lips, but such a kindly look behind the glasses, that she found both words and glance very pleasant, and answered merrily, —

"I am glad you approve of me, and much obliged for your care of my early youth. I hope to be a credit to you, and depend on your keeping me straight; for I'm afraid I shall be spoilt among you all."

"I'll keep my eye on you upon one condition," replied the youthful Mentor.

"Name it."

"If you are going to have a lot of lovers round, I wash my hands of you. If not, I'm your man."

"You must be sheep-dog, and help keep them away; for I don't want any yet awhile; and, between ourselves, I don't believe I shall have any if it is known that I am strong-minded. That fact will scare most men away like a yellow flag," said Rose: for, thanks to Dr. Alec's guardianship, she had wasted neither heart nor time in the foolish flirtations so many girls fritter away their youth upon.

"Hum! I rather doubt that," muttered Mac, as he surveyed the damsel before him.

She certainly did not look unpleasantly strong-minded, for she *was* beautiful in spite of her modest denials. Beautiful with the truest sort of beauty; for nobility of character lent its subtle charm to the bloom of youth, the freshness of health, the innocence of a nature whose sweet maidenliness Mac felt but could not describe. Gentle yet full of spirit, and all aglow with the earnestness that suggests lovely possibilities, and makes one hope that such human flowers may have heaven's purest air and warmest sunshine to blossom in.

"Wait and see," answered Rose; then, as her uncle's voice was heard in the hall, she held out her hand, adding pleasantly, "The old times are to begin again, so come soon and tell me all your doings, and help me with mine just as you used to do."

"You really mean it?" and Mac looked much pleased.

"I really do. You are so little altered, except to grow big, that I don't feel at all strange with you, and want to begin where we left off."

"That will be capital. Good-night, cousin," and to her great amazement he gave her a hearty kiss.

"Oh, but that is not the old way at all!" cried Rose, stepping back in merry confusion; while the audacious youth assumed an air of mild surprise, as he innocently asked, —

"Didn't we always say good-night in that way? I had an impression that we did, and were to begin just as we left off."

"Of course not; no power on earth would have bribed you to do it, as you know well enough. I don't mind the first night, but we are too old for that sort of thing now."

"I'll remember. It was the force of habit, I suppose; for I'm sure I must have done it in former times, it seemed so natural. Coming, father!" and Mac retired, evidently convinced that he was right.

"Dear old thing! he is as much a boy as ever, and that is such a comfort; for some of the others have grown up very fast," said Rose to herself, recalling Charlie's sentimental airs, and Archie's beatified expression while Phebe sang.

Jo's Last Scrape

From *Jo's Boys, and How They Turned Out. A Sequel to "Little Men"*
(Boston: Roberts Brothers, 1886)

*T*HE MARCH FAMILY had enjoyed a great many surprises in the course of their varied career, but the greatest of all was when the Ugly Duckling turned out to be, not a swan, but a golden goose, whose literary eggs found such an unexpected market that in ten years Jo's wildest and most cherished dream actually came true. How or why it happened she never clearly understood, but all of a sudden she found herself famous in a small way, and, better still, with a snug little fortune in her pocket to clear away the obstacles of the present and assure the future of her boys.

It began during a bad year when everything went wrong at Plumfield; times were hard, the school dwindled, Jo overworked herself and had a long illness; Laurie and Amy were abroad, and the Bhaers too proud to ask help even of those as near and dear as this generous pair. Confined to her room, Jo got desperate over the state of affairs, till she fell back upon the long-disused pen as the only thing she could do to help fill up the gaps in the income. A book for girls being wanted by a certain publisher, she hastily scribbled a little story describing a few scenes and adventures in the lives of herself and sisters, — though boys were more in her line, — and with very slight hopes of success sent it out to seek its fortune.

Things always went by contraries with Jo. Her first book, labored over for years, and launched full of the high hopes and ambitious dreams of youth, foundered on its voyage, though the wreck continued to float long afterward, to the profit of the publisher at least. The hastily written story, sent away with no thought beyond the few dollars it might bring, sailed with a fair wind and a wise pilot at the helm straight into public favor, and came home heavily laden with an unexpected cargo of gold and glory.

A more astonished woman probably never existed than Josephine Bhaer when her little ship came into port with flags flying, cannon that had been silent before now booming gayly, and, better than all, many kind faces rejoicing with her, many friendly hands grasping hers with cordial congratulations. After that it was plain sailing, and she merely had to load her ships and send them off on prosperous trips, to bring home stores of comfort for all she loved and labored for.

The fame she never did quite accept; for it takes very little fire to make a great deal of smoke nowadays, and notoriety is not real glory. The fortune she could not doubt, and gratefully received; though it was not half so large a one as a generous world reported it to be. The tide having turned continued to rise, and floated the family comfortably into a snug harbor where the older members could rest secure from storms, and whence the younger ones could launch their boats for the voyage of life.

All manner of happiness, peace, and plenty came in those years to bless the patient waiters, hopeful workers, and devout believers in the wisdom and justice of Him who sends disappointment, poverty, and sorrow to try the love of human hearts and make success the sweeter when it comes. The world saw the prosperity, and kind souls rejoiced over the improved fortunes of the family; but the success Jo valued most, the happiness that nothing could change or take away, few knew much about.

It was the power of making her mother's last years happy and serene; to see the burden of care laid down forever, the weary hands at rest, the dear face untroubled by any anxiety, and the tender heart free to pour itself out in the wise charity which was its delight. As a girl, Jo's favorite plan had been a room where Marmee could sit in peace and enjoy herself after her hard, heroic life. Now the dream had become a happy fact, and Marmee sat in her pleasant chamber with every comfort and luxury about her, loving daughters to wait on her as infirmities increased, a faithful mate to lean upon, and grandchildren to brighten the twilight of life with their dutiful affection. A very precious time to all, for she rejoiced as only mothers can in the good fortunes of their children. She had lived to reap the harvest she sowed; had seen prayers answered, hopes blossom, good gifts bear fruit, peace and prosperity bless the home she had made; and then, like some brave, patient angel, whose work was done, turned her face heavenward, glad to rest.

This was the sweet and sacred side of the change; but it had its droll and thorny one, as all things have in this curious world of ours. After the first surprise, incredulity, and joy, which came to Jo, with the ingratitude of human nature, she soon tired of renown, and began to resent her loss of liberty. For suddenly the admiring public took possession of her and all her affairs, past, present, and to come. Strangers demanded to look at her, question, advise, warn, congratulate, and drive her out of her wits by well-meant but very wearisome attentions. If she declined to open her heart to them, they reproached her; if she refused to endow pet charities, relieve private wants, or sympathize with every ill and trial known to humanity, she was called hard-hearted, selfish, and haughty; if she found it impossible to answer the piles of letters sent her, she was neglectful of her duty to the admiring public; and if she preferred the privacy of home to the pedestal upon which she was requested to pose, "the airs of literary people" were freely criticised.

She did her best for the children, they being the public for whom she wrote, and labored stoutly to supply the demand always in the mouths of voracious youth, — "More stories; more right away!" Her family objected to this devotion at their expense, and her health suffered; but for a time she gratefully offered herself up on the altar of juvenile literature, feeling that she owed a good deal to the little friends in whose sight she had found favor after twenty years of effort.

But a time came when her patience gave out; and wearying of being a lion, she became a bear in nature as in name, and retiring to her den, growled awfully when ordered out. Her family enjoyed the fun, and had small sympathy with her trials, but Jo came to consider it the worst scrape of her life; for liberty had always been her dearest possession, and it seemed to be fast going from her. Living in a lantern soon loses its charms, and she was too old, too tired, and too busy to like it. She felt that she had done all that could reasonably be required of her when autographs, photographs, and autobiographical sketches had been sown broadcast over the land; when artists had taken her home in all its aspects, and reporters had taken her in the grim one she always assumed on these trying occasions; when a series of enthusiastic boarding-schools had ravaged her grounds for trophies, and a steady stream of amiable pilgrims had worn her doorsteps with their respectful feet; when servants left after a week's trial of the bell that rang all day; when her husband was forced to guard her at meals, and the boys to cover her retreat out of back windows on certain occasions when enterprising guests walked in unannounced at unfortunate moments.

A sketch of one day may perhaps explain the state of things, offer some excuse for the unhappy woman, and give a hint to the autograph-fiend now rampant in the land; for it is a true tale.

"There ought to be a law to protect unfortunate authors," said Mrs. Jo one morning soon after Emil's arrival, when the mail brought her an unusually large and varied assortment of letters. "To me it is a more vital subject than international copyright; for time is money, peace is health, and I lose both with no return but less respect for my fellow-creatures and a wild desire to fly into the wilderness, since I cannot shut my doors even in free America."

"Lion-hunters are awful when in search of their prey. If they could change places for a while it would do them good; and they'd see what bores they were when they 'do themselves the honor of calling to express their admiration of our charming work,' " quoted Ted, with a bow to his parent, now frowning over twelve requests for autographs.

"I have made up my mind on one point," said Mrs. Jo with great firmness. "I will *not* answer this kind of letter. I've sent at least six to this boy, and he probably sells them. This girl writes from a seminary, and if I send her one all the other girls will at once write for more. All begin by saying they know they intrude, and that I am of course annoyed by these requests; but they venture to ask because I like boys, or they like the books, or it is only one. Emerson and Wittier put these things in the waste-paper basket; and though only a literary nursery-maid who provides moral pap for the young, I will follow their illustrious example; for I shall have no time to eat or sleep if I try to satisfy these dear unreasonable children;" and Mrs. Jo swept away the entire batch with a sigh of relief.

"I'll open the others and let you eat your breakfast in peace, *liebe Mutter,*" said Rob, who often acted as her secretary. "Here's one from the South;" and breaking an imposing seal, he read: —

MADAM, — As it has pleased Heaven to bless your efforts with a large fortune, I feel no hesitation in asking you to supply funds to purchase a new communion-service for our church. To whatever denomination you belong, you will of course respond with liberality to such a request.

Respectfully yours,
MRS. X. Y. ZAVIER.

"Send a civil refusal, dear. All I have to give must go to feed and clothe the poor at my gates. That is my thank-offering for success. Go on," answered his mother, with a grateful glance about her happy home.

"A literary youth of eighteen proposes that you put your name to a novel he has written; and after the first edition your name is to be taken off and his put on. There's a cool proposal for you. I guess you won't agree to that, in spite of your soft-heartedness towards most of the young scribblers."

"Could n't be done. Tell him so kindly, and don't let him send the manuscript. I have seven on hand now, and barely time to read my own," said Mrs. Jo, pensively fishing a small letter out of the slop-bowl and opening it with care, because the down-hill address suggested that a child wrote it.

"I will answer this myself. A little sick girl wants a book, and she shall have it, but I can't write sequels to all the rest to please her. I should never come to an end if I tried to suit these voracious little Oliver Twists, clamoring for more. What next, Robin?"

"This is short and sweet."

> DEAR MRS. BHAER, — I am now going to give you my opinion of your works. I have read them all many times, and call them first-rate. Please go ahead.
>
> > Your admirer,
> > BILLY BABCOCK.

"Now that is what I like. Billy is a man of sense and a critic worth having, since he has read my works many times before expressing his opinion. He asks for no answer, so send my thanks and regards."

"Here's a lady in England with seven girls, and she wishes to know your views upon education. Also what careers they shall follow, — the oldest being twelve. Don't wonder she's worried," laughed Rob.

"I'll try to answer it. But as I have no girls, my opinion is n't worth much and will probably shock her, as I shall tell her to let them run and play and build up good, stout bodies before she talks about careers. They will soon show what they want, if they are let alone, and not all run in the same mould."

"Here's a fellow who wants to know what sort of a girl he shall marry, and if you know of any like those in your stories."

"Give him Nan's address, and see what he'll get," proposed Ted, privately resolving to do it himself if possible.

"This is from a lady who wants you to adopt her child and lend her money to study art abroad for a few years. Better take it, and try your hand at a girl, mother."

"No, thank you, I will keep to my own line of business. What is that blotted one? It looks rather awful, to judge by the ink," asked Mrs. Jo, who beguiled her daily task by trying to guess from the outside what was inside her many letters. This proved to be a poem from an insane admirer, to judge by its incoherent style.

To J. M. B.

Oh, were I a heliotrope,
  I would play poet,
And blow a breeze of fragrance
  To you; and none should know it.

Your form like the stately elm
  When Phœbus gilds the morning ray;
Your cheeks like the ocean bed
  That blooms a rose in May.

Your words are wise and bright,
  I bequeath them to you a legacy given;
And when your spirit takes its flight,
  May it bloom a flower in heaven.

My tongue in flattering language spoke,
  And sweeter silence never broke
In busiest street or loneliest glen.
  I take you with the flashes of my pen.

Consider the lilies, how they grow;
  They toil not, yet are fair,
Gems and flowers and Solomon's seal.
  The geranium of the world is J. M. Bhaer.
                                      JAMES

While the boys shouted over this effusion, — which is a true one, — their mother read several liberal offers from budding magazines for her to edit them gratis; one long letter from a young girl inconsolable because her favorite hero died, and "would dear Mrs. Bhaer rewrite the tale, and make it end good?" another from an irate boy denied an autograph, who darkly foretold financial ruin and loss of favor if she did not send him and all other fellows who asked autographs, photographs, and autobiographical sketches; a minister wished to know her religion; and an undecided maiden asked which of her two lovers she should marry. These samples will suffice to show a few of the claims made on a busy woman's time, and make my readers pardon Mrs. Jo if she did not carefully reply to all.

"That job is done. Now I will dust a bit, and then go to my work. I'm all behindhand, and serials can't wait; so deny me to everybody, Mary. I won't see Queen Victoria if she comes to-day." And Mrs. Bhaer threw down her napkin as if defying all creation.

"I hope the day will go well with thee, my dearest," answered her husband, who had been busy with his own voluminous correspondence. "I will dine at college with Professor Plock, who is to visit us to-day. The *Jünglings* can lunch on Parnassus; so thou shalt have a quiet time." And smoothing the worried lines out of her forehead with his good-by kiss, the excellent man marched away, both pockets full of books, an old umbrella in one hand, and a bag of stones for the geology class in the other.

"If all literary women had such thoughtful angels for husbands, they would live longer and write more. Perhaps that would n't be a blessing to the world though, as most of us write too much now," said Mrs. Jo, waving her feather duster to her spouse, who responded with flourishes of the umbrella as he went down the avenue.

Rob started for school at the same time, looking so much like him with his books and bag and square shoulders and steady air that his mother laughed as she turned away, saying heartily, "Bless both my dear professors, for better creatures never lived!"

Emil was already gone to his ship in the city; but Ted lingered to steal the address he wanted, ravage the sugar-bowl, and talk with "Mum;" for the two had great larks together.

Mrs. Jo always arranged her own parlor, refilled her vases, and gave the little touches that left it cool and neat for the day. Going to draw down the curtain, she beheld an artist sketching on the lawn, and groaned as she hastily retired to the back window to shake her duster.

At that moment the bell rang and the sound of wheels was heard in the road.

"I'll go; Mary lets 'em in;" and Ted smoothed his hair as he made for the hall.

"Can't see any one. Give me a chance to fly upstairs," whispered Mrs. Jo, preparing to escape. But before she could do so, a man appeared at the door with a card in his hand. Ted met him with a stern air, and his mother dodged behind the window-curtains to bide her time for escape.

"I am doing a series of articles for the 'Saturday Tattler,' and I called to see Mrs. Bhaer the first of all," began the new-comer in the insinuating tone of his tribe, while his quick eyes were taking in all they could, experience having taught him to make the most of his time, as his visits were usually short ones.

"Mrs. Bhaer never sees reporters, sir."

"But a few moments will be all I ask," said the man, edging his way further in.

"You can't see her, for she is out," replied Teddy, as a backward glance showed him that his unhappy parent had vanished, — through the window, he supposed, as she sometimes did when hard bestead.

"Very sorry. I'll call again. Is this her study? Charming room!" And the intruder fell back on the parlor, bound to see something and bag a fact if he died in the attempt.

"It is not," said Teddy, gently but firmly backing him down the hall, devoutly hoping that his mother had escaped round the corner of the house.

"If you could tell me Mrs. Bhaer's age and birthplace, date of marriage, and number of children, I should be much obliged," continued the unabashed visitor as he tripped over the door-mat.

"She is about sixty, born in Nova Zembla, married just forty years ago to-day, and has eleven daughters. Anything else, sir?" And Ted's sober face was such a funny contrast to his ridiculous reply that the reporter owned himself routed, and retired laughing just as a lady followed by three beaming girls came up the steps.

"We are all the way from Oshkosh, and could n't go home without seein' dear Aunt Jo. My girls just admire her works, and lot on gettin' a sight of her. I know it's early; but we are goin' to see Holmes and Longfeller, and the rest of the celebrities, so we ran out here fust thing. Mrs. Erastus Kingsbury Parmalee, of Oshkosh, tell her. We don't mind waitin'; we can look round a spell if she ain't ready to see folks yet."

All this was uttered with such rapidity that Ted could only stand gazing at the buxom damsels, who fixed their six blue eyes upon him so beseechingly that his native gallantry made it impossible to deny them a civil reply at least.

"Mrs. Bhaer is not visible to-day, — out just now, I believe; but you can see the house and grounds if you like," he murmured, falling back as the four pressed in, gazing rapturously about them.

"Oh, thank you! Sweet, pretty place I'm sure! That's where she writes, ain't it? Do tell me if that's her picture! Looks just as I imagined her!"

With these remarks the ladies paused before a fine engraving of the Hon. Mrs. Norton, with a pen in her hand and a rapt expression of countenance, likewise a diadem and pearl necklace.

Keeping his gravity with an effort, Teddy pointed to a very bad portrait of Mrs. Jo, which hung behind the door, and afforded her much amusement, it was so dismal, in spite of a curious effect of light upon the end of the nose and cheeks as red as the chair she sat in.

"This was taken for my mother; but it is not very good," he said, enjoying the struggles of the girls not to look dismayed at the sad difference between the real and ideal. The youngest, aged twelve, could not conceal her disappointment, and turned away, feeling as so many of us have felt when we discover that our idols are very ordinary men and women.

"I thought she'd be about sixteen and have her hair braided in two tails down her back. I don't care about seeing her now," said the honest child walking off to the hall door, leaving her mother to apologize, and her sisters to declare that the bad portrait was "perfectly lovely, so speaking and poetic, you know, 'specially about the brow."

"Come, girls, we must be goin', if we want to get through to-day. You can leave your albums and have them sent when Mrs. Bhaer has written a sentiment in 'em. We are a thousand times obliged. Give our best love to your ma, and tell her we are so sorry not to see her."

Just as Mrs. Erastus Kingsbury Parmalee uttered the words her eye fell upon a middle-aged woman in a large checked apron, with a handkerchief tied over her head, busily dusting an end room which looked like a study.

"One peep at her sanctum since she is out," cried the enthusiastic lady, and swept across the hall with her flock before Teddy could warn his mother, whose retreat had been cut off by the artist in front, the reporter at the back part of the house, — for he had n't gone — and the ladies in the hall.

"They've got her!" thought Teddy, in comical dismay. "No use for her to play housemaid since they've seen the portrait."

Mrs. Jo did her best, and being a good actress, would have escaped if the fatal picture had not betrayed her. Mrs. Parmalee paused at the desk, and regardless of the meerschaum that lay there, the man's slippers close by, and a pile of letters directed to "Prof. F. Bhaer," she clasped her hands, exclaiming impressively, "Girls, this is the spot where she wrote those sweet, those moral tales which have thrilled us to the soul! Could I — ah, could I take one morsel of paper, an old pen, a postage stamp even, as a memento of this gifted woman?"

"Yes'm, help yourselves," replied the maid, moving away with a glance at the boy whose eyes were now full of a merriment he could not suppress.

The oldest girl saw it, guessed the truth, and a quick look at the woman in the apron confirmed her suspicion. Touching her mother, she whispered, "Ma, it's Mrs. Bhaer herself. I know it is."

"No? yes? it is! Well, I do declare, how nice that is!" And hastily pursuing the unhappy woman, who was making for the door, Mrs. Parmalee cried eagerly, "Don't mind us! I know you're busy, but just let me take your hand and then we'll go."

Giving herself up for lost, Mrs. Jo turned and presented her hand like a tea-tray, submitting to have it heartily shaken, as the matron said, with somewhat alarming hospitality, —

"If ever you come to Oshkosh, your feet won't be allowed to touch the pavement; for you'll be borne in the arms of the populace, we shall be so dreadful glad to see you."

Mentally resolving never to visit that effusive town, Jo responded as cordially as she could; and having written her name in the albums, provided each visitor with a memento, and kissed them all round, they at last departed, to call on "Longfeller, Holmes, and the rest," — who were all out, it is devoutly to be hoped.

"You villain, why did n't you give me a chance to whip away? Oh, my dear, what fibs you told that man! I hope we shall be forgiven our sins in this line, but I don't know what *is* to become of us if we don't dodge. So many against one is n't fair play." And Mrs. Jo hung up her apron in the hall closet, with a groan at the trials of her lot.

"More people coming up the avenue! Better dodge while the coast is clear! I'll head them off!" cried Teddy, looking back from the steps, as he was departing to school.

Mrs. Jo flew upstairs, and having locked her door, calmly viewed a young ladies' seminary camp on the lawn, and being denied the house, proceed to enjoy themselves by picking the flowers, doing up their hair, eating lunch, and freely expressing their opinion of the place and its possessors before they went.

A few hours of quiet followed, and she was just settling down to a long afternoon of hard work, when Rob came home to tell her that the Young Men's Christian Union would visit the college, and two or three of the fellows whom she knew wanted to pay their respects to her on the way.

"It is going to rain, so they won't come, I dare say; but father thought you'd like to be ready, in case they do call. You always see the boys, you know, though you harden your heart to the poor girls," said Rob, who had heard from his brother about the morning visitations.

"Boys don't gush, so I can stand it. The last time I let in a party of girls, one fell into my arms and said, 'Darling, love me!' I wanted to shake her," answered Mrs. Jo, wiping her pen with energy.

"You may be sure the fellows won't do it, but they *will* want autographs, so you'd better be prepared with a few dozen," said Rob, laying out a quire of note-paper, being a hospitable youth and sympathizing with those who admired his mother.

"They can't outdo the girls. At X College I really believe I wrote three hundred during the day I was there, and I left a pile of cards and albums on my table when I came away. It is one of the most absurd and tiresome manias that ever afflicted the world."

Nevertheless Mrs. Jo wrote her name a dozen times, put on her black silk, and resigned herself to the impending call, praying for rain, however, as she returned to her work.

The shower came, and feeling quite secure, she rumpled up her hair, took off her cuffs, and hurried to finish her chapter; for thirty pages a day was her task, and she liked to have it well done before evening. Josie had brought some flowers for the vases, and was just putting the last touches when she saw several umbrellas bobbing down the hill.

"They are coming, Aunty! I see uncle hurrying across the field to receive them," she called at the stair-foot.

"Keep an eye on them, and let me know when they enter the avenue. It will take but a minute to tidy up and run down," answered Mrs. Jo, scribbling away for dear life, because serials wait for no man, not even the whole Christian Union *en masse*.

"There are more than two or three. I see half a dozen at least," called sister Ann from the hall door. "No! a dozen, I do believe; Aunty, look out; they are all coming! What *shall* we do?" and Josie quailed at the idea of facing the black throng rapidly approaching.

"Mercy on us, there are hundreds! Run and put a tub in the back entry for their umbrellas to drip into. Tell them to go down the hall and leave them, and pile their hats on the table; the tree won't hold them all. No use to get mats; my poor carpets!" And down went Mrs. Jo to prepare for the invasion, while Josie and the maids flew about dismayed at the prospect of so many muddy boots.

On they came, a long line of umbrellas, with splashed legs and flushed faces underneath; for the gentlemen had been having a good time all over the town, undisturbed by the rain. Professor Bhaer met them at the gate, and was making a little speech of welcome, when Mrs. Jo, touched by their bedraggled state, appeared at the door, beckoning them in. Leaving their host to orate bareheaded in the wet, the young men hastened up the steps, merry, warm, and eager, clutching off their hats as they came, and struggling with their umbrellas as the order was passed to march in and stack arms.

Tramp, tramp, tramp, down the hall went seventy-five pairs of boots; soon seventy-five umbrellas dripped sociably in the hospitable tub, while their owners swarmed all over the lower part of the house; and seventy-five hearty hands were shaken by the hostess without a murmur, though some were wet, some very warm, and nearly all bore trophies of the day's ramble. One impetuous party flourished a small turtle as he made his compliments; another had a load of sticks cut from noted spots; and all begged for some memento of Plumfield. A pile of cards mysteriously appeared on the table, with a written request for autographs; and despite her morning vow, Mrs. Jo wrote every one, while her husband and boys did the honors of the house.

Josie fled to the back parlor, but was discovered by exploring youths, and mortally insulted by one of them, who innocently inquired if she was Mrs. Bhaer. The reception did not last long, and the end was better than the beginning; for the rain ceased, and a rainbow shone beautifully over them as the good fellows stood upon the lawn singing sweetly for a farewell. A happy omen, that bow of promise arched over the young heads, as if Heaven smiled upon their union, and showed them that above the muddy earth and rainy skies the blessed sun still shone for all.

Three cheers, and then away they went, leaving a pleasant recollection of their visit to amuse the family as they scraped the mud off the carpets with shovels and emptied the tub half-full of water.

"Nice, honest, hard-working fellows, and I don't begrudge my half-hour at all; but I *must* finish, so don't let any one disturb me till tea-time," said Mrs. Jo, leaving Mary to shut up the house; for papa and the boys had gone off with the guests, and Josie had run home to tell her mother about the fun at Aunt Jo's.

Peace reigned for an hour, then the bell rang and Mary came giggling up to say, "A queer kind of a lady wants to know if she can catch a grasshopper in the garden."

"A what?" cried Mrs. Jo, dropping her pen with a blot; for of all the odd requests ever made, this was the oddest.

"A grasshopper, ma'am. I said you was busy, and asked what she wanted, and says she, 'I've got grasshoppers from the grounds of several famous folks, and I want one from Plumfield to add to my collection.' Did you ever?" And Mary giggled again at the idea.

"Tell her to take all there are and welcome. I shall be glad to get rid of them; always bouncing in my face and getting in my dress," laughed Mrs. Jo.

Mary retired, to return in a moment nearly speechless with merriment.

"She's much obliged, ma'am, and she'd like an old gown or a pair of stockings of yours to put in a rug she's making. Got a vest of Emerson's, she says, and a pair of Mr. Holmes's trousers, and a dress of Mrs. Stowe's. She must be crazy!"

"Give her that old red shawl, then I shall make a gay show among the great ones in that astonishing rug. Yes, they are all lunatics, these lion-hunters; but this seems to be a harmless maniac, for she does n't take my time and gives me a good laugh," said Mrs. Jo, returning to her work after a glance from the window, which showed her a tall, thin lady in rusty black, skipping wildly to and fro on the lawn in pursuit of the lively insect she wanted.

No more interruptions till the light began to fade, then Mary popped her head in to say a gentleman wished to see Mrs. Bhaer, and would n't take no for an answer.

"He must. I shall *not* go down. This has been an awful day, and I won't be disturbed again," replied the harassed authoress, pausing in the midst of the grand *finale* of her chapter.

"I told him so, ma'am; but he walked right in as bold as brass. I guess he's another crazy one, and I declare I'm 'most afraid of him, he's so big and black, and cool as cucumbers, though I will say he's good-looking," added Mary, with a simper; for the stranger had evidently found favor in her sight despite his boldness.

"My day has been ruined, and I *will* have this last half-hour to finish. Tell him to go away; I *won't* go down," cried Mrs. Jo, fiercely.

Mary went; and listening, in spite of herself, her mistress heard first a murmur of voices, then a cry from Mary, and remembering the ways of reporters, also that her maid was both pretty and timid, Mrs. Bhaer flung down her pen and went to the rescue. Descending with her most majestic air she demanded in an awe-inspiring voice, as she paused to survey the somewhat brigandish intruder who seemed to be storming the staircase which Mary was gallantly defending, —

"*Who* is this person who insists on remaining when I have declined to see him?"

"I'm sure I don't know, ma'am. He won't give no name, and says you'll be sorry if you don't see him," answered Mary, retiring flushed and indignant from her post.

"Won't you be sorry?" asked the stranger, looking up with a pair of black eyes full of laughter, the flash of white teeth through a long beard, and both hands out as he boldly approached the irate lady.

Mrs. Jo gave one keen look, for the voice was familiar; then completed Mary's bewilderment by throwing both arms round the brigand's neck, exclaiming joyfully, "My dearest boy, where did you come from?"

"California, on purpose to see you, Mother Bhaer. Now won't you be sorry if I go away?" answered Dan, with a hearty kiss.

"To think of my ordering you out of the house when I've been longing to see you for a year," laughed Mrs. Jo, as she went down to have a good talk with her returned wanderer, who enjoyed the joke immensely.

Fiction and Autobiography

Transcendental Wild Oats

A Chapter from an Unwritten Romance

Independent, 18 December 1873

O N THE FIRST DAY of June, 184–, a large wagon, drawn by a small horse and containing a motley load, went lumbering over certain New England hills, with the pleasing accompaniments of wind, rain, and hail. A serene man with a serene child upon his knee was driving, or rather being driven, for the small horse had it all his own way. A brown boy with a William Penn style of countenance sat beside him, firmly embracing a bust of Socrates. Behind them was an energetic-looking woman, with a benevolent brow, satirical mouth, and eyes brimful of hope and courage. A baby reposed upon her lap, a mirror leaned against her knee, and a basket of provisions danced about at her feet, as she struggled with a large, unruly umbrella. Two blue-eyed little girls, with hands full of childish treasures, sat under one old shawl, chatting happily together.

In front of this lively party stalked a tall, sharp-featured man, in a long blue cloak; and a fourth small girl trudged along beside him through the mud as if she rather enjoyed it.

The wind whistled over the bleak hills; the rain fell in a despondent drizzle, and twilight began to fall. But the calm man gazed as tranquilly into the fog as if he beheld a radiant bow of promise spanning the gray sky. The cheery woman tried to cover every one but herself with the big umbrella. The brown boy pillowed his head on the bald pate of Socrates and slumbered peacefully. The little girls sang lullabies to their dolls in soft, maternal murmurs. The sharp-nosed pedestrian marched steadily on, with the blue cloak streaming out behind him like a banner; and the lively infant splashed through the puddles with a duck-like satisfaction pleasant to behold.

Thus these modern pilgrims journeyed hopefully out of the old world, to found a new one in the wilderness.

The editors of *The Transcendental Tripod* had received from Messrs. Lion & Lamb (two of the aforesaid pilgrims) a communication from which the following statement is an extract: —

"We have made arrangements with the proprietor of an estate of about a hundred acres which liberates this tract from human ownership. Here we shall prosecute our effort to initiate a Family in harmony with the primitive instincts of man.

"Ordinary secular farming is not our object. Fruit, grain, pulse, herbs, flax, and other vegetable products, receiving assiduous attention, will afford ample manual occupation, and chaste supplies for the bodily needs. It is intended to adorn the pastures with orchards, and to supersede the labor of cattle by the spade and the pruning-knife.

"Consecrated to human freedom, the land awaits the sober culture of devoted men. Beginning with small pecuniary means, this enterprise must be rooted in a reliance on the succors of an ever-bounteous Providence, whose vital affinities being secured by this union with uncorrupted field and unworldly persons, the cares and injuries of a life of gain are avoided.

"The inner nature of each member of the Family is at no time neglected. Our plan contemplates all such disciplines, cultures, and habits as evidently conduce to the purifying of the inmates.

"Pledged to the spirit alone, the founders anticipate no hasty or numerous addition to their numbers. The kingdom of peace is entered only through the gates of self-denial; and felicity is the test and the reward of loyalty to the unswerving law of Love."

This prospective Eden at present consisted of an old red farmhouse, a dilapidated barn, many acres of meadow-land, and a grove. Ten ancient apple-trees were all the "chaste supply" which the place offered as yet; but, in the firm belief that plenteous orchards were soon to be evoked from their inner consciousness, these sanguine founders had christened their domain Fruitlands.

Here Timon Lion intended to found a colony of Latter Day Saints, who, under his patriarchal sway, should regenerate the world and glorify his name for ever. Here Abel Lamb, with the devoutest faith in the high ideal which was to him a living truth, desired to plant a Paradise, where Beauty, Virtue, Justice, and Love might live happily together, without the possibility of a serpent entering in. And here his wife, unconverted but faithful to the end, hoped, and after many wanderings over the face of the earth, to find rest for herself and a home for her children.

"There is our new abode," announced the enthusiast, smiling with a satisfaction quite undampened by the drops dripping from his hat-brim, as they turned at length into a cart-path that wound along a steep hillside into a barren-looking valley.

"A little difficult of access," observed his practical wife, as she endeavored to keep her various household goods from going overboard with every lurch of the laden ark.

"Like all good things. But those who earnestly desire and patiently seek will soon find us," placidly responded the philosopher from the mud, through which he was now endeavoring to pilot the much-enduring horse.

"Truth lies at the bottom of a well, Sister Hope," said Brother Timon, pausing to detach his small comrade from a gate, whereon she was perched for a clearer gaze into futurity.

"That's the reason we so seldom get at it, I suppose," replied Mrs. Hope, making a vain clutch at the mirror, which a sudden jolt sent flying out of her hands.

"We want no false reflections here," said Timon, with a grim smile, as he crunched the fragments under foot in his onward march.

Sister Hope held her peace, and looked wistfully through the mist at her promised home. The old red house with a hospitable glimmer at its windows cheered her eyes; and, considering the weather, was a fitter refuge than the sylvan bowers some of the more ardent souls might have preferred.

The new-comers were welcomed by one of the elect precious, — a regenerate farmer, whose idea of reform consisted chiefly in wearing white cotton raiment and shoes of untanned leather. This costume, with a snowy beard, gave him a venerable, and at the same time a somewhat bridal appearance.

The goods and chattels of the Society not having arrived, the weary family reposed before the fire on blocks of wood, while Brother Moses White regaled them with roasted potatoes, brown bread and water, in two plates, a tin pan, and one mug; his table service being limited. But, having cast the forms and vanities of a depraved world behind them, the elders welcomed hardship with the enthusiasm of new pioneers, and the children heartily enjoyed this foretaste of what they believed was to be a sort of perpetual picnic.

During the progress of this frugal meal, two more brothers appeared. One a dark, melancholy man, clad in homespun, whose peculiar mission was to turn his name hind part before and use as few words as possible. The other was a bland, bearded Englishman, who expected to be saved by eating uncooked food and going without clothes. He had not yet adopted the primitive costume, however; but contented himself with meditatively chewing dry beans out of a basket.

"Every meal should be a sacrament, and the vessels used should be beautiful and symbolical," observed Brother Lamb, mildly, righting the tin pan slipping about on his knees. "I priced a silver service when in town, but it was too costly; so I got some graceful cups and vases of Britannia ware."

"Hardest things in the world to keep bright. Will whiting be allowed in the community?" inquired Sister Hope, with a housewife's interest in labor-saving institutions.

"Such trivial questions will be discussed at a more fitting time," answered Brother Timon, sharply, as he burnt his fingers with a very hot potato. "Neither sugar, molasses, milk, butter, cheese, nor flesh are to be used among us, for nothing is to be admitted which has caused wrong or death to man or beast."

"Our garments are to be linen till we learn to raise our own cotton or some substitute for woolen fabrics," added Brother Abel, blissfully basking in an imaginary future as warm and brilliant as the generous fire before him.

"Haou abaout shoes?" asked Brother Moses, surveying his own with interest.

"We must yield that point till we can manufacture an innocent substitute for leather. Bark, wood, or some durable fabric will be invented in time. Meanwhile, those who desire to carry out our idea to the fullest extent can go barefooted," said Lion, who liked extreme measures.

"I never will, nor let my girls," murmured rebellious Sister Hope, under her breath.

"Haou do you cattle'ate to treat the ten-acre lot? Ef things ain't 'tended to right smart, we shan't hev no crops," observed the practical patriarch in cotton.

"We shall spade it," replied Abel, in such perfect good faith that Moses said no more, though he indulged in a shake of the head as he glanced at hands that had held nothing heavier than a pen for years. He was a paternal old soul and regarded the younger men as promising boys on a new sort of lark.

"What shall we do for lamps, if we cannot use any animal substance? I do hope light of some sort is to be thrown upon the enterprise," said Mrs. Lamb, with anxiety, for in those days kerosene and camphene were not, and gas unknown in the wilderness.

"We shall go without till we have discovered some vegetable oil or wax to serve us," replied Brother Timon, in a decided tone, which caused Sister Hope to resolve that her private lamp should be always trimmed, if not burning.

"Each member is to perform the work for which experience, strength, and taste best fit him," continued Dictator Lion. "Thus drudgery and disorder will be avoided and harmony prevail. We shall rise at dawn, begin the day by bathing, followed by music, and then a chaste repast of fruit and bread. Each one finds congenial occupation till the meridian meal; when some deep-searching conversation gives rest to the body and development to the mind. Healthful labor again engages us till the last meal, when we assemble in social communion, prolonged till sunset, when we retire to sweet repose, ready for the next day's activity."

"What part of the work do you incline to yourself?" asked Sister Hope, with a humorous glimmer in her keen eyes.

"I shall wait till it is made clear to me. Being in preference to doing is the great aim, and this comes to us rather by a resigned willingness than a wilful activity, which is a check to all divine growth," responded Brother Timon.

"I thought so." And Mrs. Lamb sighed audibly, for during the year he had spent in her family Brother Timon had so faithfully carried out his idea of "being, not doing," that she had found his "divine growth" both an expensive and unsatisfactory process.

Here her husband struck into the conversation, his face shining with the light and joy of the splendid dreams and high ideals hovering before him.

"In these steps of reform, we do not rely so much on scientific reasoning or physiological skill as on the spirit's dictates. The greater part of man's duty consists in leaving alone much that he now does. Shall I stimulate with tea, coffee, or wine? No. Shall I consume flesh? Not if I value health. Shall I subjugate cattle? Shall I claim property in any created thing? Shall I trade? Shall I adopt a form of religion? Shall I interest myself in politics? To how many of these questions — could we ask them deeply enough and could they be heard as having relation to our eternal welfare — would the response be 'Abstain'?"

A mild snore seemed to echo the last word of Abel's rhapsody, for Brother Moses had succumbed to mundane slumber and sat nodding like a massive ghost. Forest Absalom, the silent man, and John Pease, the English member, now departed to the barn; and Mrs. Lamb led her flock to a temporary fold, leaving the founders of the "Consociate Family" to build castles in the air till the fire went out and the symposium ended in smoke.

The furniture arrived next day, and was soon bestowed; for the principal property of the community consisted in books. To this rare library was devoted the best room in the house, and the few busts and pictures that still survived many flittings were added to beautify the sanctuary, for here the family was to meet for amusement, instruction, and worship.

Any housewife can imagine the emotions of Sister Hope, when she took possession of a large, dilapidated kitchen, containing an old stove and the peculiar stores out of which food was to be evolved for her little family of eleven. Cakes of maple sugar, dried peas and beans, barley and hominy, meal of all sorts, potatoes, and dried fruit. No milk, butter, cheese, tea, or meat appeared. Even salt was considered a useless luxury and spice entirely forbidden by these lovers of Spartan simplicity. A ten years' experience of vegetarian vagaries had been good training for this new freak, and her sense of the ludicrous supported her through many trying scenes.

Unleavened bread, porridge, and water for breakfast; bread, vegetables, and water for dinner; bread, fruit, and water for supper was the bill of fare ordained by the elders. No teapot profaned that sacred stove, no gory steak cried aloud for vengeance from her chaste gridiron; and only a brave woman's taste, time, and temper were sacrificed on that domestic altar.

The vexed question of light was settled by buying a quantity of bayberry wax for candles; and, on discovering that no one knew how to make them, pine knots were introduced, to be used when absolutely necessary. Being summer, the evenings were not long, and the weary fraternity found it no great hardship to retire with the birds. The inner light was sufficient for most of them. But Mrs. Lamb rebelled. Evening was the only time she had to herself, and while the tired feet rested the skilful hands mended torn frocks and little stockings, or anxious heart forgot its burden in a book.

So "mother's lamp" burned steadily, while the philosophers built a new heaven and earth by moonlight; and through all the metaphysical mists and philanthropic pyrotechnics of that period Sister Hope played her own little game of "throwing light," and none but the moths were the worse for it.

Such farming probably was never seen before since Adam delved. The band of brothers began by spading garden and field; but a few days of it lessened their ardor amazingly. Blistered hands and aching backs suggested the expediency of permitting the use of cattle till the workers were better fitted for noble toil by a summer of the new life.

Brother Moses brought a yoke of oxen from his farm, — at least, the philosophers thought so till it was discovered that one of the animals was a cow; and Moses confessed that he "must be let down easy, for he couldn't live on garden sarse entirely."

Great was Dictator Lion's indignation at this lapse from virtue. But time pressed, the work must be done; so the meek cow was permitted to wear the yoke and the recreant brother continued to enjoy forbidden draughts in the barn, which dark proceeding caused the children to regard him as one set apart for destruction.

The sowing was equally peculiar, for, owing to some mistake, the three brethren, who devoted themselves to this graceful task, found when about half through the job that each had been sowing a different sort of grain in the same field; a mistake which caused much perplexity; as it could not be remedied; but, after a long consultation and a good deal of laughter, it was decided to say nothing and see what would come of it.

The garden was planted with a generous supply of useful roots and herbs; but, as manure was not allowed to profane the virgin soil, few of these vegetable treasures ever came up. Purslane reigned supreme, and the disappointed planters ate it philosophically, deciding that Nature knew what was best for them, and would generously supply their needs, if they could only learn to digest her "sallets" and wild roots.

The orchard was laid out, a little grafting done, new trees and vines set, regardless of the unfit season and entire ignorance of the husbandmen, who honestly believed that in the autumn they would reap a bounteous harvest.

Slowly things got into order, and rapidly rumors of the new experiment went abroad, causing many strange spirits to flock thither, for in those days communities were the fashion and transcendentalism raged wildly. Some came to look on and laugh, some to be supported in poetic idleness, a few to believe sincerely and work heartily. Each member was allowed to mount his favorite hobby and ride it to his heart's content. Very queer were some of the riders, and very rampant some of the hobbies.

One youth, believing that language was of little consequence if the spirit was only right, startled new-comers by blandly greeting them with "Good-morning, damn you," and other remarks of an equally mixed order. A second irresponsible being held that all the emotions of the soul should be freely expressed, and illustrated his theory by antics that would have sent him to a lunatic asylum, if, as an unregenerate wag said, he had not already been in one. When his spirit soared, he climbed trees and shouted; when doubt assailed him, he lay upon the floor and groaned lamentably. At joyful periods, he raced, leaped, and sang; when sad, he wept aloud; and when a great thought burst upon him in the watches of the night, he crowed like a jocund cockerel, to the great delight of the children and the great annoyance of the elders. One musical brother fiddled whenever so moved, sang sentimentally to the four little girls, and put a music-box on the wall when he hoed corn.

Brother Pease ground away at his uncooked food, or browsed over the farm on sorrel, mint, green fruit, and new vegetables. Occasionally he took his walks abroad, airily attired in an unbleached cotton *poncho,* which was the nearest approach to the primeval costume he was allowed to indulge in. At midsummer he retired to the wilderness, to try his plan where the woodchucks were without prejudices and huckleberry-bushes were hospitably full. A sunstroke unfortunately spoilt his plan, and he returned to semi-civilization a sadder and wiser man.

Forest Absalom preserved his Pythagorean silence, cultivated his fine dark locks, and worked like a beaver, setting an excellent example of brotherly love, justice, and fidelity by his upright life. He it was who helped overworked Sister Hope with her heavy washes, kneaded the endless succession of batches of bread, watched over the children, and did the many tasks left undone by the brethren, who were so busy discussing and defining great duties that they forgot to perform the small ones.

Moses White placidly plodded about, "chorin' raound," as he called it, looking like an old-time patriarch, with his silver hair and flowing beard, and saving the community from many a mishap by his thrift and Yankee shrewdness.

Brother Lion domineered over the whole concern; for, having put the most money into the speculation, he was resolved to make it pay, — as if anything founded on an ideal basis could be expected to do so by any but enthusiasts.

Abel Lamb simply revelled in the Newness, firmly believing that his dream was to be beautifully realized and in time not only little Fruitlands, but the whole earth, be turned into a Happy Valley. He worked with every muscle of his body, for *he* was in deadly earnest. He taught with his whole head and heart; planned and sacrificed, preached and prophesied, with a soul full of the purest aspirations, most unselfish purposes, and desires for a life devoted to God and man, too high and tender to bear the rough usage of this world.

It was a little remarkable that only one woman ever joined this community. Mrs. Lamb merely followed wheresoever her husband led, — "as ballast for his balloon," as she said, in her bright way.

Miss Jane Gage was a stout lady of mature years, sentimental, amiable, and lazy. She wrote verses copiously, and had vague yearnings and graspings after the unknown, which led her to believe herself fitted for a higher sphere than any she had yet adorned.

Having been a teacher, she was set to instructing the children in the common branches. Each adult member took a turn at the infants; and, as each taught in his own way, the result was a chronic state of chaos in the minds of these much-afflicted innocents.

Sleep, food, and poetic musings were the desires of dear Jane's life, and she shirked all duties as clogs upon her spirit's wings. Any thought of lending a hand with the domestic drudgery never occurred to her; and when to the question, "Art there any beasts of burden on the place?" Mrs. Lamb answered, with a face that told its own tale, "Only one woman!" the buxom Jane took no shame to herself, but laughed at the joke, and let the stout-hearted sister tug on alone.

Unfortunately, the poor lady hankered after the flesh-pots, and endeavored to stay herself with private sips of milk, crackers, and cheese, and on one dire occasion she partook of fish at a neighbor's table.

One of the children reported this sad lapse from virtue, and poor Jane was publicly reprimanded by Timon.

"I only took a little bit of the tail," sobbed the penitent poetess.

"Yes, but the whole fish had to be tortured and slain that you might tempt your carnal appetite with that one taste of the tail. Know ye not, consumers of flesh meat, that ye are nourishing the wolf and tiger in your bosoms?"

At this awful question and the peal of laughter which arose from some of the younger brethren, tickled by the ludicrous contrast between the stout sinner, the stern judge, and the naughty satisfaction of the young detective, poor Jane fled from the room to pack her trunk and return to a world where fishes' tails were not forbidden fruit.

Transcendental wild oats were sown broadcast that year, and the fame thereof has not yet ceased in the land; for, futile as this crop seemed to outsiders, it bore an invisible harvest, worth much to those who planted in earnest. As none of the members of this particular community have ever recounted their experiences before, a few of them may not be amiss, since the interest in these attempts has never died out and Fruitlands was the most ideal of all these castles in Spain.

A new dress was invented, since cotton, silk, and wool were forbidden as the product of slave-labor, worm-slaughter, and sheep-robbery. Tunics and trowsers of brown linen were the only wear. The women's skirts were longer, and their straw hat-brims wider than the men's, and this was the only difference. Some persecution lent a charm to the costume, and the long-haired, linen-clad reformers quite enjoyed the mild martyrdom they endured when they left home.

Money was abjured, as the root of all evil. The produce of the land was to supply most of their wants, or be exchanged for the few things they could not grow. This idea had its inconveniences; but self-denial was the fashion, and it was surprising how many things one can do without. When they desired to travel, they walked, if possible, begged the loan of a vehicle, or boldly entered car or coach, and, stating their principles to the officials, took the consequences. Usually their dress, their earnest frankness, and gentle resolution won them a passage; but now and then they met with hard usage, and had the satisfaction of suffering for their principles.

On one of these penniless pilgrimages they took passage on a boat, and, when fare was demanded, artlessly offered to talk, instead of pay. As the boat was well under way and they actually had not a cent, there was no help for it. So Brothers Lion and Lamb held forth to the assembled passengers in their most eloquent style. There must have been something effective in this conversation, for the listeners were moved to take up a contribution for these inspired lunatics, who preached peace on earth and good-will to man so earnestly, with empty pockets. A goodly sum was collected; but when the captain presented it the reformers proved that they were consistent even in their madness, for not a penny would they accept, saying, with a look at the group about them, whose indifference or contempt had changed to interest and respect, "You see how well we get on without money"; and so went serenely on their way, with their linen blouses flapping airily in the cold October wind.

They preached vegetarianism everywhere and resisted all temptations of the flesh, contentedly eating apples and bread at well-spread tables, and much afflicting hospitable hostesses by denouncing their food and taking away their appetite, discussing the "horrors of shambles," and "incorporation of the brute in man," and "on elegant abstinence the sign of a pure soul." But, when the perplexed or offended ladies asked what they should eat, they got in reply a bill of fare consisting of "bowls of sunrise for breakfast," "solar seeds of the sphere," "dishes from Plutarch's chaste table," and other viands equally hard to find in any modern market.

Reform conventions of all sorts were haunted by these brethren, who said many wise things and did many foolish ones. Unfortunately, these wanderings interfered with their harvest at home; but the rule was to do what the spirit moved, so they left their crops to Providence and went a-reaping in wider and, let us hope, more fruitful fields than their own.

Luckily, the earthly providence who watched over Abel Lamb was at hand to glean the scanty crop yielded by the "uncorrupted land," which "consecrated to human freedom," had received "the sober culture of devout men."

About the time the grain was ready to house, some call of the Oversoul wafted all the men away. An easterly storm was coming up and the yellow stacks were sure to be ruined. Then Sister Hope gathered her forces. Three little girls, one boy (Timon's son), and herself, harnessed to clothesbaskets and Russia-linen sheets, were the only teams she could command; but with these poor appliances the indomitable woman got in the grain and saved the food for her young, with the instinct and energy of a mother-bird with a brood of hungry nestlings to feed.

This attempt at regeneration had its tragic as well as comic side, though the world only saw the former.

With the first frosts, the butterflies, who had sunned themselves in the new light through the summer, took flight, leaving the few bees to see what honey they had stored for winter use. Precious little appeared beyond the satisfaction of a few months of holy living.

At first it seemed as if a chance to try holy dying also was to be offered them. Timon, much disgusted with the failure of the scheme, decided to retire to the Shakers, who seemed to be the only successful community going.

"What is to become of us?" asked Mrs. Hope, for Abel was heartbroken at the bursting of his lovely bubble.

"You can stay here, if you like, till a tenant is found. No more wood must be cut, however, and no more corn ground. All I have must be sold to pay the debts of the concern, as the responsibility rests with me," was the cheering reply.

"Who is to pay us for what we have lost? I gave all I had, — furniture, time, strength, six months of my children's lives, — and all are wasted. Abel gave himself body and soul, and is almost wrecked by hard work and disappointment. Are we to have no return for this, but leave to starve and freeze in an old house, with winter at hand, no money, and hardly a friend left; for this wild scheme has alienated nearly all we had. You talk much about justice. Let us have a little, since there is nothing else left."

But the woman's appeal met with no reply but the old one: "It was an experiment. We all risked something, and must bear our losses as we can."

With this cold comfort, Timon departed with his son, and was absorbed into the Shaker brotherhood, where he soon found that the order of things was reversed, and it was all work and no play.

Then the tragedy began for the forsaken little family. Desolation and despair fell upon Abel. As his wife said, his new beliefs had alienated many friends. Some thought him mad, some unprincipled. Even the most kindly thought him a visionary, whom it was useless to help till he took more practical views of life. All stood aloof, saying, "Let him work out his own ideas, and see what they are worth."

He had tried, but it was a failure. The world was not ready for Utopia yet, and those who attempted to found it only got laughed at for their pains. In other days, men could sell all and give to the poor, lead lives devoted to holiness and high thought, and, after the persecution was over, find themselves honored as saints or martyrs. But in modern times these things are out of fashion. To live for one's principles, at all costs, is a dangerous speculation; and the failure of an ideal, no matter how humane and noble, is harder for the world to forgive and forget than bank robbery or the grand swindles of corrupt politicians.

Deep waters now for Abel, and for a time there seemed no passage through. Strength and spirits were exhausted by hard work and too much thought. Courage failed when, looking about for help, he saw no sympathizing face, no hand out-stretched to help him, no voice to say cheerily,

"We all make mistakes, and it takes many experiences to shape a life. Try again, and let us help you."

Every door was closed, every eye averted, every heart cold, and no way open whereby he might earn bread for his children. His principles would not permit him to do many things that others did; and in the few fields where conscience would allow him to work, who would employ a man who had flown in the face of society, as he had done?

Then this dreamer, whose dream was the life of his life, resolved to carry out his idea to the bitter end. There seemed no place for him here, — no work, no friend. To go begging conditions was as ignoble as to go begging money. Better perish of want than sell one's soul for the sustenance of his body. Silently he lay down upon his bed, turned his face to the wall, and waited with pathetic patience for death to cut the knot which he could not untie. Days and nights went by, and neither food nor water passed his lips. Soul and body were dumbly struggling together, and no word of complaint betrayed what either suffered.

His wife, when tears and prayers were unavailing, sat down to wait the end with a mysterious awe and submission; for in this entire resignation of all things there was an eloquent significance to her who knew him as no other human being did.

"Leave all to God," was his belief; and in this crisis the loving soul clung to this faith, sure that the Allwise Father would not desert this child who tried to live so near to Him. Gathering her children about her, she waited the issue of the tragedy that was being enacted in that solitary room, while the first snow fell outside, untrodden by the foot-prints of a single friend.

But the strong angels who sustain and teach perplexed and troubled souls came and went, leaving no trace without, but working miracles within. For, when all other sentiments had faded into dimness, all other hopes died utterly; when the bitterness of death was nearly over, when body was past any pang of hunger or thirst, and soul stood ready to depart, the love that outlives all else refused to die. Head had bowed to defeat, hand had grown weary with too heavy tasks, but heart could not grow cold to those who lived in its tender depths, even when death touched it.

"My faithful wife, my little girls, — they have not forsaken me, they are mine by ties that none can break. What right have I to leave them alone? What right to escape from the burden and the sorrow I have helped to bring? This duty remains to me, and I must do it manfully. For their sakes, the world will forgive me in time; for their sakes, God will sustain me now."

Too feeble to rise, Abel groped for the food that always lay within his reach, and in the darkness and solitude of that memorable night ate and drank what was to him the bread and wine of a new communion, a new dedication of heart and life to the duties that were left him when the dreams fled.

In the early dawn, when that sad wife crept fearfully to see what change had come to the patient face on the pillow, she found it smiling at her, saw a wasted hand outstretched to her, and heard a feeble voice cry bravely, "Hope!"

What passed in that little room is not to be recorded except in the hearts of those who suffered and endured much for love's sake. Enough for us to know that soon the wan shadow of a man came forth, leaning on the arm that never failed him, to be welcomed and cherished by the children, who never forgot the experiences of that time.

"Hope" was the watchword now; and, while the last logs blazed on the hearth, the last bread and apples covered the table, the new commander, with recovered courage, said to her husband, —

"Leave all to God — and me. He has done his part, now I will do mine."

"But we have no money, dear."

"Yes, we have. I sold all we could spare, and have enough to take us away from this snow-bank."

"Where can we go?"

"I have engaged four rooms at our good neighbor, Lovejoy's. There we can live cheaply till spring. Then for new plans and a home of our own, please God."

"But, Hope, your little store won't last long, and we have no friends."

"I can sew and you can chop wood. Lovejoy offers you the same pay as he gives his other men; my old friend, Mrs. Truman, will send me all the work I want; and my blessed brother stands by us to the end. Cheer up, dear heart, for while there is work and love in the world we shall not suffer."

"And while I have my good angel Hope, I shall not despair, even if I wait another thirty years before I step beyond the circle of the sacred little world in which I still have a place to fill."

So one bleak December day, with their few possessions piled on an ox-sled, the rosy children perched atop, and the parents trudging arm in arm behind, the exiles left their Eden and faced the world again.

"Ah me! my happy dream. How much I leave behind that never can be mine again," said Abel, looking back at the lost Paradise, lying white and chill in its shroud of snow.

"Yes, dear, but how much we bring away," answered brave-hearted Hope, glancing from husband to children.

"Poor Fruitlands! The name was as great a failure as the rest!" continued Abel, with a sigh, as a frostbitten apple fell from a leafless bough at his feet.

But the sigh changed to a smile as his wife added, in a half-tender, half-satirical tone, —

"Don't you think Apple Slump would be a better name for it, dear?"

How I Went Out to Service

Independent, 4 June 1874

WHEN I WAS eighteen I wanted something to do. I had tried teaching for two years, and hated it; I had tried sewing, and could not earn my bread in that way, at the cost of health; I tried story-writing and got five dollars for stories which now bring a hundred; I had thought seriously of going upon the stage, but certain highly respectable relatives were so shocked at the mere idea that I relinquished my dramatic aspirations.

"What *shall* I do?" was still the question that perplexed me. I was ready to work, eager to be independent, and too proud to endure patronage. But the right task seemed hard to find, and my bottled energies were fermenting in a way that threatened an explosion before long.

My honored mother was a city missionary that winter, and not only served the clamorous poor, but often found it in her power to help decayed gentlefolk by quietly placing them where they could earn their bread without the entire sacrifice of taste and talent which makes poverty so hard for such to bear. Knowing her tact and skill, people often came to her for companions, housekeepers, and that class of the needy who do not make their wants known through an intelligence office.

One day, as I sat dreaming splendid dreams, while I made a series of little petticoats out of the odds and ends sent in for the poor, a tall, ministerial gentleman appeared, in search of a companion for his sister. He possessed an impressive nose, a fine flow of language, and a pair of large hands, encased in black kid gloves. With much waving of these somber members, Mr. R. set forth the delights awaiting the happy soul who should secure this home. He described it as a sort of heaven on earth. "There are books, pictures, flowers, a piano, and the best of society," he said. "This person will be one of the family in all respects, and only required to help about the lighter work, which my sister has done herself hitherto, but is now a martyr to neuralgia and needs a gentle friend to assist her."

My mother, who never lost her faith in human nature, spite of many impostures, believed every word, and quite beamed with benevolent interest as she listened and tried to recall some needy young woman to whom this charming home would be a blessing. I also innocently thought:

"That sounds inviting. I like housework and can do it well. I should have time to enjoy the books and things I love, and D——— is not far away from home. Suppose I try it."

So, when my mother turned to me, asking if I could suggest any one, I became as red as a poppy and said abruptly:

"Only myself."

"Do you really mean it?" cried my astonished parent.

"I really do if Mr. R. thinks I should suit," was my steady reply, as I partially obscured my crimson countenance behind a little flannel skirt, still redder.

The Reverend Josephus gazed upon me with the benign regard which a bachelor of five and thirty may accord a bashful damsel of eighteen. A smile dawned upon his countenance, "sicklied o'er with the pale cast of thought," or dyspepsia; and he softly folded the black gloves, as if about to bestow a blessing, as he replied, with emphasis:

"I am sure you would, and we should think ourselves most fortunate if we could secure your society, and — ahem — services for my poor sister."

"Then I'll try it," responded the impetuous maid.

"We will talk it over a little first, and let you know to-morrow, sir," put in my prudent parent, adding, as Mr. R—— arose: "What wages do you pay?"

"My dear madam, in a case like this let us not use such words as those. Anything you may think proper we shall gladly give. The labor is very light, for there are but three of us and our habits are of the simplest sort. I am a frail reed and may break at any moment; so is my sister, and my aged father cannot long remain; therefore, money is little to us, and any one who comes to lend her youth and strength to our feeble household will not be forgotten in the end, I assure you." And, with another pensive smile, a farewell wave of the impressive gloves, the Reverend Josephus bowed like a well-sweep and departed.

"My dear, are you in earnest?" asked my mother.

"Of course, I am. Why not try this experiment? It can but fail, like all the others."

"I have no objection; only I fancied you were rather too proud for this sort of thing."

"I am too proud to be idle and dependent, ma'am. I'll scrub floors and take in washing first. I do housework at home for love; why not do it abroad for money? I like it better than teaching. It is healthier than sewing and surer than writing. So why not try it?"

"It is going out to service, you know though you are called a companion. How does that suit?"

"I don't care. Every sort of work that is paid for is service; and I don't mind being a companion, if I can do it well. I may find it is my mission to take care of neuralgic old ladies and lackadaisical clergymen. It does not sound exciting, but it's better than nothing," I answered, with a sigh; for it *was* rather a sudden downfall to give up being a Siddons and become a Betcinder.

How my sisters laughed when they heard the new plan! But they soon resigned themselves, sure of fun, for Lu's adventures were the standing joke of the family. Of course, the highly respectable relatives held up their hands in holy horror at the idea of one of the clan degrading herself by going out to service. Teaching a private school was the proper thing for an indigent gentlewoman. Sewing even, if done in the seclusion of home and not mentioned in public, could be tolerated. Story-writing was a genteel accomplishment and reflected credit upon the name. But leaving the paternal roof to wash other people's tea-cups, nurse other people's ails, and obey other people's orders for hire — this, this was degradation; and headstrong Louisa would disgrace her name forever if she did it.

Opposition only fired the revolutionary blood in my veins, and I crowned my iniquity by the rebellious declaration:

"If doing this work hurts my respectability, I wouldn't give much for it. My aristocratic ancestors don't feed or clothe me and my democratic ideas of honesty and honor won't let me be idle or dependent. You need not know me if you are ashamed of me, and I won't ask you for a penny; so, if I never do succeed in anything, I shall have the immense satisfaction of knowing I am under no obligation to any one."

In spite of the laughter and the lamentation, I got ready my small wardrobe, consisting of two calico dresses and one delaine, made by myself, also several large and uncompromising blue aprons and three tidy little sweeping-caps; for I had some English notions about housework and felt that my muslin hair-protectors would be useful in some of the "light labors" I was to undertake. It is needless to say they were very becoming. Then, firmly embracing my family, I set forth one cold January day, with my little trunk, a stout heart, and a five-dollar bill for my fortune.

"She will be back in a week," was my sister's prophecy, as she wiped her weeping eye.

"No, she won't, for she has promised to stay the month out and she will keep her word," answered my mother, who always defended the black sheep of her flock.

I heard both speeches, and registered a tremendous vow to keep that promise, if I died in the attempt — little dreaming, poor innocent, what lay before me.

Josephus meantime had written me several remarkable letters, describing the different members of the family I was about to enter. His account was peculiar; but I believed every word of it and my romantic fancy was much excited by the details he gave. The principal ones are as follows, condensed from the voluminous epistles which he evidently enjoyed writing:

"You will find a stately mansion, fast falling to decay, for my father will have nothing repaired, preferring that the old house and its master should crumble away together. I have, however, been permitted to rescue a few rooms from ruin; and here I pass my recluse life, surrounded by the things I love. This will naturally be more attractive to you than the gloomy apartments my father inhabits, and I hope you will here allow me to minister to your young and cheerful nature when your daily cares are over. I need such companionship and shall always welcome you to my abode.

"Eliza, my sister, is a child at forty, for she has lived alone with my father and an old servant all her life. She is a good creature, but not lively, and needs stirring up, as you will soon see. Also I hope by your means to rescue her from the evil influence of Puah, who, in my estimation, is a *wretch*. She has gained entire control over Eliza, and warps her mind with great skill, prejudicing her against *me,* and thereby desolating my home. Puah hates *me* and always has. Why I know not, except that I will not yield to her control. She ruled here for years while I was away, and my return upset all her nefarious plans. It will always be my firm opinion that she has tried to *poison me,* and may again. But even this dark suspicion will not deter me from my duty. I cannot send her away, for both my deluded father and my sister have entire faith in her, and I cannot shake it. She is faithful and kind to them, so I submit and remain to guard them, even at the risk of my life.

"I tell you these things because I wish you to know all and be warned, for this old hag has a specious tongue, and I should grieve to see you deceived by her lies. Say nothing, but watch her silently, and help me to thwart her evil plots; but do not trust her, or beware."

Now this was altogether romantic and sensational, and I felt as if about to enter one of those delightfully dangerous houses we read of in novels, where perils, mysteries, and sins freely disport themselves, till the newcomer sets all to rights, after unheard of trials and escapes.

I arrived at twilight, just the proper time for the heroine to appear; and, as no one answered my modest solo on the rusty knocker, I walked in and looked about me. Yes, here was the long, shadowy hall, where the ghosts doubtless walked at midnight. Peering in at an open door on the right, I saw a parlor full of ancient furniture, faded, dusty, and dilapidated. Old portraits stared at me from the walls and a damp chill froze the marrow of my bones in the most approved style.

"The romance opens well," I thought, and, peeping in at an opposite door, beheld a luxurious apartment, full of the warm glow of firelight, the balmy breath of hyacinths and roses, the white glimmer of piano keys, and tempting rows of books along the walls.

The contrast between the two rooms was striking, and, after an admiring survey, I continued my explorations, thinking that I should not mind being "ministered to" in that inviting place when my work was done.

A third door showed me a plain, dull sitting-room, with an old man napping in his easy-chair. I heard voices in the kitchen beyond, and, entering there, beheld Puah the fiend. Unfortunately for the dramatic effect of the tableaux, all I saw was a mild-faced old woman, buttering toast, while she conversed with her familiar, a comfortable gray cat.

The old lady greeted me kindly, but I fancied her faded blue eye had a weird expression and her amiable words were all a snare, though I own I was rather disappointed at the commonplace appearance of this humble Borgia.

She showed me to a tiny room, where I felt more like a young giantess than ever, and was obliged to stow away my possessions as snugly as in a ship's cabin. When I presently descended, armed with a blue apron and "a heart for any fate," I found the old man awake and received from him a welcome full of ancient courtesy and kindliness. Miss Eliza crept in like a timid mouse, looking so afraid of her buxom companion that I forgot my own shyness in trying to relieve hers. She was so enveloped in shawls that all I could discover was that my mistress was a very nervous little woman, with a small button of pale hair on the outside of her head and the vaguest notions of work inside. A few spasmodic remarks and many awkward pauses brought us to teatime, when Josephus appeared, as tall, thin, and cadaverous as ever. After his arrival there was no more silence, for he preached all suppertime something in this agreeable style.

"My young friend, our habits, as you see, are of the simplest. We eat in the kitchen, and all together, in the primitive fashion; for it suits my father and saves labor. I could wish more order and elegance; but *my* wishes are not consulted and I submit. I live above these petty crosses, and, though my health suffers from bad cookery, I do not murmur. Only, I must say, in passing, that if you *will* make your battercakes green with saleratus, Puah, I shall feel it my duty to throw them out of the window. *I* am used to poison; but I cannot see the coats of this blooming girl's stomach destroyed, as mine have been. And, speaking of duties, I may as well mention to you, Louisa (I call you so in a truly fraternal spirit), that I like to find my study in order when I come down in the morning; for I often need a few moments of solitude before I face the daily annoyances of my life. I shall permit *you* to perform this light task, for *you* have some idea of order (I see it in the formation of your brow), and feel sure that *you* will respect the sanctuary of thought. Eliza is so blind she does not see dust, and Puah enjoys devastating the one poor refuge I can call my own this side the grave. We are all waiting for you, sir. My father keeps up the old formalities, you observe; and I endure them, though *my* views are more advanced."

The old gentleman hastily finished his tea and returned thanks, when his son stalked gloomily away, evidently oppressed with the burden of his wrongs, also, as I irreverently fancied, with the seven "green" flapjacks he had devoured during the sermon.

I helped wash up the cups, and during that domestic rite Puah chatted in what I should have considered a cheery, social way had I not been darkly warned against her wiles.

"You needn't mind half Josephus says, my dear. He likes to hear himself talk and always goes on so before folks. I sometimes thinks his books and new ideas have sort of muddled his wits, for he is as full of notions as a paper is of pins; and he gets dreadfully put out if we don't give in to 'em. But, gracious me! they are so redicklus sometimes and so selfish I can't allow him to make a fool of himself or plague Lizy. She don't dare to say her soul is her own; so I have to stand up for her. His pa don't know half his odd doings; for I try to keep the old gentleman comfortable and have to manage 'em all, which is not an easy job, I do assure you."

I had a secret conviction that she was right, but did not commit myself in any way, and we joined the social circle in the sitting-room. The prospect was not a lively one, for the old gentleman nodded behind his newspaper; Eliza, with her head plumed up in a little blanket, slumbered on the sofa, Puah fell to knitting silently; and the plump cat dozed under the stove. Josephus was visible, artistically posed in the luxurious recesses of his cell, with the light beaming on his thoughtful brow, as he pored over a large volume or mused with upturned eye.

Having nothing else to do, I sat and stared at him, till, emerging from a deep reverie, with an effective start, he became conscious of my existence and beckoned me to approach the "sanctuary of thought" with a melodramatic waft of his large hand.

I went, took possession of an easy chair, and prepared myself for elegant conversation. I was disappointed, however; for Josephus showed me a list of his favorite dishes, sole fruit of all that absorbing thought, and, with an earnestness that flushed his saffron countenance, gave me hints as to the proper preparation of these delicacies.

I mildly mentioned that I was not a cook; but was effectually silenced by being reminded that I came to be generally useful, to take his sister's place, and see that the flame of life which burned so feebly in this earthly tabernacle was fed with proper fuel. Mince pies, Welsh rarebits, sausages, and strong coffee did not strike me as strictly spiritual fare; but I listened meekly and privately resolved to shift this awful responsibility to Puah's shoulders.

Detecting me in gape, after an hour of this high converse, he presented me with an overblown rose, which fell to pieces before I got out of the room, pressed my hand, and dismissed me with a fervent "God bless you, child. Don't forget the dropped eggs for breakfast."

I was up betimes next morning and had the study in perfect order before the recluse appeared, enjoying a good prowl among the books as I worked and becoming so absorbed that I forgot the eggs, till a gusty sigh startled me, and I beheld Josephus, in dressing gown and slippers, languidly surveying the scene.

"Nay, do not fly," he said, as I grasped my duster in guilty haste. "It pleases me to see you here and lends a sweet, domestic charm to my solitary room. I like that graceful cap, that housewifely apron, and I beg you will wear them often; for it refreshes my eye to see something tasteful, young, and womanly about me. Eliza makes a bundle of herself and Puah is simply detestable."

He sank languidly into a chair and closed his eyes, as if the mere thought of his enemy was too much for him. I took advantage of this momentary prostration to slip away, convulsed with laughter at the looks and words of this bald-headed sentimentalist.

After breakfast I fell to work with a will, eager to show my powers and glad to put things to rights, for many hard jobs had evidently been waiting for a stronger arm than Puah's and a more methodical head than Eliza's.

Everything was dusty, moldy, shiftless, and neglected, except the domain of Josephus. Up-stairs the paper was dropping from the walls, the ancient furniture was all more or less dilapidated, and every hole and corner was full of relics tucked away by Puah, who was a regular old magpie. Rats and mice reveled in the empty rooms and spiders wove their tapestry undisturbed, for the old man would have nothing altered or repaired and his part of the house was fast going to ruin.

I longed to have a grand "clearing up"; but was forbidden to do more than to keep things in livable order. On the whole, it was fortunate, for I soon found that my hands would be kept busy with the realms of Josephus, whose ethereal being shrank from dust, shivered at a cold breath, and needed much cosseting with dainty food, hot fires, soft beds, and endless service, else, as he expressed it, the frail reed would break.

I regret to say that a time soon came when I felt supremely indifferent as to the breakage, and very skeptical as to the fragility of a reed that ate, slept, dawdled, and scolded so energetically. The rose that fell to pieces so suddenly was a good symbol of the rapid disappearance of all the romantic delusions I had indulged in for a time. A week's acquaintance with the inmates of this old house quite settled my opinion, and further developments only confirmed it.

Miss Eliza was a nonentity and made no more impression on me than a fly. The old gentleman passed his days in a placid sort of doze and took no notice of what went on about him. Puah had been a faithful drudge for years, and, instead of being a "wretch," was, as I soon satisfied myself, a motherly old soul, with no malice in her. The secret of Josephus's dislike was that the reverend tyrant ruled the house, and all obeyed him but Puah, who had nursed him as a baby, boxed his ears as a boy, and was not afraid of him even when he became a man and a minister. I soon repented of my first suspicions, and grew fond of her, for without my old gossip I should have fared ill when my day of tribulation came.

At first I innocently accepted the fraternal invitations to visit the study, feeling that when my day's work was done I had earned a right to rest and read. But I soon found that this was not the idea. I was not to read; but to be read to. I was not to enjoy the flowers, pictures, fire, and books; but to keep them in order for my lord to enjoy. I was also to be a passive bucket, into which he was to pour all manner of philosophic, metaphysical, and sentimental rubbish. I was to serve his needs, soothe his sufferings, and sympathize with all his sorrows — be a galley slave, in fact.

As soon as I clearly understood this, I tried to put an end to it by shunning the study and never lingering there an instant after my work was done. But it availed little, for Josephus demanded much sympathy and was bound to have it. So he came and read poems while I washed dishes, discussed his pet problems all meal-times, and put reproachful notes under my door, in which were comically mingled complaints of neglect and orders for dinner.

I bore it as long as I could, and then freed my mind in a declaration of independence, delivered in the kitchen, where he found me scrubbing the hearth. It was not an impressive attitude for an orator, nor was the occupation one a girl would choose when receiving calls; but I have always felt grateful for the intense discomfort of that moment, since it gave me courage to rebel outright. Stranded on a small island of mat, in a sea of soapsuds, I brandished a scrubbing brush, as I indignantly informed him that I came to be a companion to his sister, not to him, and I should keep that post or none. This I followed up by reproaching him with the delusive reports he had given me of the place and its duties, and assuring him that I should not stay long unless matters mended.

"But I offer you lighter tasks, and you refuse them," he begun, still hovering in the doorway, whither he had hastily retired when I opened my batteries.

"But I don't like the tasks, and consider them much worse than hard work," was my ungrateful answer, as I sat upon my island, with the soft-soap conveniently near.

"Do you mean to say you prefer to scrub that hearth to sitting in my charming room while I read Hegel to you?" he demanded, glaring down upon me.

"Infinitely," I responded promptly, and emphasized my words by beginning to scrub with a zeal that made the bricks white with foam.

"Is it possible?" and, with a groan at my depravity, Josephus retired, full of ungodly wrath.

I remember that I immediately burst into jocund song, so that no doubt might remain in his mind, and continued to warble cheerfully till my task was done. I also remember that I cried heartily when I got to my room, I was so vexed, disappointed, and tired. But my bower was so small I should soon have swamped the furniture if I had indulged copiously in tears; therefore I speedily dried them up, wrote a comic letter home, and waited with interest to see what would happen next.

Far be it from me to accuse one of the nobler sex of spite or the small revenge of underhand annoyances and slights to one who could not escape and would not retaliate; but after that day a curious change came over the spirit of that very unpleasant dream. Gradually all the work of the house had been slipping into my hands; for Eliza was too poorly to help or direct, and Puah too old to do much besides the cooking. About this time I found that even the roughest work was added to my share, for Josephus was unusually feeble and no one was hired to do his chores. Having made up my mind to go when the month was out, I said nothing, but dug paths, brought water from the well, split kindlings, made fires, and sifted ashes, like a true Cinderella.

There never had been any pretense of companionship with Eliza, who spent her days mulling over the fire, and seldom exerted herself except to find odd jobs for me to do — rusty knives to clean, sheets to turn, old stockings to mend, and, when all else failed, some paradise of moths and mice to be cleared up; for the house was full of such "glory holes."

If I remonstrated, Eliza at once dissolved into tears and said she must do as she was told; Puah begged me to hold on till spring, when things would be much better; and pity pleaded for the two poor souls. But I don't think I could have stood it if my promise had not bound me, for when the fiend said "Budge" honor said "Budge not," and I stayed.

But, being a mortal worm, I turned now and then when the ireful Josephus trod upon me too hard, especially in the matter of boot-blacking. I really don't know why that is considered such humiliating work for a woman; but so it is, and there I drew the line. I would have cleaned the old man's shoes without a murmur; but he preferred to keep their native rustiness intact. Eliza never went out, and Puah affected carpet-slippers of the Chinese-junk pattern. Josephus, however, plumed himself upon his feet, which, like his nose, were large, and never took his walks abroad without having his boots in a high state of polish. He had brushed them himself at first; but soon after the explosion I discovered a pair of muddy boots in the shed, set suggestively near the blacking-box. I did not take the hint, feeling instinctively that this amiable being was trying how much I would bear for the sake of peace.

The boots remained untouched; and another pair soon came to keep them company, whereat I smiled wickedly as I chopped just kindlings enough for my own use. Day after day the collection grew, and neither party gave in. Boots were succeeded by shoes, then rubbers gave a pleasing variety to the long line, and then I knew the end was near.

"Why are not my boots attended to?" demanded Josephus, one evening, when obliged to go out.

"I'm sure I don't know," was Eliza's helpless answer.

"I told Louizy I guessed you'd want some of 'em before long," observed Puah, with an exasperating twinkle in her old eye.

"And what did she say?" asked my lord with an ireful whack of his velvet slippers as he cast them down.

"Oh! she said she was so busy doing your other work you'd have to do that yourself; and I thought she was about right."

"Louizy" heard it all through the slide, and could have embraced the old woman for her words, but kept still till Josephus had resumed his slippers with a growl and retired to the shed, leaving Eliza in tears, Puah chuckling, and the rebellious handmaid exulting in the china-closet.

Alas! for romance and the Christian virtues, several pairs of boots were cleaned that night, and my sinful soul enjoyed the spectacle of the reverend bootblack at his task. I even found my "fancy work," as I called the evening job of paring a bucketful of hard russets with a dull knife, much cheered by the shoe-brush accompaniment played in the shed.

Thunder-clouds rested upon the martyr's brow at breakfast, and I was as much ignored as the cat. And what a relief that was! The piano was locked up, so were the bookcases, the newspapers mysteriously disappeared, and a solemn silence reigned at table, for no one dared to talk when that gifted tongue was mute. Eliza fled from the gathering storm and had a comfortable fit of neuralgia in her own room, where Puah nursed her, leaving me to skirmish with the enemy.

It was not a fair fight, and that experience lessened my respect for mankind immensely. I did my best, however — grubbed about all day and amused my dreary evenings as well as I could; too proud even to borrow a book, lest it should seem like a surrender. What a long month it was, and how eagerly I counted the hours of that last week, for my time was up Saturday, and I hoped to be off at once. But when I announced my intention such dismay fell upon Eliza that my heart was touched, and Puah so urgently begged me to stay till they could get some one that I consented to remain a few days longer, and wrote post-haste to my mother, telling her to send a substitute quickly or I should do something desperate.

That blessed woman, little dreaming of all the woes I had endured, advised me to be patient, to do the generous thing, and be sure I should not regret it in the end. I groaned, submitted, and did regret it all the days of my life.

Three mortal weeks I waited; for, though two other victims came, I was implored to set them going, and tried to do it. But both fled after a day or two, condemning the place as a very hard one and calling me a fool to stand it another hour. I entirely agreed with them on both points, and, when I had cleared up after the second incapable lady, I tarried not for the coming of a third, but clutched my property and announced my departure by the next train.

Of course, Eliza wept, Puah moaned, the old man politely regretted, and the younger one washed his hands of the whole affair by shutting himself up in his room and forbidding me to say farewell because he "could not bear it." I laughed, and fancied it done for effect then; but I soon understood it better and did not laugh.

At the last moment, Eliza nervously tucked a sixpenny pocketbook into my hand and shrouded herself in the little blanket with a sob. But Puah kissed me kindly and whispered, with an odd look: "Don't blame us for anything. Some folks is liberal and some ain't." I thanked the poor old soul for her kindness to me and trudged gayly away to the station, whither my property had preceded me on a wheel-barrow, hired at my own expense.

I never shall forget that day. A bleak March afternoon, a sloppy, lonely road, and one hoarse crow stalking about a field, so like Josephus that I could not resist throwing a snowball at him. Behind me stood the dull old house, no longer either mysterious or romantic in my disenchanted eyes; before me rumbled the barrow, bearing my dilapidated wardrobe; and in my pocket reposed what I fondly hoped was, if not a liberal, at least an honest return for seven weeks of the hardest work I ever did.

Unable to resist the desire to see what my earnings were, I opened the purse and beheld *four dollars*.

I have had a good many bitter minutes in my life; but one of the bitterest came to me as I stood there in the windy road, with the sixpenny pocket-book open before me, and looked from my poor chapped, grimy, chill-blained hands to the paltry sum that was considered reward enough for all the hard and humble labor they had done.

A girl's heart is a sensitive thing. And mine had been very full lately; for it had suffered many of the trials that wound deeply yet cannot be told; so I think it was but natural that my first impulse was to go straight back to that sacred study and fling this insulting money at the feet of him who sent it. But I was so boiling over with indignation that I could not trust myself in his presence, lest I should be unable to resist the temptation to shake him, in spite of his cloth.

No, I would go home, show my honorable wounds, tell my pathetic tale, and leave my parents to avenge my wrongs. I did so; but over that harrowing scene I drop a veil, for my feeble pen refuses to depict the emotions of my outraged family. I will merely mention that the four dollars went back and the reverend Josephus never heard the last of it in that neighborhood.

My experiment seemed a dire failure and I mourned it as such for years; but more than once in my life I have been grateful for that serio-comico experience, since it has taught me many lessons. One of the most useful of these has been the power of successfully making a companion, not a servant, of those whose aid I need, and helping to gild their honest wages with the sympathy and justice which can sweeten the humblest and lighten the hardest task.

Recollections of My Childhood

Youth's Companion, 24 May 1888

ONE OF MY EARLIEST memories is of playing with books in my father's study. Building towers and bridges of the big dictionaries, looking at pictures, pretending to read, and scribbling on blank pages whenever pen or pencil could be found. Many of these first attempts at authorship still exist, and I often wonder if these childish plays did not influence my after life, since books have been my greatest comfort, castle-building a never-failing delight, and scribbling a very profitable amusement.

Another very vivid recollection is of the day when running after my hoop I fell into the Frog Pond and was rescued by a black boy, becoming a friend to the colored race then and there, though my mother always declared that I was an abolitionist at the age of three.

During the Garrison riot in Boston the portrait of George Thompson was hidden under a bed in our house for safe-keeping, and I am told that I used to go and comfort "the good man who helped poor slaves" in his captivity. However that may be, the conversion was genuine, and my greatest pride is in the fact that I have lived to know the brave men and women who did so much for the cause, and that I had a very small share in the war which put an end to a great wrong.

Being born on the birthday of Columbus I seem to have something of my patron saint's spirit of adventure, and running away was one of the delights of my childhood. Many a social lunch have I shared with hospitable Irish beggar children, as we ate our crusts, cold potatoes and salt fish on voyages of discovery among the ash heaps of the waste land that then lay where the Albany station now stands.

Many an impromptu picnic have I had on the dear old Common, with strange boys, pretty babies and friendly dogs, who always seemed to feel that this reckless young person needed looking after.

On one occasion the town-crier found me fast asleep at nine o'clock at night, on a door-step in Bedford Street, with my head pillowed on the curly breast of a big Newfoundland, who was with difficulty persuaded to release the weary little wanderer who had sobbed herself to sleep there.

I often smile as I pass that door, and never forget to give a grateful pat to every big dog I meet, for never have I slept more soundly than on that dusty step, nor found a better friend than the noble animal who watched over the lost baby so faithfully.

My father's school was the only one I ever went to, and when this was broken up because he introduced methods now all the fashion, our lessons went on at home, for he was always sure of four little pupils who firmly believed in their teacher, though they have not done him all the credit he deserved.

I never liked arithmetic or grammar, and dodged these branches on all occasions; but reading, composition, history and geography I enjoyed, as well as the stories read to us with a skill which made the dullest charming and useful.

"Pilgrim's Progress," Krummacher's "Parables," Miss Edgeworth, and the best of the dear old fairy tales made that hour the pleasantest of our day. On Sundays we had a simple service of Bible stories, hymns, and conversation about the state of our little consciences and the conduct of our childish lives which never will be forgotten.

Walks each morning round the Common while in the city, and long tramps over hill and dale when our home was in the country, were a part of our education, as well as every sort of housework, for which I have always been very grateful, since such knowledge makes one independent in these days of domestic tribulation with the help who are too often only hindrances.

Needle-work began early, and at ten my skilful sister made a linen shirt beautifully, while at twelve I set up as a doll's dress-maker, with my sign out, and wonderful models in my window. All the children employed me, and my turbans were the rage at one time to the great dismay of the neighbors' hens, who were hotly hunted down, that I might tweak out their downiest feathers to adorn the dolls' head-gear.

Active exercise was my delight from the time when a child of six I drove my hoop round the Common without stopping, to the days when I did my twenty miles in five hours and went to a party in the evening.

I always thought I must have been a deer or a horse in some former state, because it was such a joy to run. No boy could be my friend till I had beaten him in a race, and no girl if she refused to climb trees, leap fences and be a tomboy.

My wise mother, anxious to give me a strong body to support a lively brain, turned me loose in the country and let me run wild, learning of nature what no books can teach, and being led, as those who truly love her seldom fail to be,

Through nature up to nature's God.

I remember running over the hills just at dawn one summer morning, and pausing to rest in the silent woods saw, through an arch of trees, the sun rise over river, hill and wide green meadows as I never saw it before.

Something born of the lovely hour, a happy mood, and the unfolding aspirations of a child's soul seemed to bring me very near to God, and in the hush of that morning hour I always felt that I "got religion" as the phrase goes. A new and vital sense of His presence, tender and sustaining as a father's arms, came to me then, never to change through forty years of life's vicissitudes, but to grow stronger for the sharp discipline of poverty and pain, sorrow and success.

Those Concord days were the happiest of my life, for we had charm-

ing playmates in the little Emersons, Channings, Hawthornes and Good-
wins, with the illustrious parents and their friends to enjoy our pranks and
share our excursions.

Plays in the barn were a favorite amusement, and we dramatized the
fairy tales in great style. Our giant came tumbling off a loft when Jack cut
down the squash vine running up a ladder to represent the immortal bean.
Cinderella rolled away in a vast pumpkin, and a long, black pudding was
lowered by invisible hands to fasten itself on the nose of the woman who
wasted her three wishes.

Little pilgrims journeyed over the hills with scrip and staff and cockle-
shells in their hats; elves held their pretty revels among the pines, and
"Peter Wilkins' " flying ladies came swinging down on the birch tree-tops.
Lords and ladies haunted the garden, and mermaids splashed in the bath-
house of woven willows over the brook.

People wondered at our frolics, but enjoyed them, and droll stories
are still told of the adventures of those days. Mr. Emerson and Margaret
Fuller were visiting my parents one afternoon, and the conversation having
turned to the ever interesting subject of education, Miss Fuller said:

"Well, Mr. Alcott, you have been able to carry out your methods in
your own family, and I should like to see your model children."

She did in a few moments, for as the guests stood on the door steps
a wild uproar approached, and round the corner of the house came a wheel-
barrow holding baby May arrayed as a queen; I was the horse, bitted and
bridled and driven my elder sister Anna, while Lizzie played dog and
barked as loud as her gentle voice permitted.

All were shouting and wild with fun which, however, came to a sudden end as we espied the stately group before us, for my foot tripped, and
down we all went in a laughing heap, while my mother put a climax to
the joke by saying with a dramatic wave of the hand:

"Here are the model children, Miss Fuller."

My sentimental period began at fifteen when I fell to writing romances, poems, a "heart journal," and dreaming dreams of a splendid
future.

Browsing over Mr. Emerson's library I found "Goethe's Correspondence with a Child," and was at once fired with the desire to be a second
Bettine, making my father's friend my Goethe. So I wrote letters to him,
but was wise enough never to send them, left wild flowers on the doorsteps of my "Master," sung Mignon's song in very bad German under his
window, and was fond of wandering by moonlight, or sitting in a cherry-
tree at midnight till the owls scared me to bed.

The girlish folly did not last long, and the letters were burnt years ago, but Goethe is still my favorite author, and Emerson remained my beloved "Master" while he lived, doing more for me, as for many another young soul, than he ever knew, by the simple beauty of his life, the truth and wisdom of his books, the example of a good, great man untempted and unspoiled by the world which he made nobler while in it, and left the richer when he went.

The trials of life began about this time, and my happy childhood ended. Money is never plentiful in a philosopher's house, and even the maternal pelican could not supply all our wants on the small income which was freely shared with every needy soul who asked for help.

Fugitive slaves were sheltered under our roof, and my first pupil was a very black George Washington whom I taught to write on the hearth with charcoal, his big fingers finding pen and pencil unmanageable.

Motherless girls seeking protection were guarded among us; hungry travellers sent on to our door to be fed and warmed, and if the philosopher happened to own two coats the best went to a needy brother, for these were practical Christians who had the most perfect faith in Providence, and never found it betrayed.

In those days the prophets were not honored in their own land, and Concord had not yet discovered her great men. It was a sort of refuge for reformers of all sorts whom the good natives regarded as lunatics, harmless but amusing.

My father went away to hold his classes and conversations, and we women folk began to feel that we also might do something. So one gloomy November day we decided to move to Boston and try our fate again after some years in the wilderness.

My father's prospect was as promising as a philosopher's ever is in a money-making world, my mother's friends offered her a good salary as their missionary to the poor, and my sister and I hoped to teach. It was an anxious council; and always preferring action to discussion, I took a brisk run over the hill and then settled down for "a good think" in my favorite retreat.

It was an old cart-wheel, half hidden in grass under the locusts where I used to sit to wrestle with my sums, and usually forget them scribbling verses or fairy tales on my slate instead. Perched on the hub I surveyed the prospect and found it rather gloomy, with leafless trees, sere grass, leaden sky and frosty air, but the hopeful heart of fifteen beat warmly under the old red shawl, visions of success gave the gray clouds a silver lining, and I said defiantly, as I shook my fist at fate embodied in a crow cawing dismally on the fence near by, —

"I *will* do something by-and-by. Don't care what, teach, sew, act, write, anything to help the family; and I'll be rich and famous and happy before I die, see if I won't!''

Startled by this audacious outburst the crow flew away, but the old wheel creaked as if it began to turn at that moment, stirred by the intense desire of an ambitious girl to work for those she loved and find some reward when the duty was done.

I did not mind the omen then, and returned to the house cold but resolute. I think I began to shoulder my burden then and there, for when the free country life ended the wild colt soon learned to tug in harness, only breaking loose now and then for a taste of beloved liberty.

My sisters and I had cherished fine dreams of a home in the city, but when we found ourselves in a small house at the South End with not a tree in sight, only a back yard to play in, and no money to buy any of the splendors before us, we all rebelled and longed for the country again.

Anna soon found little pupils, and trudged away each morning to her daily task, pausing at the corner to wave her hand to me in answer to my salute with the duster. My father went to his classes at his room down town, mother to her all-absorbing poor, the little girls to school, and I was left to keep house, feeling like a caged sea-gull as I washed dishes and cooked in the basement kitchen where my prospect was limited to a procession of muddy boots.

Good drill, but very hard, and my only consolation was the evening reunion when all met with such varied reports of the day's adventures, we could not fail to find both amusement and instruction.

Father brought news from the upper world, and the wise, good people who adorned it; mother, usually much dilapidated because she *would* give away her clothes, with sad tales of suffering and sin from the darker side of life; gentle Anna a modest account of her success as teacher, for even at seventeen her sweet nature won all who knew her, and her patience quelled the most rebellious pupil.

My reports were usually a mixture of the tragic and the comic, and the children poured their small joys and woes into the family bosom where comfort and sympathy were always to be found.

Then we youngsters adjourned to the kitchen for our fun, which usually consisted of writing, dressing and acting a series of remarkable plays. In one I remember I took five parts and Anna four, with lightning changes of costume, and characters varying from a Greek prince in silver armor to a murderer in chains.

It was good training for memory and fingers, for we recited pages without a fault, and made every sort of property from a harp to a fairy's spangled wings. Later we acted Shakespeare, and Hamlet was my favorite hero, played with a gloomy glare and a tragic stalk which I have never seen surpassed.

But we were now beginning to play our parts on a real stage, and to know something of the pathetic side of life with its hard facts, irksome duties, many temptations and the daily sacrifice of self. Fortunately we had the truest, tenderest of guides and guards, and so learned the sweet uses of adversity, the value of honest work, the beautiful law of compensation which gives more than it takes, and the real significance of life.

At sixteen I began to teach twenty pupils, and for ten years learned to know and love children. The story writing went on all the while with the usual trials of beginners. Fairy tales told the Emersons made the first printed book, and "Hospital Sketches" the first successful one.

Every experience went into the chauldron to come out as froth, or evaporate in smoke, till time and suffering strengthened and clarified the mixture of truth and fancy, and a wholesome draught for children began to flow pleasantly and profitably.

So the omen proved a true one, and the wheel of fortune turned slowly, till the girl of fifteen found herself a woman of fifty with her prophetic dream beautifully realized, her duty done, her reward far greater than she deserved.